Elements of
Language

Program

First Course

Elements of
Language
First Course

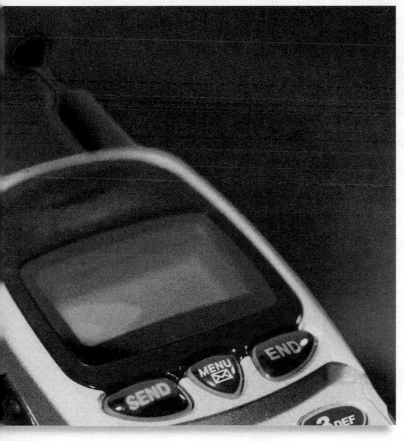

Lee Odell

Richard Vacca

Renée Hobbs

Judith L. Irvin

Grammar, Usage, and Mechanics
Instructional Framework by

John E. Warriner

HOLT, RINEHART AND WINSTON
A Harcourt Classroom Education Company

Austin • New York • Orlando • Atlanta • San Francisco • Boston • Dallas • Toronto • London

STAFF CREDITS

EDITORIAL

Director
Mescal Evler

Manager of Editorial Operations
Bill Wahlgren

Executive Editor
Kristine E. Marshall

Program Editors
Marcia L. Kelley
Amy Strong

Project Editors
Ann Michelle Gibson
Julie Barnett Hoover

Writing and Editing
Roger Boylan, Randy Dickson, Eric Estlund, Peggy Ferrin, Jim Hynes, Kevin Lemoine, Carla C. Robinson, Tressa Sanders, Jennifer R. Schwan

Quality Assurance—Grammar, Mechanics, and Usage
Robert H. Hoyt
Kathryn Rogers

Copyediting
Michael Neibergall, *Copyediting Manager;* Mary Malone, *Senior Copyeditor;* Joel Bourgeois,
Gabrielle Field, Suzi A. Hunn, Jane Kominek, Millicent Ondras, Theresa Reding, Désirée Reid, Kathleen Scheiner, *Copyeditors*

Project Administration
Marie Price, *Managing Editor;* Lori De La Garza, *Editorial Operations Coordinator;* Tracy DeMont, Heather Cheyne, Mark Holland, Marcus Johnson, Jill O'Neal, Joyce Rector, Janet Riley, Kelly Tankersley, *Project Administration;* Gail Coupland, Elizabeth Dickson, Ruth Hooker, Margaret Sanchez, *Word Processing*

Editorial Permissions
Janet Harrington

ART, DESIGN, AND PHOTO

Book Design
Senior Design Director
Diane Motz

Robin Bouvette, Candace Moore, *Senior Designers*
John Harrison, Dave Hernandez, *Designers;* Mercedes Newman, Charlie Taliaferro, *Design Associates*

Photo Studio
Lauren Eischen, Victoria Smith

Graphic Services
Kristen Darby, *Manager;*
Jane Dixon, Linda Wilbourn

Image Acquisitions
Joe London, *Director*
Elaine Tate, *Supervisor;* Erin Cone, Sunday Patterson, *Art Buyers*
Jeannie Taylor, Tim Taylor, *Photo Research Supervisors;* Rick Benavides, *Assistant Photo Researcher*

Book and Media Design
Joe Melomo, *Design Director*

Cover Design
Joe Melomo
Jane Dixon

PRODUCTION
Simira Davis, Joan Lindsay, Beth Prevelige

MANUFACTURING
Michael Roche, *Senior Manufacturing Coordinator*

▶ **LEE ODELL** helped establish the pedagogical framework for the composition strand of *Elements of Language.* In addition, he guided the development of the scope and sequence and pedagogical design of the Writing Workshops. Dr. Odell is Professor of Composition Theory and Research and, since 1996, Director of the Writing Program at Rensselaer Polytechnic Institute. He began his career teaching English in middle and high schools. More recently he has worked with teachers in grades K–12 to establish a program that involves students from all disciplines in writing across the curriculum and for communities outside their classrooms. Dr. Odell's most recent book (with Charles R. Cooper) is *Evaluating Writing: The Role of Teachers' Knowledge about Text, Learning, and Culture* (1999). He is Past Chair of the Conference on College Composition and Communication and of the NCTE's Assembly for Research.

▶ **RICHARD VACCA** helped establish the conceptual basis for the reading strand of *Elements of Language.* In addition, he guided the development of the pedagogical design and the scope and sequence of skills in the Reading Workshops. Dr. Vacca is Professor of Education at Kent State University. He recently completed a term as the forty-second President of the International Reading Association. Originally a middle school and high school teacher, Dr. Vacca served as the project director of the Cleveland Writing Demonstration Project for several years. He is the co-author of *Content Area Reading; Reading and Learning to Read;* and articles and chapters related to adolescents' literacy development. In 1989, Dr. Vacca received the College Reading Association's A. B. Herr Award for Outstanding Contributions to Reading Education. Currently, he is co-chair of the IRA's Commission on Adolescent Literacy.

▶ **RENÉE HOBBS** helped develop the theoretical framework for the viewing and representing strand of *Elements of Language.* She guided the development of the scope and sequence; served as the authority on terminology, definitions, and pedagogy; and directed the planning for the video series. Dr.

Hobbs is Associate Professor of Communication at Babson College in Wellesley, Massachusetts, and Director of the Media Literacy Project. Active in the field of media education, Dr. Hobbs has served in the following capacities: Director of the Institute on Media Education, Harvard Graduate School of Education; Director of the "Know TV" Project, Discovery Networks and Time Warner Cable; and Board Member, The New York Times Newspaper in Education Program. She works actively in staff development in school districts nationwide. Dr. Hobbs has contributed articles and chapters on media, technology, and education to many publications.

▶ **JUDITH L. IRVIN** also helped establish the conceptual basis for the reading strand of *Elements of Language.* Dr. Irvin taught middle school for several years before pursuing graduate studies in Reading-Language Arts. She now teaches courses in curriculum, middle school education, and educational leadership at Florida State University. She chaired the Research Committee of the National Middle School Association and was the editor of *Research in Middle Level Education Quarterly* for six years. Dr. Irvin writes a column, "What Research Says to the Middle Level Practitioner," for the *Middle School Journal.* Her many publications include *What Research Says to the Middle Level Practitioner* and *Reading and the Middle School Student: Strategies to Enhance Literacy.*

▶ **JOHN E. WARRINER** was a high school English teacher when he developed the original organizational structure for his classic *English Grammar and Composition* series. The approach pioneered by Mr. Warriner was distinctive, and the editorial staff of Holt, Rinehart and Winston have worked diligently to retain the unique qualities of his pedagogy. For the same reason, HRW continues to credit Mr. Warriner as an author of *Elements of Language* in recognition of his groundbreaking work. John Warriner also co-authored the *English Workshop* series and was editor of *Short Stories: Characters in Conflict.* Throughout his career, however, teaching remained Mr. Warriner's major interest, and he taught for thirty-two years in junior and senior high schools and in college.

Continued

v

Geri-Lee DeGennaro
Tarpon Springs High School
Tarpon Springs, Florida

Karen Dendy
Stephen F. Austin Middle School
Irving, Texas

Dianne Franz
Tarpon Springs Middle School
Tarpon Springs, Florida

Doris F. Frazier
East Millbrook Magnet Middle
  School
Raleigh, North Carolina

Shayne G. Goodrum
C. E. Jordan High School
Durham, North Carolina

Bonnie L. Hall
St. Ann School
Lansing, Illinois

Doris Ann Hall
Forest Meadow Junior High
  School
Dallas, Texas

James M. Harris
Mayfield High School
Mayfield Village, Ohio

Lynne Hoover
Fremont Ross High School
Fremont, Ohio

Patricia A. Humphreys
James Bowie High School
Austin, Texas

Jennifer L. Jones
Oliver Wendell Holmes Middle
  School
Dallas, Texas

Kathryn R. Jones
Murchison Middle School
Austin, Texas

Bonnie Just
Narbonne High School
Harbor City, California

Vincent Kimball
Patterson High School #405
Baltimore, Maryland

Nancy C. Long
MacArthur High School
Houston, Texas

Carol M. Mackey
Ft. Lauderdale Christian School
Ft. Lauderdale, Florida

Jan Jennings McCown
Johnston High School
Austin, Texas

Alice Kelly McCurdy
Rusk Middle School
Dallas, Texas

Elizabeth Morris
Northshore High School
Slidell, Louisiana

Victoria Reis
Western High School
Ft. Lauderdale, Florida

Dean Richardson
Scarborough High School
Houston, Texas

Susan M. Rogers
Freedom High School
Morganton, North Carolina

Sammy Rusk
North Mesquite High School
Mesquite, Texas

Carole B. San Miguel
James Bowie High School
Austin, Texas

Jane Saunders
William B. Travis High School
Austin, Texas

Gina Sawyer
Reed Middle School
Duncanville, Texas

Laura R. Schauermann
MacArthur High School
Houston, Texas

Stephen Shearer
MacArthur High School
Houston, Texas

Elizabeth Curry Smith
Tarpon Springs High School
Tarpon Springs, Florida

Jeannette M. Spain
Stephen F. Austin High School
Sugar Land, Texas

Carrie Speer
Northshore High School
Slidell, Louisiana

Trina Steffes
MacArthur High School
Houston, Texas

Andrea G. Freirich Stewart
Freedom High School
Morganton, North Carolina

Diana O. Torres
Johnston High School
Austin, Texas

Jan Voorhees
Whitesboro High School
Marcy, New York

Ann E. Walsh
Bedichek Middle School
Austin, Texas

Mary Jane Warden
Onahan School
Chicago, Illinois

Beth Westbrook
Covington Middle School
Austin, Texas

Char-Lene Wilkins
Morenci Area High School
Morenci, Michigan

CONTENTS IN BRIEF

PART 1

Communications

PART 2

Sentences and Paragraphs

PART 3

Grammar, Usage, and Mechanics

PART 4

Quick Reference Handbook

CONTENTS

CHAPTER

2

Exposition

Explaining a Process 48

Previewing a Novel................ 116

Finding and Reporting Information 156

Convincing Others 200

Advertising 232

Contents **xvii**

Parts of Speech Overview
Verb, Adverb, Preposition, Conjunction, Interjection 356

CHAPTER 12

Complements
Direct and Indirect Objects,

The Phrase
Prepositional and Verbal Phrases 400

The Clause
Independent and Subordinate Clauses **422**

CHAPTER **15**

Using Verbs Correctly
Principal Parts, Regular and Irregular Verbs, Tense, Voice **484**

CHAPTER

18

Using Pronouns Correctly
Nominative and Objective Case Forms

Using Modifiers Correctly
Comparison and Placement

Punctuation

End Marks, Commas, Semicolons, and Colons..... 596

Punctuation

Underlining (Italics), Quotation Marks, Apostrophes, Hyphens, Parentheses, Brackets, and Dashes 626

Spelling
Improving Your Spelling **654**

CHAPTER

25

Correcting Common Errors

Key Language Skills Review **684**

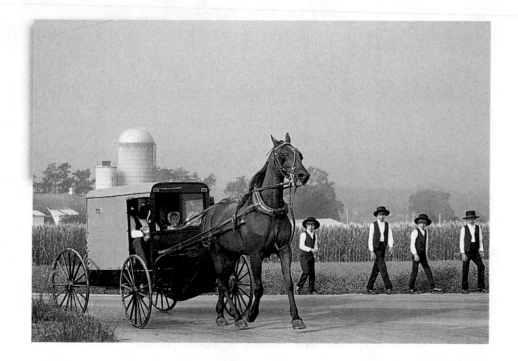

PART 4 | **Quick Reference Handbook** **718**

MODELS

TO OUR STUDENTS

On any given day, you probably watch TV, surf the Internet, read magazines, and listen to CDs. Each day you probably also write papers in school, send e-mails, and talk on the phone. The world of language around you is expanding rapidly. To keep up, you need to become a skilled language user. *Elements of Language* can be an important resource by helping you use language more effectively as you communicate in the twenty-first century.

Elements of Language is divided into four major parts:

PART 1 Communications shows you how to develop the skills you use to **receive** communications through **reading, listening,** and **viewing** and to **send** communications through **writing, speaking,** and **representing.**

PART 2 Sentences and Paragraphs shows you how to develop interesting, clear **sentences** and **paragraphs.**

PART 3 Grammar, Usage, and Mechanics provides instruction and practice with the **building blocks of language**—words, phrases, and clauses—so you can convey meaning clearly and correctly.

PART 4 Quick Reference Handbook is a one-stop **reference guide** to a variety of skills and concepts—in a concise, easily accessible form.

Think of *Elements of Language* as your personal communication resource. As you use this resource, remember that everything is here for a reason. For example, **boldface** type and color draw your attention to important words or ideas; **charts** present information in an easy-to-read form; and **headings** show the organization of ideas.

PART 1 chapters include the following sections:

▶ **Reading Workshop**—to show you how to develop and improve your reading skills

▶ **Writing Workshop**—to show you how to use the writing process to develop a piece of your own writing

▶ **Focus on Speaking and Listening** or **Focus on Viewing and Representing**—to help you master either the skills of speaking and listening or of viewing and representing

You will also encounter the following features in PART 1.

- **Mini-Lessons**—vocabulary and test-taking strategies, as well as writing or critical thinking skills
- **A Writer's Model**—a model of how you might write your own paper
- **A Student's Model**—a paper written by a real student
- **Content and Organization Guidelines for Peer and Self-Evaluation** and **Style Guidelines**—questions, tips, and techniques to help you evaluate and revise *what* you say as well as *how* you say it
- **Designing Your Writing**—pointers on how to present ideas and information visually so your readers can grasp them more easily
- **Connections to Literature** and **Connections to Life**—communication activities related to literature or to the world at large

Here are some of the features you will meet in PART 2 and PART 3.

- **Rules**—the grammar, usage, and mechanics concepts in each Part 3 chapter, numbered in each chapter
- **Exercises**—practice for skills and concepts
- **Tabs**—colored corners on the Part 3 pages that show rule numbers
- **Tips & Tricks**—easy-to-use hints about grammar, usage, and mechanics
- **Style Tips**—information about formal and informal uses of English
- **Help**—pointers to help you understand concepts and complete exercises
- **Computer Tips**—hints for using a computer to help you write better
- **Writing Applications**—activities that link grammar, usage, and mechanics skills and concepts with writing activities

go.hrw.com
Elements of Language on the Internet

At the *Elements of Language* Internet site, you can dissect the prose of professional writers, crack the codes of the advertising industry, and find out how your communication skills can help you in the real world. You can also submit your work for publication in one of our online galleries. As you move through *Elements of Language*, you will find the best online resources at **go.hrw.com**.

Let this book be your guide to developing your skill as an effective and critical language user—a communicator—in the twenty-first century.

The Authors and Editors

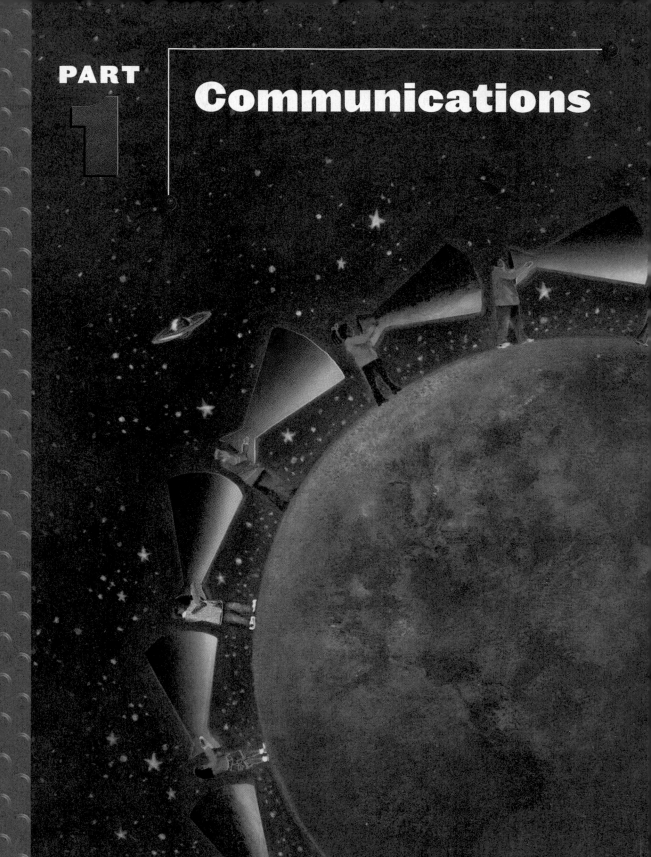

PART
1
Communications

Introduction

READING WRITING

Thinking About Reading and Writing

You have probably been in situations like this: You read a scary detective story straight through without stopping, or you write to a friend about a terrific movie you just saw. These kinds of reading and writing are easy and fun to do. Why is it that in other situations, especially in school, reading and writing can seem difficult?

Practice the Process

If you are an athlete (or a painter, computer whiz, singer, or guitarist), you already know that you have to keep working to improve your skills. Similarly, even if you are already a pretty good reader and writer, you need to keep getting better, because as you get older, the reading and writing you are expected to do become more and more complex.

The good news is, you *can* do many things to improve your reading and writing skills. Both reading and writing are processes made up of a series of steps. For each step, you can learn activities and thinking strategies that will help you understand what you read and improve the quality of what you write. Good readers and writers use some of the same basic strategies before, during, and after reading or writing.

Looking at the Reading and Writing Processes

- Bring to class an essay you wrote within the last year. Try to list each separate step you had to do to get from the first idea in your head to your finished piece of writing.
- Now, exchange essays with a partner. After reading, talk about each other's essays. Did you get the message the writer intended to send? Brainstorm all of the separate things you had to do in order to get from looking at the words on the page to understanding the writer's message.

TIP Sometimes it is helpful to write down your thoughts and feelings about what you are reading and writing. Get in the habit of carrying a **learning log** with you. A learning log can be a simple, spiral-bound notebook. You use a learning log to summarize what you have read, to make prewriting notes, or to work out problems you are having with something you are reading or writing.

TIP With a partner or small group, brainstorm some of the powers reading gives you.

- Think about the kinds of texts you can read and what you can learn through reading.
- Think about the people you can meet through reading.

Reading as a Process

When you were young you figured out that letters stood for sounds and that clumps of letters made words. Then, you learned that the words formed sentences that communicate a message. To understand those messages, you need to use the thinking strategies listed in the chart below *before, while,* and *after* you read.

What You Do During the Reading Process	
Before You Read: Prereading	■ **Preview** the text and **make predictions** about what it contains. ■ Build **background knowledge** for what you will read by thinking about what you already know about the topic. ■ Set your **purpose** for reading by asking questions. ■ **Focus your mind** on what you are about to do.
While You Read: Reading	■ **Make connections** between what you are reading and what you already know. ■ **Adjust** your reading rate. ■ Look for **patterns of organization**. ■ Revise your **predictions** about the text. ■ Ask yourself **questions** about the text, and **use fix-it strategies** when you become confused.
After You Read: Exploring and Extending Your Reading	■ Decide whether you achieved your **purpose** for reading. ■ **Confirm your understanding** of the text's meaning. ■ **Draw conclusions** and **form generalizations**. ■ **Extend** and use the ideas you encountered while reading.

Getting Ready

If you were a relief pitcher called into a game with the bases loaded and a tie score, would you skip your chance to practice a few pitches from the mound? Reading without getting ready is like trying to step in and save a ballgame without warming up. This getting-ready stage is called prereading. Use these prereading warm-ups:

- **Preview the text.** To get an idea of what is coming, **skim** (read quickly) the first few paragraphs. Consider how difficult the vocabulary is and what the writer's style is like. **Scan** (look specifically) for headings, subheadings, and boldface or italicized terms. See what the graphics (charts, maps, and time lines) and illustrations show.

- **Make predictions.** Based on your preview, what do you think the text will be about? What are the main ideas, and where will you find them? Take a guess. Also, try to determine the audience that the author has in mind. Thinking about these things will help you figure out whether you should start reading quickly or slowly.

- **Build background.** Suppose you are looking through a magazine. A photo of a kangaroo makes you recall a number of things: a movie you saw about Australia, the kangaroos you saw in a zoo, the words *marsupial* and *joey*. Before you begin any kind of reading, get in touch with your **prior knowledge.** Ask yourself, "What background knowledge do I already have about this topic, based on my experiences and other things I have read?"

- **Set your purpose.** When you read a short story just for fun, you probably read quickly to find out what happens next. When you read for a school assignment, though, you read much more slowly, looking for important information. Any time you read, think about your predictions, and ask yourself what you think you will find in the text. Before you read, ask yourself whether you are reading for fun or information. Reading with a purpose will help you focus on and remember what is important in a text.

- **Focus your mind.** If your mind starts wandering to last night's sitcoms, try to drum up some interest in what you are reading. Look for the buried treasure by asking, "What important things will I discover as I read? How can I use what I find?"

TIP Make these strategies a before-you-read habit. They take only a few minutes, and they are a sure way to turn you into a better reader. Try the strategies out on a textbook chapter or on the pages of a Web site.

While Reading

Making Sense

When you read a magazine article about animal camouflage, a Greek myth, and a math textbook, the reading experiences are very different. Whatever you read, though, your goal is the same: to understand and interpret what the writer is saying. The strategies below will help you.

- **Make connections.** If you read that a walrus uses its whiskers as a rake to comb for food, connect that to the documentary you saw about how bears search for food. Find a hook in your mind on which to hang each new piece of information you read.

- **Adjust your reading rate.** When you read for enjoyment, you may read quickly; however, when you read for information, you should slow down. You may race through texts with simple sentences and familiar words, but read more slowly texts with complicated sentences and unfamiliar words. The more you already know about the subject of a text, the faster you may be able to read it.

- **Look for patterns of organization.** Once you notice that an article about soccer leagues has an advantages/disadvantages organization, you will be on the lookout for pros and cons. When you understand how a writer organizes ideas, you will be able to tell the more important ideas from the less important ones.

- **Adjust your predictions.** Be aware of whether the text is matching your original predictions about topic and organization. Say you predicted a piece of writing was going to compare the fairy tale *Cinderella* with a Chinese fairy tale. After reading the first few paragraphs, though, you do not see any further mention of Cinderella. At this point, you might scan ahead to see if the word *Cinderella* comes up again. If not, you might predict that the article is really only about the Chinese fairy tale, and that each paragraph is going to deal with a different aspect of that fairy tale. Avoid getting stuck in a rut; revising your predictions as you read will help you find the most important ideas in a piece of writing.

- **Ask yourself questions as you read.** Keep up a dialogue with the writer. Ask questions, make comments, and note whatever puzzles you. If you become lost, try **fix-it strategies** such as those on the next page.

- Slow down.
- Brainstorm the meaning of a difficult word.
- Put a difficult sentence into your own words.
- Read a difficult passage aloud.
- Sketch the ideas in the text in a graphic organizer.
- Take notes, perhaps using sticky notes that you can put on the pages.

The marginal notes below are one reader's thoughts on the following magazine article.

The room is pitch dark. The floor is littered with toys. Furniture is scattered throughout. The challenge: Find your way across the room to the door. You have no flashlight and you can't see a thing. How will you do it? Probably by shuffling slowly, hands stretched out in front of you. Hopefully, you won't stub your toe on the sofa or trip over a toy.

It's too bad you don't have whiskers. Whiskers allow cats and other animals to move through darkness, avoiding every obstacle as if they could see. That's because whiskers—special hairs—are very sensitive to touch.

Thicker than normal hairs, whiskers are rooted deeper in the skin. The base of each whisker rests in a tiny sac of fluid underneath the skin. Each whisker rotates at the skin's surface, like a straw in a soda bottle. When something brushes the tip of the whisker, a sensation zips down the hair shaft to the nerves in the fluid sac. The sensation transmits valuable information such as which way the wind is blowing or what food or obstacle lies ahead.

Scientists conducted an experiment to see if cats could find their way relying on their whiskers. They blindfolded domestic cats and released them into a large cage full of toys and other cats. The blindfolded cats walked around as normally as the cats that could see. They knew where the "invisible" objects were because their whiskers sensed the air currents moving around the objects.

"It's Touch and Go with Whiskers," *National Geographic World*

> I've been in this situation before.

> So that's what whiskers are for.

> I don't understand how this works— I'll try reading this part aloud.

> Here's support proving that whiskers help animals move in the dark.

After Reading

Exploring and Extending

You have just finished reading a magazine article about the discovery of a new solar system. "What a cool story!" you think. You are eager to talk with someone, to exchange ideas about the article.

The reading process does not end when you read the final sentence. That is the time to explore the ideas you encountered and extend them further. Here are some postreading strategies you can use.

- **Decide whether you have achieved your purpose for reading.** Consider which of your questions were answered. Compare what you expected to get out of the text with what you actually got.

- **Confirm your understanding of the text.** Sometimes you do not know just what you got out of a text until you capture your thoughts on paper. Try summarizing what you read in a *learning log,* or confirm your understanding by sharing your ideas with other readers.

- **Draw conclusions and form generalizations.** Sometimes the most important ideas in a text are not directly stated. Merge the facts and details from the text with your own experience to form new ideas, or *conclusions.* Then, form *generalizations* by broadening the meaning of the text to apply to many people or situations.

- **Extend and use the ideas in your reading.** Try these activities.

  1. Be creative. Use the text as a springboard—and take off. Write a character's journal entry, draw a map, or set a poem to music.

  2. Read on. One idea often leads to another. Use any questions that come up as you read as your purpose to read other resources.

  3. Connect your reading to the real world. A text may help you solve a problem or give you a new view of an issue or event. Consider how the ideas in a text apply to real life, and put them to work.

When you examine the reading process, consider the role that writers play in helping readers to make sense of the text. In the next few pages, you will look closely at the writing process.

Writing as a Process

WHAT'S AHEAD?

In this section, you will learn how effective writers
- prewrite
- write
- revise
- publish

"Genius," wrote Thomas Edison, "is 1 percent inspiration and 99 percent perspiration." He was talking about inventing, but the same goes for writing. Writing is a process made up of many steps, and it takes effort. The chart below summarizes the stages that usually take place during the writing process.

What You Do During the Writing Process	
Prewriting	■ Choose a **form** and a manageable **topic**. ■ Identify your **purpose** and **audience**. ■ Draft a sentence that expresses your **main idea**. ■ **Gather information** about the topic. ■ Begin to **organize** the information.
Writing a Draft	■ Draft an **introduction** that gets your reader's attention and states your main idea. ■ Provide **background information**. ■ State your **supporting points** and **elaborate** on them. ■ Follow a **plan** or order. ■ Wrap things up with a **conclusion**.
Revising	■ **Evaluate** your draft. ■ **Edit** to improve content, organization, and style.
Publishing	■ **Proofread** the draft to find and correct spelling, punctuation, and grammar mistakes. ■ **Share** your finished writing with readers. ■ **Reflect** on your writing experience.

TIP The writing process is flexible: You can always go back to an earlier stage or even (if a topic does not work out) start all over again. Suppose you are revising a report on the history of skateboards. You decide paragraph three is too skimpy. It needs some elaboration to drive home the paragraph's main idea. You go to the library, research more information, add it to paragraph three, and then return to revising and editing your draft.

Prewriting

Getting Ready

Most of the 99 percent perspiration that Edison talked about takes place before you begin writing. The following prewriting steps will help prepare you to write your first draft.

- **Choose a form.** Writing comes in all different shapes and sizes. Your choices of forms include essays, reports, poems, letters, editorials, memoirs, stories, pamphlets, or instructions.

Reference Note

For more on **freewriting, clustering,** and **brainstorming,** see page 803 in the Quick Reference Handbook.

- **Choose and narrow your topic carefully.** Try *freewriting, clustering,* and *brainstorming* to come up with topic ideas that interest you. Then, think about the amount of space you have to present your information. For example, a topic like "cars" is too large. However, a manageable topic might be "the latest developments in the design of electric cars."

Reference Note

For more on **author's purpose,** see page 53.

- **Identify your purpose and audience.** Why are you writing? Who will read your work? The answers to these questions will focus your ideas. For example, if you were creating a short story to share with your classmates, you would write differently than if you were writing a persuasive letter to a city council member.

COMPUTER TIP

Word processors are not just for final drafts. You can also use word-processing tools to shape your message. For example, you might plan to include some of the information you find in a chart or present a series of instructions in a bulleted list.

- **Decide what point you want to make.** Even if you change your mind later, draft one sentence (your **main idea statement,** or **thesis**) that sums up your main point. It will help keep you on track. If you are writing to entertain readers or to express yourself, you probably will not include a main idea statement. Even so, you should figure out the meaning of the specific story you want to tell or what you want readers to understand about you.

- **Gather lots of information.** Maybe you will look for information in books and magazines. You might do a Web search or interview someone who knows about your subject. Take notes. If you are writing about a personal experience, jot down every detail you can remember.

- **Think about organizing.** It is time to arrange the information you have discovered. Keep your audience in mind as you try to find a **logical progression,** or helpful order, for your ideas. You may consider writing a formal or informal outline or using a chart or conceptual map to organize your information.

Making a Start

Like most good writers, you probably keep your best pieces of writing—and maybe your worst—in a collection or **portfolio.** Take some time now to review this portfolio and set some goals. Try to make this new piece at least as good as your best work. Focus on improving weaknesses you see in your past writing. Here are things you need to do as you write your first draft.

- **Grab your readers' attention.** Your introduction should make your readers *want* to read your work. In an essay, you might start with a surprising statement, a question, a brief story, or another way of hooking your audience's interest.

- **Give them some background.** What do your readers need to know about your topic in order to understand what you are going to tell them? Help them by defining important terms, identifying people and places, or giving a little history.

- **Get to the point.** State your main idea as clearly as you can. Your readers should not be wondering what you mean. In a multiparagraph work, each paragraph after the introduction should also include a main point.

- **Elaborate.** You know a lot about your topic, and you have worked hard to find facts, specific details, and quotations to back up your ideas. Do not just give your opinion: "Students should have to take showers after gym class." Elaborate by citing statistics, by explaining the rules in other schools, or by quoting experts.

- **Organize.** Organizing involves arranging ideas and information in an overall pattern, or order. If you are writing a story, for example, you probably will try to create a clear chronological order (first this happened, then this . . .). You will learn in this book about other orders for organizing ideas. Use them in your writing.

- **Wrap things up.** It is important to give readers a satisfying ending. You might write a sentence or two that restates your basic point in a new way or gives a clear sense of the impression you have been trying to create. You might add a final thought or comment on your topic.

TIP You can use a variety of resources and reference materials as you write your first draft. For example, you might use a thesaurus to find the exact word you need to express yourself. Refer to "The Library/Media Center" beginning on page 735 in the Quick Reference Handbook for help in selecting other resources.

Reference Note

For more information and practice on **elaboration,** see page 304.

Revising

Going Back Over Your Draft

TIP One of the most helpful things you can do to improve your writing is to have a peer evaluate it. **Peer evaluation** makes you a better writer and a better reader.

Follow these steps when you evaluate a peer's draft.

- Ask the writer what he or she would like to know.
- Give the paper two careful readings, looking for what works as well as what doesn't.
- Be specific when you give feedback, and always start out by telling the writer what you liked about his or her composition.
- Specific Guidelines for Peer Evaluation and Self-Evaluation appear in the Revising section of each Writer's Workshop in this book.

Good writers are good editors. An editor works on a draft until it is as good as he or she can make it. Editing involves evaluating (deciding what needs fixing), revising (making changes), and proofreading (correcting grammar, punctuation, and spelling errors). Since it is impossible to focus on all three of these processes at once, most writers focus on evaluating and revising first.

- **Evaluate your draft.** Re-read your draft carefully at least twice. First, focus on content and organization; then, focus on sentence style and word choice. Peer editors may make suggestions and point out weak or confusing parts of your draft.

- **Revise the content and organization.** Use these five strategies.

  1. **Add.** If your writing seems skimpy, add a paragraph that looks at your composition's main idea from another angle. Consider adding transitions, such as *therefore, for instance,* and *finally,* to help readers follow your thoughts.

  2. **Delete.** Cut words, sentences, and even whole paragraphs that stray from your composition's main idea. Eliminate unnecessary repetition and wordiness and get to the point.

  3. **Replace.** Look for weak spots. Replace any weak support with something stronger.

  4. **Rearrange.** Try out different arrangements for words in sentences or paragraphs in compositions. You can easily rearrange using a word-processing program—or you can cut portions of your paper and then paste them onto new paper. Keep your readers in mind as you search for the clearest, most logical order.

  5. **Elaborate.** Be sure that the main idea of every paragraph is supported by specific details, facts, examples, illustrations, sensory images, figurative language, quotations, or anecdotes.

- **Revise the style.** Consider these strategies.

  1. **Eliminate** slang, clichés, and tired verbs.

  2. **Avoid** using the passive voice.

  3. **Vary** sentence length and sentence beginnings.

  4. **Combine** sentences to add variety or complexity.

Going Public

Congratulations! You have created a piece of writing that no one else has ever written or read before. Now there is only one bit of tidying up to do before you go public with your work.

■ **Proofread your final draft.** The last step in the editing process is making your paper error-free. Proofreading demands a close and careful reading. Hunt down every mistake in spelling, capitalization, punctuation, grammar, and usage—and fix them all. Sometimes you are so familiar with what you meant to say that your eye skips over mistakes, so ask one or more partners to proofread, too.

Here is a chart of the guidelines you can use to edit your final draft before you make a final copy. Use the proofreading symbols found on page 809 of the Quick Reference Handbook to mark your edits.

TIP You can find a variety of resources and **reference materials** that will help you eliminate errors. A word processor's spell-checker or dictionary will help you correct spelling errors. Part 3 of this book will help you eliminate grammar mistakes.

Guidelines for Proofreading
❶ Is every sentence a complete sentence, not a fragment or run-on? (See page 268.)
❷ Does every sentence begin with a capital letter? Does every sentence end with the correct punctuation mark? Are punctuation marks used correctly within sentences? (See page 574 and Chapters 23 and 24.)
❸ Do plural subjects have plural verbs? Do singular subjects have singular verbs? (See page 458.)
❹ Are verb forms and verb tenses used correctly? (See pages 485 and 496.)
❺ Are adjective and adverb forms used correctly in comparisons? (See page 532.)
❻ Are the forms of personal pronouns used correctly? (See page 511.)
❼ Does every pronoun agree with its antecedent (the word it refers to) in number and gender? Are pronoun references clear? (See page 475.)
❽ Is every word spelled correctly? (See page 655.)

- **Publish what you have written.** Most writers want someone else to learn what they have learned and to experience what they have experienced. You began writing with an audience and purpose in mind; now consider ways to share your writing with that audience. You might submit your writing to a school newspaper or magazine. You might read it aloud, enter it in a contest, or post it on the Web. Brainstorm other publishing ideas with your classmates, and get your writing out there.

- **Reflect on your experience.** Ask yourself some questions about what you learned from your writing experience: What will I do differently next time? What are the strengths and weaknesses of this piece? What was easy for me to do, and what was difficult? Write your responses in a learning log or place them in your portfolio with your latest piece of writing.

In this chapter, you have examined the reading and writing processes. The chart below compares these two processes step by step.

The Reading-Writing Connection		
	Reading Process	**Writing Process**
Before	• Think about what you already know about the topic. • Set a purpose for reading. • Scan the text to make predictions about what the text will include.	• Think about what you already know about the topic. Do some research to find out more. • Identify your purpose and audience. • Make notes or an outline to plan what the text will include.
During	• Take notes on important ideas and details. • Notice how the writer has organized the text. Look for clue words that help you find the writer's main idea and supporting details.	• Follow your prewriting notes or outline. • Organize your writing and use transitions as clue words so that readers can easily follow your main idea and supporting details.
After	• Evaluate how well you met your purpose for reading. • Connect what you have read with the real world and to your own experiences. • Reflect on what you have read. You might ask questions about what you have learned.	• Evaluate and revise the text to make sure you achieve your purpose for writing. • Connect your writing with the real world by publishing your ideas. • Reflect on what you have written. You might ask questions about what you have learned about yourself as a writer.

Choices

Choose one of the following activities to complete.

▶ WRITING

1. Exploring New Forms As a class, brainstorm as long a list as possible of the different forms of writing. (Here is a head start for your list: poem, letter, TV script, and directions.) Think of all the other kinds of writing that people do in the working world. Then, create a classroom **poster** as a reminder of the many forms from which a writer can choose. Now, **write** in a form you have never used before.

▶ SPEAKING AND LISTENING

2. Thinking About Listening In this chapter you have examined reading and writing as processes. Is listening a process, too? In a small group, plan to listen to the same speech, radio talk show, lecture, or news report. Take notes on what you do *before* you listen, *while* you listen, and *after* you listen. Then compare notes with the other members of the group and decide whether listening, too, is a process. Report your findings to your class in an **oral presentation.**

▶ READING

3. Dialogue with a Writer Get together with two or three other students. Choose a text none of you have read before— a letter to the editor, an article, or a book review. Read it independently, and in a **reading log** try to work out problems you have in understanding the text. (As an example, look back at the reader's notes on page 7.) Then, compare your notes with the notes of the other members of your group.

▶ CAREERS

4. Team Spirit TV writers and other professional writers often work in teams. In collaborative writing, a pair or a small group of writers get together to decide on a topic or to develop a story idea. Then, they decide what roles each will play in doing research, writing drafts, and editing the drafts. With your teacher's permission, try working with a team of classmates to produce a piece of **collaborative writing.**

 PORTFOLIO

1

Witnessing
an Event

Reading Workshop

Reading an Eyewitness Account
PAGE 18

Writing Workshop

Writing an Eyewitness Account
PAGE 27

Focus on Viewing and Representing

Examining News
PAGE 44

Have you ever seen huge explosions of fireworks at a festival? Have you watched a famous Hollywood director shutting down the streets of your hometown to make a new film? Even if you have not seen events like these, someone somewhere has, and has probably written about them in an *eyewitness account*. An **eyewitness account** is a **narrative,** or story, that tells about something interesting, unusual, or exciting that the writer has seen. It gives facts and details about an event so that the reader can picture it clearly.

Reading an eyewitness account can put you at the scene of the action. You can also write your own eyewitness account that will pull a reader into your world. Writing an eyewitness account is one of the best ways you and other writers can share what you have seen with the rest of the world.

internet**connect**

go.
hrw
.com

GO TO: go.hrw.com
KEYWORD: EOLang 7-1

YOUR TURN 1 Discovering an Eyewitness Account

Think of an exciting or unusual event you have seen lately, and then briefly discuss it with a partner. Answer these questions.

- What was the event?
- Why does this event stand out in your mind?
- What details of the event can you recall most easily? Why do you think you can recall these details?

Reading an Eyewitness Account

You are hiking along a path when you hear a distinctive sound, like bacon sizzling in a pan. It could be a camper cooking breakfast, but more likely it is a rattlesnake. You look down and see the long, legless creature, whose body—marked with a blotched diamond pattern—coils tightly around itself. Bright yellow eyes with vertical slits gaze out at you, and the snake shakes its rattle as if to say, "Watch out! I don't want to have to use my fangs!"

Snakes may scare you or fascinate you. People's views of snakes may differ, but these creatures always seem to create a strong reaction. The author of the following eyewitness account saw an extraordinary event involving snakes. As you read the selection, try to picture the event she is describing.

Preparing to Read

READING FOCUS

Descriptive Language   Author Jennifer Owings Dewey wants to do more than give a list of the events she witnessed. She wants to create in your mind a clear picture of those events. As you read, look for ways the author uses language to create a picture for you.

READING SKILL

Implied Main Idea   The main idea in a reading reveals the point that the writer is trying to make. The author of "Hopi Snake Ceremonies" never clearly states the main idea of her eyewitness account. Instead, the main idea is *implied*. The author gives the reader clues to figure out the main idea by supporting and building on the idea throughout the account. Watch for clues as you read to decide what you think the main idea is.

Read the following article. In a notebook, jot down answers to the numbered active-reading questions in the shaded boxes. The underlined words will be used in the Vocabulary Mini-Lesson on page 25.

from Rattlesnake Dance

HOPI SNAKE CEREMONIES

BY JENNIFER OWINGS DEWEY

1   **D**eath is not the automatic result of a snakebite. I learned this when I was nine. But the mystery of snakebite and venom, and the human response to these, deepened for me when I was ten and my father took me to the Hopi snake ceremonies in Arizona.

> **1. What do you think this piece will be about?**

2   For more than two weeks in August the Hopi Indians held secret rituals that concluded with the snake dance. On those days non-Indians were allowed to watch the dance, although they probably understood little of what they saw. My father did his best to explain what he knew.

3   The Hopi live in a bone-dry region of the desert Southwest. They depend on rain to water their crops. The Hopi believe snakes have unique powers, that they are messengers between humans and spirits—especially the spirits that bring the rain.

4   For the Hopi, the snake ceremony is a time to make a plea to the spirits for the water the Indians badly need to survive. . . .

5   The dancers, all men, filed into the dance plaza of the town. They had shoulder-length hair as sleek and black as raven wings. Bunches of eagle feathers were tied into the thick strands.

6   The men were painted black and white, with zigzag lines to represent lightning. They wore knee-length kilts and woven belts. Each of the dancers had a tortoise-shell rattle tied to his right leg below the thigh.

7   The men moved in a shuffling circle, their buckskin moccasins kicking up puffs of white dust. Their movements were accompanied by a chant, a low, humming sound that rose and fell like the wind. With this came the rattling of the tortoise shells, not unlike the noise a rattlesnake makes when it shakes the hinged buttons at the end of its tail.

> **2. How does the author help you see the dancers?**

8   After several turns around the dance area, a few of the dancers reached into a hole in the ground, a pit that had a shelter of cottonwood boughs over it. They came up with serpents in their hands. They gave these to other dancers, who put them in their mouths and carried them that way, moving in rhythm with the chant. . . .

9   Many of the snakes were coachwhips, bull snakes, and other harmless reptiles. Some were full-grown rattlesnakes, their rattles buzzing furiously. . . .

10   For a long time I kept my eyes on one dancer, a short, stocky man with hair that flew up when he moved. As he made his circle he faced me for as long as a minute. He came close, and I could plainly see the sun shining on the scales of the snakes he carried. On one turn he had a rattlesnake in his mouth.

11   I stared in horror as the snake arched itself around and attached its jaw to the dancer's cheek. The man went on dancing.

> 3. Why do you think the author includes the detail about the snake biting the dancer?

12   When it came time to change snakes, the man following with the prayer stick unhooked the rattlesnake's mouth from the dancer's face. Two spots of blood remained.

13   "Did you see?" I asked my father in a whisper. "Did you see what that snake did?"

14   "Quiet," my father said. "No talking now."

15   Later, when the dance was over, the two of us sat in the cab of the truck watching fat drops of rain spatter the windshield. . . .

16   "Did you see what that rattlesnake did? How it bit the dancer on the cheek?"

17   "Yes," my father said. "I saw it. It's a mystery, how they do it. . . . Perhaps the dancers have a special way with snakes. The Hopi are protective of their rituals. There are questions we can't answer, because we're not Hopi."

18   We drove across the desert obscured by sheets of rain. My mind returned to what I'd seen that afternoon.

19   Figures of Hopi dancers, snakes of all kinds dangling from their mouths, passed through my imagination like the rain sweeping across the land. I believed the Hopi kept mysterious secrets in their hearts, knowledge of how to cajole a rattlesnake into withholding its venom.

> 4. Why do you think the author believes the Hopi keep "mysterious secrets"?

Descriptive Language

READING FOCUS

Do You See What I See?   Do you see anything when you read the following list of events? "We camped. . . .We saw some people dance with snakes. . . . It rained. . . .We were interested." You probably do not see much because this list lacks descriptive language. The writer of an eyewitness account uses descriptive language to help the reader experience an event. Three types of description that a writer relies on are **sensory language, figures of speech,** and **precise words.**

The following chart defines these three types of description and provides examples of how they can be used to help a reader "see" an event.

Types of Descriptive Language		
Types of Description	**Definition**	**Example**
Sensory Language	words and descriptions that appeal to one or more of the five senses—sight, hearing, touch, taste, smell	The fire crackled and the smell of pine filled the air as I watched the sparks leave trails of light.
Figures of Speech	words or phrases that describe one thing by comparing it to something else—*similes* and *metaphors* are two common figures of speech	**Simile:** The snow fell *like* a whisper. [a comparison that uses the word *like* or the word *as*] **Metaphor:** When he is embarrassed his face *is* a ripe tomato. [a direct comparison that says one thing *is* another thing]
Precise Words	specific words that make a description as clear and sharp as possible	**Inexact words:** He walked across the court to receive the trophy. **Precise words:** The 6'4" basketball player strutted across the court to receive the MVP trophy.

Finding Descriptive Language

■ Re-read "Hopi Snake Ceremonies" on pages 19–20 and find at least two examples each of sensory language, figures of speech, and precise words.

■ In a small group, tell what examples of descriptive language you found and discuss how they helped you picture the events clearly.

| READING SKILL ▶

Implied Main Idea

What Does It All Mean? Suppose you want to tell someone that you are afraid of snakes. You could state your main idea, "I am afraid of snakes." You could also **imply** it by explaining your reaction to seeing a snake: "When I saw the snake, I froze; my heart was pounding and echoing in my ears. My hands were damp and clammy, and sweat was running down my back. My friends were carefully walking around the snake, but I still could not move." To figure out an implied main idea, you need to *read the entire passage* and then put the clues together.

When a writer implies a main idea, he or she gives clues throughout the reading to help you find the main idea.

In the following paragraph, the main idea is implied. Can you identify it? If you have trouble, use the steps on the next page.

TIP The details and description in a reading may help you understand the main idea, but they do not state the main idea directly. To understand the main idea, you must add up all the details and descriptions in the entire passage.

When I visited northern Arizona I went to the Hopi Indian Reservation. I visited a very old village; many of the houses had been built more than four hundred years ago. The houses sat around a central plaza, which served as a meeting place as well as the site of ceremonies and celebrations. One of the houses that I saw was falling apart, but the villagers were working to rebuild it. Newer houses were made of stone carved so the pieces fit together, a traditional Hopi construction technique. Solar panels located on the roofs of the houses provided their power. Solar power allowed the people to have modernized homes, but it did not disrupt the villagers' traditional way of life.

Identifying the Implied Main Idea

Not every paragraph that you read will have a main idea, but you can still figure out the point an author is making by looking at several paragraphs instead of one. These same steps can help.

Follow these steps to find a paragraph's implied main idea:

▶ **STEP 1** Read the paragraph. Ask yourself, "What is the general topic?"

The paragraph tells me about a Hopi village.

▶ **STEP 2** Look at the details and descriptions to decide what points the writer is making about the general topic.

The village is old. There are celebrations and ceremonies in the village. The houses have solar panels.

▶ **STEP 3** Sum up the details in a statement that tells what the paragraph is about. This is the **implied main idea.**

The Hopi villagers live in traditional homes with modern conveniences.

▶ **STEP 4** Confirm the implied main idea with details from the paragraph.

I know tradition is important because the Hopi have ceremonies in the village and use old ways to build new homes. They use solar panels for electricity, which is a modern convenience.

Mapping It Out   The steps for figuring out the implied main idea of a paragraph can also help you find the implied main idea of a longer reading selection. Follow these steps.

1. Divide the reading selection into multi-paragraph sections.

2. Look at the details in each section and ask yourself, "What is the general idea of this section?"

3. Use the ideas from each section to figure out the implied main idea of the whole reading selection.

4. Compare your main idea with the details to confirm your answer.

When you are hunting for the implied main idea of a passage, you need a place to keep track of information. A graphic organizer can help you keep the information in order and see how it all fits together. Suppose the paragraph about the Hopi village on page 22 were part of a longer selection. The following graphic organizer shows how ideas throughout the longer selection would add up to the implied main idea.

Implied Main Idea for a Multi-paragraph Selection

1st Section: The Hopi still perform ceremonies their people have had for hundreds of years.

2nd Section: Hopi villagers live in traditional homes equipped with modern conveniences.

3rd Section: The Hopi use both traditional and modern farming techniques.

Many Hopi are trying to maintain a traditional way of life in the modern world.

YOUR TURN 3 **Mapping the Implied Main Idea**

With three other students, find the implied main idea of "Hopi Snake Ceremonies" by completing the following steps. It may help to create a map like the one above.

■ Assign each group member one of the following parts of the selection: Paragraphs 1–4, 5–9, 10–14, 15–19. Some of the paragraphs in the reading have main ideas, and some do not. Each group member should use the steps in Mapping It Out on page 23 to come up with a main idea statement for his or her section.

■ As a group, look at all of your main idea statements. What do they say about the Hopi snake ceremony? Sum up these main ideas into one overall statement that tells the main idea of the whole reading. This is the reading's implied main idea.

■ Confirm the overall main idea your group has identified by checking it against details from the reading.

Parts of Speech and Context Clues

As you read eyewitness accounts, you may find words you do not know. To figure out a word's meaning, you can think about what is happening in the story and look at other words around it—its **context**. Context clues can come from all the sentences around a word, not just the sentence in which the word appears.

You can also use a word's **part of speech** to understand the word's meaning. The part of speech tells you the word's job in a sentence.

If the word . . .	you know it is . . .
names a person, place, thing, or idea	a noun
shows an action or state of being	a verb
describes something	an adjective

The steps below can help you figure out a word's meaning.

THINKING IT THROUGH — Using Parts of Speech and Context Clues

The following example uses the word *plea* from "Hopi Snake Ceremonies."

Context: "For the Hopi, the snake ceremony is a time to make a *plea* to the spirits for the water the Indians badly need to survive."

▶ **STEP 1** Identify the word's part of speech.

The sentence says, "to make a plea." You make things, so a plea is probably a noun.

▶ **STEP 2** Get clues about the word's meaning from its context.

The plea is made "to the spirits." The Hopi are making a plea because they need rain.

▶ **STEP 3** Use what you may already know to figure out the word's meaning. Check your definition by plugging it into the original sentence.

The Hopi are having a ceremony to ask the spirits for rain. A plea must be a very serious request.

PRACTICE

Use the parts of speech and context clues to find the meanings of these words. They are underlined in "Hopi Snake Ceremonies."

1. rituals (page 19)
2. coachwhips (page 20)
3. stocky (page 20)
4. obscured (page 20)
5. cajole (page 20)

Identifying an Implied Main Idea

When taking a reading test, you will often be asked to identify a reading selection's main idea. Read the following passage and the test item after it. How would you respond to this item on a reading test?

I have had close encounters with snakes. Most snakes are shy and do not want to be around people; however, sometimes they come around houses looking for water. Snakes hide in rock piles, broken logs, or areas with tall grass. When I am walking in an area I think may have snakes, I take a long stick with me. I go slowly and hit the ground with the stick to make noise, so the snakes know I am coming. Then the snakes can get out of the way or warn me that they are there. I have seen many snakes. Many of them are poisonous, but I've never been bitten.

The main idea of this paragraph is that

A. snakes come to houses to find food and water

B. if you shake a stick at a snake, it will not bite you

C. if you take precautions, you do not need to fear snakes

D. people should be terrified of snakes

THINKING IT THROUGH

Identifying an Implied Main Idea

▶ **STEP 1** Read the passage and determine the topic. Then, consider all the details. What one main idea do all of the details support?

The topic is snakes. I think the writer is saying that snakes are not always dangerous.

▶ **STEP 2** Find the answer choice that best matches the main idea you have decided on. Confirm your answer choice by checking to see whether details in the passage support it. Remember that details will help you confirm the main idea, but the answer itself should not be a specific detail.

A. This answer is mentioned in the passage, but it is only a detail.

B. The passage doesn't say this, so it can't be the answer.

C. I think this is the best answer. The writer talked about precautions to take when you think snakes may be around.

D. The writer did not seem to be afraid of snakes at all. This is not the answer.

Writing an Eyewitness Account

An account of the *Titanic* disaster in the words of a survivor…The story of a calf being born, told by the 4-H member who witnessed it…These firsthand observations are called *eyewitness accounts.* Through an **eyewitness account,** a writer can share an experience with someone who has never seen the event. A writer's vivid retelling of an experience can create something like a movie in the reader's mind, allowing him or her to imagine every detail and action.

It is your turn to create a mental movie for your reader. In this workshop you will write a **letter** giving an eyewitness account of a memorable event. You will use detail and sensory language to show your reader an event.

WHAT'S AHEAD?

In this workshop you will write an eyewitness account. You will also learn how to

- **narrate an experience by using details and chronological order**
- **describe by showing rather than telling**
- **choose exact nouns and adjectives**
- **punctuate dialogue**

Prewriting

Choose an Experience

Seeing the World   Have you ever had an experience like this? You are walking through the park when you come across a dog show. You are thrilled to be seeing dogs of every breed. Mainly though, you wish someone were there to witness the event with you. If you have ever witnessed something that you wanted to share with a friend or family member, write about that experience now. Choose an event that you think is interesting. Your goal will be to communicate your interest and enthusiasm to your reader.

An eyewitness account takes the form of a **narrative,** or story. Therefore, **choose an event you saw from beginning to end and can recall clearly.** Your reader should be able to see the account as you did, so be sure you can remember plenty of details.

TIP When choosing experiences, focus on events that you observed rather than participated in. For example, you would write about the soccer game you saw instead of the basketball game you played in.

THINKING IT THROUGH ● Choosing an Experience

Use these steps to choose an event for your eyewitness account.

▶ **STEP 1** Brainstorm a list of events you have witnessed. You might consider

- sports events such as a soccer game or track meet
- school events such as a science fair or art exhibit opening
- natural events such as a flood or sunset
- neighborhood events such as a parade or street festival

▶ **STEP 2** Decide which events

- you find most interesting
- you remember most clearly
- you saw from beginning to end
- you observed without participating in

▶ **STEP 3** Choose the event you most want to write about.

The writer whose example appears below chose the snowboarding exhibition because she had the most fun watching it and remembered the most details from that event.

state championship track meet   Cinco de Mayo parade

my brother's soap-box car race   snowboarding exhibition ✓

 Choosing an Experience

Use the Thinking It Through steps above to brainstorm and evaluate events you have seen and to choose an experience for your eyewitness account.

Think About Purpose and Audience

Share Your Vision   Your **purpose,** or reason for writing, is to share a memorable experience. You would not need to write a letter describing a snowboarding exhibition to a friend who saw it with you. Instead, you would want to tell a friend who was not there about the thrill of watching people glide on the snow and flip through the air.

 Identifying Your Audience

To identify the audience for your eyewitness-account letter, think about a person who would be interested in the event but who did not get to see it.

Gather Events and Details

What Happened?   You are thinking about the snowboarding exhibition and all you can remember is the woman who amazed you by flipping through the air. Your mind may jump to the most exciting moments or to your favorite part of the experience. However, there is more to an eyewitness account than the big moments. You are telling a story, so **think about and list the small events that made up the experience from beginning to end.**

Who, What, Where, How   A good eyewitness account will give plenty of specific information to create a complete picture of the event for the reader. You can flesh out details from the events by asking yourself these four questions.

 KEY CONCEPT

TIP Check your list for unnecessary events—those that don't really add to the narrative. Think about these questions: *Does each event add something to my story? Can I make each event vivid for my audience?*

Who?	questions about **people,** such as *Who took part in this event? Who caught my attention?*
What?	questions that get at **sensory details,** such as *What did I hear* (including **dialogue**), *see, smell, feel, or taste?*
Where?	questions about **places,** such as *Where did this event take place?*
How?	questions about **feelings,** such as *How did I feel watching this event?*

As you list details, you may include terms or information that your reader may not know. Support your descriptions and details with definitions or background information.

KEY CONCEPT

Order Up Once you list the events and details involved in your experience, you'll need to put them in order. **The best order for an eyewitness account is chronological** (or time) **order.** Tell the events in the order they happened—first, second, third, and so on. Chronological order helps the reader follow the story.

To make the chart below, the writer first listed the events that made up the experience. Then, for each event, she listed details that answered the Who, What, Where, and How questions.

Snowboarding Exhibition

Events	Details: Who, What, Where, How?
1. arrived and waited for the competition to begin	who: crowd of people what: cold; people stamping feet to keep warm; crunchy snow where: around the exhibition area; overlooking the half-pipe how: surprised at how many people were there definition: a half-pipe is a U-shaped snow structure, about 10 feet high and 360 feet long; it is like a pipe cut in half
2. half-pipe jam session	what: cheers of the crowd and crunch of the snow how: amazed by the skill of the athletes
3. big air session	what: a woman doing an inverted 720; riders framed by the sky when they were in the air how: impressed by the tricks; want to take more lessons background info: riders fly off a jump and do tricks in the air
4. drove home	how: asked Dad to let me take more snowboarding lessons

 Gathering and Organizing Ideas

- Create a chart like the one above for your event. In the first column, write the events of your experience in chronological order.
- In the second column, include details for each event. Use the questions on page 29 to find details.

Showing Instead of Telling

The stomach flu keeps you away from the state championship basketball game. Later, when you ask a friend about the game, he says, "It was fun. We won." "That's it?" you think. "I want to hear more!"

What you want is a dazzling **description.** You want to hear the stomping of the crowd's feet, smell the sweat of the packed gym, and sense the thrill of cheering your team on to victory. You want your friend to *show* you the victory, not tell you, "We won."

Showing rather than telling allows your **style,** the way *you* express ideas, to come through. Showing lets the reader see through your eyes and hear your **voice,** which indicates your attitude toward the event.

There are several ways to show an event rather than tell it. Show by adding

- dialogue—actual words of the people involved in the events
- precise words—strong verbs, vivid adjectives, precise nouns

You can also show details through **figures of speech,** expressions that describe one thing in terms of another. Two figures of speech you can use are *similes* and *metaphors.*

A **simile** uses *like* or *as* to compare two unlike things.

The runner looked as graceful as a cheetah.

A **metaphor** says directly that one thing *is* another thing.

Her eyes were a well of disappointment.

Here is an example of the difference showing can make.

Telling: Betsy is a clumsy girl.

Showing: Betsy usually trips through a doorway, her arms flailing toward any object that might keep her from falling. "My mom keeps telling me to wear more sensible shoes," she says to cover up the near fall. She then teeters along, looking like a flamingo with a twisted ankle.

This example *shows* by using strong verbs *(trips, flailing, teeter),* a simile *(looking like a flamingo),* and dialogue.

PRACTICE

Turn the following *telling* statements into descriptive *showing* passages.

1. I look forward to lunch every day.

2. Anna-Marie was fascinated as she watched the play.

3. Jordan was angry that his parents had taken him to the symphony.

4. My dog misses me when I am at school all day.

5. Paco looks happy today.

Eyewitness Account

Framework	Directions and Explanations

Introduction
- Salutation
- Attention-grabbing opener
- Statement of the event

■ Open with a greeting, or salutation. (For more on letter form, see page 798 of the Quick Reference Handbook.)

■ Use a question, a story, or a personal note to get your reader's attention. Try two different attention grabbers. Then, ask a peer which is better.

Body
- First event and details
- Second event and details and so on

■ Put each event of your experience in a paragraph. Combine two or more short events into one paragraph.

■ **Elaborate** on each detail from your prewriting chart by using descriptive language that **shows, rather than tells,** what the experience was like. Provide additional **background information,** including definitions, for anything that might be unfamiliar to your audience.

Conclusion
- Your feelings or questions about what you observed
- Importance of the event
- Closing for the letter

■ Leave your reader with an understanding of the importance of the event. You might summarize why you liked the event and wanted to share it. Remember the reason you decided to write this letter. Then, close with a **personal note** to your reader.

 Writing Your Eyewitness Account

Now it is your turn to write a letter about an eyewitness account. As you write, refer to the framework above and the Writer's Model on the next page.

A Writer's Model

The final draft below follows the framework for a letter relating an eyewitness account.

1825 E. Avenue B
Salt Lake City, UT 84103
January 21, 2000

Dear Jake,

    Have you ever seen a snowboarding exhibition? I have been wanting to see one ever since I took a lesson a month ago. This past Saturday, my dad and I went to see a competition. I had a great time, and I got to see some of my favorite professional riders.

    When we arrived, we were surprised by how many people were there. We worked our way through a crowd around the exhibition area and waited for the first session to begin. People were stamping their feet to keep warm in the twenty-degree weather. The gray snow crunching under our feet sounded like pieces of plastic foam rubbing together. My skin felt tight and prickly, and I could see my breath in puffs of fog on the chilly air. As we waited, we talked about how good the half-pipe looked. A half-pipe is snow packed into a U-shape, about 10 feet high and 360 feet long. It is like a big pipe that has been cut in half. Riders drop in from the top at one side and glide down and then up the other side and perform tricks in the air above the pipe. The tricks involve twisting and flipping in the air, usually while grabbing the board with at least one hand.

    As the half-pipe jam session began, I could sense a rush of excitement from the crowd. The whooshing and crunching sounds of the boards in the snow were soon muted by the whooping cheers of the crowd. We were all amazed by how graceful the athletes looked. Once in a while, a rider would fall. One rider missed the edge of

(continued)

Salutation
Attention-grabbing beginning

First and second events

Descriptive language
Details (sensory)

Definition

Precise words

Third event
Details (sensory)

Detail (feelings)

Detail (dialogue)

Fourth event

Detail (sensory)

Descriptive language

Last event

Importance of experience

Closing

the pipe and fell to the other side of the wall. "Ouch!" Dad said, "Did you see that fall? You know that hurt."

The second part of the competition was a "big air" session. In this event, riders go off a jump to perform tricks in the air. Sometimes the riders would hang in the air with one arm extended. It looked like they were holding on to a handle in the sky. The last woman in the exhibition performed an inverted 720, which means she rotated twice in the air while flipping!

I was so excited that I talked the whole ride home, trying to convince my dad to let me take more snowboarding lessons. He must have been impressed, too, because he is going to let me. Next winter when you visit, I will show you what I have learned.

All my best,

Samantha

PEANUTS reprinted by permission of United Feature Syndicate, Inc.

A Student's Model

When you write an eyewitness account you want to *show* the event to your reader. Matthew Hutter, a student from Lansing, Illinois, uses vivid descriptions and dialogue to pull readers into a snowy morning event. The following excerpts are from a letter he wrote.

It was 6:30 in the morning, and I was in dreamland. Suddenly, my dad threw open my bedroom door with a loud bang and started tickling me until I got all tangled up in my covers and fell out of bed.

First event

"Gosh Dad, how can you be so energetic at 6:30 on a Monday morning?" I asked with a bit of an attitude.

Detail (dialogue)

"Look outside and that will answer your question," he said. It was amazing! There were snowflakes of every imaginable size. Some were as big as two inches, and some were as small as an eraser on a pencil. I could hear the wind howling past my window, as the snowflakes flew in every direction. . . .

Second event

Descriptive language

Dad drove slowly to the school because he couldn't see. On the way we saw fallen trees and damaged houses. About a block away from school we saw a tree that had fallen on a car. The whole back of the car was smashed. As we turned the corner to school, I noticed that the whole east side of the school was covered with snow and ice. . . .

Third event

Descriptive language

I put my book on my desk and sat down. I kept the lights off because I liked to listen to the silence of an empty school.

Fourth event

For some odd reason, I was counting the lines on the chalkboard when all of a sudden I heard a buzzing sound and a green glowing light filled the room. I whirled around and to my astonishment, I saw a power box outside, exploding. After about four seconds, the explosion stopped as abruptly as it had started. I walked to Mrs. Hall's room where it was also dark. She was sitting at her desk.

Fifth event

Details (sensory)

"Pretty cool huh," I said. . . .

"Very cool," she said. . . .

Revising

Evaluate and Revise Content, Organization, and Style

Checking It Twice   When revising your first draft or evaluating a peer's, read through it at least twice. In the first reading, look at the content and organization of the letter, using the guidelines below. In the second reading, examine the letter at the sentence level, using the Focus on Word Choice on page 38.

▷ **First Reading: Content and Organization**   Use the chart below to evaluate and revise your eyewitness account so it is clear and interesting.

Eyewitness-Account Letter: Content and Organization Guidelines for Self-Evaluation and Peer Evaluation

Evaluation Questions	▸ Tips	▸ Revision Techniques
❶ Does the introduction include an attention-grabber?	▸ **Underline** the personal note, question, or story that grabs the reader's attention.	▸ **Add** an interesting question or brief story, if necessary.
❷ Does the account provide background information to help the reader understand unfamiliar terms and ideas?	▸ **Put stars** next to terms that might be unfamiliar to readers. **Circle** information that helps the reader understand the terms.	▸ **Add** information or **replace** unclear information with more helpful details.
❸ Are the events retold in chronological order?	▸ **Number** each event in the letter. Check that the numbers match the order in which the events happened.	▸ **Rearrange** events in the order they happened, if necessary.
❹ Are there enough details to make the experience real for the reader?	▸ With a colored marker, **highlight** details and vivid descriptions.	▸ **Elaborate** on the experience by adding descriptive language to help the reader "see" it.
❺ Does the letter's conclusion show why the experience was important?	▸ **Put a check mark** next to statements that explain why the event was important.	▸ **Add** thoughts or feelings that will show the importance of the event.

ONE WRITER'S REVISIONS This revision is an early draft of the letter on page 33.

People were stamping their feet to keep warm in the
gray
twenty-degree weather. The snow ~~was~~ crunching under   **add**
    sounded like pieces of plastic foam rubbing together.   **add**
our feet. My skin felt tight and prickly, and I could see my
in puffs of fog   **add**
breath on the chilly air. As we waited, we talked about how

good the half-pipe looked. A half-pipe is snow packed into
                                    It is like a big   **add**
a U-shape, about 10 feet high and 360 feet long.
pipe that has been cut in half.

Responding to the Revision Process

1. Why do you think the writer added a sentence to the end of this passage?

2. What is the effect of the other additions the writer made to the passage?

PEER REVIEW

If you are evaluating a peer's eyewitness account, ask yourself:

- Can I picture the events the writer is describing?
- Does the order of the account make sense?

▶ **Second Reading: Style** You have already evaluated and revised *what* you say in your letter. Now look at *how* you say it. Look closely at each of your sentences to polish your writing. For this assignment, focus on using precise nouns and adjectives to create clear and descriptive writing. Use the following guidelines and the Focus on Word Choice on the next page to see if you need more exact words in your writing.

Reference Note

For more on **precise words,** see page 31.

Style Guidelines

Evaluation Question	▶ Tip	▶ Revision Technique
Does the account use precise nouns or adjectives that clearly describe the event?	▶ Draw a wavy line under precise nouns and adjectives.	▶ If you see few wavy lines, look through your letter for dull nouns or adjectives. Replace them with descriptive ones.

Word Choice

Precise Nouns and Adjectives

"How was that thing you went to?"

"It was nice."

That brief dialogue did not tell you much, did it? Nouns like "thing" and adjectives like "nice" are *vague*. **Vague words**—words that are not clear or precise—cannot give the reader of an eyewitness account enough information to understand what happened. Precise words quickly tell a reader exactly what a writer means.

■ **Precise nouns** illustrate *particular* persons, places, or things. A *noise* can become a *clank, squeak, clatter, shriek,* or *rattle*.

■ **Precise adjectives** describe nouns specifically. A *fun* amusement-park ride can be transformed into a *thrilling, exhilarating, pulse-pounding* ride.

Do not settle for vague, dull words in your eyewitness accounts. Make an impression with precise words.

TIP If you cannot think of the precise noun or adjective for what you are describing, use a **thesaurus**. Look up the word you want to change and you will find many *synonyms*— different ways of expressing a similar idea.

ONE WRITER'S REVISIONS

The ~~loud~~ *whooshing and crunching* sounds of the boards in the snow were soon
muted by the ~~loud sounds~~ *whooping cheers* of the ~~people~~ *crowd.*

Responding to the Revision Process

How did adding precise words improve the sentence above?

 Evaluating and Revising Your Eyewitness Account

■ First, evaluate and revise the content and organization of your letter following the guidelines on page 36.

■ Next, use the Focus on Word Choice above to help you use more precise nouns and adjectives.

■ Finally, have a peer evaluate your paper. Think carefully about your peer's comments as you revise.

Proofread Your Eyewitness Account

Second Opinions   Errors in your final letter will distract your reader. If you ask another person to proofread the letter after you have gone through it, you will be more likely to find all the mistakes.

Punctuating Dialogue

You may include **dialogue,** exact words spoken by people, in your account. Punctuate dialogue correctly so your reader can tell the dialogue from the rest of the text.

Use quotation marks to enclose a person's exact words.

Incorrect	Ouch Dad said did you see that fall?
Correct	"Ouch!" Dad said. "Did you see that fall?"

■ A direct quotation begins with a capital letter. Commas, a question mark, or an exclamation point can separate the dialogue from the rest of the sentence.

Examples:
The weather person said, "There is a seventy-percent chance of snow today."

"Should I wear boots?" Grace asked.

■ When the expression identifying the speaker interrupts a quotation, commas set off the expression. The second part of the quotation then begins with a small letter.

Example:
"I like to ski," Ian said, "but I don't like to wait in the lines."

■ A period or comma always goes inside the closing quotation marks.

Examples:
"The snowboarding exhibition begins at 9:00 A.M.," said the ticket taker.

Dad remarked, "We have time to get some hot apple cider."

PRACTICE

Punctuate the dialogue in each of the following sentences.

1. It's too bad that snowboarding can be expensive said Henry.

2. When you think about it Isabel sighed everything can be expensive.

3. Do you think individual lessons are less expensive Naomi wondered.

4. Let's take lessons during the winter break Roshanda suggested.

5. I really like the clothes snowboarders wear Cesar added especially the hats.

For more information and practice on **punctuating dialogue,** see pages 630–635.

COMPUTER TIP

If you choose to e-mail your letter, you do not have to write it in one sitting. Most e-mail programs will let you save a draft, so you can work on your letter in stages.

Publish Your Eyewitness Account

Show the World   It is finally time to send your letter. You can now put it in an envelope and mail it, or you can e-mail it in a flash. However, with a few changes you can also use your letter in other ways. Take off the salutation and cut out any direct references to your audience, and you simply have an eyewitness account. What are some things you can do with an eyewitness account?

- Submit your eyewitness account to your local or school newspaper as an article describing the event.

- Submit it to your school's yearbook as a historical record of events in your area, or include it in a class chronicle of the year's events.

- Narrative and descriptive writing are often read aloud. You might read your eyewitness account to classmates.

PORTFOLIO

Reflect on Your Eyewitness Account

Building Your Portfolio   Take time to reflect on your finished letter. Reflecting will help you strengthen your narrative and descriptive writing skills. Think about how you can use this kind of writing for other projects.

- What was the best description in your paper? Why do you think it was effective?

- How did you use sensory language, precise words, dialogue, and figures of speech in your writing? How could you use these types of descriptive language in other forms of writing?

- In what other forms of writing could you use narration? In what kinds of writing assignments would chronological organization be helpful?

Proofreading, Publishing, and Reflecting on Your Eyewitness Account

- Correct any grammar, usage, and mechanics errors. Be especially careful to punctuate dialogue correctly.

- Publish your eyewitness account.

- Answer the Reflect on Your Eyewitness Account questions above. Write your responses in a learning log, or include them in your portfolio.

Connections to Literature

Writing a Descriptive Essay

Eyewitness accounts and descriptive essays are both based on observation. A descriptive essay focuses on an object, such as a statue or car; on a place, such as a room or park; or on a person.

Two important skills to master in preparing to write a descriptive essay are making **observations** and using **spatial organization.**

What You See Is What They'll Get

Close, accurate observation is essential to writing a descriptive essay. After all, how can you describe something unless you know exactly what it looks like? Once you choose the subject of your essay, you should spend at least twenty minutes observing it.

When you write the essay, you'll want to use **descriptive language:** sensory details, figures of speech, and exact words. You will *show* your object rather than tell about it. Asking questions about your subject can help you **develop** and **record** specific details for your essay.

- What colors do you see?
- What size is the object, person, or place in relation to the surroundings?
- What shape or shapes do you see?
- What specific adjectives describe the object, person, or place?
- Can you create a simile or metaphor by comparing the object, person, or place to something else?

As you observe, focus on the special characteristics that draw your attention to the object, person, or place.

Filling Up Space   An effective way to organize a descriptive essay is by describing items according to their location. Using this **spatial organization** technique, you will start your description at a certain point and then move in a logical way around your subject. For example, if you were describing a dog, you might start with the dog's face and then move along his body to his tail. Organize the description in your essay so that it moves

- from top to bottom or bottom to top
- from near to far or far to near
- from left to right or right to left
- from inside to out or outside to in

Words Showing Spatial Organization		
next to	across from	between
down	up	around
close	far	near

Picture This   As you read the description on the next page, notice how author Jamaica Kincaid uses specific details and spatial organization when describing a child's bedroom.

Description of important objects in room

Description moves from wall down to corner

Lying there in the half-dark of my room, I could see my shelf, with my books—some of them prizes I had won in school, some of them gifts from my mother—and with photographs of people I was supposed to love forever no matter what, and with my old thermos, which was given to me for my eighth birthday, and some shells I had gathered at different times I spent at the sea. In one corner stood my washstand and its beautiful basin of white enamel with blooming red hibiscus painted at the bottom and an urn that matched. In another corner were my old school shoes and my Sunday shoes. In still another corner, a bureau held my old clothes. I knew everything in the room, inside out and outside in. I had lived in this room for thirteen of my seventeen years. I could see in my mind's eye even the day my father was adding it onto the rest of the house. Everywhere I looked stood something that had meant a lot to me, that had given me pleasure at some point, or could remind me of a time that was a happy time. But as I was lying there my heart could have burst open with joy at the thought of never having to see any of it again.

Description moves from corner to corner

Explanation of the room's meaning to the writer

Jamaica Kincaid, *Annie John*

Now You Try Think of the object, person, or place you want to describe. Choose a subject with plenty of details.

After you have written a first draft, revise your essay by following the suggestions in the next column.

- Add details about the subject's shape, size, or color.
- Include information about its overall appearance or atmosphere.
- Rearrange information to make the spatial organization clearer.

 Writing a Descriptive Essay

Before you write your descriptive essay, observe your subject for at least twenty minutes and record details. Then, use spatial organization to organize your observations and write your essay. Finally, revise your essay to make it clearer and more descriptive.

Literature

A Descriptive Poem

An eyewitness account captures an event. A *haiku* captures a moment. A **haiku** is a special form of poetry that vividly describes a moment in nature.

Short and Sweet   Japanese poets began writing haiku hundreds of years ago to capture a quick, clear image from nature.

The elements of haiku are simple. The poem has only three lines with a total of seventeen *syllables*. A **syllable** is part of a word that can be pronounced by itself. For example, the word *thunder* has two syllables, *thun–* and *–der*. In a haiku, the first and last lines contain five syllables each. The middle line has seven syllables. Notice the syllables in the following haiku.

> The light•ning flash•es! (5)
> And slash•ing through the dark•ness (7)
> A night-her•on's screech. (5)
>
> Matsuo Bashō, translated by Earl Minor

It's Natural   The traditional topic for a haiku is a moment in nature. Possible topics include a scene, such as a park or nature trail; an event, such as a tornado or a sunrise; an action, such as a bird flying; a feeling, such as an ocean breeze.

Choose a moment that you can describe vividly. Then, brainstorm details about the moment. You can use the senses of smell, hearing, taste, or touch, as well as sight.

Not all details are equal, though. A detail such as *a pretty beach* doesn't paint a specific picture for readers. However, the words *pebbled sand, scattered footprints,* and *abandoned sand castles* do. Notice the precise details in the example haiku. See page 38 for help in using precise words.

Get Choosy   To write your haiku, choose your best details and arrange them into three lines. Then, rearrange and replace words until you have re-created the moment and the feeling you want.

Once you have written a first draft of your haiku, revise it to make sure it

- clearly describes a moment in nature
- uses precise words
- captures a feeling
- contains five syllables in the first and last lines and seven in the middle line

 YOUR TURN 11   Writing a Haiku

Follow the steps above to write and revise a haiku. Share your haiku by reading it aloud or illustrating it and putting it on display.

Examining News

In this workshop you will examine two types of news media. You will also learn how to

- recognize elements of news stories
- compare a TV and print news story

Reference Note

For more on **newsworthiness,** see page 791 in the Quick Reference Handbook.

Reference Note

For more on **hard news** stories, see page 793 in the Quick Reference Handbook.

"**I** saw it on the news, so it must be important." People gather information in many ways, but watching TV news and reading the newspaper are two of the most common ways of gaining information about the world. TV news and newspapers share the goal of presenting true and balanced information, but they differ in their choices of topics and in their presentations.

Look at the News

Writing an eyewitness account is similar to reporting the news. What is the news? It is information about current events. However, it is not an exact copy of those events. Just as your eyewitness account was *your* interpretation of the event, the news is only a *representation* of an actual event, created by the people who report it. It is a representation because we do not experience the actual event; we get information about the event through the words and images that someone else has pieced together.

Get Your News Here   One purpose of producers and editors is to provide the community with a news service. To stay in business, however, commercial news producers need to attract an audience for advertisers, who help the service stay in business. With these purposes in mind, producers and editors consider the following values when they choose what to call news.

- Timeliness   Is the event something people are interested in now? **Hard news** stories usually tell about what has just happened or what is about to happen.

- Impact   Does the event affect the audience? People pay attention to issues that have a direct effect on their lives or issues that they believe will affect them soon, such as their country's security or world conflicts. **Investigative reports,** which expose something most people do not know and are reported with great detail, are often chosen for impact. Another type of story chosen for impact is a **news analysis,** a detailed look at a major issue in which a reporter will draw a conclusion and give opinions.

- Human Interest   Most people like to hear stories about their basic needs, such as food, shelter, and affection. They also like stories about ordinary people experiencing unusual circumstances. **Feature stories,** which profile everyday events, concerns, and interests of the audience, are almost always human interest stories. **Hard news** stories can also show elements of human interest.

- Celebrity Angle   People like to know about celebrities. A story is often more interesting to an audience if it features a movie star or other celebrity. **Features** and **investigative reports** are often about famous people.

Reference Note

For more on **feature news** stories, see page 793 in the Quick Reference Handbook.

 Looking at the News

In a small group, look through newspapers to find news stories that show each one of the news values listed above and on page 44. Then, explain how each story shows that value.

TV News Versus Newspaper News

A news story will usually include the *who, what, where, when, why,* and *how* of an event. How this information is delivered will depend on the form of the news.

Turn It On or Read All About It?   Newspapers and TV news differ in the number of details and visuals used. The audience's emotional reactions may also differ based on the form of the news.

Details   A newspaper article typically provides more in-depth details than a TV news story does. Descriptions, quotations, background information, and narration support the basic information in a newspaper article. The typical TV news story, on the other hand, provides only a quick summary of an event with limited details.

Visuals   Images are important in TV news; they tell half the story. Words—spoken or printed on the screen—form the other half. Because newspapers focus on written details, newspaper editors limit the use of photos. In both TV news and newspapers, the visuals that accompany a story influence our perception of the story.

> **TIP**   The way news is presented affects your reaction to it. A news report can create an emotional reaction such as outrage, happiness, a desire to help, or an urge to change habits. Because the impact of visual images can be intense, TV news tends to create a stronger emotional response than print news.

Here are some ways in which television and newspaper reports might present the same story about a fire differently.

	Newspaper story	TV news story
What kinds of details are in the story?	■ detailed description of the damage done by the fire ■ quotations from fire department officials and the people who were in the building ■ a narration of how the fire started and how it was put out	■ talk of the damage done by the fire ■ clips from interviews with people at the scene of the fire
What are the visuals in the story?	■ a still photo of the scene	■ video footage of the fire burning and interviews at the scene

 Comparing a TV and Print News Story

Collect newspapers for two or three days, and watch the evening news for the same days. Then, find a news story that was covered in both the TV news and the newspaper. Compare the TV and newspaper stories, making a chart like the one above. Then, present your findings orally to the class, answering these questions:

■ Which story gave you the better understanding of the issue or event?

■ Which story had the greater emotional effect? Why?

■ In each case, what do you think was the producer's or editor's purpose in running the story?

1 *Choices*

Choose one of the following activities to complete.

▶ CROSSING THE CURRICULUM: ART

1. Create a World Closely observe an object, such as a machine, a leaf, or a coin, and make a **drawing** of it. You might draw the object you observed for your descriptive essay, an element from your haiku, or another object. Be sure to include as many of the details of your subject as you can.

▶ CONNECTING CULTURES

2. Once upon a Time Folk tales, fairy tales, and other narratives from the **oral tradition** show up in all cultures, often as different versions of the same story. The story "Cinderella," for example, is "Aschenputtel" in Germany and "Yeh-Shen" in China. Think of a folk tale or fairy tale that you enjoy, and research similar stories in other cultures. In a **presentation**, share the stories with your classmates and describe the differences.

▶ CAREER: JOURNALISM

3. On the Beat Think like a reporter for a week. Carry a notebook with you and go out looking for an interesting or unusual story that you could write for your school newspaper. Get together with a few other students, compare observations, and write a **collaborative news story.**

▶ WRITING

4. Do You See Eye to Eye? With a partner, choose an event or object to observe. Observe it at the same time, but do not talk to each other. Write separate **descriptions** of the event or object. Compare your two essays to see if your partner's observation is different from your own. Talk about your differences.

▶ DRAMA

5. The Way I See It Writing is not the only way to present an eyewitness account. Communicate what you witnessed in a **dramatic interpretation.** Assemble a cast to act out the events from the experience you wrote about in the Writing Workshop, or star in a monologue presenting your descriptive essay aloud.

PORTFOLIO

2

Explaining a Process

Reading Workshop

Reading Instructions
PAGE 50

Writing Workshop

Writing Instructions
PAGE 59

Focus on Listening

Following Oral Instructions
PAGE 76

T he blue light blinks at you: "12:00, 12:00, 12:00." With VCR manual in hand, you try to follow the instructions for setting the clock. You punch buttons until, finally, you have completed every step in the directions. You have conquered the VCR! No, wait! It is still blinking "12:00, 12:00, 12:00." In frustration, you howl, "My little sister could write better instructions!"

Instructions are all around us. They come with the electronic gadgets, frozen dinners, and games we buy. When you tell a friend how to bait a fishhook or how to get to your house, you are giving **instructions.** Reading and listening to instructions helps you learn new skills. Writing your own instructions lets you share what you know.

internet**connect**

go. hrw .com

GO TO: go.hrw.com
KEYWORD: EOLang 7-2

YOUR TURN 1 Looking at Instructions

Find several examples of instructions that tell how to do something or how to make something. Look in manuals, books, or magazines. Then, working with a partner, discuss the following questions.

■ Do the instructions tell how to *do* or how to *make* something?

■ Which instructions are the clearest and easiest to follow? Why?

■ In general, do you think it is easier to tell how to *do* something or how to *make* something? Why do you think so?

Reading Instructions

WHAT'S AHEAD?

In this section you will read part of a book chapter that gives instructions. You will also learn how to

- identify an author's purpose for writing
- map out the order of events in a process

You hear the sound faintly at first, but gradually it becomes louder. It sounds like a voice, but it is coming from . . . the chimney? People have been amazed and confused by ventriloquism for centuries. In the following reading selection, Ormond McGill explains how to "throw" your voice so that it sounds like it is coming from an attic or chimney. The selection is a chapter from a book on *ventriloquism*, the art of disguising the real source of a voice.

Preparing to Read

READING SKILL

Identifying Author's Purpose Every time a writer sits down to write, he or she has a *purpose* in mind. **Purpose** is the reason for writing a particular article or paper. As you read the following chapter from Mr. McGill's book on ventriloquism, think about his purpose for writing.

READING FOCUS

Order of a Process In order to learn a process, you need to know what to do and when to do it. As you read the selection and learn how to "throw" your voice, notice the **order** of steps that the author uses. If you drew a map of the steps in the chapter, it might look something like this:

As you read, see if you can identify the separate steps in the process and figure out how they fit together.

Read the following selection about ventriloquism. In your notebook, jot down answers to the numbered active-reading questions in the shaded boxes. Underlined words will be used in the Vocabulary Mini-Lesson on page 57.

from VOICE MAGIC

The Voice in the Attic

BY ORMOND MCGILL

You look up at the ceiling and call out to an imaginary person in the attic. The person answers you! To the amazement of the audience, you carry on a conversation with this mysterious person.

> **1.** What activity is the author describing?

You can choose to direct your conversation toward someone up in the attic or toward someone down in the basement, if you like. The key to this performance is that you stand with your back to the audience. Your mouth movements can then be less restricted when you speak in the voice of the distant person.

Be sure to direct the audience's attention to the attic by pointing to the ceiling and looking up at it. Call out loudly and distinctly in your natural voice. Ask some questions, as though you know there is a person up there. Remember that the success of the illusion depends on convincing the audience you believe in this imaginary presence.

> **2.** What is the main point of this paragraph?

Now, in exactly the same tone and pitch of voice, make the distant voice answer. But, this time, form the words at the back part of the roof of your mouth. Draw your lower jaw back and hold it there. Keep your mouth open. Inhale deeply before you speak. Then, as you speak, exhale in little jerks, using a bit of air for each word. This action will produce a sound that is subdued and muffled, just a little louder than a whisper.

> **3.** Do you have any trouble following each step? Rewrite the steps in your own words.

You can make this distant voice appear to come gradually nearer, too. To do this, call loudly in your natural voice and say, "Come down here!" At the same time, gesture downward with your hand to increase the illusion.

> **4.** What two actions happen at once in the second-to-last paragraph? How do you know?

Have the voice answer, "I'm coming" or "I'm getting closer now," being sure to speak a little louder as the imaginary person approaches.

Here is an example of a conversation you might have with a person who is up inside a chimney:

You: (Look up the chimney.) *Are you up there?*

Voice: *Yes, I'm up here sweeping the chimney.*

You: *What for? The chimney has already been cleaned.*

Voice: *I'm looking for birds' nests.*

You: *That's ridiculous! There aren't any birds' nests up there. . . . Now, come down out of there. . . .*

Voice: *All right. I'm coming . . . . I'm coming.*

5. Why do you think the author includes a sample conversation?

You can then continue your <u>ventriloquial</u> conversation with the voice as the person seemingly comes down the chimney. At every supposed step closer, alter the place from which the person's voice comes. Gradually open the <u>cavity</u> of your mouth and produce the sounds closer to your lips. You will create a larger space inside your mouth so that the voice will appear to come nearer and nearer by degrees.

6. If the author were writing for eight-year-olds, what changes in vocabulary might he need to make here?

By the time the person reaches the bottom of the chimney, your lips should be drawn into a circle, as though you were whistling. This movement enlarges the cavity of your mouth as much as possible.

Here is another conversation you could have with a person on the roof. Start by directing the attention of the audience upward.

You: *Are you up there on the roof, Frank?*

Voice: *Hello down there! What did you say?*

You: (shouting louder) *I said, are you up there on the roof?*

Voice: *I sure am. I'm putting on some shingles.*

You: *Good. Are you almost finished?*

Voice: *I'm just putting on the last one now.*

You: *Fine. Please come on down then. I want to see you.*

Voice: *Okay. I'll come right down.*

You: *Which way are you coming, Frank? . . .*

Keep the conversation going as long as you wish. Make the voice get closer and closer, and use gestures to show that Frank is descending. Finally, as the voice approaches the door, speak in the near ventriloquial voice that you learned in the previous section. Practice hard, and the illusion will be complete.

7. Is the last paragraph a good wrap-up for this selection? Why or why not?

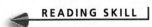

Identifying Author's Purpose

Tell Me Why   No piece of writing happens by accident. Whenever you write a report, story, or essay, you have a *purpose* in mind. An **author's purpose** for writing is the reason he or she writes a particular piece. Sometimes the author's purpose is obvious. After all, the author of an owner's manual for a CD player is not writing to express a love of electronics. That author's purpose is to give information about how to use the CD player.

At other times, the author's purpose will not be as clear. In every kind of writing, however, there are clues to help readers determine the author's purpose (or purposes) for writing. The chart on the next page explains each of the four main purposes for writing and gives examples of clues that point to each purpose.

TIP   Sometimes authors have more than one purpose. For example, an author who writes a story about tigers may write both to entertain readers and to inform them that tigers are endangered.

Purpose for Writing	Explanation	Clues
To inform	Informative writing may teach *how to* or it may teach *what, how,* or *why.* The author's purpose in **"how-to"** writing is to teach readers how to do or make something. **"What-how-or-why"** writing may explain what a paramecium is, how bees make honey, or why the Egyptians built pyramids.	*"How-to" Writing* ▪ step-by-step instructions ▪ numbered steps, lists, or diagrams ▪ words such as *first, next,* and *last* *"What-how-or-why Writing"* ▪ facts, statistics, examples, or definitions explaining what, how, or why ▪ illustrations, diagrams, maps, charts ▪ headings and subheadings
To express	This type of writing expresses an emotion or belief, but does not try to change your beliefs. Poems and personal essays are written to express.	▪ emotional words and expressions ▪ frequent use of the word *I* ▪ words that show value, such as the adjectives *worst, best, terrible, great*
To entertain	Entertaining writing often tells a story, uses drama or humor, or features playful language. Stories, novels, poems, and plays are all written to entertain.	▪ a story that has a beginning, middle, and end ▪ dialogue ▪ rhymes ▪ drama or humor
To influence	Persuasive writing tries to convince the reader to share the writer's opinion.	▪ statements of opinion, backed up by facts, statistics, and examples ▪ words like *should, must,* and *have to* ▪ words that show value, such as the adjectives *worst, best, terrible, great*

Try identifying the author's purpose in the following paragraph. If you get stuck, use the Thinking It Through on the next page.

Over two thousand schools use peer-mediation programs. How does peer mediation work? Starting as early as the third grade, students can be trained to mediate, or help work out, other students' conflicts. Student mediators help peers to understand the source of the conflict, to listen to each other, and to arrive at a "win-win" solution.

Identifying an Author's Purpose

▶ **STEP 1** Read the passage carefully, and look for clues to the author's purpose. Narrow the possible purposes based on the clues.

I see a statistic, "Over two thousand schools. . . ." The purpose could be to inform or to influence.

▶ **STEP 2** Re-read the passage. Look for specific statements to help you confirm the author's main purpose. Make a final decision about purpose.

The statistics don't seem to back an opinion. They seem to explain peer mediation, because the author also says, "How does peer mediation work?" I think the writer is mainly trying to inform me about what and how.

YOUR TURN 2 Identifying an Author's Purpose

Using the chart on page 54 and the Thinking It Through steps above, jot down your thoughts as you figure out the author's purpose in "The Voice in the Attic." Then, complete these sentences:

The author's purpose is _____. I know this because _____.

Order of a Process

READING FOCUS

Take It One Step at a Time Have you ever taught a young child to do something? If you have, you probably had to show the child how to proceed step by step—explaining the first step first, the second step second, and so on, to the end. When you explain something this way, you are following **chronological order** (or **time order**). Most "how-to" writing uses chronological order because it is the clearest way to explain a process.

As you read "how-to" explanations, certain clue words let you know that the steps are listed in chronological order. Some of these clue words appear below.

as	before	finally	next	then
at the same time	during	first	second	while

Charting a Path   One way to make sure you understand the order of instructions is to create a *flowchart*. A **flowchart** is a map that shows the steps in a process. Flowcharts use arrows to indicate the order of steps. Read the following paragraph and the flowchart below it. Notice how you can use a flowchart to show that two steps happen at the same time.

> Veggie pizza is a tasty, nutritious snack. First, you need to make or buy pizza dough. Then, preheat the oven. While the oven heats, put toppings like tomato sauce, mushrooms, onions, and cheese on the dough. Pop it in the oven, and soon you'll have a great snack to share with your friends.

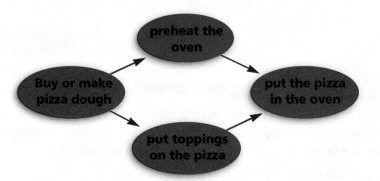

TIP   Some instructions can be hard to follow. Occasionally, writers *omit*, or leave out, details or entire steps because they assume that readers already know them. In the example above, the writer did not tell you to take the pizza out of the oven. However, you would know that in order to eat the pizza, you need to remove it from the oven. Missing steps can be frustrating, but if you draw on your experience, you can often figure out what to do.

YOUR TURN 3   Mapping the Order of a Process

- Re-read "The Voice in the Attic" on pages 51–52. Then, make a flowchart like the one above. Use clue words like those on page 55 to help you figure out the order of the steps necessary to "throw" your voice. Fill in each step as it is listed in the reading selection.

- Would you have added any steps or details about steps? If so, what types of information would you have added? Write your additions below your flowchart.

Identifying Greek and Latin Word Roots

Instructions may define unfamiliar words. If they do not, you can figure out the meanings of some words by using common *word roots*. The **word root** is the main part of a word. Many English roots come from ancient Greek and Latin.

Greek Root	Meaning	Examples
–bio–	life	biology
–cycl–, –cyclo–	circle, wheel	bicycle
–graph–	writing	biography
–ton–, –tonos–	sound	monotone

Latin Root	Meaning	Examples
–aud–, –audi–	hear	audible
–cav–, –cava–	hollow	cave
–lud–, –lus–	trick	elude
–strict–	draw tight	constrict

THINKING IT THROUGH Identifying Greek and Latin Word Roots

The steps below show how word roots can help you define the word *ventri-loquial* from "The Voice in the Attic."

▶ **STEP 1** Separate any roots from the rest of the word, and define them.

–Ventri– means "stomach" or "belly," and –loqui– means "speaking."

▶ **STEP 2** Use the meanings of the roots to guess the word's meaning. Then, see if your meaning makes sense in the word's original context.

–Ventri– plus –loqui– means "belly speaking." The reading selection is about talking without moving your lips, which seems like speaking from the belly.

PRACTICE

Based on their roots, define these words from "The Voice in the Attic."

1. audience (page 51)   **2.** restricted (page 51)   **3.** illusion (page 51)   **4.** tone (page 51)   **5.** cavity (page 52)

Reference Note

For more on **word roots,** see page 754 in the Quick Reference Handbook.

Identifying Sequence of Events

When you take reading tests, you may find questions about the **sequence,** or order, of events in a reading selection. Read the following passage and the question after it. If this were a reading test, how would you go about answering this question?

When you use your imagination, you can create an exercise program for yourself that is fun and healthy. First, decide whether you want to work out for a particular sport or just for overall improved health. If you want to focus on one sport, talk to the coaches at your school to find out which kind of exercises are best for that sport. Then, think about how much time you would like to spend exercising each week. After you have determined when and how often to exercise, try to add a little variety. For example, if you usually work out in a gym, try taking your exercise routine outside. Adding variety to your workout will help you stick with it and be a happier, healthier person.

According to the reading passage, what should you do after you decide when and how often to exercise each week?

A. Choose a type of workout to do.

B. Add variety to your workout.

C. Talk to your coach.

D. Stick with your workout routine.

THINKING IT THROUGH **Identifying Sequence of Events**

▶ **STEP 1** Look for clues in the question to figure out what it is asking.

The question asks what step comes <u>after</u> another step. "After" tells me it is asking about chronological order.

▶ **STEP 2** Scan the passage, looking only for chronological-order clue words or phrases.

I found "first," "then," and "after."

▶ **STEP 3** Re-read the text around each clue word to find the part of the passage referred to in the question.

"<u>After</u> you have determined when and how often to exercise, try to add a little variety." There's my answer.

▶ **STEP 4** Match your response to one of the answer choices available.

Answers **A** and **C** both happen before you decide when and how often to exercise. **D** is the last step mentioned. **B** matches my response best. It must be correct.

Writing Instructions

"Show me how to shoot a free throw," a little boy says to his older sister. To him, she is an expert. Like the boy's big sister, you, too, are an expert on something, no matter who you are or where you live. You have unique skills and talents. Do not keep all of that knowledge to yourself—share it with the world!

One way to share what you know is by writing instructions that teach your reader how to do something. In this workshop you will explore your expert knowledge to write instructions for a process. As you develop your ideas, you may learn even more about that process than you knew when you started.

WHAT'S AHEAD?

In this workshop you will write instructions that tell how to do something. You will also learn how to

- map the sequence of your activity
- identify relevant and Irrelevant detalls
- use transitional phrases
- use commas after introductory phrases

Prewriting

Choose a Topic

How to . . . What? You know how to do so many things. To write your instructions, however, you need to choose just one thing to explain. Instructions can either tell how to make something or how to do something. For example, a recipe for banana bread tells how to make something, while a Web site on dog training tells how to do something.

In this workshop, you will focus on writing instructions for an activity or process that you *do*, rather than for something you *make*. **The topic you decide to write about should be something you know how to do well enough to explain.** After all, you cannot tell someone else how to play the guitar if you have never played a note yourself.

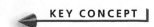 KEY CONCEPT

Brainstorm about things you enjoy doing. If you need help coming up with ideas, think about these questions.

■ If I could do any activity I wanted to right now, what would it be?
■ Am I proud of any special skill, talent, or trick? If so, what?

Evaluate Your Topic

Testing the Water   Before you begin writing, make sure you have picked the right topic. The chart that follows shows how one student evaluated three topics based on these questions.

■ Is the topic something I *do* or something I *make*?
■ Do I know how to do it? How well?
■ Is the topic interesting or unusual?

Topic	Something I do or make?	Can I do it? How well?	Is it interesting or unusual?
✓Flying a kite	Do	Yes. I won third place in a kite contest.	Yes. It's a lot of fun.
Making bread	Make	Kind of. I only made it once.	Yes. Fresh bread tastes great!
Tying my shoes	Do	Yes, I've been doing it since I was four or five.	No. I tie my shoes all the time.

Because the assignment calls for something to *do,* not *make,* the student chose not to write about making bread. He settled on flying a kite as the more interesting topic of the two remaining.

 Choosing and Evaluating a Topic

Make a list of possible topics for your instructions. Then, evaluate your topics by making a chart like the one above. Choose a topic that is something you know how to do well and find interesting.

Reflect on Your Audience and Purpose

Who and Why   Before you start writing, think about your audience and your purpose. First, ask yourself, "Who will be reading my instructions?" It may be your classmates, a teacher, or a younger brother or sister. In any case, you should write for readers who do not know how to do the activity you have picked but want to learn.

Next, think about your purpose. Your purpose answers the question, "Why am I writing?" You are writing for a very specific reason: to teach someone how to do something. **To make your instructions effective, make them as clear and simple as possible.** Notice how the student writing about kite flying analyzed his audience in the Thinking It Through below.

TIP   Be sure that your **voice,** or the sound of your writing, is clear and straightforward. Use vocabulary that your audience will understand, and avoid humor that may not come across in writing.

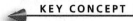 **KEY CONCEPT**

THINKING IT THROUGH

Writing for a Specific Audience

▶ **STEP 1** Ask yourself:

- Who is my audience?

    students my age who have no experience with kites

- What is my purpose?

    to explain how to fly a kite

▶ **STEP 2** Consider any special words or names that go with your topic. Decide how you might make these ideas clear to a beginner.

There aren't any special words or names I know of in kite flying. Someone might need to know where to get a kite, though.

▶ **STEP 3** Identify any parts of this activity that are easier to show than tell. Decide how you can make these parts clearer to your audience.

It's easier to show than to tell how a kite takes off. I can write down the steps as I imagine getting a kite off the ground to make this action clear.

Thinking About Your Audience and Purpose

With your topic in mind, consider the audience for your "how-to" paper and the purpose for which you are writing it. To figure out how to match your instructions to your audience, use the Thinking It Through steps above.

TIP Since you already know each step of the process, you probably have all the information you need. However, if you have any questions, use **reference materials and resources,** such as books, articles, videotapes, or the World Wide Web.

Gather and Organize Information

Pretend You Are Talking to a Two-Year-Old   Even if your audience does not include young children, pretend for a moment that it does. Then, jot down every single thing a small child would need to know. Make two lists: one for the materials needed to complete your activity and the other for the steps. Later, as you put the steps in order, you can decide whether you have included more steps than your audience will need.

Order Put Directions In   Re-read the heading to the left. It does not make sense because it was written in the wrong order. Putting steps in the correct order helps your audience successfully follow your instructions. Most instructions are written in **chronological** (or time) **order.** They explain what comes first, what comes second, and so on.

You can organize your list of steps by numbering each step to show its place in the process. To decide the order of your steps, ask yourself the following questions.

■ Is one step a better place to start than the others? What is the very first thing a beginner should do? Make this step the first step.

■ Is there any step on which other steps depend? If so, this step must come before the ones that depend on it.

The following example shows one student's list of steps and materials. First, the student wrote down all the steps. Then, he added numbers showing the correct order of the steps.

Topic: how to fly a kite

Materials: a kite and string

Steps: 2. Hold the kite so the wind can pick it up.
3. When the wind catches the kite, let out string so the kite won't crash.
1. Find out what direction the wind is blowing.
5. Walk backwards to keep the string tight.
6. When you're done, roll up string slowly and the kite will come down.
4. As the kite gets higher, gradually let out more string.

Did You Leave Something Out?   Remember that your audience members are counting on you to teach them about this activity, so **make your instructions as complete as possible.** Remember to define words that your audience might not understand. Also, look back over your steps while you imagine doing the activity. Then, add any missed steps and adjust your numbering. Notice how the student writing about kite flying put his first three steps in order but then realized he needed to add a new step one.

◄ KEY CONCEPT

> **1.** Find an open space.
> Steps: **2** ~~1.~~ Find out what direction the wind is blowing.
> **3** ~~2.~~ Hold the kite so the wind can pick it up.
> **4** ~~3.~~ When the wind catches the kite, let out string so the kite won't crash.

TIP   As you look over the list of steps that you brainstormed, think about your audience. Take out any steps that seem unnecessary for your particular audience. For example, you may need to tell a younger audience how to find out which way the wind is blowing, but you probably would not need to provide this information for adults.

Map It Out   Another way to make sure you have included each step in the correct order is to create a *flowchart*. A **flowchart** is a map of an activity or process. Most flowcharts are linear; that is, they go from step to step in chronological order. Seeing each step in the order it happens helps you make sure your instructions are complete.

How to Fly a Kite

| Step 1: Find an open space. | → | Step 2: Find out what direction the wind is blowing. | → | Step 3: Hold the kite so the wind can pick it up. | → | (and so on) |

YOUR TURN 6   **Planning Your Instructions**

Follow the examples on pages 62–63 as you complete these steps.

- Make a list of the materials your activity requires.
- Make a list of the steps in your activity. Put the steps in chronological order by writing numbers next to them.
- Check for steps you may have left out, and add them. Renumber your steps if necessary.
- Finally, create a flowchart of the activity.

TIP   Have a classmate or parent look over your flowchart before you start to write. Tell that person to imagine doing the activity described, and then ask if any of the steps were unclear or if you left out important information.

Writing

Instructions for a Process

Framework	**Directions and Explanations**

Introduction
- Interesting opening
- Statement of topic
- Reason for learning

You may grab your reader's attention with advice about when to use the process or do the activity. Include a **statement of the topic** so your audience knows what you are teaching them to do. Make your reader pay attention by giving a **reason for learning** this skill—perhaps it is fun, useful, or impressive.

Body
- Materials
- Step 1 explanation (with relevant details)
- Step 2 explanation (with relevant details)
and so on

Start by giving a **list of materials** needed. Make sure you support this list with explanations and examples. To organize the body of your paper, use these tips:

- Think back to when you learned the process or activity. Were there steps that confused you? Elaborate on those steps with relevant details.
- If any step requires a long explanation, put that step in its own paragraph.
- Use transition words such as *first, next,* and *finally,* and prepositional phrases such as *at the same time.* (For more on **transitions,** see page 302.)

Conclusion
- Restatement of reason for learning
- Advice for doing process

Summarize the reason for learning the activity. Finally, give your reader some parting **advice,** such as a general tip on how to be successful or how to enjoy doing the activity.

 Writing Your First Draft

Now it is your turn to draft instructions. As you write, refer to the framework above, the Writer's Model on the next page, and the Critical Thinking Mini–Lesson on page 68.

A Writer's Model

Go Fly a Kite!

Get up off the couch! Outside it is a beautiful, windy day. It is far too nice to sit and watch reruns on television. Windy days are made for flying kites. Learning how to fly a kite is simple, and flying kites can be a fun form of exercise. Nothing beats seeing a kite sail high into the clouds.

Interesting opening

Statement of topic
Reason for learning

Of course, the first thing you need is a kite and a ball of string. You can buy your kite and string at a toy or hobby shop. Most kites need to be assembled before you can fly them. Follow the instructions in the package to put your kite together. Then tie the loose end of the string to the hole in the middle of the kite and wait for a windy day.

Materials

When the perfect day arrives, one with wind that is not too strong, find an open space, such as a field, where you can fly your kite. It is important not to fly it near trees or power lines because the kite can get caught, and you might not get it back. Then you will be back to watching reruns on TV.

Step 1
Explanation

Before flying your kite, figure out which way the wind is blowing. You can do this by observing the way the trees are bending or by throwing a few blades of grass into the air. To begin flying your kite, stand with your back to the wind and hold the kite up so the wind can catch it. Let out about three feet of string or else your kite will just crash after the wind hits it. If the day is not very windy, you may need to get your kite started by running while holding the kite up with a little string let out.

Step 2
Explanation

Step 3
Explanation/Step 4
Explanation

Once the wind catches your kite, gradually let out more and more string so the kite can climb higher into the air. At the same time, walk backwards a few steps to keep the string tight. If the string has too much slack, the kite may start to dip or act as though it is going to crash. Now

Step 5
Explanation
Step 6
Explanation

(continued)

(continued)

that your kite is up in the air, you can decide how long to fly it and how high you want it to go.

Eventually, you will need to bring your kite down. After all, you will probably need to do your homework sometime! To bring your kite back in, slowly wind up the string. Try not to pull your kite in too fast or it may crash. If your kite does start to crash, slowly let out more string and wait for the wind to catch the kite. Then, start winding up the string again, more slowly and carefully this time.

Flying a kite is a great way to spend a breezy afternoon. If you follow these steps carefully, you will have something more fun to do than sitting inside and watching reruns. You may even decide to form a kite club with some friends and trade or build kites. So on the next windy day, get up off of the couch. Go fly a kite!

Step 7

Explanation

Restatement of reason for learning

Advice

A Student's Model

Stephanie Pearl wrote these instructions as a student at Randolph Middle School in Randolph, New Jersey. Notice that the following excerpt from her paper gives clear, step-by-step instructions in chronological order.

How to Choose a Puppy

Everyone knows that puppies are cute. What some people don't know is that a puppy requires planning and responsibility, even before you bring it home. By following the steps below, you can find the puppy that is right for you and make a home that is right for your puppy.

Before adopting a puppy, you must prepare for one. Make sure you have a crate or area set aside in your home for the puppy to stay in when you are not around. Have all the supplies you will need before you bring the puppy home. You should have a collar and leash, some toys, and puppy food. You may want to consider fencing in a part of your yard.

After you have decided to get a puppy, and you are prepared and have all necessary supplies, you need to decide where to get one. The best place to go adopt a puppy is an animal shelter. Animal shelters usually have a wide variety of puppies that people have abandoned.

When choosing a puppy, you should look for one with good qualities. The puppy should not be too timid or too aggressive. It should respond to noises and allow you to pet it. It should appear healthy and have all necessary vaccinations.

After picking out a puppy you like, take that puppy into a separate room. Sit down on the floor, and call it. The puppy should come, or at least look at you. If it does not come, walk over and pet the puppy, letting it smell your hand first. If it cringes or snarls, you may want to think twice about adopting it. Overly aggressive or submissive puppies require a lot of patience to train. . . .

Interesting opening

Statement of topic

Step 1
Explanation

Step 2
Explanation

Step 3
Explanation

Step 4

Explanation

Relevant and Irrelevant Details

"So then, at the end of the movie, the aliens landed on earth, and they had these really spiffy spaceships, but they weren't shaped like flying saucers. They were more like garbage cans. Oh, I got grounded today because I didn't take out the garbage. Anyway, the aliens came down and…"

Have you ever had friends who rambled this way about anything that popped into their heads? People ramble when they talk or write because they can't separate relevant and irrelevant details.

A **relevant detail** is one that gives information about the main idea. In instructions, relevant details are ones that help explain the process and provide **logical support** for ideas and explanations. **Irrelevant details** are just fluff. They do not give necessary information, and they may distract and annoy your reader. Look at the examples in the following paragraph.

There *is* a right way to make a peanut butter sandwich **(main idea)**. First, you should use a butter knife or some other dull knife so that you can easily spread the peanut butter without cutting yourself **(relevant detail)**. Once, when I made a sandwich, I almost cut my hand, but I didn't **(irrelevant detail)**.

To identify relevant and irrelevant details, ask yourself these questions.

- What is the main idea of the paragraph?
- Does this detail help me understand the main idea?

For instructions, you should also ask,

- Does this information tell me how to do the task better?

Reference Note

For more on **main idea,** see page 289.

PRACTICE

The following sentences are instructions for shooting a basketball free throw. On a piece of paper, number from 1 to 5. Write *R* if the sentence following the number in brackets contains relevant details. Write *I* if the sentence contains irrelevant details.

> You can shoot free throws much better if you learn the technique. [1] Before you shoot, help yourself relax by following a routine, such as bouncing the ball or taking a deep breath. [2] My brother likes to play basketball, but he's a lousy free-throw shooter. [3] Hold the ball out in front of you with your hands on the sides. [4] Basketball is one of the most popular sports in America today. [5] As you release the ball, push the ball off your hands with a flip of your wrist.

Revising

Evaluate and Revise Content, Organization, and Style

Doing a Double Take   Whether you are evaluating and revising your own paper or evaluating a peer's, read the paper twice. The first time, look at big issues, such as content and organization. The second time, ask whether each sentence is as clear as it can be.

▶ **First Reading: Content and Organization**   Use this chart to evaluate and revise your paper so your instructions are effective and easy to follow.

COMPUTER TIP

If you are using a computer, you can format your paper to make **editing** (revising and proofreading) easier. Double-space your text and leave wide margins so you will have room for comments and corrections.

Instructions for a Process: Content and Organization Guidelines for Self-Evaluation and Peer Evaluation

Evaluation Questions	▶ Tips	▶ Revision Techniques
❶ Does the introduction clearly state what the activity or process is?	▶ **Put a star** next to the statement that tells what activity or process will be explained.	▶ If needed, **add** a sentence telling what the activity or process is.
❷ Does the introduction give the reader a reason to learn the activity or process?	▶ **Underline** the reason for learning the activity or process.	▶ **Add** a reason why the reader should learn to do the activity or process.
❸ Do the steps show a logical progression of ideas?	▶ Write a **number** in the margin next to each step and compare the numbers to the flow chart from prewriting.	▶ **Rearrange** steps that are confusing or out of order, if necessary.
❹ Do any steps need additional explanation?	▶ Use a **highlighter** to mark any explanation that follows a step.	▶ **Elaborate** any step that needs more explanation.
❺ Are all details relevant to the instructions?	▶ Look at the highlighted explanations. **Write** an *R* by relevant details and an *I* by irrelevant ones.	▶ **Delete** all irrelevant details, and **replace** them with helpful, relevant details and examples.
❻ Does the conclusion restate the reason for learning this process and end with advice?	▶ **Put a check mark** next to the sentence that restates the reason for learning the process. **Draw a wavy line** under the advice for using the process.	▶ **Add** a restatement of the reason for learning the process. **Add** some advice for using the process successfully.

ONE WRITER'S REVISIONS Study this revision of an early draft of the essay on pages 65–66.

delete

elaborate

> Before flying your kite, figure out which way the wind is blowing. You can do this by observing the way the trees are bending or by throwing a few blades of grass into the air. ~~I like the grass method because when I throw the blades in the air, my dog jumps up and tries to catch them. It is very funny to watch.~~ To begin flying your kite, stand with your back to the wind and hold the kite up so the wind can catch it. Let out about three feet of string or else your kite will just crash after the wind hits it. ∧ *If the day is not very windy, you may need to get your kite started by running while holding the kite up with a little string let out.*

PEER REVIEW

As you read a peer's instructions, ask yourself, Does this paper make me want to try out the activity or process it explains? Why or why not?

Responding to the Revision Process

1. Why do you think the writer deleted two sentences?

2. Why do you think the writer added a sentence?

▶**Second Reading: Style** Now you are ready to begin fine-tuning the individual sentences in your instructions. One way to improve your sentences is by using **transitional phrases,** phrases that connect ideas.

Style Guidelines

Evaluation Question	▶ Tip	▶ Revision Technique
Are there any phrases that help the reader move from one step to another?	▶ **Circle** each transitional phrase.	▶ **Add** transitional phrases to paragraphs without any circled phrases.

Prepositional Phrases

Some transitional phrases are *prepositional phrases*. A **prepositional phrase** consists of a preposition followed by a noun or pronoun and any modifiers of the noun or pronoun. Prepositional phrases can help you show the order of steps involved in a process. Prepositional phrases help you improve the **coherence,** or connectedness, of your instructions by showing how all of your ideas relate to one another. Using a tightly knit style will help you achieve your purpose for writing instructions.

Below are a few examples of prepositional phrases. In each example, the preposition is in boldface.

about 3:00	**at** the same time	**during** this step
after lunch	**before** finishing	**until** dawn

Reference Note

For more on **coherence,** see page 297.

Reference Note

For more information and practice on **prepositional phrases,** see page 371.

ONE WRITER'S REVISIONS

> Once the wind catches your kite, gradually let out more and more string so the kite can climb higher into the air. *At the same time,* ∧ Walk backwards a few steps to keep the string tight.

Responding to the Revision Process

How did adding a prepositional phrase improve the instructions?

YOUR TURN

Evaluating and Revising Your Instructions

- First, evaluate and revise the content and organization of your essay using the guidelines on page 69.
- Next, use the Style Guidelines on page 70 and the Focus on Sentences above to help you add transitional phrases to your instructions.
- If a peer evaluated your paper, think carefully about each of your peer's comments as you revise.

Publishing

Proofread Your Instructions

Reference Note
For more on **proofreading**, see page 13.

Catching Your Mistakes   Errors in the final draft of your instructions will be distracting to your readers. Mistakes may even steer your readers in the wrong direction as they try to learn from your instructions. Have a peer help you find mistakes.

Grammar Link

Commas with Introductory Prepositional Phrases

A **prepositional phrase** includes a preposition, a noun or pronoun, and any modifiers of the noun or pronoun. An introductory phrase is one that comes at the beginning of a sentence.

You need a comma after two or more introductory prepositional phrases.

Example:
At the ends of the basketball court, you should see the two backboards.

Use a comma after a single introductory prepositional phrase only if you need the comma to avoid confusing your reader.

Example:
After breakfast, sausage production begins. [A comma is needed so that the reader does not read "breakfast sausage production."]

Reference Note
For more information and practice on using commas with **introductory prepositional phrases,** see page 613.

PRACTICE

Decide whether a comma should follow any of the introductory prepositional phrases in each sentence. Rewrite the sentence on your paper with the comma in the correct place, or write *C* on your paper for correct sentences. The introductory prepositional phrases have been underlined for you.

Example:
1. By the mid-twenties advertising was a mainstay of American society.
1. C

1. After World War I soldiers returned home to a booming economy, and advertising became a billion-dollar business.

2. To many consumers in the twenties a product endorsement by a famous person was as good as a guarantee.

3. At this time even Eleanor Roosevelt promoted a breakfast food.

4. Across the nation during this decade new stores were built to fill the demand created by the advertisers.

5. In the mid-twenties one grocery chain had 14,000 stores.

Using illustrations   Illustrations can make your instructions clearer for your audience. You can draw diagrams, maps, or illustrations by hand and add them to your final draft.

If you prefer, you can take photographs of a friend following your instructions. Then, paste the photos onto your final paper. If available, use a scanner to put photos into a computer file, or use a digital camera. Using any of these techniques will help you create an impressive, illustrated final draft.

Reference Note
For more on **illustration,** see page 789 in the Quick Reference Handbook.

Publish Your Instructions

Putting It All Together   Now your instructions are ready to be used. How can you get those instructions into the hands of people who need them?

■ Make an illustrated book of your instructions to present to your school library. You might get together with several classmates and combine your instructions into one handy manual.

■ Give your instructions to a class in a different grade. Arrange a demonstration of your activity or process for the class.

Reflect on Your Instructions

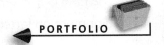
PORTFOLIO

Building Your Portfolio   Finally, it is time to reflect on your instructions. Reflecting can help you improve on future assignments.

■ Which details and explanations in your instructions are the most effective? Why do you think they are more effective than others?

■ Think about how you planned the order of steps in your instructions. Did you use any techniques that you might use in another type of writing? What are these techniques?

YOUR TURN 9   Proofreading, Publishing, and Reflecting on Your Instructions

■ Proofread to correct grammar, usage, and mechanics errors. In particular, look for comma errors.

■ Publish your instructions so that they can be used.

■ Answer the Reflect on Your Instructions questions above. Record your responses in a learning log, or include them in your portfolio.

TIP   As you proofread your instructions, you may find **reference materials,** such as language handbooks, dictionaries, and Part 3 of this book, helpful.

Explaining "How-to" for Tests

Sometimes a prompt on a writing test asks you to explain how to make something or the process involved in doing something. The essay that you write for this type of prompt is called a **"how-to" paper.** To the right is a "how-to" prompt from a writing test. How would you answer this prompt?

Making arts and crafts is a popular hobby. Think about something you like to make, such as a model airplane or tie-dyed T-shirts. Write a letter to a friend explaining how to make your favorite craft. Be sure to include examples and specific details to explain your steps.

THINKING IT THROUGH **Explaining "How-to" for Tests**

▶ **STEP 1**

- First, decide exactly what the prompt is asking you to do.
  I need to explain how to make a craft, such as a model airplane.

- Then, figure out who the audience for your paper is.
  The audience is a friend.

- Finally, decide on the form of your paper.
  The form is a letter.

  (For more on **letters,** see page 798 in the Quick Reference Handbook.)

▶ **STEP 2** Decide the topic of your "how-to" paper.

▶ **STEP 3** Brainstorm a list of the steps that readers will need to follow or understand. Then, put the steps in order by using a flowchart or some other graphic organizer.

▶ **STEP 4** Use your brainstorming notes to write your "how-to" paper. Write an introductory paragraph that tells readers what to expect from your paper. Then, write other paragraphs that thoroughly explain each step. Make each major step its own paragraph, and include a list of the materials needed.

▶ **STEP 5** Re-read your "how-to" paper, and add details and explanations if you need to make steps clearer.

TIP When writing a process explanation for a test, do not use illustrations to explain your steps. Also, write in essay format, without numbered lists. Your essay will be evaluated only on the way you express yourself in words, not numbers or illustrations.

Giving Directions

Oral Directions   Have you ever given someone directions to get somewhere and wound up explaining the steps over and over again to a confused listener? Giving directions orally is difficult because you usually do not have an opportunity to plan what you will say. Remembering a few steps can make you a better guide when someone asks for your help.

■ Ask questions to make sure you understand where the person asking for directions wants to go.

■ Visualize the route in your mind and explain it step by step.

■ Mention well-known landmarks to help the lost person get oriented. A landmark does not have to be an important building or historical place. Often, the best landmarks are signs for businesses, colorful buildings, or places with odd names.

Written Directions   Of course, many times you need to give written directions. For example, if you throw a birthday party for your best friend, you might include directions in the invitation to help your friends find your house. When you give written directions, you should follow the same steps for oral directions, with the following additions.

■ Write the instructions in numbered or bulleted steps or other manageable chunks instead of in paragraph form.

■ Write legibly. You may choose to write **cursive** or **manuscript,** but be sure that your audience will be able to read the directions.

■ Draw a map on the same page. The combination of written directions and a map will make it more likely that people will easily find your party.

YOUR TURN 10   Giving Directions

Think of a place close to your home or school, and explain to a classmate how to get there. Then, write down directions to the same place and show them to your classmate. Switch roles, and then discuss these questions with your partner.

■ Which was easier: giving oral or written directions? Why?

■ Which is more effective when you ask for directions: getting them orally or having them written down? Why?

Talk

Listen

Following Oral Instructions

WHAT'S AHEAD?

In this workshop you will learn how to follow oral instructions. You will also learn how to

- practice active listening skills
- take notes as you listen
- ask questions for understanding

"**A**ttention, students! All students with last names beginning with A through M should report to Room 206 at 10:15 A.M. for school pictures. Students with names beginning N through Z report to Room 208 at 10:45 A.M. Afterwards, please turn in order forms in Room 315."

Do announcements like this make your head spin? You probably hear oral instructions every day. For example,

- in class when your teacher gives an assignment
- when your sister explains how to get to the museum
- when your uncle explains how to bait a hook and clean a fish

You can improve your ability to follow oral instructions by learning to listen.

Learning to Listen

The ability to follow oral instructions is a skill you need for life. Why is it sometimes hard to follow spoken instructions? Maybe you "tune out" for a minute, only to realize later that you have missed something important. Maybe the speaker uses terms that you do not understand.

Most people *hear* what is being said, but they may not really *listen*. Listening is an active process. It involves trying to interpret the main points, as well as *verbal* and *nonverbal cues*. **Cues** are hints or clues a speaker gives to help listeners follow speech. **Verbal cues** are spoken hints, while **nonverbal cues** are unspoken hints such as movements, facial expressions, and gestures. The chart on the next page shows some common verbal and nonverbal cues.

Verbal Cues	Nonverbal Cues
clue words such as *first, next, last,* and *in conclusion* to help the listener follow along	"body language," or movements and facial expressions that show the speaker's mood or attitude
repetition of important phrases or ideas	demonstrating the activity or using hand movements to emphasize important points
emphasis on important information, such as speaking more loudly or stressing certain words	facial expressions or movements that ask for questions or encourage the listener's participation

Tricks for Tuning In   In addition to using verbal and nonverbal cues, you should focus on the speaker to get the main points. You will miss important information if you are gazing out the window or doodling instead of taking notes. To keep yourself from "tuning out," try to avoid such distractions.

Taking Notes

As you listen to oral instructions, you may need to take notes. Jotting down a few key phrases and steps can help you remember what was said. As you take notes, keep the following points in mind.

- Do not try to write down every word. Instead, focus on key words and phrases.
- Abbreviate frequently used words or phrases. Just remember to make a key so you do not forget what your abbreviations mean.
- Jot down questions or put question marks by steps that confuse you. Look back to your notes if the speaker asks for questions.

Asking Questions

As you listen, think about whether you are understanding what you hear. Ask questions to clarify anything you do not fully understand. You ask questions all the time, but you might not realize that there are "dos and don'ts" when it comes to asking questions. The chart on the next page lists some of the most important "dos and don'ts" to remember when you need to ask a question.

Reference Note
For more on **eliminating barriers to effective listening,** see page 767 in the Quick Reference Handbook.

TIP   Ask the speaker to listen to you summarize his or her instructions to ensure that you have understood them.

If it is not possible to confirm your understanding through summarizing or questioning, take a moment to organize your notes. Remember, it is much easier to organize your notes while the instructions are still fresh in your mind than it will be if you put if off.

What to Do	What Not to Do
Wait until the speaker pauses before you ask a question.	Do not blurt out a question while the speaker is still talking.
Ask specific questions that show you have been listening.	Do not ask vague questions such as "What are you talking about?"
Ask in a clear, loud voice.	Do not mumble the question.
Read notes back to the speaker to make sure they are correct.	Do not assume you can figure out anything you did not understand.

 Following Oral Instructions

For this activity, work in groups of three or four students. Each of you will need several sheets of paper and a pen or pencil.

1. Draw a simple picture. Do not let anyone else in your group see it.

2. Describe your picture. Each of the other group members should listen, take notes, ask questions, then draw the picture.

3. Share your picture with the group. Discuss the similarities and differences of the pictures each group member created.

4. Complete the steps above using a picture and oral instructions from each member of the group. Then, talk about what group members learned about giving and listening to instructions.

Reference Note

For more on speaking and listening in a **group discussion,** see page 763 in the Quick Reference Handbook.

2 *Choices*

Choose one of the following activities to complete.

▶ CROSSING THE CURRICULUM: ART

1. That Covers It Create a **cover for a "how-to" video** based on the paper you wrote. Remember that a cover should catch people's attention and give them information about the video. Include pictures, eye-catching headlines and titles, and a brief summary of the contents of the program.

▶ CAREERS

2. What Goes on in Your Mind? Do you ever wonder how your favorite author develops ideas for his or her books? Get together with two or three classmates and write a **letter** asking an author about his or her creative process. Compare the response you receive with those received by your classmates.

▶ CROSSING THE CURRICULUM: HISTORY

3. How It Was Done Choose an activity, such as mummification or shipbuilding, and find out how it was performed in an ancient civilization. Research the step-by-step process used in the activity. Create a **flowchart** of the process, including important steps and explanations. Share what you have learned with a small group of classmates.

▶ CROSSING THE CURRICULUM: SCIENCE

4. What Makes It Tick? Are you the kind of person who likes to figure out what makes things work? Choose a simple mechanical device like a doorknob or a kitchen tool, and figure out what makes it work. Explain the process in a **technical drawing,** or write a short **essay** explaining how this device works.

▶ CREATIVE WRITING

5. How to Create a Snicker Poetry is a form of writing that is meant to entertain or express, often through humor. A process with missed steps, or a simply ridiculous process, can be funny. Tickle someone's funny bone by writing a **humorous "how-to" poem.**

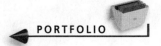
PORTFOLIO

3 Looking at Both Sides

Reading Workshop

Reading an Advantages/ Disadvantages Article
PAGE 82

Writing Workshop

Writing an Advantages/ Disadvantages Essay
PAGE 91

Focus on Viewing and Representing

Making a Documentary Video
PAGE 111

W hen you walk into a supermarket, you know that similar types of foods are grouped together. For example, if you need an orange, you know that you should go to the produce section. Sorting items into different categories is known as **classification.** The supermarket organizes the items in a way that makes sense so you can find them quickly and easily.

Classification is a good way to sort not just things but also ideas. For example, when you need to make a decision, you can sort out the pros and cons, or advantages and disadvantages, of a topic.

internetconnect

go.
hrw
.com
GO TO: go.hrw.com
KEYWORD: EOLang 7-3

YOUR TURN 1   Understanding Classification

On your own paper, brainstorm the pros and cons, or advantages and disadvantages, of being a seventh-grader or of having an older/younger sibling. Here is an example.

Having a Little Brother

Advantages	Disadvantages
Someone looks up to me.	Sometimes I have to baby-sit instead of being with my friends.

Compare your responses with those of another student.

Reading an Advantages/ Disadvantages Article

Would you like to attend an all-girls or all-boys school? The article on the next page investigates the advantages and disadvantages of all-girls schools. The writer's goal is to present a balanced look at the topic of single-sex schools. Once you have read about the advantages and disadvantages of all-girls schools, you can make your own decision about the topic.

Preparing to Read

READING FOCUS

Advantage/Disadvantage Structure   The author of the following article organizes her discussion of **advantages** and **disadvantages,** or pros and cons, in a certain way. As you read, watch for clues the author gives to let you know whether she is discussing an advantage or a disadvantage.

READING SKILL

Making Inferences: Drawing Conclusions   Sometimes, instead of fully explaining *every* point in an article, an author leaves some "blanks" for the reader to fill. In order to fill in these blanks, the reader must *draw conclusions.* Readers **draw conclusions** by combining the details found in an article with what they already know about the topic. As you read the following article, look for places where the author leads you to draw your own conclusions.

Read the following magazine article. In your notebook, jot
down answers to the numbered active-reading questions in
the shaded boxes. You will refer to the underlined words
when you complete the Vocabulary Mini-Lesson on page 89.

from Junior Scholastic

FOR GIRLS ONLY?

Do girls get a better education in all-girls schools?
Would you want to go to a school where there were no
students of the opposite sex?

by Alexandra Hanson-Harding

1 Thirteen-year-old Maryam Zohne
used to be shy. "I always used
to try to sneak out of giving presentations in school,"
she says. In sixth
grade, she never
spoke up in class.
Not any more.
Now in the eighth
grade, she is the president of the
student body at her school. What
made the difference? For the past
two years, Maryam has gone to an
all-girls public school—the Young
Women's Leadership School of East
Harlem, in New York City. "I feel
more open," says Maryam. "The
girls here are like sisters."

2 Nicole Flores, who goes to the
same school, agrees. "You gain
more confidence in this school,"
she says. "We've learned how to
speak in a strong, respectful way."

3 In 1992, the American Association of University Women (AAUW)
published a study called *How
Schools Fail Girls*. It said that
girls often do not get the same educational opportunities as boys.
When boys and girls are in the
same classroom, the report said,
boys speak out more and teachers
call on them more often to answer
questions.

4 What can be done? One solution, say some experts, is to
establish more single-sex public
schools—such as the Young
Women's Leadership School. Today,
however, there are only a handful
of such public schools. By contrast,
there are hundreds of private and

1. How does the writer get your attention in the first few sentences?

parochial (church-related) schools just for girls or just for boys.

Changed Its Mind

5 Last month, the AAUW released a new study. It said that girls in single-sex schools tend to be more confident in traditionally male subjects such as math and science. The new study found, however, that girls in single-sex schools do not make higher test scores in those subjects.

6 As a result of this study, some people are changing their minds about the benefits of single-sex schools. As Janice Weinman of the AAUW says: "What the report says is that single-sex education is not the silver bullet [magical solution that solves a problem]."

7 Are single-sex schools a good idea—especially for girls? Or is there a better solution? Here are some of the arguments on both sides.

Yes! Single-Sex Schools Help

8 Many experts say that single-sex schools are a good thing, especially for girls. They point to studies that show that teachers tend to call on boys more and take the work of girls less seriously. "Too often, girls receive praise for how they look and how they behave rather than for

> **2. According to this paragraph, is being called on in the classroom a good thing or a bad thing? Why do you think so?**

what they accomplish and what ideas they have," says Whitney Ransome, executive director of the National Coalition of Girls Schools.

9 All-girls schools can make girls more confident at crucial times of their lives, says Ransome—especially during the middle school and high school years.

10 Maryam Zohne agrees. "This school isn't for all girls," she says. "It's for girls who want the confidence to move on in life. Some girls have the tools they need already."

> **3. Is this section discussing advantages or disadvantages? How do you know?**

11 Whitney Ransome says that all-girls schools work because, "When there are all girls in the classroom, the culture changes. You're not a second-class citizen because of your gender. . . . You're surrounded by people who look like you, think like you, and empower you."

No! Not the Solution

12 Chris Dunn, a lawyer for the New York Civil Liberties Union (NYCLU), is opposed to the idea of single-sex public schools. The NYCLU fought against the opening of the Young Women's Leadership School. Dunn says that the idea of "separate but equal" schools is unconstitutional.

> **4. What word(s) tell you that this paragraph discusses the disadvantages of single-sex education?**

"If a person can't go to a public school just because he's a boy, that's discrimination," he told JS. When the government runs schools, it needs to provide an excellent educational environment for *all* students."

13 Would the NYCLU still object if New York City opened a separate all-boys school with equal facilities? Yes, says Dunn. "If a school district has four hundred buses and they won't let white students on ten of them, that's still discrimination," he says.

5. Would the NYCLU object if New York City opened a separate all-boys school? Why or why not?

14 Some educators say that single-sex schools fix only part of the problem. "What the research shows is that boys and girls both thrive when the elements of good education are there—elements like smaller classes, focused academic curriculum, and gender-fair instruction," says the AAUW's Janice Weinman.

The problem of unequal treatment will not be solved by putting girls in all-girls classes, say these educators. The solution, they say, is to make the classroom a better place to learn for everyone. Since 95 percent of all girls in the U.S. are in mixed-sex classes, that is where the problem should be solved. 15

How? By emphasizing "equality, better coeducation, and an end to discrimination against girls in the classroom," says Ann Connor of the National Organization for Women (NOW). "To be a leader, you have to interact with both sexes. You have to learn to be a leader of both men and women." 16

6. Based on this paragraph and on what you know, are boys and girls treated differently in the classroom? Explain your answer.

What Kind of School for You?

Students at the Young Women's Leadership School think that they are learning plenty about leadership. "I've learned to speak up for myself, voice my opinion, and not to be negative," says Melique Birks, thirteen. 17

Contrary to what students in coed classes may think, Melique does not feel that she is missing out on the chance to meet people of the opposite sex. "You're focused on your work during the day, and after school you can meet boys," she says. 18

Nicole Flores agrees: "The school's not responsible for your meeting boys—it's responsible for teaching you to learn." 19

READING FOCUS ➤

TOPIC
↓

Cons
↓

Pros

TIP One way to decide quickly whether the writer is going to discuss an advantage or a disadvantage is to look at any **headings** included in the piece. These headings may include **clue words** that hint at a paragraph's purpose.

Advantage/Disadvantage Structure

What Are the Pros and Cons?   The purpose of advantages/disadvantages writing is to present both the advantages *and* the disadvantages of a topic so that a reader can get information to make a decision. To help the reader, the writer **classifies,** or groups, the advantages and disadvantages in a pattern that makes them easy for the reader to understand.

Many writers choose to discuss all of a topic's advantages together in one block and all of its disadvantages together in another block. Just as the drawers in your dresser separate your socks from your shirts, this block structure helps the reader separate a topic's advantages (pros) from its disadvantages (cons).

"Cluing" In   How does the reader decide whether the writer is discussing an advantage or a disadvantage? One way is to look for **clue words.** Words such as *benefit, pro, positive,* and *plus* point to advantages, while words such as *drawback, con, negative,* and *downside* point to a topic's disadvantages. Look at the following sentences and decide whether the writer is discussing an advantage or a disadvantage in each one. How do you know?

> Another benefit of teaching at an all-boys school is that I have more opportunities to boost a young man's self-confidence.

> The downside to teaching boys only is that the boys miss out on the opportunity to hear girls' views on certain subjects.

Mapping the Advantages and Disadvantages   Writing the ideas from an article into a graphic organizer will help you understand the relationships between those ideas. The **fishbone** is a graphic organizer you can use to list advantages and disadvantages. Notice how the sample fishbone on page 87 clearly organizes the pros and cons of the topic "coed sports."

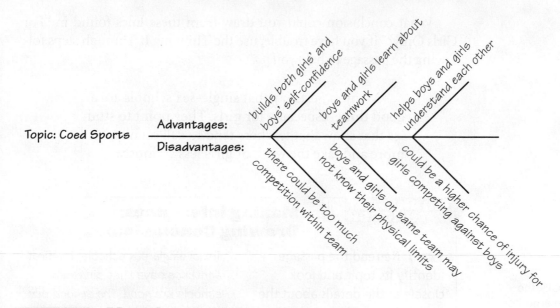

Topic: Coed Sports

Advantages:
- builds both girls' and boys' self-confidence
- boys and girls learn about teamwork
- helps boys and girls understand each other

Disadvantages:
- there could be too much competition within team
- boys and girls on same team may not know their physical limits
- could be a higher chance of injury for girls competing against boys

Mapping the Advantages and Disadvantages

On your own paper, draw a fishbone organizer like the one above. Fill in the advantages and disadvantages discussed in "For Girls Only?" on pages 83–85. If you have trouble locating the advantages and disadvantages, look for clue words such as those on page 86.

Making Inferences: Drawing Conclusions

READING SKILL

I Think . . . While reading about a topic's advantages and disadvantages, you may have to fill in information that the writer has left out. You fill in those "blanks" in the text by making *inferences*. An **inference** is an educated guess about information in the text. A **conclusion** is a type of inference based on details in the text *and* on what you already know. A conclusion applies only to the text on which it is based.

> **What you read:** Mara passed the ball to Howard, who scored the winning basket.
>
> + **What you already know:** I know that passing a ball and shooting a basket are things you do when playing basketball.
> ---
> **Conclusion:** Mara and Howard are playing basketball on the same team.

TIP A conclusion applies only to the text on which it is based. A **generalization** is an inference based on a text that applies to the world in general. From the details about Mara and Howard, you might generalize that girls and boys sometimes play basketball on the same teams.

What conclusion could you draw from these lines found in "For Girls Only?" If you have trouble, use the Thinking It Through steps following the passage to help you.

> Many experts say that single-sex schools are a good thing, especially for girls. They point to studies that show that teachers tend to call on boys more and take the work of girls less seriously.

Making Inferences: Drawing Conclusions

▶ **STEP 1** Re-read the passage. Identify its topic and look closely at the details about the topic.

Topic: single-sex schools. The first sentence says that single-sex schools are good. The second sentence says that teachers in coed schools call on boys more.

▶ **STEP 2** Think about what you already know. What are your experiences with the topic or the details?

I know that in many of my classes, some boys are called on a lot because they raise their hands first or even shout out answers to the teachers' questions. So, in a way, boys get more attention.

▶ **STEP 3** Connect your experiences from Step 2 with the details in Step 1 to draw a conclusion about the topic.

Girls might get more attention—participate more and be taken more seriously—if there were no boys in class.

TIP Usually, the author of an expository advantages/disadvantages article like the one on pages 83–85 will not favor one side of an issue over the other. However, after hearing both the pros and the cons, most readers will like one option better than the other. For example, after reading "For Girls Only?" you may decide that the disadvantages to single-sex schools outweigh the advantages.

YOUR TURN 3 Making Inferences: Drawing Conclusions

Working in pairs, use the steps in the Thinking It Through above to answer the following questions about "For Girls Only?" For each question, explain what led you to your conclusion.

- Read paragraphs 15 and 16 on page 85. Which type of school would help a student become a better leader?
- Read paragraph 18 on page 85. Is Melique for or against focusing on schoolwork during the day?

Denotation and Connotation

Advantages/disadvantages writing has one purpose—to inform the reader by giving the facts. Even when you are reading for facts, be aware that some words can influence your feelings. In addition to a **denotation,** or dictionary definition, many words have strong *connotations.* A word's **conno-** tation includes the feelings and associations connected with that word. For example, you know the denotation of the word *leader:* someone who is in charge. The connotations of *leader* may include *power, pride, strength, role model, determination,* and *wisdom.*

THINKING IT THROUGH | **Understanding Denotation and Connotation**

Take a look at this example using the word *equality* from "For Girls Only?" to understand how a word's connotations can affect a reader.

Context: ". . . make the classroom a better place to learn for everyone . . . [by] emphasizing 'equality, better coeducation, and an end to discrimination against girls in the classroom.'"

▶ **STEP 1** Write down the word's **denotation.** Use your own definition, or check the word's definition in a dictionary.

Equality means "fair treatment for everyone."

▶ **STEP 2** Think about the word's **connotation.** What feelings or ideas do you associate with this word?

The word equality makes me think of freedom and fairness. In the excerpt above, it tells me girls need to be treated fairly in the classroom so they can succeed.

▶ **STEP 3** Ask yourself, "What if the author had used a synonym? What are its connotations?"

Sameness is a synonym with more negative connotations. "Emphasizing sameness" doesn't sound very attractive.

PRACTICE

Use the Thinking It Through steps above to figure out the denotations and connotations of these words from "For Girls Only?" Each word has been underlined in the article.

1. respectful (page 83) 2. second-class (page 84) 3. empower (page 84) 4. thrive (page 85) 5. focused (page 85)

Drawing Conclusions

When taking a reading test, you may be asked to draw conclusions about a selection. Read the following passage and the test item that follows it. How would you tackle this test question?

Last weekend Isabell's service club helped rebuild a home destroyed by floods. Over two days, the group made noticeable progress in restoring the family's home. In just a few days, six young men and women made a great difference to a family who had lost nearly everything. In addition, club members learned to work together as a team.

You can tell from the passage that the service club members

A. will help rebuild other homes in the future

B. found that teamwork can be rewarding

C. encouraged the family to participate in the rebuilding

D. helped repair other homes in the same town

TIP The answer to a conclusion question will not be in the passage word-for-word. You will have to use details in the passage and your own knowledge to figure out the correct answer.

THINKING IT THROUGH
Drawing Conclusions in a Reading Test

▶ **STEP 1** See what information you can get from the question.

The question tells me that I need to make a decision about the service club. I should look for details in the passage.

▶ **STEP 2** Use what you know and the details from the passage to examine each answer choice.

Choice A is wrong; they may rebuild more homes, but the passage does not mention what they will do next. Choice B sounds reasonable; the passage said they learned to work together as a team and they made a difference, and I know that can feel good. Choice C is not right because there is no mention of the family working. Choice D is not supported. Other homes may have been destroyed by floods, but the passage doesn't mention other homes.

▶ **STEP 3** Choose the answer that is supported by details from the passage *and* that makes sense.

Choice B makes sense and can be supported by details in the passage. Choice B must be the answer.

Writing an Advantages/ Disadvantages Essay

When you decide which electives to take, what helps you settle on fine art instead of industrial technology, or Spanish instead of band? Chances are, you investigate the advantages and disadvantages of each class to see which one better suits your needs. When you group ideas into categories, such as "advantages" and "disadvantages," you are **classifying** information.

Classifying information not only helps you make decisions, but also gives you the opportunity to help someone else make a decision. When you write about advantages and disadvantages, you provide readers with the facts they need to make well-informed decisions.

Prewriting

Think of Possible Topics

What Do You Know?   Finding a topic for your advantages/disadvantages essay can be a snap if you stick with what you know. Think about topics that relate to your school, hobbies, or home life. Following are more suggestions for discovering a topic for your essay.

- Think of a time when you made a big decision. List the pros and cons that you thought about in order to make your decision.

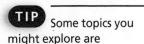
- Refer to **resources,** such as TV news programs, local newspapers, magazines, or the World Wide Web for current topics. Then, freewrite about the topics, answering these questions: What topics are familiar to me? Can I list these topics' advantages and disadvantages?

As you search, **remember that you are looking for topics with both advantages *and* disadvantages.** To help keep your essay focused and informative, you should look for topics that are specific and narrow. For example, instead of discussing the advantages and disadvantages of owning pets, investigate the advantages and disadvantages of adopting a pet from the local animal shelter.

TIP Some topics you might explore are
- a school dress code
- summer vacations
- after-school jobs, such as baby-sitting or paper routes
- a particular hobby or sport

Evaluate Your Topics

Finding the Right One   Which topic will work best for this essay? To find out, ask yourself these questions: Can I think of at least three advantages and three disadvantages for this topic? Are the advantages and disadvantages balanced?

A topic with advantages or disadvantages that are too obvious will not tell your reader anything new. On the other hand, a topic that has advantages but no disadvantages (or vice versa) will result in a lopsided essay. Instead of discussing the advantages of getting regular exercise, explore the pros and cons of exercising at an indoor gym.

Consider Your Purpose and Audience

KEY CONCEPT

Discovering the "Why" and the "Who"   You know your purpose for writing this essay: to inform your audience about the advantages and disadvantages of an important topic. Since your purpose for writing is to provide information, you can assume your audience's purpose for reading will be to get information, possibly to make a decision. It is up to you to give the audience the whole picture. That means you will have to **be careful not to leave out an important advantage or disadvantage.**

The next step is to think about your audience. Ask yourself who can use information about the advantages and disadvantages of your topic to make a decision: your classmates? younger students? your teacher? After you have identified your audience, answer the following questions to help you think about their needs.

- What will this audience need to know to get a balanced picture of the advantages and disadvantages of my topic?

- What does this audience already know about my topic?

A Matter of Style   Once you know your audience, consider your writing **style**. Different readers understand different levels of writing. For example, when writing for teachers, sentences can be longer and more complex, and your words can be more difficult. For an audience of third-graders, however, you would have to use shorter, simpler sentences and easier words.

Evaluating Possible Topics and Considering Your Audience

Jot down several topics that you might write about in your advantages/disadvantages essay. Then, evaluate each possible topic, and choose one that is interesting and has a balance of advantages and disadvantages. Next, identify your target audience. Make notes about the audience you have identified using the questions on page 92.

State Your Main Idea

The Game Plan   Tell your reader early on what your essay will discuss. A **main idea statement** gives your topic and your plan for discussing it. Your main idea statement may be a single sentence or a few sentences. Here is how one student developed his main idea statement.

Topic: extracurricular activities

Plan: to discuss the advantages and disadvantages

Main idea statement: Deciding whether or not to participate in an extracurricular activity can be a challenge. Before signing up to sing in the choir or play on the volleyball team, first consider the advantages and disadvantages of such a decision.

TIP   Remember that your job in this essay is to present the facts so your reader can make a decision. Do not let your own feelings about the topic become part of your main idea statement.

List the Advantages and Disadvantages

Getting the Picture   You chose a topic with at least three advantages and at least three disadvantages. Making a fishbone graphic organizer like the one on the next page will help you list those advantages and disadvantages and any others you can think of for your topic. Later you will evaluate these advantages and disadvantages to see which ones you will use in your essay.

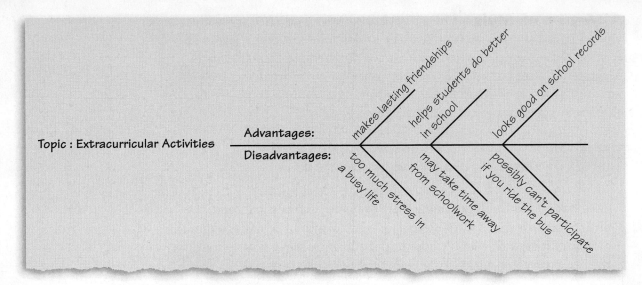

Topic : Extracurricular Activities

Advantages:
- makes lasting friendships
- helps students do better in school
- looks good on school records

Disadvantages:
- too much stress in a busy life
- may take time away from schoolwork
- possibly can't participate if you ride the bus

 Listing Your Advantages and Disadvantages

Make a fishbone organizer like the one shown above. List at least three advantages and three disadvantages that relate to your topic.

TIP Good support for your pros and cons requires **elaboration.** When you elaborate on a point, you extend it a little bit more, often by giving an example. See how elaboration helps the following point.

Advantage: Extracurricular activities help students get to know certain teachers better.

Support: I got to know Mrs. Ashton, the art teacher, better through the Art Club.

Elaborated Support: Mrs. Ashton helped me work on my entry for an art contest even though I was not in her class.

KEY CONCEPT

Gather Support

Finding the Facts To help your audience make a decision about your topic, you will need to provide support for each pro and con. Support can take the form of

- facts: statements that can be proved true
- expert opinions: opinions of people with expert knowledge in a field
- examples or anecdotes: instances or brief stories that illustrate a point

To find support for your advantages and disadvantages, you may brainstorm examples or anecdotes from your own life that show a specific advantage or disadvantage; research in your school or public library; look in magazines, newspapers, or school databases; and interview experts for their opinions or read about what they think.

Making the Right Choices Your support will help you choose which advantages and disadvantages to keep and which to cut. Specifically, **favor advantages and disadvantages with strong support and eliminate advantages and disadvantages not supported by facts, expert opinions, or examples.**

Mapping It Out   Study the **conceptual map** below and notice that the student recorded the support for each advantage and disadvantage. He also decided *not* to use one advantage and one disadvantage. See if you can figure out why.

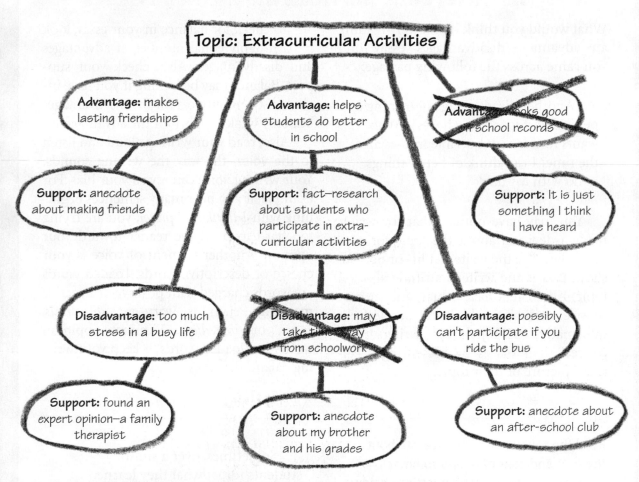

Choosing the Advantages and Disadvantages

YOUR TURN 6

- Refer to the fishbone organizer you made in Your Turn 5 on page 94. List each advantage and disadvantage in a conceptual map like the one above. Add the support you found for each advantage and disadvantage. Note whether each piece of support is a fact, an expert opinion, an example, or an anecdote.

- Look over the information and cross out any advantage or disadvantage you could not support well.

Telling the Difference Between Balance and Bias

What would you think if you were reading an advantages/disadvantages essay and you came across the following passage:

> Another disadvantage of owning a pet is that it is too much work. Who wants to clean up horrible messes all the time? I can think of better things to do with my day!

You may have noticed that the writer made a decision about the topic for you. That's because the writer let his or her *bias* show. **Bias** is the writer's attitude about a topic. All writers have a bias, and in persuasive writing the bias will be clear. In informative writing, though, writers try to conceal their biases by presenting a balanced picture of their topic.

To check for balance in your essay, look for a roughly equal number of advantages and disadvantages. Also, check your support. Balance may be lacking if you have included strong support for the disadvantages but only weak support for the advantages.

Also, read your writing aloud and listen to the **voice,** the way the writing sounds. Your writing voice can reveal your bias. For example, if you hear many sentences beginning with *I think* or *I prefer,* you are trying too hard to push the reader toward your opinion. Another element of voice is your choice of descriptive words. **Loaded words** are words charged with positive or negative meanings, such as *worn-out, disastrous, super,* or *incredible.* Eliminate opinion words and loaded words to keep your writing balanced.

PRACTICE

Read the following essay excerpt about the pros and cons of a long summer vacation, and answer the questions below the excerpt.

> I think summertime is fabulous. Children and parents can use a long vacation to participate in educational activities. Every summer, my family and I learn a lot about our city's history and culture.

> Sometimes, over a summer, students forget what they learned during the last school year. When school starts, teachers have to refresh the students' memories.

1. Find two ways in which the writer's discussion of the advantages and disadvantages of summer vacation is unbalanced.

2. Jot down the words or phrases in the passage that show bias.

Plan Your Essay

Arranging Information   When you write your essay, should you discuss the advantages or the disadvantages first? If a topic has obvious advantages or disadvantages, you may choose to discuss what the reader is familiar with first. Your reader will want to read the entire essay to find out what he or she *does not* know. **The key point is to discuss *all* the advantages together and *all* the disadvantages together.** These separate chunks of information make it easier for the reader to navigate your essay.

 KEY CONCEPT

Order in the Court   Get organized by jotting down the advantages and disadvantages in the order in which you would like them to appear in your essay. In the example below, notice how one writer organized the advantages and disadvantages of his topic.

Order of My Essay

I'll discuss the advantages of extracurricular activities first because they are more familiar to my audience.

Advantages	Disadvantages
1. helps students do better in school (a strong advantage with good impact—will grab the reader's attention)	1. too much stress in a busy life (begin with an unexpected disadvantage—this is unexpected because the reader may not think this is stressful)
2. makes lasting friendships (put second—not as strong as first advantage)	2. possibly can't participate if you ride the bus (place second—has less impact on reader)

COMPUTER TIP

You may need to try several different orders for the advantages and disadvantages in your essay before you find the order that makes the most sense. To make your job easier, type your prewriting notes into a word-processing program. Then, use the program's cut and paste commands to try out different orders for your advantages and disadvantages. When you finally decide on an order, you can use the prewriting notes document to help you write your first draft.

 Organizing Your Essay

Answer the following questions. Use the information from the graphic organizer you created for Your Turn 6 on page 95.

- Will I discuss advantages or disadvantages first? Why?
- In what order will I discuss each advantage and disadvantage *within* the paragraphs? Why is this a good order?

Writing

Advantages/Disadvantages Essay

Framework	**Directions and Explanations**

Introduction
- Attention-grabbing opening
- Main idea statement

Include an **engaging quotation** or piece of **dialogue** that makes the reader curious about your topic. In a **main idea statement,** state your topic and inform readers that you plan to discuss advantages and disadvantages. This statement may be one sentence or more.

Body
- *First paragraph:*
  Advantage (or disadvantage) #1
  Support for #1
- *Second paragraph:*
  Advantage (or disadvantage) #2
  Support for #2 and so on
- *Third paragraph:*
  Disadvantage (or advantage) #1
  Support for #1

  and so on

For each paragraph, be sure to
- clearly state and explain the advantage or disadvantage
- support the advantage or disadvantage with a fact, an expert opinion, or an anecdote
- **elaborate** by extending your support with examples

Conclusion
- Restatement of an advantage and a disadvantage

Pick a strong advantage and a strong disadvantage from the body of your paper. **Restate both** in a way that allows your reader to draw his or her own conclusions about the topic. **Do not include your opinion.**

Drafting Your Advantages/Disadvantages Essay

It is your turn to draft an advantages/disadvantages essay. As you write, refer to the framework above and the Writer's Model on page 99.

A Writer's Model

The final draft below closely follows the framework for an advantages/disadvantages essay on the previous page.

To Join or Not to Join?

"Hey, Juan, did you hear about the new multicultural club? Why don't you come with us?"

"I don't know—I have to finish my homework, practice the saxophone, *and* do my chores. It sounds like a great club, but I already have so much to do! I'll have to get back to you about it."

Many students are overwhelmed by all the things they have to do. Can students juggle their time between school, home, friends, and extracurricular activities such as sports or clubs? Deciding whether or not to participate in an extracurricular activity can be a challenge. Before signing up to sing in the choir or play on the volleyball team, first consider the advantages and disadvantages of such a decision.

Participating in extracurricular activities has many advantages. Students are successful when they participate in many activities. They do well in their classes and feel more connected to school. Research shows that students in extracurricular activities have better attendance and grades. Research also shows that these students have higher goals for their education after high school.

Extracurricular activities also help students make new friends and lasting relationships. I met my best friend when we were on the YMCA swim team. We were both in the eight-and-under age group, and we swam on the same relay team. Even though we became friends a long time ago, we are still close today.

While these activities have many advantages, students should consider the negative side as well. One drawback to participating in extracurricular activities is the stress it

(continued)

Attention-grabbing opening

Main idea statement

Advantage #1

Support (fact)

Advantage #2

Support (anecdote)

Disadvantage #1

(continued)

Support (expert opinion)

can add to a student's life. Extracurricular activities can be too much for students who do not practice good time management. Students need to be good at budgeting their time between different activities, such as homework, instrument practice, and sports. Kathleen Glenn Doyle, a family therapist, says that a child needs a healthy balance between structured time (time spent in class or in extracurricular activities) and free time (time spent with friends or family or time to unwind).

Disadvantage #2

Another downside to extracurricular activities involves transportation. What if you ride the bus to school, or a parent picks you up right after school? Some clubs or sports meet before or after school. This situation limits students' extracurricular choices to those outside of school and closer to home. A few of my classmates joined

Support (anecdote)

the school's multicultural club. They later discovered that it met after school. These students dropped out of the club after the first meeting because they had to catch their buses.

Restatement of advantage and disadvantage

Only you can decide if extracurricular activities are right for you. Activities outside of school can help you be successful in many areas of your life. However, you need good time-management skills to avoid stress that comes with a busy life. Are you up for a challenge?

FOR BETTER OR FOR WORSE

A Student's Model

Jenna Arndt, a student at Labay Middle School in Houston, Texas, wrote about the advantages and disadvantages of being a teenager. Below are excerpts from her essay.

TIP Jenna used the acronym SCORE to support and elaborate on her ideas. SCORE stands for *source/statistic, compare, outcome, relate,* and *example.*

Advantages and Disadvantages of Being a Teenager

. . . One significant asset of being a teen is having fewer worries. "When I was a teenager, I didn't have the family's needs to take care of," claims my uncle Bob Arndt. "I also didn't have bills to pay." Having fewer of these problems to worry about results in more overall free time, extra-curricular activities, and additional time to spend with friends. When I asked my mother and brother if they would like to ride bikes, my brother immediately agreed to join. My mother, on the other hand, shook her head no because she was "much too busy sorting out the bank books." Besides having to worry about paying the bills, adults constantly have to worry about how much they spend. They are usually very resourceful shoppers, so as not to spend more money than they need to. Having fewer worries is a definite plus of being a teenager.

Although there are benefits of being a teenager, there are also drawbacks. One certain disadvantage is the fact that we get fewer privileges than the average adult. One of the significant privileges teens miss out on is voting. Not being able to vote is like being blocked from the political world. Because teens have not been introduced to politics sooner, many make mistakes when they *can* vote. Another privilege that the younger teens miss out on is driving. Since I am not able to drive, I constantly have to bother my parents. Just the other night I had to get to soccer practice. With my father at work and my mother at a party, I was in a tight spot. I had to wait until my father arrived home and was over a half hour late. Having fewer privileges is definitely a minus to being a teenager. . . .

Source

Outcome
Relate

Example

Compare

Outcome

Relate

Revising

Evaluate and Revise Content, Organization, and Style

Play It Again, Sam As you evaluate your own essay or a peer's, make sure to read the essay twice. In the first reading, keep an eye out for content and organization problems, using the guidelines below. During your second reading, focus on strengthening each sentence by using the guidelines on page 103.

➤ **First Reading: Content and Organization** Use the following chart to evaluate and revise your essay so the advantages and disadvantages of your topic are clear to your reader.

Advantages/Disadvantages Essay: Content and Organization Guidelines for Self-Evaluation and Peer Evaluation		
Evaluation Questions	▶ **Tips**	▶ **Revision Techniques**
❶ Does the introduction include a main idea statement?	▶ **Circle** the main idea statement.	▶ If needed, **add** a sentence or two to state the topic and explain that the topic's advantages and disadvantages will be discussed.
❷ Are all the advantages together? Are all the disadvantages together?	▶ **Put a star** next to each advantage and **put a check mark** next to each disadvantage.	▶ **Rearrange** the advantages and disadvantages so that all the advantages are together and all the disadvantages are together.
❸ Is each advantage and disadvantage explained and supported?	▶ **Highlight** the explanation and support for each advantage and disadvantage.	▶ **Elaborate** on advantages and disadvantages with facts, anecdotes, or expert opinions.
❹ Does the conclusion include a restatement of both an advantage and a disadvantage?	▶ **Put brackets** around the restated advantage and disadvantage in the conclusion.	▶ **Add** a restatement of the strongest advantage and disadvantage from the essay, if needed.
❺ Does the essay present a balanced discussion of the topic?	▶ **Put exclamation points** next to statements of opinion and biased words. Count the advantages and disadvantages.	▶ **Delete** personal opinions and biased language. If necessary, **add** more advantages or disadvantages.

ONE WRITER'S REVISIONS Study this revision of an early draft of the essay on pages 99–100.

Another ~~really big~~ downside to extracurricular activities involves transportation. What if you ride the bus to school, or a parent picks you up right after school? Some clubs or sports meet before or after school. This ~~pitiful~~ situation limits students' extracurricular choices to those outside of school and closer to home. A few of my classmates joined the school's multicultural club. They later discovered that it met after school. *These students dropped out of the club after the first meeting because they had to catch their buses.*

delete

delete

elaborate

Responding to the Revision Process

1. Why do you think the writer cut out words in the first and fourth sentences?

2. Why do you think the writer added a sentence to the passage? How does it improve the passage?

PEER REVIEW

As you evaluate a peer's essay, ask yourself the following questions:

■ Which advantages and disadvantages were presented clearly? Which were not?

■ How many advantages and disadvantages were discussed?

▶ **Second Reading: Style** Now, take a look at your sentence style. Your readers can become confused if you include long, drawn-out sentences, called **stringy sentences.** Improve your style by eliminating stringy sentences from your writing. Use the following guidelines, and study the Focus on Sentences on page 104.

Style Guidelines

Evaluation Question	▶ Tip	▶ Revision Technique
Are there any sentences made up of several ideas connected with *and, but, or,* or *so*?	▶ **Draw a wavy line** under each sentence that connects more than two ideas using *and, but, or,* or *so.*	▶ If necessary, **break** the stringy sentences into separate sentences.

Focus on Sentences

Stringy Sentences

The reader of an advantages/disadvantages essay should not have to pick apart sentences to get to the meat of the topic. Having many ideas in a sentence connected with *and*, *but*, *or*, or *so* results in a **stringy sentence.** Stringy sentences don't give the reader a chance to pause before each new idea. One way to fix a stringy sentence is to break it up into separate sentences as in the example below.

> **Stringy:** I have to finish cleaning my room so we'll have to wait to go to a movie, but I will call you when I'm done.

> **Revised:** I have to finish cleaning my room, so we'll have to wait to go to a movie. I will call you when I'm done.

TIP When you break apart a stringy sentence, you may need to add punctuation or a word to make the new sentence clear.

ONE WRITER'S REVISIONS

I met my best friend when we were on the YMCA swim team. and we were both in the eight-and-under age group, and we swam on the same relay team.

Responding to the Revision Process

How did breaking the stringy sentence above into two parts improve the flow of the writing?

 ### Evaluating and Revising Your Advantages/Disadvantages Essay

- First, evaluate and revise the content and organization of your essay, using the guidelines on page 102.
- Next, use the Focus on Sentences above to see if you need to revise any stringy sentences in your essay.
- If a peer evaluated your essay, think carefully about each of your peer's comments as you revise.

Proofread Your Essay

Striving for Perfection Avoid including any errors in the final draft of your essay. Remember, your goal is to inform the reader. Edit your essay to eliminate grammar and spelling errors. Enlist the help of a peer to read your essay and check for mistakes.

Reference Note
For more on **proofreading,** see page 13.

Grammar Link

Correcting Run-ons When Combining Sentences

An **independent clause** expresses a complete thought and can stand alone as a sentence. However, when you identify a pair of advantages or disadvantages, you may find that you want to combine sentences. Be careful, though. Combining two sentences without proper punctuation or a conjunction results in a **run-on sentence.**

Run-on: One benefit of bringing your own lunch to school is that you have more control over what you eat another benefit is that you may save money.

You can correct a run-on sentence by inserting a semicolon or a comma and a conjunction between the independent clauses.

One benefit of bringing your own lunch to school is that you have more control over what you eat**;** another benefit is that you may save money.

One benefit of bringing your own lunch to school is that you have more control over what you eat**, and** another benefit is that you may save money.

PRACTICE

Decide whether each sentence below is a run-on sentence. If it is a run-on, revise it by inserting a semicolon or a comma and a conjunction in the correct place. If the sentence is not a run-on, write C on your paper.

Example:
1. The bell rings at noon the students fill the cafeteria.
1. *The bell rings at noon; the students fill the cafeteria.*

1. I start to smell cafeteria food my stomach begins to growl.
2. I packed a big and nutritious lunch.
3. We have only twenty minutes for lunch I eat very quickly.
4. The cafeteria serves fresh fruit and sandwiches until they sell out.
5. Lunch is fun I enjoy spending the time with my friends.

For more information and practice on **punctuating independent clauses,** see page 618.

TIP Before you make design decisions, such as adding boldface heads, check with your teacher to be sure that your choice is acceptable.

Designing Your Writing

Boldface Heads In an advantages/disadvantages essay, it is sometimes hard for readers to tell whether you are discussing the advantages or the disadvantages of a topic. To help readers, you can use **boldface heads** that include clue words.

Advantages **The Pros of Participating in Extracurricular Activities**
Disadvantages **Why You Should Not Join**

Publish Your Essay

Sounding the Trumpets It is time to share your work with an audience. Try one of these ideas.

- Add your essay to a class collection of advantages/disadvantages pieces, and post the collection on a school bulletin board or Web page. Invite students and teachers to view your class's essays.

- Make a quick-reference booklet for readers. Fold a piece of paper in half. On one side, print the advantages from your essay. On the other side, print the disadvantages.

PORTFOLIO

Reflect on Your Essay

Building Your Portfolio We all learn from our experiences. Reflecting on your advantages/disadvantages essay gives you a chance to think about what you wrote and how you wrote it.

- What was the strongest support in your essay? Why?

- How did you find the best topic ideas for your essay?

- Review your writing portfolio. What strengths and weaknesses do you notice? Set goals to use your writing strengths and improve upon your weaknesses in future assignments.

YOUR TURN 10
Proofreading, Publishing, and Reflecting on Your Essay

- Correct grammar, usage, and mechanics errors in your essay.
- Publish your essay so that others can learn more about your topic.
- Answer the Reflect on Your Essay questions above. Record your responses in your learning log, or include them in your portfolio.

Explaining Advantages and Disadvantages for Tests

An essay test may ask you to discuss the advantages and disadvantages of a specific topic. Some tests may ask you to discuss what is good and bad about a topic. "The good points and bad points" is another way of saying "the advantages and disadvantages." How would you respond to the prompt to the right from a writing test?

Your school is considering adding girls' field hockey to its athletic program. Write an essay for your principal that reports the good points and bad points of adding a new sport to the school's current athletic program. Include solid support for each advantage and disadvantage you discuss.

THINKING IT THROUGH   Explaining Advantages and Disadvantages for Tests

▶ **STEP 1** Analyze the test prompt to identify the

- topic [the good and bad points of adding a new sport to the school athletic program]
- audience [the school principal]
- format [an essay]

▶ **STEP 2** To find out what you know about the topic, ask yourself the following questions.

- Have I seen or read anything positive or negative about the topic on TV or in magazines?
- What do I know about the pros and cons from firsthand experience?
- What are some of the good and bad things about the topic that I can figure out for myself? (**MoTiVate** yourself to find the pros and cons by thinking about **m**oney, **t**ime, and hidden **v**alues relating to the topic.)

In a fishbone organizer, jot down the good and bad points of the topic.

▶ **STEP 3** Use an outline or a conceptual map to organize your good and bad points. Support the points with examples or anecdotes from your own experiences or experiences of people you know.

▶ **STEP 4** Write your essay. Then, verify that you have supported each good point and bad point, and check your essay for correct grammar and spelling.

Life

Comparing "TV Life" to "Real Life"

The classification skills you learned by writing an advantage/disadvantage essay can help you with many other types of writing and thinking. For example, comparing and contrasting also requires you to place information into two categories. In the following activity, instead of pointing out pros and cons, you will examine similarities and differences between life on television and life in the real world.

It Looks Like . . .   What you watch on television is not real life. That may sound obvious, but it is an important point for you to remember as a knowledgeable, critical viewer of television. What you watch on television is created by people who choose *what* activities and events to show and *how* to show them.

For example, think of hospitals on television. TV hospitals are exciting places brimming with extremely young and attractive doctors and patients. These TV hospitals might not match your own experience of hospitals, where perhaps you found that you spent a lot of time waiting, that most of the patients were older, and that your doctors were no more attractive, on average, than anyone else. On the other hand, perhaps you have never been in a hospital. TV hospitals might have shaped your idea of what a hospital is like.

Get Real   This is the question: Is TV life realistic? You may get many answers to this question. People have different **points of view,** or ways of seeing "real life," so people also have different ideas about whether events on TV are realistic. After all, everyone has had different experiences and ways of doing things. Your experience with hospitals may be limited to your trip to the emergency room of a small community hospital. Perhaps you know someone who volunteers at a large city hospital (with many young interns) and sees more of what goes on behind the scenes. *Your* ideas are based on *your* experiences, just as your friend's ideas are based on his or her experiences.

Call It As You See It   To explore the differences between TV life and real life, you will compare how an activity such as doing homework or eating dinner looks on TV with how it happens in your own life.

In the example on the next page, one student compared a classroom discussion on TV to classroom discussions from his own experiences. The student watched a television program and made a Venn diagram based on what he saw. On the left side, he recorded how the activity looked on TV. On the right side, he recorded how the activity looks in his class. In the center, he listed similarities between the two. The student used the information in the diagram to make a decision about how realistic the TV activity was.

Program: Junior High Blues   Activity: a classroom discussion

| TV | Similarities | My Experiences |

- The students sat in neat rows.
- All students paid attention.
- All students raised their hands.
- Every student that spoke sounded smart.

- Some students get really involved during discussions.
- Most students raise their hands and wait to be called on.
- Some students add something intelligent to a discussion.

- We sit in grouped tables.
- Not all students participate in discussions.
- Some students shout out comments during a discussion.

The class discussion on TV was not realistic. It was too smooth and orderly. While my class does have good discussions, sometimes we are not as focused as the show's class, and we do not always raise our hands.

Comparing an Activity on TV to an Activity in Your Life

Pick an everyday activity or event from a TV show and think about what it looks like. What point of view about that activity is reflected? Next, think about what that same activity looks like in your own life, from your point of view. (You should choose an activity you are comfortable sharing.) In a journal make a Venn diagram like the one above to compare the TV activity to your own experience. Then, answer the following questions in a **journal entry**.

- Was the activity portrayed on TV in a realistic way? Explain.
- Remember that someone chooses the way you see things on TV. Why do you think the show portrayed the activity as it did?

Connections to Life

Comparing Informative TV or Video Presentations

When you compare and contrast, you place information into categories, much as you organized your advantages/disadvantages essay. Comparing and contrasting requires you to look at the similarities and differences between two subjects. To compare two informative television or video presentations, you might use the following points of comparison:

Video: What do you see? Do the producers include documentary (or actual) footage, animation (cartoons), or still photography? Does the program use actors in dramatizations (pre-scripted scenes)?

Audio: From whose **point of view** is the "talk" delivered? Is there an unseen narrator, or do people on-screen do the talking? How is music used?

Overall Effect: How do the audio and video add up? Does the program succeed in informing? Does it have any other purposes or goals besides informing?

Study the following comparison.

Bugs are everywhere, even on your TV screen. Two good television pro-

grams about bugs are "The Giant Bug Invasion!" (*Kratt's Creatures,* 1995) and *Insect* (Eyewitness Video, 1994). Each program uses different techniques, resulting in different overall effects.

Insect features rapid cuts of stills, animation, and documentary footage. The producers used 3-D animation. These visuals force the viewer to look at the insect world in a fresh, new way. For the audio, narrator Martin Sheen stays off-screen and remains in the background, accompanied by soothing background music.

Like *Insect,* "The Giant Bug Invasion!" uses rapid editing to present documentary footage of bugs. The program entertains as it informs by mixing facts with funny scenes involving the hosts. Music plays a big role. Different styles of upbeat dance music accompany each image, creating an energetic mood.

Both programs are informative and highly entertaining.

YOUR TURN 12

Comparing Informative TV or Video Presentations

View two informative TV or video presentations about the same subject, and make notes about the audio and video elements used in each. Then, write a comparison-contrast essay like the one above.

Making a Documentary Video

You are watching a TV show when one scene makes you do a doubletake. It shows a school hallway full of teenagers. At first it seems normal, but then you notice something: These students do not look like the students at your school. First, they seem older. They are also gorgeous and dressed in the trendiest clothes. In fact, these "students" do not look like students at all.

Is this portrayal of teenagers typical of what you see on TV and in movies or magazines? Are the teens you see in the media like you, your friends, or the people you see at school? How realistically do the media portray groups of people? You will answer this question by examining how TV classifies teenagers, just as you classified advantages and disadvantages in your essay.

WHAT'S AHEAD?

In this section you will make a video about how teens are shown in the media. You will also learn how to

- identify stereotypes
- classify the way teens are shown
- create a documentary video

Identifying Stereotypes

The way groups of people are portrayed by the media is often *not* realistic. More often, what we see on TV and in movies or magazines are *stereotypes*. **Stereotypes** are limited, fixed ideas about groups of people. For instance, the media often imply that all teens can be classified as one of a few "types." Some of these types are

- the bully
- the popular kid
- the troublemaker
- the lonely, sensitive kid

- the "good kid"
- the jock
- the outcast
- the brain

What is the purpose of media stereotypes? Stereotypes are a kind of shortcut, a quick and easy way to introduce the characters in

TIP Think of a TV or movie character who fits one of these "types." What makes that character a stereotype?

TIP To evaluate the purposes and effects of stereotypes in TV shows or movies, discuss these questions with your classmates. When is it all right to use stereotypes? When is it not all right? How do media stereotypes influence viewers? What are the effects of having stereotypes in media?

a TV show or movie. Viewers quickly recognize the jock, the brain, and the bully in a typical TV or movie classroom scene. When showing students in stereotypical roles, the media are saying, "You know people like these." Real people, however, are well-rounded and much more complex than stereotypes. For example, a real teen can have a sense of humor, be intelligent, *and* rule the basketball court at the same time.

Many TV and movie characters fall somewhere between the stereotype and the complex people you know in real life. Think about rating TV and movie characters on a scale such as this one.

You may give a "one" to the "brain" character who wears glasses, always carries books, and does homework for all the other students. On the other hand, you may give a "seven" to the "bully" character who is occasionally kind. A "ten" would go to the character who seems real to you—like someone you might know.

YOUR TURN 13 Classifying TV Teens

Watch one or two TV shows with several teenage characters. If possible, record the shows on a VCR as you watch; you will use the recording in Your Turn 14. As you watch the shows, decide which characters are stereotypes and which are more complex—like real teenagers. Use a scale like the one above to rate the characters. Record your observations in a chart like the one below.

TV Show: Jimmy's World

Character	Rating and Type of Character	Why I Think So
Steve	1—stereotype (a "jock")	Steve's attitude, his muscles, and the fact that he wore sweats all the time made him a stereotype. Not all athletes look like athletes, have an attitude, and always wear sweats.
Ling	9—well-rounded character	Ling was both smart and popular. She also had friends from several different groups.

Making a Documentary

A **documentary film** or **video** explains or interprets some aspect of reality. It creatively presents and analyzes a topic through words and through images related to the topic. For example, a documentary may explore the life of the first astronaut, the Brazilian rain forests, or how teens are shown in the media.

In a group, you will create a documentary to discuss how teens are shown on television. Your group will select and analyze a short scene (two to three minutes) from one of the TV shows you and other group members watched for Your Turn 13. Your video will show a narrator standing next to a television set. As a recording of the scene plays (with its sound off), the narrator will present your group's analysis of the scene.

Put It on Film   Making a documentary video requires planning and preparation. The chart below shows the first steps for creating an informative documentary video.

Preproduction (everything you do before using the camera)	
Step	**Helpful Hints**
1 **Make decisions** about the main idea your group wants to communicate to your audience.	Answer these questions: • Who will make up our audience? • What do we think about how teens are shown on TV? • How can we support our ideas?
2 **Select** a scene from the TV show you taped.	• Look for a scene with a variety of characters. • Look for a scene that will help you support your ideas.
3 **Storyboard** the scene.	• Draw a sketch of each shot in the scene. Under each sketch, write notes on the events, actions, and language in the shot.
4 **Analyze** the scene.	• What types of characters are present in the scene? Discuss what those characters reveal about how teens are shown in the media.
5 **Write** a script.	• Use your storyboard to match your words to the action. Remember to introduce the TV show you are discussing.
6 **Choose** roles for group members.	• Narrator: presents the group's analysis and conclusions while discussing the selected scene • Cameraperson: shoots the video • Producer: directs the narrator and the cameraperson; signals the cameraperson when to start and stop shooting

It is action time! Once your group has finished planning the video, you can begin producing the final product.

Depending on your school's policy, you may need to use your school's video equipment during class time, or you may be able to check it out to record your documentary. Either way, be sure you understand how to operate the equipment before you begin. Ask your teacher, librarian, or someone else experienced with using the equipment to show you how to use it. If no video equipment is available, skip step 3 in the chart below.

Production	
Step	**Helpful Hints**
❶ **Rehearse** your documentary video.	Rehearsing gives you a chance to work out problems and polish a performance. Rehearse off-camera first. Have the **narrator** practice speaking at the proper volume for recording. The **cameraperson** should decide the correct distance for recording to get a clear image of both the narrator and the television program being analyzed. The **producer** should hold cue cards to help the narrator with the script and practice signaling the cameraperson when to start and stop shooting. Then, using the video camera, record one rehearsal.
❷ **Revise** the documentary, if necessary.	As a group, evaluate your taped rehearsal. Decide whether you should revise your script to make your main idea easier to understand. Then, consider other elements of the video, such as the narrator's voice and gestures and the quality of the recording. Note where improvements are needed.
❸ **Record** the video.	Most video cameras allow you to view what you have just recorded. Look for problems with the sound or camera work in your recording. Reshoot your documentary if you find problems.

 Making a Documentary Video

Use the guidelines on pages 113–114 to create a documentary. Then present the documentary to your class, and discuss these questions with your audience:

■ How well did the script fit the video images?

■ Could the same information have been presented as effectively through a medium other than video? Why or why not?

3 *Choices*

Choose one of the following activities to complete.

▶ CONSUMER EDUCATION

1. Do You Buy This? Think of a product that interests you, such as a game or stereo equipment. List the advantages and disadvantages of buying this particular product. Then, write a brief **review** of the product. Explain in detail why you would or would not buy the product. With other students, create **database records** of product reviews for the class to use.

▶ CROSSING THE CURRICULUM: ART

2. Picture This Create a **chart** using pictures rather than words to represent the advantages and disadvantages of your essay topic. Use symbols such as + or – to label the columns on your chart. In each column, draw or paste pictures showing the good and bad points of your topic.

▶ SPEECH

3. Hear Me Roar Present a **speech** about the topic of your advantages/disadvantages essay. This time, however, include a persuasive slant. Try to convince your audience that one option *is* better than the other. See page 758 for information on formal speaking.

▶ CROSSING THE CURRICULUM: HISTORY

4. From the Past Making comparisons requires you to categorize information, just as considering advantages and disadvantages does. Compare two accounts, or perspectives, of a historic event. For example, you might read about the sinking of the *Titanic* from a survivor's standpoint and from a rescuer's standpoint. List the similarities between the two accounts, and then list the differences. In a **paragraph,** explain the similarities and the differences between the accounts.

▶ CAREERS

5. The Results Are In Pick a workplace topic such as shorter work hours, longer lunch breaks, or a change of the dress code. Discuss its advantages and its disadvantages in an **oral report.** To research your topic, ask an adult how such a change might affect his or her workplace.

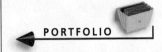

PORTFOLIO

4 Previewing a Novel

Reading Workshop

Reading a Novel's Book Jacket
PAGE 118

Writing Workshop

Creating a Jacket for a Novel
PAGE 128

Focus on Viewing and Representing

Analyzing and Designing a Book Cover
PAGE 148

Focus on Speaking and Listening

Performing a Dramatic Reading
PAGE 152

I magine that you are standing in the library with a book in each hand. You read the back cover of each book. You look at the writing on the inside flaps. Then, you put one book back on the shelf and confidently tuck the other under your arm as you walk toward the check-out desk.

How did you decide which book to take and which to leave on the shelf? When you read the book jackets, you used a method called *previewing*. **Previewing** is an activity that helps you gather information about a book. After previewing a book, you can predict what the book is about and decide whether you want to read it. Writers and editors create book jackets to let readers preview books—in the hope that those readers will buy (or borrow) the book.

GO TO: go.hrw.com
KEYWORD: EOLang 7-4

Previewing a Book

Go to the library and check out a book with a book jacket that has flaps. Only hard-backed books will have an entire book jacket. Bring the book to class and discuss it with a few classmates. Be sure to

- decide what the image on the cover says about the book
- read the back cover and inside flaps and see if they change what you thought about the book based on the cover image
- tell whether the book jacket makes you want to read the book

Reading a Novel's Book Jacket

WHAT'S AHEAD?

In this section you will read a novel's book jacket. You will also

■ learn how to preview a novel

■ learn how to generate questions and make predictions about a novel

John "Crash" Coogan is the star athlete of his seventh-grade class and is a better athlete than most eighth-graders, too. He is the high-energy main character of the novel *Crash*, whose covers and inside flaps appear on the following pages. As you look at the cover and flaps of *Crash*, try to notice what information you can learn about a novel just by looking at its jacket.

Preparing to Read

READING FOCUS

Preview Information When you take stock of the details on a novel's jacket, you are *previewing*. **Previewing** happens before you read or view something, and it helps you decide whether you are interested in the story. For this lesson, you will preview a novel—a long, fictional story. You will gather information from the book jacket of *Crash* to help you guess about the plot of the novel and decide whether you would like to read it.

READING SKILL

Questioning and Predicting As you gather information from a book jacket, you can make some educated guesses about what might happen in the novel and what the characters might be like. You can also draw upon your own experience and knowledge of stories to ask questions such as, "What will happen to the main character?" To the left is a picture of what a book jacket looks like when laid flat.

CRASH

KNOPF

Jerry Spinelli

FRONT COVER

Look at the covers and inside flaps of *Crash*. In your notebook, answer the numbered active-reading questions that appear in the margins. The underlined words appear in the Vocabulary Mini-Lesson on page 126.

1. What is unusual about the photo and drawing that appear together on the front cover?

2. What sort of expression does the baby have? What do you think the expression says about his character?

My real name is John. John Coogan. But everybody calls me Crash, even my parents.

It started way back when I got my first football helmet for Christmas. I don't really remember this happening, but they say that when my uncle Herm's family came over to see our presents, as they were coming through the door I got down into a four-point stance, growled, "Hut! Hut! Hut!" and charged ahead with my brand-new helmet. Seems I knocked my cousin Bridget clear back out the doorway and onto her butt into a foot of snow. They say she bawled bloody murder and refused to come into the house, so Uncle Herm finally had to drag his whole family away before they even had a chance to take their coats off.

Like I said, personally I don't remember the whole thing, but looking back at what I do remember about myself, I'd have to say the story is probably true. As far as I can tell, I've always been crashing—into people, into things, you name it, with or without a helmet.

3. What aspect of Crash's character makes him interesting to you? Is he like anyone you know?

9 780679 879572

51600>

ISBN 0-679-87957-9

NB21

BACK COVER

4. What does this novel seem to be about?

6. Is Jerry Spinelli an experienced writer? What makes you think so?

What's it like to be Crash Coogan? You might think you know him already—the big jock, star of the football team. Huge shoulders, smallish brain. Basically <u>mows</u> down everything in his path, including kids like Penn Webb, the dweeby, puny, button-wearing vegetable-eater who moved onto Crash's block when they were little—and has been a <u>prime</u> target ever since.

But there's more to Crash than the touchdown-scoring kid every seventh grader sees. And it's not the predictable sob story that's supposed to make you feel sorry for the poor bully. It's the story of a kid with overworked parents, an ecology-minded smart-aleck little sister, a <u>crush</u> on an activist cheerleader, and a best buddy named Mike Deluca, who helps Crash pull off hilarious pranks at Webb's <u>expense</u>.

Until one day Mike goes too far, maybe even for Crash, and the football hero has to choose which side he's really on.

Jerry Spinelli won the Newbery Medal for *Maniac Magee*, the sixth of his more than fifteen acclaimed books for young readers, which include *There's a Girl in My Hammerlock* and *Who Put That Hair in My Toothbrush?* Growing up, he played no less than five different sports—from football and track to basketball. He wanted to be a shortstop in the majors long before it occurred to him to be a writer.

Crash came out of his desire to include the beloved Penn Relays of his home state of Pennsylvania in a book. And, of course, to show the world a little bit of what jocks are made of.

http://www.randomhouse.com/

Jacket illustration © 1996 by Eleanor Hoyt
Jacket photo © 1996 by Stan Reis

Also available in Gibraltar Library Binding
Printed in the United States

5. What do you think will happen to make Crash "choose which side he's really on"?

Alfred A. Knopf
New York

FRONT FLAP

BACK FLAP

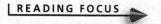
READING FOCUS

Preview Information

You *Can* Judge a Book by Its Cover!

The first step to understanding a novel is gathering information from its front and back covers and inside flaps. The information you gather from a book jacket will help you decide whether you want to read the novel. Reading the book jacket to get an idea of the contents is a technique that works for any type of book—novels, photography books, sports books, or cookbooks. Use this chart to see what the parts of a book jacket can tell you about a novel.

Part of the Book Jacket	Information You Might Find
Front Cover	▪ Title ▪ Author ▪ An illustration or picture that tells something about the novel ▪ Awards the novel has received
Back Cover	▪ Quotations from the novel ▪ Summary of the novel ▪ Reviews of the novel or reviews of other novels by the same author
Front Flap	▪ A summary of the novel ▪ A reason for people to read the novel
Back Flap	▪ Information about the author

TIP Movie previews are called **trailers.** Like a novel's book jacket, a movie trailer will summarize the story and give you an idea of who the characters are.

The text from parts of the jacket of another novel, *Where the Red Fern Grows* by Wilson Rawls, is shown on the next page. Read over the information, and look at the chart on page 124 to see how one reader recorded the information he found.

Back Cover:

My eyes were wide, my throat dry, and my heart thumping. One judge stopped in front of Little Ann. My heart stopped, too. Reaching over, he patted her on the head.

Turning to me, he asked, "Is this your dog?"
I couldn't speak. I just nodded my head.
He said, "She's a beautiful hound."
He walked on down the line. My heart started beating again.

There were eight dogs left. Little Ann was still holding her own. Then there were four. I was ready to cry.

Front Flap:

Growing up in the Ozark Mountains of northeastern Oklahoma, Billy Colman wants nothing more than to own the pair of coonhound pups he saw advertised in a sportsman's magazine. Although the sum is tremendous, Billy is determined, and after two years of hard work and saving, the two puppies become his.

Billy's pups are his "shadow," following his every move through the dark hills and icy river bottoms in search of the elusive raccoons. The three gain a fine reputation as an inseparable team when they win the coveted gold cup in the annual coon-hunt contest, capture the deceptive ghost coon, and, in the most difficult battle of all, put up a fierce struggle against a mountain lion.

But the victory over the mountain lion turns to tragedy, and Billy's days of freedom and innocent boyhood rapidly end. Yet much remains for Billy: He not only has his wonderful memories, but he learns a beautiful old Indian legend which gives them sacred meaning.

As it has for generations, this modern classic is sure to warm the hearts of young and old alike.

Part of the Book Jacket	Information I Found
Front Cover	The book is <u>Where the Red Fern Grows</u>, written by Wilson Rawls. The front cover shows two dogs and a boy who is carrying a lantern.
Back Cover	The long quotation tells me that a character enters his dog in a contest. The judge praises the dog.
Front Flap	The front flap tells me about Billy Colman, a boy who saves his money and buys two puppies. Billy and the puppies win a gold cup in a hunting contest and go on many adventures. The flap mentions an Indian legend, which makes me curious to read the book.

 Gathering Preview Information

In your notebook create a chart like the one above. Then, using the book jacket from *Crash* on pages 119–121, fill in the chart. (Note: You will need to add a row titled "Back Flap" to your chart.)

Questioning and Predicting

What's Happening?   Previewing a book leads a reader to **ask questions**. After looking at a book jacket, you probably find yourself asking several questions. For example, you may ask why a character acts a certain way, or you may wonder what will happen next.

What Happens Next?   Once a reader begins to ask questions, he or she also begins to make *predictions*. A **prediction** is an educated guess about what will happen in the future based on what you have read and what you know. When reading a book jacket, you base your predictions on the parts of the novel you have examined closely. You also draw from your own life experience and your knowledge of how stories generally work.

text: what you read

+ prior knowledge: what you already know based on your life

prediction: an educated guess about what will happen

Asking questions and making predictions will give you a **purpose** for reading. As you read, you will look for answers to questions and see whether your predictions are correct.

THINKING IT THROUGH

Questioning and Predicting

Here is how one student used the book jacket of Rawls's novel to generate questions and make predictions.

▶ **STEP 1** Review the information you gathered while previewing the book jacket, and ask questions about what you want to know.
Why are the dogs and the boy out in the woods at night with a lantern? Will something bad happen to the dogs or to the boy?

▶ **STEP 2** Think about your own experiences that relate to your questions.
I know that people hunt in the woods and that some people, like my uncle, bring their dogs. Also, it seems like a lot of the stories I've read about dogs, like Old Yeller, end with something bad happening.

▶ **STEP 3** Make predictions that answer your questions by considering preview information and your own experiences.
I bet the boy and his dogs are hunting for the "ghost coon" or the mountain lion mentioned on the front flap. I also think the dogs will get hurt saving the boy's life because the front flap says "the victory over the mountain lion turns to tragedy."

▶ **STEP 4** Confirm or revise your predictions as you read the novel.

TIP You can ask questions and make predictions *before* you read a novel by previewing its jacket, but you can also do so *as* you are reading a novel. These questions and predictions can be about the characters' personalities, the events in the story, or problems the characters may face.

YOUR TURN 3

Questioning and Predicting

Using the Thinking It Through steps above, ask questions and make predictions about *Crash*. Use the information you gathered from the book jacket in Your Turn 2 and your own experience to help you.

Multiple-Meaning Words

Sometimes when you read, you find familiar words used in ways you do not understand. Such words are **multiple-meaning words.** For instance, the word *bank* often means a place that keeps money, but what does it mean in the following sentences?

We all sat on the *bank* of the river.

The basketball player made a *bank* shot.

When you see a multiple-meaning word, you have to decide which meaning is the right one.

TIP The difference between word meanings can depend on a word's part of speech. For example, many of the words we recognize as nouns may also be used as verbs. *Elbow, staple,* and *ice* are examples of nouns that have meanings as verbs, too. The following sentences show how the same word can be used as a verb and as a noun. Note how the meaning changes.

She *cut* her hand. [the *action* of cutting, which is a verb]

It was a bad *cut*. [the *result* of the cutting, which is a noun]

THINKING IT THROUGH   **Multiple-Meaning Words**

The following steps can help you find the correct definition of multiple-meaning words. The example is a word from the book jacket of *Crash*.

Example: *bawled*

▶ **STEP 1** Consider all meanings of a word. Rule out definitions that are not the correct part of speech. You may need to use a dictionary.

(1) v.: to shout out noisily; (2) v.: to weep loudly (3) n.: an outcry. The word is a verb in the sentence, so definition #3 is wrong.

▶ **STEP 2** Examine the context of the word or passage.

"They say she bawled bloody murder. . . ." She does not sound sad, so #2 must be wrong.

▶ **STEP 3** Substitute your definition into the sentence. You may have to adjust the wording of your definition.

"They say she shouted noisily bloody murder . . . ." It works!

PRACTICE

These words are underlined on the book jacket of *Crash*. Follow the steps above to define the words as they are used on the book jacket.

1. stance (page 120) **4.** crush (page 121)
2. mows (page 121)   **5.** expense (page 121)
3. prime (page 121)

Making Predictions About Future Outcomes

On many reading tests, you will find questions that ask you to predict future actions or events. You will not find answers to the questions in the selection, but you will find hints. You can also draw on your own experience and knowledge to predict the future event. Read the following passage and answer the question after it.

Karen, a seventh-grader, was very nervous on the first day that she went to tutor a group of third-graders. She did not know how they would respond to her. With a queasy feeling in her stomach, she knocked on the door to Mrs. Warren's classroom.

Mrs. Warren opened the door and led her inside. Karen could see that most of the third-graders were sitting quietly at their desks with their books open.

"Class, this is Karen," Mrs. Warren announced. "She will be helping you with your math problems. Who would like Karen's help?"

Several students quickly raised their hands. Karen was glad she had an hour to spend with them.

During the next hour, the children will

A. argue about who gets to go first

B. work with Karen only because their teacher expects it

C. be glad Karen is helping them with their math problems

D. convince Karen that she does not want to tutor them after all

Predicting Future Outcomes

▶ **STEP 1** Read the test item and turn the incomplete sentence into a question, if necessary.

▶ **STEP 2** Gather clues about what will happen from information in the text and from your own experience.

▶ **STEP 3** Eliminate answers that are obviously wrong, and choose the answer to which the clues in the passage lead you.

"During the next hour, the children will . . ." becomes "During the next hour, what will the children do?"

In the passage, the children were working quietly. Many of them raised their hands so they could work with Karen. In my experience, a lot of children welcome help on math problems.

The children seem ready and willing to work with Karen, so answers B and D must be wrong. The children seem well behaved, so choice A is probably wrong, too. I choose answer C. It matches the information in the passage.

Creating a Jacket for a Novel

Do you remember the last time you liked a book so well that you told someone else about it? Creating a book jacket is a way to promote the book to hundreds of people at once. Professional publishers and designers create book jackets as *marketing* tools. **Marketing** is the process of promoting and selling a product.

In this workshop you will create a book jacket for a novel you have read. You will give readers important information about the novel and help them decide for themselves whether they want to read it.

Prewriting

Select a Novel

TIP Make sure you read the novel you choose before you start the project, even if you have read it before. Otherwise, you might not be able to remember important details needed to create a good book jacket.

Find Your Inspiration   For this workshop you need to choose a novel that you really like or that you think you will like. Your enthusiasm for the novel you choose should come through in your writing. The best way to make sure that happens is to write about a novel you enjoyed reading. You can also choose a new novel based on your interests.

To select a novel, complete these sentences.

My favorite kinds of novels are about _____.

The most exciting moment I remember from a novel is _____.

One student chose a novel this way:

> The most exciting moment I remember from a novel is . . . the scene where Ponyboy gets his head held underwater by a member of the Socs. That was in a novel called The Outsiders. I would like to read that novel again. I think I'll use it for my book jacket.

Think About Purpose and Audience

Be Reasonable   If you think about your reasons for creating this book jacket, you will realize that you really have three goals:

- to tell people what the novel is about
- to give your audience a **reason to read** the novel
- to attract the readers' attention

   Since you are writing a book jacket for a young-adult novel, young adults are your primary audience. To create an effective book jacket, you will need to include information that will appeal to readers your own age. Keep in mind, however, that parents and librarians also select novels for young adults to read. Include for this secondary audience information such as awards the novel has received.

> My primary audience will be young adults. They would be interested in the rivalry and what happens between groups of teens who think they are tough. I will include information about that for them.
>
> My secondary audience will be parents and librarians. They might worry about the rivalry, so I will mention on the jacket that the book is really about how violence is bad.

TIP   Since you have two audiences for your book jacket, you should avoid words and phrases that sound too formal as well as words and phrases that are considered to be slang. In other words, make sure the **tone** of your writing **voice** fits both your primary *and* secondary audiences.

Selecting a Novel and Thinking About Audience

To select a novel and target your audience, complete the following.

- Think of possible novels by completing one of the sentences at the bottom of page 128. Choose a novel you would be interested in reading or re-reading.
- Identify information you should include to get your primary and secondary audiences interested in the novel.

Select the Front Cover Image

TIP Your goal is to create an entirely *new* jacket for a novel, not to copy the original one. If you choose a novel that already has a jacket, look for a chance to show your unique views about the novel. You will pick the characters and scenes *you* like best for your jacket, not the ones another person chose.

A Picture Is Worth a Thousand Words Which book are you more likely to pick up from the shelf: a plain book with the title written across it, or a book with a big picture on the cover? No contest, right? The picture on the front cover makes the book instantly interesting. Deciding on the picture for your book jacket may be difficult because there are so many images that come to mind. How do you pick just one?

Think about the story. Make a list of all the times the main character runs into trouble or does something unusual. Briefly describe the scene. For example, the student writing about *The Outsiders* chose the following scenes. Notice that he was careful to make sure the scene did not give away too much of the story. After completing the chart, the student ranked the scenes to determine which one would make the best cover for the novel.

Rank	Scene	Analysis
3	A member of the Socs dunks Ponyboy's head in a fountain and holds it there.	I think this would be a bad choice because you can't see the main character's face, and it gives away a big surprise in the story.
1	Ponyboy and Johnny run away to an abandoned church and wait for Dallas to come and help them.	I like this one because it shows that these "tough guys" are really just scared kids, and it does not give the story away.
2	Ponyboy saves several children in a burning church.	I like this picture, but it has lots of characters that aren't important. Plus, the fire was less important than some of the other events.

Just Close Your Eyes When you have decided on a scene to use for your cover, sit back for a minute with your eyes closed and get a clear picture of it. Then, start describing the scene on paper. Take a pen or pencil, and write down everything you can about the picture in your head. After deciding which scene to illustrate, the student whose example is shown above used the steps on the next page to decide which elements to include in his cover image.

Choosing the Elements for the Cover Image

▶ **STEP 1** Determine who or what the major focus of the scene is.

The major focus of the scene is on the characters Ponyboy and Johnny.

▶ **STEP 2** Identify the action that takes place during this scene.

They are sitting on the steps of an abandoned church.

▶ **STEP 3** Think about the emotions or feelings that are present in this scene.

They must be experiencing feelings of fear, uncertainty, and disbelief.

▶ **STEP 4** Identify the setting of the scene. What does the place look like?

It is sunrise as the boys sit on the old, stone steps outside the church. The church is crumbling and sitting in the middle of a field.

Once you have a good idea of the elements you will include in your scene, you can draw a rough sketch of it. Decide where you will place the title of the novel and the name of the author. Also decide where you will list any awards the book has won. Because this is only an early sketch, stick figures are fine. You will create your final cover image later in the chapter.

Reference Note

For more on **analyzing and designing book covers,** see page 148.

Select the Back Cover Quotation

Listen to the Characters   A common element on the back cover of a novel is a quotation. **Quotations help readers learn more about the story and the characters in the novel.** To select a quotation for the back cover, you need to remember important things that the characters or narrator said. A sentence from the book that reveals something important about the novel's conflict or about one of its main characters makes a good cover quotation. Use sticky notes to mark potential quotations as you read or re-read the novel. Looking back at the novel will help you decide on a good quotation. Notice how the writer of the example on the next page chose a quotation from *The Outsiders*.

KEY CONCEPT

There are two big moments in the book—when Ponyboy meets a Soc girl who is actually nice to him and when Ponyboy and Johnny are confronted by the girl's boyfriend late at night. I don't see a good quotation during the scene with the boyfriend. I'll use this quote from the scene with the girl.

"I figured it was all right to be sitting there with them. Even if they did have their own troubles. I really couldn't see what Socs would have to sweat about—good grades, good cars, good girls, madras and Mustangs and Corvairs—Man, I thought, if I had worries like that, I'd consider myself lucky. I know better now."

When you pick a quotation, consider whether your audience will understand it. Some quotations make sense only as part of a longer passage. Be sure you choose a quotation that people will understand without knowing what happened before and after it.

TIP When choosing a cover quotation, consider whether a quotation gives away too much of the story. Make sure the quotation you choose sparks the audience's interest without giving anything away.

 Selecting a Cover Image and a Quotation

Use the following suggestions to select a front cover image and a quotation for the back cover.

■ List possible scenes and determine which would work best.

■ Use the Thinking It Through steps on page 131 to determine what to include in your cover image.

■ Create a mental picture of the scene, and sketch it on paper.

■ Choose a quotation from one of the most important moments in the book. Choose carefully, and do not give away the whole story.

Plan Your Summary

Make a Long Story (or Novel) Short   The front flap of your book jacket will contain a *summary*. When you write a **summary**, you briefly state the main ideas of a piece of writing. Because a novel is a special type of writing, its summary is special, too. **The summary for a novel must include details about characters, setting, plot, and theme.** The Critical Thinking Mini-Lesson on the next page will explain these key elements of novels and other fictional pieces.

KEY CONCEPT ➤

Elements of Fiction

Even though novels can be about many different kinds of characters and subjects, all novels share four key elements: character, plot, setting, and theme. These key elements appear not only in novels but also in other types of stories, such as short stories and fairy tales. The following chart lists, defines, and gives an example from the fairy tale "Cinderella" for each element.

Element	Definition	Example
Character	A person or animal that takes part in the action. This includes the main character, called the **protagonist.**	Cinderella, prince, stepmother, stepsisters, fairy godmother
Setting	Setting is the time and place in which the events occur.	A kingdom long, long ago
Plot	Plot is the series of events that make up a story. The plot events of a story indicate the **conflict** (the problem the main character faces), the **climax** (the highest point of action), and the **resolution** (the solution of the problem). Note: Leave the resolution out of your book jacket summary—you want your readers to enjoy reading the novel's ending themselves.	**Event 1:** Jealous of her beauty and kindness, Cinderella's cruel stepfamily leaves her at home to do housework on the eve of the ball (conflict). **Event 2:** However, Cinderella's fairy godmother magically cleans the house and helps Cinderella get to the ball. **Event 3:** At the ball, the prince falls in love with Cinderella, but at midnight Cinderella disappears (climax). **Event 4:** The prince conducts a search and finds her. They marry (resolution).
Theme	A **theme** is the author's message about life that is revealed in the story.	Kind people will be rewarded.

PRACTICE

Choose a novel you have read or a familiar fairy tale such as "The Three Little Pigs." Then, identify the characters, setting, plot, and theme of the story.

Put It All Together   To write a summary of a novel, you must include information about all the important elements of the novel—characters, setting, plot, and theme. In addition to a summary, your book jacket's front flap should begin with a piece of information to "hook" your reader, and end with a reason to read the novel. The questions in the following charts will help you identify the information your readers will want as they read your summary. Be sure to include all these elements. In the right column are the notes one reader took about the novel *The Outsiders*.

Hook	
What small bit of information would make the reader want to know more about the novel?	Ponyboy's friends often get mugged.

Summary		
Characters	Who is the main character? What is he or she like? What is that character interested in or concerned about?	Ponyboy is the main character. He's a tough member of the greasers but a good guy overall. He's worried about the conflict between the greasers and the Socs.
Setting	Where does the story take place? Is it set in the past, present, or future?	The setting is a big town in the mid-1960s.
Plot	What major problem does the main character face? In general, how does he or she respond to that problem? (Be careful; do not give away too much of the plot.)	Ponyboy gets in trouble when he talks to a Soc cheerleader, and her boyfriend wants to get back at him.
Theme	What idea about life do you think the author is trying to give you? What does he or she want readers to learn from this novel?	Violence is senseless.

Reasons for Reading	
Why should people read this novel? What will they get out of it?	Readers will understand that the novel's message about violence is as important to today's readers as it was to readers in the 1960s.

 ## Writing the Front Flap

Create charts like the ones on page 134 and the one above to help you gather information for your summary and front flap.

Research the Author

"Let Me Introduce You to . . ." The back flap often includes a short biography or other information about the author of the novel. If you have read other novels by the same author, you can say a little bit about the topics about which he or she likes to write. The back flap often includes interesting information about the author. To find author information, visit a library or use the Internet.

- **Library** In your school or local library, you will find many books that tell you about authors. One source is *Contemporary Authors,* a book that tells about authors' lives, careers, and awards. Some books such as *The Junior Book of Authors* and *Authors of Books for Young People* are geared toward young-adult readers. Also, the library's catalog will list other books, stories, and articles the author has written.

- **Internet** The World Wide Web offers many Web sites about authors. Browse on a search engine using the author's name or keyword combinations, including the words *young adult, literature, authors,* and *biographies.* You may even find an author's personal Web page.

 KEY CONCEPT

TIP As you read about authors, think about what other people will want to know about them. Look for details that surprise or interest you. Other people will want to know that information, too.

Reference Note
For more on **searching the World Wide Web,** see page 740 in the Quick Reference Handbook.

 ## Researching the Author

Conduct a search for information about the author of your novel. Take notes on any important or interesting details that you can use in creating your book jacket.

Writing

Framework

Back Flap
- Author biography *or*
- Information about the author

Back Cover
- Catchy quotation or passage

Directions and Explanations

Show your audience what makes this writer interesting. Tell them about other books by the author, the author's career, or where the author lives.

Choose a **quotation** or **passage** that grabs the reader's attention. A good quotation or passage usually introduces an important character or conflict in the novel.

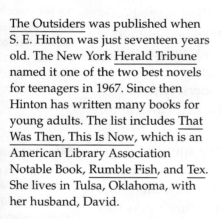

The Outsiders was published when S. E. Hinton was just seventeen years old. The New York Herald Tribune named it one of the two best novels for teenagers in 1967. Since then Hinton has written many books for young adults. The list includes That Was Then, This Is Now, which is an American Library Association Notable Book, Rumble Fish, and Tex. She lives in Tulsa, Oklahoma, with her husband, David.

"I figured it was all right to be sitting there with them. Even if they did have their own troubles. I really couldn't see what Socs would have to sweat about—good grades, good cars, good girls, madras and Mustangs and Corvairs—Man, I thought, if I had worries like that, I'd consider myself lucky. I know better now."

Book Jacket

Here is the front cover and flap of a book jacket created by Christopher C. Stone, a student at Chenery Middle School in Belmont, Massachusetts.

Front Cover

- Author and title
- Meaningful image

Front Flap

- Hook
- Summary and reason for reading

Be sure to include the **author** and **title** of the book. You will create the cover in detail later. For now, use your rough sketch.

Begin this section with a quotation or phrase that will **hook** the reader. Your **summary** and **reason for reading** should not give away the novel's ending.

THE OUTSIDERS

S. E. Hinton

Ponyboy cannot walk home from the movies without being mugged. He is one of the greasers and an enemy of the Socs, the rich kids from the other side of town. Most people think that the only thing the greasers and Socs have in common is their hatred of each other. When Ponyboy meets a Soc cheerleader, Cherry Valence, he begins to wonder whether greasers and Socs are really so different after all.

When Cherry's boyfriend finds out about her innocent conversation with a greaser, he sets off a frightening chain of events that adds to Ponyboy's anger at the Socs. It also leads Ponyboy to get over old grudges. He learns that people are pretty much the same and that things are rough all over.

The Outsiders is set in the mid-1960s, and it deals with the senselessness of violence. The novel is as important today as it was in 1967, when it was first published.

A Student's Model

Here is the front cover and flap text of a book jacket created by Artemese C. Evans, a student at Chemawa Middle School in Riverside, California.

Setting
Character

Hook

Summary

Setting

Theme
Reason for reading

The Sign of the Chrysanthemum

During the twelfth century, a young boy named Muna yearns to know his father, a proud samurai warrior. When his mother dies, Muna has only one clue to his father's identity: a chrysanthemum tattoo on his father's left shoulder.

Muna stows away on a ship and goes to the capital city of Japan, where he meets a swordsmith named Fukuji. Muna becomes a servant for the well-known swordsmith and has to fight temptations such as the temptation of stealing a sword from Fukuji. However, Muna never gives up his dream of claiming his father's name and becoming a man.

The Sign of the Chrysanthemum tells about a boy with fantastic goals and courage. Muna dreams about finally belonging in the world, but he realizes there are more important things in life. This story will teach its readers to overcome their fears and become individuals.

YOUR TURN 8 Creating a Book Jacket

As you create your book jacket, keep both your primary and secondary audience in mind. Also, refer to the framework and Writer's Model on pages 136–137.

Evaluate and Revise Content, Organization, and Style

It's as Easy as One, Two . . . Read over your draft at least twice. In the first reading, follow the guidelines below to check content and organization. In the second reading, work on the style of your writing by following the instructions on page 140.

▶ **First Reading: Content and Organization** Use this chart to evaluate and revise your book jacket so the message is clear.

Novel Book Jacket: Content and Organization Guidelines for Self-Evaluation and Peer Evaluation

Evaluation Questions	▶ Tips	▶ Revision Techniques
❶ Does the cover image grab the audience's attention?	▶ **Use sticky notes** to mark three things in the illustration that would interest readers.	▶ **Elaborate** with details to make the illustration more interesting, or choose a more interesting scene for the cover.
❷ Does the front flap hook the reader?	▶ **Circle** a statement that should make readers want to read the entire novel.	▶ If needed, **add** a hook to the beginning of the summary.
❸ Does the summary include details about character, setting, plot, and theme?	▶ **Underline** these details in the summary and label the element each describes.	▶ If necessary, **add** details about character, setting, plot, or theme to the summary.
❹ Does the summary provide a reason for reading that will encourage people to read the novel?	▶ **Place a star** by the reason for reading, and consider whether you would read the novel based on the information provided.	▶ As needed, **elaborate** with additional information that will help readers understand how the novel will relate to them and why they should read it.
❺ Does the back cover quotation make sense, and does it make audiences want to read the novel?	▶ Ask a friend who has not read the novel to **evaluate the quotation.**	▶ If necessary, **replace** the quotation with one that is easier to understand or more interesting.
❻ Does the biography include interesting facts and details about the author?	▶ Review the biography and **highlight** each of the interesting facts or details.	▶ **Elaborate** with more details about the writer's books, career, or life, if needed.

ONE WRITER'S REVISIONS Examine this revision of an early draft of the book jacket on pages 136–137.

add

cannot walk home from the movies without being mugged. He
Ponyboy is one of the greasers and an enemy of the Socs,

the rich kids from the other side of town. Most people

think that the only thing the greasers and Socs have in

common is their hatred of each other. When Ponyboy

a Soc cheerleader,

elaborate

meets Cherry Valence, he begins to wonder whether

greasers and Socs are really so different after all.

PEER REVIEW

As you evaluate a peer's book jacket, ask yourself these questions:

- Does this jacket make me want to read the novel? Why?
- What parts could be made more interesting?

Responding to the Revision Process

1. Why do you think the writer added a sentence to the beginning of the passage?
2. Why do you think the writer elaborated on information in the third sentence?

▶ **Second Reading: Style**   *How* you say something is just as important as *what* you say and *when* you say it. Look at each sentence in your book jacket. Do any of those sentences seem too short to you? Does the paragraph sound choppy? You can improve your writing by combining short, choppy sentences into longer ones. Use the following guidelines.

Style Guidelines

Evaluation Question	▶ Tip	▶ Revision Technique
Are there short, choppy sentences in the paper?	▶ Read each sentence of the book jacket aloud. **Put an X** by each sentence that contains only five to eight words.	▶ **Combine** some of the short, choppy sentences that are related. Put a comma and a conjunction between them or simply join them with a semicolon.

Combining Sentences

Since your purpose for creating a book jacket is to inform potential readers quickly and clearly, your book jacket has to read smoothly. One way to improve the flow of your writing is to vary your sentence length. Too many short, choppy sentences will make your jacket less readable.

Example:
The Pearl was written over fifty years ago. Its message is still true today.

Revised:
The Pearl was written over fifty years ago, but its message is still true today.

Short sentences that have the same subject can be combined to form a compound sentence. To create a compound sentence, place a comma after the first sentence and add a conjunction such as *and, but*, or *or*.

ONE WRITER'S REVISIONS

The Outsiders is set in the mid-1960s. ~~It~~ , and it deals with the senselessness of violence.

Responding to the Revision Process
Why do you think the writer combined the two sentences above?

Evaluating and Revising Your Book Jacket

- First, use the guidelines on page 139 to evaluate and revise the content and organization of your book jacket.

- Next, use the Focus on Sentences section above to help you decide whether you need to combine any choppy sentences.

- If a peer evaluated your jacket, think carefully about those comments and how they might help you improve your jacket.

Focus on Sentences

TIP When you combine your sentences, be careful not to create a *run-on sentence*. A **run-on sentence** is actually two complete sentences punctuated as one sentence. In a run-on, the thoughts just run into each other.

Reference Note
For more information on **combining sentences,** see page 273.

Publishing

Proofread Your Book Jacket

The Home Stretch   Before you finalize your book jacket, proofread by reading your entire book jacket out loud slowly. Make **edits,** or corrections, as you find errors in spelling and grammar in the draft. If possible, repeat the same exercise with a classmate's book jacket.

Grammar Link

Hyphenation

Have you ever noticed how narrow the inside flaps of a book jacket really are? To make good use of that cramped space, you may need to divide some words at the end of a line by using **hyphens**. It is important to learn how to use hyphens properly. Read each rule below, and notice how *not* following the rule makes a sentence hard to understand. For more on **hyphenation,** see page 646.

■ Never divide a word that has only one syllable.

Incorrect
Ponyboy cannot walk home from the movies without being mug-ged.

Correct
Ponyboy cannot walk home from the movies without being mugged.

■ Divide a word only between syllables.

Incorrect
When Ponyboy meets a Soc cheerle-ader, Cherry Valence . . .

Correct
When Ponyboy meets a Soc cheer-leader, Cherry Valence, he . . .

■ Make sure you do not divide a word so that one letter stands alone.

Incorrect
Since then she has written many books for young adults. . . including an A-merican Library Association Notable Book.

Correct
Since then she has written many books for young adults. . . including an American Library Association Notable Book.

PRACTICE

Show how you would divide the following words if they did not fit on the end of a line.

1. different	**6.** practice
2. movies	**7.** following
3. conversation	**8.** innocent
4. important	**9.** consider
5. through	**10.** amend

Publish Your Book Jacket

Check It Out!   To make your book jacket available to people who will benefit from it, try one of these ideas.

- Help put all the information from your classmates' book jackets into a book-preview *spreadsheet*. A **spreadsheet** is a document that is arranged into rows and columns. See the tip to the right.

- With your classmates, talk to the school librarian about laminating your book jackets and displaying them in your library.

COMPUTER TIP

To start a spreadsheet, create columns labeled "title," "author," "summary," "quotation," and "author information." Then, have your classmates type in their book jacket information.

Designing Your Writing

Book Jacket Layout   After you have finished writing and editing the text for your book jacket, you will need to create the final version. You can do this either by hand or on a computer. The diagram to the right shows you how to place your covers and flaps on paper so that it will fold into a book jacket. You will need two sheets of 8½- × 11-inch paper and tape.

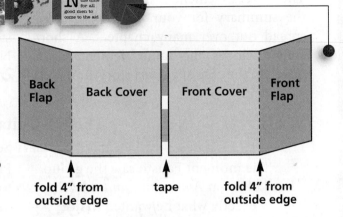

Back Flap | Back Cover | Front Cover | Front Flap

fold 4" from outside edge   tape   fold 4" from outside edge

Reflect on Your Book Jacket

Building Your Portfolio   Reflect on your work by answering the following questions.

- How well did you achieve your purpose for creating a book jacket? Explain.

- What did you learn while writing your summary? How could you use those summary-writing techniques in other types of writing?

PORTFOLIO

YOUR TURN 10 Proofreading, Publishing, and Reflecting on Your Book Jacket

- Correct grammar, usage, and mechanics errors.
- Publish your book jacket so that it will reach your target audience.
- Answer the questions from Reflect on Your Book Jacket above. Record your responses in a learning log, or include them in your portfolio.

Writing a Short Story

In a novel like the one you read for this chapter, readers spend a long time with the characters and follow a complex plot. The novel's elements, which you used in the summary for your book jacket, are spread out over many chapters. A **short story** includes the same elements as a novel. In the case of a short story, however, the **characters, plot, and setting** of the story are given in only a few pages. In this workshop, you will write a short story using all of these fiction elements.

Read the first few paragraphs of the short story "The No-Guitar Blues" by Gary Soto. Notice how quickly he introduces the main character and sets the plot events in motion.

The No-Guitar Blues

by Gary Soto

The moment Fausto saw the group Los Lobos on *American Bandstand*, he knew exactly what he wanted to do with his life—play guitar. His eyes grew large with excitement as Los Lobos ground out a song while teenagers bounced off each other on the crowded dance floor.

He had watched *American Bandstand* for years and had heard Ray Camacho and the Teardrops at Romain Playground, but it had never occurred to him that he too might become a musician. That afternoon Fausto knew his mission in life: to play guitar in his own band; to sweat out songs and prance around the stage; to make money and dress weird.

Fausto turned off the television set and walked outside, wondering how he could get enough money to buy a guitar. . . .

The main **character** of this story is Fausto. The **plot** begins with him wondering how he will be able to buy a guitar. You have a hint at the **setting** for the beginning of the story—he is at home watching television.

A Flash of Inspiration

Before you write a short story of your own, you must come up with an idea for the story. Some-times a story idea springs into your mind immediately, but other times you have to search for one. You might try

- writing about a person you know who is interesting or unusual

- telling about an experience you have had

One student decided that his friend's desire to play hockey might make a good story. He decided to change parts of the story to create **suspense,** the uncertainty a reader feels about what will happen.

Critical Elements

Once you have a story idea, consider each of the fiction elements and decide how they will take shape in your story. Creating a story map like the one below will help you. Do not forget that your plot events should indicate the conflict, climax, and resolution of your story. (For more on the **elements of fiction,** see page 133.)

Put It in Words

Once your story map is complete, you are ready to begin writing a draft of the story. Remember to use **dialogue** to show character and to use concrete **description** to explain your setting. (For more on **dialogue,** see page 31. For more on **description,** see page 21.) The following is the beginning of the student's story about his friend.

Characters: John, his mom

Plot event: Mother is looking for John and finds him at a skating rink watching a hockey team. (setting)

Plot event: He explains that he really wants to be on the team. She won't let him because she thinks it's dangerous. (conflict)

Plot event: A game is about to start, and John convinces his mom to watch.

Plot event: She gets very excited cheering for the team. (climax)

Plot event: She decides hockey might be a good thing for John to do after all. (resolution)

John lived for hockey. Every day after school, he would walk to the town's only ice rink and watch the local youth teams practice. Often when the teams were packing up, he would borrow some skates and a stick and zoom around on the ice, perfecting his turns or slamming the puck into the net.

"Come on, John!" someone would almost always say. "Why don't you join the team?"

"Naw," he would answer. "My mom's scared I'll get hurt. She won't sign the papers."

 Writing a Short Story

Brainstorm a story idea, and fill in a story map like the one above. Then, use the information in your story map to write a short story.

Literature

Analyzing a Poem

When you made the cover of your book jacket, you created a picture that quickly gave readers an idea about the novel you chose. Poets also create pictures for their readers by using descriptive language.

Figuratively Speaking A **figure of speech** is a descriptive word or expression that is not meant to be taken literally. Two figures of speech commonly used in poetry are *simile* and *metaphor*.

A **simile** is a comparison between two unlike things, using a word such as *like* or *as*.

> The windblown children dashed across the field like scattered leaves.

A **metaphor** is a comparison between two unlike things in which one thing is said to *be* another thing.

> Our feet became hot potatoes roasting in the sand.

Sense or Sensibility While figures of speech describe by making comparisons, **imagery** uses vivid language to help the reader feel like a part of the poem. Imagery appeals to the senses—sight, touch, hearing, taste, and smell.

> The buzzing of bees in the garden broke the morning's silence.

Read the poem "Construction" by Patricia Hubbell, paying attention to its descriptive language.

Construction
by Patricia Hubbell

The house frames hang like spider webs
Dangling in the sun,
While up and down the wooden strands
The spider workers run.
They balance on the two-by-fours,   5
They creep across the beams,
While down below, the heap of wood,
A spider-stockpile, gleams.
The spider-workers spin the web
And tack it tight with nails.   10
They ready it against the night.
When all work ends.

A Closer Look When you analyze a poem, you should read it several times and take notes on what you find. The notes below were taken by a student who analyzed the descriptive language in "Construction."

- simile—house frames compared to spider webs (line 1)
- imagery—"Dangling in the sun" (line 2)
- imagery—"They creep across the beams" (line 6)
- metaphor—workers compared to spiders spinning a web (line 9)

The Big Picture Once you have identified a poem's figures of speech and imagery, decide what message the descriptive language seems to support. You will use this message as the main idea of your paper.

Put It in Words Before writing your essay, you will need to organize your ideas. Your poem analysis should include the parts listed in the following chart.

Introduction	■ the author and title of the poem
	■ the types of descriptive language used
	■ the writer's message
Body	■ examples of descriptive language
	■ explanation of how the descriptive language points to the writer's message
Conclusion	■ restatement of the descriptive language used and the writer's message

The student analyzing the poem "Construction" wrote the following essay. Notice that the student includes quotes from the poem when discussing examples of figurative language. According to the essay, what is the poet's message?

In her poem "Construction," Patricia Hubbell uses similes, metaphors, and imagery to show the similarities between workers building a house and spiders spinning a web.

Hubbell uses a simile and a metaphor to make the comparisons between the efforts of the workers and spiders. In this poem, the "house frames hang like spider webs." She also describes "spider-workers" who "spin the web." The imagery supports these comparisons as well. The house frames are "dangling in the sun." The description of the workers makes them sound like spiders when the poet writes, "They creep across the beams." All these descriptions help the reader picture the workers and spiders at the same time.

The figures of speech and imagery point to the message that a construction site is very similar to a spider web. The workers and spiders work the same way and both build houses.

YOUR TURN 12 Analyzing a Poem

Find a poem you like that contains figures of speech and vivid imagery. Follow the guidelines in this lesson to write an essay analyzing the poem's descriptive language.

Analyzing and Designing a Book Cover

WHAT'S AHEAD?

In this section you will analyze book covers and design your own. You will also learn how to:

- recognize the effect of color, font, and kind of illustration on a book's cover
- analyze a cover for effectiveness
- finalize your book jacket using appropriate media, color, and type

Can you judge a book by its cover? People do all the time. Sometimes a person will read or buy a book simply because of the cover, so the cover can be very important. If you know how to analyze a book cover, you can gather much more information than the title and author's name. A good book cover presents images, colors, and words in a way that reveals something about the book's content.

To analyze and interpret a book's cover, pay attention to three important elements: illustration, color, and font.

Illustration

TIP *Media* is the plural form of *medium*.

Tools of the Trade   An illustration is an image; a **medium** is the way an artist chooses to present that image. An artist has many media to choose from when presenting an illustration. For instance, an artist who wants to show a sailboat on an ocean could draw it with pencils, paint it with acrylic paint, use a computer-generated design, or take a photograph of a real sailboat. The artist could also use scraps of paper to create a collage of a sailboat.

Reference Note

For more on **illustration,** see page 789 in the Quick Reference Handbook.

Get It Covered   No matter what medium an artist uses, the illustration on a book's cover should tell readers something about the book. It can reveal something about the characters, setting, or action.

- **Characters**   Are they male or female, young or old, rich or poor?

- **Setting** Is the story set in the past, present, or future? Is it set in the city, the country, the United States, or somewhere else?
- **Action** Is there a chase scene or an important discovery?

Color

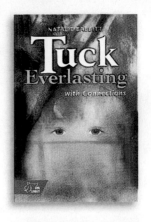

Color is an important element of an illustration. Colors can be described as warm or cool. Warm colors, such as red or yellow, tend to create a feeling of excitement. On the other hand, cool colors, such as blue or green, often create feelings of calmness or moodiness. The feeling an artist creates through his or her use of color is part of the artist's own style. Artists can also use color, however, to tell the reader something about the mood of the novel. An artist might also use a combination of warm and cool colors to emphasize important information. For example, in an illustration full of cool colors, the artist can use a warm color to draw the reader's eye to an important aspect of the novel. For more on **color,** see page 728 in the Quick Reference Handbook.

Examine the covers in the right margin and decide whether the colors are warm or cool. What do you think the artist is trying to achieve by using these colors?

Font

Most computers allow you to change the **font,** or the size and design of the type. Fonts can look like newsprint or handwriting. The font can look heavy and dark or light and thin. In addition, most fonts are available in styles such as bold or italic, and come in any number of sizes. Like colors, different fonts can suggest different meanings. For more on **font,** see page 726 in the Quick Reference Handbook.

Look at the examples below. What makes each font match the subject?

Romance **Old-fashioned**
Children **FUN!**
Scary Technology

Put It All Together

Using illustration, color, and font, the artist gives a general understanding of a book's content. Read the example on the next page of how one student analyzed the cover of the book *Hatchet.*

Illustration

Does the illustration clearly show the main character, setting, and action?	The illustration shows a boy—maybe the main character. The setting seems to be underwater, since there are fish and bubbles. The action is pretty clear—the boy must be trying to get to the surface.
What medium was used, and how does that medium help convey meaning?	The medium could be paint or computer. Bright painting or computer-generated art like this looks clean and crisp. It shows the setting, character, and action clearly.

Color

Are the colors in this cover warm or cool? What emotions could they represent?	The purple and green (cool colors) make me think that the novel might be moody and emotional. Because the boy's shirt is yellow, it really stands out against the green water. The ripped shirt might be important. Maybe the boy faces a dangerous or difficult situation.

Font

What meanings do the font styles reveal?	The word "hatchet" has pointed edges, just like a blade. The hatchet must be an important part of the story. I think the hatchet is going to help the boy.

TIP You might classify an illustrator's style as *literal* or *symbolic*. A more **literal** style of illustration might show actual scenes from the book. A more **symbolic** style of illustration may hint at an important idea or emotion in the book, rather than show an actual scene.

How would you describe the style of each cover shown on page 149 and on this page?

Interpreting a Book Cover

Make a chart like the one above to interpret the cover of a book. If you have trouble, review the information on pages 148–149.

Design Your Cover

Reference Note

To review how to get ideas for your cover illustration, see the Thinking It Through on page 131.

Now that you know how book covers provide information about a book, you should create your own. Look at the rough sketch of the cover you began earlier in the chapter. To complete your cover, use the same elements other artists use: illustrations, color, and font. Remember, the cover should convince people to read the novel. Make sure it gives readers interesting hints about the action, characters, or setting of the novel you have chosen.

A Rave Review   Do you think that the characters, setting, and action you have chosen to illustrate represent the novel well? Review your choices in the chart you created on page 150. Once you are sure about the content of your image, pick the medium that best helps you express something important about the novel.

The mood of the novel will help you decide on the colors to use. Determine the primary emotions portrayed in the novel, and use warm or cool colors to emphasize those emotions.

Finally, decide how the title should look on the page. Experiment with different fonts on a computer or flip through a magazine, tracing any fonts that fit the subject or mood of your novel.

Improve Your Drafts

Like writers, artists need to make drafts before they create a finished product. Few cover illustrators convey the true meaning of a book on their first try. Experiment with different images, media, colors, and fonts until you feel you have captured the point of the novel. Sketch several ideas, and choose one that you will fully develop as your final cover image.

YOUR TURN 14   Designing Your Book Cover

Follow the guidelines beginning on page 148 to finalize the book cover you began as part of your book jacket project. Remember to include the title of the book and the author's name on the cover. After you complete a rough sketch of your cover design, ask a classmate to look at it and give you suggestions for improving it.

Performing a Dramatic Reading

WHAT'S AHEAD?

In this section you will perform a dramatic reading. You will also learn how to

- choose a reading selection
- edit a selection for a dramatic reading
- analyze a selection for its mood and the characters' personalities
- use facial expressions, gestures, and different voices to portray different characters

TIP You may also choose a dramatic reading from a play. Be sure the scene you choose still follows these guidelines.

You are in an auditorium. On stage, a young man begins to speak, but he does not sound like a young man. He stomps his foot, and in a little girl's voice he demands a snack. Then, suddenly, his tone changes: "Honey, you can't have a snack now. It'll spoil your dinner." You are watching a *dramatic reading*. A **dramatic reading** is a presentation of a reading selection in which the reader acts out the characters and action as he or she reads aloud.

In one way, a dramatic reading from a novel is just like a novel's book jacket. They both give audiences a taste of a longer piece of literature. A dramatic reader brings the reading to life by using voices, facial expressions, and hand gestures. In this section you will have the opportunity to become a dramatic reader by dramatizing a scene from a novel.

Choose Your Selection

Choose Wisely   Use these questions to help you pick a passage for your dramatic reading.

- **Is it interesting?** Avoid long, descriptive passages. They are not easy to dramatize, especially for a young-adult audience. Instead, choose a passage with interesting dialogue or action. Focus on scenes that are full of suspense, action, or emotion.
- **Is it easy to understand?** If you have trouble understanding your passage, your audience will, too. Make sure your reading will make sense to people who have not read the whole book.
- **What is your time limit?** Make sure you know what your time limit is, and stick to it. Test the length of your passage by reading it slowly.

Prepare for Reading

From the Page to the Stage   After you choose a selection, you need to adapt it for performance. Follow these three steps.

- **Edit the Selection.** Some parts of a novel do not sound right in performance. To keep your reading interesting, cut dialogue tags such as "he said" and "she said," long descriptive passages, and references to characters and events that are not important to the passage you selected. All these things break the flow of your performance and distract your audience. To make editing easy, make a copy of your selection. Then, cross out the parts that will not sound right in a performance.

"Honey, you can't have a snack now. It'll spoil your dinner."
~~Maggie's mother said firmly.~~

After you have crossed out unnecessary parts, you can add background information from other parts of the novel as needed. Sometimes this is necessary to make sure the audience understands what is happening in the passage.

- **Analyze the Selection.** What happens in your selection? How do the characters feel? Is the tone of the piece happy, sad, or suspenseful? Go through the passage and make notes on the overall scene and on each character. You can show what the characters are like in general, as well as how they act in your selection.

Maggie: She is stubborn and likes to get her own way. In this passage about the snack, she's having a temper tantrum. She pouts. She takes her anger out on her brother.

Maggie's mother: She is gentle, but firm. She has a soothing voice.

Little brother: He is afraid. He seems to get picked on by Maggie a lot.

Overall tone: The tension rises when Maggie confronts her brother.

- **Plan Your Delivery.** Have you ever noticed that when you are happy or excited, the **pitch** of your voice gets higher and your speaking **rate** gets faster? If you are serious or sad, the pitch of your voice becomes lower and your speaking rate gets slower. Using your notes, figure out what kind of voice will fit the moods of the narrator and each of the characters. Most important, keep a character's voice consistent until the selection is over or until his or her feelings change. Also, use gestures. When people speak, they move. Most people emphasize their words with gestures. Some even have certain mannerisms, like raising their eyebrows or waving their hands. Your reading will look more realistic if you act out unique gestures for each character.

To figure out the best way to add voices and actions to your reading script, you can add notes to remind you how to perform your edited selection. Retype or rewrite your edited reading selection with the acting notes in parentheses.

Example:
(Maggie's mom, medium-low voice, soft but firm)
"Honey, you can't have a snack now. It'll spoil your dinner."

(Maggie, high voice, yelling. Face in a pout.)
"But I want a snack NOW!" (stomp)

Practice Delivery

Practice Makes Perfect   To make your reading the best it can be, you need to practice many times. Think of practicing as a series of steps, each one a little different from the one before it.

Step 1	Practice reading until you are comfortable and familiar with the characters and story.
Step 2	Practice your delivery several times, each time adding another element, including ■ voice changes, pauses, and adjustments in how fast or slow you talk ■ gestures and facial expressions (practice with a mirror)
Step 3	Rehearse in front of a friend or relative, or tape your rehearsal with a video camera or a tape recorder. Ask your listener for feedback, or play back the tape, noting parts you need to improve. Watch especially for how fast you are reading, how you use gestures, and how your facial expressions change.

 Performing a Dramatic Reading

Prepare for a performance of your own dramatic reading by

■ choosing a scene with few characters and clear action

■ editing the scene to remove any unnecessary parts

■ analyzing the scene to get a feel for the characters and their voices and gestures

■ practicing the scene until you know it well

4 Choices

Choose one of the following activities to complete.

▶ SPEAKING

1. Lights, Camera, Action!
Imagine you are a movie director and want to make a movie from a book. Just as your book jacket previewed a book, you will need a preview for the movie. Use the book you read earlier in the chapter for your **movie preview.** Use the same information as you did for your book-jacket summary—character, setting, plot, and theme. This time, however, make a three-minute presentation of your summary as if you were the narrator for the preview. You may want to include a few visuals showing scenes that you would include in your preview.

▶ DRAMA

2. Acting Out Choose a poem and give a **dramatic interpretation** of it. Read it for an audience, using gestures, pauses, and voice changes to dramatize the poem. Ask your teacher or librarian for assistance in finding the perfect poem to read aloud.

▶ CAREERS

3. Meet the Author Authors often visit bookstores to talk to readers and to autograph books. Call a bookstore nearby and ask when the next author of young-adult books will be having a book signing. Using the author research skills you learned in this chapter, learn more about the author. After researching, generate a list of questions you still have. Then, go to the book signing and ask your questions. When you get home, write a **journal entry** about your experience.

▶ CROSSING THE CURRICULUM: SCIENCE

4. Experience Laboratory Life Choose an experiment by reading a science book for young adults or by asking your science teacher for ideas. Study how the experiment works. Then, write a **hypothesis,** or a prediction about what will happen when you conduct the experiment. Then, conduct the experiment with a teacher or other adult and record the results. Write a **paragraph** explaining why your hypothesis was or was not correct.

PORTFOLIO

Finding and Reporting Information

Reading Workshop	Writing Workshop	Focus on Speaking and Listening	Focus on Viewing and Representing
Reading an Informative Article **PAGE 158**	*Writing a Report of Information* **PAGE 168**	*Giving and Listening to an Informative Speech* **PAGE 191**	*Interpreting Graphics and Web Sites* **PAGE 194**

Who decided that people need to go to school? What does a manatee eat? How do computers work? Questions like these probably run through your mind all the time.

You may begin finding answers to the questions *Who? What? When? Where? Why?* and *How?* by doing research. Look around and you will find many sources of informative writing to help you answer your questions: textbooks, newspapers, and other media sources such as the Internet and documentaries. When you have a question about a particular topic, look for informative books or articles to help you find the answer.

internet connect

go.
hrw
.com

GO TO: go.hrw.com
KEYWORD: EOLang 7-5

YOUR TURN 1 · Exploring Informative Articles

Find an informative article on a topic that interests you. After you read it, answer the following questions.

- Where did you find the article?
- Did the article give you all the information you wanted? Explain.
- Was the information in the article easy to understand? Explain.
- Where else might you look for information on this topic?
- How might you share what you have learned?

Reading an Informative Article

WHAT'S AHEAD?

In this section you will read an excerpt from a science textbook. You will also learn how to

- identify textbook features

- summarize information

Have you ever wondered why people sneeze, or why some people seem to get sick all the time while others never do? Our bodies have several ways to defend themselves when germs and viruses are around. In the following textbook selection, you will read more about the human body's defense system. As you read, notice how the author makes the information in this section easy to understand.

Preparing to Read

READING FOCUS

Textbook Features Imagine that you are writing a letter to your best friend (during lunch, of course), and you really want to get a certain point across. What do you do? You probably underline it, circle it, or draw a big arrow pointing to it. Without realizing it, you have used some of the same types of features that textbook authors use to communicate their points. **Textbook features** include bold or italic print, definitions and notes in the side and bottom margins, and special headings. As you read the following textbook selection, pay attention to the way the author uses text features to present information.

READING SKILL

Summarizing Information Textbooks are loaded with information. Even when you read a short selection, you may feel like you are experiencing an information overload. Putting information in your own words by *summarizing* can help you get a handle on it. When you **summarize** information, you state only the most important ideas. Summarizing a reading selection is a great study strategy that can help you remember what you read.

Read the following textbook selection. In your notebook, jot down answers to the numbered active-reading questions in the shaded boxes. The underlined words will appear in the Vocabulary Mini-Lesson on page 166.

from SciencePlus

THE BODY'S DEFENSES

The boy in the photo to the right has spent his entire life inside a plastic bubble. He is not allowed to touch anyone, not even his mother or father, because he was born with no natural defense against <u>infectious</u> diseases. As a result, even a simple cold could endanger his life. Fortunately, most of us have a defense system that automatically fights off most of the bacteria and viruses that could harm us. This system consists of several lines of defense.

> **1. Which sentence indicates the main idea of this selection?**

The First Line of Defense
Skin and Mucus

Under normal conditions, the skin stops microorganisms from entering the body. However, when the skin is broken, cut, or damaged, germs can enter. That is why it is very important to clean cuts and

> **2. What role does skin play in your body's defense system?**

scrapes. But skin does not cover every surface of the body.

Mucus stops germs from attacking tissue not covered by the skin. For example, the inside of the nose is covered by tiny hairs and mucus. These hairs and mucus trap dust and germs from the air you breathe. Sometimes extra mucus is made by the body in response to the presence of foreign substances such as dust, pollen, or germs. . . . Blowing your nose and sneezing help remove trapped microorganisms. It

> **3. What is your body doing when you sneeze?**

Mucus A thick, sticky fluid covering many surfaces inside the body and its natural openings.

is important to cover your mouth and nose when you sneeze to <u>prevent</u> the spread of these microorganisms. . . .

The Second Line of Defense
White Blood Cells

What happens if you cut your skin and germs enter the cut? Then your second line of defense, the *white blood cells*, becomes active.

White blood cells are one part of your blood. They are made inside some of your bones. Many of them are found in structures called lymph nodes and in the tonsils.

It is believed that damaged tissue, such as a cut, and invading germs both release chemicals. These chemicals attract white blood cells. At the same time, the area around the cut becomes warm and appears red, indicating that the cut has become infected.

White blood cells, like the one shown here, are the body's second line of defense.

White blood cells surround and destroy germs and damaged tissue. This action is similar to the way that an amoeba surrounds its food. The activity of white blood cells stops infection and cleans the area so that proper healing can take place.

4. How could you put the main details in this paragraph in your own words?

The Third Line of Defense
The Immune System

. . . Some kinds of white blood cells make special chemicals called **antibodies.** Antibodies help in the destruction of microorganisms and other foreign substances. Your body is capable of producing antibodies for just about every kind of germ or foreign substance that exists on earth.

The <u>production</u> of antibodies is a relatively quick process. A few days after an <u>invader</u> has entered the body, a large number of antibodies can usually be found in the blood. This process of antibody production

5. What does "invader" refer to in this paragraph?

Antibodies Chemicals that are made by the body and that fight germs or other foreign substances.

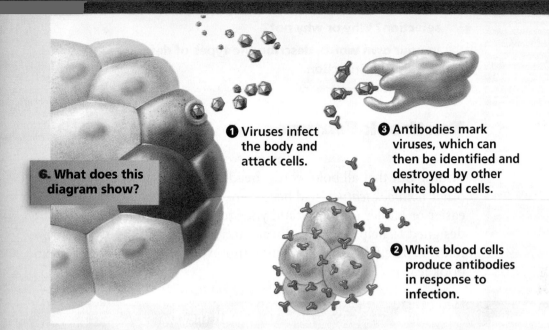

❶ Viruses infect the body and attack cells.

❸ Antibodies mark viruses, which can then be identified and destroyed by other white blood cells.

6. What does this diagram show?

❷ White blood cells produce antibodies in response to infection.

is a function of the **immune system,** the body's third line of defense.

Soon after a disease is successfully stopped, the level of the antibody that fought against it drops. For example, a person who has <u>recovered</u> from chickenpox will have only a small amount of chickenpox antibody left in his or her bloodstream. But a few of the white blood cells that made the chickenpox antibody remain in the bloodstream to fight the chickenpox virus if it returns. These white blood cells "remember" how to make the antibody for

chickenpox. If the virus that causes chickenpox enters the body again, these cells will make a lot of new antibodies in a very short time. They will eliminate the virus before it can do any damage and before you become ill. That is why a person usually gets diseases like measles, mumps, whooping cough, scarlet fever, and chickenpox only once. This <u>resistance</u> to a disease is called **acquired immunity.** Acquired immunity to some diseases lasts a lifetime.

7. Why is "acquired immunity" in bold print?

Immune system Body system that uses antibodies to seek out and destroy invading microorganisms.

Acquired immunity Resistance to reinfection by a disease after the body has recovered from the original infection.

First Thoughts on Your Reading

1. Did the headings and definitions help you understand this selection? Why or why not?

2. In your own words, describe the types of defenses our bodies use against infection.

Textbook Features

Information, Please Imagine opening up your textbook and finding out that all bold words, headings, definitions, graphics, and other *textbook features* had been removed. Do you think it would be easier or harder to understand your textbook? **Textbook features** are designed to help you easily locate and understand important information. The following table lists and explains some common textbook features.

Types of Features	Examples	What They Do
Features within the main reading (or chapter)	■ titles, subtitles, headings, and subheadings ■ boldface and italic type ■ charts, graphs, and diagrams	■ break information into chunks to make it clearer ■ point to important ideas or add emphasis ■ present information found in the text in a visual way
Features in the margins	■ definitions ■ questions ■ reference notes	■ provide meanings of important words ■ give readers clues to important information ■ tell readers where to find more information about a topic
Features after the main reading	■ end-of-selection questions	■ emphasize information from the main text

Using Textbook Features Recognizing textbook features is important. However, textbook features are meaningless unless you use them to help you learn. Learning to use textbook features before, during, and after you read will make informative writing easier to understand and remember.

Before You Read If you spend a few minutes making predictions about the chapter *before you read*, you will find that the details of the chapter will easily fall into place *as you read*. For example, after reading the chapter title "The Body's Defenses," you could predict that the chapter is about how the body defends itself. Then, if you studied the first main heading (The First Line of Defense) and the subheading beneath this heading (Skin and Mucus), you could conclude that skin and mucus are part of the first line of defense.

As You Read As you read a textbook, pay close attention to boldface and italic type. **Boldface** and *italic* type call attention to important vocabulary you will need to know to understand a certain concept. When you read a word in boldface or italics, look for the meaning or definition within the passage or in the margin.

Many textbooks also include questions or reference notes in the side or bottom margins. The questions help you check your understanding. If you cannot answer a question, you should re-read the passage or ask your teacher for help. The reference notes tell you where to find more information about an important idea.

After You Read Answering end-of-chapter questions is a great way for you to check your understanding. If you are able to answer these questions correctly, you can be confident that you understand the main points of the chapter. After you have successfully answered end-of-chapter questions, you can use text features to make a *study guide* to help you remember what you have read. A **study guide,** like the partial example below, contains only the most important information from the selection, such as the main headings and important vocabulary.

TIP Some textbooks provide questions at the beginning or end of a chapter. If so, you should take a moment to read them. These questions often stress the main points of the chapter. Of course, when you first read these questions, you might not know the answers. However, you will be surprised to find that some of the answers may "jump out" of the book as you read.

TIP If a book does not have end-of-chapter questions, you might want to make your own. You can do this by turning headings or subheadings into questions. For example, for the heading "The First Line of Defense," you would ask "What is the body's first line of defense?"

Chapter Title: The Body's Defenses

Heading one: The First Line of Defense

Subheading one: Skin and Mucus

Relationship of heading to subheading: The first line of defense is the skin and mucus.

Boldface or italicized words with definitions: Mucus is a sticky substance that helps keep germs out of the body.

Explanation of graphic: no graphic in this section

Summary of information in subheading one:

Using Textbook Features to Make a Study Guide

Make a study guide like the one on page 163 for the second and third headings of "The Body's Defenses." Be sure to use the chapter's textbook features to help you. (Do not fill in the "summary" section for either heading. You will do this in Your Turn 3.)

Summarizing Information

TIP Summarizing as you read will help you remember what you have read.

Say It Your Way   You have probably heard teachers and librarians say this a thousand times: "Put it in your own words!" When you **summarize,** you put only the most important information you have read or heard into your own words.

A good summary covers the main ideas of a selection, not every detail. For this reason, a summary is always much shorter than the original material. Think of a summary in terms of a sportscast: A summary includes only the highlights, such as the key plays and final results; it does not include a lengthy play-by-play account with every name and statistic.

How would you summarize the following passage? If you have trouble, use the Thinking It Through steps on the next page.

> . . . Some diseases, such as various types of heart disease and arthritis, are caused by malfunctions of the immune system. Like other systems in the body, the immune system can malfunction or even break down altogether. Such a breakdown is called an immune disease or disorder. There are three basic types of *immune disorders:* allergies, autoimmune disorders, and immune deficiency disorders.
>
> An **allergy** is a condition in which the immune system reacts to a normally harmless foreign substance, such as pollen or certain foods. In an allergic reaction, the immune system produces antibodies that attack the foreign substance, causing a variety of symptoms: runny nose, sneezing, red and watery eyes, swelling, rashes, and so on. In a few cases, severe allergic reactions can be fatal.
>
> "The Body's Defenses," *SciencePlus*

Summarizing Information

▶ **STEP 1** Find the main idea of each paragraph. For each paragraph, ask yourself, "What do all of the sentences have in common?"

In the first paragraph, all of the sentences are about the immune system.

The second paragraph is about allergies.

Reference Note

For more on **identifying implied main ideas,** see page 745 in the Quick Reference Handbook.

▶ **STEP 2** In your own words, write the most important supporting details necessary for understanding each main idea. In other words, explain what the author is saying about each main idea. Do not include most examples, anecdotes, or sensory language in your summary.

Diseases are sometimes caused by problems with the immune system. When the immune system stops working right, it's called an immune disorder. One type of immune disorder is an allergy. An allergy is a reaction to something that is normally harmless. Antibodies attack this substance, which causes an allergic reaction. Allergic reactions are usually minor, but they can be deadly.

▶ **STEP 3** Check that you did not copy any sentences or long phrases from the original text. If you did, replace them with original words and phrases that have the same meaning as those you copied.

Summarizing Information

■ Re-read "The Body's Defenses" on pages 159–161. Then, working with a small group, orally summarize the section titled "The First Line of Defense." Be sure to state the main idea and only the most important supporting details.

■ On your own, write summaries for the two remaining sections of "The Body's Defenses," and add these summaries to the study guide that you began earlier. Remember to write your summaries using your own words.

MINI-LESSON VOCABULARY

Prefixes and Suffixes

When reading a textbook, you may come across unfamiliar words that are not defined for you. Learning to take these words apart can help you determine their meanings.

The main part of a word, the root, contains the word's core meaning. When a prefix or a suffix such as those shown in the charts below is added to a root, the meaning of the word changes.

Prefix	Meaning	Example
anti–	against	antibiotic
pre–	before	preview
re–	back, again	replay

Suffix	Meaning	Example
–ion	action, result	selection
–ous	characterized by	joyous
–er	doer, action	catcher

THINKING IT THROUGH — Using Prefixes and Suffixes

Here is how to use a word's parts to understand its meaning.

▶ **STEP 1** Separate word parts until you get to a word you know.

resistance = resist + –ance

▶ **STEP 2** Find the meaning of each part.

Resist means "to oppose."
The suffix –ance means "the condition of."

▶ **STEP 3** Combine the meanings to define the unfamiliar word.

Resistance means "the condition of opposing something."

▶ **STEP 4** Adjust your definition to fit the context of the sentence.

Sentence: "This resistance to a disease is called acquired immunity." Resistance is "the condition of being able to oppose diseases."

PRACTICE

Use the charts and steps above to define these words, which are underlined in "The Body's Defenses."

1. infectious (page 159)

2. prevent (–vent: to come) (page 160)

3. production (page 160)

4. invader (page 160)

5. recovered (page 161)

Answering Questions That Include Graphs

Like textbooks, many reading tests include graphs. However, a graph on a reading test usually does not have a paragraph that explains it. Instead, the reading test will probably ask you to answer a series of questions about the graph. Study the graph below and the question that follows it.

How would you answer the question?

A local charity is starting a campaign to get more teens to volunteer for its program, which builds housing for families in need. According to the graph at left, which of the following approaches might be most successful in attracting teenage volunteers?

Reasons Teens Give for Not Volunteering

Number of Teens

"I'm too busy with school." — No Time During School Year

"None of my friends do this." — Peer Pressure

"I've got other things to do." — Lack of Interest

A. Have "Teen Volunteer Days" during the summer.

B. Hold training classes for volunteers.

C. Distribute informational videos to get teens interested.

D. Start a "Be Brave—Don't Cave" program to combat negative peer pressure.

THINKING IT THROUGH **Answering Questions That Include a Graph**

▶ **STEP 1** Read the question to determine what it is asking.

It is asking how the charity can get more teens to volunteer.

▶ **STEP 2** Read the title of the graph.

It is about why teens don't volunteer.

▶ **STEP 3** Find and interpret each of the intersections of the graph. An **intersection** in a bar graph is the point at which the top end of a bar rising from the floor of the graph meets with a number from the left side.

25 teens decline to volunteer because they don't have enough time during the school year; about 21 because of peer pressure; and around 17 because of a lack of interest.

▶ **STEP 4** Use the question and the graph to find the correct answer.

Most (25) don't volunteer because they have no time. Because they might have more time in the summer, answer "A" is the best choice.

Writing a Report of Information

WHAT'S AHEAD?

In this workshop you will write a report of information. You will also learn how to

■ focus a subject

■ find and evaluate sources

■ take notes

■ add sentence variety to your writing

■ format sources

I f you have ever sought answers to the questions *Who? What? When? Where? Why?* or *How?* you have done research. After all, seeking answers to questions is the whole point of doing research. In this workshop you will write a report of information. The subject of your report is up to you, but it should be something that sparks your curiosity. Finding information and writing a report about it is your chance to answer your own questions about your subject as well as the questions of your readers.

Prewriting

Choose and Focus a Subject

I Wonder . . . What will you write about in your report of information? If you have ever said, "I wonder," about something, that something might be a good subject for research. After all, the best subject for a research report is one that really interests you.

You may already know what you want to research. However, if you still need a subject, try one of these ideas and see if you become inspired.

■ Thumb through an informative magazine to get ideas. Scientific discoveries and historical events make good research subjects.

■ Think about your favorite class. Then, list the subjects from this class that you like. Choose one of these subjects to explore.

At the top of the next page is one student's list of possible subjects.

Favorite class: (science,) math, history, English

I like when we talk about (animals,) volcanoes, and inventions.

Animals that interest me: elephants, wolves, tigers, (eagles)

Get Focused   From avalanches to zebras, you can choose almost anything for a subject. However, unless you plan on pitching a tent and living in the library for the next year or two, **you should limit your subject. You can do this by focusing on something specific about your subject.** For example, instead of writing everything about zebras, you could limit your report to how zebras raise their young.

Begin focusing your subject by making a **conceptual map.** Draw an oval in the center of a piece of paper and write your subject within it. As you think of specific topics, write them in connecting ovals.

◄ KEY CONCEPT |

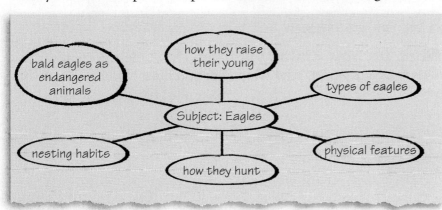

TIP Once you start researching, you may not be able to find enough information on your specific topic. If so, you might have focused your subject too narrowly. On the other hand, if you find *too much* information about your specific topic, it may still be too broad. Talk to your teacher about getting the best focus.

YOUR TURN 4 Choosing and Focusing a Subject

Choose a subject and focus it by making a map like the one above. Then, choose the specific topic that is most interesting to you.

Think About Audience and Purpose

What's My Motivation?   Every time you write, you should remind yourself why you are writing. **The purpose of a report of information is to find information and share it with other people.** Who are those people? Your audience will probably include your teacher and

◄ KEY CONCEPT |

TIP Be sure to write in your own **voice**. Because your purpose is to inform, you should be as clear as possible by using standard, formal English. However, you should avoid trying to sound like an adult scientist or someone you are not. In other words, your writing voice should sound like you—a knowledgeable and serious you.

classmates, but anyone who is interested in your topic could be your audience. Ask yourself the following questions about the audience you identify.

Question	Explanation
What do my readers already know about my topic?	If you repeat information that your readers already know, they might become bored with your report.
What do my readers need to know about my topic?	Give your readers enough information to understand your topic by thoroughly explaining important ideas.
What can they do with the information?	Explain why the information is important for readers to know.

Ask Questions

What Do You Know?   To think about the information you need for your report, start with what you already know about your topic. Use a graphic organizer, or make a list like the one below.

- There are fewer bald eagles now than there used to be.
- I know that there are laws to protect other animals.
- I think bald eagles used to be hunted.

What Do You Need to Know?   After brainstorming what you already know about your topic, make a list of the questions you still have. **These questions will guide your research later.** Also, write down questions your audience might have. Start with the *5W-How?* **questions:** *Who? What? Where? When? Why?* and *How?*

| KEY CONCEPT ▶

TIP Your list of research questions may change as you do your research. As more questions occur to you, add them to your list.

Who is trying to help endangered eagles?

What are they doing to help endangered eagles?

Where are bald eagles most endangered?

When did bald eagles first become endangered?

Why are they endangered?

How many bald eagles are living today?

Thinking About Audience and Purpose and Asking Questions

- Think about your purpose and audience. Answer the questions in the chart on page 170 to identify your audience's needs.

- List the information you already know about your topic. Then, write a list of questions that you still have or that your audience might have. Title this list "Research Questions."

Find Sources

Get the Facts! Start finding answers to your questions by researching sources. A **source** gives you information about your topic. Where can you find sources?

The Library The library is a great resource for print sources such as encyclopedias, books, magazines, and newspapers. Many libraries also contain nonprint sources such as videotapes, audiotapes, slides, microfiche, CD-ROMs, and Internet access.

Television Some TV channels broadcast informative documentaries and biographies as well as programs about science and nature. To find programs about your topic, check a television guide.

The Web The World Wide Web is a resource for information on almost any subject. If you use a Web site, be sure it is a reliable source of information. A reliable Web site should include information on the author's professional background, the date the site was last updated, and a list of the sources the author used.

Experts You may find experts on your topic at a local museum, university, hospital, or government office. If you arrange an **interview** with an expert, be sure you prepare for it by bringing a list of questions and paper on which to write down all of the answers.

Make a Source List

Hey, Where Did You Get That? After you find sources for your report, you need to make a *source list*. A **source list** is a sheet of paper on which you write all of the sources you use for your report. There are several different styles for listing sources. The chart on the next page shows the style the Modern Language Association recommends.

COMPUTER TIP

To find information for your report, try conducting a *key word search* on a search engine. A **key word search** limits your search results to those pages that contain a specific word or words related to your topic. For example, to research the history of television, you could enclose in quotation marks the key words *television history*. This would bring up a list of sites that contained these words.

Reference Note

For more on **evaluating Web sites,** see page 742 in the Quick Reference Handbook.

MLA Guide for Listing Sources

Book

Author/editor. Title. City: Publisher, year.

Grambo, Rebecca L., ed. Eagles: Masters of the Sky. Stillwater, OK: Voyageur Press, 1997.

Electronic Sources

Online: Author (if known). "Document Title." Web Site or Database Title. Date of electronic publication. Name of Sponsoring Institution. Date information was accessed <url>.

Martell, Mark, and MaryBeth Garrigan. "Bald Eagle." The Raptor Center. Sept. 1994. U of Minnesota. 18 Nov. 1998 <http://www.raptor.cvm.umn.edu/>.

CD-ROM: Author (if known). "Title of Article." Title of Database. Title of Medium (CD-ROM). City of Electronic Publication: Electronic Publisher, Date of electronic publication.

"Eagle." 1997 Grolier Multimedia Encyclopedia. CD-ROM. Danbury: Grolier Interactive, 1997.

Encyclopedia Article

Author (if known). "Title of Article." Name of Encyclopedia. Edition (if known) and year.

Grier, James W. "Eagle." The World Book Encyclopedia. 1998.

Interview

Speaker. The words *Personal interview, Telephone interview,* or *Guest speaker.* Date.

Sullivan, Vanessa. Personal interview. 17 Nov. 1998.

Magazine or Newspaper Article

Author. "Title of Article." Publication Name Date: page number(s).

Gerstenzang, James. "Eagle May Fly From Nest of Endangered." Los Angeles Times 6 May 1998: A1.

Movie or Video Recording

Title. Name of Director or Producer. The words *Videocassette, Videodisc, or Movie.* Name of Distributor, year released.

Amazing Birds of Prey. Dir. Ann Neale. Videocassette. DK Vision, 1997.

Television or Radio Program

Title of Program. Name of Host (if any). Network. Station Call Letters, City. Date of broadcast.

Jaws & Claws: Flying Assassins. Discovery Channel. DISC, Austin. 26 July 1998.

Finding Sources and Making a Source List

Find at least three different types of sources for your report of information. Then, make a source list, and number each source on your list. You will need these numbers when you take notes.

Evaluating Sources

Newspapers, magazines, books, the Internet, and television shower us with information every day. Unfortunately, not all of the information available is reliable. Use the following guidelines to evaluate the reliability of the sources you find.

- **Identify the writer or creator of the source.** Look for an "About the Author" page that lists the writer's qualifications. In general, the more experience and education a writer has on the subject, the more reliable he or she will be. Also, sources that are endorsed by reputable nonprofit or educational organizations are generally reliable.

  Preferred source: *a book on endangered animals written by an environmental scientist and endorsed by the World Wildlife Federation*

  Less reliable source: *a Web page created by a nine-year-old as a class project on endangered tigers*

- **Locate the date the information was published.** Although older sources can be helpful for historical topics, up-to-date information is usually best for a report, especially one on a scientific topic.

  Preferred source: *a recent magazine article on the state of endangered animals in Guatemala*

  Less reliable source: *a book about Central American animals published in 1934 by an explorer and hunter*

- **Identify the purpose of the source.** Some books and articles are written to inform and do not include many of the author's opinions or feelings. If the author of your source includes too many opinions and too few facts, don't use it as a main source.

  Preferred source: *a newspaper article citing statistics on endangered animals*

  Less reliable source: *a fund-raising brochure describing the plight of a certain species*

PRACTICE

Below are several descriptions of sources for a research paper on the moon. Identify each description as either a **preferred** source or a **less reliable** source. Be prepared to defend your answer.

1. a book published in 1910 on the geography of the moon

2. a Web page on moon rocks published by the National Aeronautics and Space Administration (NASA)

3. a 1999 edition encyclopedia article on geographical formations on the moon

4. a book of poetry about the moon

5. a report on the moon published on the Web by a high school student

Take Notes

Unforgettable   The Great Lakes have an area of 94,600 square miles. Light travels at 186,000 miles per second. Jasmine is a plant in the olive family. So many facts and ideas can be hard to remember. To remember the facts and information you gather while researching, you should write them down.

Use note cards, small sheets of paper, or computer files to record your notes. Here are some suggestions for taking notes.

- Write a short label on the top line of each card, sheet of paper, or computer file to identify the subject of the note.
- Make sure that each note contains only one main idea.
- Summarize information, using your own words. If you do write an author's exact words, use quotation marks. Using an author's words or ideas without giving credit is called *plagiarism*. **Plagiarism** is a form of cheating and can result in disciplinary action.
- Write the source number you are using in the top right corner of your card, file, or piece of paper. For example, if you are using source five from your source list, write "5" in the top right corner.
- Write the number of the page where you found the information at the bottom of your card, file, or piece of paper.

TIP Sometimes a quotation from a writer or speaker lends interest and believability to your report. If you use a quotation, give the person credit by using the person's name or the title of the book in which the quotation appears.

Example:
In an interview Babbitt said, "The eagle is doing splendidly. It's making a wonderful comeback everywhere."

TIP If your teacher asks you to show your sources in the body of your paper, use **parenthetical citations**. A parenthetical citation includes the author's last name or, if no author is given, the first major word of the source title followed by the page number.

Example:
The territory of Alaska paid a bounty for every eagle that was shot (Grambo 78).
    The Writer's Model on pages 179–181 includes parenthetical citations.

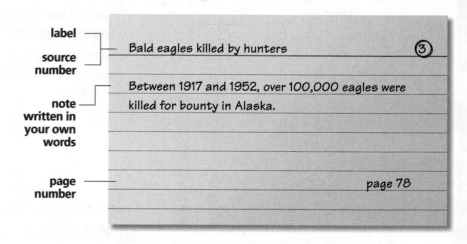

label
source number
note written in your own words
page number

Bald eagles killed by hunters   ③

Between 1917 and 1952, over 100,000 eagles were
killed for bounty in Alaska.

page 78

YOUR TURN 7   Taking Notes

Read your sources to find answers to your research questions. Take notes when you find useful information. Refer to the suggestions for taking notes above, if necessary.

Plan Your Report

Get It Together   Making an early plan and an outline can help you make sure none of the information you gathered falls through the cracks.

Early Plan   First, group the notes that deal with similar information into separate sets. Then, give each group of notes a **heading**—a word or phrase that describes the information in that set. **The headings for your groups are the main ideas of your report.** Here is a list of headings for a student's report on bald eagles. Notice that each of her headings represents a single idea. In what order would you discuss the following headings?

KEY CONCEPT

- General facts about endangered eagles
- Reasons eagles were endangered
- Eagles' recovery
- Ways eagles were helped

TIP   You can also use a graphic organizer, such as a **conceptual map** or a **time line,** to organize your notes into groups or categories. For more information on these and other graphic organizers you can use for prewriting, see page 806 in the Quick Reference Handbook.

 Making an Early Plan

Sort your notes into sets and give each set a heading. Then, decide the order in which you will discuss each heading in your report.

Mapping It Out   Before you begin writing your report, you should make an *outline* using the headings you created for your early plan. An **outline** shows how the ideas in a composition are related to each other. Study the following excerpt from a student's outline. Notice that she listed related details beneath her heading.

TIP   When making your outline, you may notice that some of your subheadings can be grouped together. If this happens, think of a word or phrase that describes these subheadings. This word or phrase will become your new subheading. Compare Roman numeral two in the example to the left with the Roman numeral two in the outline on the next page.

II. Reasons eagles were endangered
   A. Belief that eagles were destroying crops and livestock
   B. Bounties that encouraged hunting
   C. Loss of trees
   D. New homes and businesses

The main heading in the example above is "Reasons eagles were endangered." The specific causes for their low numbers are underneath the heading. These are called **subheadings.**

To make your own outline, use the following steps. If you have trouble, study the outline that follows.

- Write your main headings on a sheet of paper in the order you want to discuss them. Label each heading with a Roman numeral.
- Under each main heading, write subheadings. Label each subheading with a capital letter. Number each detail that explains a subheading.

Bald Eagles as Endangered Animals

I. General facts about endangered eagles
   A. Drop in numbers in the 1940s and '50s
   B. Enormous decline in 1960s

II. Reasons eagles were endangered
   A. Hunters
      1. Belief that eagles were destroying crops and livestock
      2. Bounties that encouraged hunting
   B. Demand for lumber and land
      1. Lumber mills
      2. New homes and businesses
   C. Pesticides
      1. Effect on eagles' food
      2. Effect on offspring

III. Ways eagles were helped
   A. Laws
      1. 1940—the Bald Eagle Protection Act
      2. 1972—banning of DDT
      3. 1973—the Endangered Species Protection Act
   B. Captive breeding programs
      1. Description of program
      2. Effect on eagle population

IV. Eagles' recovery
   A. Statistics about recovery
   B. Eagles' removal from the endangered species list

TIP Since the Roman numerals from your outline will be the main sections of your report, you might want to include these headings in your final draft. Providing a clear heading before each major part of your report can help the reader understand the organization of your report.

Outlining Your Report

Create an outline for your report based on your notes and on the headings you created in Your Turn 8. Use the example outline and the instructions on pages 175–176 to help you make your own outline.

Write Your Main Idea Statement

What's the Big Idea? Now that you have done your research and taken notes, you are ready to write a main idea statement about your specific topic. **The main idea statement, also known as a *thesis statement*, appears in the introductory paragraph of your report and tells what you will say about your topic.** A good main idea statement serves as an umbrella for the main headings from your outline.

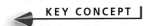

Focused Topic: Eagles as Endangered Animals

Headings from outline:

I. General facts about endangered eagles

II. Reasons eagles were endangered

III. Ways eagles were helped

IV. Eagles' recovery

Main idea statement: Although bald eagles were in danger of becoming extinct in the 1950s, the efforts of many groups over the last ten years have helped them make an amazing comeback.

Anyone who reads your report should understand what it is about after reading the main idea statement. In the example above, the reader could guess that the report would cover eagles as endangered animals, the reasons eagles were once endangered, and how people helped them to recover.

 10

Writing Your Main Idea Statement

Use the example above to help you write your main idea statement. Remember that this statement should serve as an umbrella for the Roman numeral headings of your outline.

Writing

Report of Information

Framework	**Directions and Explanations**

Introduction
- Attention-grabbing beginning
- Main idea statement

To catch the reader's interest, start with an **attention-grabber,** or hook, such as an interesting fact, quotation, or question. Then, state the **main idea,** or **thesis,** of your paper.

Body
- Heading #1
  Supporting details
- Heading #2
  Supporting details
  and so on

- Use the information from your outline and notes to write the body of your report. In general, each paragraph should address one heading or subheading from your outline. However, you may need to use more than one paragraph to explain a particular heading or subheading.

- Make sure that the main point in each paragraph has **logical support,** including all of the relevant **details** (facts, examples, and statistics) you found during research. **Elaborate** on each detail by asking yourself, "Why is this detail important?" or "What does this detail mean?"

Conclusion
- Restatement of main idea

In your conclusion, sum up the ideas in your report. **Restate your main idea** and bring your report to a close. You can bring your report to a close by drawing a conclusion about your research or by referring to something specific in your introduction.

Works Cited
- List of sources used

End with a list of the works you used. In this list, show your sources in alphabetical order by the author's last name. If there is no author for a source, alphabetize by the first word in the title of the source. If you did not use nonprint sources, such as videos or sound recordings, your teacher may ask you to title your list of sources "Bibliography," rather than "Works Cited."

A Writer's Model

The final draft below closely follows the framework for a report of information on the previous page.

Flying High—Again

You see its picture every time you look at a quarter. You even see it when the letter carrier delivers your mail. The bald eagle has been a symbol of the United States since 1782. Not long ago, though, the bald eagle seemed headed for extinction. Although bald eagles were in danger of becoming extinct in the 1950s, the efforts of many groups over the last ten years have helped them make an amazing comeback .

In the 1950s, nature watchers noticed there were fewer bald eagles in the skies. Charles Broley, a volunteer eagle watcher, was one of the first to notice the decline of eagles in Florida. Broley counted one hundred fifty eaglets, or baby eagles, in 1939. In 1952, he counted only fifteen in the same area. Broley thought something was keeping adult birds from raising babies (Grambo 82).

Broley was right. The National Foundation to Protect America's Eagles estimated that 10,000 nesting pairs of eagles lived in the continental United States in the 1950s. In the 1960s, the number of eagles fell to fewer than 500 pairs. Eagles moved closer to extinction every day (Bald).

Many things caused the decline of the bald eagle. One of the most obvious was hunting. Farmers once thought of eagles as pests. They believed that bald eagles harmed livestock and crops (Tucker 58). To decrease its number of eagles, the territory of Alaska paid a bounty for every eagle that was shot. It is estimated that more than 100,000 bald eagles were shot while this policy was in effect (Grambo 76–78).

The demand for lumber and land also hurt eagles. When America was first being settled, it had over a billion acres of forest land where eagles and other animals could

Attention-grabbing beginning

Main idea statement

Heading #1: General facts about endangered eagles

Heading #2: Reasons eagles were endangered

(continued)

make their homes. However, as lumber mills cut more and more trees, eagles lost their forest homes. Eagles also suffered as people built houses, roads, and businesses in their nesting areas. As early as 1930, much of America's forest land was becoming unsuitable for many animals (Tucker 62–69).

The major cause of the eagles' endangerment was the use of pesticides such as DDT. Farmers used pesticides to kill unwanted insects and plants. Sadly, other animals and plants also absorbed the poisons. When bald eagles ate the poisoned animals, they became poisoned too. Eagles that consumed DDT laid thin-shelled eggs that broke easily when the mother sat on them (Dudley 54–55).

Heading #3: Ways eagles were helped

Fortunately, lawmakers realized that eagles could become extinct. In 1940, Congress passed a law to protect bald eagles: the Bald Eagle Protection Act. Under this act, people who killed eagles could be punished by a fine and time in jail (Tucker 69). The bald eagle was also helped by the Endangered Species Act of 1973. Under this act, the government protected millions of acres where bald eagles could live without being threatened by hunting or construction. The passage of these laws, along with the ban of the pesticide DDT in 1972, provided much-needed protection for the bald eagle (Tucker 75; Bald).

Scientists also helped bald eagles. To help increase the number of mature eagles, scientists developed a captive breeding program. In this program, injured eagles that could not survive in the wild laid eggs in a laboratory. After hatching, the eaglets were returned to the wild. Captive breeding successfully increased the number of bald eagles (Tucker 85).

Heading #4: Eagles' recovery

With the help of many people all over the United States, eagles are slowly recovering. From a low point of fewer than 500 nesting pairs in the 1960s, the numbers have grown to an estimated 4,500 nesting pairs in the continental United States. If you count eaglets and young adults, there are about 55,000 bald eagles in the United States today (Bald). In 1998, Secretary of the Interior Bruce Babbitt took steps to remove the bald eagle from the endangered species list. In an interview, Babbitt said, "The eagle is doing splendidly. It's making a wonderful comeback everywhere" (qtd. in Gerstenzang).

The bald eagle is not completely out of danger yet, but its future looks better every day. If eagles keep making a comeback, our national symbol should be around for a long time to come.

Restatement of main idea

Works Cited

Bald Eagle: The U.S.A.'s National Symbol. 1997. The National Foundation to Protect America's Eagles. 16 Nov. 1998 <http://www.eagles.org/moreabout.html>.

Dudley, Karen. Bald Eagles. Austin: Raintree Steck-Vaughn, 1998.

Gerstenzang, James. "Eagle May Fly from Nest of Endangered." Los Angeles Times 6 May 1998: A1.

Grambo, Rebecca L., ed. Eagles: Masters of the Sky. Stillwater, OK: Voyageur Press, 1997.

Tucker, Priscilla. The Return of the Bald Eagle. Mechanicsburg, PA: Stackpole Books, 1994.

TIP Reports of information and their *Works Cited* lists are normally double-spaced. Because of limited space on these pages, A Writer's Model and A Student's Model are single-spaced. The *Elements of Language* Internet site provides a model of a report of information in the double-spaced format. To see this interactive model, go to **go.hrw.com** and enter the keyword **EOLang 7-5.**

Writing Your Report of Information

Write the first draft of your report of information. Be sure to

- put information you gathered from sources into your own words
- write each paragraph using a separate heading or subheading from your outline
- support each paragraph with details, such as facts and statistics
- refer to the Writer's Model on pages 179–181 and framework on page 178

A Student's Model

Writing a research report is your opportunity to be a teacher. In the following report excerpt, J.D. Brannock, a student at Davis Drive Middle School in Apex, North Carolina, teaches his readers about the interesting subject of caves.

Caves

Attention-grabbing beginning

In Mark Twain's book <u>The Adventures of Tom Sawyer</u>, Tom and Becky spend three dreadful days in a winding, confusing cave. No matter how they try, they cannot find a way out until the last minute. Today spelunking, the American word for exploring caves, is a popular pastime around the world. Experienced guides lead adventure-seeking groups of people through these mystifying underground worlds, pointing out anything of interest and leading them to magnificent caverns.

Main idea statement

Before you dive headfirst into these wonderlands, you might want to know a little bit about them.

Fact

Caves are usually formed out of limestone by surface water leaking through cracks in the rock.

Elaboration

Above the surface the water gathers carbon dioxide from the air, making a weak acid that eats away at the rock. Over the centuries the water hollows out the rock, leaving behind a cave.

Example

The largest cave chamber in the world is the Sarawak Chamber in the Gunung Mulu National Park in Malaysia.

Elaboration

It is 2,300 feet long, has an average width of about 985 feet, and at no point is it less than 230 feet high.

Fact

Some caves are one chamber. Other caves consist of a series of chambers that are all connected in some way, known as a cave system.

Example

The longest known cave system is the Mammoth-Flint Ridge cave system in Kentucky.

Fact

When people think of caves, they think of caverns filled with pillars protruding from the floor and ceiling. The pillars protruding from the ceiling are sta-

Elaboration

lactites. Stalactites form when water droplets containing limestone sediments drip from the ceiling. . . .

Evaluate and Revise Content, Organization, and Style

"Making a list and checking it twice . . ." Whether you are evaluating a peer's paper or revising your own report, it is a good idea to read the paper twice. The first time, think about both the content, or information, and the organization of the draft. Use the guidelines below to help you. During your second reading, focus on each sentence using the Focus on Sentences on page 185.

TIP Use reference materials to help you revise and edit your final draft. Dictionaries, composition textbooks, and reference handbooks (like Part 4 of this book) can help you improve your writing.

▶ **First Reading: Content and Organization** Use this chart to evaluate a peer's report or to evaluate and revise your own paper.

Report of Information: Content and Organization Guidelines for Self-Evaluation and Peer Evaluation

Evaluation Questions	▶ Tips	▶ Revision Techniques
❶ Does the main idea statement cover all of the report's important ideas?	▶ **Match** each part of the main idea statement with a paragraph or section of the report.	▶ **Revise** the main idea statement so that it covers the important ideas of the report.
❷ Is the main point in each paragraph clear? Does all the information in the paragraph support that main point?	▶ **Write** each paragraph's main point in the paper's margin. **Write N** next to information that does not support the main point.	▶ If needed, **add** a sentence that states the main point. **Delete** or **rearrange** information that does not support the main point.
❸ Is the information in each paragraph properly summarized or quoted?	▶ **Circle** sentences that sound as if someone else wrote them. **Underline** information in quotation marks.	▶ **Revise** by summarizing information or adding quotation marks.
❹ Does the conclusion restate the report's main idea?	▶ **Put a check** next to the restatement of the main idea.	▶ **Add** a restatement of the report's main idea if needed.
❺ Does a list of sources in the correct form end the report?	▶ **Check the format and punctuation** by referring to the guide on page 172.	▶ **Add** correct format and punctuation as needed.
❻ Does the list of sources contain at least three different types of sources?	▶ **Count** the number of different types of sources on the list.	▶ **Add** information from another reliable source to the report if needed.

ONE WRITER'S REVISIONS Study this revision of an early draft of the report on page 179.

> To decrease its number of eagles, the territory of Alaska paid a bounty for every eagle that was shot. It is estimated that more than 100,000 bald eagles were shot while
>
> *rearrange*   this policy was in effect. Eagles also suffered as people built houses, roads, and businesses in their nesting areas.
>
> *The demand for lumber and land also hurt eagles.*
>
> *add*   When America was first being settled, it had over a billion acres of forest land where eagles and other animals could make their homes. However, as lumber mills cut more and more trees, eagles lost their forest homes. As early as 1930, much of America's forest land was becoming unsuitable for many animals.

PEER REVIEW

As you read your classmate's report, ask yourself these questions:

- What part of the report is the best?
- What new information did I learn about the report's topic?

Responding to the Revision Process

1. Why do you think the writer moved a sentence from the first paragraph to the second paragraph?
2. Why do you think the writer added to the second paragraph?

▶ **Second Reading: Style** One thing you can do to make sure your report flows smoothly is to vary how your sentences begin. Adding variety to your sentence beginnings can also help ensure that the reader will remain interested in what you are saying.

Sentence Style Guidelines

Evaluation Question	▶ Tip	▶ Revision Technique
Does the report contain a variety of sentence beginnings?	▶ **Draw a wavy line** under the first five words of each sentence.	▶ If several sentences begin the same way, change one or more of these sentences by moving a phrase from the end of a sentence to the beginning of the sentence.

Varying Sentence Beginnings

To add variety to your writing, look for places where you can move a phrase from the end of the sentence to the beginning. When you move a phrase to the beginning of a sentence, you may need to add a comma after the phrase. The following chart gives some examples.

Reference Note

For more information and practice on **prepositional phrases** and **infinitive phrases,** see pages 402 and 415.

Original Sentence	Revision Strategy	Revised Sentence
People depended on candlelight *before the invention of the light bulb.*	Move the *prepositional phrase* to the beginning.	*Before the invention of the light bulb,* people depended on candlelight.
You need skill *to repair a watch.*	Move the *infinitive phrase* to the beginning.	*To repair a watch,* you need skill.

ONE WRITER'S REVISIONS

Scientists also helped bald eagles. ~~Scientists~~ developed a captive breeding program to help increase the number of mature eagles.

Responding to the Revision Process

How did the revision above affect the flow of the sentence?

 Evaluating and Revising Your Report of Information

Use the guidelines on page 183 to revise the content and organization of your report. Next, add variety by using the Focus on Sentences above. Finally, consider feedback from your peers as you revise your report.

Publishing

Proofread Your Report

Get It Right Before you write your final draft, proofread your paper for mistakes in spelling, usage, or punctuation. Having a peer **edit** your report will help you find and correct errors that might distract your readers.

Grammar Link

Formatting Sources

One of the most difficult parts of research is correctly formatting your sources on the Works Cited list. Not only do you have to indent your sources a certain way, but you also have to mark titles correctly and use correct punctuation.

- **Periods:** Place a period after the author's name and after the title of the book or article. The end of the entry is also punctuated with a period.

- **Titles:** Titles of books, magazines, newspapers, encyclopedias, television or radio programs, or Web pages are underlined if handwritten and usually *italicized if typed on a word processor*. Titles of magazine, newspaper, or encyclopedia articles are placed in quotation marks.

- **Indentations:** Always indent the second and all following lines of a citation five spaces.

    Here is the correct format for citing a book.

Horton, Casey. Eagles. Tarrytown, N.Y.:
    Benchmark Books, 1996.

PRACTICE

Each of the following citations has two or more problems. Refer to the guide on page 172, and rewrite each citation with the correct punctuation and format.

1. (Book)

> MacGuire, Spunky Baseball's Favorite Heroes. Boston: Home Base Publications, 1983.

2. (Magazine article)

> Aliki, Malik, Watch Out for the Bird Lady. Birdwatching Today. August 1998: 67–70.

3. (Online source)

> Wark, Lori. Mummies in the Midst Discovery Channel Online 16 Oct. 1998. 5 Apr. 1999 <http://www.discovery.com/stories/history/mummies/mummies.html>.

Text features If you have access to a word-processing program, you can use **text features** to help you create interesting, eye-catching reports.

    Fonts: Use a **text font,** such as Times or Palatino, for formal papers. Decorative fonts, such as *Mistral,* are often difficult to read.

    Size: For your report, make sure your print size is set at twelve points. Experiment with larger sizes for headings, if your teacher allows.

    Numbering or Bulleting Features: Most word-processing programs can automatically number lists. If you have a list that does not require numbers, consider using a decorative "bullet," such as a point (•) or check mark (✓) to separate items in the list.

Reference Note

For more on **text features,** see page 162.

TIP Your teacher might ask you to create a title page for your report. A **title page** tells your name, the title of the report, and the date. Also include any other information your teacher recommends.

Publish Your Report

Spread the News Now is the time to teach others what you have learned. Here are some publishing ideas.

- Publish your report on a personal or school Web page.
- Turn your report into an illustrated book for children.
- Send your report to a teacher with an interest in your topic.

Reflect on Your Report

Building Your Portfolio Think back on the process of researching and writing your report. Reflect on what you wrote and how you wrote it by answering the questions below.

- What information did you not include in your paper? Why? What information was the most difficult to find?
- What research techniques did you use? Would you use them again?

YOUR TURN 13 Proofreading, Publishing, and Reflecting

- Correct grammar, usage, and mechanics errors.
- Publish your report for your target audience.
- Answer the Reflect on Your Report questions above. Record your responses in a learning log, or include them in your portfolio.

Writing to Explain

Some writing test prompts ask you to inform your readers by explaining your thoughts on a topic. The informative essay that you write for such a prompt is sometimes called a **clarification essay**. The best thing about writing this kind of essay is that you get to explain what a topic means to you. Read the following prompt and think about how you would answer it.

> Think about your favorite food. Then, write an essay that explains why that food is your favorite. Be sure to explain each of your reasons fully.

THINKING IT THROUGH — Writing an Informative Essay to Explain

STEP 1 Read the prompt and decide what it is asking you to do.

The prompt asks me to think about my favorite food and write an essay that explains why it is my favorite.

STEP 2 Identify your answer to the prompt.

My favorite food is Chinese food.

STEP 3 Brainstorm a list of reasons that tell why you chose your answer.

Reason 1: Chinese food is sometimes spicy.
Reason 2: It is so different from what I usually eat.
Reason 3: You also get good soup.

STEP 4 Think about the support you will give for each of your reasons. Ask *What do I mean*? *How do I know*? You can use examples, descriptions, and facts.

Support for Reason 1: I could explain why I like spicy food. I could also give an example of a spicy Chinese dish, like garlic chicken with peppers, and I could describe the taste of it.
Support for reason 2: I could explain that Chinese food contains ingredients that I normally don't eat, such as bamboo shoots.
Support for reason 3: I could list different kinds of soup. Then, I could describe my favorite soup, which contains tofu and seafood.

STEP 5 Write your essay, making sure that you thoroughly explain your answer to the prompt. After you complete your essay, read it at least once to check for errors.

Life

Writing a Personal Narrative

Everybody has a story to tell. In fact, you probably have a good story to tell about writing your research report. You might think at first that you have nothing else to say about your topic. After all, you *did* just write a report about it. However, for this assignment, you will not focus on the facts you learned about your research subject. Instead, you will write a *personal narrative* about the experiences you had while writing the report. A **personal narrative** is a true story with a beginning, middle, and end, told from your point of view. The writer's purpose in a personal narrative is to **express** his or her thoughts and feelings and to **reflect on ideas.**

Less Is More?   When you write a narrative about writing your research report, you might be tempted to include everything. However, by focusing on a single event, you can make your narrative more interesting. To help you focus the **topic** of your narrative, think about an event associated with a specific person or place. You can also think about a particular problem you solved.

- **Person:** Who helped you with your report? A librarian? A friend? How did he or she help? Did you interview an interesting expert? Can you tell about an interaction with this person?
- **Place:** Where did you go to get information for your report? Did you have a funny or interesting experience at the library? Did you go somewhere unique, such as a museum? Did you get information by sending e-mail?
- **Problem:** Did you experience a problem while you were writing or researching your report of information? How did you solve this problem?

Express Yourself After you have focused the subject of your personal narrative, think about the **thoughts and feelings** you experienced while writing your research report. Were you glad? relieved? frustrated? confused? excited? One way to relate your thoughts and feelings to the reader is to state them **directly**. For example, the student whose example is given below directly states that he experienced panic and a sense of defeat on finding the library closed.

> I tried to go to the library to get the sources I needed. However, when I got there, it was closed. Needless to say, I began to panic. I felt defeated because I thought that I would never get my research report done.

A more interesting way to express your thoughts and feelings is to do so **indirectly** through action and dialogue. In the following example, the same student uses action and dialogue to reveal his thoughts and feelings.

On reaching the entrance, I realized that the library was already closed. I desperately shook the immovable doors. The only thing separating me from the sources I needed was a thin sheet of glass! "How can I do research without books?" I murmured as I walked from the building with my head down.

The following excerpt from another student's personal narrative focuses on one important event: choosing a research subject. Does the student express feelings about this topic directly, indirectly, or both?

The Research Subject That Swooped Down from the Sky

. . . I went to school the next morning with a sense of dread at showing up for English without the assignment. As a last effort, I tried to come up with a subject during free time that morning while the rest of my science class watched a video on birds. Then, just as I was about to give up and choose something like "the history of yarn," it happened. I looked up at the television screen just in time to see a majestic bald eagle swoop down and grab a fish out of the water with its talons. What an awesome sight! The eagle made catching a fish look so easy. Suddenly, all sorts of questions began to pop into my head. "How can they swoop down like that and grab fish out of the lake?" "Do eagles eat anything else besides fish?" "How big do eagles get?" "Why don't we see more bald eagles?" I was so excited that I accidentally exclaimed "Woo-hoo!" during the video. I had to stay after class because of the disturbance, but I finally had a good subject for my report.

I was happy to go to English class that day with my homework in hand. I was even happier to discover that I had chosen a subject that I really wanted to research. Over the next few weeks, I worked hard on the report. I went to the library several times and even spent a couple of hours after school talking to my science teacher, Mr. Newton. He let me borrow a book about birds of prey. He also helped me understand an article I found on the Internet about eagles. Researching was hard, but I am glad I did it.

 Writing a Personal Narrative

Write a personal narrative about your research report. Be sure to focus on key events or problems as the topic of your narrative. Also, make sure to express your thoughts and feelings on your topic directly, indirectly, or both.

Giving and Listening to an Informative Speech

A hush falls over the crowd as you approach the podium. You can feel the tension in the audience as everyone waits for you to begin. Delivering a speech can be a nerve-racking experience. However, if you prepare well, delivering a speech can also be fun. After all, when you deliver a speech, you are the center of attention. The audience is in your control.

WHAT'S AHEAD?

In this workshop you will give an informative speech. You will also learn how to

- adapt a research report for a speech
- use visuals
- listen to get the most out of an informative speech

Adapting a Report for a Speech

What makes a good speech? As you get ready to make a speech based on the topic you chose in the Writing Workshop, focus on these elements:

- **Think about the purpose and occasion.** Are you giving an informal speech to your class, or is your speech part of a formal evaluation? Think about how these factors affect your word choice and delivery.

- **Limit your speech to your report's major ideas and the evidence you need to clarify and support** those ideas. When giving evidence, make sure you tell your audience where you found that information.

- **Adjust your word choice** so that your audience can easily understand your ideas and learn from your speech.

- **Use a simple outline** to deliver your speech, rather than simply reading your report. Speaking from a simple outline will make your speech sound more conversational and natural.

- **Avoid speaking too fast or too slow or too loud or too soft.** In other words, use an effective **rate** and **volume** for your audience.

TIP Use elaborations to explain your main ideas. **Elaborating,** or explaining your points in more detail, will make your speech easier to understand.

Reference Note
For more information and practice on **elaboration,** see page 304.

TIP Running through your entire presentation—visuals and all—a few times will help you avoid making mistakes on speech day. Practice delivering your speech as if you were in front of the class. If you are using note cards or visuals, practice using them, too. Keep practicing until you are able to get through the speech once without stopping.

Reference Note

For more on giving a **formal speech,** see page 758 in the Quick Reference Handbook.

- Use the pitch, or the highs and lows, of your voice to create an enthusiastic tone. If the tone of your voice suggests that you do not care about your speech, your audience is likely to feel the same.

Using Visuals in an Informative Speech

Avoid getting caught up in "chartmania," the mysterious disease that affects speakers who use too many visuals. Having one or two well-chosen visuals is better than having too many. Whatever the number of visuals you decide to use, each one should have the same purpose: to complement and extend the meaning of an important point.

Posters, Pictures, Charts, and Graphs If you decide that using a poster, picture, chart, or graph is essential to your presentation, follow these tips.

- Make sure all words and pictures are large enough to be seen clearly from the back of the room.
- Be sure to describe in words what the visual means.
- When explaining a visual, face the audience.

Overhead Projectors or Presentation Software One of the best ways to use visuals that everyone can see is to use a projector. By creating transparencies of your visuals, you can make them large or small by moving the projector away from or closer to the screen. Some projectors even project images from a word-processing program or presentation software. If you choose to use a projector, consider these tips.

- Use dark colors for your text and pictures.
- Make your graphic simple. A cluttered design is confusing.
- Have a backup plan in case the projector breaks or is unavailable.

Video- or Audiotaped Segments Sometimes the best way to demonstrate your point is by using a video- or audiotaped segment. Here are some tips for using a video or audio clip.

- The clip should be fairly short; it should support your presentation, not replace it.
- Have your tape cued up before you speak so that the audience does not have to wait for you to rewind or fast forward it.
- Test your equipment before your audience arrives.

Listening to an Informative Speech

An informative speech often contains so much information that you might have trouble absorbing it all. To make the most of the informative speeches you hear, follow these steps.

Before the Speech

- **Determine your purpose.** Identify what you want to learn from listening to this speech.
- **Make predictions.** Identify two or three points you expect the speaker to cover.
- **Get ready.** Have pen or pencil and paper ready for taking notes.

Reference Note

For more on **listening purpose** see page 767 in the Quick Reference Handbook.

During the Speech

- **Devote your full attention to the speaker.** Looking around the room or doing another assignment is discourteous and will prevent you from learning all you can.
- **Listen for cues that signal main points,** such as the speaker's slightly changing the volume or tone of his or her voice. Cues can also include these words and phrases: *first, second,* and *finally; there are many reasons* or *causes; the most important thing is;* and *in conclusion.* Hearing these cues is the key to understanding, interpreting, and organizing the information you hear in the speech.
- **Summarize the main points of the speech.** As you listen, take notes by summarizing the speaker's main points and supporting details.

Reference Note

For more on **eliminating barriers to effective listening,** see page 767 in the Quick Reference Handbook.

Reference Note

For more on **summarizing,** see pages 164–165.

After the Speech

- **Monitor,** or note, your understanding of this speaker's message by asking yourself if the speaker covered all of the points you expected. If not, what did he or she leave out? Ask the speaker to clarify.

YOUR TURN 15   Giving and Listening to an Informative Speech

Now it is your turn to make an informative speech with visuals.

- First, adapt your report, using the suggestions on pages 191–192.
- Next, choose a visual that will help your audience understand your topic and practice with it. Use the guidelines on page 192.
- Finally, practice your listening skills when your classmates present their speeches.

WHAT'S AHEAD?

In this workshop you will learn how to

■ understand data contained in graphics

■ use a Web site as a source of information

Interpreting Graphics and Web Sites

How are compact discs made? Who was the first female astronaut? The answers to these and many other questions await you in books, on the Internet, and even on TV. However, just knowing where to find information is only half of the battle. You must also understand how to interpret the graphics and other features, such as hyperlinks, that writers use to communicate information.

Interpreting Information from Graphics

I See!   You see them in books, on television, and on the Internet. Graphics, like words, communicate information. When words alone are not enough, writers often use tables, maps, and other graphics to help you visualize difficult concepts and ideas. Most graphics contain one or more of the elements in the table below.

Element	Use
Title	gives the subject or main idea of the graphic
Body	presents the main information in the form of a chart, map, graph, time line, or other graphic
Legend	includes special symbols, codes, and other features needed to understand the graphic
Source	lists where the information is from

Maps Maps give geographical information, such as the streets and landmarks in a city, state, or country. However, some maps contain other useful information. To read a map, such as the one to the right, first study the title. Then, study the legend for special symbols and definitions or color codes. By studying the title and the symbols of this map, you learn that one of the colonial products in the 1700s was fish. By looking for the symbol of the fish on the map, you can determine that fish was an important product from the Boston and Portsmouth areas in the 1700s.

Tables Tables organize written information into categories, or groups. Textbooks often contain tables that organize and summarize important ideas. Whenever you see a table, such as the one on the previous page, first look for the capitalized or boldface words that identify the categories. The two categories in this table are "Element" and "Use." By reading from left to right, you can easily identify each element and its use.

Line Graphs Line graphs usually show how something changes over time. For example, the line graph to the right shows how the reindeer population of Saint Paul Island changed over a period of forty years. The first step in reading this graph is to find the intersections. An **intersection** is the point at which a number from the bottom of the graph intersects, or meets with, a number from the left side of the graph. By finding the first intersection in the line graph to the right, you learn that the reindeer population in 1940 was about two thousand. Once you find and interpret all of the intersections of a line graph, you can usually draw a conclusion from the data. What trend occurred between 1925 and 1940?

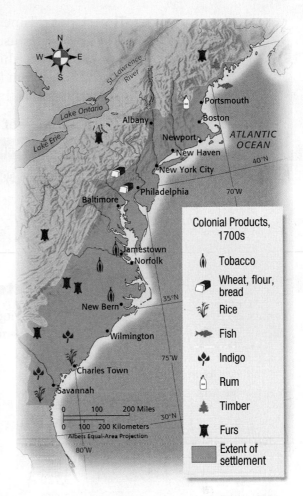

Colonial Products, 1700s

- ⚱ Tobacco
- 🍞 Wheat, flour, bread
- 🌾 Rice
- 🐟 Fish
- ✿ Indigo
- 🍾 Rum
- 🌲 Timber
- 🐾 Furs
- ▨ Extent of settlement

The Population of Reindeer on Saint Paul Island Between 1910 and 1950

Time Lines Time lines illustrate when important events occur in time. Time lines usually have a beginning date and an ending date. You know when things occur by their placement on the time line, which is read from left to right. The following time line shows some important events that occurred between 900 and 1500.

The Age of Discovery

	Crusades		Commercial Revolution	
900	1000	1100	1200	1300	1400	1500

982 Eric the Red founds settlement on Greenland

1000 Vikings reach America

1095 Crusades begin

1271 Polo travels to China

1488 Dias sails around southern tip of Africa

1492 Columbus sails to America

 Interpreting Graphics

Study the following graphics. Then, answer the questions at the bottom of the page.

Major Rivers of the World

River and Location	Length (mi)
Nile (Africa)	4,145
Amazon (S. America)	4,000
Mississippi-Missouri (N. America)	3,740
Yangtze (Asia)	3,720
Yenisey-Angara (Asia)	3,650
Amur-Argun (Asia)	3,590
Ob-Irtysh (Asia)	3,360
Plata-Paraná (S. America)	3,030
Huang (Asia)	2,903
Congo (Africa)	2,900

Source: U.S. Dept. of Commerce, National Oceanic and Atmospheric Admin., Principal Rivers and Lakes of the World

Unemployment,* 1925–35

*Government estimates   Source: U.S. Bureau of Labor Statistics

1. What are the categories in the table to the left?
2. Which continent has the greatest number of major rivers?
3. Around what year was unemployment at its lowest point?
4. What trend do you see taking place between 1926 and 1932?

Interpreting Web Sites

Where Is It?   How would you go about finding information on plant reproduction in your biology book? One way would be to turn each page, one-by-one, until you found it. Of course, the more efficient way would be to look in the **index,** which is a listing of the major topics in a work. An index—whether for a book or for a Web site—can help you find answers to your questions more efficiently.

A Web site's index can usually be found on the site's home page and is usually a list of *hyperlinks*. A **hyperlink** might look like a button, or it may be an underlined word, phrase, or sentence. In the home page below, the underlined words and phrases are all hyperlinks.

Clicking on a hyperlink in the index will take you to another page that contains more information on that subject; it can also take you to a page that contains another, more specific index.

Making good predictions about the hyperlinks in an index can help you narrow the number of links to explore. After all, when you have a question, you want to get the answer as soon as possible. To make predictions about where the hyperlinks in an index will take you, follow these steps.

- Read each hyperlink in the index.

- Ask yourself if the information you want could logically fit in the category of the hyperlink.

- If your answer is "yes," explore the link until you find your answer. If you run into a dead end, go back to the home page and try another link.

For example, a student who wanted biographical information about former astronaut Alan Shepard visited the NASA home page that appears on the previous page. He studied the home page index and decided to explore two hyperlinks, "Human Exploration and Development of Space" and "History." Both of these links seem as if they might contain information about Alan Shepard. However, after clicking on the "Human Exploration and Development" link, the student found that it only led to a page that explained NASA's purpose. He then returned to the home page and clicked on the "History" link, which eventually led him to a page with a link to astronaut biographies.

 Interpreting Information from a Web Site

Use the NASA home page on page 197 to complete the following.

1. If you were trying to find information on how NASA began, which hyperlink(s) would you follow? Why?

2. If you wanted to find general information about space, which two links might you follow? Why?

5 *Choices*

Choose one of the following activities to complete.

▶ CAREERS

1. Get a Job! Pick a career you would like to have ten years from now. Then, write a **letter** to someone who has this career to discover how much education you will need and what the daily activities are. After getting a response, pretend that ten years have passed and that you have just finished your first day on the job. Write a **journal entry** describing your work activities and the way you feel about landing your dream job.

▶ CROSSING THE CURRICULUM: SOCIAL STUDIES

2. Where Did I Come From? Do some family research to find out more about your relatives. Create a **family tree** to share with your class that includes information you find about your relatives. Then, write a **memoir** about a special event you experienced with one or more of the relatives on your tree.

▶ CROSSING THE CURRICULUM: MATH

3. Learning to Count Find out about different methods of counting that have existed, or research the "invention" of mathematical symbols and ideas such as zero, percentages, and signs. Then, report your findings in an **oral report** for your math class.

▶ DRAMA

4. Let's Put on a Show Many children's programs use puppet shows to break down difficult concepts into easy-to-understand "edutainment." Adapt the information you learned in your research project into a **puppet show** for young children. Then, create your own puppets and arrange for a show at a local elementary school or day-care center.

▶ CONNECTING CULTURES

5. You Say Potato Pancake, I Say Latke All over the world, people love to celebrate, but we all celebrate in different ways. Read about how people in other cultures celebrate birthdays and holidays. Make a **report** that compares and contrasts the celebrations of other cultures with your own culture's celebrations.

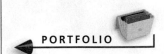
PORTFOLIO

6 | Convincing Others

SUPPORT AFTER-SCHOOL PROGRAMS

SCHOOL NEWS
Vote "Yes"
On School
Uniforms

Reading Workshop

Reading a Persuasive Article
PAGE 202

Writing Workshop

Writing a Persuasive Essay
PAGE 211

Focus on Viewing and Representing

Analyzing an Editorial Cartoon
PAGE 228

"Wait until you grow up." "You can do that when you're an adult." Do these comments sound familiar? Sometimes it must seem as if you have little or no say in the issues that affect your life. This can be frustrating, especially when you have a strong opinion. Fortunately, there *is* a way you can express your opinion effectively: through *persuasion*.

Persuasion is a type of communication that offers an opinion and supports it with reasons and evidence. Some persuasive communication even asks readers or listeners to take a specific action. You have probably come across persuasion in newspapers and magazines, or on TV or the radio. You can use persuasion to try to make a change in your world—begin by writing your own persuasive piece.

internetconnect

go. hrw .com

GO TO: go.hrw.com
KEYWORD: EOLang 7-6

YOUR TURN 1 · Discovering Persuasion

In your local newspaper or in a magazine, find an example of persuasive writing. Share the article you find with a few classmates, and discuss these questions:

- Why do you think the article is an example of persuasion?
- What reasons or examples does the author use to try to persuade you to share his or her opinion?
- Which article in your group is most persuasive? Why?

Reading a Persuasive Article

They cause young people to huddle over their game pads for hours. They mean big business for software developers. They ping, zap, and explode in arcades across the country. What are they? You guessed it: video games—the topic of the persuasive article on the next page. If you have an opinion about video games, you probably find reasons to back it up. Do you try to convince people to share your opinion? Or do you talk with those who already share it? As you read the article, remember the author's purpose: to persuade you to accept his point of view. Will he succeed? Read on and find out.

Preparing to Read

READING SKILL → **Point of View**   A **point of view** is a person's opinion on an issue. The author of the following article, Lloyd Garver, has a very definite point of view on video games. He may not announce it in the first paragraph, but he does provide certain clues that will help you figure it out.

READING FOCUS → **Logical Support**   Mr. Garver does not just expect people to accept his point of view without question. He supports his opinion. As you read, think about how *well* he supports it. If he wants to persuade a thoughtful reader—like you—he will use *logical appeals*. That means he will support his point of view with *reasons* and *evidence*. **Logical appeals** can include stories, facts, and expert opinions—support you can weigh carefully and confirm.

Read the following article. In a notebook, jot down answers to the numbered active-reading questions in the shaded boxes. Underlined words will be discussed in the Vocabulary Mini-Lesson on page 209.

from Newsweek®

A Veto on Video Games

A parent speaks out on why he has barred TV video games from his home.

BY LLOYD GARVER

My wife and I are the kind of mean parents whom kids grumble about on the playground. We're among that ever-shrinking group of parents known as video game holdouts. We refuse to buy a video game set. Around Christmastime, my son made a wish list, and I noticed that Nintendo was No. 1. I said, "You know you're not going to get Nintendo." He said, "I know I'm not going to get it from *you*. But I might get it from *him*." Alas, Santa, too, let him down.

I don't think that playing a video game now and then is really harmful to children. But the children I know are so obsessed with these games that they have prompted at least one second-grade teacher (my son's) to ban the word *Nintendo* from the classroom. When I asked my seven-year-old if the teacher wouldn't let the kids talk about the games because that's all they were *talking* about, he said, "No. That's all we were *thinking* about."

Our society is already so computerized and dehumanized that kids don't need one more reason to avoid playing outside or going for a walk or talking with a friend. I'd still feel this way even if there were nothing wrong with games whose objectives are to kill and destroy.

I know, I know. There are games other than those like Rampage, Robocop, Motor Cross Maniacs, Bionic Commando, Dr. Doom's Revenge, Guerrilla War, and Super Street Fighter. But aren't the violent games the ones the kids love to play for hours? And hours. And hours. My son told me he likes the "killing games" the best, hasn't had much experience with

> **1. What is the author for or against? What specific words tell you?**

> **2. Why does the author tell us this story about his son's teacher?**

> **3. Why do you think the author quotes his young son?**

"sports games," and likes "learning games" the least because they are "too easy." (Manufacturers take note.) My five-year-old daughter told me she enjoyed playing Duck Hunt at a friend's house. The beauty of this game is that even very young players can have the fun of <u>vicariously</u> shooting animals. And then there's the game with my favorite title—an obvious attempt to combine a graceful sport with exciting action—Skate or Die.

'Promote habituation'[1]: The January issue of the Journal of the American Academy of Child and Adolescent Psychiatry featured an article entitled "Pathological Preoccupation with[2] Video Games." The author believes that some game manufacturers try to develop programs that "deliberately promote habituation," and the goal of some of the people who make up these games is "to <u>induce</u> an altered level of concentration and focus of attention in the gamester."

> **4. Are you confused by the last quotation in this paragraph? Try reading on to the next paragraph for an explanation.**

If you have children, or know any, doesn't this "altered level of concentration and focus" sound familiar? If not, try talking to a child while he is staring at that screen, pushing buttons. He won't hear you unless the words you happen to be saying are, "I just bought a new game for you."

In case you couldn't tell, I'm worried that electronic games are dominating children's lives. There are games that <u>simulate</u> sports like baseball and basketball, and that's all some kids know about the sports. Someday soon, a young couple will take their children to their first baseball game and hear the kids exclaim, "This is great. It's almost like the *real baseball* we play on our home screen." When I took my son to a recent Lakers basketball game, the thing that seemed to excite him most was a video game in the lobby. You see, if a kid didn't want to be bored watching some of the greatest athletes in the world play, he could just put a quarter in the machine and watch lifeless electronic images instead.

> **5. What is the main point of this paragraph?**

My son's teacher was right. Kids do play and talk about these games too much. They even have books and magazines that kids can study and classes so they can get better at the games. And that's what's got me worried. I'm just concerned that this activity is so <u>absorbing</u>, kids are going to grow up thinking that the first people to fly that airplane at Kitty Hawk were the Super Mario Brothers.

> **6. In this paragraph, where does the author's point of view come across most strongly?**

I don't like to discourage children from doing something they're good at; in this case, I must. ■

---

1. **'Promote habituation':** cause addiction.
2. **"Pathological Preoccupation with . . .":** total focus of attention on, to the point of obsession.

Point of View

What Does the Author *Really* Think?   One step in understanding persuasive writing is figuring out the author's point of view on the issue. Sometimes persuasive writers announce their point of view in an *opinion statement*. An **opinion statement** is made up of an issue plus the writer's point of view on the issue.

Example: **Issue:** video games on library computers

+ **Point of view:** they should be included
_____

Opinion statement: Video games should be included on the library's computers.

Unfortunately, writers don't always include an opinion statement—especially if they think you will disagree with it. You can figure out the writer's point of view on an issue, though, from clues in the article.

Try figuring out the point of view in the paragraph below. The issue is video games as learning tools. The steps on the next page will help you if you get stuck.

> ### From the Game Room to the Operating Room
>
> There is a lot of talk about violence in some video games. Few people, however, stop to think about the positive benefits of the games. The workers of the future will need to know how to operate computers, concentrate on complicated tasks, and do several tasks at once. Does this sound familiar? I, for one, have marveled at the concentration of a child playing a video game. Last night, watching a documentary about microsurgery, I could not help noticing how much the surgeon's skilled movements resembled those of a child playing a video game. . . .

TIP   Notice that the sentence containing the word *violence* is followed by a sentence containing the word *however*. A sentence that includes *however* tends to weaken the meaning of what came before. That means the impact of the word *violence* is not so negative after all.

Identifying Point of View

▶ **STEP 1** Scan the title and the first few sentences. Look for positive and negative words and comments related to the issue.

Positive: positive benefits, marveled, skilled
Negative: violence

▶ **STEP 2** Look for patterns. Are the words and comments you identified mostly positive or mostly negative?

Most of the words are positive. Also, the author compares a video game player to a surgeon— that has to be good.

▶ **STEP 3** Based on what you have found, make a decision about the author's point of view.

The author thinks video games are good learning tools.

YOUR TURN 2 **Identifying the Author's Point of View**

Using the three steps shown above, figure out the author's point of view in "A Veto on Video Games." Then complete this sentence:

The author's point of view is _____.

| READING FOCUS →

Logical Support

A Show of Support We all need a little support now and then, and so does a point of view. As a critical reader, you should always look at how well a writer supports his or her point of view in a persuasive article.

Remember, good writers always support their points of view logically, using *reasons* and *evidence*. Using this kind of support is called making a **logical appeal.** Logical appeals require readers to use their heads (that is, their logic) to decide whether they agree or disagree with the author.

Reasons A **reason** explains *why* the writer takes a certain point of view. In a persuasive article, the main point of each body paragraph is likely to be a reason. In "A Veto on Video Games" the first body paragraph begins this way:

> I don't think that playing a video game now and then is really harmful to children. But the children I know are so obsessed with these games that they have prompted at least one second-grade teacher (my son's) to ban the word *Nintendo* from the classroom. . . .

The author begins by saying that video games played "now and then" are not harmful. Is that his main point in this paragraph, though? He goes on to say that children are obsessed with the games. That is the author's reason for having the point of view on video games that he does—and the main point of the paragraph.

Evidence   Since reasons alone are not always convincing, persuasive writers support them with evidence. There are several different kinds of evidence a writer can use. (One example from the following chart comes from "A Veto on Video Games." Can you identify it?)

Types of Evidence	Definition	Example
Fact	a statement that can be proven true	"While playing a video game, a person's heart rate, blood pressure, and oxygen intake all increase."
Anecdote	a brief story that illustrates a point	"When I asked my seven-year-old if the teacher wouldn't let the kids talk about the [video] games because that's all they were *talking* about, he said, 'No. That's all we were *thinking* about.'"
Expert Opinion	the opinion of someone with expert knowledge	"Psychologists say that playing video games helps children learn skills that will prepare them for the work force."

TIP   Persuasive writers often try to capture their readers' *hearts* as well as their *heads*. They choose support that has **emotional appeal** as well as logical appeal.

Example:
Today's video game players could be tomorrow's lifesavers. Many young surgeons who grew up playing video games show incredible skill in microsurgery.

?   Why would the example above appeal to readers' emotions?

Mapping the Logical Appeal Sorting out the reasons and evidence as you read a persuasive essay is hard work. You can keep track of a writer's support in a conceptual map like the one below. Think of the map as a mental filing cabinet: each space represents a folder in which you can file information. Mapping the information will help you in two ways: It will (1) help you think critically about the author's point of view and (2) help you learn how to organize a persuasive essay of your own.

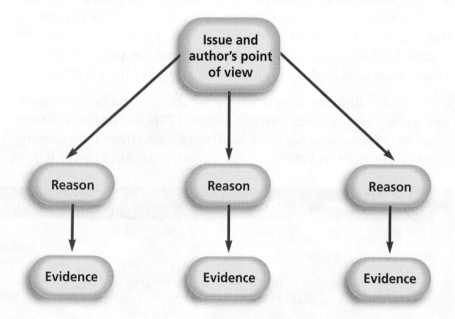

YOUR TURN 3 **Mapping the Logical Appeal**

- Re-read the selection "A Veto on Video Games" on pages 203–204. Then, fill in a map like the one above with the issue, the author's point of view, and the reasons and evidence from the article. Identify each piece of evidence you find as a fact, an anecdote, or an expert opinion. (**Hint:** Look for reasons near the beginning of each body paragraph. Look for supporting evidence in those same paragraphs.)

- Now that you have had a chance to think carefully about the author's views on video games, do you agree with him? Why or why not? Explain your answer in a sentence or two.

Wordbusting Strategy (CSSD)

Words have power—power to persuade. It is important, then, to understand the words you read. **Wordbusting** is a strategy for figuring out the meanings of unfamiliar words. The strategy has four parts, but you only need to use as many as it takes to understand a word. The letters *CSSD* can help you remember the parts of the strategy.

- **Context** You may get clues to an unfamiliar word's meaning from its context— the words, sentences, or paragraphs around the unfamiliar word.

- **Structure** Look at the word to see if you recognize any roots, prefixes, or suffixes.

- **Sound** Say the word aloud; you may hear a root or another word part you recognize and can define.

- **Dictionary** If necessary, look up the word.

Using the Wordbusting Strategy

Here is an example of Wordbusting, using a word from "A Veto on Video Games."

Word: simulate

My Best Guess:

▶ **STEP 1 Context:** "There are games that *simulate* sports like baseball and basketball, and that's all some kids know about the sports."

The author says "that's all some kids know about the sports." I think those words have something to do with the meaning, but I'm not sure.

▶ **STEP 2 Structure:** sim + u + late

I know a simile is a comparison using "like" or "as." Maybe sim means the same thing in both words.

▶ **STEP 3 Sound:** sim′ yoo lāt′

Sounds like similar, which means "kind of like." Based on all of these clues, I think simulate means "to be like something else."

Figure out the meanings of the words on the right. The words are underlined in "A Veto on Video Games," so you can see each word's context. Write the steps of CSSD that you actually use to define each word, using the example above as a model.

1. dehumanized (page 203)
2. objectives (page 203)
3. vicariously (page 204)
4. induce (page 204)
5. absorbing (page 204)

Identifying Author's Purpose and Point of View

When you read a selection on a reading test, you may be asked to identify the author's point of view. You may also be asked to identify the author's *purpose*: to inform, to entertain, or to persuade the reader. Suppose the following passage and test item were on a reading test. How would you approach them?

> Educational software, or kidware, grabs a child's attention through color, sound, and motion. In this way, kidware is like many video games. Many video games, however, are violent. Kidware, on the other hand, involves children in acts of learning, not in acts of destruction.

The author probably wrote this passage to

A. inform readers about a new video game on the market

B. tell a funny story about kidware and video games

C. explain how to use both kidware and video games

D. convince readers that kidware is better than video games

TIP Most writing in which the author has a strong point of view is *persuasive.* If you find a strong point of view in a test passage, the **author's purpose** is probably to persuade.

THINKING IT THROUGH   Identifying Author's Purpose

▶ **STEP 1** Turn the first part of the item into a question.

"The author probably wrote this passage to" means the same as "Why did the author write this passage?" ("What was the author's purpose?")

▶ **STEP 2** Try to answer the question in your own words.

The author uses negative words to describe video games. However, he or she says you can learn from kidware. I think the author wants to show that kidware is good.

▶ **STEP 3** Eliminate answer choices that are clearly wrong. Look for a choice that best matches your own answer.

Answer A is wrong because the author does not mention a particular video game. The author is not telling a story, so Answer B is not right. Answer C is wrong because the author is not giving an explanation. Answer D sounds most like my answer. This is the right choice.

Writing a Persuasive Essay

"That is *not* fair!" "We shouldn't let that happen!" Have you ever said those words? When you feel strongly about an issue, you want to *do* something about it. One way you might change a situation is to write about it. You can write something that might persuade other people to share your opinion. You may even convince people to help you bring about the change you want.

Here is your chance to make the world a better place. In this workshop you will write a persuasive essay on an issue about which you feel strongly. Using reasons and evidence, you will try to convince your readers to share your opinion.

WHAT'S AHEAD?

In this workshop you will write a persuasive essay. You will also learn how to

- **take a stand on an issue**
- **use reasons and evidence effectively**
- **distinguish between fact and opinion**
- **eliminate clichés from your writing**
- **use comparatives correctly**

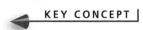

Prewriting

Choose an Issue

Picking Your Battles   Persuasive writing is about convincing your readers to share your point of view on an issue. So, the first step in writing a persuasive essay is to choose an issue. **An issue is a subject, situation, or idea about which people disagree,** such as the best way to raise money for the band trip, or whether television is harmful to children.

Your issue should be important to you. It should also be important enough for other people to have strong feelings and opinions about it. Avoid matters of personal preference, such as clothing styles or food. **Focus on issues that have a real impact on people's lives,** such as school rules or current social issues.

KEY CONCEPT |

KEY CONCEPT |

Choosing an Issue

Here is how to choose an issue for your persuasive essay.

▶ **STEP 1** Brainstorm several issues about which you feel strongly. To come up with an issue, you may **quickwrite** using the starter sentences below. You won't use these sentences in your essay, but you may use the ideas they help you generate.

If I were president, the first thing I'd change is _____.

One thing that really bothers me about _____ is _____.

▶ **STEP 2** Decide which issues are most important to you and create strong feelings and opinions in others.

▶ **STEP 3** Check off the single issue you want to address.

> **Issues**
>
> ✔ having to pay for athletes' autographs
> chores—should parents pay kids?
> bad-tasting school lunches

State Your Opinion

Taking a Stand   Every issue has at least two sides—for it and against it. What is your point of view? As a writer, you need to take a stand and tell your reader which side of the issue you support. In other words, **state your point of view clearly in an opinion statement.**

KEY CONCEPT ▶

An **opinion statement** is made up of an issue plus a writer's point of view on the issue.

TIP   An opinion statement serves the same purpose as a **main idea statement,** or **thesis.** It tells your readers the topic of your essay and what you are going to say about the topic.

> **Issue:** having to pay for athletes' autographs
> **+ Point of view:** fans shouldn't have to
>
> **Opinion statement:** Fans shouldn't have to pay for athletes' autographs.

Choosing an Issue and Stating Your Opinion

Use the Thinking It Through steps on page 212 to choose an issue for your persuasive essay. Then, write an opinion statement. Make sure your opinion statement shows your readers the stand you have taken—for or against the issue.

Consider Your Audience

Who Cares?   You probably would not write a persuasive essay about the school cafeteria to your college-age brother. Since problems with the school cafeteria don't affect his life, he probably would not be very interested in them. Persuasive writing works best when it is directed at the right group, or audience. You can identify the audience for your persuasive essay in two steps.

1. Figure out what groups of people are interested in your issue.

2. Choose one group to focus on, and analyze that group.

Finding Your Audience   To identify the right audience for your essay, think about the issue you have chosen. Remember that any issue is likely to affect more than one group of people. Ask yourself these questions.

■ Who is interested in this issue?

After identifying at least two of the groups who might care about your issue, ask,

■ For which group do I want to write?

The student writing about athletes charging for autographs identified baseball card collectors and professional baseball players as groups interested in that issue. She then decided to write to baseball card collectors. As a collector herself, she feels she understands them and knows what is important to them.

Identifying Your General Audience

To identify your general audience,
■ think of at least two groups interested in your issue
■ choose a group to address

TIP   Your **voice** shows your attitude about the issue in your persuasive essay. Not all attitudes are right for all audiences, so take your audience into account when you choose a writing voice.

For example, it might be okay to use humor and a lighthearted tone in a school newspaper piece about outdated science lab equipment. However, if you wrote to your principal or the school board on the same issue, your tone would have to be more serious and formal.

Putting Your Audience in Focus Now you can zero in on the group you picked. **Focus on the members of that group who might be undecided or might disagree with you, because they are the ones you have to convince.** (You don't need to convince people who already share your opinion.) To get them on your side, you will have to understand their concerns.

The group I'm addressing: baseball card collectors

Why might people in this group disagree with me? They might think that signed cards aren't that expensive. Some collectors my age get a bigger allowance than I do, so the price of the cards won't matter.

How old are people in this group? They are all ages, but I know more about the ones my age.

What else do I know about this group? They all have their favorite players, but most of them love Hank Aaron.

Specific audience: baseball card collectors my age who admire Hank Aaron and think it's okay for athletes to charge money for autographs

 Identifying Your Specific Audience

Zero in on your audience by answering the questions that appear in the example above. Then, identify your specific audience by completing this sentence:

My specific audience is _____.

Gather Support

Putting Your Money Where Your Mouth Is It is not enough to state your opinion on an issue. You also have to convince your reader that your opinion is logical, or that it makes sense. To do this, **you must provide support, reasons, and evidence that back up your opinion. Reasons** tell why you believe as you do. **Evidence**—in the form of anecdotes, facts, or expert opinions—backs up each reason.

Opinion Statement: The school lunchroom should offer vegetarian meals.

Reason: Many students at King Middle School are vegetarians.

Reason with Evidence: Many students at King Middle School are vegetarians. A poll shows that 30% of the students here do not eat meat. (fact)

To find support for your opinion, try the following sources:

- **Interview experts, friends, or other people who are interested in the issue.** For example, if you are writing about the school lunchroom, you might interview students, teachers, cafeteria workers, or the cafeteria manager.

- **Research the issue.** For example, find magazine articles, Web pages, or electronic newsgroup postings about other young people who are vegetarians. Taking a poll—to see how many students at a school are vegetarian, for instance—is another way to do research.

Reference Note

For more on **reasons,** see page 206. For more on **evidence,** see page 207.

Designing Your Writing

Using Numbers   Statistical evidence—numbers—can be very persuasive. You can create visuals to show graphically the statistical evidence in your essay. A pie chart is a good choice when you want to show how a whole breaks down into percentages or parts. For example, the writer who created the pie chart below wanted to show the percentages of all students at King Middle School who do and do not eat meat.

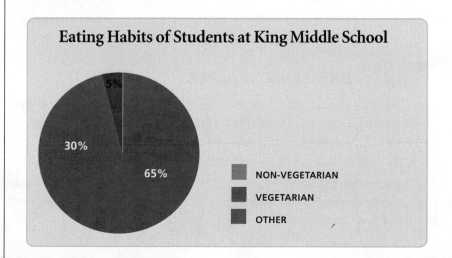

Eating Habits of Students at King Middle School

5%

30%

65%

- NON-VEGETARIAN
- VEGETARIAN
- OTHER

COMPUTER TIP

Many software programs allow you to create visuals such as pie charts on your computer. If you have access to a color printer, you can make each section of your pie chart a different color. This will help your reader see the different amounts represented by each part of the chart.

In the support chart below, a student lists several reasons why professional athletes should not charge fans for autographs. In the second column, she gives evidence to support each reason. In the third column, the writer evaluates her evidence, and in the fourth column, she rates the strength of each item ("Good," "Best," "Okay"), based on her audience's concerns. Knowing which evidence is strongest will help you organize your support before you write.

Support Chart

Reasons	Supporting Evidence	How Strong?	Rating
Players should be grateful for their fans' interest.	**Expert Opinion:** Hank Aaron's biographer says he was flattered to have kids look up to him.	Pretty strong. My audience still thinks of Hank Aaron as the greatest.	Good
The fans help the players get huge salaries.	**Fact:** The most popular major league baseball players earn millions of dollars a year in salaries.	Very strong. This example will make readers think, "Players already make so much money. They shouldn't take any more from us."	Best
Kids don't have enough money to spend on things like autographs.	**Anecdote:** A friend of mine spent his entire month's allowance on one card.	Not as strong as the other support—it depends on who's paying for the card.	Okay

 Gathering Support

- Create a support chart like the one above, listing **reasons** and **evidence** to support your opinion statement. With your audience's concerns in mind, use the fourth column to rate the overall strength of each piece of evidence.
- Replace any evidence you decide is too weak to convince your audience. You should have at least two reasons, each supported by evidence.

Telling the Difference Between Facts and Opinions

Picture this: A student you have never met tells you that you should buy a can of popcorn for a cheerleading fund-raiser.

"Why should I?" you ask.

"Because the cheerleaders need new uniforms," she says.

"What makes you say that?" you ask.

"Well, their old uniforms look really sad!" the student replies.

Are you persuaded? Probably not. The student stated her opinion and gave you a reason. What she did not do was support her reason with convincing evidence. Where she could have given you facts, she only gave you another opinion (". . . their old uniforms look really sad!"). In most cases, opinions do not make persuasive evidence.

Persuasive evidence should be based on fact, not on an opinion. An **opinion** expresses a personal belief. It can't be proved true or false. It may be *reasonable*, but it is not a fact.

Opinion: The uniforms we want to buy are more attractive than those we have currently.

Words that evaluate—*greatest, best, worst,* and of course, *sad*—often signal an opinion.

Opinion: Cotton is the *best* fabric for athletic wear.

When a writer begins *I believe, I feel, I think,* an opinion usually follows. Opinions may also contain words like *should* and *ought to.*

Opinion: *I think* the cheerleaders *should* wear the school colors.

A **fact,** on the other hand, can be proved true. You can look it up, ask witnesses, or measure it yourself.

Fact: The cheerleaders' current uniforms are blue and white.

Fact: Blue and red are our school colors.

Fact: In the majority of the middle schools in our district, the cheerleaders wear their school colors.

TIP The only opinions you should use as evidence are *expert opinions.* An **expert opinion** comes from someone with expert knowledge in his or her field.

PRACTICE

Identify each of the following statements as either a fact or an opinion. Explain your answers in a sentence.

1. Every student should have a locker.
2. Taft Middle School has 500 students and 450 lockers.
3. The U.S. women's ice hockey team won gold in the 1998 Olympics.
4. Michael Jordan is the greatest basketball player of all time.
5. Figure skating requires more talent than gymnastics does.

Writing

Persuasive Essay

Framework	Directions and Explanations

Introduction
■ Attention-grabbing opening
■ Opinion statement

Grab your reader's attention with an **interesting beginning.** Also include a **clear opinion statement** so your audience knows what you are supporting. (For more on writing **interesting beginnings,** see page 795 in the Quick Reference Handbook.)

Body
■ Reason #1
  (evidence supporting reason #1)
■ Reason #2
  (evidence supporting reason #2)
and so on

Choose the most convincing reasons and evidence from your support chart. Here is one effective way to organize your reasons:

■ Start with your **second strongest reason** to attract your reader to your side.

■ Leave your audience with a strong impression by using your **strongest reason last.**

■ Sandwich any **other reasons in the middle.**

This organization makes the most of your strongest support and downplays your weaker support.

Conclusion
■ Restatement of opinion
■ Summary of reasons and/or
  call to action

Leave your audience convinced that you are right. **Restate your opinion** in a new way. Then, **summarize your reasons** in a single sentence or **call on your audience** to take some kind of action. (You can do either or both).

 Writing Your Persuasive Essay

Now it is your turn to write a persuasive essay. As you write,

■ keep your audience in mind
■ use the strongest reasons and evidence from your chart
■ refer to the framework above and the Writer's Model on page 219

A Writer's Model

The final draft below closely follows the framework for a persuasive essay on the previous page.

What Is a Fan's Loyalty Worth?

Last week at a baseball card show, I asked a well-known baseball player for his autograph. Imagine my surprise when his agent said I would have to pay fifteen dollars before the player would sign his name! Fans should not have to pay to get a baseball player's autograph.

Baseball players should be satisfied that their fans love them. Hank Aaron's biographer states that Aaron was flattered just to have kids look up to him. He would not have dreamed of asking people to pay for his autograph. Today's players should follow Hank Aaron's example.

Kids, who might grow up to be lifelong fans of a player, cannot afford to pay fifteen dollars for an autograph. A friend of mine spent his entire month's allowance on a single autographed card. His experience is not unusual. The average allowance of the twenty-five Eagle Middle School students I surveyed is five dollars a week. For these students, buying one card would leave little money for any other recreation for the month.

Athletes should not charge fans for autographs. After all, the fans help many athletes receive huge salaries in the first place. Popular players—the ones fans ask for autographs most—already make millions. In 2000, according to *USA Today*'s Internet site, these were the salaries of some popular players: Mike Piazza, $12,000,000; Pedro Martinez, $11,500,000; and Sammy Sosa, $11,000,000. Top players make more in a year than most of us will make in a lifetime.

Instead of taking our money, athletes should repay our loyalty by freely signing their beloved names to our tattered cards. Do not pay for autographs. Show players that an autograph should be a way of saying "thank you" to a loyal fan, and thank yous should not cost money.

Attention-grabbing opener

Opinion statement

Reason #1

Evidence (expert opinion)

Reason #2

Evidence (anecdote)

Reason #3

Evidence (fact)

Restatement of opinion

Call to action

A Student's Model

When you write a persuasive essay, remember to pick a topic about which you feel strongly. There is no doubt where David Stamas, a junior high school student from Oak Bluffs, Massachusetts, stands on the issue of snack time in school.

Hungry Students Can't Study

Opinion statement

"Grrr! Oh, I'm hungry! When is lunch?" If you have ever walked down the junior high halls, this is something you will definitely hear. All kids should be able to have a snack time, or at least be allowed to keep food in their lockers.

Reason #1

When I asked why we couldn't have a snack time, one teacher I asked just said, "Why? You're not little kids anymore." That is just the point; we need food because we are growing now more than we ever will in our lives. Being hungry can have a big effect on the performance of a student. We just can't work or concentrate when all we can hear is the rumbling of our stomachs. We count down the seconds till lunch.

Reason #2

Getting a snack time really wouldn't change things all that much. All we need is five minutes. Trust me, if we can cram blueberry muffins down our throats in a two-minute hall period, we can definitely do it in five. All we have to do is take off a minute from each class and we will have more than enough time to eat.

Reason #3

No one can work on an empty stomach and be focused at the same time. Teachers certainly have figured that out. That is why they have a vending machine in the teachers' room, and why you will find a box of crackers in almost every teacher's desk. . . .

Restatement of opinion

It is not that we just want a snack time; it is that we need a snack time to keep us focused in class. The way I feel is that kids aren't looked upon as regular people the way we should be. We need a snack during the day just as much as everyone else. As I say, "Let us eat cake!"

Writing a Position Paper

A position paper is similar to a persuasive essay. Both require you to state your opinion and convince readers to take action. In a **position paper,** though, you discuss the benefits of both sides of an issue *before* you state your position and request that your readers take action. If the prompt to the right appeared on a writing test, how would you approach it?

> Your school is overcrowded. The school board is debating whether it is better to enlarge your school or build a new one that half the students would attend. Write a letter to your school board president discussing both sides of the issue. Then, state your position and give convincing support for it.

THINKING IT THROUGH   Writing a Position Paper

▶ **STEP 1** Read the prompt and identify the issue, the two options, the purpose, and the audience.

Issue: crowded school; Option #1: enlarge our school; Option #2: build a new school; Purpose: to persuade; Audience: school board president

▶ **STEP 2** To generate a list of the benefits of each option, use the memory strategy THEMES: **t**ime, **h**ealth, **e**ducation, **m**oney, **e**nvironment, and **s**afety.

Option 1: friends will continue to go to the same school, our community will not be divided, the school will look better since some parts will be new

Option 2: will still know everyone since the school will not be that big, traffic will be better since students will attend two different schools

▶ **STEP 3** Decide which option you support. Then, using THEMES again, list the drawbacks of the option you do not support.

I do not want a new school. These are the drawbacks: Friendships may be broken. A new school would cost a lot. Competition between the "old school" and the "new school" may cause problems.

▶ **STEP 4** Write your essay, elaborating on each benefit and drawback.

Introduction: Identify the issue and the two choices.
Body Paragraph #1: Discuss benefits of the first option.
Body Paragraph #2: Discuss benefits of the second option.
Body Paragraph #3: State position; give drawbacks of other option.
Conclusion: Restate position; ask audience to act.

Revising

Evaluate and Revise Content, Organization, and Style

Giving Your Essay the Twice Over   As you evaluate a peer's paper or evaluate and revise your own draft, you should do at least two readings. In the first reading, consider the content and organization of your draft, using the guidelines below. In your second reading, get down to the sentence level, using the Focus on Word Choice on page 224.

▶ **First Reading: Content and Organization**   Use this chart to evaluate and revise your paper so your message is persuasive.

Persuasive Essay: Content and Organization Guidelines for Self-Evaluation and Peer Evaluation		
Evaluation Questions ▶	**Tips** ▶	**Revision Techniques**
❶ Does the introduction grab the audience's attention?	▶ **Put stars** next to questions, anecdotes, or statements that would interest the audience.	▶ If needed, **add** an attention-grabber to the beginning of the introduction.
❷ Does the introduction have a clear opinion statement?	▶ **Underline** the opinion statement. Ask a friend to read it and to identify the point of view.	▶ **Add** an opinion statement, or, if necessary, **replace** the opinion statement with a clearer one.
❸ Does the essay include at least two reasons that logically support the opinion statement?	▶ With a colored marker, **highlight** the reasons that support the opinion statement.	▶ **Add** reasons that support the opinion statement as needed.
❹ Does at least one piece of evidence support each reason?	▶ **Circle** evidence that supports each reason in the essay. **Draw a line** from the evidence to the reason it supports.	▶ If necessary, **add** evidence to support each of the reasons. **Elaborate** evidence by adding details or explaining its meaning.
❺ Does the conclusion include a restatement of the opinion?	▶ **Put a check mark** next to the restatement.	▶ **Add** a restatement of the opinion if it is missing.
❻ Does the conclusion include a summary of reasons or a call to action?	▶ **Draw a wavy line** under the summary of reasons or call to action.	▶ **Add** a summary of reasons, a call to action, or both.

ONE WRITER'S REVISIONS This revision is an early draft of the essay on page 219.

> *Baseball players should be satisfied that their fans love them.*
> ∧Hank Aaron's biographer states that Aaron was flattered just to have kids look up to him. He would not have dreamed of asking people to pay for his autograph. Today's players should follow Hank Aaron's example.
>
> Kids, who might grow up to be lifelong fans of a player, cannot afford to pay fifteen dollars for an autograph. A friend of mine spent his entire month's allowance on a single autographed card. His experience is not unusual. The average allowance of ∧*the twenty-five* Eagle Middle School students∧*I surveyed* is *five dollars a week.* ∧~~pretty low.~~ For these students, buying one card would leave little money for any other recreation for the month.

add

elaborate

Responding to the Revision Process

1. Why did the writer add a sentence to the first paragraph?

2. How did elaborating the evidence improve the writing?

PEER REVIEW

As you evaluate a peer's persuasive essay, ask yourself these questions:

- What is the *most* convincing part of this essay? Why?

- What is the *least* convincing part? Why?

➤ **Second Reading: Style** Now you will look at *how* you say what you say, and that means looking closely at each of your sentences. One way to improve sentence style is to eliminate **clichés,** or overused expressions. Use the following guidelines.

Style Guidelines

Evaluation Question	▶ Tip	▶ Revision Technique
Have I used any expressions I have heard many times?	▶ **Put an X** through every word or phrase you think is a cliché.	▶ **Delete** each cliché and **replace** it with your own original words.

Focus on

Word Choice

Clichés

When you are writing persuasively, it is easy to reach for a familiar expression—called a **cliché**—to help you make your point. Clichés, though, are expressions that have been used so many times they have lost their meaning and freshness. If you use clichés in a persuasive paper, you run the risk of weakening the effect of your ideas on your audience.

Examples: cool as a cucumber   tough as nails
                to run like the wind   on top of your game

You probably know many more overused expressions.

Replacing clichés with your own original, forceful words will help you get your opinion across in a more convincing way. Remember: *that* is the purpose of persuasive writing.

ONE WRITER'S REVISIONS

> Instead of taking our money, athletes should repay
> our loyalty by freely signing their ~~John Hancocks.~~ *beloved names to our tattered cards.*

Responding to the Revision Process

How did replacing "John Hancocks" with another phrase improve the sentence above?

 Evaluating and Revising Your Essay

■ First, evaluate and revise the content and organization of your essay, using the guidelines on page 222.

■ Next, use the Focus on Word Choice above to see if you need to eliminate any clichés from your paper.

■ If a peer evaluated your paper, think carefully about each of your peer's comments as you revise.

Proofread Your Essay

A Finishing Touch Errors in your final essay will distract your reader from the persuasive point you are trying to make. If you have another person proofread your essay, you'll be much less likely to miss mistakes.

Reference Note
For more on **proofreading,** see page 13.

Grammar Link

Using Comparatives

When you write a persuasive paper, you sometimes want to compare one thing with another. For example, you may want to convince your readers that your candidate for class president is *more experienced* than other candidates.

Most one-syllable words and many two-syllable modifiers form the comparative by adding *–er*.

closer   cheaper   likelier

Some two-syllable modifiers (and all modifiers with more than two syllables) form the comparative by using *more*.

more polite   more recklessly

Do not use the word *more* if the modifier is already in the comparative form.

Incorrect	Powermax batteries last **more longer** than batteries from other companies. [The word *longer* doesn't need *more* added to it, because *longer* already means "more long."]
Correct	Powermax batteries last **longer** than batteries from other companies.

Some words, such as *good* and *bad*, have special comparative forms.

good ➤ better   bad ➤ worse

PRACTICE

For each of the following sentences, identify the incorrect modifier. Then, give the correct form of the modifier.

Example:
1. Video games are more cheaper than ever.
1. cheaper

1. Some video games are more harder than others. harder
2. Is a video game more bad than a TV crime drama? worse
3. Playing real basketball is more slower *slower* than playing the video game version.
4. The more I play this video game, the more better I get. better
5. The more I play real sports, the more good I get. better

For more information and practice on **comparatives,** see page 532.

Publish Your Essay

Get the Word Out   Now is the time for your essay to do what it was written to do—persuade people. Think about the audience you identified before you wrote your first draft. What are some ways to get your persuasive essay in front of that audience?

- Send your essay to the opinion page editor of a magazine, your local or school newspaper, or another publication.
- Think about other ways to go public with your work. You might convert your essay to a speech and present it to your audience directly. (For more on **formal speaking,** see page 758.)

PORTFOLIO

Reflect on Your Essay

Building Your Portfolio   Take time to reflect on your essay. Think about *what* you wrote and *how* you wrote. Reflecting will help you improve your next persuasive essay.

- What was the strongest piece of support in your essay? Why was it the strongest?
- What was your purpose for writing your essay? Do you think you achieved your purpose? Why or why not?

Proofreading, Publishing, and Reflecting on Your Essay

- Correct grammar, usage, and mechanics errors.
- Publish your essay to your target audience.
- Record your responses to the Reflect on Your Essay questions above in a learning log, or include them in your portfolio.

Life

Evaluating a Persuasive Speech

When you listen to a friend give advice or watch a TV ad, you are listening to persuasive messages. When you evaluate a persuasive speech, consider these basic elements:

- **Content**   A persuasive speech will contain an opinion and support for that opinion. In addition, a speaker may try to convince listeners by using *persuasive techniques*, such as the bandwagon approach. (For more on **persuasive techniques,** see page 246.) A careful listener needs to be able to identify a speaker's opinion and must not confuse it with fact. (For more on **fact and opinion,** see page 217.) Listen actively by asking questions. You may bring up points with which you agree, or challenge those with which you disagree. Responding to the speaker in this way will help you understand the speaker's message.

- **Delivery**   The speaker's delivery contributes to the persuasiveness of the speech. To evaluate delivery, consider whether the speaker's voice has good volume, rate, and clarity. Also, notice gestures and eye contact.

- **Believability**   Both content and delivery contribute to a speaker's believability. You should also analyze the speaker's purpose and perspective, or **bias**—the beliefs that affect his or her thinking.

To evaluate a persuasive speech, you need to develop **criteria,** or standards for judging. Follow the steps below.

1. **Look at the main elements of a persuasive speech**—content, delivery, believability. Ask yourself how the speaker could persuade using each element. Ask, for example, "What makes a persuasive voice?" You might decide that a loud, clear speech would persuade more effectively than soft, mumbled speech.

2. **Make a chart that lists your criteria in one column and space for notes in the other.** Get down as much information as possible as you listen to the speech. You will use these notes when you make your final evaluation of the speech. For more on **taking notes while you listen,** see page 775.

Evaluating a Persuasive Speech

Develop criteria for the content, delivery, and believability of a speech. Then, listen to a persuasive speech and take notes about how well the speaker meets your criteria. In a short presentation, evaluate the speech. Explain why you were or were not persuaded based on your criteria.

Analyzing an Editorial Cartoon

WHAT'S AHEAD?

In this section you will analyze an editorial cartoon. You will also learn how to

- identify symbolism
- understand exaggeration and caricature
- find and interpret analogies

"Where are the funnies?" This question is heard the moment the newspaper arrives in homes. Reading the "funnies" or the comics page of your newspaper may be your favorite way to start the day. Have you ever noticed that the comics page is not the only place in the newspaper where you can find cartoons? On the editorial page of most newspapers you will find a special type of cartoon, known as an **editorial** or **political cartoon**.

What Is an Editorial Cartoon?

Editorial cartoons are different from the cartoons you find in a comic book. These cartoons are designed to persuade their readers. They reflect the cartoonist's opinion on an issue or current event.

To make their points, editorial cartoonists use several techniques in their words and images. To understand the cartoonist's point, you need to understand these tools of the trade.

Symbolism	using a concrete picture or idea to stand for a more abstract one
Exaggeration/ Caricature	overstating a problem or issue to draw attention to it, or exaggerating someone's physical features to make sure viewers will recognize that person
Analogy	a comparison of two things (in editorial cartoons, directly or indirectly comparing a situation or event with a historical or fictional event)

Symbolism

The cartoon at the right uses symbolism to make its point. Uncle Sam, the symbol of the United States, is in a stalled car that symbolizes the troubled economy. The elephant (the symbol of the Republican political party) and the donkey (the symbol of the Democratic political party) are both claiming that they can fix Uncle Sam's car. However, we see that they are about to pull the car apart. The cartoonist uses symbols to persuade readers that the two political parties have conflicting goals that could hurt the country.

Exaggeration/Caricature

The cartoon at the bottom of this page uses exaggeration to make its point. The cartoonist is exaggerating the trend in professional basketball for high school players to go straight into professional sports instead of going to college first. What statement do you think the cartoonist is trying to make about this trend?

Frequently, cartoons also exaggerate the physical characteristics of famous people. This kind of exaggeration is called caricature. Caricatures add humor and help readers to recognize the cartoon's subject. On the right is a caricature of President George Washington. Presidents and political leaders are often the subjects of caricature.

Analogy

By using an analogy, a cartoonist can say a lot with very few words. The cartoon above makes an analogy, or a comparison, between the effort to balance the budget and the *Titanic*, the "unsinkable" ship that sank on its first voyage after it hit an iceberg. What is the cartoonist's opinion about the effect tax cuts will have on the balanced budget? (Notice that the iceberg is labeled "tax cuts.") Does the cartoonist want to persuade his readers that tax cuts are a good thing or a bad thing?

 Looking at an Editorial Cartoon

Find an editorial cartoon that you would like to analyze. You might look in a newspaper or newsmagazine from home or the school library. Then, ask yourself the following questions about your cartoon.

- What is the issue or topic the cartoon addresses?
- What symbols, if any, are used in the cartoon? What do they represent?
- What exaggeration or caricature, if any, is used in the cartoon?
- What effect does the exaggeration or caricature have?
- What analogies, if any, are used in the cartoon? How do the analogies help tell the story?
- What do you think is the cartoonist's opinion on the issue or current event?

Write down your answers and be prepared to share them with a few classmates. Try to find similarities and differences in the topics, attitudes, and techniques of the cartoonists each of you chose.

6 *Choices*

Choose one of the following activities to complete.

▶ SPEECH

1. Lay It on the Line Write a **persuasive speech** on an issue that is important to you. You might explore an interesting new issue, one that is a hot topic at your school or in your town. You might also turn the essay you wrote for the Writing Workshop into a speech. If you do, be aware that your speech's audience may not be the same as your essay's audience—you may have to adapt some or all of your reasons and evidence.

▶ CAREERS

2. Tools of the Trade Law, politics, advertising: These are just a few career fields that use persuasion. Research one of these fields or a different field. Then, write a **paragraph** describing a specific example of how a person in that field uses persuasion.

▶ ART

3. See You in the Funny Papers Create a cartoon reflecting the issue you wrote about in your essay. You may want to use it as an illustration to accompany your essay, but your cartoon's message should also be able to stand alone.

▶ CROSSING THE CURRICULUM: SOCIAL STUDIES

4. Time Traveling Write a **persuasive letter** from the point of view of someone living in the time and place you are studying in social studies. For example, if you were studying the pyramids of ancient Egypt, you could write a letter to the Pharaoh trying to convince him that your workers need more food and better living conditions.

▶ WRITING

5. What Is Your Problem? Think of a problem in your school or community—perhaps an overcrowded school or a lack of bike trails. Then, come up with a solution to the problem. You may need to brainstorm and write about several solutions before you decide which is best. Then, write a **problem-solution** composition in the form of an **editorial.**

PORTFOLIO

PORTFOLIO

Reading Workshop

Reading a Print Advertisement
PAGE 234

Writing Workshop

Creating a Print Advertisement
PAGE 242

Focus on Viewing and Representing

Analyzing Visual Effects in Ads
PAGE 261

A giant face looms on a billboard, smiling and suggesting that a particular brand of bread will make you happy, too. The scent of a flowery perfume drifts up as you open a magazine. Colorful signs on taxis and buses tell you to eat at certain restaurants.

Print advertisements are everywhere. These ads combine words, images, and sometimes even smells to convince people to buy or support a product or service. Print ads persuade people by appealing to their wants and needs. They often interest readers by using clever slogans and attractive images.

internetconnect

GO TO: go.hrw.com
KEYWORD: EOLang 7-7

YOUR TURN 1 — Exploring Advertising

Think about memorable print advertisements you have seen. Make a list of three or four advertisements you have seen on a billboard or in a newspaper or magazine, and answer these questions about them.

- Where did you see the advertisement?
- What product or service was being advertised?
- What in the advertisement caught your attention?
- Did the ad make you interested in buying the product or service? If so, how did it persuade you?

Then, share your list in a small group and decide what made each advertisement so memorable.

Reading a Print Advertisement

WHAT'S AHEAD?

In this section you will read a print advertisement. You will also learn how to

- form generalizations
- identify persuasive techniques

Companies that share a common goal, such as fighting a dangerous illness, sometimes band together to create a joint advertising campaign. These companies have more than one goal for their advertising. They want to get the public's support for their efforts, and they want to enhance their images in the public's eye. Advertising is one way that organizations can work toward these goals. Ads like the one on the next page are designed to persuade the public that there is more to business than simply selling products or services.

Preparing to Read

READING SKILL

Making Inferences: Forming Generalizations   A generalization is a statement that applies to many different individuals or situations. When you form a generalization, you combine what you know with specific information you read to make a judgment about the world in general. The following advertisement contains information from which you can make several generalizations. As you read, think about what generalizations the advertisers are leading you to make.

READING FOCUS

Persuasive Techniques   Advertisers aim to persuade an audience to buy a product, support a cause, or view an organization in a certain way. They do this through *persuasive techniques*. **Persuasive techniques** are ways of adding to the appeal of information presented to support a persuasive argument. An advertiser may try to choose the one persuasive technique that best fits the audience for an ad. The advertisement on the following page uses persuasive techniques to convince readers to support pharmaceutical companies' efforts to fight leukemia, a type of cancer that often strikes children.

Read the following advertisement. In a notebook, answer the numbered active-reading questions located in the shaded boxes. The underlined words will be used in the Vocabulary Mini-Lesson on page 240.

LEUKEMIA MADE HIM A PATIENT. WE HELPED HIM BECOME A KID AGAIN.

"Your child has leukemia." The most devastating news a parent could hear. It used to mean there was little chance of survival. Now, 80 percent of kids diagnosed with leukemia not only survive—but lead normal lives. How? New breakthrough medicines, discovered and developed by pharmaceutical company researchers, have given many leukemia patients and their parents a second chance. The new medicines our researchers are discovering are giving families hope—and patients a chance to be kids again.

America's Pharmaceutical Companies

Leading the way in the search for cures

1. How does the picture contrast with the word *leukemia?*

2. Why do you think the advertiser used a dog in this ad?

3. What does the ad mean by "become a kid again"?

4. To what emotion does the first sentence below the picture appeal?

5. Why do you think the text below the picture repeats "be kids again" at the end?

6. Who are the advertisers trying to persuade? Why do you think so?

READING SKILL ➤

Making Inferences: Forming Generalizations

Generally Speaking   As you read new information, you constantly make *inferences*. An **inference** is an educated guess based on what you read plus what you already know about the subject. One specific type of inference is a *generalization*. **Generalizations** are statements that apply to many individuals or situations.

Example: **What you read:** The Guadalupe River flooded several houses near its banks during recent heavy rains.

+ **What you know:** The Mississippi River also flooded houses near its banks during heavy rains a few years ago.

Generalization: Rivers often flood houses near their banks during heavy rains.

TIP Generalizations tend to use clue words such as *most, many, often, generally, overall,* and *usually.*

?   What clue word does the generalization in the example to the right use?

Faulty generalizations may use clue words such as *none, no one, never, always, everyone, every,* and *all.*

Example:
Rivers *always* flood houses near their banks during heavy rains.

Advertisers expect the reader to make generalizations about the kinds of people who use their products and about what those products will do. Frequently, the generalizations that a reader makes from an ad are faulty. **Faulty generalizations** are either not true or do not apply in all cases. Questions like these can help you evaluate a generalization.

■ What would *really* happen if you did or did not use this product or service?

■ Do the people in the ad represent *everyone* who uses this product or service, or do they represent just *some* people?

■ Do the claims in the ad make sense?

   Study the advertisement on the following page. What generalization does the ad lead you to make about the product and the people who buy it? Is that generalization a sound one, or is it faulty? If you need help answering these questions, use the Thinking It Through steps that follow the ad.

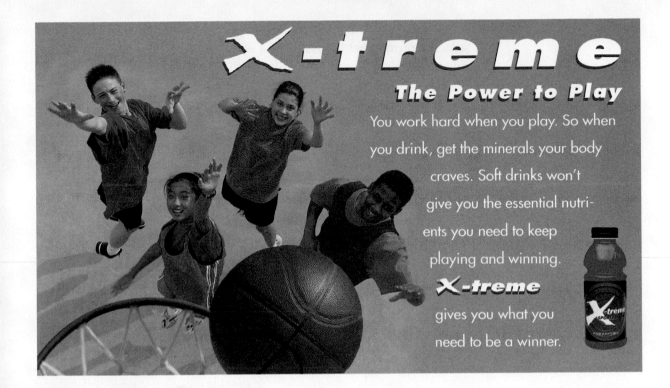

X-treme
The Power to Play

You work hard when you play. So when you drink, get the minerals your body craves. Soft drinks won't give you the essential nutrients you need to keep playing and winning. **X-treme** gives you what you need to be a winner.

THINKING IT THROUGH

Forming and Evaluating Generalizations from Advertisements

▶ **STEP 1** Look at the text and image in the advertisement. What does the ad *say* about the product or company? What does the ad *suggest*?

The ad <u>says</u> that the drink gives you the nutrients you need to be a winner. It <u>suggests</u> that the drink made the people in the picture more energetic.

▶ **STEP 2** Consider what you already know about the topic.

The football team drinks a special sports drink during games.

▶ **STEP 3** Make a generalization that extends to individuals or situations outside the ad.

Generalization: People who drink sports drinks will have more energy and be better athletes.

▶ **STEP 4** Evaluate the generalization you have made to see if it is faulty or not. You may use the questions on page 236.

I think this is a faulty generalization. You could drink all the sports drinks in the world and still not be a better athlete.

The X-treme Sports Drink ad led the reader to form the faulty generalization that sports drinks will improve the performance and energy levels of people who drink them. Even though the generalization is not true, the ad may still accomplish its purpose: to persuade the reader to buy the product. As a reader, you should evaluate the generalizations you make from advertisements so that you do not buy a product or service based on a faulty generalization.

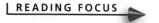
Forming and Evaluating Generalizations from Advertisements

Look again at the advertisement on page 235. Use the Thinking It Through steps on page 237 to form and evaluate a generalization about

- the pharmaceutical companies that sponsored the ad
- the children who use those companies' treatments for leukemia

Then, find a print ad in a magazine. Form and evaluate a generalization about the company or product advertised.

READING FOCUS

Persuasive Techniques

Jump on the Bandwagon   Advertisers aim to get their audiences to believe in something or to take some action. The way ads accomplish this is by using specific **persuasive techniques**. Some people call these techniques *propaganda techniques*. **Propaganda** is a systematic approach to influencing many people at once. Propaganda is not only used in advertising, however. You may find propaganda in speeches, editorials, or any other form of persuasive communication.

Many people have negative feelings about propaganda. History is full of examples of how individuals, governments, or companies have used propaganda to deceive others. For example, advertisers might use propaganda to get the public to support an unworthy cause or to buy a product out of fear.

Still, propaganda is also used for good purposes. For example, a public service announcement could convince people to exercise more often. In that case, propaganda is being used to help people lead healthier lives.

The chart on the next page shows common persuasive techniques. You can find these techniques in all types of persuasive messages.

Common Persuasive Techniques		
Bandwagon	You are urged to do or believe something because everyone else does.	"Be where the action is. Shop at Hangout Mall."
Testimonial	Famous people endorse a product or idea.	"I'm professional football player Marcus Browning, and I use Wash Out window cleaner."
Emotional Appeal	Words or images that appeal to the audience's emotions are used. The appeal may be to positive emotions, such as desire for success, or to negative ones, such as fear.	"What would you do if all your possessions were lost in a fire? Get the Save-All fireproof safe and protect your valuables."
Plain Folks	Ordinary people sell a message. You are to believe that because these people are like you, they can be trusted.	"As a construction worker, I often get headaches on the job. That's why I use PainAway aspirin."
Snob Appeal	This technique suggests that you can be like the expensively dressed, perfectly shaped people who use this product.	"I accept only the best, and that's why I buy Aloft perfume."

When you read an advertisement, think about how the advertiser is trying to persuade you. Ask yourself these questions.

■ What is the ad trying to persuade me to do, think, or feel?

■ What persuasive words and images appear in the ad?

■ Which technique would use those types of words and images?

Finally, ask yourself whether the ad gives any logical or concrete support that can persuade you. An ad that relies solely on the persuasive techniques above may not persuade a critical reader at all. For example, the X-treme Sports Drink ad says the drink gives you the nutrients you need to be a winner, but it doesn't name any specific nutrients. Should you really be persuaded by such an ad?

TIP Ads may use more than one persuasive technique at a time. The ad for X-treme Sports Drink on page 237 uses a bandwagon approach by showing a group of active teenagers who supposedly drink X-treme. The ad also uses an emotional appeal—"X-treme gives you what you need to be a winner"—which makes readers feel good about the product.

 Identifying Persuasive Techniques

Re-read the pharmaceutical company advertisement on page 235. Ask yourself the questions above to identify how the advertiser is trying to convince you. Write your responses on a piece of paper, and provide examples from the ad to support your answers.

Dictionaries, Glossaries, and Other References

A print ad may contain words that you do not understand. You can use many types of reference sources to find the meanings of unfamiliar words in print ads and other written works.

- **Dictionary:** Dictionaries tell how to pronounce a word, explain the word's usage, define all of the word's meanings, provide synonyms, and give information about a word's history.

- **Thesaurus:** A thesaurus lists **synonyms,** or words that have the same meaning, and **antonyms,** words with the opposite meaning of a word.

- **Glossary:** Glossaries list the important or difficult words used in a textbook. They only include the meaning of the word as it is used in the book.

- **Software:** Some computer software programs include an electronic dictionary or thesaurus. These resources list only the most common definitions or synonyms of each word.

Using a dictionary can be particularly challenging because dictionaries list several definitions for each word. You may have to decide which definition fits the word's context. The steps below can help.

THINKING IT THROUGH   Choosing the Right Definition

Here is an example using the word *breakthrough* from the reading selection on page 235.

▶ **STEP 1** Look up the unfamiliar word in the dictionary. Read the entire definition.

Breakthrough: 1. the act of breaking through resistance 2. an important discovery

▶ **STEP 2** Use each of the meanings in the context of the reading selection. Decide which meaning makes the most sense.

"New breaking through resistance medicines. . . ." That doesn't sound right. "New important discovery medicines. . . ." That sounds better. The second definition is correct here.

PRACTICE

Use a dictionary to look up these words from the reading selection on page 235. Write the correct definition of each word as it is used in the ad, and write a sentence using each word. The words are underlined in the ad.

1. devastating   **2.** diagnosed   **3.** pharmaceutical   **4.** cures

Identifying Causes and Effects

Advertisements are built on cause-and-effect relationships. Readers are supposed to believe that a certain cause, such as buying a specific brand of toothpaste, will lead to a certain effect, such as having many friends.

When you read a selection on a reading test, you may be asked to identify a cause-and-effect relationship within the passage. Read the following text and question. How would you answer the question?

Cancer can attack many parts of the human body. Cancer of the white blood cells is known as leukemia. Human blood contains both red and white blood cells. Normally, the body produces white blood cells only to replace those that die off. In patients with leukemia, however, the body produces abnormal white blood cells at an increased rate. Leukemia negatively affects the function of organs such as the liver, spleen, and brain. Eventually, leukemia can cause serious infections and even death.

What effect does leukemia have on the body?

A. increases the number of red blood cells

B. harms the liver, spleen, and brain

C. causes sore throats and fever

D. decreases the number of white blood cells

THINKING IT THROUGH — Answering a Cause-and-Effect Question

▶ **STEP 1** Read the question. Does it ask about a cause or an effect?

The question is asking about the effect of leukemia.

▶ **STEP 2** Look in the passage for clue words such as *cause, effect, affect, because, impact, influences, leads to,* or *results in.*

The passage says that leukemia "negatively <u>affects</u> the function of organs" and can "<u>cause</u> serious infections and even death."

▶ **STEP 3** Make a cluster diagram or a conceptual map that shows which event caused the other.

▶ **STEP 4** Choose an answer choice that closely matches your diagram.

Answer B matches one part of my diagram. The other answer choices aren't mentioned in the passage. I'll choose answer B.

Creating a Print Advertisement

WHAT'S AHEAD?

In this workshop you will create a print advertisement. You will also learn how to

- identify a target market for your ad
- analyze ads for their target markets
- choose a persuasive technique
- use emotional words
- correctly punctuate possessive nouns

After a hard day at school, you head home, hit the couch, and flip open your favorite magazine. Turning the pages, you see an advertisement that shows your favorite actor eating a sandwich. Suddenly you realize how hungry you are. You amble off to the kitchen for something, but as you peer into the refrigerator, you wish you had that big sandwich instead.

There is no doubt about it. Advertisements are persuasive. Print ads in magazines and newspapers influence what readers buy, how they vote, and even what social causes they support. Now is your chance to create an advertisement that will persuade a specific audience to buy a product or service of your own creation.

Prewriting

Pick a Product or Service

> **TIP** A **product** is a thing, such as blue jeans, bottled fruit juice, or ballpoint pens. **Services** are tasks, such as housecleaning, car washing, or lawn mowing, done for another person.

Something You Can't Live Without Brainstorm a product or service for your print advertisement. Try one of these methods to help you choose.

- **Think of an improvement for an existing product or service,** such as a computer program, a pair of shoes, or a pencil. How could you improve the way it works or looks? Create a new product based on your ideas for improving an existing one.

- **Come up with a totally new product or service.** Think about chores you do by hand that could be done with a machine. Invent a new snack. Offer a service for a task others might not like to do.

Once you have a product or service in mind, you can think of a name for it. You can think of a catchy, memorable name, or you can use a descriptive name that explains a key feature of the product or service. Either way, be careful not to choose a name that already exists.

Find a Target Market

Who Will Buy It? In any ad, the advertiser focuses on a specific group of people called the *target market*. **A target market is made up of the people who *might* use or buy a certain product or service.** For example, the target market for a new dog food would only include people who own a dog. The advertiser's job is to convince those people who *might* need the product that they *do* need it. To determine your target market, ask yourself these questions.

- Who might use the product or service?
- Who might actually buy the product or service?

The people who might use the product or service and the people who might actually buy it are not always the same. For example, small children ride tricycles, but adults buy them. In that case, decide which group to focus on in your ad. Here is how one student identified the target market for his product, an improved organizer for school lockers.

KEY CONCEPT

TIP *Target market* is a special advertising term. Choosing a **target market** in an advertisement is similar to considering your **audience** in other types of writing.

Product: Magnetic Attraction Locker Organizer

Who will use the product? My locker organizers are for middle school and high school students.

Who will buy it? Parents will most likely buy the organizers, but probably only when the students pick them out.

Who is the focus? Students should be the focus. Even if they don't buy the organizers, they do tell their parents what they need.

YOUR TURN 4

Choosing a Product and Finding a Target Market

- Identify a product or service for your advertisement.
- Name your new product or service by thinking of a catchy name or a descriptive name that highlights a key feature.
- Answer the questions above to determine your target market.

Analyzing Target Markets in Advertisements

Imagine picking up your favorite music magazine and seeing an advertisement for baby food. You would probably think "Wow! That ad is sure out of place!" The target market for baby food is probably not the same as the audience for the music magazine.

Every advertisement has a target market. If you can determine who the target market is, you can begin to analyze that ad. The more you analyze advertising, the smarter you will be as a consumer. To determine the target market of an advertisement, ask questions about these four parts of the ad.

Product or service
Who would use this product or service? Who would buy it?

People
What people are shown using the product or service? How old are they? Are they male or female?

Other images
Aside from the people using the product, what other pictures are in the ad? Who would be interested in these types of pictures?

Text
Does the ad address certain people? Does it use language that would appeal to a particular group?

If these questions have different answers, you will need to look closely at people, images, and text in the ad to figure out whom it really targets.

The following ad seems to target more than one group. Use the questions in the chart on the left side of the page to determine the real target market of the Dino Pockets ad.

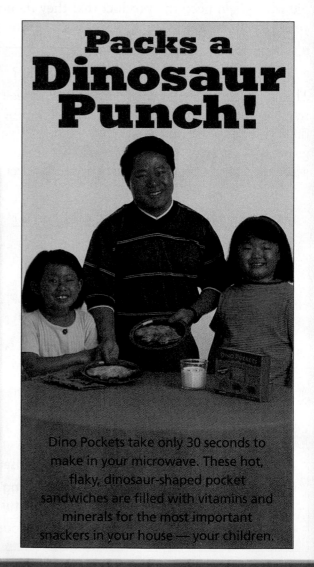

Packs a **Dinosaur Punch!**

Dino Pockets take only 30 seconds to make in your microwave. These hot, flaky, dinosaur-shaped pocket sandwiches are filled with vitamins and minerals for the most important snackers in your house — your children.

Now, compare your answers to the questions on product, people, other images, and text to the answers below. Did you identify the correct target market?

- **Product** Pocket sandwiches shaped like dinosaurs are designed to be eaten by children. However, the people who will buy these sandwiches at the grocery store are parents.

- **People** The people pictured in the ad are a father and his two children. They represent two different age groups. The father represents the parents who buy the sandwiches. The two children represent the people who eat the sandwiches.

- **Other images** Besides the people, the ad shows a sunny kitchen and a neat table. This setting would appeal to parents who want a safe, orderly home for their children.

- **Text** The large text "Packs a Dinosaur Punch" probably appeals more to children. However, the smaller text addresses parents directly by saying "your house—your children."

The target market of this ad is not obvious at first. Looking only at the product and people, you might conclude the market is either parents or children. The other images and the text, though, suggest that the primary, or main, target market is parents. It is possible that the slogan "Packs a Dinosaur Punch" is an attempt to get children's attention. However, that slogan would also capture the attention of the parents whose children are interested in anything to do with dinosaurs. An ad like this might appear in a magazine geared towards parents and families.

PRACTICE

Use the questions on page 244 to help you identify the target market of each advertisement part shown below.

1.

2.

Be cool with our new high-top sneaker that makes crashing noises with every step.

3.

Analyze Your Target Market

Give 'Em What They Want   To convince your target market to spend hard-earned pay (or allowance) on your product or service, you have to give them a good reason.

To analyze your target market and what your product or service can do for them, you will brainstorm a list of this group's needs and wants, as in the example below.

Product: locker organizer

Target market: students who use lockers

Needs: to be more organized
      to have more room in their lockers
      to find things fast and have more time between classes

Wants: to have other students admire their lockers

I think the most important need or want that my locker organizer can help fulfill is the need to be organized.

YOUR TURN 5   Analyzing the Target Market

Analyze your target market by brainstorming a list of their needs and wants. Pick the most important need to focus on in your advertisement and circle it. You will use the most important need to choose your persuasive technique in the next section.

Choose a Persuasive Technique

Make Your Pitch   Advertisers use persuasive techniques to influence their audience. **Persuasive techniques can help convince people to buy the product or service.** Although some advertisements use more than one technique, they usually choose a single technique as the main focus. As you choose the main persuasive technique for your print advertisement, pick one that will appeal to your target market's wants and needs. The chart on the next page summarizes the most common persuasive techniques: bandwagon, testimonial, emotional appeal, plain folks, and snob appeal.

Reference Note
For more on **persuasive techniques,** see page 238.

Common Persuasive Techniques	
Technique	**Example**
Bandwagon—says that everyone else is buying the product or service	"More people buy our basketball shoes than buy any other brand."
Testimonial—uses famous people to support the product or service	"Even basketball superstar Bob Tallman wears our shoes."
Emotional Appeal—promotes fear, hope, or other emotions	"Are you getting left behind on the courts? Our shoes can help."
Plain Folks—shows people like you	"My basketball shoes helped me make the basketball team at my school."
Snob Appeal—suggests you will be fashionable or trendy	"Our shoes are for the athletes who want only the best."

Choosing a Persuasive Technique

Here is how to choose a persuasive technique for your print ad.

▶ **STEP 1** Pick a persuasive technique to address the main need of your target market.

Students' main need is to be organized. I'll use an emotional appeal. The use of an emotional situation, such as the frustration of having a messy locker, might make students think they need my product.

▶ **STEP 2** Test the persuasive technique by filling in these blanks: "Will (technique) make the target market believe they will (need)?"

Will an emotional appeal make the target market believe they will be more organized? Yes. Showing a frustrated student with a messy locker will show students that they need to buy my product to get organized.

 Choosing a Persuasive Technique

Use the chart and Thinking It Through steps above to choose a persuasive technique to use in your advertisement.

TIP Test several persuasive techniques to make sure you choose the one that best matches the needs of your target market.

Think About a Slogan

Stuck on You   What do you think of when you hear, "Got milk?®" You may think of famous faces sporting milk mustaches. This is just one example of the power of *slogans*.

A **slogan** is a short, catchy phrase or motto that attracts attention. **Slogans help advertising stick in the minds of the target market.** Think about your product or service. How can you tell something about it while using the persuasive technique you have chosen? Here is how one student thought of his slogan.

TIP Many slogans use rhyme or alliteration (the repetition of an initial consonant sound). Rhyming slogans like "For the best construction tools, buy Ruhl" create a singsong rhythm that is easy for people to remember. Alliteration such as "Cecil's sandwiches are always served with a smile" repeats the *s* sound to make the slogan memorable.

> Since I am using an emotional appeal, I want to point out what a difference my locker organizer will make in students' lives when they have more time between classes to talk to friends. My slogan will be: "What a difference three shelves make!"

YOUR TURN 7 Writing a Slogan

Keeping the persuasive technique that you have chosen in mind, write a catchy slogan for your product or service. You might use alliteration or rhyme to make your slogan easy to remember.

Choose an Image

Get the Picture   The most persuasive elements of a print advertisement are often the images that accompany the words, so to illustrate your ad, select a visual that stands out from the crowd. You may draw your own art, create pictures on a computer, take a photograph, cut out magazine photos, or trace other illustrations and adjust them for your advertisement.

TIP Use professional ads as a **resource** to get ideas about images, colors, and arrangement of subjects. Other resources such as a dictionary or thesaurus will help you write and revise the text of your ad.

As you choose a **subject** for your image, remember to make it match the persuasive technique you chose. If you picked a plain folks approach, you should not choose a person wearing expensive clothes as your subject. Also, choose your colors carefully. In general, bright, **warm colors** stir strong emotions, and light, **cool colors** create calm feelings. Tie your use of color to the type of emotion you want to create in your reader.

Choosing an Image

Choose an image for your print ad that fits the persuasive technique you have chosen. Sketch a draft of the image after you

- choose a subject and decide what the subject will be doing
- decide what else will be included in the image with the subject
- choose colors to convey strong or soothing emotions

Plan the Text

The Ad Game You have already planned parts of your ad, but you still need to write the main text. The chart below explains the three main parts of an ad's text and shows a student's example.

Description Describe the product or service completely. Give basic information, such as sizes, colors, business hours, or key features. Also explain what makes your product special.	The Magnetic Attraction Locker Organizer features ■ three sturdy metal shelves ■ adjustable widths to fit any locker ■ magnets for hanging pictures and notes
Reasons to Buy Mention any reasons to buy your product or service that you have not already included in your slogan or description.	Why spend the entire break between classes looking for homework in a messy locker? Get Magnetic Attraction and get organized!
Action Finally, your print advertisement needs to tell your target market what they should do. Where can they buy the product or service? What is their next step?	The Magnetic Attraction Locker Organizer is available wherever school supplies are sold. Get our organizer before <u>your</u> locker becomes a disaster.

Play Fair In the Reading Workshop, you learned how to avoid being persuaded by persuasive techniques alone. Assume that your target market knows enough to demand **logical support** and **concrete evidence.** Give important facts about your product or service in your product description. Be sure the reasons you give are logical.

 Planning the Text

Plan the text of your ad by using the chart and example above. Be sure to include a description of your product or service, reasons to buy it, and information that tells readers what action they should take.

TIP Use a voice that fits your **purpose,** which is to persuade. One way to win over your audience is to use vivid language, including precise adjectives and verbs. Instead of saying a pen "writes smoothly," say it "glides like silk across the page."

Writing

Advertisement

Framework	Directions and Explanations
Slogan	**Slogans** should be short, catchy, and to the point. Since you want people to remember your slogan, **write it in large print** at the top of your ad.
Image	The most noticeable part of your ad should be an **attractive image** geared toward your target market. Use an **interesting subject** that supports your persuasive technique, and choose **colors** thoughtfully.
Text ■ Tie-in ■ Description ■ Reasons ■ Action	■ Start out with a statement that **ties the product or service to the persuasive technique** you use. ■ Include the **name** of your product or service at the beginning. ■ **Describe the product or service vividly.** Use words with punch and impact. ■ **Give logical reasons** to buy the product or service. ■ Provide **important facts** about your product or service. ■ Tell the customer **where to buy** the product or service.

YOUR TURN 10 Drafting Your Print Advertisement

Now it is your turn to write a first draft of your print advertisement. As you draft,

■ keep your persuasive technique in mind
■ use vivid, precise language and important facts in the description
■ refer to the framework above and the Writer's Model on page 251

A Writer's Model

The final draft below closely follows the framework for a print advertisement on the previous page.

Slogan

Image

Do you want more time to talk to friends between classes? The Magnetic Attraction Locker Organizer can help.

Tie-in

The Magnetic Attraction Locker Organizer features

Description

- three sturdy metal shelves
- adjustable widths to fit any locker
- magnets for hanging pictures and notes

Why spend the entire break between classes looking for homework in a messy locker? Get Magnetic Attraction and get organized!

Reasons

The Magnetic Attraction Locker Organizer is available wherever school supplies are sold. Get our organizer before <u>your</u> locker becomes a disaster.

Action

A Student's Model

Chris Cheung, a student at Davidson Middle School in Crestview, Florida, created the following print ad. His ad achieves most of the goals of the framework plus something else: It makes a funny comment about advertising and logos. What is that comment?

Evaluate and Revise Content, Organization, and Style

Once Is Not Enough   When you evaluate a classmate's advertisement or revise your own, you should always read the entire advertisement at least twice. The first reading gives you an opportunity to evaluate the content and organization of the advertisement. Use the guidelines below to help you during your first reading. In your second reading, use the Focus on Word Choice on page 255 to improve your style.

▶ **First Reading: Content and Organization**   Use this chart to evaluate and revise your advertisement so that it is more persuasive. If you need help answering the questions, use the tips in the center column. Then, use the revision techniques in the right-hand column to make necessary changes.

Print Advertisement: Content and Organization Guidelines for Self-Evaluation and Peer Evaluation		
Evaluation Questions ▶	**Tips** ▶	**Revision Techniques**
❶ Would the image catch a reader's attention?	▶ **Note** two things about the image that would make a reader look at it, such as color or subject.	▶ **Delete** the image and replace it with one that is more visually interesting, unusual, or colorful, if needed.
❷ Is the slogan catchy and memorable?	▶ **Underline** words that have rhyme, alliteration, or some other catchy element.	▶ If necessary, **add** words that are memorable, or that use rhyme or alliteration.
❸ Does the ad have a clearly defined target market?	▶ **Write down** two specific things that point to the ad's target market.	▶ If needed, **add** to the image, slogan, or text to identify clearly the target market.
❹ Does the ad provide a clear description of the product or service?	▶ **Put a number** next to each fact about the product or service.	▶ **Elaborate** by adding facts about the product or service, if needed.
❺ Does the ad clearly tell readers what action to take to buy the product or service?	▶ **Place a check mark** by the information that tells the readers what action to take.	▶ **Add** an action or clarify what the reader should do.

ONE WRITER'S REVISIONS This revision is from an early draft of the print advertisement on page 251.

add

between classes

Do you want more time to talk to friends? The ∧

Magnetic Attraction Locker Organizer can help.

The Magnetic Attraction Locker Organizer features

elaborate

∧
- three sturdy metal shelves
- *adjustable widths to fit any locker*
- magnets for hanging pictures and notes

Why spend the entire break between classes looking for

homework in a messy locker? Get Magnetic Attraction and

get organized!

add

∧ *The Magnetic Attraction Locker Organizer is available wherever school supplies are sold. Get our organizer before your locker becomes a disaster.*

As you evaluate a peer's print advertisement, ask yourself these questions:
- What is the most persuasive part of this advertisement? What is the least persuasive? Why?

PEER REVIEW

Responding to the Revision Process

1. Why did the writer add words to the first sentence?

2. Why did the writer elaborate on the description?

3. Why do you think the writer added the last two sentences?

▶ **Second Reading: Style** During your first reading, you revised what you said and the order in which you said it. The second reading focuses on your style, or the way you say things in your advertisement. One method of improving your style is to make sure you use words that have a strong emotional impact on your readers.

Style Guidelines

Evaluation Question	▶ Tip	▶ Revision Technique
Does the body of the ad use emotional language?	▶ **Circle** words that create an emotional response.	▶ If the ad contains few emotional words, **delete** some ordinary words and replace them with more emotional ones.

Using Emotional Language

When you write an advertisement, you should make your product or service descriptions create an emotional response in your target audience. Consider the following two descriptions.

The Abracadab Circus will be fun!

The Abracadab Circus will make you giggle and gasp!

The second sentence, which would probably appeal to a young audience, is more emotional than the first one. You feel more interested in the circus because the description suggests an emotional response. You want to go to the circus and see what will make you giggle and gasp.

You can find more emotional words by looking in a thesaurus or by brainstorming a whole new way of describing your subject. You should think carefully about your ad's descriptions and determine what type of emotional response you want your reader to have.

ONE WRITER'S REVISIONS

Get our organizer before your locker becomes ~~cluttered~~ *a disaster*.

Responding to the Revision Process

Why do you think the writer changed a word? Do you think the change improves the advertisement? Why or why not?

YOUR TURN 11 Evaluating and Revising Your Ad

- First, evaluate and revise the content and organization of your advertisement by using the guidelines on page 253.

- Next, use the Focus on Word Choice above to add emotional impact to your words.

- If a peer evaluated your print ad, carefully consider each of your peer's comments as you revise.

Publishing

Proofread Your Ad

Reference Note

For information on **proofreading guidelines,** see page 13.

Getting It Right Before you create the final draft of your ad, have someone else **edit,** or proofread, it for you. Mistakes in your advertisement might make your target market wonder whether your product is also flawed.

Grammar Link

Punctuating Possessives

Advertisements often talk about the features of certain products. For example, an ad for a vacuum cleaner might list its attachments. To explain these features, you will use the possessive form of a noun.

To form the possessive of a singular noun, add an apostrophe and an *s*.

Examples:
the computer**'s** software
the vacuum cleaner**'s** brushes

If the noun ends in *s*, it will still take both the apostrophe and the *s*. If the extra *s* would make the noun awkward to say, you may use only the apostrophe.

Examples:
Jonas**'s** house [*Jonas's* is not awkward to say.]
the Netherlands**'** exports [*Netherlands's* is awkward to say.]

To form the possessive of a plural noun, add only an apostrophe if the noun ends in an *s*.

Examples:
the brushes**'** bristles
four days**'** work

If the plural noun does not end in an *s*, add an apostrophe and an *s*.

Examples:
the teeth**'s** enamel
children**'s** games

Make sure nouns are possessive, not simply plural, before adding apostrophes.

| Incorrect | The girl's left their bicycles. |
| Correct | The girls left their bicycles. |

PRACTICE

For each sentence, identify the word that needs an apostrophe. Then, write the word correctly.

Example:
1. The beanbags stuffing is nontoxic.
1. beanbag's

1. Remove the air conditioners filter.
2. The two quilts stitching is excellent.
3. The womens team won both races.
4. Mrs. Rogers garden is blooming.
5. Everyone believed the four girls story.

For more information and practice on **punctuating possessives,** see page 638.

Sixteen-year-old swimmer Kristin Ziemke learned how to perform CPR for her

other buddies on the swim team. But little did she know that during one meet,

the one who needed it would be a spectator up in the stands. He collapsed

with a heart attack, and Kristin climbed into the bleachers and saved his life.

The American Red Cross gives a helping hand to people who urgently need it.

We are not a government agency. We depend on you. Please give us

your time and support. Because help can't wait.

American Red Cross

Adding a Background

In this ad for the American Red Cross, the words are printed in white over the illustration. This "reverse" type over a background of the girl's face draws the reader's attention right away.

Look at your print advertisement. Can you use a background behind your text? If you use a computer, you can format the background as a color or as a simple pattern. If your background is dark, use reverse type to keep your words readable. Look for these options under the format menu, or use drawing tools if they are available. If you are drawing your ad by hand, use colored pencils to color in a light background.

Publish Your Ad

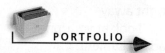

Showing Your Stuff   Now it is time to see whether your advertisement works. Will your target audience really be influenced by your ad? Try one of these methods to share your powers of persuasion.

■ Create a class magazine with all of your print advertisements. You might even group advertisements together by the type of product or service.

■ Show your ad to a member of the ad's target market. Would this person be persuaded to buy your product or service? Ask for comments about the techniques you used.

■ Show your print ad to friends and family. What do they like about the product or service you advertised? What do they think are the most effective parts of your advertisement?

Reflect on Your Ad

Building Your Portfolio   Take some time now to reflect on your advertisement. Think about *what* you wrote and *how* you wrote it. As you reflect on your print advertisement, consider what skills you can improve for future assignments.

■ What was the most difficult task you faced in creating an advertisement? Why do you think so?

■ How did analyzing your target market help you create your advertisement? Do you think learning about your readers could help you on other writing assignments?

■ Examine all the written works in your portfolio to set goals for yourself as a writer. What are three things you could do to improve your writing?

YOUR TURN 12 Proofreading, Publishing, and Reflecting on Your Ad

■ Correct grammar, usage, and mechanics errors in your ad.

■ Publish your ad by following one of the suggestions above.

■ Answer the questions from Reflect on Your Ad above. Record your responses in a learning log, or include them in your portfolio.

Creating Your Own Commercial

Now that you have created a print advertisement, bring it to life in a commercial. In this section you will adapt your print ad to create a television commercial.

Making a Plan   Follow these steps to convert a print ad into a commercial.

Fill in the Details   Many effective commercials are like little stories—stories in which a problem is solved by buying a product. Brainstorm a story for your own ad by answering the following questions.

Characters: Who will be in your commercial? How will they appeal to your target audience?

Setting: Where and when will your commercial take place?

Action: What will your characters do? How will that action tie in with your persuasive technique? How will the action appeal to your target audience?

Draw a Storyboard   A storyboard is like a graphic organizer for your commercial. It includes the **dialogue, narration,** and images showing the **major actions** that will take place in your commercial. Your storyboard will help you plan all of the props and other supplies you will need.

To make a storyboard, sketch the basic action of each scene in your commercial. Below each sketch, write the dialogue for your characters. Look at the following example.

GIRL 1: I never get a chance to talk to anybody between classes! And now I can't find my math homework!
GIRL 2: Your locker is out of control. Haven't you heard of the Magnetic Attraction Locker Organizer?
GIRL 1: The what?
GIRL 2: Look at MY locker.

GIRL 1: Wow! How did you manage that?
GIRL 2: Easy. I just installed the adjustable Magnetic Attraction Locker Organizer. It comes with three shelves and these cool little magnets to hang pictures with. Now I have all the time I need between classes.

GIRL 1: What a difference three shelves make!

Prepare Your Commercial Before you can rehearse your commercial, you must pick out the scenery, the actors, and the props the actors will use. Once these are in place, rehearse your commercial all the way through several times. Doing a complete run-through will help you see problems in the script and adjust your commercial to run more smoothly.

Lights, Camera, Action If you have access to a video camera, you can tape your commercial for all to see. By using a process called "in-camera editing," you can create a commercial by taping each shot in the correct order so that special editing equipment is not necessary.

First, use your storyboard to plan each shot. Then, tape your shots in the order they happen according to your storyboard. If you make a mistake, stop, rewind, and try it again. Once you finish a shot exactly the way you want it, stop or pause the camera and set up the next shot. Repeat the process until your commercial is complete.

The suggestions in the next column can also help as you videotape your TV commercial.

- Watch the lighting of your scenes. The light should be bright enough for the action to show up well on camera. It should not come from behind the actors.
- Eliminate background clutter from your scenes. Extra furniture, backdrops, or people will only distract your viewers.
- Use a tripod if possible so the camera will not shake during recording. If you do not have access to a tripod, make sure the cameraperson practices holding the camera still.
- Remind your actors to face partway toward the camera. If your actors face each other, your audience will not be able to hear their voices or see their facial expressions as well.
- Your actors should speak clearly and slowly. Many people speak quickly when they get nervous, so have the actors talk more slowly than they normally would.

If you do not have access to a video camera, perform your commercial live. Once you get up in front of your audience, all of your hard work will pay off as you convince the whole class that your product is better than anything they could buy in a store.

 Creating a TV Commercial

Use the suggestions on pages 259–260 to turn your print advertisement into a TV commercial. Remember to

- create a storyboard
- choose characters and props
- videotape your commercial or perform it live

Analyzing Visual Effects in Ads

Has a television commercial ever made you say, "Wow, did you see that?" Perhaps a three-dimensional object seemed to hurtle out of the screen. A dog might have dunked a basketball like a pro. Advertisers will do anything they can to keep potential customers from turning the page or changing the channel when an advertisement appears. One of their most powerful weapons is the *visual effect.* **Visual effects** are ways of changing an image to add to its message or create a certain impression in a viewer's mind.

WHAT'S AHEAD?

In this section you will analyze visual effects used in mass-media advertising. You will also learn how to

- recognize the visual effects used by print and television ads
- compare the ways effects are used
- find examples of print and television ads with visual effects

The Purpose of Visual Effects

Not only are visual effects fun and interesting, but they also keep viewers looking at an advertisement. The longer a viewer looks at an ad, the more likely the product or service being advertised will stick in the viewer's mind. Visual effects naturally hold our attention because they combine reality with the fantastic. Which image would be more likely to grab your attention: a giant bug invading a house or a real bug walking across a kitchen floor?

Visual effects also help shape a viewer's feelings about the product or service in the ad. For example, if an ad shows the giant bug retreating and finally dying after being sprayed with bug spray, the viewer might feel confident that the product can get rid of *any* insect. After all, the bug spray successfully killed the giant bug.

Types of Visual Effects

Print advertisements and television commercials each use unique visual effects. These effects make an ad more interesting so it can attract the most readers or viewers possible.

TIP Visual effects also hold viewers' attention in film, television shows, newspapers, magazines, and news programs.

A print ad can include a collage of images and text—words and pictures that, when combined, create an overall effect on the readers. Unless a print ad runs for several pages, it usually focuses on one image which creates an unfinished story. Important information about what happened before the product was used or what happened afterward is missing. The readers become involved because they must fill in the blanks to finish the story.

Television commercials contain movement. They can fade in and out or dissolve from one scene to another. Instead of one primary image to develop, a television commercial has many. Action sequences can tell a story.

While some effects are limited to either television or print advertisements, most of the visual effects advertisers use are available to both. Visual effects can be divided into two catagories: **photographic** (made with a camera) or **digital** (made with a computer).

Common Visual Effects

Photographic Effects

Camera Angle (point of view)	■ Tilting the camera up makes the subject seem large and dominating. ■ Tilting the camera down makes the subject seem small.
Lighting	■ Dark, shadowy lighting can add mystery or gloom. ■ Bright lighting can create a shiny, happy appearance. ■ Soft lighting suggests pleasant feelings.
Filters	■ Filters alter the image as it gets to the camera, making it fuzzy, sharp, dull, or sparkling.

Digital Effects

Digital Editing	■ Images can be converted to digital computer versions and then altered.
Digital Reality	■ Images such as babies that dance and animals that talk can be made completely by computer animation.

Both

Miniaturization	■ Small models of props or settings can be used to make a subject a giant in comparison.
Superimposing	■ Two images can be cut or digitally placed on top of each other, making people look as if they are in a jungle or in the air, for example.

Analyze Visual Effects in Advertisements

As a viewer of print ads and commercials, you should know that visual effects are used to capture your attention and to convince you to think a certain way. Just flip through any magazine or watch a TV commercial, and see how advertisers use visual effects. When you create your own advertisements, you should know that visual effects are a valuable tool to help you persuade a target market. Whether you are a viewer or a creator of advertisements, you can become more aware of visual effects by analyzing the different ways they are used.

The following print ad and the television commercial storyboard on the next page use the same visual effect. As you read these ads, identify the visual effect and determine how the effect is used differently in the two different media.

Are you going to tell him you bought a generic lotion for his itchy bug bites? Use **Dr. Shay's Anti-Itch Lotion** to tame the toughest itch.

NARRATOR:

Tell HIM you plan to use generic lotion on his bug bites.

NARRATOR:

Dr. Shay's Anti-Itch Lotion soothes and calms itches caused by most bites and rashes.

NARRATOR:

Bring the toughest itches down to size with Dr. Shay's Anti-Itch Lotion.

TIP Some commercials deliberately omit information so that you become involved filling in the rest of the story.

? Can you think of a commercial for which you have to fill in the missing action?

The visual effect used in both of these ads is **camera angle**. Notice that in the print ad and in the first TV storyboard, the boy looks large and imposing because the camera looks up into his face, making him seem huge. However, the print ad could only hint that the lotion would bring the boy back down to size, but the television ad was able to tell the whole story. In the storyboard, you can see the boy getting the lotion and then returning to a more normal size through the use of a different camera angle.

Analyzing Print and Television Ads

Find a print ad and a television commercial that both use at least one of the following visual effects. You may choose an ad and a commercial that use the same visual effects or different effects. The effects are explained in the chart on page 262.

- camera angle (point of view)
- lighting
- filters
- digital editing
- digital reality
- miniaturization
- superimposing

Record the commercial, if possible, or draw a storyboard for it. Cut out the print advertisement if you have permission. Then, identify the visual effect used in each advertisement and explain what message or impression the effect communicates. Finally, compare the overall effectiveness of both ads.

7 *Choices*

Choose one of the following activities to complete.

▶ COMMUNITY SERVICE

1. For a Good Cause A little publicity can help good causes. Choose a cause that is important to you, such as a tutoring or recycling program. Create a **poster,** or record a **TV or radio ad** to advertise this cause to your classmates. Include information telling how your friends and teachers can get involved with this issue to make a difference.

▶ CROSSING THE CURRICULUM: MATH

2. Charting the Course With two classmates, collect twelve print ads. Then, identify the main persuasive technique used in each ad. (See chart on page 239.) Make a **record** for each ad on a sheet of paper or in a database that has separate fields for a description of the ad and the technique. Then, make a **pie chart** that shows what percentage of the ads used each persuasive technique. Which techniques are the most common? Present your results to your class.

▶ CROSSING THE CURRICULUM: SOCIAL STUDIES

3. History Hall of Fame Use your new knowledge of advertising to create an entire advertising campaign for a historical figure you admire. Design a **campaign** of three or four **print and TV ads** nominating him or her for the History Hall of Fame. If you have access to a video camera, you can even record a television commercial to share with the rest of your class.

▶ CAREERS

4. The Ad Game The fields of advertising, marketing, and public relations are rapidly growing. Find out more about these careers by contacting companies such as advertising and public relations firms. Develop a list of questions and schedule a phone interview to get information about these career fields. Use your interview notes to write a **report** of your findings.

PORTFOLIO

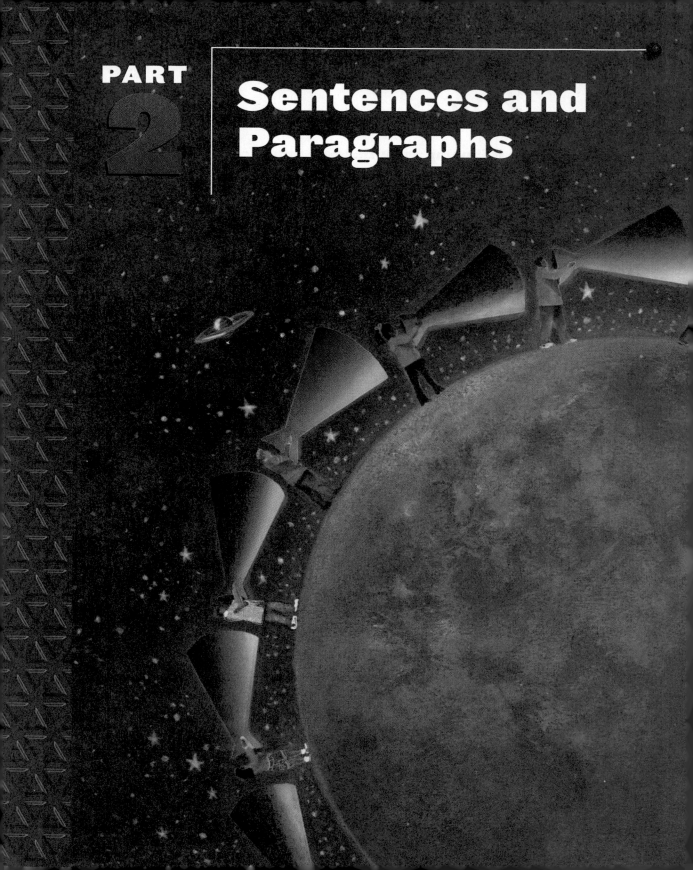

PART 2

Sentences and Paragraphs

8 | Writing Effective Sentences

GO TO: go.hrw.com
KEYWORD: EOLang

Writing Complete Sentences

One of the best ways to make your writing clear is to use complete sentences. A *complete sentence*

- has a subject
- has a verb
- expresses a complete thought

EXAMPLES   Trees help absorb excess carbon dioxide in the atmosphere.

Some species are in danger of dying out.

Get involved!

Each of the example word groups above expresses a complete thought. Each has a verb. The last example may not appear to have a subject in it, but it actually has the understood subject *you:* (You) Get involved!

Two common errors get in the way of writing complete sentences: *sentence fragments* and *run-on sentences.* Once you learn how to recognize fragments and run-ons in your writing, you can revise them to form clear, complete sentences.

Sentence Fragments

A *sentence fragment* is a word group that has been capitalized and punctuated as if it were a complete sentence. Because it is incomplete, a sentence fragment can confuse your reader.

FRAGMENT   Was the first African American man to win the Wimbledon tennis championship. [The subject is missing. *Who* was the first African American man to win Wimbledon?]

SENTENCE   Arthur Ashe was the first African American man to win the Wimbledon tennis championship.

FRAGMENT   Ashe the Wimbledon singles title in 1975. [The verb is missing. What is the connection between Ashe and the singles title?]

SENTENCE   Ashe won the Wimbledon singles title in 1975.

FRAGMENT   While he was a student at the University of California. [This group of words has a subject and a verb, but it does not express a complete thought. *What happened* while Ashe was a student?]

SENTENCE   Ashe also won several championships in college tennis while he was a student at the University of California.

As you can see from the first two examples, you can correct some sentence fragments by adding a subject or verb. Other times a sentence fragment just needs to be attached to the sentence next to it.

NOTE Be careful not to create a fragment by putting in a period and a capital letter too soon.

FRAGMENT   The crowd cheered wildly. When Leon scored the winning touchdown. [The second word group is a fragment and belongs with the sentence before it.]

SENTENCE   The crowd cheered wildly when Leon scored the winning touchdown.

Exercise 1 Identifying Sentence Fragments

Decide whether the following groups of words are sentence fragments or complete sentences. If the word group is a

---

TIPS & TRICKS

Some words look like verbs but really aren't. These "fake" verbs can fool you into thinking a group of words is a sentence when it is really a fragment. A word that ends in *–ing* cannot stand as a verb unless it has a helping verb (such as *is, are,* or *were*) with it.

FRAGMENT
The children playing on the swings. [Without the helping verb, this is not a complete thought.]

SENTENCE
The children **were playing** on the swings.

fragment, write *F*. If it is a sentence, write *S*. Remember that a complete sentence meets three requirements: It has a subject, it has a verb, and it expresses a complete thought.

1. A flying squirrel a squirrel that can gracefully glide through the air.
2. Some Asian flying squirrels three feet long.
3. Skillfully leaps from one tree to another.
4. The squirrel glides downward, then straight, and finally upward.
5. Some flying squirrels more than fifty feet.
6. If they use a higher starting point.
7. Flying squirrels live in the forests of Asia, Europe, and North America.
8. To eat berries, birds' eggs, insects, and nuts.
9. Nesting in the hollows of trees.
10. Notice how this squirrel stretches out its legs to help it glide.

Exercise 2 **Finding and Revising Fragments**

Some of the following groups of words are sentence fragments. Revise each fragment by (1) adding a subject, (2) adding a verb, or (3) attaching the fragment to a complete sentence. You may need to change the punctuation and capitalization, too. If an item is already a complete sentence, write *S*.

EXAMPLE 1. As soon as we finished eating breakfast.

1. *We left for our camping trip as soon as we finished eating breakfast.*

1. As the whole family loaded into the car.
2. We traveled for hours.
3. When we arrived at the campground.
4. My sister and I down to the river.
5. Took our fishing gear with us.
6. We cast our lines the way our aunt had taught us.
7. Because we didn't have the best bait.
8. We headed back to the campsite at sunset.
9. Dad cooking bean soup over the fire.
10. While Mom and my sister pitched the tent.

Run-on Sentences

A *run-on sentence* is actually two complete sentences punctuated like one sentence. In a run-on, two separate thoughts run into each other. The reader cannot tell where one idea ends and another one begins.

RUN-ON	Researchers have created a "virtual frog" it will allow students to see the inside of a frog on the computer.
CORRECT	Researchers have created a "virtual frog**.**" **I**t will allow students to see the inside of a frog on the computer.

RUN-ON	The software allows students to peel back the frog's muscles, another option makes the skin invisible.
CORRECT	The software allows students to peel back the frog's muscles**. A**nother option makes the skin invisible.

NOTE A comma does mark a brief pause in a sentence, but it does not show the end of a sentence. If you use just a comma between two sentences, you create a run-on sentence.

RUN-ON	Scientists have discovered ice on the moon, the discovery is great news for people who study space exploration.
CORRECT	Scientists have discovered ice on the moon**. T**he discovery is great news for people who study space exploration.

Revising Run-on Sentences

Here are two ways you can revise run-on sentences.

1. You can make two sentences.

RUN-ON	Asteroids are tiny planets they are sometimes called planetoids.
CORRECT	Asteroids are tiny planets**. T**hey are sometimes called planetoids.

2. You can use a comma and a coordinating conjunction such as *and, but,* or *or.*

RUN-ON	Some asteroids shine with a steady light, others keep changing in brightness.
CORRECT	Some asteroids shine with a steady light**, but** others keep changing in brightness.

Reference Note

For more information and practice on **coordinating conjunctions,** see page 374.

Exercise 3 Identifying and Revising Run-on Sentences

Decide which of the following groups of words are run-on sentences. Then, revise each run-on by (1) making it into two separate sentences or (2) using a comma and *and, but,* or *or.* If the group of words is already correct, write *C.*

1. Saturn is a huge planet it is more than nine times larger than Earth.
2. Saturn is covered by clouds, it is circled by bands of color.
3. Some of the clouds are yellow, others are off-white.
4. Saturn has about twenty moons Titan is the largest.
5. Many of Saturn's moons have large craters the crater on Mimas covers one third of its diameter.
6. Saturn's most striking feature is a group of rings that circles the planet.
7. The rings of Saturn are less than two miles thick, they spread out from the planet for a great distance.
8. The rings are made up of billions of tiny particles.
9. Some of the rings are dark, but others are brighter.
10. You can use a telescope to view Saturn, you can visit a planetarium.

Review A Correcting Sentence Fragments and Run-on Sentences

The following paragraph is confusing because it contains some sentence fragments and run-on sentences. First, identify the sentence fragments and run-on sentences. Then, revise each sentence fragment and run-on sentence to make the paragraph clearer.

```
    Many deserts have no plant life,
some desert regions have a variety of
plants. Many plants can survive. Where
the climate is hot and dry. Cacti,
Joshua trees, palm trees, and wild-
flowers grow in deserts those plants
do not grow close together. They are
spread out, each plant gets water and
minerals from a large area.
```

Combining Sentences

Although short sentences can sometimes express your ideas well, using only short sentences will make your writing sound choppy and dull. For example, read the following paragraph, which has only short sentences.

```
Thomas Edison invented the phono-
graph. He also experimented with
mechanical toys. Many people do not
know this. Edison created a talking
doll. He created the talking doll in
1894. The doll would recite a nursery
rhyme or poem. It said the words when
a crank in its back was turned. The
talking doll was very popular. Edison
opened a factory. The factory made
five hundred of the dolls every day.
```

Now read the revised paragraph. Notice how the writer has combined some of the short sentences to make longer, smoother sentences.

```
Thomas Edison invented the phono-
graph. Many people do not know that
he also experimented with mechanical
toys. Edison created a talking doll
in 1894. When a crank in its back was
turned, the doll would recite a nurs-
ery rhyme or poem. The talking doll
was very popular, and Edison opened a
factory that made five hundred of the
dolls every day.
```

Sentence combining also helps to reduce the number of repeated words and ideas. The revised paragraph is clearer, shorter, and more interesting to read. The following pages contain strategies for combining sentences. Once you learn these strategies, you can apply them to your own writing.

Combining Sentences by Inserting Words

One way to combine short sentences is to take a key word from one sentence and insert it into another sentence. Sometimes you will need to change the form of the key word before you can insert it. You can change the forms of some words by adding an ending such as *–ed, –ing, –ful,* or *–ly.* In its new form, the key word can describe or explain another word in the sentence.

ORIGINAL   Easter lily plants have leaves. The leaves have points.

COMBINED   Easter lily plants have **pointed** leaves.

Exercise 4 Combining Sentences by Inserting Words

Each of the following items contains two sentences. To combine the two sentences, take the italicized key word from the second sentence and insert it into the first sentence. The directions in parentheses will tell you how to change the form of the key word if you need to do so.

EXAMPLE   1. Peanuts are the tiny fruit of the peanut plant. They have a good *taste.* (Change *taste* to *tasty.*)

1. *Peanuts are the tiny, tasty fruit of the peanut plant.*

1. This picture shows peanuts underground. They *grow* underground. (Add *–ing.*)
2. Peanuts are a crop of many warm regions. They are a *major* crop.
3. Peanuts are a food for snacking. Peanuts are good for your *health.* (Add *–ful.*)
4. The oil from peanuts is used in many dressings. The dressings are for *salad.*
5. Grades of peanut oil are used to make soap and shampoo. The *low* grades are used for these products.
6. Many countries grow peanuts solely for their oil. This oil is *versatile.*
7. The peanut-producing countries include China, India, and the United States. These countries *lead* the world in peanut production. (Add *–ing.*)
8. Some soils will stain the peanut shells. *Dark* soils are responsible for the stains.

9. After peanuts are harvested, the plants are used for feed. The feed is for *livestock.*

10. Peanuts are a good source of vitamins. Peanuts contain *B* vitamins.

Combining Sentences by Inserting Phrases

A *phrase* is a group of words that acts as a single part of speech and that does not have both a subject and a verb. You can combine sentences by taking a phrase from one sentence and inserting it into another sentence.

ORIGINAL	Arachne is a famous figure. She is a figure in Greek mythology.
COMBINED	Arachne is a famous figure **in Greek mythology**.

NOTE Some phrases need to be set off by commas. Before you insert a phrase into a sentence, ask yourself whether the phrase renames or identifies a noun or pronoun. If it does, it is an **appositive phrase,** and you may need to set it off with a comma (or two commas if the phrase is in the middle of the sentence).

ORIGINAL	Arachne challenged Athena to a weaving contest. Athena was the goddess of wisdom.
COMBINED	Arachne challenged Athena**, the goddess of wisdom,** to a weaving contest. [The phrase in boldface type renames the noun *Athena.*]

Reference Note

For more information and practice on using commas to set off **appositive phrases,** see page 609.

Another way to combine sentences is to change the verb and create a new phrase. Just add *–ing* or *–ed* to the verb, or put the word *to* in front of it. You can then use the new phrase to describe a noun, verb, or pronoun in a related sentence.

ORIGINAL	The name *Inuit* refers to several groups of people. These people live in and near the Arctic.
COMBINED	The name *Inuit* refers to several groups of people **living in and near the Arctic**.

ORIGINAL	Early Inuit followed a special way of life. They did this so they could survive in a harsh environment.
COMBINED	**To survive in a harsh environment,** early Inuit followed a special way of life.

NOTE When you combine sentences by adding a word or phrase from one sentence to another sentence, the resulting sentence may contain a compound phrase. Be sure to keep the compound elements **parallel,** or matching in form. Otherwise, instead of making your writing smoother, combining may actually make it more awkward.

ORIGINAL	Ana likes to hike. Ana also likes cycling.
NOT PARALLEL	Ana likes to hike and cycling. [*To hike* is an infinitive; *cycling* is a gerund.]
PARALLEL	Ana likes hiking and cycling. [*Hiking* and *cycling* are both gerunds.]

Exercise 5 **Combining Sentences by Inserting Phrases**

Each of the following items contains two sentences. Combine the sentences by taking the italicized word group from the second sentence and inserting it into the first sentence. The hints in parentheses tell you how to change the forms of words if you need to do so. Remember to insert commas where they are needed.

EXAMPLE   1. The Inuit followed their traditional way of life. They followed this way of life *for thousands of years.*

   1. *The Inuit followed their traditional way of life for thousands of years.*

1. The Inuit built winter shelters in a few hours. They *stacked blocks of snow.* (Change *stacked* to *stacking.*)
2. They used harpoons. This is how they *hunted seals.* (Change *hunted* to *to hunt.*)
3. The Inuit also hunted and ate caribou. Caribou are *a type of deer.*
4. Whalers and fur traders came to the region and affected the Inuit way of life. They arrived *in the 1800s.*

5. The Inuit often moved several times a year. They moved so that they could *find food.* (Change *find* to *to find.*)
6. During the summer, traditional Inuit lived in tents. The tents were *made from animal skin.*
7. In the 1800s, many Inuit began to trap animals. They trapped animals *for European fur traders.*
8. Some Inuit worked on whaling ships. They *needed to find other ways to provide for their families.* (Change *need* to *needing.*)
9. The Inuit have survived for thousands of years. They have survived *in the harsh Arctic climate.*
10. Most Inuit today follow a modern way of life. They are *like the Canadian Inuit seen in the photo on the opposite page.*

Combining Sentences Using *And, But,* or *Or*

You can also use the coordinating conjunctions *and, but,* and *or* to combine sentences. With these connecting words, you can make a *compound subject,* a *compound verb,* or a *compound sentence.*

Compound Subjects and Verbs

Sometimes two sentences have the same verb with different subjects. You can combine the sentences by linking the two subjects with *and* or *or* to make a **compound subject.**

ORIGINAL   Dolphins look a little like fish. Porpoises look a little like fish.

COMBINED   **Dolphins and porpoises** look a little like fish.

Two sentences can also have the same subject with different verbs. You can use *and, but,* or *or* to connect the two verbs. The result is a **compound verb.**

ORIGINAL   Dolphins live in water like fish. They breathe like other mammals.

COMBINED   Dolphins **live** in water like fish **but breathe** like other mammals.

┌TIPS & TRICKS┐

When you use the coordinating conjunction *and* to link two subjects, your new compound subject will be a plural subject. Remember to make the verb agree with the subject in number.

ORIGINAL
  Zach likes watching the sea mammals. Briana likes watching the sea mammals.

COMBINED
  Zach and Briana like watching the sea mammals. [The plural verb *like* is needed with the plural subject *Zach and Briana.*]

For more information and practice on **agreement of subjects and verbs,** see page 458.

- *And* shows equality. Use it if you mean *both.*

  Katie **and** Tyrone are my friends.

- *But* shows contrast. Use it to point out something *different.*

  Katie likes to play tennis, **but** Tyrone does not.

- *Or* shows a choice. Use it if you have *options.*

  Usually either Katie **or** Tyrone waits for me after school.

Exercise 6 Combining Sentences by Creating Compound Subjects and Verbs

Combine each of the following pairs of short, choppy sentences by using *and, but,* or *or.* If the two sentences have the same verb, make a compound subject. If they have the same subject, make a compound verb. Remember to keep the ideas in parallel forms.

EXAMPLE   1. Dolphins belong to a group of mammals called cetaceans. Porpoises belong to a group of mammals called cetaceans.

1. *Dolphins and porpoises belong to a group of mammals called cetaceans.*

1. Dolphins are warm-blooded. Porpoises are warm-blooded.
2. Common dolphins live in warm waters. Common dolphins swim in large schools.
3. Porpoises are similar to dolphins. Porpoises generally live in cooler water.
4. Dolphins have beak-like snouts. Dolphins use sonar to locate objects under water.
5. Dolphins hunt fish. Dolphins eat fish.
6. Dolphins swim by moving their tails up and down. Porpoises swim by moving their tails up and down.
7. Porpoises can swim fast. Dolphins can swim fast.
8. A porpoise could outswim most sharks. A tuna could outswim most sharks.
9. Bottle-nosed dolphins can measure up to fifteen feet in length. Bottle-nosed dolphins can weigh over four hundred pounds.
10. Sharks sometimes attack porpoises. Sharks sometimes kill porpoises.

Compound Sentences

Sometimes you will want to combine two sentences that express equally important ideas. You can connect two closely related, equally important sentences by using a comma plus the coordinating conjunction *and, but,* or *or.* Doing so creates a ***compound sentence.***

ORIGINAL   My brother entered the Annual Chili Cook-off. His chili won a prize.

COMBINED   My brother entered the Annual Chili Cook-off**, and** his chili won a prize.

ORIGINAL	I did not help him cook the chili. I helped him clean up the kitchen.
COMBINED	I did not help him cook the chili, **but** I helped him clean up the kitchen.

NOTE A compound sentence tells the reader that the two ideas are closely related. If you combine two short sentences that are not closely related, you may confuse your reader.

UNRELATED	Fernando mowed the grass, and I brought a broom.
RELATED	Fernando mowed the grass, and I swept the sidewalk.

Exercise 7 Combining Sentences by Forming a Compound Sentence

Each of the following pairs of sentences is closely related. Make each pair into a compound sentence by adding a comma and a coordinating conjunction such as *and* or *but*.

EXAMPLE   1. The Pueblos have lived in the same location for a long time. They have strong ties to their homeland.

1. *The Pueblos have lived in the same location for a long time, and they have strong ties to their homeland.*

1. Some Pueblos built villages in the valleys. Others settled in desert and mountain areas.
2. Desert surrounded many of the valleys. The people grew crops with the help of irrigation systems.
3. Women gathered berries and other foods. Men hunted game.
4. Their adobe homes had several stories. The people used ladders to reach the upper levels.
5. Today, each Pueblo village has its own government. The Pueblo people still share many customs.

Combining Sentences Using Subordinate Clauses

A *clause* is a group of words that contains a subject and a verb. *Independent clauses* can stand alone as a sentence. *Subordinate* (or *dependent*) *clauses* cannot stand alone because they do not express a complete thought.

Reference Note

For more information and practice on **independent clauses** and **subordinate clauses,** see page 424.

Reference Note

For more information and practice on **complex sentences,** see page 445.

| INDEPENDENT CLAUSE | Gertrude Ederle swam the English Channel. [This clause can stand alone.] |
| SUBORDINATE CLAUSE | when she was nineteen years old [This clause cannot stand alone.] |

If two sentences are related, you can combine them by using a subordinate clause. The resulting sentence is called a *complex sentence.* The subordinate clause in a complex sentence will give information about a word or idea in the independent clause.

| TWO SIMPLE SENTENCES | Theresa traveled to Rome. She saw the Sistine Chapel. |
| ONE COMPLEX SENTENCE | Theresa traveled to Rome, **where she saw the Sistine Chapel.** |

Making Clauses That Begin with *Who, Which,* or *That*

You can make a short sentence into a subordinate clause by inserting *who, which,* or *that* in place of the subject.

| ORIGINAL | The Everglades is an area of swamps. It covers the southern part of Florida. |
| COMBINED | The Everglades is an area of swamps **that covers the southern part of Florida.** |

Making Clauses with Words of Time or Place

Another way to turn a sentence into a subordinate clause is to add a word that tells time or place. Words that begin this type of clause include *after, before, where, wherever, when, whenever,* and *while.* You may need to delete some words to insert the clause into another sentence.

| ORIGINAL | No humans lived in the Everglades until 1842. In 1842, Seminoles fled to the area. |
| COMBINED | No humans lived in the Everglades until 1842, **when Seminoles fled to the area.** |

NOTE If you put your time or place clause at the beginning of the sentence, use a comma after the clause.

| ORIGINAL | People began draining the swamps to make farmland. The Everglades was in danger. |
| COMBINED | **When people began draining the swamps to make farmland,** the Everglades was in danger. |

Reference Note

For more information and practice on the use of **commas with introductory clauses,** see page 613.

Combining Sentences by Using Subordinate Clauses

Combine each sentence pair by making the second sentence into a subordinate clause and attaching it to the first sentence. You may need to cut a word or two from the second sentence.

1. The pearl is a gem. It is made by certain kinds of oysters and clams. (Use *that.*)
2. Beautiful pearls are found in tropical seas. The best pearl oysters live there. (Use *where.*)
3. A valuable pearl has a shine. The shine comes from below its surface. (Use *that.*)
4. A pearl becomes round. It is formed in the soft part of the oyster. (Use *after.*)
5. Pearls should be wiped clean with a soft cloth. They are worn as jewelry. (Use *after.*)

Review B **Revising a Paragraph by Combining Sentences**

The following paragraph sounds choppy because it has too many short sentences. Use the methods you have learned in this section to combine sentences in the paragraph.

    Dr. James Naismith invented the game
of basketball over one hundred years ago.
He probably never guessed the sport would
become so popular. He just wanted a new
game that could be played indoors. The
original basketball teams started in
1891. They had nine players instead of
five. The first basket was a peach basket. A player had to climb up and
retrieve the ball after each score. Some
parts of the game have stayed the same.
Players still cannot hold the ball while
they run. They must dribble. Thousands of
teams across the world now play Dr.
Naismith's game.

Improving Sentence Style

In addition to combining some sentences, you can also make your writing more effective by revising *stringy* and *wordy sentences* to make them shorter and clearer. Your reader will stay involved if you mix long and short sentences and include simple, compound, and complex sentences in your writing.

Revising Stringy Sentences

A *stringy sentence* is made up of several complete thoughts strung together with words like *and* or *but*. Stringy sentences just ramble on and on. They don't give the reader a chance to pause before each new idea.

To fix a stringy sentence, you can

- break the sentence into two or more sentences
- turn some of the complete thoughts into phrases or subordinate clauses

STRINGY   Martina climbed the stairs of the haunted house, and she knocked on the door several times, but no one answered, and she braced herself, and then she opened the door.

REVISED   Martina climbed the stairs of the haunted house. She knocked on the door several times, but no one answered. Bracing herself, she opened the door.

Reference Note

For more information and practice on **compound sentences,** see page 441.

NOTE   When you revise a stringy sentence, you may decide to keep *and* or *but* between two closely related independent clauses. If you do this, be sure to use a comma before the *and* or *but*.

EXAMPLE   She knocked on the door several times**,** **but** no one answered.

Exercise 9 Revising Stringy Sentences

Some of the following sentences are stringy and need to be improved. First, identify the stringy sentences. Then, revise them by (1) breaking each sentence into two or more sentences or (2) turning some of the complete thoughts into phrases or subordinate clauses. If the sentence is effective and does not need to be improved, write *C* for *correct*.

1. Mercedes O. Cubría was born in Cuba, but her mother died, and she moved to the United States, and she moved with her two sisters.
2. She worked as a nurse, and then she joined the Women's Army Corps, and she soon became an officer in the army.
3. Cubría was the first Cuban-born woman to become an officer in the U.S. Army.
4. Her job during World War II was to translate important government papers into a secret code.
5. The war ended, and she was promoted to captain, and later her official rank rose to major.
6. Then there was the Korean War, and she worked as an intelligence officer, and she studied information about the enemy.
7. Cubría retired from the army in 1953 but was called to duty again in 1962.
8. After the Castro revolution, thousands of Cubans fled to the United States, and Cubría interviewed many of these refugees, and she also prepared reports on Cuba.
9. In her spare time, she helped people from Cuba find jobs and housing.
10. She retired again in 1973, and she settled in Miami, Florida, and she was surrounded by friends and family there.

┌HELP──
As you revise these sentences, keep in mind that there is often more than one correct way to revise a sentence.

Revising Wordy Sentences

Sometimes you use more words in a sentence than you really need. Extra words do not make writing sound better and, in fact, they can even interfere with your message. Revise **wordy sentences** in these three ways.

1. Replace a phrase with one word.

WORDY   **In a state of exhaustion,** Tony slumped across the bus seat and fell asleep.

REVISED   **Exhausted,** Tony slumped across the bus seat and fell asleep.

WORDY   **As a result of what happened when** the tire went flat, we were late.

REVISED   **Because** the tire went flat, we were late.

| COMPUTER TIP

The grammar-checking option on a computer will often alert you if you have written a sentence that is too long. Review the sentence and see if you can break it into parts or edit out unnecessary words.

2. Take out *who is* or *which is*.

WORDY   Yesterday I went for a long hike with Sonya, **who is my best friend.**

REVISED   Yesterday I went for a long hike with Sonya, **my best friend.**

WORDY   Afterward, we drank some apple juice, **which is a good thirst quencher.**

REVISED   Afterward, we drank some apple juice, **a good thirst quencher.**

3. Take out a whole group of unnecessary words.

WORDY   I spent a lot of time writing this report because I **really** want people to learn about manatees **so they can know all about them.**

REVISED   I spent a lot of time writing this report because I want people to learn about manatees.

Exercise 10 Revising Wordy Sentences

Some of the following sentences are wordy and need improvement. Decide which of the sentences are wordy; then, revise them. You can (1) replace a phrase with one word, (2) take out *who is* or *which is,* or (3) take out a whole group of unnecessary words. If a sentence is effective as it is, write *C* for *correct.*

1. Our science class has been learning about the starfish, which is a strange and beautiful animal.
2. What I want to say is that starfish are fascinating creatures.
3. A starfish has little feet tipped with suction cups that have suction power.
4. At the end of each arm is a sensitive eyespot.
5. In spite of the fact that the eyespot cannot really see things, it can tell light from dark.
6. The starfish's mouth is in the middle of its body.
7. When it uses its arms, it can pull at the shells of clams.
8. At the point at which the clam's shell opens, the starfish can feed on the clam.
9. Starfish come in a variety of colors, shapes, and sizes, and some are bigger than others.
10. This photograph shows a blue sea star holding onto a soft coral by holding it with its suction cups.

Varying Sentence Structure

An important way to keep your readers' attention is to mix sentences of different lengths and structures. Think like a movie director. If you were making a movie, you would include long, complex scenes; but you would mix those scenes with shorter, simpler scenes to keep your audience's attention. A movie made up entirely of long scenes or short scenes would be difficult for your audience to follow. Apply the same ideas to your writing.

For example, the writer of the following paragraph uses only short sentences.

> Jim Knaub lost the use of his legs in a motorcycle accident. He decided he would not let that slow him down. He started racing wheelchairs. All the other racers were using standard wheelchairs. Those wheelchairs were not fast enough for Jim. He began to design his own. Soon, his light-weight, ultrafast wheelchair was winning races. He became a well-known wheelchair-racing champion. Jim now designs wheelchairs for others to use.

Now read the revised paragraph. Notice how the writer has varied the sentence structure to include different sentence lengths and a mixture of simple, compound, and complex sentences.

> When Jim Knaub lost the use of his legs in a motorcycle accident, he decided he would not let that slow him down. He started racing wheelchairs. All the other racers were using standard wheelchairs, but those wheelchairs were not fast enough for Jim. He began to design his own. Soon, his light-weight, ultrafast wheelchair was winning races. He became a well-known wheelchair-racing champion and began to design wheelchairs for others to use.

Varying sentence length keeps the reader interested in the story. By changing the sentence structure, the writer avoids starting each sentence the same way, which would make the paragraph boring and repetitive.

HELP
When adding variety to sentences in a paragraph, first look for words that are repeated. Sentences with repeated words can often be combined or rewritten to improve the paragraph.

Exercise 11 Adding Variety to Sentences

The following paragraph is uninteresting because it includes only compound sentences. Rewrite the paragraph to include a variety of sentence structures. Mix short, simple sentences; compound sentences; and longer sentences with subordinate clauses in your version. Remember, you are the director of this piece of writing. Use variety to keep your audience involved.

My friends and I have been talking, and we have made a decision. We should have a day off, and we could go on a class picnic. We could do it right before winter break, or we could go near the end of the school year. We could each bring a sack lunch, or we could each bring something to share with the rest of the class. The park near the school has picnic tables, and it has playing fields and a pool. We don't all know how to swim, so the students who can't swim can play soccer or baseball instead. It might seem bad to take a free day, but we work hard the rest of the year. We would enjoy the picnic, and we would have a fun day. We would return to school, and we would have smiles on our faces.

Review C Revising a Paragraph by Improving Sentence Style

The paragraph on the following page is hard to read because it contains stringy and wordy sentences. Identify the stringy and wordy sentences, and use the methods you have learned to revise them. Try to mix simple, compound, and complex sentences in your improved version.

The movie *Anastasia* is based on a real story about a real girl from history. Her name was Anastasia Romanov and she was born in 1901 and lived in Russia. The movie is about some historical events in Russia's history, and many things in the movie are not true. For example, the movie says that Anastasia was eight years old when the revolutionaries came to overthrow and defeat her father, who was the czar, but the real Anastasia was a teenager in real life. The movie shows Anastasia and her grandmother, who was the Grand Duchess Marie, escaping together, but in reality her grandmother was already safely in Denmark when the family was seized and captured. Unlike the character in the movie, the real Anastasia did not get away, her remains were found with her family's remains when they were found in 1991. Although *Anastasia* is an interesting movie, people who see it should also know the real story that happened.

STYLE TIP

When planning your own writing assignments, save time to edit your composition for style. Many writers revise first for content and organization; then they look at style elements like sentence variety.

Learning About Paragraphs

What Is a Paragraph?

A *paragraph* is a section of text focused on a *main idea*. Usually a paragraph is part of a longer piece of writing. In an essay about summer camp, for example, one paragraph might focus just on the meals. Other paragraphs in the essay would each focus on another aspect of camp, such as the outdoor activities, adding up to create an overall picture of the experience.

Why Use Paragraphs?

As writers and readers, we often seem to take paragraphs for granted. Imagine, though, a piece of writing with no paragraphs. As a reader, you would face huge blocks of uninterrupted text, giving your eyes no chance for a break until the end. As a writer, you might think it would be nice not to worry about where to start a new paragraph or when to indent; however, paragraphs help you get your message across to readers. They show readers that you are moving from one idea (or setting, or speaker) to another. Showing where paragraphs begin and end is like holding the reader's hand and walking him or her through your piece. Paragraphs make it easier for readers to get where you want to take them.

What Are the Parts of a Paragraph?

Most paragraphs that focus on a *main idea* have a *topic sentence* and *supporting sentences*. Many also include a *clincher sentence*.

The Main Idea

Whether they stand alone or are part of a longer piece of writing, paragraphs usually have a main idea. The **main idea** is the overall point of the paragraph. The following paragraph is from an article about the United States 2000 census, on which nearly seven million people identified themselves as belonging to more than one race. In this paragraph the main idea is in the first sentence.

> Many multiracial kids glide easily between their mixed cultures. Kelly Dubé, 12, of Los Angeles is half Korean and half French Canadian. His mother takes him to a Buddhist temple, where he has learned how to meditate. He can understand and speak some Korean and knows a little French. Most of the time, though, he doesn't think about his bi-racial status: "If anything, I think I'm more American."
>
> Ritu Upadhyay, "We, the People…,"
> *TIME for Kids*

The Topic Sentence
Location of the Topic Sentence

The main idea of a paragraph is often stated in a **topic sentence.** You may find it at the beginning of the paragraph, in the middle, or even at the end. In the paragraph above, the topic sentence is the first sentence: *Because Hopis have no written language, kachina dolls are used to pass tribal lore and religion down through generations.*

In the following paragraph, the topic sentence is last. This sentence makes clear that the villagers are preparing for a battle. The other sentences lead up to that point.

> Quickly, quickly we gathered the sheep into the pens. Dogs barked, and people shouted out orders to one another. Children rushed through the village gathering firewood to pile inside the homes. Men and women scooped up pots and pots of water, filling cisterns and containers as rapidly as possible. People pulled the last ears of corn from the fields and turned their backs on the dry stalks. Finally, we all stood together in the plaza in the center of the village for just a moment before the fighters went to stand near the walls and the wide-eyed children were coaxed inside the houses. We were prepared for the coming battle.

Importance of a Topic Sentence

Although not all paragraphs have topic sentences, it is helpful to use them when you are writing. Topic sentences may help you focus on your main idea. They also help the reader find the main idea and know what to expect from the paragraph. However, paragraphs that relate a series of events or that tell a story often lack a topic sentence. When a paragraph has no topic sentence, the reader must figure out the main idea by determining what all of the sentences have in common. Read the following paragraph. Although it has no topic sentence, all the sentences are about one main idea—the unexpected reactions of a poor woman toward her wealthy friend.

> "Oh, Lottie, it's good to see you," Bess said, but saying nothing about Lottie's splendid appearance. Upstairs Bess, putting down her shabby suitcase, said, "I'll sleep like a rock tonight," without a word of praise for her lovely room. At the lavish table, top-heavy with turkey, Bess said, "I'll take light and dark both," with no marveling at the size of the bird, or that there was turkey for two elderly women, one of them too poor to buy her own bread.
>
> Dorothy West, *The Richer, the Poorer*

NOTE When a writer includes no topic sentence, readers must determine the main idea of a paragraph from its supporting details. In paragraphs like the one from *The Richer, the Poorer*, the main idea is *implied*, rather than directly stated.

Exercise 1 Identifying Main Ideas and Topic Sentences

Finding a main idea is like detective work: Both require a keen eye for detail. Look for the main idea in each of the following paragraphs by looking for a topic sentence and by studying the paragraph's details. Remember that the main idea is the overall point of the paragraph. If the selection has a topic sentence, write it down. If the paragraph has no topic sentence, write the main idea of the paragraph in your own words, using details from the paragraph.

1. He turned and looked back at the stand of raspberries. The bear was gone; the birds were singing; he saw nothing that could hurt him. There was no danger here that he could sense, could feel. In the city, at night, there was sometimes danger. You could not be in the park at night, after dark, because of the danger. But here, the bear had looked at him and had moved on and—this filled his thoughts—the berries were so good.

   Gary Paulsen, *Hatchet*

2. Like lots of other kids her age, eight-year-old Auralea Moore plays baseball, swims, and skis. She also has a favorite plaything: a 19-inch doll named Susan, who was handcrafted to look like her. Auralea was born with spina bifida, a birth defect that has left her paralyzed from the waist down. Her look-alike doll, equipped with a pair of blue and silver "designer" braces, helps her remember that although she may be handicapped, she is definitely not out of the action.

   "A Doll Made to Order," *Newsweek*

3.   Personally, I thought Maxwell was just
about the homeliest dog I'd ever seen in my
entire life. He looked like a little old man
draped in a piece of brown velvet that was too
long, with the leftover cloth hanging in thick
folds under his chin. Not only that, his long
droopy ears dragged on the ground; he had sad
wet eyes and huge thick paws with splayed toes.
I mean, who could love a dog like that, except
my brother Joji, aged nine, who is a bit on the
homely side himself.

Yoshiko Uchida, *A Jar of Dreams*

COMPUTER TIP

Use a word-processing program's cut and paste com-
mands to find the best
placement of a topic sen-
tence within a paragraph.
You can always move or
replace the sentence if you
change your mind.

Exercise 2   Writing a Topic Sentence

For each of the following paragraphs, write a topic sentence that
communicates the main idea.

1.   A bottle of nail polish can cost as
little as a dollar and last for months,
depending on how much you use. You can
find it in every color in nature and any
unnatural color you can imagine. Best of
all, if you get tired of a color, you
can easily change it.

2.   This movie is packed with action.
I have never seen so many chases and
explosions before. It also has an
important lesson about friendship. The
two main characters always look out for
each other. Maybe the best thing about
it is the music. The soundtrack will
certainly be a bestseller.

3.   First, you need some supplies. These
include a roller or brush, a ladder tall
enough to reach the roof, and enough
paint to cover the whole house. You
should have already scraped off the old
paint. Start at the top of a section and
work your way down to avoid dripping wet
paint on a finished part.

Supporting Sentences

Supporting sentences are the details that expand on, explain, or prove a paragraph's main idea. These details can include *sensory details, facts,* or *examples.*

- *Sensory details* are what we experience through our five senses—sight, hearing, touch, taste, and smell.

- *Facts* give information that can be proved true by direct observation or by checking a reliable reference source. For instance, it is a fact that great herds of buffalo once roamed the western plains. You can prove this fact by checking an encyclopedia or history book.

- *Examples* give typical instances of an idea. An example of a creature with protective coloration is a chameleon, a lizard whose coloring changes with its surroundings.

The following chart shows the kinds of details you can use to support the main idea of a paragraph.

Kinds of Details	Supporting Sentences
Sensory Details	
Sight	The bright sun glared off the front windshield of the car.
Hearing	Thunder boomed down the canyon, echoing off the walls.
Touch	My hands felt frozen to the cold, steel handlebars.
Taste	Thirstily, she gulped down the sweet orange juice.
Smell	The sharp, unpleasant odor of asphalt met his nose.
Facts	In 1998, Mark McGwire slammed seventy home runs in one season to break the record of sixty-one held by Roger Maris.
Examples	Fierce windstorms occur worldwide. For example, tornadoes have wind speeds over 200 miles per hour.

Reference Note

Supporting details help you elaborate on your ideas. For more information and practice on **elaboration,** see page 304.

When you write paragraphs, you have to collect details that support your main idea. You can practice with the following topic sentences. List at least two details to support each topic sentence.

EXAMPLE   **1.** The appliance that toasts our bread has changed over the years.

            1. Details: It originated in the early 1900s. It consisted of bare wires with no thermostat. The first pop-up toaster appeared in 1926.

1. The time I spend with my friends on Saturday nights is my favorite time of the week.
2. My dream is to spend two days in a shopping mall.
3. One person's actions can make a difference in the lives of others.
4. When I feel hungry, I can just imagine my favorite meal.

The Clincher Sentence

Once you have written a topic sentence and developed well-organized details that support your main idea, the only thing left to do is to wrap it all up. Some writers do this by using a ***clincher sentence,*** also known as a ***concluding sentence.*** Notice how the last sentence of the following paragraph pulls together the preceding information by echoing the topic sentence.

> Helping the homeless helps the community. When homeless people are given housing assistance and job training, they can become our neighbors, co-workers, and friends. Not only do they find work and learn to support themselves, but they also pay taxes and share their skills with others. Every person we help out of homelessness is one more person who can enrich our neighborhood and community.

Although many paragraphs have no clincher sentence, you may want to use one to cement your main idea in readers' minds.

Exercise 4 Developing a Clincher Sentence

For each of the following short paragraphs, write a sentence that can serve as its clincher, wrapping up the information presented in the paragraph, but not repeating it.

EXAMPLE   1. Even though ferns grow everywhere in the forest, I can't seem to keep them alive at home. My shriveled brown ferns have the benefits of frequent waterings, plant food, and careful lighting. Nothing seems to help.

        1. *Clincher: I guess nature knows how to take care of ferns better than people do.*

1. Eating food in the library is a bad idea. Crumbs get on the floor and between pages when you eat, even if you are careful. These tiny bits of food may be impossible for you to see, but insects know they are there and will raid the books to find them. These insects will eventually harm the pages.

2. Computers have made getting information faster and easier. Almost all schools use them now, and they are very helpful in doing homework or typing papers. Before computers were available, most students had to do research by going to libraries, which might not be open. Now students can use computers any time of day in their own homes or at a friend's house.

What Makes a Good Paragraph?

Unity

A paragraph has *unity* when all the sentences support, or tell something about, one main idea. A paragraph that does not have unity may confuse your readers. For example, in a paragraph about Bonnie St. John Deane, you might tell how she became a skiing champion despite losing a leg. However, if

People Weekly/Time Inc., ©1986 Richard Howard.

you mentioned a friend who is also a skier, you would destroy the unity. The information about the friend is not related to your main idea.

Notice how all the sentences in the following paragraph tell something more about the paragraph's main idea.

> Technology has changed the ways of the ranch. While cowboys continue to drive cattle to the corral on horseback, a pickup truck—air-conditioned, of course—also helps. And though they don't plug branding irons into electrical outlets, propane tanks make lighting fires and heating branding irons easier. Computers log inventory and keep track of wildlife. Hal Hawkins, King Ranch's animal physiologist, monitors herd research and development with a laptop computer.
>
> Johnny D. Boggs, "Home on the Range," *Boys' Life*

Exercise 5 Identifying Sentences That Destroy Unity

Each of the following paragraphs has one sentence that destroys the unity. Try your skill at finding the unrelated sentences.

1. It felt like an oven to Tamara as she walked up the street toward the park. It was a hot day for baseball practice. She wondered if the Cardinals game would be on television that evening. Tamara told herself she couldn't let the heat slow her down, though. Today the coach would be deciding who would start in the season's first game. Tamara wanted to be playing third base.

2. Canoes are made for many purposes. White-water canoes are made for use in fast, rock-filled streams. They can turn quickly to avoid obstacles. Other canoes are made for lakes and quiet rivers. Unable to turn quickly, they are poor

HELP

The first step in completing Exercise 5 is to decide what the main idea is. Next, find the sentence that is not closely connected to the main idea.

choices for use on a river with lots of
rapids. On the other hand, they are easy
to paddle in a straight line. White-water
canoes can be very expensive. Before
choosing a canoe, think about what kind of
water you will ride.

Coherence

What goes into a paragraph is only part of the picture.
Supporting details need to be clearly connected and
arranged. A paragraph has **coherence** when readers can tell
how and why ideas are connected. To create coherence you
can do two things. First, you can arrange your details in an
order that makes sense to the reader. Then, you can link
those ideas together with transitional words or phrases (like *first*
and *then* in this paragraph).

Order of Details

To help your readers follow your ideas, use one of the following
patterns to organize your ideas.

- *Chronological order* presents details in the order in which
  they happen.
- *Spatial order* presents details according to their location.
- *Logical order* groups related ideas together.

Chronological Order   What happens when a character
lost in the Arctic wilderness cannot build a fire? How is soccer
played? To answer these questions, you must tell about an event
or an action as it changes over time. To tell about changes in
time, you usually use chronological, or time, order.

You can use chronological order to tell a story (what happens
to the character in the Arctic), to explain a process (how to play
soccer), or to explain causes and effects (why the *Titanic* sank).

- **Using chronological order to tell a story**   On the following
  page is a story, passed down from one generation to the next,
  about some curious escapes from slavery before the Civil War.

Uncle Mingo's forehead wrinkled like a mask in the moonlight. "Don't make light of what old folks tell you, son," he warned. "If the old folks say they seen slaves pick up and fly back to Africa, like birds, just don't you dispute them. If they tell you about a slave preacher what led his whole flock to the beach and sat down on the sand with them, looking across the ocean toward home, don't ask no questions. Next morning nobody could find trace of that preacher or his people. And no boat had been there neither. One day when I was chopping cotton in the field, I looked up and the old fellow working in the row next to mine was gone. He was too feeble to run away, and I couldn't see no place for him to hide. None of the others in the field saw him leave either, but later on an old woman drinking water at a well told us she noticed something pass in front of the sun about that time, like a hawk or a buzzard maybe, but she didn't pay it much mind."

Arna Bontemps, *Chariot in the Sky: A Story of the Jubilee Singers*

- **Using chronological order to explain a process** When you tell how to do something or how something works, you are explaining a process. Often, this means telling how to do something step by step—what is done first, then next, and so on. The following paragraph tells how kites may have developed.

No one is quite sure how kite flying started. Perhaps an ancient Chinese first noticed big leaves of certain plants fluttering at the end of long vines. Then, after watching "leaf-kites" for a while, he tied his straw hat to a string just for fun and happily found that the wind kept it flying. Later, he may have stretched a piece of animal skin over a bamboo frame and flown that from the end of a line.

Dan Carlinsky, "Kites," *Boys' Life*

- **Using chronological order to explain causes and effects**
  Chronological order is also used to explain a *cause-and-effect chain*. A **cause-and-effect chain** is a set of events that starts with a cause, and the effect that follows causes yet another event to occur. The chain continues with each event triggering yet another event, just as a stone thrown in the water causes a series of ripples. The following paragraph shows a cause-and-effect chain that started with some dogs getting sick.

Dogs may be man's best friend. But to the lions of Serengeti National Park in Tanzania, dogs unintentionally have been worst enemies. In 1994, distemper, a deadly disease, started spreading to the lions from pet dogs living in villages near the park.	Cause
Then it spread to lions in nearby Masai Mara Reserve in Kenya.	Effect/Cause
Eventually distemper killed about 1,200 lions, reports biologist Craig Packer, who studies lions in Africa.	Effect/Cause
In response, wildlife agents inoculated thousands of dogs against distemper.	Effect/Cause
Now few animals catch the disease.	Effect/Cause
Packer happily reports that the area's lion population has rebounded to 3,000, about as many as there were before the epidemic began.	Effect

Scott Stuckey, "Lions Recover from Dog Disease," *National Geographic*

Exercise 6 Arranging Details by Using Chronological Order

Follow the directions for each item on the next page to practice telling about events in the order in which they happen.

1. **Tell a story.** Select one of the following topics, and make up three or more events to include in a story about it. Arrange the events in chronological order.
   a. A mysterious light follows you down an empty street one night.
   b. A tall, shy new student enters your school. He has trouble fitting in at first, but soon the situation changes.
2. **Explain a process.** Pick one of the following activities. Then, list three or more steps involved in performing this activity. Arrange the steps in chronological order—that is, the order in which they should happen.
   c. how to wash a car
   d. how to clean up your room
3. **Explain cause and effect.** Create a cause-and-effect chain for one of the following situations.
   e. missing the school bus
   f. finding a litter of puppies

Spatial Order   When you describe something, you often use *spatial order.* Spatial order organizes details according to their location. Think of a video camera shooting a scene. The camera acts as a roving eye, beginning in one place, then moving around to show viewers other parts of the scene. Writers use spatial order in much the same way. In the following paragraph, notice how the writer uses spatial order to describe her father's farm.

> The farm my father grew up on, where Grandpa Welty and Grandma lived, was in southern Ohio in the rolling hills of Hocking County, near the small town of Logan. It was one of the neat, narrow-porched, two-story farmhouses, painted white, of the Pennsylvania-German country. Across its front grew feathery cosmos and barrel-sized peony bushes with stripy heavy-scented blooms pushing out of the leaves. There was a springhouse to one side, down a little walk only one brick in width, and an old apple orchard in front, the barn and the pasture and fields of corn
>
> *(continued)*

(continued)

and wheat behind. Periodically there came sounds from the barn, and you could hear the crows, but everything else was still.

Eudora Welty, *One Writer's Beginnings*

Exercise 7 Arranging Details by Using Spatial Order

How would you describe an insect, a rock star, or a movie set? Working with one or two others, choose a subject below, and list details that describe it. Arrange the details in spatial order.

1. the most unusual animal you have ever seen
2. your favorite car
3. the best setting for a science fiction movie
4. your classroom, moments before a vacation break

Logical Order When you write about information that fits into categories, you will use *logical order.* For example, an informative paragraph about sea otters might group together details about where they live, then explain what they eat, and finally tell how they act. When you *compare and contrast,* it is logical to group related ideas together.

Comparison

Contrast

It is easy to confuse frogs with toads. After all, they have a similar body shape and are basically the same size, and both are amphibious. There are some observable differences, though, that can help you tell them apart. The first is their skin texture. Frogs have smooth skin, while toads' skin is more bumpy. Their body shapes are slightly different, too. Frogs look leaner and sleeker than toads. Finally, they move differently. Most frogs can leap long distances, while toads will usually take only small hops.

Think about two subjects that are alike enough to be compared yet different enough to be interesting. Write down three ways that these subjects are alike and three ways that they are different. You might compare and contrast the following items:

1. being a child and being a teenager
2. live-action movies and animated movies
3. living in a large city and living in a small community

Transitional Words and Phrases

The second way of creating coherence in paragraphs is to use *transitional words* or *phrases* to connect ideas. These are words and phrases such as *for example, mainly,* and *in addition.* They connect ideas and tell why and how they are related.

The following chart shows examples of some of the common transitional words and phrases that help to create coherence.

Transitional Words and Phrases			
Comparing and Contrasting Ideas	also although and another but	however in the same way like likewise moreover	on the other hand similarly too unlike yet
Showing Cause and Effect	as a result because	consequently since	so therefore
Showing Time	about after at at last before during eventually	finally first, second, etc. immediately later meanwhile next	often soon then thereafter until when while

Transitional Words and Phrases

Showing Place	above	beneath	into
	across	beside	near
	among	between	next
	around	by	over
	before	down	there
	behind	here	under
	below	in	
Showing Support	for example	for instance	in fact

The following paragraph tells how American Indians are recognized everywhere they go. The writer uses transitional words to show how ideas are connected. Notice, for example, how "at first" kids pretend not to see him. "Then," they turn and look.

> <u>When</u> I go someplace, most of the time those little people see me. At <u>first</u> they'll pretend not to see me. They go past me a little ways, and <u>then</u> they will turn back and look at me. <u>Then</u> they'll nudge their mama or daddy or grandma or grandpa, and I'll hear them say, "There's an Indian back there." So the Indians are still here. We never phased away. We didn't just blend into society and vanish. <u>In fact</u>, we're appearing more and more and more.
>
> Wallace H. Black Elk and William S. Lyon,
> *Black Elk: The Sacred Ways of a Lakota*

STYLE TIP

Another way to create coherence is to repeat key or similar words and phrases in your writing. For example, in the first few sentences of the paragraph to the left, the writer uses the words *look* and *see* to create a clear connection between ideas.

Exercise 9 Identifying Transitional Words and Phrases

Using the chart on pages 302–303 as a guide, make a list of all the transitional words and phrases in the paragraph that follows on the next page.

When she was elected principal chief of the Cherokee Nation in 1987, Wilma Mankiller took on a huge job. She was used to challenges, though. For example, she had developed many needed projects for Cherokees in rural Oklahoma in 1976. First, she taught people how to build their own homes. Next, she installed new water supply lines. Finally, she started new rural health clinics. Then, she had to overcome serious injuries she suffered in an auto accident in late 1979. While others were impressed with the new chief's dedication, no one who really knew her well found her leadership ability surprising. Once elected chief, Mankiller continued her work to improve Cherokee communities. She focused on housing and education needs, and she encouraged her people to be proud of their language and culture. After serving two terms as chief, Wilma Mankiller continued to work for the Cherokee Nation by speaking across the country.

Elaboration

Reference Note

For more information and practice on adding **supporting details,** see page 293.

A good paragraph does not give just bare facts. It *elaborates,* or expands, on the supporting details so that readers get enough information to understand the subject. To elaborate, you must expand an idea by using *details, facts,* or *examples.* A writer who does not elaborate risks leaving the reader with an unclear or incomplete picture of the subject.

The paragraph below has a main idea and supporting details, but the supporting details need more elaboration.

```
    Cheetahs are the fastest animals
on land. A typical cheetah runs faster
than a car moving at average speed.
Cheetahs can sprint so well because their
bodies are adapted for speed. Cheetahs
use this incredible speed to hunt prey
and to outrun predators.
```

Now read the elaborated paragraph. Notice how the writer has expanded on the supporting details by adding several new facts, a new example, and a new detail. Does this new information give you a clearer picture of the subject?

Cheetahs are the fastest animals on land. A typical cheetah runs faster than a car moving at average speed. In **New fact** fact, cheetahs can move from a standstill to 45 miles per **New fact** hour in two seconds. Their top speed has been clocked at 70 miles per hour, as fast as many highway speed limits. Cheetahs can sprint so well because their bodies are adapted for speed. They have **New** small heads, short ears, and **example** long sleek bodies. Unlike other cats, they also have **New detail** claws that do not retract. Their nonretractable claws **New fact** enable them to turn corners quickly and maintain good traction. Cheetahs use this incredible speed to hunt prey and to outrun predators.

Exercise 10 **Elaborating Details**

The following paragraph does not have enough elaboration. Add details, facts, or examples to improve the paragraph. Be ready to explain the elaboration strategies you used.

Getting to school on time is not easy. I usually have to wait in line to get in the bathroom. Then, I have to pick out something to wear. Finally, I have to make my own breakfast. Sometimes I think school should start an hour later.

What Are the Types of Paragraphs?

There are four different types of paragraphs.

Narrative	used to tell a story or a sequence of events
Descriptive	used to describe a scene or an object
Expository	used to provide information, including facts, instructions, and definitions
Persuasive	used to share opinions and convince others to agree or take action

The type of paragraph you use will depend on your *purpose for writing*. To **entertain** readers or **express** themselves, writers use narration or description. Exposition and narration are used to **inform** readers about something. Writers use persuasion to **influence** people. Several paragraphs written about the same subject might be very different, depending on why the writers wrote them. The four paragraphs that follow all talk about roller coasters, but in different ways.

Narrative paragraphs tell about an event or series of events, usually in chronological order. Most short stories and newspaper articles are examples of narrative writing.

Reference Note

For more information and practice on **chronological order,** see page 297.

> Your knuckles are white, your palms are drenched, and it feels like your dentist has just switched on the drill. Worse still, as the click of the chain pulls the train skyward, you glance back at the gum-chewing guy who strapped you in and wonder what possessed you to put your life in the hands of a kid you wouldn't trust to wrap your sandwich. That's when you realize: This is all a big mistake. Only now you're at the top, staring into the air, the track seems to have vanished, and the car teeters on the edge of nothingness. Then gravity takes hold and whoooooaa . . . you're hurtling
>
> *(continued)*

(continued)

earthward. Faster, faster. Suddenly you're upside down, spinning around corners, praying for it all to end. Minutes later the shoulder bar rises, you stagger out on wobbly knees . . . and hey, where's that kid? Maybe he'll let us ride up front this time.

Anne-Marie O'Neill, "On a Roll," *People Weekly*

Descriptive paragraphs do exactly what you think they do; they describe a person, an object, or a scene in detail.

Reference Note

For more information and practice on **spatial order,** see page 300.

Rising ominously from the frozen Muskegon landscape, it is a sight both exhilarating and unnerving, this man-made mountain range of wood. Under a cold grey sky, the soul of this creation waits in silent hibernation for the warmth of spring. Then, when the clouds part, the snows melt, and the earth awakens, *it shall be silent no more*. A gorgeous, textbook example of the classic "out-and-back" roller coaster, Shivering Timbers will be Michigan's largest coaster. Even more, this humongous lumber wonder will rank as the third longest wooden coaster in the United States.

"1998 Preview," Thrillride! Web site

Expository paragraphs are used for explanation. They can list facts, give directions, or explain ideas. Writers also use expository paragraphs to define terms, make comparisons, and show cause and effect. Since information in expository writing can usually be put into categories, it often uses logical order.

Reference Note

For more information and practice on **logical order,** see page 301.

In the Nickel Empire, attractions grew bigger, faster, weirder: horses diving from platforms; "guess men" who guessed your weight, age, occupation; clowns with cattle prods who mildly shocked innocent bystanders. Every amusement park had its Ferris wheel, but only Coney Island

(continued)

Reference Note

For more on **order of importance,** see page 218.

(continued)

had the Wonder Wheel, with cages that rocked and slid along tracks inside the 135-foot disk. In 1920 the Wonder Wheel replaced the Statue of Liberty as the first sight immigrants saw as they sailed into New York Harbor. Pumping up the adrenaline, Coney's showmen built roller coasters with hair-raising names like the Tornado, the Thunderbolt, and in 1927, the Cyclone. With its 60-mile-per-hour plunge, the Cyclone soon drew lines five hours long. Charles Lindbergh has been quoted as calling the coaster "a greater thrill than flying an airplane at top speed."

Bruce Watson, "Three's a Crowd, They Say, But Not at Coney Island!" *Smithsonian*

Persuasive paragraphs are used to share an opinion about a particular subject. Writers of persuasive paragraphs try to convince readers to agree with the opinions in the paragraphs and, sometimes, to take action. A persuasive paragraph often uses *order of importance.*

Going on amusement park rides is one of the safest forms of recreation. According to the International Association of Amusement Park Attractions, you are more likely to be injured when you play sports, ride a horse, or even ride a bicycle. Statistics show the occurrence of death to be approximately one in 250 million riders. This group's statistics are supported by those of the National Consumer Product Safety Commission. It estimates that more than 270 million people visit amusement parks each year, and that 7,000 people out of those 270 million go to emergency rooms for injuries they receive on amusement park rides—that's only 0.00259 percent of riders.

"Amusement Park Physics," *Learner on Line* Web site

Exercise 11 **Identifying Types of Paragraphs**

With two or three other students, find an example of each of the four paragraph types in magazines, newspapers, books, or on Web sites. Then, answer the following questions for each paragraph.

1. Do you think the paragraph is narrative, descriptive, expository, or persuasive? How can you tell?
2. How are the details organized in each paragraph (chronologically, spatially, logically)? How do you know? Could the information have been organized in a different way? How?
3. What was the writer's purpose for writing each piece (to entertain, inform, influence, express)? Does your group feel that the writer achieved his or her purpose? Why?

How Are Paragraphs Used in Longer Pieces of Writing?

So far, you have had practice with paragraphs that can stand on their own or are part of the body of a longer piece of writing. There are two other kinds of paragraphs you will need to use in your writing: *introduction* and *conclusion* paragraphs. The body paragraphs in a composition are like the supporting details in a paragraph—they serve as the filling for your "idea sandwich." Introduction and conclusion paragraphs are the bread for that sandwich. They are like larger versions of your topic and clincher sentences.

Reference Note

For more on **introductions** and **conclusions,** see "Writing" in the Quick Reference Handbook.

Dividing a Piece into Paragraphs

When you write a longer piece, you need to divide the body into paragraphs to give your readers' eyes a rest and to switch to a new main idea. To help your readers understand changes in a longer piece of writing, start a new paragraph when

- you express a new or different main idea
- you explain another part of your subject or step in a process
- you provide another kind of support for your opinion
- the setting—time or location—of your piece changes
- a different person or character speaks

┌HELP─

As you complete
Exercise 12, keep in mind
that there may be more
than one correct way to
divide the piece into
paragraphs.

Exercise 12 Dividing a Piece into Paragraphs

The paragraph indentations from the following selection have
been removed. Read the selection with a small group of classmates and decide where to start and end each paragraph.

It was supposed to be a simple nature walk. In
August 1995, eight middle school students and their
teacher were hiking in a field near Henderson,
Minnesota, as part of their study of the region's
environment. But then they saw the frogs. "At first,
when we saw that some of their back legs were
twisted and bent or sticking straight out, we thought
we had broken their legs," says Jack Bovee, now 16.
"Then we found three or four that were missing one
leg." The students abandoned their planned walk
and headed to nearby Ney Pond to search for more
frogs. "It seemed like the closer we got to the pond,
the grosser the deformities," Jack says. "We saw one
with three legs. It was like, Great, there's a problem
here. Cool." By the end of the day, the students had
caught twenty-two frogs. Half of them were seriously deformed. Their discovery generated much
more than a couple of freaky frog jokes. The case of
the deformed frogs has alarmed scientists across the
country and turned into one of the nation's greatest
environmental mysteries. Scientists want to know
what happened to the frogs, and whether what's
affecting them could affect us.

Susan Hayes, "The Celebrated Deformed Frogs of
Le Sueur County," *Scholastic Update*

Review A Writing a Narrative Paragraph

Write a narrative paragraph on one of the following topics. Use
chronological (time) order to organize details in your supporting
sentences.

- an event you saw recently
- a story you have heard before

Review B — Writing a Descriptive Paragraph

Apply what you have learned to write a descriptive paragraph on one of the following topics. Use plenty of sensory details to describe what your subject looks like, sounds like, smells like, and so on. Organize the details using spatial (place) order.

- a favorite pet or place
- a park you have visited

Review C — Writing an Expository Paragraph

This is the type of writing you will use most often, whether answering an essay test question or sharing your favorite recipe. Use an expository paragraph to explain what you know about a topic. Remember to support your main idea using facts, examples, and sensory details. Here are some ways you might approach your expository paragraph.

- Explain how to do something simple, such as tying shoelaces. (Use time order.)
- Compare and contrast two things, for example, dogs and cats. (Use logical order.)
- Provide information about a topic you know well, such as the history of hip-hop music or types of aquarium fish. (Use chronological order for history topics and logical order when explaining types of things.)

Review D — Writing a Persuasive Paragraph

You have probably used spoken persuasion since you were old enough to talk. Putting persuasion into writing gives you an edge, because you can better plan what you want to say. Remember that the supporting sentences of your persuasive paragraph should give good *reasons* for your opinion. Choose one of the following prompts and write a persuasive paragraph.

- Express your opinion about a school or community issue. For example, you might propose making passing periods between classes longer or building a new city park.
- Ask a parent for a privilege, such as a later bedtime.

Grammar

Usage

Mechanics

internet**connect**

go.hrw.com

GO TO: go.hrw.com
KEYWORD: EOLang

The Sentence
Subject and Predicate, Kinds of Sentences

Diagnostic Preview

A. Identifying Sentences

Identify each of the following word groups as a *sentence* or a *sentence fragment*. If a word group is a sentence, write it in the correct form, using a capital letter at the beginning and adding the appropriate punctuation mark at the end.

EXAMPLES   **1.** having forgotten their homework

         1. sentence fragment

        2. how strong the wind is

         2. sentence—How strong the wind is!

1. after we visit the library and gather information for the research paper
2. are you ready for the big game next week
3. listen closely to our guest speaker
4. have read the first draft of my paper
5. an excellent short story, "The Medicine Bag," is in that book
6. that we helped Habitat for Humanity to build
7. Mrs. Chin, our math teacher this year
8. be prepared to give your speech tomorrow
9. fishing, skiing, and swimming in the lake
10. what a good idea you have, Amy

B. Identifying Simple Subjects and Simple Predicates

Write the simple subject and the simple predicate in each of the following sentences.

EXAMPLE   **1.** A computer can be a wonderful tool for people with disabilities.

       1. computer—simple subject; can be—simple predicate

11. Specially designed machines have been developed in the past several years.

12. Have you ever seen a talking computer?

13. It is used mainly by people with visual impairments.

14. Most computers display writing on a screen.

15. However, these special models can give information by voice.

16. Closed-captioned television is another interesting and fairly recent invention.

17. Subtitles appear on the television screens of many hearing-impaired viewers.

18. These viewers can read the subtitles and enjoy their favorite television shows.

19. With a teletypewriter (TTY), people can type messages over phone lines.

20. Many new inventions and devices make life easier.

C. Punctuating and Classifying Sentences

Copy the last word of each of the following sentences, and then punctuate each sentence with the correct end mark. Classify each sentence as *declarative, interrogative, imperative,* or *exclamatory.*

EXAMPLE   **1.** Flowers and insects depend on one another for life

       1. life.—declarative

21. Have you ever watched a honeybee or a bumblebee in a garden

22. The bee flies busily from one flower to another, drinking nectar

23. Notice the yellow pollen that collects on the legs and body of the bee

24. The bee carries pollen from flower to flower, helping the plants to make seeds

25. What a remarkable insect the bee is

The Sentence

10a. A *sentence* is a word or word group that contains a subject and a verb and that expresses a complete thought.

A sentence begins with a capital letter and ends with a period, a question mark, or an exclamation point.

EXAMPLES   **S**he won a prize for her book**.**

Why did you stop running**?**

Wait**!** [The understood subject is *you*.]

Sentence or Sentence Fragment?

A *sentence fragment* is a group of words that looks like a sentence but does not contain both a subject and a verb or does not express a complete thought.

SENTENCE FRAGMENT   Sailing around the world. [The word group lacks a subject.]

SENTENCE   They are sailing around the world.

SENTENCE FRAGMENT   The hike through the Grand Canyon. [The word group lacks a verb.]

SENTENCE   The hike through the Grand Canyon was long and hard.

SENTENCE FRAGMENT   After they pitched the tent. [The word group contains a subject and a verb, but does not express a complete thought.]

SENTENCE   After they pitched the tent, they rested.

Exercise 1   Identifying Sentences

Identify each of the following word groups as a *sentence* or a *sentence fragment*. If a word group is a sentence, write it in the correct form, using a capital letter at the beginning and adding the appropriate punctuation mark at the end.

EXAMPLES   1. during her vacation last summer

1. *sentence fragment*

2. my friend Michelle visited Colorado

2. *sentence—My friend Michelle visited Colorado.*

Reference Note

For information on the use of **capital letters,** see page 572. For information on **end marks,** see page 598.

Reference Note

For information on **the understood subject,** see page 331.

STYLE   TIP

Sentence fragments are common and acceptable in informal situations. However, in formal writing, you should avoid using sentence fragments.

COMPUTER TIP

Many grammar-checking software programs can help you identify sentence fragments. If you have access to such a program, use it to help you evaluate your writing.

Reference Note

For information on **revising sentence fragments,** see pages 269 and 685.

1. do you know what happened during Michelle's boat trip
2. down the rapids on the Colorado River
3. at first her boat drifted calmly through the Grand Canyon
4. then the river dropped suddenly
5. and became foaming rapids full of dangerous boulders
6. many of which can break a boat
7. Michelle's boat was small
8. with one guide and four passengers
9. some passengers prefer large inflatable boats with outboard motors
10. carrying eighteen people

Subject and Predicate

Sentences consist of two basic parts: subjects and predicates.

The Subject

10b. The *subject* tells *whom* or *what* the sentence is about.

EXAMPLES   **Nicholasa Mohr** is a writer and an artist.

           The girls on the team were all good students.

           He shared his lunch with the boy on the other team.

           Swimming is good exercise.

To find the subject, ask *who* or *what* is doing something or *whom* or *what* is being talked about. The subject may come at the beginning, middle, or end of a sentence.

EXAMPLES   **The pitcher** struck Felicia out. [*Who* struck Felicia out? *The pitcher* did.]

           After practicing for hours, **Timmy** bowled two strikes. [*Who* bowled two strikes? *Timmy* did.]

           How kind **you** are! [*Who* is kind? *You* are.]

           When will **the afternoon train** arrive? [*What* will arrive? *The afternoon train* will.]

           Hiding in the tall grass was **a baby rabbit**. [*What* was hiding? *A baby rabbit* was.]

Reference Note

A compound noun, such as *Nicholasa Mohr*, is considered one noun. For information on **compound nouns,** see page 337.

Writing Subjects and Punctuating Sentences

Add subjects to fill in the blanks in the following sentences. Use a different subject in each sentence. Begin each sentence with a capital letter, and end it with a punctuation mark.

EXAMPLE   1. _____ is very heavy.

          1. *This is very heavy.*

1. _____ is a difficult game to play
2. _____ works in the post office
3. Luckily for me, _____ was easy to read
4. Tied to the end of the rope was _____
5. Did _____ help you
6. _____ eventually became President of the United States
7. Have _____ always wanted to visit Peru
8. Luis, _____ was the score
9. Before the game, _____ will meet in the gym
10. _____ has always been one of my favorite books
11. What a great basketball player _____ is
12. Has _____ called you yet
13. In the afternoon _____ takes a nap
14. _____ is playing at the theater this weekend
15. When did _____ start making that sound
16. In a minute _____ will feed you, Spot
17. Under the pile of leaves in the front yard was _____
18. _____ is the group's best-known song
19. In my opinion _____ is a better goalie than Alex
20. Where in the world did _____ get that hat

TIPS & TRICKS

Here is a test you can use to find the simple subject of most sentences: If you leave out the simple subject, a sentence does not make sense.

EXAMPLE
The four new . . . arrived early.

Simple Subject and Complete Subject

10c. The *simple subject* is the main word or word group that tells *whom* or *what* the sentence is about.

The ***complete subject*** consists of all the words that tell *whom* or *what* a sentence is about.

EXAMPLES   The four new students arrived early.

          Complete subject   The four new students

          Simple subject   students

Is the winner of the go-cart race present?

Complete subject   the winner of the go-cart race

Simple subject   winner

A round walnut table with five legs stood in the middle of the dining room.

Complete subject   A round walnut table with five legs

Simple subject   table

A simple subject may consist of one word or several words.

EXAMPLES   **Jets** often break the sound barrier. [one word]

Does **Aunt Carmen** own a grocery store? [two words]

On the library shelf was ***The Island of the Blue Dolphins.*** [six words]

NOTE In this book, the simple subject is usually referred to as the *subject.*

Exercise 3 Identifying Subjects

Write the subject of each of the following sentences.

EXAMPLE   1. A book by N. Scott Momaday is on the table.

          1. book

1. Born in 1934 in Oklahoma, Momaday lived on Navajo and Apache reservations in the Southwest.
2. Momaday's father was a Kiowa.
3. As a young man, Momaday attended the University of New Mexico and Stanford University.
4. In *The Way to Rainy Mountain,* he tells about the myths and history of the Kiowa people.
5. The book includes poems, an essay, and stories about the Kiowa people.
6. *The Way to Rainy Mountain* was published in 1969.
7. After Momaday's book came works by other modern American Indian writers.
8. William Least Heat-Moon traveled in a van across the United States and wrote about his journey.
9. Was he inspired to write by his travels?
10. Readers of this Osage writer enjoy his beautiful descriptions of nature.

 Link to Literature

Exercise 4 Identifying Complete Subjects and Simple Subjects

Write the complete subject in each of the following sentences. Then, underline the simple subject.

EXAMPLES 1. Stories about time travel make exciting reading.
1. *Stories* about time travel

2. Samuel Delany writes great science fiction.
2. *Samuel Delany*

Link to Literature

1. Ray Bradbury is also a writer of science fiction.
2. *The Golden Apples of the Sun* is a collection of Bradbury's short stories.
3. Is your favorite story in that book "A Sound of Thunder"?
4. The main character in the story is called Mr. Eckels.
5. For ten thousand dollars, Mr. Eckels joins Time Safari, Inc.
6. He is looking for the dinosaur *Tyrannosaurus rex*.
7. With four other men, Bradbury's hero travels more than sixty million years back in time.
8. On the safari, trouble develops.
9. Because of one mistake, the past is changed.
10. Do the results of that mistake affect the future?

The Predicate

10d. The *predicate* of a sentence tells something about the subject.

EXAMPLES The phone **rang.**

Old Faithful **is a giant geyser in Yellowstone National Park.**

Jade Snow Wong **wrote about growing up in San Francisco's Chinatown.**

Like the subject, the predicate may be found anywhere in a sentence.

EXAMPLES **Outside the tent was** a baby bear.

Late in the night we **heard a noise.** [The predicate in this sentence is divided by the subject, *we*.]

Has the dough **risen enough**? [The predicate is divided by the subject, *the dough*.]

Stop right there! [The subject in this sentence is understood to be *you*.]

Exercise 5 **Identifying Predicates**

Write the predicate in each of the following sentences.

EXAMPLES   **1.** My favorite sports poster is this one of Roberto Clemente.

   1. is this one of Roberto Clemente

   2. Have you heard of this famous sports hero?

   2. Have heard of this famous sports hero

1. Also among my baseball treasures is a book about Clemente's life and career.
2. Clemente played right field for the Pittsburgh Pirates, my favorite team.
3. During his amazing career, he won four National League batting titles.
4. In 1966, he was named the league's Most Valuable Player.
5. Twice Clemente helped lead the Pirates to World Series victories.
6. In fourteen World Series games, Clemente never went without a hit.
7. Roberto Clemente died in a plane crash off the coast of his homeland, Puerto Rico.
8. The plane crash occurred on a flight to Nicaragua to aid earthquake victims.
9. After his death, Clemente was elected to the National Baseball Hall of Fame.
10. In New York, a park has been named for this beloved ballplayer.

Exercise 6 Writing Predicates

Make a sentence out of each of the following word groups by adding a predicate to fill the blank or blanks.

EXAMPLES   **1.** A flock of geese _____

         1. A flock of geese flew high overhead.

    2. _____ a poster of Nelson Mandela.

         2. Over Kim's desk hung a poster of Nelson Mandela.

1. My favorite food _____.

2. A course in first aid _____.

3. _____ our car _____?

4. Rock climbing _____.

5. Spanish explorers in the Americas _____.

6. Several computers _____.

7. _____ a new pair of roller skates.

8. The skyscrapers of New York City _____.

9. Some dogs _____.

10. _____ my family _____.

11. Winning the championship _____.

12. _____ all sorts of birds _____.

13. The new store at the mall _____.

14. _____ a small, brown toad.

15. The flowers in Mr. Alvarez's garden _____.

16. _____ my chores _____.

17. Gerry's allowance _____.

18. _____ we _____?

19. The cool of the morning _____.

20. The tiny kittens _____.

Simple Predicate and Complete Predicate

10e. The *simple predicate*, or *verb*, is the main word or word group that tells something about the subject.

The ***complete predicate*** consists of a verb and all the words that describe the verb and complete its meaning.

EXAMPLES   The pilot broke the sound barrier.

         Complete predicate   broke the sound barrier

         Simple predicate (verb)   broke

We should have visited the diamond field in Arkansas.

Complete predicate	should have visited the diamond field in Arkansas
Simple predicate (verb)	should have visited

The telephone on the table rang.

Complete predicate	rang
Simple predicate (verb)	rang

NOTE In this book, the simple predicate is usually referred to as the *verb.*

Exercise 7 Identifying Complete Predicates and Verbs

Write the complete predicate of each of the following sentences. Then, underline the verb.

EXAMPLE   1. Who created the U.S. flag?

          1. <u>created</u> the U.S. flag

1. Many scholars are unsure about the history of the Stars and Stripes.
2. The Continental Congress approved a design for the flag.
3. The flag's design included thirteen red stripes and thirteen white stripes.
4. The top inner quarter of the flag was a blue field with thirteen white stars.
5. The name of the designer has remained a mystery.
6. During the American Revolution, the colonists needed a symbol of their independence.
7. George Washington wanted flags for the army.
8. Unfortunately, the flags did not arrive until the end of the Revolutionary War.
9. According to legend, Betsy Ross made the first flag.
10. However, most historians doubt the Betsy Ross story.

The Verb Phrase

Some simple predicates, or verbs, consist of more than one word. Such verbs are called *verb phrases* (verbs that include one or more helping verbs).

EXAMPLE   Kathy **is riding** the Ferris wheel.

Reference Note

For information on **helping verbs,** see page 361.

EXAMPLES   The carnival **has been** in town for two weeks.

Should Imelda **have gotten** here sooner?

NOTE The words *not* and *never* are not verbs; they are adverbs. They are never part of a verb or verb phrase.

EXAMPLES   She **has** not **written** to me recently.

I **will** never **forget** her.

They **do**n't **know** my cousins. [*Don't* is the contraction of *do* and *not*. The *n't* is not part of the verb phrase *do know.*]

Exercise 8 Identifying Verbs and Verb Phrases

Write the verb or verb phrase in each of the following sentences.

EXAMPLES   1. Look at these beautiful pictures of Hawaii.
       1. *Look*

       2. They were taken by our science teacher.
       2. *were taken*

1. Hawaii is called the Aloha State.
2. It was settled by Polynesians about 2,000 years ago.
3. The musical heritage and rich culture of the original Hawaiians have contributed to the islands' popularity.

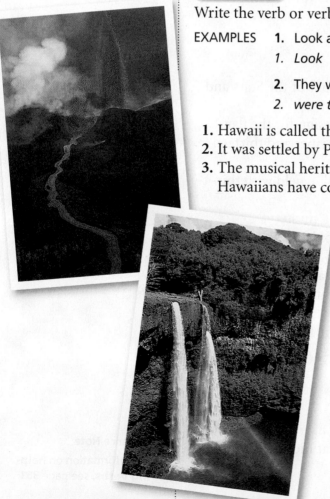

4. Have you ever seen a traditional Hawaiian dance, one with drums and chants?
5. The Hawaiian islands are also known for their lush, exotic scenery.
6. I can certainly not imagine anything more spectacular than an active volcano at night.
7. Would you like a helicopter ride over misty waterfalls like those in Hawaii?
8. What an incredible sight that surely is!
9. Those Hawaiian dancers must have been practicing for years.
10. Save me a place on the next flight!

Finding the Subject

To find the subject of a sentence, find the verb first. Then, ask "Who?" or "What?" before the verb.

EXAMPLES   In high school we will have more homework. [The verb is *will have. Who* will have? *We* will have. *We* is the subject of the sentence.]

Can you untie this knot? [*Can untie* is the verb. *Who* can untie? *You* can untie. *You* is the subject of the sentence.]

The peak of Mount Everest was first reached by Sir Edmund Hillary and Tenzing Norgay. [The verb is *was reached. What* was reached? *Peak* was reached. *Peak* is the subject of the sentence.]

Ahead of the explorers lay a vast wilderness. [The verb is *lay. What* lay? *Wilderness* lay. *Wilderness* is the subject of the sentence.]

Where are the Canary Islands located? [*Are located* is the verb. *What* are located? *Canary Islands* are located. *Canary Islands* is the subject of the sentence.]

Pass the salad, please. [*Pass* is the verb. *Who* should pass? *You* pass. Understood *you* is the subject of the sentence.]

Compound Subjects and Compound Verbs

Compound Subjects

10f. A *compound subject* consists of two or more subjects that are joined by a conjunction and that have the same verb.

The conjunctions most commonly used to connect the words of a compound subject are *and* and *or.*

EXAMPLES   **Paris** and **London** remain favorite tourist attractions. [The two parts of the compound subject have the same verb, *remain.*]

Nelson Mandela or **Archbishop Desmond Tutu** will speak at the conference. [The two parts of the compound subject have the same verb, *will speak.*]

Among my hobbies are **reading, snorkeling,** and **painting.** [The three parts of the compound subject have the same verb, *are.*]

GRAMMAR

| TIPS & TRICKS |

When you are looking for the subject of a sentence, remember that the subject is never part of a prepositional phrase. Cross through any prepositional phrases; the subject will be one of the remaining words.

EXAMPLE
  Several ~~of the puzzle pieces~~ are ~~under the sofa.~~

SUBJECT
  Several

VERB
  are

Reference Note

| For information on **prepositional phrases,** see page 371.

Reference Note

| For information on **conjunctions,** see page 374.

| TIPS & TRICKS |

In sentences with a compound subject joined by *or*, the verb agrees with the subject closest to it. Here is a quick test you can use. (1) Cover the part of the subject that is farther from the verb. (2) Decide whether the remaining part of the compound subject agrees with the verb.

EXAMPLE
Janie or her parents (is, are) coming. [*Her parents is coming* or *her parents are coming*? *Her parents are coming* is correct.]

ANSWER
Janie or her parents **are** coming.

Exercise 9 **Identifying Compound Subjects**

Write the compound subject in each of the following sentences.

EXAMPLE   1. The shapes and sizes of sand dunes are determined by the wind.

         1. *shapes, sizes*

1. The national parks and monuments of the United States include many of the world's most spectacular landforms.
2. The Grand Canyon and the waterfalls of Yosemite are examples of landforms shaped by erosion.
3. Water, wind, and other natural forces are continuing the age-old erosion of landforms.
4. On the Colorado Plateau, for example, natural bridges and arches, like the one in the photograph on the left, have been produced by erosion.
5. Likewise, Skyline Arch and Landscape Arch in Utah are two natural arches formed by erosion.
6. Underground, caves and immense caverns are created by rushing streams and waterfalls.
7. Stalagmites and stalactites, such as the ones in the photograph on the right, are formed by lime deposits from drops of water seeping into these caverns.

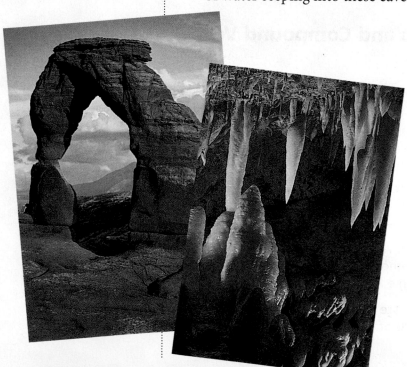

8. In river systems throughout the world, canyons and gorges are cut into the earth by erosion.
9. Many rapids and waterfalls have also originated through the process of erosion.
10. Do steep areas with heavy rainfall or dry regions with few trees suffer more from erosion?

Exercise 10   Writing Compound Subjects

Add a compound subject to each of the following predicates. Use *and* or *or* to join the parts of your compound subjects.

EXAMPLE   1. _____ were at the bottom of my locker.

           1. *My bus pass and a pair of gym socks were at the*
             bottom of my locker.

1. Yesterday _____ arrived in the mail.
2. _____ make loyal pets.
3. On the beach _____ spotted a dolphin.
4. _____ will present their report on the adventures of Álvar Núñez Cabeza de Vaca.
5. In the attic were piled _____ .
6. Ever since first grade, _____ have been friends and neighbors.
7. Is _____ coaching the tennis team this year?
8. For Indian food, _____ always go to the Bombay Cafe in the shopping center nearby.
9. To our great surprise, out of my little brother's pockets spilled _____ .
10. Both _____ may be seen on the African plains.

Compound Verbs

10g. A *compound verb* consists of two or more verbs that are joined by a conjunction and that have the same subject.

The conjunctions most commonly used to connect the words of a compound verb are *and*, *or*, and *but*.

EXAMPLES   The rain **has fallen** for days and **is** still **falling.**

           The team **played** well but **lost** the game anyway.

           Will Rolando **mop** the floor or **wash** the dishes?

A sentence may contain both a *compound subject* and a *compound verb*. Notice in the following example that both subjects carry out the action of both verbs.

EXAMPLE   A few **vegetables** and many **flowers sprouted** and **grew** in the rich soil. [The vegetables sprouted and grew, and the flowers sprouted and grew.]

STYLE	TIP

Using compound subjects and verbs, you can combine ideas to make your writing less wordy. Compare the examples below.

WORDY
  Orville and Wilbur Wright built one of the first airplanes. Orville and Wilbur Wright flew it near Kitty Hawk, North Carolina.

REVISED
  Orville and Wilbur Wright **built** one of the first airplanes and **flew** it near Kitty Hawk, North Carolina.

┌HELP┐
Be sure to
include all parts of each
verb phrase in Exercise 11.

Exercise 11 Identifying Compound Verbs

Write each compound verb or verb phrase in the following sentences.

EXAMPLE   1. Have you heard of the game Serpent or learned the game Senet?

   1. *have heard, learned*

1. Just like children today, children in ancient Egypt played games and enjoyed toys.
2. For the Egyptian board game Serpent, players found or carved a serpent-shaped stone.
3. Players placed the serpent in the center of the board and then began the game.
4. They used place markers and threw bones or sticks as dice.
5. The players took turns and competed with one another in a race to the center.
6. Senet was another ancient Egyptian board game and was played by children and adults alike.
7. Senet looked like an easy game but was actually difficult.
8. Players moved their playing pieces toward the ends of three rows of squares but sometimes were stopped by their opponents.
9. Senet boards were complex and had certain squares for good luck and bad luck.
10. These squares could help players or could block their pieces.

Exercise 12 Identifying Subjects and Verbs

Identify the subject and verb in each of the following sentences.

EXAMPLE   1. American pioneers left their homes and traveled to the West.

   1. *pioneers—subject; left, traveled—verbs*

┌HELP┐
Some of the
subjects and verbs in
Exercise 12 are compound.

1. Settlers faced and overcame many dangers.
2. Mount McKinley and Mount Whitney are two very high mountains.
3. Sacagawea of the Shoshone people helped open the West to explorers and settlers.
4. Every winter many skiers rush to the Grand Tetons.

5. Did all of the mountaineers successfully ascend and descend Mount Everest?

6. Valleys and dense forests cool and refresh travelers in the Appalachian Mountains.

7. On Beartooth Highway in Montana, excellent campgrounds and scenic overlooks provide many views of distant glaciers.

8. Mount Evans is west of Denver and can be reached by the highest paved road in the United States.

9. Is the view from the top slopes of Mount Evans breathtaking?

10. Thick forests cover the Great Smoky Mountains and help form the peaks' smoky mist.

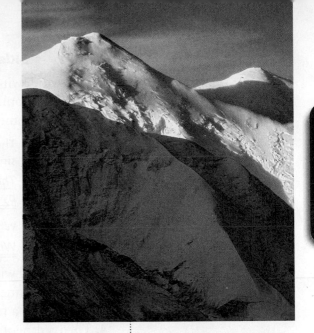

Review A **Identifying Subjects and Predicates**

Write the simple subject and the verb or verb phrase in each of the following sentences.

EXAMPLE   1. Even the ancient Incas and the Aztecs paid and collected taxes.

          1. *Incas, Aztecs; paid, collected*

1. Among the obligations of citizens in large cities is the prompt payment of taxes.

2. The ancient citizens of Mesoamerica were no exception to this rule.

3. Are some of these taxes also known today as "tribute"?

4. Bowls, blankets, honey, or even warriors' shields were given and accepted as tribute.

5. High officials and the sick did not, however, pay taxes.

6. In the interest of fairness, taxes must be counted and recorded in some way by accountants.

7. As a record, Incas knotted a string or cord and counted the number of knots.

8. The Codex Mendoza is a formal record of the Aztecs' taxes.

9. Both the Incas and the Aztecs used the number *20* as the base of their mathematics.

10. Might roads, buildings, or emergency supplies have been paid for with the tribute, or taxes?

┌─HELP─
Some of the subjects and verbs in Review A are compound.

Subject and Predicate   **329**

HELP

Some of the subjects and verbs in Review B are compound.

Review B Identifying Subjects and Predicates

Write the following sentences. Underline the complete subjects once and the complete predicates twice. Then, circle each simple subject and each verb.

EXAMPLES 1. The entire continent of Australia is occupied by a single country.

1. <u>The entire (continent) of Australia</u> <u>(is occupied) by a single country.</u>

2. What do you know about this continent?

2. <u>What (do) (you) (know) about this continent?</u>

1. It is located within the Southern Hemisphere.
2. Can you name the capital of Australia?
3. Australia is a federation of six states and two territories.
4. The continent of Australia was claimed for Britain by Captain James Cook.
5. The native people of Australia live mainly in the desert regions and, traditionally, have a very close bond with their environment.
6. A large number of British colonists settled in cities and towns on the coast.
7. Many ranchers raise sheep and export wool.
8. In addition, large quantities of gold and uranium are mined in Australia.
9. The country is also highly industrialized and produces a variety of goods, ranging from shoes to airplanes.
10. Among Australia's most unusual animals are the platypus and the anteater.

Kinds of Sentences

10h. A _declarative sentence_ makes a statement and ends with a period.

EXAMPLES   Amy Tan was born in Oakland, California.

I couldn't hear what Jason said.

10i. An _imperative sentence_ gives a command or makes a request. Most imperative sentences end with a period. A strong command ends with an exclamation point.

Reference Note

For information about how **sentences can be classified according to their structure,** see Chapter 16.

EXAMPLES   Be quiet during the play. [command]

Please give me another piece of melon. [request]

Stop! [strong command]

The subject of a command or a request is always *you,* even if *you* doesn't appear in the sentence. In such cases, *you* is called the **understood subject.**

EXAMPLES   (You) Be quiet during the play.

(You) Please give me another piece of melon.

(You) Stop!

The word *you* is the understood subject even when the person spoken to is addressed by name.

EXAMPLE   Miguel, (you) please answer the phone.

10j. An *interrogative sentence* asks a question and ends with a question mark.

EXAMPLES   When did you return from your camping trip?

Did the surfboard cost much?

10k. An *exclamatory sentence* shows excitement or expresses strong feeling and ends with an exclamation point.

EXAMPLES   Gabriella won the match!

How terrifying that movie was!

Exercise 13   **Classifying Sentences by Purpose**

Label each of the following sentences *declarative, imperative, interrogative,* or *exclamatory.*

EXAMPLE   1. Ask Yoshiko for the address.

        1. imperative

1. Will your grandfather compete in the Kansas City Marathon again this year?
2. Our school's project, cleaning up the Silver River Nature Preserve, was a success.
3. Bring more sandbags over here now!
4. Is the Rig-Veda the oldest of the Hindu scriptures?
5. Read this poem by Naomi Shihab Nye.

6. How huge this library is!
7. Origami is the fascinating Japanese folk art of folding paper into shapes.
8. How did you make that paper crane?
9. Please line up alphabetically.
10. After we eat supper, we're going to my aunt's house down the block.

Review C **Classifying and Punctuating Sentences**

Write the last word of each of the following sentences, adding the correct end mark. Then, label each sentence as *declarative*, *imperative*, *interrogative*, or *exclamatory*.

EXAMPLE   **1.** Are prairie dogs social creatures
           1. creatures?—interrogative

1. Many of these small mammals live together in underground "towns" like the one shown below
2. Look at how prairie dogs dig family burrows
3. How large are the burrows
4. The burrows sometimes cover several acres
5. These creatures can usually be seen at night or in the early morning
6. What alert animals prairie dogs are
7. At least one prairie dog always keeps a lookout for threats to the community
8. Look at how it sits up to see better
9. It then dives headfirst into the burrow and alerts the colony
10. How shrill the prairie dog's whistle of alarm is

10

Chapter Review

A. Identifying Sentences

Identify each of the following groups of words as a *sentence* or a *sentence fragment*.

1. Trying a double somersault.

2. She barely caught her partner's hands!

3. As she began the triple.

4. She fell into the net.

5. The crowd gasped.

6. Even the clowns turned and looked.

7. Was she hurt?

8. Rolled off the net to the ground.

9. Smiling as she waved to the crowd.

10. She was fine!

B. Identifying Subjects

Identify the complete subject of the following sentences. Then, underline the simple subject. The simple subject may be compound.

HELP

Remember that the subject may be the understood *you*.

11. Foods and beverages with large amounts of sugar can contribute to tooth decay.

12. The lava from a volcano hardens when it cools.

13. The earthquake survivors camped on blankets in the rubble.

14. In Beijing, bicyclists weave through the busy streets.

15. By 1899, many gold prospectors had rushed to Alaska.

16. The weather during an Alaskan summer can be hot.

17. Have you read this collection of Claude McKay's poems?

18. In the center of the table was a huge bowl of fruit.

19. Linked forever in legend are Paul Bunyan and Babe the Blue Ox.

20. Have many famous racehorses been trained in Kentucky?

21. The bright lights and the tall buildings amaze and delight most visitors to New York City.

22. Are Lita and Marisa going to give their presentation?
23. After soccer practice tomorrow afternoon, please come to my house for dinner.
24. Inside the box were letters and postcards written around the turn of the century.
25. The book *Come a Stranger* was written by the award-winning author Cynthia Voigt.

C. Identifying Predicates

Identify the complete predicate of the following sentences. Then, underline the simple predicate (verb or verb phrase). The simple predicate may be compound.

26. Teenagers need a balanced diet for good health.
27. A balanced diet improves student performance in school.
28. Students are sometimes in a hurry and skip breakfast.
29. For a nutritious breakfast, they can eat cereal and fruit.
30. Cheese and juice also provide good nutrition.
31. The cheese contains calcium, an important mineral.
32. People need protein as well.
33. Protein builds body tissue.
34. Protein can be supplied by eggs, dried beans, red meat, fish, and poultry.
35. Carbohydrates include whole grains, vegetables, and fruits.
36. Junk foods can ruin your appetite.
37. Sweets cause tooth decay and contain many calories.
38. According to nutritionists, sweets are low in nutrients and fill the body with "empty" calories.
39. Good eating habits keep you healthy and help you live longer.
40. Start eating right!

D. Classifying and Punctuating Sentences

Classify each of the following sentences as *declarative, interrogative, imperative,* or *exclamatory.* Then, write each sentence with the correct end punctuation.

41. In ancient times, the Julian calendar was used

42. Why was it called Julian

43. It was named after the Roman leader Julius Caesar

44. I thought so

45. Because the Julian calendar was not perfect, the Gregorian calendar was invented

46. In 1752, the calendar was changed in England

47. Tell me the result

48. Eleven days in September were lost

49. That's the strangest thing I've ever heard

50. Were those days lost forever

Writing Application
Writing a Letter

Using Complete Sentences   Yesterday, you went to a birthday party. Write a letter describing the party to a friend or relative who lives far away. Include details about the activities you enjoyed and about the other people who were there. Use complete sentences to make sure your thoughts are clear.

Prewriting   Make a list of the details that you would like to include in your letter. At this stage, you do not have to use complete sentences. Simply jot down your thoughts.

Writing   Use your prewriting list of details as you write your rough draft. Choose details that would be interesting to your friend or relative. You might organize your letter chronologically (describing events in the order in which they occurred).

Revising   Read your letter aloud. As you read, mark any parts of the letter that seem unclear. Add, cut, or rearrange details to make your letter clear and interesting to your reader.

Publishing   Check your work to make sure you have used only complete sentences. Read your letter for any errors in spelling and punctuation. You and your classmates may want to collect the letters in a booklet. Make a copy for each member of the class.

Reference Note

For information on **writing a letter,** see "Writing" in the Quick Reference Handbook.

11

Parts of Speech Overview

Noun, Pronoun, Adjective

Diagnostic Preview

Identifying Nouns, Pronouns, and Adjectives

Identify each italicized word in the following paragraphs as a *noun*, a *pronoun*, or an *adjective*.

EXAMPLES The [1] *achievements* of the [2] *native* peoples of
North America have sometimes been overlooked.

1. noun
2. adjective

Recent [1] *studies* show that the Winnebago people developed a [2] *calendar* based on careful observation of the [3] *heavens*. An [4] *archaeologist* has found that markings on an old [5] *calendar* stick are the precise records of a [6] *lunar* year and a solar year. These records are remarkably accurate, considering that at the time the [7] *Winnebagos* had neither a [8] *written* language nor a system of [9] *mathematics*.

[10] *The* calendar stick is a carved [11] *hickory* branch with [12] *four* sides. [13] *It* is worn along the [14] *edges* and shows other signs of frequent use. A [15] *similar* stick appears in a portrait of an early chief of the Winnebagos. In the portrait, the chief holds a calendar stick in [16] *his* right hand. [17] *One* current theory is that the chief went out at [18] *sunrise* and

sunset to observe the sun and the moon. [19] *He* then marked on the stick what he saw. According to one researcher, this calendar is the [20] *oldest* indication we have that native North American peoples recorded the year day by day.

The Noun

11a. A *noun* is a word or word group that is used to name a person, a place, a thing, or an idea.

Persons	Jessye Norman, teacher, chef, Dr. Ling
Places	Grand Canyon, city, Namibia, kitchen
Things	lamp, granite, Nobel Prize, Golden Gate Bridge
Ideas	happiness, self-control, liberty, bravery

Notice that some nouns are made up of more than one word. A *compound noun* is a single noun made up of two or more words used together. The compound noun may be written as one word, as a hyphenated word, or as two or more words.

One Word	grandmother, basketball
Hyphenated Word	mother-in-law, light-year
Two Words	grand piano, jumping jack

TIPS & TRICKS

To find the correct spelling of a compound noun, look it up in a recent dictionary.

Exercise 1 Identifying Nouns

Identify the nouns in the following sentences.

EXAMPLE
    1. We have been reading about patriotic heroines in our textbook.

    1. heroines, textbook

1. Rebecca Motte was a great patriot.
2. During the Revolutionary War, British soldiers seized her mansion in South Carolina.
3. General Harry Lee told Motte that the Americans would have to burn her home to smoke out the enemy.

HELP

In Exercise 1, some nouns are used more than once.

4. Motte supported the plan and was glad to help her country.
5. She even supplied flaming arrows and a bow for the attack.
6. The house was saved after the enemy raised the white flag of surrender.
7. Other people might not have been so generous or patriotic.
8. Afterward, Motte invited soldiers from both sides to dinner.
9. How their laughter must have filled the air!
10. The colonies and all citizens of the United States are in her debt.

Proper Nouns and Common Nouns

Reference Note

For more information about **capitalizing proper nouns,** see page 574.

A *proper noun* names a particular person, place, thing, or idea and begins with a capital letter. A *common noun* names any one of a group of persons, places, things, or ideas and is generally not capitalized.

Common Nouns	Proper Nouns
girl	Kay O'Neill
writer	Octavio Paz
country	Morocco
monument	Eiffel Tower
compact disc	*A Long Way Home*
book	*Tiger Eyes*
religion	Buddhism
language	Arabic
city	Ottawa

Exercise 2 Identifying Common Nouns and Proper Nouns

HELP

In Exercise 2, some nouns are used more than once.

Write the nouns in each of the following sentences. Then, identify each noun as a *common noun* or *proper noun.*

EXAMPLE   1. Mark visited an interesting museum in Colorado last month.

         1. *Mark—proper; museum—common; Colorado—proper; month—common*

1. Mark and his parents went to the Black American West Museum and Heritage Center in Denver.
2. The museum displays many items that cowboys used.
3. These items are from the collection of Paul Stewart, the man who founded the museum.
4. Mark saw saddles, knives, hats, and lariats.
5. He also saw many pictures of African American cowboys.
6. The museum is located in an old house that is listed in the National Register of Historic Places.
7. The house once belonged to Dr. Justina L. Ford.
8. She was the first black female physician in Colorado.
9. Mark was amazed by all of the old medical instruments in one display.
10. He said he was glad doctors don't use equipment like that anymore.

Exercise 3 Revising Sentences by Using Proper Nouns

Revise the following sentences by substituting a proper noun for each common noun. You might have to change some other words in each sentence. You may make up proper names.

EXAMPLE   1. An ambassador visited a local school and spoke about his country.

           1. *Ambassador Rios visited Jackson High School and spoke about Brazil.*

1. That painting is in a famous museum.
2. The police officer cheerfully directed us to the building on that street.
3. My relatives, who are originally from a small town, now live in a large city.
4. The librarian asked my classmate to return the book as soon as possible.
5. That newspaper is published daily; this magazine is published weekly.
6. The girl read a poem for the teacher.
7. That state borders the ocean.
8. The owner of that store visited two countries during a spring month.
9. A man flew to a northern city one day.
10. Last week the mayor visited our school and talked about the history of our city.

Exercise 4 Identifying and Classifying Nouns

Identify the nouns in the following sentences, and label each noun as a *common noun* or a *proper noun.*

EXAMPLE   **[1]** Lillian Evanti performed in Europe, Latin America, and Africa.

       1. Lillian Evanti—proper noun; Europe—proper noun; Latin America—proper noun; Africa—proper noun

[1] Evanti was the first African American woman to sing opera professionally. **[2]** Her talent was recognized early; when she was a child, she gave a solo concert in Washington, D.C. **[3]** As an adult, she performed in a special concert at the White House for President Franklin Roosevelt and his wife, Eleanor. **[4]** Evanti also composed a musical piece titled "Himno Panamericano," which was a great success. **[5]** Her career inspired many other African American singers.

[6] A few years later Marian Anderson stepped into the limelight. **[7]** Always a champion of the arts, Mrs. Roosevelt again aided a great performer. **[8]** With the assistance and encouragement of the former First Lady, Anderson sang at a most appropriate site—the Lincoln Memorial. **[9]** Like Evanti, Anderson broke barriers, for before her, no other African American had sung at the famous Metropolitan Opera House in New York City. **[10]** Honors Anderson earned include a place in the National Arts Hall of Fame.

Concrete Nouns and Abstract Nouns

A *concrete noun* names a person, place, or thing that can be perceived by one or more of the senses (sight, hearing, taste, touch, smell). An *abstract noun* names an idea, a feeling, a quality, or a characteristic.

Concrete Nouns	photograph, music, pears, filmmaker, sandpaper, rose, Brooklyn Bridge
Abstract Nouns	love, fun, freedom, self-esteem, beauty, honor, wisdom, Buddhism

Writing Sentences with Concrete and Abstract Nouns

Identify each noun in the following list as *concrete* or *abstract*. Then, use each noun in an original sentence.

EXAMPLE   **1.** truth

         1. abstract—People should always tell the truth.

1. soy sauce   **4.** ice   **7.** motor   **9.** pillow

2. brotherhood   **5.** excitement   **8.** health   **10.** honor

3. laughter   **6.** kindness

Collective Nouns

A *collective noun* is a word that names a group.

audience	committee	herd	quartet
batch	crew	jury	swarm
class	family	litter	team

Reference Note

For more information about **collective nouns,** see pages 468 and 477.

Using the Different Kinds of Nouns

Complete the following poem, which is based on this painting. Add common, proper, concrete, abstract, or collective nouns as directed. For proper nouns, you'll need to make up names of people and places. Be sure you capitalize all proper nouns.

Meet my **[1]** (*common*), the really amazing,
Truly tremendous **[2]** (*proper*), that's who.
You can see what **[3]** (*abstract*) he gives
The **[4]** (*collective*) of fans who hang on him
    like glue.

The walls of his gym on **[5]** (*proper*)
Are covered with **[6]** (*concrete*) that show
The muscled, tussled **[7]** (*common*) aplenty,
Who work out there, come rain or come snow.

Eduardo, **[8]** (*proper*), and I really enjoy
The **[9]** (*abstract*) of hanging on tight
Way above the **[10]** (*concrete*) and swinging,
Held up by the muscleman's might.

Jacob Lawrence, *Strong Man*. Gouache on paper, 22" x 17". Photo by Chris Eden, Francine Seders Gallery.

The Pronoun

11b. A *pronoun* is a word that is used in place of one or more nouns or pronouns.

EXAMPLES   Ask Dan if Dan has done Dan's homework.

Ask Dan if **he** has done **his** homework.

Both of Lois's friends said both would help Lois find Lois's missing books.

Both of Lois's friends said **they** would help **her** find **her** missing books.

The word or word group that a pronoun stands for (or refers to) is called its *antecedent.*

           antecedent   pronoun   pronoun
EXAMPLES   **Frederick,** have **you** turned in **your** report?

           antecedent   pronoun
           Walking the dog is fun, and **it** is good exercise.

Sometimes the antecedent is not stated.

EXAMPLES   **Who** asked that question?

I did not understand what **you** said.

Someone will have to clean up the mess.

Reference Note

For information about choosing **pronouns that agree with their antecedents,** see page 475.

Personal Pronouns

A *personal pronoun* refers to the one speaking (*first person*), the one spoken to (*second person*), or the one spoken about (*third person*).

Personal Pronouns		
	Singular	**Plural**
First Person	I, me, my, mine	we, us, our, ours
Second Person	you, your, yours	you, your, yours
Third Person	he, him, his, she, her, hers, it, its	they, them, their, theirs

┌─HELP─

Some authorities prefer to call possessive pronouns (such as *my, your,* and *their*) possessive adjectives. Follow your teacher's directions when you are labeling these words.

Reflexive and Intensive Pronouns

A *reflexive pronoun* refers to the subject and is necessary to the meaning of the sentence. An *intensive pronoun* emphasizes a noun or another pronoun and is unnecessary to the meaning of the sentence.

Reflexive and Intensive Pronouns	
First Person	myself, ourselves
Second Person	yourself, yourselves
Third Person	himself, herself, itself, themselves

REFLEXIVE   Tara enjoyed **herself** at the party.
             The team prided **themselves** on their victory.

INTENSIVE   I **myself** cooked that delicious dinner.
             Did you redecorate the room **yourself**?

TIPS & TRICKS

If you are not sure whether a pronoun is reflexive or intensive, use this test: Read the sentence aloud, omitting the pronoun. If the basic meaning of the sentence stays the same, the pronoun is intensive. If the meaning changes, the pronoun is reflexive.

EXAMPLES
The children amused **themselves** all morning. [Without *themselves*, the sentence doesn't make sense. The pronoun is reflexive.]

Mark repaired the car **himself.** [Without *himself*, the meaning stays the same. The pronoun is intensive.]

Demonstrative Pronouns

A *demonstrative pronoun* points out a person, a place, a thing, or an idea.

Demonstrative Pronouns			
this	that	these	those

EXAMPLES   **This** is the book I bought for my sister.

               Are **those** the kinds of plants that bloom at night?

NOTE *This, that, these,* and *those* can also be used as adjectives. When they are used in this way, they are called *demonstrative adjectives.*

DEMONSTRATIVE PRONOUN   **Those** are very sturdy shoes.
DEMONSTRATIVE ADJECTIVE   **Those** shoes are very sturdy.

DEMONSTRATIVE PRONOUN   Did you order **this**?
DEMONSTRATIVE ADJECTIVE   Did you order **this** salad?

Reference Note
For more about **demonstrative adjectives,** see page 348.

Interrogative Pronouns

An *interrogative pronoun* introduces a question.

Interrogative Pronouns				
what	which	who	whom	whose

EXAMPLES   **What** is the best brand of frozen yogurt?

                     Who wrote *Barrio Boy*?

Indefinite Pronouns

An *indefinite pronoun* refers to a person, a place, a thing, or an idea that may or may not be specifically named.

Common Indefinite Pronouns				
all	each	many	nobody	other
any	either	more	none	several
anyone	everything	most	no one	some
both	few	much	one	somebody

EXAMPLES   **Both** of the girls forgot their lines.

                     I would like **some** of that chow mein.

NOTE   Most indefinite pronouns can also be used as adjectives.

      PRONOUN   **Some** are bored by this movie.
      ADJECTIVE   **Some** people are bored by this movie.

Relative Pronouns

A *relative pronoun* introduces a subordinate clause.

Common Relative Pronouns				
that	which	who	whom	whose

EXAMPLES   Thomas Jefferson, **who** wrote the Declaration of Independence, was our country's third president.

                     Exercise is something **that** many people enjoy.

TIPS & TRICKS

The indefinite pronouns *some, any, none, all, more,* and *most* may be singular or plural. Look closely at any prepositional phrase that follows these pronouns. The object of the preposition determines whether the pronoun is singular or plural.

SINGULAR
None of the milk **is** sour. [*Milk* is singular.]

PLURAL
None of the grapes **are** sweet. [*Grapes* is plural.]

Reference Note

For information on **indefinite pronouns and subject-verb agreement,** see page 463.

Reference Note

For information on **subordinate clauses,** see page 424.

Exercise 6 Identifying Pronouns

Identify each pronoun in the following sentences. Then, tell what type of pronoun each one is.

EXAMPLES   **1.** The drama coach said he would postpone the rehearsal.

       1. he—personal

      2. Does Pamela, who is traveling to Thailand, have her passport and ticket?

      2. who—relative; her—personal

1. "I want you to study," Ms. Gaines said to the class.
2. The firefighter carefully adjusted her oxygen mask.
3. The children made lunch themselves.
4. Jenny and Rosa decided they would get popcorn, but Amy didn't want any.
5. Who will be the next president of the school board?
6. Mr. Yoshira, this is Mrs. Volt, a neighbor of yours.
7. Ralph Bunche, who was awarded the Nobel Peace Prize, was a diplomat for his country at the United Nations.
8. Of all United States Olympic victories, perhaps none were more satisfying than Jesse Owens's 1936 triumphs in the 200-meter dash and broad jump.
9. Oh, yes, the puppy taught itself how to open the gate.
10. Only one of seventy-five fine boys and girls will win the grand prize.

Exercise 7 Writing Appropriate Pronouns

Rewrite each sentence, replacing the repeated nouns with pronouns.

EXAMPLE   **1.** The boy forgot the boy's homework.

      1. The boy forgot his homework.

1. Put the flowers in water before the flowers' petals droop.
2. The canoe capsized as the canoe neared the shore.
3. The players convinced the players that the players would win the game.
4. Lorraine oiled the bicycle before Lorraine put the bicycle in the garage.
5. Tim said, "Tim answered all six questions on the quiz."
6. Ben folded the newspapers for Ms. Glinsmann, and then Ben stuffed the newspapers in plastic bags for Ms. Glinsmann.

┌HELP─

Some sentences in Exercise 6 have more than one pronoun.

GRAMMAR

7. Sarah, Keith, and I arrived early so that Sarah, Keith, and I could get good seats.

8. Her wheelchair was amazingly fast, and her wheelchair was lightweight, too.

9. Grandpa just graduated from college, and Grandpa is now working as a computer programmer.

10. Because Japan fascinates Ron and Ron's brother, this film will interest Ron and Ron's brother.

The Adjective

11c. An *adjective* is a word that is used to modify a noun or a pronoun.

COMPUTER TIP

Using a software program's thesaurus can help you choose appropriate adjectives. To make sure that an adjective has exactly the connotation you intend, check the word in a dictionary.

To *modify* a word means to describe the word or to make its meaning more definite. An adjective modifies a noun or a pronoun by telling *what kind*, *which one*, *how much*, or *how many*.

What Kind?	Which One or Ones?	How Much or How Many?
Korean children	**seventh** grade	**several** days
busy dentist	**these** countries	**five** dollars
braided hair	**any** book	**no** marbles

Sometimes an adjective comes after the word it modifies.

EXAMPLES   A woman, **kind** and **helpful,** gave us directions. [The adjectives *kind* and *helpful* modify *woman*.]

The box is **empty.** [The predicate adjective *empty* modifies *box*.]

Reference Note

For more about **predicate adjectives,** see page 393.

Articles

The most commonly used adjectives are *a, an,* and *the.* These adjectives are called **articles.** *A* and *an* are called **indefinite articles** because they refer to any member of a general group. *A* is used before a word beginning with a consonant sound. *An* is used before a word beginning with a vowel sound.

EXAMPLES   **A** frog croaked.

           An orange is **a** good source of vitamin C.

           My cousin Jimmy wears **a** uniform to school. [Even though *u* is a vowel, the word *uniform* begins with a consonant sound.]

           This is **an** honor. [Even though *h* is a consonant, the word *honor* begins with a vowel sound. The *h* is not pronounced.]

The is called the **definite article** because it refers to someone or something in particular.

EXAMPLES   **The** frog croaked.

           Where is **the** orange?

Nouns or Adjectives?

Many words that can stand alone as nouns can also be used as adjectives modifying nouns or pronouns.

Nouns	Adjectives
bean	**bean** soup
spring	**spring** weather
gold	**gold** coin
football	**football** game
Labor Day	**Labor Day** weekend
Super Bowl	**Super Bowl** party
Milan	**Milan** fashions
White House	**White House** security
Persian Gulf	**Persian Gulf** pearls

Reference Note

For more about **words used as different parts of speech,** see pages 351 and 379.

Demonstrative Adjectives

This, that, these, and *those* can be used both as adjectives and as pronouns. When they modify a noun or pronoun, they are called *demonstrative adjectives.* When they are used alone, they are called *demonstrative pronouns.*

Reference Note

For more about **demonstrative pronouns,** see page 343.

DEMONSTRATIVE ADJECTIVES	**This** drawing is mine, and **that** drawing is his. **These** soccer balls are much more expensive than **those** soccer balls are.
DEMONSTRATIVE PRONOUNS	**This** is mine and **that** is his. **These** are much more expensive than **those** are.

Exercise 8   Identifying Adjectives

Identify the adjectives in the following sentences, and give the noun or pronoun each modifies. Do not include the articles *a, an,* and *the.*

EXAMPLE   1. Why don't you take the local bus home from school on cold days?

　　　　　1. *local—bus; cold—days*

1. On winter afternoons, I sometimes walk home after band practice rather than ride on a crowded, noisy bus.
2. I hardly even notice the heavy traffic that streams past me on the street.
3. The wet sidewalk glistens in the bright lights from the windows of stores.
4. The stoplights throw green, yellow, and red splashes on the pavement.
5. After I turn the corner away from the busy avenue, I am on a quiet street, where a jolly snowman often stands next to one of the neighborhood houses.
6. At last, I reach my peaceful home.
7. There I am often greeted by my older brother, Kenny, and my sister, Natalie.
8. I know they are glad to see me.
9. Delicious smells come from the kitchen where Mom and Dad are cooking dinner.
10. This quiet, private walk always makes me feel a little tired but also happy.

Exercise 9 Writing Appropriate Adjectives

Complete the following story by writing an appropriate adjective to fill each blank.

EXAMPLES   **[1]** ____ parks have **[2]** ____ trails for hikers.
1. *Many*
2. *wooded*

The hikers went exploring in the **[1]** ____ forest. Sometimes they had difficulty getting through the **[2]** ____ undergrowth. On **[3]** ____ occasions they almost turned back. They kept going and were rewarded for their **[4]** ____ effort. During the **[5]** ____ hike through the woods, they discovered **[6]** ____ kinds of **[7]** ____ animals. In the afternoon the **[8]** ____ hikers pitched camp in a **[9]** ____ clearing. They were **[10]** ____ for supper and rest.

Proper Adjectives

A *proper adjective* is formed from a proper noun.

Proper Nouns	Proper Adjectives
Thanksgiving	**Thanksgiving** dinner
Catholicism	**Catholic** priest
Middle East	**Middle Eastern** country
Africa	**African** continent

Reference Note
For more about **capitalizing proper adjectives,** see page 584.

Notice that a proper adjective, like a proper noun, is capitalized. Common adjectives are generally not capitalized.

NOTE Some proper nouns, such as *Thanksgiving,* do not change spelling when they are used as adjectives.

Exercise 10 Identifying Common and Proper Adjectives

Identify the adjectives in the sentences on the next page. Then, tell whether each is a *common* or *proper* adjective. Do not include the articles *a, an,* and *the.*

EXAMPLE   1. We have been studying how various animals protect themselves.

        1. *various—common*

1. Many small animals defend themselves in unusual ways.
2. For example, South American armadillos wear suits of armor that consist of small, bony scales.
3. Armadillos seem delicate, with their narrow faces.
4. However, their tough armor protects them well.
5. Likewise, the Asian anteater has scales that overlap like the shingles on a roof.
6. Unlike anteaters, armadillos are a New World animal.
7. *Armadillo* is a Spanish word that can be translated as "little armor."
8. Texas and Florida residents as well as Mexican citizens are familiar with these shy creatures.
9. At early twilight, look for armadillos, energetic and ready for a meal of unlucky spiders or insects.
10. Like tortoises, armadillos can pull in their noses and all four of their feet for better protection.

┌HELP──
Use a dictionary to help you spell the adjectives in Exercise 11.

Exercise 11   Writing Proper Adjectives

Change the following proper nouns into proper adjectives.

EXAMPLE   1. Spain

        1. *Spanish*

1. Rome
2. Victoria
3. Memorial Day
4. Korea
5. Congress

6. New Year's Day
7. Inca
8. Shakespeare
9. Judaism
10. Celt

Review B   Identifying Nouns, Pronouns, and Adjectives

Identify each italicized word in the following paragraph as a *noun*, a *pronoun*, or an *adjective*.

EXAMPLE   Four [1] *forces* govern the flight of an aircraft.

        1. *noun*

Lift and thrust must overcome [**1**] *drag* and weight. If an airplane is very [**2**] *heavy,* it cannot lift off unless it has great thrust or speed. If the craft is slow, [**3**] *it* may not have enough thrust to achieve lift. By 1783, the [**4**] *French* Montgolfiers had learned how to beat gravity and achieve lift in their hot-air balloon. However, it had little thrust and didn't steer well. Nevertheless, [**5**] *Parisians* didn't mind the unpredictability. In fact, everybody [**6**] *who* was anybody wanted to hitch a ride on a balloon. With a rudder and propellers, airships (also known as blimps, dirigibles, and Zeppelins) achieved enough thrust to be steered but became unpopular after the [**7**] *Hindenburg* met [**8**] *its* fiery fate. Not until Orville and [**9**] *Wilbur Wright* put an engine on their famous craft and made its wings slightly [**10**] *movable* was the quest for thrust and lift achieved. As you know, the rest is history.

Determining Parts of Speech

Remember, the way a word is used in a sentence determines what part of speech it is. Some words may be used as nouns or as adjectives.

NOUN	The helmet is made of **steel.**
ADJECTIVE	It is a **steel** helmet.

Some words may be used as pronouns or as adjectives.

PRONOUN	**That** is a surprise.
ADJECTIVE	**That** problem is difficult.

Review C **Identifying Nouns, Pronouns, and Adjectives**

Identify the nouns, pronouns, and adjectives in the following sentences. Do not include the articles *a*, *an*, and *the*.

EXAMPLE   1. We walked along the empty beach at sundown.

1. *We—pronoun; empty—adjective; beach—noun; sundown—noun*

1. When the tide comes in, it brings a variety of interesting items from the sea.
2. When the tide ebbs, it leaves behind wonderful treasures for watchful beachcombers.
3. Few large creatures live here, but you almost certainly will find several small animals if you try.
4. Some live in shallow burrows under the wet sand and emerge in the cool evening to dine on bits of plants and other matter.
5. A number of different species of beetle like this part of the beach.
6. Around them you can find bristly flies and tiny worms.
7. You might also come across old pieces of wood with round holes and tunnels in them.
8. These holes are produced by shipworms.
9. If you watch the shoreline carefully, you will see many signs of life that casual strollers miss.
10. Low tide is a marvelous time to search along the shore.

"Now! ... *That* should clear up a few things around here!"

CHAPTER

GRAMMAR

Chapter Review

A. Identifying Types of Nouns

For each of the following sentences, identify the noun of the type indicated in parentheses. There may be more than one type of noun in the sentence.

1. No one understands why whales sometimes strand themselves. (*common*)
2. Since 1985, people in a group called Project Jonah have used an inflatable pontoon to rescue stranded whales and other marine mammals. (*proper*)
3. The people in Project Jonah find fulfillment in helping stranded mammals. (*abstract*)
4. More than two thousand marine mammals have been helped in recent years. (*concrete*)
5. The group has rescued mammals ranging in size from dolphins to whales. (*collective*)

B. Identifying Types of Pronouns

For each of the following sentences, identify the pronoun of the type indicated in parentheses. There may be more than one type of pronoun in the sentence.

6. Which of all the animals do you think has the worst reputation? (*interrogative*)
7. I believe the skunk is the animal that most people want to avoid. (*relative*)
8. The skunk can easily protect itself from others. (*reflexive*)
9. It can spray those nearby with a bad-smelling liquid. (*personal*)
10. This is a repellant that drives away predators. (*demonstrative*)
11. What do you think a skunk uses as its warning? (*interrogative*)
12. It warns possible predators by stamping its feet, which is intended to frighten the predator. (*relative*)
13. When the skunk needs to "attack" some other animal, it sprays in the direction of the victim. (*personal*)

14. Anyone who has ever been sprayed by a skunk will never forget the smell. (*indefinite*)
15. I myself would prefer never to upset a skunk. (*intensive*)

C. Identifying Adjectives

Identify the adjectives in each of the following sentences. Then, write the word the adjective modifies. Do not include the articles *a, an,* and *the.* A sentence may have more than one adjective.

16. Chapultepec is the name of a historic castle on a hill in Mexico City.
17. This word means "hill of the grasshopper" in the language of the early Aztecs.
18. Aztec emperors used the park area for hunting and relaxation.
19. In 1783, the hilltop was chosen as the location for the castle of the Spanish viceroy.
20. Even though the castle was never finished, it was used as a fortress during the colonial period of Mexican history.
21. After several decades of neglect, the unfinished castle became the home of the National Military Academy in 1842.
22. In 1847, during a war with the United States, this castle was captured by enemy troops.
23. The emperor of Mexico, Maximilian, converted the castle into an imperial residence.
24. After the downfall of Maximilian in 1867, it became the summer residence of Mexican presidents.
25. In 1937, the property was converted into a national museum.

D. Identifying Nouns, Pronouns, and Adjectives

The following paragraph contains twenty numbered, italicized words. Identify each italicized word as a *noun,* a *pronoun,* or an *adjective.*

In [26] *this* country [27] *mangroves* grow along the coasts of [28] *Florida.* [29] *They* form a [30] *wonderland* where land, water, and [31] *sky* blend. [32] *The* lush, green [33] *mangrove* islands and [34] *shoreline* are both beautiful and valuable. Mangroves are important to [35] *our* [36] *environment.* They produce [37] *tons* of valuable [38] *vegetable* matter and are an [39] *essential* part of [40] *tropical* biology. So far as [41] *we* know, the [42] *first* reference to mangroves dates back to [43] *Egyptian* times. A [44] *South African* expert has also discovered evidence of mangrove islands along the [45] *Red Sea.*

Writing Application
Using Pronouns in a Report

Clear Pronoun Reference Your class is creating a bulletin board display for the school's Special People Day. For the display, write a brief report about someone you think is special. Tell why you think so. Be sure that the pronouns you use refer clearly to their antecedents.

Prewriting First, you will need to select your subject. Make a list of the different people you know. Which of these people do you find really remarkable? After you choose a subject, jot down notes about this person. Tell what this person has done to earn your respect and admiration.

Writing As you write your first draft, refer to your notes. Your thesis statement should briefly state what is special about your subject. In the rest of your paragraphs, give specific examples that illustrate why the person is special.

Revising Now, read through your report and imagine that you do not know the subject. What do you think about him or her? Does the person sound special? If not, you may want to add or cut details or rearrange your report. Read your report aloud. Combine short, related sentences by inserting prepositional phrases or appositive phrases.

Reference Note
For more about **combining sentences,** see page 273.

Publishing Look closely at your use of pronouns. Be sure that each pronoun has a clear antecedent. You may need to correct some sentences to make the antecedents clear. You and your classmates may want to use your reports to make a classroom bulletin board display. If possible, include pictures or drawings of your subjects. You may also wish to send a copy of your report to the special person.

Parts of Speech Overview
Verb, Adverb, Preposition, Conjunction, Interjection

Diagnostic Preview

Identifying Verbs, Adverbs, Prepositions, Conjunctions, and Interjections

Identify each italicized word or word group in the following paragraphs as a *verb*, an *adverb*, a *preposition*, a *conjunction*, or an *interjection*.

EXAMPLES   Some [1] *very* unusual words [2] *are used* [3] *in* crossword puzzles.

    1. adverb
    2. verb
    3. preposition

The first crossword puzzle was published [1] *in* 1913. It [2] *appeared* on the Fun Page [3] *of* a New York City newspaper, [4] *and* readers [5] *immediately* [6] *asked* the editors [7] *for* more. [8] *Almost* every newspaper in the United States [9] *now* publishes a daily crossword puzzle.

Every day, millions of Americans [10] *faithfully* work crossword puzzles. Many people take puzzles [11] *quite* seriously. For many, solving puzzles [12] *is* a competitive game.

I [13] *do* puzzles [14] *strictly* for fun. Best of all, I can work on them [15] *by* myself. That way, no one knows whether I succeed [16] *or* fail. I [17] *occasionally* [18] *brag* about my successes. [19] "*Aha!*" I exclaim. "That was a tough one, [20] *but* I filled in every space."

The Verb

12a. A *verb* is a word that expresses action or a state of being.

EXAMPLES   We **celebrated** the Chinese New Year yesterday.

The holiday **is** usually in February.

NOTE In this book, verbs are classified as action or linking verbs, as helping or main verbs, and as transitive or intransitive verbs.

Action Verbs

12b. An *action verb* is a verb that expresses either physical or mental activity.

EXAMPLES   The owls **hooted** all night. [physical action]

Gloria **plays** volleyball. [physical action]

She **thought** about the problem. [mental action]

I **believe** you. [mental action]

NOTE Action verbs may be transitive or intransitive.

Reference Note

For more information about **transitive and intransitive verbs,** see page 364.

Exercise 1 Classifying Verbs

Tell whether each of the following action verbs expresses physical or mental action.

EXAMPLE   **1.** visualize

1. mental

1. pounce	**5.** rest	**9.** shout
2. consider	**6.** remember	**10.** nibble
3. wish	**7.** dash	
4. want	**8.** anticipate	

Exercise 2 Identifying Action Verbs

Identify each action verb in the following sentences.

EXAMPLE 1. I saw that movie last week.
        1. saw

┌HELP──
Sentences in
Exercise 2 may contain
more than one action verb.

1. For a science project, Elena built a sundial.
2. Mr. Santos carefully explained the word problem to each of the students.
3. I enjoy soccer more than any other sport.
4. This waterfall drops two hundred feet.
5. Mike's bicycle suddenly skidded and fell hard on the wet pavement.
6. Mrs. Karras showed us the way to Johnson City.
7. Mix the ingredients slowly.
8. The heavy traffic delayed us.
9. For the Jewish holiday of Purim, Rachel and her sister Elizabeth gave a party.
10. The early Aztecs worshiped the sun.

Linking Verbs

12c. A _linking verb_ is a verb that expresses a state of being. A linking verb connects, or links, the subject to a word or word group that identifies or describes the subject.

EXAMPLES Denzel Washington **is** an actor. [The verb _is_ connects _actor_ with the subject _Denzel Washington_.]

The children **remained** quiet. [The verb _remained_ links _quiet_ with the subject _children_.]

Reference Note
For more information about **transitive and intransitive verbs,** see page 364.

NOTE Linking verbs never have objects (words that tell who or what receives the action of the verb). Therefore, linking verbs are always intransitive.

Some Forms of the Verb _Be_			
am	were	will be	can be
is	has been	shall be	should be
are	have been	may be	would have been
was	had been	might be	

Other Linking Verbs			
appear	grow	seem	stay
become	look	smell	taste
feel	remain	sound	turn

NOTE *Be* is not always a linking verb. *Be* can express a state of being without having a complement (a word or word group that identifies or describes the subject). In the following sentences, forms of *be* are followed by words or word groups that tell *where*.

Reference Note

For information about **complements,** see Chapter 13.

EXAMPLES   We **will be** there.

The apples **are** in the bowl.

Some words may be either action verbs or linking verbs, depending on how they are used.

ACTION   Amy **looked** through the telescope.

LINKING   Amy **looked** pale. [The verb *looked* links *pale* with the subject *Amy.*]

ACTION   **Stay** in your seats until the bell rings.

LINKING   **Stay** calm. [The verb *stay* links *calm* with the understood subject *you.*]

Reference Note

For more about **understood subjects** in imperative sentences, see page 331.

Exercise 3   **Identifying Linking Verbs**

Identify the linking verb in each of the following sentences.

EXAMPLE   1. A radio station can be the voice of a community.

          1. *can be*

1. This is Roberto Martínez, your weather forecaster.
2. Unfortunately, the forecast looks bad today.
3. Outside the window here at Station WOLF, the skies appear cloudy.
4. It certainly felt rainy earlier this morning.
5. According to the latest information, it should be a damp, drizzly day with an 85 percent chance of rainfall.
6. Our sportscaster this morning is Marta Segal.
7. Things have been quiet here around Arlington for the past few days.

8. Stay alert for sports action tonight.
9. It should be an exciting game between our own Arlington Angels and the visiting Jackson City Dodgers.
10. The team looked great at practice today, and I predict a hometown victory.

Review A Identifying Action Verbs and Linking Verbs

Identify the verbs in the following sentences. Then, label each verb as either an *action verb* or a *linking verb*.

EXAMPLE 1. I always enjoy field trips.
1. enjoy—action verb

1. Last spring, our earth science class visited the Hayden Planetarium.
2. It is a wonderful place, full of amazing sights.
3. We wandered slowly through the various displays and saw a collection of fascinating exhibits.
4. One space vehicle seemed like something from a science fiction movie.
5. Another amazing and interesting display showed a thirty-four-ton meteorite.
6. When this meteorite fell to earth many years ago, it made a huge crater.
7. After a delicious lunch, we stayed for the show in the observatory.
8. As the room became darker, the picture of a galaxy appeared on the ceiling of the dome above us.
9. The lecturer said that the galaxy is so far away from here that its light reaches us centuries after its first appearance.
10. When we look at such stars, we actually see the ancient past!

Exercise 4 Identifying Action Verbs and Linking Verbs

Identify the verb in each of the following sentences. Then, label each verb as either an *action verb* or a *linking verb*. If the verb is a linking verb, give the words that it connects.

EXAMPLES 1. We sent our dog to obedience school.
1. *sent—action verb*

2. Some breeds are extremely nervous.
2. *are—linking verb; breeds, nervous*

1. Everyone felt sorry about the misunderstanding.
2. In daylight, we looked for the lost ring.
3. The temperature plunged to ten degrees below zero.
4. The local museum exhibited beautiful Inuit sculptures.
5. Loretta felt her way carefully through the dark, quiet room.
6. The city almost always smells musty after a heavy summer thunderstorm.
7. Dakar is the capital of Senegal.
8. The firefighter cautiously smelled the burned rags.
9. Antonia Novello was the first female surgeon general of the United States.
10. They looked handsome in their party clothes.

Helping Verbs and Main Verbs

12d. A *helping verb* (*auxiliary verb*) helps the main verb express action or a state of being.

EXAMPLES **can** speak   **has been** named

were sent   **should have been** caught

A *verb phrase* contains one main verb and one or more helping verbs.

EXAMPLES Many people in Africa **can speak** more than one language.

The packages **were sent** to 401 Maple Street.

Kansas **has been named** the Sunflower State.

The ball **should have been caught** by the nearest player.

Commonly Used Helping Verbs			
Forms of *Be*	am are be	been being is	was were
Forms of *Do*	do	does	did
Forms of *Have*	have	has	had
Other Helping Verbs	can could may	might must will	would shall should

Some verbs can be used as either helping verbs or main verbs.

HELPING VERB	**Do** you like green beans?
MAIN VERB	Did you **do** this math problem?

HELPING VERB	She **is** arriving at noon.
MAIN VERB	Her luggage **is** over there.

HELPING VERB	**Have** they arrived yet?
MAIN VERB	They **have** a dog.

HELPING VERB	Where **has** he gone?
MAIN VERB	He **has** his homework in his backpack.

Sometimes a verb phrase is interrupted by another part of speech. Often the interrupter is an adverb. In a question, however, the subject often interrupts the verb phrase.

EXAMPLES   Our school **has** always **held** a victory celebration when our team wins.

Did you **hear** Jimmy Smits's speech?

Should Anita **bring** her model airplane to class?

Ken **does** not [*or* **doesn**'t] **have** a new desk.

Notice in the last example that the adverb *not* [or its contraction *–n't*] is not included in the verb phrase.

Exercise 5 Identifying Verb Phrases and Helping Verbs

Identify the verb phrases in the following sentences. Underline the helping verbs.

EXAMPLE
1. You can recognize redwoods and sequoias by their bark.

1. *can recognize*

1. Have you ever visited Redwood National Park?
2. The giant trees there can be an awesome sight.
3. For centuries, these trees have been an important part of the environment of the northwest United States.
4. Surely, these rare trees must be saved for future generations.
5. More than 85 percent of the original redwood forest has been destroyed over the years.
6. Because of this destruction, the survival of the redwood forest is being threatened.
7. With proper planning years ago, more of the forest might already have been saved.
8. Unfortunately, redwood forests are still shrinking rapidly.
9. According to some scientists, redwood forests outside the park will disappear within our lifetime.
10. However, according to other experts, the redwood forests can still be saved!

Review B Identifying Action Verbs and Linking Verbs

Identify the verbs in the following sentences. Then, label each verb as an *action verb* or a *linking verb*.

EXAMPLE
1. Have you ever seen a play in Spanish?

1. *Have seen—action verb*

1. The Puerto Rican Traveling Theatre performs plays about Hispanic life in the United States.
2. Over the past twenty years, this group has grown into a famous Hispanic theater group.
3. Sometimes, a production has two casts—one that speaks in English and one that speaks in Spanish.
4. In this way, speakers of both languages can enjoy the play.
5. In recent years many young Hispanic playwrights, directors, and actors have begun their careers at the Traveling Theatre.

┌HELP─
Some sentences
in Review B contain more
than one verb. Also, be sure
to include all parts of each
verb phrase.

6. Some became well-known at the Puerto Rican Traveling Theatre and then moved on to Broadway or Hollywood.
7. Others remain happy at the Traveling Theatre, where they enjoy the warm, supportive atmosphere.
8. Each production by the Traveling Theatre has its own style.
9. Some shows are musicals, full of song and dance, while other plays seem more serious.
10. Light or serious, Puerto Rican Traveling Theatre productions present a lively picture of Hispanic life today.

Transitive and Intransitive Verbs

12e. A *transitive verb* is a verb that expresses an action directed toward a person, a place, a thing, or an idea.

With transitive verbs, the action passes from the doer—the subject—to the receiver of the action. Words that receive the action of a transitive verb are called *objects.*

Reference Note

For more about **objects** and their uses in **sentences,** see page 386.

EXAMPLES   Derrick **greeted** the visitors. [The action of the verb *greeted* is directed toward the object *visitors.*]

When **will** Felicia **paint** her room? [The action of the verb *will paint* is directed toward the object *room.*]

12f. An *intransitive verb* expresses action (or tells something about the subject) without the action passing to a receiver, or object.

EXAMPLES   The train **stopped.**

Last night we **ate** on the patio.

A verb may be transitive in one sentence and intransitive in another.

EXAMPLES   The children **play** checkers. [transitive]
The children **play** quietly. [intransitive]

Mr. Lopez **is baking** bread. [transitive]
Mr. Lopez **is baking** this afternoon. [intransitive]

Have Roland and Tracy **left** their coats? [transitive]
Have Roland and Tracy **left** yet? [intransitive]

Identifying Transitive and Intransitive Verbs

Identify the italicized verb in each of the following sentences as either *transitive* or *intransitive*.

EXAMPLE   1. She *runs* early in the morning.
          1. intransitive

1. If you do different kinds of exercises, you *are exercising* in the correct way.
2. When you exercise to improve endurance, flexibility, and strength, your body *develops*.
3. Aerobic exercise *builds* endurance and strengthens the heart and lungs.
4. When you *walk* quickly, you exercise aerobically.
5. Many active people in the United States *attend* classes in aerobics.
6. They *enjoy* the fun of exercising to popular music.
7. Exercises that *improve* flexibility require you to bend and stretch.
8. *Perform* these exercises slowly to gain the maximum benefit from them.
9. Through isometric and isotonic exercises, your muscle strength *increases*.
10. These exercises *contract* your muscles.

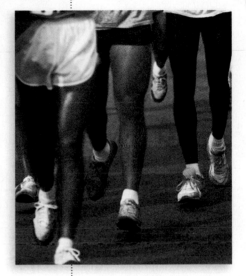

Writing Sentences with Transitive and Intransitive Verbs

For each verb given below, write two sentences. In one sentence, use the verb as a *transitive* verb and underline its object. In the other, use the verb as an *intransitive* verb. You may use different tenses of the verb.

EXAMPLE   1. write
          1. *Alex is writing a research <u>report</u>. (transitive)*
             Alex writes in his journal every day. (intransitive)

1. fly	5. drive	9. climb	13. turn	17. skip
2. leave	6. jump	10. watch	14. pay	18. read
3. return	7. hear	11. visit	15. row	19. help
4. draw	8. answer	12. shout	16. run	20. sing

The Adverb

12g. An *adverb* is a word that modifies a verb, an adjective, or another adverb.

Just as an adjective makes the meaning of a noun or a pronoun more definite, an adverb makes the meaning of a verb, an adjective, or another adverb more definite.

Adverbs answer the following questions:

> Where?   How often? *or* How long?
>
> When?   To what extent?
>
> How?   *or* How much?

EXAMPLES   The sprinter ran **swiftly.** [The adverb *swiftly* modifies the verb *ran* and tells *how.*]

I read the funny pages **early** on Sunday morning. [The adverb *early* modifies the verb *read* and tells *when.*]

Jolene was comforting a **very** small child. [The adverb *very* modifies the adjective *small* and tells *to what extent.*]

The fire blazed **too wildly** for anyone to enter. [The adverb *too* modifies the adverb *wildly* and tells *to what extent.* The adverb *wildly* modifies the verb *blazed* and tells *how.*]

Dad will **sometimes** quote from Archbishop Desmond Tutu's speech. [The adverb *sometimes* modifies the verb *will quote* and tells *how often.*]

Put the apples **there,** and we will eat them **later.** [The adverb *there* modifies the verb *put* and tells *where.* The adverb *later* modifies the verb *will eat* and tells *when.*]

Words Often Used as Adverbs	
Where?	away, here, inside, there, up
When?	later, now, soon, then, tomorrow
How?	clearly, easily, quietly, slowly

Words Often Used as Adverbs	
How often? or *How long?*	always, usually, continuously, never, forever, briefly
To what extent? or *How much?*	almost, so, too, more, least, extremely, quite, very, not

NOTE The word *not* is nearly always used as an adverb modifying a verb. When *not* is part of a contraction, as in *hadn't, aren't,* and *didn't,* the *–n't* is still an adverb and is not part of the verb.

Reference Note
For more about **contractions,** see page 641.

Adverb or Adjective?

Many adverbs end in *–ly*. These adverbs are generally formed by adding *–ly* to adjectives.

Adjective	+	–ly	=	Adverb
clear	+	–ly	=	clearly
quiet	+	–ly	=	quietly
convincing	+	–ly	=	convincingly

However, some words ending in *–ly* are used as adjectives.

Adjectives Ending in *–ly*		
daily	friendly	lonely
early	kindly	timely

NOTE The adverb *very* is often overused. In your writing, try to use adverbs other than *very* to modify adjectives. You can also revise sentences so that other words carry more of the descriptive meaning.

EXAMPLE Chloe is very tall.
REVISED Chloe is **amazingly** tall.

or

Chloe is **5'11"** tall and **is a guard on the varsity basketball team.**

TIPS & TRICKS

If you aren't sure whether a word is an adjective or an adverb, ask yourself what it modifies. If a word modifies a noun or a pronoun, it is an adjective.

EXAMPLE
She gave us a **friendly** hello. [*Friendly* modifies the noun *hello* and is used as an adjective.]

If a word modifies a verb, an adjective, or an adverb, then it is an adverb.

EXAMPLE
People from many nations have come to the United States **recently.** [The adverb *recently* modifies the verb *have come.*]

Reference Note
For more about **adjectives,** see page 346.

Exercise 8 Identifying Adverbs

Identify each adverb and the word or words it modifies in each of the following sentences.

EXAMPLE   1. Today, many Cherokee people make their homes in Oklahoma.

        1. *Today—make*

1. Oklahoma is not the Cherokees' original home.
2. The Cherokees once lived in Georgia, North Carolina, Alabama, and Tennessee.
3. A number of Cherokees still live in the Great Smoky Mountains of North Carolina.
4. Settlers often ignored the Cherokees' right to the land.
5. Feeling threatened by the settlers, the Cherokees readily supported the British during the Revolutionary War.
6. In 1829, people hurried excitedly to northern Georgia for the first gold rush in the United States.
7. Many white settlers of the region were extremely eager to find gold.
8. Later, the Cherokees were forced by the United States government to leave their land.
9. The Cherokee people were hardly given a chance to collect their belongings.
10. Many Cherokees will never forget the Trail of Tears, which led their ancestors to Oklahoma.

Statue of Cherokee mourning those who died on the Trail of Tears.

The Position of Adverbs

One of the characteristics of adverbs is that they may appear at various places in a sentence. Adverbs may come before, after, or between the words they modify.

EXAMPLES   We **often** study together.

           We study together **often.**

           Often we study together.

When an adverb modifies a verb phrase, it frequently comes in the middle of the phrase.

EXAMPLE   We have **often** studied together.

An adverb that introduces a question, however, appears at the beginning of a sentence.

EXAMPLES   **When** does your school start? [The adverb *When* modifies the verb phrase *does start*.]

How did you spend your vacation? [The adverb *How* modifies the verb phrase *did spend*.]

┌HELP┐
Some sentences in Exercise 9 contain more than one adverb.

Exercise 9 Identifying Adverbs

Identify the adverbs and the words they modify in the following sentences.

EXAMPLE   1. "To Build a Fire" is a dramatically suspenseful short story.

   1. *dramatically—suspenseful*

1. In this story, a nameless character goes outdoors on a terribly cold day in the Yukon.
2. Except for a dog, he is traveling completely alone.
3. Soon both the dog's muzzle and the man's beard are frosted with ice.
4. Along the way, the man accidentally falls into a stream.
5. Soaked and chilled, he desperately builds a fire under a tree.
6. The flames slowly grow stronger.
7. Unfortunately, he has built his fire in the wrong place.
8. A pile of snow suddenly falls from a tree limb and kills the small fire.
9. Unable to relight the fire, the man again finds himself in serious trouble.
10. Based on what you now know about the story, what kind of ending would you write for "To Build a Fire"?

Link to   Literature

Exercise 10 Writing Adverbs

Write ten different adverbs to fill the blanks in the following sentences.

EXAMPLE   I have **[1]** _____ been a music lover.

   1. *always*

Every Friday I **[1]** _____ go to the record store. I can **[2]** _____ wait to see what new cassettes and CDs have arrived. As soon as school is out, I bicycle [3] _____ to the store and join the other [4] _____ enthusiastic customers. [5] _____ I stroll through the aisles and [6] _____ study the selections. I listen [7] _____ as the loudspeaker announces the day's specials. When I have decided what I want, I [8] _____ figure out which items I can afford. Then I walk [9] _____ to the cash register. I grin [10] _____ as I think of how much I will enjoy the music.

The Preposition

12h. A *preposition* is a word that shows the relationship of a noun or pronoun to another word.

Notice how changing the preposition in these sentences changes the relationship of *walked* to *door* and *kite* to *tree*.

> The cat walked **through** the door.
> The cat walked **toward** the door.
> The cat walked **past** the door.

> The kite **in** the tree is mine.
> The kite **beside** the tree is mine.
> The kite **in front of** the tree is mine. [Notice that a preposition may be made up of more than one word. Such a preposition is called a *compound preposition*.]

Commonly Used Prepositions				
aboard	before	for	off	toward
about	behind	from	on	under
above	below	in	out	underneath
across	beneath	in front of	out of	unlike
after	beside	inside	over	until
against	between	instead	past	up
along	beyond	into	since	up to
among	by	like	through	upon
around	down	near	throughout	with
as	during	next to	till	within
at	except	of	to	without

Exercise 11 **Writing Prepositions**

Write two prepositions for each blank in the following sentences. Be prepared to tell how the meanings of the two resulting sentences differ.

EXAMPLE   1. The car raced _____ the highway.
                1. *along, across*

1. We practiced karate _____ dinner.
2. She jumped up and ran _____ the park.
3. A boat with red sails sailed _____ the river.
4. The hungry dog crawled _____ the fence.
5. The marathon runner jogged easily _____ the track at the stadium.
6. Put the speakers _____ the stage, Cody.
7. Brightly colored confetti streamed _____ the piñata when it burst open.
8. Why does Roseanne always sit _____ the door?
9. Excuse me, but the blue fountain pen _____ your chair is mine, I believe.
10. Parrots _____ the South American jungle squawked all through the hot afternoon.

The Prepositional Phrase

A *prepositional phrase* includes a preposition, a noun or pronoun called the *object of the preposition,* and any modifiers of that object.

EXAMPLES   You can press those leaves **under glass.** [The noun *glass* is the object of the preposition *under.*]

Fred stood **in front of us.** [The pronoun *us* is the object of the compound preposition *in front of.*]

The books **in my new pack** are heavy. [The noun *pack* is the object of the preposition *in.* The words *my* and *new* modify *pack.*]

A preposition may have more than one object.

EXAMPLES   Thelma's telegram to **Nina** and **Ralph** contained good news. [The preposition *to* relates its objects, *Nina* and *Ralph,* to *telegram.*]

┌HELP┐
In the example for Exercise 11, the car was on the highway. In the second sentence, the car crossed the highway.

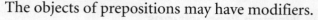

The objects of prepositions may have modifiers.

EXAMPLE   It happened during **the last** examination. [*The* and *last* are adjectives modifying *examination,* which is the object of the preposition *during.*]

Reference Note
For more about **infinitives,** see page 414.

NOTE   Be careful not to confuse a prepositional phrase beginning with *to* (*to the park, to him*) with an infinitive beginning with *to* (*to sing, to be heard*).

┌HELP─

Some sentences in Exercise 12 contain more than one prepositional phrase.

Exercise 12   Identifying Prepositional Phrases

Identify the prepositional phrases in the following sentences. Underline the preposition once and its object twice.

EXAMPLES   1. Commander Robert Peary claimed that he reached the North Pole in 1909.
   1. *in 1909*

   2. Peary and Matthew Henson searched for the North Pole for many years.
   2. *for the North Pole, for many years*

1. Henson traveled with Peary on every expedition except the first one.
2. However, for a long time, Henson received no credit at all for his role.
3. Peary had hired Henson as an assistant on a trip Peary made to Nicaragua.
4. There, Peary discovered that Henson had sailing experience and could also chart a path through the jungle.
5. As a result, Peary asked Henson to join his Arctic expedition shown in the photograph on this page.
6. The two explorers became friends during their travels in the North.
7. On the last three miles to the North Pole, Henson did not go with Peary.
8. Because he was the leader of the trip, Peary received the credit for the achievement.
9. Finally, after many years, Henson was honored by Congress, Maryland's state government, and two U.S. presidents.
10. Both Peary and Henson wrote books about their experiences.

Preposition or Adverb?

Some words may be used either as prepositions or as adverbs. Remember that a preposition always has an object. An adverb never does. If you can't tell whether a word is used as an adverb or a preposition, look for an object.

ADVERB   I haven't seen him **since.**

PREPOSITION   I haven't seen him **since** Thursday. [*Thursday* is the object of the preposition *since.*]

ADVERBS   The bear walked **around** and then went **inside.**

PREPOSITIONS   The bear walked **around** the yard and then went **inside** the cabin. [*Yard* is the object of the preposition *around. Cabin* is the object of *inside.*]

┌ **TIPS** & **TRICKS** ┐

When you are looking for the object of a preposition, be careful. Sometimes the object comes before, not after, the preposition.

EXAMPLES
Here is the CD **that** I was looking for yesterday. [*That* is the object of the preposition *for.*]

She is the speaker **whom** we enjoyed listening to so much. [*Whom* is the object of the preposition *to.*]

GRAMMAR

Exercise 13   Identifying Adverbs and Prepositions

Identify the italicized word in each of the following sentences as either an *adverb* or a *preposition.*

EXAMPLE   1. He watches uneasily as the hunter slowly brings the pistol *up.*

     1. *up—adverb*

1. "The Most Dangerous Game" is the story of Rainsford, a famous hunter who falls *off* a boat and comes ashore on a strange island.
2. Rainsford knows that this island is feared by every sailor who passes *by.*
3. In fact, *among* sailors, the place is known as Ship-Trap Island.
4. After looking *around* for several hours, Rainsford can't understand why the island is considered so dangerous.
5. Finally, he discovers a big house *on* a high bluff.
6. A man with a pistol *in* his hand answers the door.
7. Putting his pistol *down,* the man introduces Rainsford to the famous hunter General Zaroff.
8. Zaroff invites Rainsford *inside.*
9. Soon, however, Rainsford wishes he could get *out* and never see Zaroff again.
10. Rainsford has finally discovered the secret *about* the island—Zaroff likes to hunt human beings!

┌ Link to   Literature ┐

STYLE **TIP**

The conjunction *so* is often overused. In your writing, revise sentences as needed to avoid overusing *so*.

EXAMPLE
Traffic is bad, so we'll probably be late.

REVISED
Because traffic is bad, we'll probably be late.

TIPS & TRICKS

You can remember the seven coordinating conjunctions as FANBOYS:

For
And
Nor
But
Or
Yet
So

Reference Note

For more about **using commas between independent clauses**, see page 605.

The Conjunction

12i. A *conjunction* is a word that joins words or word groups.

(1) *Coordinating conjunctions* join words or word groups that are used in the same way.

Coordinating Conjunctions						
and	but	for	nor	or	so	yet

EXAMPLES   Jill **or** Anna [*Or* joins two nouns.]

strict **but** fair [*But* joins two adjectives.]

over the river **and** through the woods [*And* joins two prepositional phrases.]

Alice Walker wrote the book, **yet** she did not write the movie script. [*Yet* joins two independent clauses.]

The word *for* may be used either as a conjunction or as a preposition. When *for* joins word groups that are independent clauses, it is used as a conjunction. Otherwise, it is used as a preposition.

CONJUNCTION   He waited patiently, **for** he knew his ride would be along soon.

PREPOSITION   He waited patiently **for** his ride.

NOTE   Coordinating conjunctions that join independent clauses are almost always preceded by a comma. When *for* is used as a conjunction, there should always be a comma in front of it.

EXAMPLES   She has read the book, **but** she has not seen the movie.

We can bathe the dog, **or** you can do it when you get home from school.

Did Nazir call her, **and** has she called him back?

We asked Jim to be on time, **yet** he isn't here.

I'll be home late, **for** I have basketball practice until 4:30 or 5:00 today.

(2) Correlative conjunctions are pairs of conjunctions that join words or word groups that are used in the same way.

Correlative Conjunctions	
both . . . . and	not only . . . . . . but also
either . . . . or	whether . . . . or
neither . . . . . . nor	

EXAMPLES **Both** Bill Russell **and** Larry Bird played for the team. [The pair of conjunctions joins two nouns.]

She looked **neither** to the left **nor** to the right. [The pair of conjunctions joins two prepositional phrases.]

Not only did Wilma Rudolph overcome her illness, **but** she **also** became an Olympic athlete. [The pair of conjunctions joins two independent clauses.]

NOTE A third kind of conjunction—the **subordinating conjunction**—introduces an adverb clause.

EXAMPLES Meet me in the park **after** the bell chimes.

Before I washed the dishes, I let them soak in the sudsy water.

Reference Note

For more information about **subordinating conjunctions,** see page 431. For more on **adverb clauses,** see page 430.

Exercise 14 Identifying Conjunctions

Identify the conjunction or conjunctions in each of the following sentences. Be prepared to tell what words or word groups each conjunction or pair of conjunctions joins.

EXAMPLE 1. Both she and her mother enjoy sailing.

1. *Both . . . and*

┌HELP┐

In the example in Exercise 14, the conjunction joins *she* and *her mother*.

1. I wanted to see Los Lobos in concert, but I didn't have the money.
2. Our class is recycling not only newspapers but also glass bottles and aluminum cans.
3. He set the table with chopsticks and rice bowls.
4. Have you seen either LeAnn Rimes or Janet Jackson in person?

5. We learned to use neither too many adjectives nor too few.
6. That diet is dangerous, for it does not adequately meet the body's needs.
7. Both the Mohawk and the Oneida are part of the famous Iroquois Confederacy.
8. It rained all day, yet we enjoyed the trip.
9. Shall we walk home or take the bus?
10. Revise your paper, and proofread it carefully.

Exercise 15 Writing Conjunctions

Provide an appropriate conjunction for each blank in the following sentences.

EXAMPLES
    1. ____ solve the problem yourself, ____ ask your teacher for help.
    1. *Either . . . or*

    2. Would she prefer juice ____ iced tea?
    2. *or*

1. We will visit ____ the Johnson Space Center ____ Astroworld in Houston, Texas.
2. Alaska ____ Hawaii were the last two states admitted to the Union.
3. Those two students are twin sisters, ____ they do not dress alike.
4. They were ____ hungry ____ thirsty.
5. ____ turn that radio down, ____ take it into your room while I'm studying.
6. These nails aren't long enough, ____ I'm going to buy some others.
7. You could put the chair in the living room, in your bedroom, ____ even in the dining room.
8. Their weather forecaster isn't sure ____ it will rain ____ not.
9. In the delicate ecosystem of the river, ____ motorboats ____ personal watercraft are allowed.
10. His bike is old, ____ it takes him anywhere he needs to go.

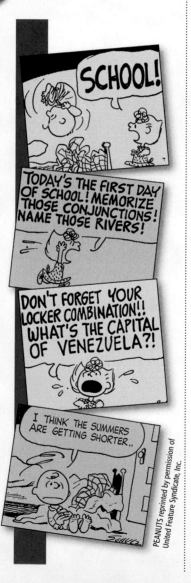

PEANUTS reprinted by permission of United Feature Syndicate, Inc.

Exercise 16 **Writing Sentences with Conjunctions**

Follow the directions given below to write sentences using conjunctions.

| EXAMPLE | **1.** Use *and* to join two verbs. |
| | **1.** *Jessye Norman smiled at the audience and bowed.* |

1. Use *and* to join two adverbs.
2. Use *or* to join two prepositional phrases.
3. Use *for* to join word groups that are sentences.
4. Use *but* to join two linking verbs.
5. Use *either . . . or* in an imperative sentence.
6. Use *or* to join two nouns.
7. Use *both . . . and* to join two subjects.
8. Use *neither . . . nor* to join two adverbs.
9. Use *yet* to join two adjectives.
10. Use *whether . . . or* in an interrogative sentence.

The Interjection

12j. An *interjection* is a word that expresses emotion.

Commonly Used Interjections			
aha	my	ouch	wow
hey	oh	rats	yikes
hurray	oops	well	yippee

An interjection has no grammatical relationship to the rest of the sentence.

Usually an interjection is followed by an exclamation point.

EXAMPLES	**Ouch!** That hurts!
	Goodness! What a haircut!
	Aha! I know the answer.

Sometimes an interjection is set off by a comma.

| EXAMPLES | **Oh,** I wish it were Friday. |
| | **Well,** what have you been doing? |

Exercise 17 Writing Interjections

Choose an appropriate interjection for each blank in the following sentences. Use a variety of interjections.

EXAMPLE   1. _____ , I'd love to go to your party.

    1. Hey, I'd love to go to your party.

1. _____! The heel just fell off my shoe.
2. There's, _____, about seven dollars in the piggy bank.
3. _____, finally we're finished raking those leaves.
4. _____! You squirrels, stop eating the birds' food!
5. Young Eric, _____, you certainly have grown!
6. _____! I sprained my ankle during the obstacle course!
7. Weren't the special effects in the movie amazing? _____!
8. _____, there's only one round left in the tournament.
9. _____! I knew you were planning a surprise!
10. _____, what a relief it is to have that term paper finished.

Review C Identifying Parts of Speech

Label each italicized word or word group in the following sentences as a *verb*, an *adverb*, a *preposition*, a *conjunction*, or an *interjection*.

EXAMPLE   1. *Both* otters *and* owls hunt *from* dusk to dawn.

    1. Both . . . and—conjunction; from—preposition

1. *Oh!* I *just* spilled tomato soup on the new white tablecloth!
2. Luis Alvarez *closely* studied atomic particles *for* many years.
3. *Did* Toni Morrison *or* Toni Cade Bambara write the book that you are reading?
4. The Inuit hunters *ate* their meal *inside* the igloo.
5. They were tired, *yet* they did *not* quit working.
6. I *like* Persian carpets, *for* they are beautiful and wear well.
7. The plane from Venezuela *nears* the terminal and taxis *down* the runway.
8. *Either* geraniums *or* daisies would grow *well* in that sunny corner of the garden.
9. Put your pencils *down,* class, *during* the instructions for this test.
10. Computers and, *oh,* all that electronic stuff seem *so* easy for you, Brittany.

Determining Parts of Speech

12k. The way a word is used in a sentence determines what part of speech it is.

The same word may be used as different parts of speech.

NOUN	The **play** had a happy ending.
VERB	The actors **play** their roles.

NOUN	The **outside** of the house needs paint.
ADVERB	Let's go **outside** for a while.
PREPOSITION	I saw the birds' nest **outside** my window.

NOUN	The **well** has run dry.
ADVERB	Did you do **well** on the quiz?
ADJECTIVE	I don't feel **well** today.
INTERJECTION	**Well,** that's a relief.

Review D Identifying Verbs, Adverbs, Prepositions, Conjunctions, and Interjections

For each of the following sentences, identify the italicized, numbered word or word group as a *verb*, an *adverb*, a *preposition*, a *conjunction*, or an *interjection*.

EXAMPLE **[1]** *Hey,* I recognize that place!
1. *interjection*

Though you might recognize the scene at right from the movies, it is **[1]** *not* a fake movie set. Khasneh al Faroun, or the "Pharaoh's Treasury," is the name of this magnificent structure, and it is **[2]** *quite* real. Located south of Jerusalem **[3]** *and* west of the Jordan River, the Pharaoh's Treasury is one of many sites in the ancient city of Petra. The word *Petra* **[4]** *means* "rock," and the city is carved out of solid sandstone. Petra served as a busy center of trade, and thousands of people strolled its streets **[5]** *or* sat in its outdoor theater. The theater seats **[6]** *about* four thousand people and is so old that the Romans had to repair it in A.D. 106. After a short occupation by Crusaders, the city was forbidden to Europeans **[7]** *for* about seven hundred years.

[8] *Well,* you're probably wondering about the "treasury" part of the name. For many years, the large urn atop the dome over the statue [9] *was believed* to be full of gold. However, as Bedouin treasure hunters [10] *discovered* long ago, the urn is just rock.

Review E Writing Sentences

Write ten sentences, following the directions given below. Underline the given word in each sentence, and identify how it is used.

EXAMPLE   1. Use *yet* as an adverb and as a conjunction.

1. Are we there <u>yet</u>?—adverb

   The sky grew somewhat brighter, <u>yet</u> the rain continued falling.—conjunction

1. Use *walk* as a verb and as a noun.
2. Use *like* as a preposition and as a verb.
3. Use *well* as a noun and as an adjective.
4. Use *inside* as an adverb and as a preposition.
5. Use *fast* as an adjective and as an adverb.

Chapter Review

A. Identifying Types of Verbs

Identify each italicized verb in the following sentences as a *linking verb*, a *transitive action verb*, or an *intransitive action verb*.

1. A land survey *is* a method of measuring land.
2. When he was cutting lumber, my father *used* a table saw.
3. Each concert in the series *was* an hour long.
4. The water *became* ice when the temperature dropped.
5. *Hang* the banner from the ceiling.
6. The astronomer *calculated* the distance to the galaxy.
7. Mr. Lurie and Ms. Modeski *walked* hand in hand.
8. The cook *multiplied* the ingredients of the stew by three.
9. Substitute teachers *work* hard!
10. *Are* they weary at the end of the day?

B. Identifying Verb Phrases

Identify the verb phrase in each of the following sentences, and underline the helping verb.

11. Have you ever heard of a mongoose?
12. Do these small carnivores inhabit parts of Africa and Asia?
13. In captivity they have lived for more than twenty years.
14. They will attack even the largest snakes.
15. The mongoose was made famous by a Rudyard Kipling story.

┌HELP┐
There may be
more than one adverb
in each sentence in
Chapter Review C.

C. Identifying Adverbs

Identify the adverb in each of the following sentences. Then, write the word it modifies.

16. The lonely boy looked longingly across the street.
17. "I'm going there after I've graduated," Rochelle said decisively, as she pointed to a map of Malaysia.
18. It is always easier for a child than for an adult to learn a second language.

19. I unfailingly read the newspaper at breakfast.

20. Did Joni remember the details of the accident later?

D. Identifying Prepositions and Prepositional Phrases

Identify the prepositional phrases in each of the following sentences. Underline the preposition once and its object twice. A sentence may have more than one prepositional phrase.

21. Will I find the broom beside the refrigerator?

22. My cat Sam likes to sit upon the television.

23. Mr. Takei used tofu in the recipe instead of chicken.

24. My mom gets upset when people talk throughout the film.

25. During the storm the windowpane streamed with rain.

E. Identifying Conjunctions

Identify the conjunctions in each of the following sentences.

26. Are you coming to the party, or are you staying home?

27. Not only did he produce the film, but he also wrote it.

28. I didn't finish the *Odyssey*, but I enjoyed what I did read.

29. We will have beans and rice for dinner.

30. Both Taj Mahal and B.B. King performed at the blues festival.

F. Identifying Verbs, Adverbs, Prepositions, Conjunctions, and Interjections

The following paragraphs contain twenty numbered, italicized words and word groups. Identify each of these italicized words as a *verb*, an *adverb*, a *preposition*, a *conjunction*, or an *interjection*.

Have you ever [31] *hiked* into the wilderness [32] *with* a pack on your back? Have you ever [33] *camped* under the stars? Backpacking [34] *was* once popular only with mountaineers, [35] *but* now almost anyone who loves the outdoors [36] *can become* a backpacker.

First, however, you [37] *must be* able to carry a heavy pack long distances [38] *over* mountain trails. To get in shape, start with short walks and [39] *gradually* increase them to several miles. Exercising [40] *and* going on practice hikes can [41] *fur-ther* build your strength. [42] *After* a few short hikes, you [43] *should* be ready for a longer one.

[44] *Oh,* you [45] *may be thinking,* what equipment and food should I take? Write [46] *to* the International Backpackers Association [47] *for* a checklist. The first item on the list will [48] *usually* be shoes with rubber [49] *or* synthetic soles. The second item on the list will [50] *certainly* be a sturdy backpack.

Writing Application
Using Prepositions in Directions

Prepositional Phrases   Your class has decided to provide a "how-to" manual for seventh-graders. The manual will have chapters on crafts and hobbies, personal skills, school skills, and other topics. Write an entry for the manual, telling someone how to do a particular activity. In your entry, be sure to use preposi-tional phrases to make your directions clear and complete. Underline the prepositional phrases that you use.

Prewriting   First, picture yourself doing the activity you are describing. As you imagine doing the activity, jot down each step. Then, put each step in the order it is done.

Writing   Refer to your prewriting notes as you write your first draft. You may find it necessary to add or rearrange steps to make your directions clear and complete.

Revising   Ask a friend or a classmate to read your paragraph. Then, have your reader repeat the directions in his or her own words. If any part of the directions is unclear, revise your work. Make sure you have used prepositional phrases correctly.

Publishing   Read your entry again to check your spelling, grammar, and punctuation. You may want to share your how-to hints with other students.

Reference Note

See page 540 for more about the **correct placement of phrase modifiers.**

13

Complements
Direct and Indirect Objects, Subject Complements

Diagnostic Preview

Identifying Complements

Identify the complement or complements in each of the following sentences. Then, label each complement as a *direct object*, an *indirect object*, a *predicate nominative*, or a *predicate adjective*.

EXAMPLE   1. A respirator pumps oxygen into the lungs.
            1. *oxygen—direct object*

1. Our cat avoids skunks and raccoons.
2. Jim Thorpe was an American Indian athlete.
3. The teacher showed us a film about the Revolutionary War.
4. The television commercials for that new product sound silly.
5. Who put the tangerines in that basket?
6. I sent my grandparents a gift for their anniversary.
7. During her interview on television, Zina Garrison-Jackson appeared relaxed and confident.
8. At first the colt seemed frightened.
9. Mrs. Constantine offered us olives and stuffed grape leaves.
10. The DJ played songs by Will Smith, Shania Twain, and Paula Cole.
11. The newspaper story prompted an investigation by the mayor's office.
12. My sister has become a computer-repair technician.
13. Write your name and address on the envelope.

14. The weather forecasters haven't issued a tornado warning.
15. Before long, the mistake became obvious to nearly everyone.
16. The sky looked gray and stormy.
17. The Irish poet Seamus Heaney won the Nobel Prize in literature in 1995.
18. The consumer group wrote the senator a letter about this type of airbag.
19. *Red Azalea* is the autobiography of Anchee Min.
20. The presidential candidate and his running-mate seem ambitious and sincere.

Recognizing Complements

13a. A *complement* is a word or word group that completes the meaning of a verb.

Every sentence has a subject and a verb. In addition, the verb often needs a complement to complete its meaning. A complement may be a noun, a pronoun, or an adjective.

	S V	
INCOMPLETE	Dr. Charles Drew made [what?]	

	S V C
COMPLETE	Dr. Charles Drew made **advances** in the study of blood plasma.

	S V
INCOMPLETE	Medical societies honored [whom?]

	S V C
COMPLETE	Medical societies honored **him.**

	S V
INCOMPLETE	Dr. Drew's research was [what?]

	S V C
COMPLETE	Dr. Drew's research was **important.**

An adverb is never a complement.

ADVERB	The package is **here.** [*Here* modifies the verb *is* by telling where the package is.]
COMPLEMENT	The package is **heavy.** [The adjective *heavy* modifies the subject *package* by telling what kind of package.]

Reference Note

For information on **adverbs,** see page 366.

Reference Note

For information on **prepositional phrases,** see page 371.

A complement is never in a prepositional phrase.

PREPOSITIONAL PHRASE	Erin is painting **in the garage.** [The prepositional phrase *in the garage* is an adverb phrase telling where Erin is painting.]
COMPLEMENT	Erin is painting her **room.** [The noun *room* completes the verb by telling what she is painting.]

Direct Objects

13b. A *direct object* is a noun, pronoun, or word group that tells *who* or *what* receives the action of the verb.

A direct object answers the question *Whom?* or *What?* after a transitive verb.

Reference Note

For information on **transitive verbs,** see page 364.

EXAMPLES   I met **Dr. Mason.** [I met *whom*? I met *Dr. Mason. Dr. Mason* receives the action of the verb *met.*]

Did Bill hit a **home run**? [Bill did hit *what*? Bill did hit a *home run. Home run* receives the action of the verb *hit.*]

Please buy **fruit, bread,** and **milk.** [Please buy *what*? Please buy *fruit, bread,* and *milk. Fruit, bread,* and *milk* receive the action of the verb *buy.*]

My uncle repairs **engines** and sells **them.** [My uncle repairs *what*? My uncle repairs *engines. Engines* receives the action of the verb *repairs.* My uncle sells *what*? He sells *them. Them* receives the action of the verb *sells.*]

Because a linking verb does not express action, it cannot have a direct object.

Reference Note

For information on **linking verbs,** see page 358.

LINKING VERB   Augusta Savage **was** a sculptor during the Harlem Renaissance. [The verb *was* does not express action; therefore, it has no direct object.]

A direct object is never in a prepositional phrase.

PREPOSITIONAL PHRASE	She worked **with clay.** [*Clay* is not the direct object of the verb *worked*; it is the object of the preposition *with.*]
DIRECT OBJECT	She worked the **clay** with her hands. [She worked *what*? She worked the *clay. Clay* receives the action of the verb *worked.*]

A direct object may be a compound of two or more objects.

EXAMPLE   We bought **ribbon, wrapping paper,** and **tape.** [The compound direct object *ribbon, wrapping paper,* and *tape* receives the action of the verb *bought.*]

Exercise 1   Identifying Direct Objects

Identify the direct object in each of the following sentences.

EXAMPLE   1. Many sports test an athlete's speed and agility.
           1. *speed, agility*

1. Long-distance, or marathon, swimming requires strength and endurance.
2. A swimmer in training may swim five or six miles every day.
3. Marathon swimmers smear grease on their legs and arms for protection against the cold water.
4. During a marathon, some swimmers may lose several pounds.
5. Fatigue, pain, and huge waves challenge marathon swimmers.
6. As they swim, they endure extreme isolation from the rest of the world.
7. Toward the end of the marathon, swimmers hear the loud applause and shouts of encouragement from their fans.
8. Spectators generally watch only the finish of a marathon.
9. Nevertheless, they know the long distance traveled by the accomplished athletes.
10. Emerging from the cold water, the exhausted swimmers have successfully completed another marathon.

HELP

In Exercise 1, direct objects may be compound.

Exercise 2 ▸ Identifying Direct Objects

Identify the direct object in each of the following sentences. If a sentence does not contain a direct object, write *no direct object.*

EXAMPLES   1. Have you ever flown a hang glider?
         1. *hang glider*

         2. Hang gliding has become a popular sport.
         2. *no direct object*

1. Many adventurous people enjoy the thrill of gliding through the air.
2. As you can see, a hang glider can carry a full-grown person in its harness.
3. The hang glider has a lightweight sail with a triangular control bar underneath.
4. At takeoff, the pilot lifts the glider shoulder-high and runs hard down a slope into the wind.
5. The wind lifts the hang glider and the pilot off the ground.
6. Because of wind currents, takeoffs from a hilltop or a cliff are the easiest.
7. Once airborne, the glider pilot directs the path of flight.
8. He or she also controls the glider's speed by either pushing or pulling on the control bar.
9. For example, a gentle pull increases speed.
10. To land, the pilot stalls the glider near the ground and drops lightly to his or her feet.

Indirect Objects

13c. An *indirect object* is a noun, pronoun, or word group that sometimes appears in sentences containing direct objects.

Indirect objects tell *to whom* or *to what,* or *for whom* or *for what,* the action of the verb is done. If a sentence has an indirect object, it always has a direct object also.

EXAMPLES   The waiter gave **her** the bill. [The pronoun *her* is the indirect object of the verb *gave.* It answers the question "To whom did the waiter give the bill?"]

Pam left the **waiter** a tip. [The noun *waiter* is the indirect object of the verb *left*. It answers the question "For whom did she leave a tip?"]

Did she tip **him** five dollars? [The pronoun *him* is the indirect object of the verb *Did tip*. It answers the question "For whom did she tip five dollars?"]

If the word *to* or *for* is used, the noun or pronoun following it is part of a prepositional phrase and cannot be an indirect object.

Reference Note

For information on **prepositional phrases** and **objects of prepositions,** see page 371.

OBJECTS OF PREPOSITIONS

The ship's captain gave orders to the **crew.**

Vinnie made some lasagna for **us.**

INDIRECT OBJECTS

The ship's captain gave the **crew** orders.

Vinnie made **us** some lasagna.

Like a direct object, an indirect object can be a compound of two or more objects.

EXAMPLE   Felicia threw **David, Jane,** and **Paula** slow curveballs. [The compound indirect object *David, Jane,* and *Paula* tells to whom Felicia threw curveballs.]

MOTHER GOOSE & GRIMM © Tribune Media Services, Inc. All rights reserved. Reprinted with permission.

Exercise 3 Identifying Direct Objects and Indirect Objects

Identify and label the direct objects and the indirect objects in the following sentences. Make sure that you include all parts of compound objects.

EXAMPLE   1. Did you buy Mom a calculator for her birthday?
           1. *Mom—indirect object; calculator—direct object*

1. The usher found us seats near the stage.
2. I'll gladly lend you my new Garth Brooks CD.

HELP

In Exercise 3, you may find it easier to identify the direct object first and then to look for the indirect object.

3. The Nobel Foundation awarded Octavio Paz the Nobel Prize in literature.

4. Please show me your beaded moccasins.

5. They owe you and me an apology.

6. Our teacher taught us some English words of American Indian origin.

7. After the ride to Laramie, I fed the horse and the mule some hay and oats.

8. My secret pal sent me a birthday card.

9. Mai told the children stories about her family's escape from Vietnam.

10. Will you please save Ricardo a seat?

—HELP—

Some sentences in Review A do not contain an indirect object.

Review A **Identifying Objects of Verbs**

Identify and label the direct objects and the indirect objects in the following sentences. Make sure that you include all parts of compound objects.

EXAMPLES
1. Did you bring the map?
   1. *map—direct object*

2. My parents gave me a choice of places to go on our camping vacation.
   2. *me—indirect object; choice—direct object*

1. I told them my answer quickly.

2. I had recently read a magazine article about the Flathead Reservation in Montana.

3. A Salishan people known as the Flatheads governs the huge reservation.

4. We spent five days of our vacation there.

5. We liked the friendly people and the rugged land.

6. I especially liked the beautiful mountains and twenty-eight-mile-long Flathead Lake.

7. My sister and I made camp beside the lake.

8. Someone gave my father a map and some directions to the National Bison Range, and we went there one day.

9. We also attended the Standing Arrow Pow-Wow, which was the highlight of our stay.

10. The performers showed visitors traditional Flathead dances and games.

Subject Complements

13d. A *subject complement* is a word or word group in the predicate that identifies or describes the subject.

EXAMPLES   Julio has been **president** of his class since October. [*President* identifies the subject *Julio*.]

Was the masked stranger **you**? [*You* identifies the subject *stranger*.]

The racetrack looks **slippery**. [*Slippery* describes the subject *racetrack*.]

A subject complement is connected to the subject by a linking verb.

Common Linking Verbs					
appear	become	grow	remain	smell	stay
be	feel	look	seem	sound	taste

There are two kinds of subject complements—*predicate nominatives* and *predicate adjectives*.

Predicate Nominatives

13e. A *predicate nominative* is a word or word group in the predicate that identifies the subject.

A predicate nominative may be a noun, a pronoun, or a word group that functions as a noun. A predicate nominative is connected to its subject by a linking verb.

EXAMPLES   A dictionary is a valuable **tool.** [*Tool* is a predicate nominative that identifies the subject *dictionary*.]

This piece of flint could be an old **arrowhead.** [*Arrowhead* is a predicate nominative that identifies the subject *piece*.]

The winner of the race was **she.** [*She* is a predicate nominative that identifies the subject *winner*.]

Is that **what you ordered**? [*What you ordered* is a predicate nominative that identifies the subject *that*.]

┌ **TIPS** & **TRICKS** ┐

To find the subject complement in a question, rearrange the sentence to make a statement.

EXAMPLE
Is Reagan the drummer in the band?

Reagan is the **drummer** in the band.

Reference Note

For more about **linking verbs,** see page 358.

┌ **STYLE** **TIP** ┐

Expressions such as *It is I* and *That was he* may sound awkward even though they are correct. In conversation, many people say *It's me* and *That was him.* Such expressions may one day become acceptable in formal writing and speaking as well as in informal situations. For now, however, it is best to follow the rules of standard, formal English, especially in your writing.

Like other sentence complements, a predicate nominative may be compound.

EXAMPLES   The discoverers of radium were **Pierre Curie** and **Marie Sklodowska Curie**.

The yearbook editors will be **Maggie, Imelda,** and **Clay.**

Be careful not to confuse a predicate nominative with a direct object. A predicate nominative always completes a linking verb. A direct object always completes an action verb.

PREDICATE NOMINATIVE   We are the **delegates** from our school.

DIRECT OBJECT   We elected the **delegates** from our school.

A predicate nominative is never part of a prepositional phrase.

PREPOSITIONAL PHRASE   Bill Russell became famous **as a basketball player.**

PREDICATE NOMINATIVE   Bill Russell became a famous basketball **player.**

Reference Note

For more information about **prepositional phrases,** see page 371.

Exercise 4   Identifying Predicate Nominatives

Identify the linking verb and the predicate nominative in each of the following sentences.

EXAMPLE   1. Are whales mammals?

1. *Are—mammals*

┌HELP──

Sentences in Exercise 4 may contain a compound predicate nominative.

1. Kilimanjaro is the tallest mountain in Africa.
2. The kingdom of Siam became modern-day Thailand.
3. Dandelions can be a problem for gardeners.
4. Sue Mishima should be a lawyer or a stockbroker when she grows up.
5. When will a woman be president of the United States?
6. Reuben has become a fine pianist.
7. The team captains are Daniel, Mark, and Hannah.
8. At the moment, she remains our choice as candidate for mayor.
9. Is Alaska the largest state in the United States?
10. According to my teacher, *philately* is another name for stamp collecting.

Predicate Adjectives

13f. A *predicate adjective* is an adjective that is in the predicate and that describes the subject.

A predicate adjective is connected to the subject by a linking verb.

EXAMPLES   Cold milk tastes **good** on a hot day. [*Good* is a predicate adjective that describes the subject *milk.*]

The pita bread was **light** and **delicious.** [*Light* and *delicious* form a compound predicate adjective that describes the subject *bread.*]

How **kind** you are! [*Kind* is a predicate adjective that describes the subject *you.*]

> **Exercise 5**   **Identifying Predicate Adjectives**

Identify the linking verbs and the predicate adjectives in the following sentences.

EXAMPLES   1. The crowd became restless.
       1. *became—restless*

       2. Do the waves seem high and rough today?
       2. *Do seem—high, rough*

1. Everyone felt good about the decision.
2. The milk in this container smells sour.
3. Don't the black beans mixed with rice and onions taste delicious?
4. The situation appears dangerous and complicated.
5. Everyone remained calm during the emergency.
6. Why does the water in that pond look green?
7. During Annie Dillard's speech, the audience grew thoughtful and then enthusiastic.
8. Jan stays cheerful most of the time.
9. She must be happy with her excellent results on the science midterm.
10. From my seat in the stadium, I thought the big bass drums sounded too loud.

| STYLE   TIP |

As you review your writing, you may get the feeling that nothing is *happening,* that nobody is *doing* anything. That feeling is one sign that your writing may contain too many *be* verbs. Wherever possible, replace a dull *be* verb with a verb that expresses action.

BE VERB
   Behind the door **was** a hideous monster.

ACTION VERB
   Behind the door **lurked** a hideous monster.

┌HELP──

Sentences in Exercise 5 may contain a compound predicate adjective.

COMPUTER TIP

The overuse of *be* verbs is a problem that a computer can help you solve. Use the computer's search function to highlight each occurrence of *am, are, is, was, were, be, been,* and *being.* For each case, decide whether the *be* verb can be replaced with an action verb for greater variety.

Review B   **Identifying Predicate Nominatives and Predicate Adjectives**

Identify each subject complement in the following sentences. Then, label each complement as a *predicate nominative* or a *predicate adjective.*

EXAMPLE   1. Are these your shoes, Janelle?

1. *shoes—predicate nominative*

1. This tasty eggplant dish is a favorite in Greece.
2. The twins are tired after the long flight.
3. How beautiful that kimono is, Keiko!
4. This perfume smells sweet and almost lemony.
5. When will the piñata be ready?
6. The winners of the race are Don, Shelby, and she.
7. Vijay Singh is a professional golfer.
8. What good dogs they are!
9. Why is your little brother acting so shy?
10. Loyal and true are the royal bodyguards.

Review C   **Writing Predicate Nominatives and Predicate Adjectives**

Choose an appropriate predicate nominative or predicate adjective for each blank in the following sentences. Then, label each answer as a *predicate adjective* or *predicate nominative.*

EXAMPLES   1. The currents looked _____ than they were.

1. *slower—predicate adjective*

2. Should I become a _____?

2. *veterinarian—predicate nominative*

1. He remained a _____ in the army for more than twenty years.
2. My sister became a _____ after many years of study.
3. In the night air, the jasmine smelled _____.
4. The Navajo way of life was sometimes _____.
5. Peggy seemed _____ with her new kitten.
6. For many travelers, a popular vacation spot is _____.
7. My favorite season has been _____ ever since I was five.
8. Don't these Japanese plums taste _____, Alex?
9. How _____ Grandpa will be to see us!
10. One of the most dangerous animals in the ocean is the _____.

Review D Identifying Complements

Identify the complement or complements in each of the following sentences. Then, label each complement as a *direct object*, an *indirect object*, a *predicate nominative*, or a *predicate adjective*.

┌HELP─
Complements
in Review D may be
compound.

┌ Link to ▓▓ Literature ┐

EXAMPLES   1. Our teacher read us stories from *The Leather-Stocking Tales*.
            1. *us—indirect object; stories—direct object*

            2. James Fenimore Cooper is the author of these tales.
            2. *author—predicate nominative*

1. Leather-Stocking is a fictional scout in Cooper's popular novels.
2. He is also a woodsman and a trapper.
3. He cannot read, but he understands the lore of the woods.
4. To generations of readers, this character has been a hero.
5. He can face any emergency.
6. He always remains faithful and fearless.
7. Leather-Stocking loves the forest and the open country.
8. In later years he grows miserable.
9. The destruction of the wilderness by settlers and others greatly disturbs him.
10. He tells no one his views and retreats from civilization.

Review E Identifying Complements

Identify the complement or complements in each of the following sentences. Then, label each complement as a *direct object*, an *indirect object*, a *predicate nominative*, or a *predicate adjective*.

┌HELP─
Complements
in Review E may be
compound.

EXAMPLES   1. Sean, my brother, won three medals at the Special Olympics.
            1. *medals—direct object*

            2. Are the Special Olympics an annual event?
            2. *event—predicate nominative*

1. Sean was one of more than one hundred special-education students who competed in the regional Special Olympics.

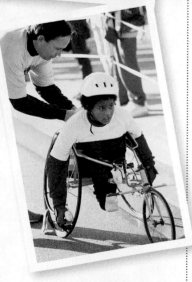

2. The games brought students from many schools to our city.
3. The highlights of the games included track events such as sprints and relay races.
4. These were the closest contests.
5. Sean's excellent performance in the relays gave him confidence.
6. The softball throw and high jump were especially challenging events.
7. Sean looked relaxed but determined as he prepared for the broad jump.
8. He certainly felt great after his winning jump, shown in the top photograph.
9. Mrs. Duffy, one of the coaches, told us the history of the Special Olympics.
10. Eunice Kennedy Shriver founded the program in 1968.
11. To begin with, the program was a five-week camp.
12. Several years later, the camp became an international sports event with contestants from twenty-six states and Canada.
13. Today, the organizers of the Special Olympics sponsor regional and international games.
14. The Special Olympics are exciting and inspiring.
15. Many of the contestants have physical impairments; some cannot walk or see.
16. Teachers and volunteers train contestants in the different events.
17. However, the young athletes themselves are the force behind the program.
18. The pictures on the left give you a glimpse of the excitement at the Special Olympics.
19. In the middle photograph, a volunteer guides a runner.
20. In the photo on the left, this determined boy prepares himself for the wheelchair race.

13

Chapter Review

A. Classifying Complements

Classify each italicized complement in the following sentences as a *direct object*, an *indirect object*, a *predicate adjective*, or a *predicate nominative*.

1. Pamela was the *star* of the play.
2. The guidebook gave the lost *tourists* the wrong directions.
3. Monet is *famous* for the way his paintings captured light.
4. Manuel offered *Anita* some good advice.
5. Ms. Benton is our next-door *neighbor.*
6. Bring *me* the cutting board, please.
7. The box was *big* and awkward to handle.
8. The library receives many new *books* each week.
9. Mexico celebrates its *independence* on September 16.
10. The new president of the bank will be *Ms. Morales.*
11. Angel became a professional jai alai *player.*
12. Amelia Earhart flew her *plane* across the Atlantic in 1932.
13. The glow from the diamond is *dazzling*!
14. Thomas Edison provided *people* with electric light bulbs.
15. New York City was briefly the *capital* of the United States.
16. The Simpsons showed *him* slides of China.
17. My chair was hard and *uncomfortable.*
18. The machine can produce two *crates* a day.
19. Have you seen Akiho's yellow *sweater*?
20. The house appeared *empty.*

B. Identifying Complements

Write the complement or complements in each sentence. Then, identify each complement as a *direct object*, an *indirect object*, a *predicate adjective*, or a *predicate nominative*. Write *none* if the sentence does not contain a complement.

21. American Indian peoples taught the English colonists many useful skills for survival.

22. Steven Spielberg is a famous director and producer of motion pictures.

23. A hurricane of immense power lashed the Florida coast a few years ago.

24. The fans became very anxious during the final minutes of the game.

25. This winter was colder and drier than most.

26. Nora sent postcards from Argentina to her friends.

27. The new homeowners found some rare photographs in the back of the attic.

28. Although many eggshells are white, others are brown, and still others are light green.

29. Lita and Trenell studied until seven o'clock.

30. During this month, Mars is too close to the sun to be seen easily from Earth.

31. Both the House and the Senate gave the President their support on the bill.

32. The movers carried the sofa and dining room table up the front stairs.

33. Armand worked all day with his grandfather.

34. That gigantic reflector is considered the world's most powerful telescope.

35. Our dog Spike is both a good watchdog and an affectionate family pet.

36. *A Raisin in the Sun* was certainly Lorraine Hansberry's most successful play.

37. Why do animals seem nervous during a storm?

38. The theater manager will pay each usher an extra five dollars this week.

39. Luis Alvarez won a Nobel Prize for his important research in nuclear power.

40. Our neighbor has offered my mother and father a good price for their car.

Writing Application
Using Subject Complements to Write Riddles

Predicate Nominatives and Predicate Adjectives

A magazine for young people is sponsoring a riddle-writing contest. Whoever writes the best riddle will win the most advanced computer game on the market. You are determined to write the best riddle and win. Write two riddles to enter in the contest. In each one, use at least two subject complements.

Prewriting   The best way to make up a riddle is to begin with the answer. List some animals, places, and things that suggest funny or hidden meanings. For each animal, place, or thing, jot down a description based on the funny or hidden meaning. Then, choose the two topics that you think will make the best riddles.

Writing   Use your prewriting notes as you write your first draft. In each riddle, make sure that your clues will help your audience guess the answer. Be sure that you use a subject complement (a predicate nominative or a predicate adjective) in the riddle.

Revising   Ask a friend to read your riddles. If the riddles are too difficult or too simple, revise them. You may want to add details that appeal to the senses. Linking verbs such as *appear, feel, smell, sound,* and *taste* can help you add such details.

Reference Note

For a longer **list of linking verbs,** see page 359.

Publishing   Read through your riddles again to check for errors in spelling, punctuation, and capitalization. Pay special attention to the capitalization of proper nouns. You and your classmates may want to publish a book of riddles. Collect your riddles and draw or cut out pictures as illustrations. Make photocopies for all the members of the class.

The Phrase
Prepositional and Verbal Phrases

Diagnostic Preview

A. Identifying and Classifying Prepositional Phrases

Identify the prepositional phrase in each of the following sentences. Then, classify each phrase as an *adjective phrase* or an *adverb phrase,* and write the word that the phrase modifies.

EXAMPLE   1. The chairs in the kitchen need new cushions.

         1. *in the kitchen—adjective phrase—chairs*

1. I wish I were better at tennis.
2. The Rio Grande is the boundary between Texas and Mexico.
3. Those apples come from Washington State.
4. The most popular name for the United States flag is the Stars and Stripes.
5. The pony with a white forelock is Sally's.
6. Through the window crashed the baseball.
7. Cathy Guisewite is the creator of that comic strip.
8. During the last presidential election, we watched the national news often.
9. The first United States space shuttle was launched in 1981.
10. Outside the door the hungry cat waited patiently.

B. Identifying and Classifying Verbal Phrases

Identify the verbal phrase in each of the following sentences. Then, classify each phrase as a *participial phrase* or an *infinitive phrase*.

EXAMPLE   1. The snow, falling steadily, formed huge drifts.
           1. *falling steadily—participial phrase*

11. We expect to do well on the test.
12. The bus, slowed by heavy traffic, arrived at our stop later than it usually does.
13. Breaking the eggs into the wok, he made egg foo yong.
14. To remain calm is not always easy.
15. She wants to study Japanese in high school.
16. The magazine featuring that article is in the school library.
17. Chilled to the bone, the children finally went inside.
18. Who are the candidates that they plan to support in the election?
19. Bethune-Cookman College, founded by Mary McLeod Bethune, is in Daytona Beach, Florida.
20. Teresa called to ask about tonight's homework assignment.

What Is a Phrase?

14a. A *phrase* is a group of related words that is used as a single part of speech and that does not contain both a verb and its subject.

VERB PHRASE	could have been hiding [no subject]
PREPOSITIONAL PHRASE	in the kitchen [no subject or verb]
INFINITIVE PHRASE	to go with them [no subject or verb]

NOTE If a word group has both a subject and a verb, it is called a *clause.*

EXAMPLES   The wind howled. [*Wind* is the subject of the verb *howled.*]

           when the Wilsons left [*Wilsons* is the subject of the verb *left.*]

Reference Note
For information on **clauses,** see Chapter 15.

Identifying Phrases

Identify each of the following word groups as a *phrase* or *not a phrase*.

EXAMPLES 1. on the paper   2. after we eat
1. *phrase*   2. *not a phrase*

1. when you know
2. as they walked in
3. in the garden
4. is sleeping
5. how she remembered

6. smiling brightly
7. to the supermarket
8. where the car is
9. to laugh at myself
10. if he says so

Prepositional Phrases

Reference Note

For a list of commonly used **prepositions**, see page 370.

14b. A *prepositional phrase* includes a preposition, the object of the preposition, and any modifiers of that object.

EXAMPLES   under the umbrella   for ourselves
among good friends   next to them

Notice that an article or another modifier may appear in a prepositional phrase. The first example above contains the article *the*. In the second example, *good* modifies *friends*.

The noun or pronoun that completes a prepositional phrase is called the ***object of the preposition.***

Reference Note

For more about the **object of a preposition,** see page 371.

EXAMPLES   Linh Phan has the lead in the school **play.** [The noun *play* is the object of the preposition *in.*]

Standing between **them** was the Russian chess champion. [The pronoun *them* is the object of the preposition *between.*]

Any modifier that comes between the preposition and its object is part of the prepositional phrase.

EXAMPLE   **Into the thick mist** vanished the carriage. [The adjectives *the* and *thick* modify the object *mist.*]

An object of a preposition may be compound.

EXAMPLE   Come with **Rick** and **me** to the concert. [Both *Rick* and *me* are objects of the preposition *with.*]

GRAMMAR

NOTE Be careful not to confuse an infinitive with a prepositional phrase beginning with *to.* A prepositional phrase always has an object that is a noun or a pronoun. An infinitive is a verbal that usually begins with *to.*

Reference Note

For more information about **infinitives,** see page 414.

PREPOSITIONAL PHRASE	Send the package **to them.**
INFINITIVE	Are you ready **to go**?

Exercise 2 Identifying Prepositional Phrases

Identify the prepositional phrases in each of the following sentences.

EXAMPLE   1. Many soldiers fought bravely during the Vietnam War.

       1. *during the Vietnam War*

┌─**HELP**─

The sentences in Exercise 2 may contain more than one prepositional phrase apiece.

1. One of these soldiers was Jan C. Scruggs.
2. When the war was over, he and other veterans wondered why there was no national memorial honoring those who had served in Vietnam.
3. Scruggs decided he would raise funds for a Vietnam Veterans Memorial.
4. The memorial would include the names of all American men and women who were missing in action or who had died.
5. Organizing the project took years of great effort.
6. Many different people contributed their talents to the project.
7. Maya Ying Lin, a college student, designed the memorial that now stands in Washington, D.C.
8. This picture shows the V-shaped, black granite wall that was built from Lin's design.
9. A glass company from Memphis, Tennessee, engraved each name on the shiny granite.
10. Now the names of those who died in Vietnam will never be forgotten by the American people.

Adjective Phrases

A prepositional phrase used as an adjective is called an *adjective phrase.*

ADJECTIVE   Rosa chose the **blue** one.

ADJECTIVE PHRASE   Rosa chose the one **with blue stripes.**

14c. An *adjective phrase* modifies a noun or a pronoun.

Adjective phrases generally come after the words they modify and answer the same questions that single-word adjectives answer.

> What kind?   Which one?
>
> How many?   How much?

EXAMPLES   The store **with the neon sign** is open. [The prepositional phrase *with the neon sign* is used as an adjective modifying the noun *store.* The phrase answers the question *Which one?*]

     We bought a CD **by Janet Jackson.** [*By Janet Jackson* is used as an adjective modifying the noun *CD.* The phrase answers the question *What kind?*]

Exercise 3   Identifying Adjective Phrases

Identify the adjective phrase in each of the following sentences, and write the word that each phrase modifies.

EXAMPLE   1. Marie Sklodowska Curie, a scientist from Poland, was awarded the Nobel Prize in 1911.

     1. *from Poland—scientist*

HELP

Remember, an adjective phrase must modify a noun or a pronoun.

1. While she was a student in France, Marie met Pierre Curie.
2. Pierre had already gained fame as a scientist.
3. Paris was where the two of them became friends.
4. Their enthusiasm for science brought them together.
5. The marriage between the two scientists was a true partnership.
6. The year after their marriage another scientist discovered natural radioactivity.
7. The Curies began researching the radioactivity of certain substances.
8. Their theories about a new element were proved to be true.

9. Their research on the mineral pitchblende uncovered a new radioactive element, radium.

10. In 1903, the Curies and another scientist shared a Nobel Prize for their discovery.

More than one adjective phrase may modify the same noun or pronoun.

EXAMPLE   Here's a gift **for you from Uncle Steve.** [The prepositional phrases *for you* and *from Uncle Steve* both modify the noun *gift.*]

An adjective phrase may also modify the object in another adjective phrase.

EXAMPLE   A majority **of the mammals in the world** sleep during the day. [The adjective phrase *of the mammals* modifies the noun *majority.* The adjective phrase *in the world* modifies the noun *mammals,* which is the object of the preposition in the first phrase.]

Exercise 4 **Identifying Adjective Phrases**

Identify the adjective phrases in the following sentences. Then, write the word that each phrase modifies.

EXAMPLE   1. R.I.C.E. is the recommended treatment for minor sports injuries.

1. *for minor sports injuries—treatment*

1. The first letters of the words *Rest, Ice, Compression,* and *Elevation* form the abbreviation *R.I.C.E.*

2. Total bed rest is not necessary, just rest for the injured part of the body.

3. Ice helps because it deadens pain and slows the loss of blood.

4. Ice also reduces swelling of the injured area.

5. Compression with a tight bandage of elastic cloth prevents further strain on the injury.

6. This photograph shows an ice pack treating the injured knee of the athlete Robert Horry.

7. The last step in the treatment is elevation of the injured area.

8. The effect of gravity helps fluid drain away.

┌HELP┐
The sentences in Exercise 4 may contain more than one adjective phrase apiece.

9. If pain continues, someone with medical training should be called to examine the injured person.
10. Even injuries of a minor nature need proper attention.

Exercise 5 **Using Adjective Phrases**

Write an adjective phrase for each blank in the following sentences. Then, write the word that the phrase modifies.

EXAMPLE   1. A flock _____ flew overhead.

           1. of small gray birds—flock

1. The sound _____ suddenly filled the air.
2. The theater _____ often shows kung-fu movies.
3. May I have some more _____?
4. Our vacation _____ was relaxing.
5. Her photograph _____ looks like a prizewinner.
6. Andrea found the answer _____.
7. He put the flowers in a vase _____.
8. A boy _____ hung a piñata in the tree.
9. The nest is in the top branch _____.
10. Someone _____ shouted for quiet.

Adverb Phrases

A prepositional phrase used as an adverb is called an *adverb phrase.*

ADVERB   The cavalry will reach the fort **soon.**

ADVERB PHRASE   The cavalry will reach the fort **by noon.**

14d. An *adverb phrase* modifies a verb, an adjective, or an adverb.

Adverb phrases answer the same questions that single-word adverbs answer: *When? Where? How? Why? How often? How long? To what extent?*

EXAMPLES   We got our new puppy **at the animal shelter.** [The adverb phrase *at the animal shelter* modifies the verb *got,* telling *where.*]

              A puppy is always ready **for a game.** [The adverb phrase *for a game* modifies the adjective *ready,* telling *how.*]

              He barks loudly **for a puppy.** [The adverb phrase *for a puppy* modifies the adverb *loudly,* telling *to what extent.*]

GRAMMAR

┌HELP┐
Remember, an adjective phrase must modify a noun or a pronoun.

Unlike adjective phrases, which generally follow the word or words they modify, adverb phrases may appear at various places in sentences.

EXAMPLES   **At dusk,** we went inside to eat dinner.

We went inside **at dusk** to eat dinner.

We went inside to eat dinner **at dusk.**

Exercise 6 **Identifying Adverb Phrases**

Identify the adverb phrase in each of the following sentences. Then, write the word that each phrase modifies. Do not list adjective phrases.

EXAMPLE   1. Pecos Bill will live forever in the many legends about him.

        1. *in the many legends—will live*

1. When he was only a baby, Pecos Bill fell into the Pecos River.
2. His parents searched for him but couldn't find him.
3. He was saved by coyotes, who raised him.
4. He thought for many years that he was a coyote.
5. After a long argument, a cowboy convinced Bill that he was not a coyote.
6. During a drought, Bill dug the bed of the Rio Grande.
7. On one occasion he rode a cyclone.
8. A mountain lion once leaped from a ledge above Bill's head.
9. Bill was always ready for trouble and soon had the mountain lion tamed.
10. Stories like these about Pecos Bill are common in the West.

Like adjective phrases, more than one adverb phrase may modify the same word.

EXAMPLES   She drove **for hours through the storm.** [Both adverb phrases, *for hours* and *through the storm,* modify the verb *drove.*]

The library is open **during the day on weekends.** [Both adverb phrases, *during the day* and *on weekends,* modify the adjective *open.*]

On Saturday we will rehearse our drill routine **before the game.** [Both adverb phrases, *On Saturday* and *before the game,* modify the verb phrase *will rehearse.*]

TIPS & TRICKS

If you are not sure whether a prepositional phrase is an adjective phrase or an adverb phrase, remember that an adjective phrase almost always follows the word it modifies. If you can move the phrase without changing the meaning of the sentence, the phrase is probably an adverb phrase.

Link to   Literature

GRAMMAR

NOTE An adverb phrase may be followed by an adjective phrase that modifies the object in the adverb phrase.

EXAMPLE   The boat landed **on an island near the coast.** [The adverb phrase *on an island* modifies the verb *landed*. The adjective phrase *near the coast* modifies the noun *island.*]

Exercise 7 Identifying Adverb Phrases

Identify the adverb phrases in the following sentences. Then, write the word or words that each phrase modifies. Do not list adjective phrases.

EXAMPLE   1. Never before had a blizzard struck the coastal area with such force.

    1. *with such force—had struck*

1. Andrea saw the dark clouds and turned toward home.
2. The raging wind blew the eleven-year-old over a sea wall near the shore.
3. She found herself trapped in a deep snowdrift.
4. No one could hear her shouts over the howling wind.
5. Andrea's dog charged through the snow toward the beach.
6. He plunged into the snow around Andrea and licked her face, warming the skin.
7. Then the huge dog walked around Andrea until the snow was packed down.
8. The dog pulled her to an open area on the beach.
9. With great effort, Andrea and her dog made their way home.
10. Grateful to their dog, Andrea's family served him a special steak dinner.

┌─HELP─
The sentences in Exercise 7 may contain more than one adverb phrase apiece.

Review A Identifying and Classifying Prepositional Phrases

Identify the prepositional phrase in each of the following sentences, and classify it as an *adjective phrase* or an *adverb phrase.* Then, write the word or words the phrase modifies.

EXAMPLE   1. Here is some information about sharks.

    1. *about sharks—adjective phrase; information*

Greenland
ARCTIC OCEAN
ATLANTIC
OCEAN
Mako
Dogfish
PACIFIC OCEAN
PACIFIC OCEAN
Hammerhead
Goblin
Tiger
INDIAN
OCEAN
Bull
Blue
Thresher
Basking

1. Did you know that there are hundreds of shark species?
2. Scientists group these species into twenty-eight families.
3. Sharks within the same family share many traits.
4. The body shape, tail shape, and teeth determine the differences among families.
5. Sharks are found throughout the world's oceans.
6. As the map shows, some sharks prefer cold waters, and others live mostly in warm tropical oceans.
7. Only thirty kinds of sharks are dangerous.
8. The huge whale shark, however, falls under the "not dangerous" category.
9. Divers can even hitch a ride on its fins.
10. Beautiful yet frightening to most people, sharks are perhaps the world's most awesome creatures.

Review B Writing Sentences with Prepositional Phrases

For each of the following items, write a sentence using the given prepositional phrase. Then, tell whether you have used each phrase as an *adjective phrase* or an *adverb phrase*.

EXAMPLE   1. through the tollbooth

1. *A car passed through the tollbooth.—adverb phrase*

1. in the movie theater
2. for the party
3. along the water's edge
4. about Madeleine
5. into the department store
6. underneath the bed
7. with chopsticks
8. of the equipment
9. in front of city hall
10. at the campsite

Verbals and Verbal Phrases

A *verbal* is a word that is formed from a verb but is used as a noun, an adjective, or an adverb.

The Participle

14e. A *participle* is a verb form that can be used as an adjective.

Two kinds of participles are *present participles* and *past participles.*

(1) *Present participles* end in *–ing.*

EXAMPLES   Mr. Sanchez rescued three people from the **burning** building. [*Burning* is the present participle of the verb *burn.* The participle modifies the noun *building.*]

        Chasing the cat, the dog ran down the street. [*Chasing* is the present participle of the verb *chase.* The participle modifies the noun *dog.*]

(2) *Past participles* usually end in *–d* or *–ed.* Some past participles are formed irregularly.

Reference Note
For a list of **irregular past participles,** see page 489.

EXAMPLES   Well **trained,** the soldier successfully carried out her mission. [The past participle *trained* modifies the noun *soldier.*]

        We skated on the **frozen** pond. [The irregular past participle *frozen* modifies the noun *pond.*]

NOTE Be careful not to confuse participles used as adjectives with participles used in verb phrases. Remember that the participle in a verb phrase is part of the verb.

ADJECTIVE   **Discouraged,** the fans went home.
VERB PHRASE   The fans **were discouraged** by the string of losses.

ADJECTIVE   **Singing** cheerfully, the birds perched among the branches of the trees.
VERB PHRASE   The birds **were singing** cheerfully among the branches of the trees.

Exercise 8 Identifying Participles and the Nouns They Modify

Identify the participles used as adjectives in the following sentences. Then, write the noun that each participle modifies.

EXAMPLE   1. The deserted cities of the Anasazi are found in the Four Corners area of the United States.

       1. *deserted—cities*

1. Utah, Colorado, New Mexico, and Arizona are the bordering states that make up the Four Corners.
2. Because of its natural beauty, Chaco Canyon is one of the most visited sights in this region of the Southwest.
3. Among the remaining ruins in Chaco Canyon are the houses, public buildings, and plazas of the Anasazi.
4. What alarming event may have caused these people to leave their valley?
5. Historians are studying the scattered remains of the Anasazi culture to learn more about these mysterious people.
6. Woven baskets were important to the earliest Anasazi people, who were excellent basket weavers.
7. On the floors of some caves are pits for stored food and other vital supplies.
8. Surviving descendants of the Anasazi include today's Zuni, Hopi, and some of the Pueblo peoples.
9. Programs protecting archaeological sites help ensure the preservation of our nation's heritage.
10. There are several national parks and monuments commemorating the Pueblo's past.

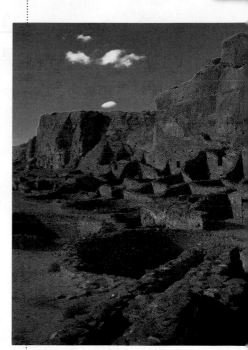

Exercise 9 Identifying Participles and the Words They Modify

Identify the participles used as adjectives in the following sentences. Then, write the noun or pronoun each participle modifies.

EXAMPLE   1. Buzzing mosquitoes swarmed around me.

       1. *Buzzing—mosquitoes*

1. Annoyed, I went inside to watch TV.
2. I woke my sleeping father to ask about mosquitoes.
3. Irritated, he directed me to an encyclopedia.

4. I learned that some flying insects carry diseases.
5. Biting mosquitoes can spread malaria.
6. Bites make the skin swell, and the swollen skin itches.
7. Sucking blood for food, mosquitoes survive in many different climates.
8. Sometimes you can hear mosquitoes buzzing.
9. Their beating wings make the sound.
10. Mosquitoes, living only a few weeks, may go through as many as twelve generations in a year.

The Participial Phrase

14f. A *participial phrase* consists of a participle together with its modifiers and complements. The entire phrase is used as an adjective.

Reference Note

For information on **modifiers,** see Chapter 20. For information on **complements,** see Chapter 13.

EXAMPLES   **Stretching slowly,** the cat jumped down from the windowsill. [The participle *Stretching* is modified by the adverb *slowly.* The phrase modifies *cat.*]

The tornado **predicted by the meteorologist** did not hit our area. [The participle *predicted* is modified by the prepositional phrase *by the meteorologist.* The whole participial phrase modifies *tornado.*]

Reading the assignment, she took notes carefully. [The participle *Reading* has the direct object *assignment.* The phrase modifies *she.*]

A participial phrase should be placed close to the word it modifies. Otherwise, the phrase may appear to modify another word, and the sentence may not make sense.

Reference Note

For information on **how to place participial phrases correctly,** see page 544.

MISPLACED   Hopping along the fence, I saw a rabbit. [Was *I* hopping along the fence?]

CORRECTED   I saw a rabbit **hopping along the fence.**

Exercise 10 Identifying Participial Phrases and the Words They Modify

Identify the participial phrases in the following sentences. Then, write the word or words each phrase modifies.

EXAMPLE   1. Living over four hundred years ago, Leonardo da Vinci kept journals of his ideas and inventions.

           1. *Living over four hundred years ago—Leonardo da Vinci*

1. The journals, written backwards in "mirror writing," are more than five thousand pages long.
2. Leonardo drew many pictures showing birds in flight.
3. He hoped that machines based on his sketches of birds would enable humans to fly.
4. Shown here, his design for a helicopter was the first one in history.
5. Studying the eye, Leonardo understood the sense of sight.
6. He worked hard, filling his journals with sketches like the ones on this page for a movable bridge.
7. The solutions reached in his journals often helped Leonardo when he created his artworks.
8. He used the hands sketched in the journals as models when he painted the hands in the *Mona Lisa.*
9. Painting on a large wall, Leonardo created *The Last Supper.*
10. Leonardo, experimenting continually, had little time to paint in his later years.

The Granger Collection, New York.

Exercise 11 Writing Sentences with Participial Phrases

For each of the following items, write a sentence using the given participial phrase. Make sure the participial phrase modifies a noun or pronoun.

EXAMPLE   1. cheering for the team

           1. *Cheering for the team, we celebrated the victory.*

1. confused by the directions
2. gathering information on the Hopi
3. practicing my part in the play
4. followed closely by my younger brother

—HELP—

In Exercise 11, place a comma after a participial phrase that begins a sentence.

Reference Note

For more information about **punctuating participial phrases,** see pages 607 and 613.

5. searching through the crowd
6. shaped by wind and water
7. freshly painted at the shop
8. born in Tahiti
9. reading a book by the window
10. holding the Ming vase

The Infinitive

14g. An *infinitive* is a verb form that can be used as a noun, an adjective, or an adverb. Most infinitives begin with *to*.

Infinitives	
Used as	**Examples**
Nouns	**To succeed** is my goal. [*To succeed* is the subject of the sentence.]
	My ambition is **to teach** Spanish. [*To teach* is a predicate nominative.]
	She tried **to win.** [*To win* is the direct object of the verb *tried.*]
Adjectives	The place **to meet** tomorrow is the library. [*To meet* modifies the noun *place.*]
	She is the one **to call.** [*To call* modifies the pronoun *one.*]
Adverbs	Tamara claims she was born **to surf.** [*To surf* modifies the verb *was born.*]
	This math problem will be hard **to solve** without a calculator. [*To solve* modifies the adjective *hard.*]

NOTE   *To* plus a noun or a pronoun (*to Washington, to her*) is a prepositional phrase, not an infinitive.

PREPOSITIONAL PHRASE   I am going **to the mall** today.

INFINITIVE   I am going **to shop** for new shoes.

Reference Note

For more information about **prepositional phrases,** see page 371.

Exercise 12 **Identifying Infinitives**

Identify the infinitives in the following sentences. If a sentence does not contain an infinitive, write *none*.

EXAMPLE　　1.　I would like to go to New York City someday.

　　　　　　1. to go

1. My first stop would be to visit the Statue of Liberty.
2. Thousands of people go to see the statue every day.
3. They take a boat to Liberty Island.
4. The statue holds a torch to symbolize freedom.
5. The idea of a statue to represent freedom came from a French historian.
6. France gave the statue to the United States in 1884.
7. The statue was shipped to this country in 214 cases.
8. It was a gift to express the friendship between the two nations.
9. In the 1980s, many people helped to raise money for repairs to the statue.
10. The repairs were completed in time to celebrate the statue's hundredth anniversary on October 28, 1986.

The Infinitive Phrase

14h. An *infinitive phrase* consists of an infinitive together with its modifiers and complements. The entire phrase may be used as a noun, an adjective, or an adverb.

EXAMPLES　　**To be a good gymnast** takes hard work. [The infinitive phrase is used as a noun. The infinitive *To be* has a complement, *a good gymnast.*]

　　　　　　The first person **to fly over both the North Pole and the South Pole** was Richard Byrd. [The infinitive phrase is used as an adjective modifying the noun *person.* The infinitive *to fly* is modified by the prepositional phrase *over both the North Pole and the South Pole.*]

　　　　　　Are you ready **to go to the gym now**? [The infinitive phrase is used as an adverb modifying the adjective *ready.* The infinitive *to go* is modified by the prepositional phrase *to the gym* and by the adverb *now.*]

Reference Note

For information on **modifiers,** see Chapter 20. For information on **complements,** see Chapter 13.

Exercise 13   Identifying Infinitive Phrases

Identify the infinitive phrase in each of the following sentences.

EXAMPLE   1. We went to the park to watch birds.

     1. *to watch birds*

1. A bird is able to control many of its feathers individually.
2. Birds use their feathers to push their bodies through the air.
3. Human beings learned to build aircraft by carefully studying the way birds fly.
4. A bird sings to claim its territory.
5. To recognize the songs of different birds takes many hours of practice.
6. By molting (or gradual shedding), birds are able to replace their feathers.
7. Eagles use their feet to catch small animals.
8. Since they have no teeth, many birds have to swallow their food whole.
9. In many cases both parents help to build a nest.
10. Most birds feed their young until the young are ready to fly from the nest.

Exercise 14   Writing Sentences with Infinitive Phrases

For each of the following items, write a sentence using the given infinitive phrase. Try to vary your sentences as much as possible.

EXAMPLE   1. to see the carved masks of the Haida people

     1. *Terry wants to see the carved masks of the Haida people.*

1. to sing with the Boys Choir of Harlem
2. to ask a question about the test
3. to write a poem to his girlfriend
4. to understand the assignment
5. to give a report on the Spanish exploration of California
6. to learn a little Japanese over the summer
7. to predict accurately the weather patterns
8. to imitate that style
9. to be the best at everything
10. to dry in the sun

Review C Identifying and Classifying Participial Phrases and Infinitive Phrases

Identify the participial phrase or the infinitive phrase in each sentence of the following paragraph. Classify each phrase as a *participial phrase* or an *infinitive phrase*.

EXAMPLES
[1] My family is proud to celebrate our Jewish holidays.

   1. *to celebrate our Jewish holidays—infinitive phrase*

[2] Observing Jewish traditions, we celebrate each holiday in a special way.

   2. *Observing Jewish traditions—participial phrase*

[1] During Rosh Hashana we hear writings from the Torah read in our synagogue. [2] Celebrated in September or October, Rosh Hashana is the Jewish New Year. [3] On this holiday, our rabbi chooses to wear white robes instead of the usual black robes. [4] Representing newness and purity, the white robes symbolize the new year. [5] My favorite food of Rosh Hashana is the honey cake baked by my grandmother. [6] During this holiday everyone eats a lot, knowing that Yom Kippur, a day of fasting, is only ten days away. [7] Yom Kippur, considered the holiest day of the Jewish year, is a serious holiday. [8] To attend services like the one you see here is part of my family's Yom Kippur tradition. [9] I am always pleased to see many of my friends and neighbors there. [10] Sunset, marking the end of the day, brings Yom Kippur to a peaceful close.

Review D Writing Phrases for Sentences

For each of the following sentences, write the kind of phrase that is called for in parentheses.

EXAMPLE   **1.** _____, the audience cheered Yo-Yo Ma's performance. (participial phrase)

       1. *Clapping loudly, the audience cheered Yo-Yo Ma's performance.*

1. We walked slowly _____. (adverb phrase)
2. The people _____ applauded Mayor Garza's speech. (adjective phrase)
3. My little brother is afraid _____. (adverb phrase)
4. The water _____ dripped steadily. (adjective phrase)
5. _____ we saw many beautiful Navajo rugs. (adverb phrase)
6. _____, the principal entered the classroom. (participial phrase)
7. Suddenly, _____, the lion pounced. (participial phrase)
8. My friends and I like _____. (infinitive phrase)
9. _____ is my greatest ambition. (infinitive phrase)
10. She wrote a poem _____. (participial phrase)

Chapter Review

A. Identifying Prepositional Phrases

Identify each prepositional phrase in the following sentences. Then, write the word each phrase modifies. There may be more than one prepositional phrase in a sentence.

1. The view from Mount Fuji is spectacular.
2. Boulder Dam was the original name of Hoover Dam.
3. Eat something before the game.
4. We heard stories about our Cherokee ancestors.
5. The coach paced nervously on the sidelines.
6. The second-longest river in Africa is the Congo.
7. For the costume party, Jody dressed as a lion tamer.
8. Has the hiking party returned to the campsite?
9. The Hudson River was once the chief trading route for the western frontier.
10. Hearing a loud noise, Rita stopped the car and looked underneath it.

B. Identifying Adjective and Adverb Phrases

Classify each italicized prepositional phrase in the following sentences as an *adjective phrase* or an *adverb phrase*. Then, write the word the phrase modifies.

11. The jacket *with the gray stripes* is mine.
12. The man *across the aisle* is sleeping.
13. Mai spoke *with confidence* at the leadership conference.
14. A young woman *in a blue uniform* answered the phone.
15. Nobody *except Alicia* was amazed at the sudden downpour.
16. Were you upset *about the delay*?
17. Does your doctor work *at Emerson Hospital*?
18. *Along the Appalachian National Scenic Trail,* you will find painted rocks that indicate the route.
19. Masud's friends *from New Jersey* are coming to visit.
20. He is tall *for his age.*

C. Classifying Verbal Phrases

Identify each italicized verbal phrase in the following sentences as an *infinitive phrase* or a *participial phrase*.

21. *Returning her library books,* Janelle chose two more.
22. Commander Scott, *chilled by the brisk wind,* pulled on her gloves.
23. *To become a park ranger* is Keisha's dream.
24. The awards dinner *planned for this evening* has been canceled because of a snowstorm.
25. A soufflé can be difficult *to prepare properly.*
26. *Organized in 1884,* the first African American professional baseball team was the Cuban Giants.
27. Guillermo hopes *to visit us soon.*
28. My brother was the first person *to see a meteor* last evening.
29. Stella did not disturb the cat *sleeping in the window.*
30. How do you plan *to tell the story*?

D. Identifying Verbal Phrases

Identify the verbal phrase in each of the following sentences. Then, classify each phrase as an *infinitive phrase* or a *participial phrase.*

31. To skate around the neighborhood was Lee's favorite pastime.
32. Racing around on his in-line skates, he felt as if he were flying.
33. Then one afternoon, prevented from skating by the rain, Lee wondered about the history of skates.
34. He decided to search the Internet for information.
35. Lee learned that Joseph Merlin, an eighteenth-century Dutchman, was the first person to adapt ice skates for use on dry land.
36. Merlin's idea was to attach wooden spools to a plate that supported them.
37. First fashioned in 1763, skates with metal wheels were in use for a century.
38. Appearing in 1863, the first modern skates were invented by an American.

39. Skates with more durable ball-bearing wheels, introduced later in the nineteenth century, popularized roller skating.

40. At the end of the afternoon, Lee exclaimed, "It's fun to know the history of skates!"

Writing Application
Using Prepositional Phrases in a Note

Adjective and Adverb Phrases   You are writing a note to a friend explaining how to care for your pet while you are away on vacation. In your note, use a combined total of at least ten adjective phrases and adverb phrases to give detailed instructions to your friend.

Prewriting   Begin by thinking about a pet you have or would like to have. Then, make a chart or list of the pet's needs. If you need more information about a particular pet, ask a friend or someone else who owns such a pet.

Writing   As you write your first draft, focus on giving information about each of your pet's needs. Tell your friend everything he or she needs to know to care for your pet properly.

Revising   Ask a family member or friend to read your note. Add any missing information and take out any unnecessary instructions. Be sure that you have used both adjective phrases and adverb phrases and that you have used a total of at least ten phrases.

Publishing   Read over your note again to check the grammar, punctuation, and spelling. You and your classmates may wish to create a pet care guide. Gather your notes in a three-ring binder and group your instructions by type of pet.

The Clause

Independent and Subordinate Clauses

Diagnostic Preview

A. Identifying and Classifying Independent and Subordinate Clauses

Identify each of the following clauses as either *independent* or *subordinate*.

EXAMPLE   1. when I was eleven years old
          1. *subordinate*

1. because I have lived in Chile and Ecuador
2. his writing has improved
3. although Gullah is still spoken on South Carolina's Sea Islands
4. when the Philadelphia Phillies baseball team won the National League pennant
5. she served as secretary of labor
6. which we brought to the Juneteenth picnic
7. everyone laughed
8. whose mother you met yesterday
9. during the storm the power failed
10. to whom his mother explained the reason for the delay

B. Identifying and Classifying Subordinate Clauses

Identify the subordinate clause in each of the following sentences. Then, classify each as either an *adjective clause* or an *adverb clause.*

EXAMPLES   **1.** Today is the day that you are eating at my house.

          1. that you are eating at my house—adjective clause

         2. I will give you a map so that you can find my house.

          2. so that you can find my house—adverb clause

11. If you have never had Caribbean food, you are in for a treat.

12. My mother, who was born and raised in Jamaica, really knows how to cook.

13. Whenever I have a chance, I try to learn her secrets.

14. My grandmother, whose cooking is spectacular, is making her special sweet potato pone for dessert.

15. Some of the fruits and vegetables that grow in Jamaica are hard to find in the markets around here.

16. Today we are shopping for coconuts, avocados, and callaloo greens, which were introduced to the Caribbean by Africans.

17. We must also remember to buy the fresh hot peppers, onions, and spices that are needed for seasoning the meat.

18. Although my mother never uses measuring spoons, she seems to know just how much of each spice to add.

19. As soon as we pay for these items, let's take them home.

20. Part of your treat will be to smell the delicious aroma from the kitchen before you even begin eating.

What Is a Clause?

15a. A *clause* is a word group that contains a verb and its subject and that is used as a sentence or as part of a sentence.

Every clause contains a subject and a verb. However, not all clauses express complete thoughts. A clause that does express a complete thought is called an *independent clause.* A clause that does not make sense by itself is called a *subordinate clause.*

> NOTE   A subordinate clause that is capitalized and punctuated as if it were a sentence is a ***sentence fragment.***

Reference Note

For information about **correcting sentence fragments,** see page 269.

The Independent Clause

15b. An *independent* (or *main*) *clause* expresses a complete thought and can stand by itself as a sentence.

EXAMPLES   I woke up late this morning.

Do you know Joseph?

When an independent clause stands alone, it is called a sentence. Usually, the term *independent clause* is used only when such a clause is joined with another clause.

EXAMPLES   **My mother drove me to school.** [This entire sentence is an independent clause.]
My mother drove me to school, but **my brother rode his bicycle.** [This sentence contains two independent clauses.]
Since I missed the bus, **my mother drove me to school.** [This sentence contains one subordinate clause and one independent clause.]

Reference Note

For information on using **commas and coordinating conjunctions to join two independent clauses,** see page 605. For information about **using commas to join independent and subordinate clauses,** see page 607.

The Subordinate Clause

15c. A *subordinate* (or *dependent*) *clause* does not express a complete thought and cannot stand by itself as a complete sentence.

Words such as *because, if, since, that, until, which,* and *whom* signal that the clauses following them may be subordinate. *Subordinate* means "lesser in rank or importance." A subordinate clause must be joined with at least one independent clause to make a sentence and express a complete thought.

SUBORDINATE   **if** the dress is too long
CLAUSES
that the veterinarian recommended

SENTENCES   **If the dress is too long,** we will hem it.

The new food **that the veterinarian recommended** is good for our hamster.

Subordinate clauses may appear at the beginning, in the middle, or at the end of a sentence.

Exercise 1 Identifying Independent and Subordinate Clauses

Identify the italicized clause in each of the following sentences as *independent* or *subordinate*.

EXAMPLE   1. *If you know any modern music history,* then you are probably familiar with the Motown sound.

1. subordinate

1. Do you recognize the entertainers *who are shown in the photographs on this page and the next?*
2. These performers had hit records in the 1950s and 1960s *when the music business in Detroit (the Motor City, or "Motown") was booming.*
3. Berry Gordy, *who founded the Motown record label,* began his business in a small office in Detroit.
4. He was a songwriter and producer, and *he was able to spot talent.*
5. Gordy went to clubs to hear local groups *whose sound he liked.*
6. The Miracles, *which was the first group discovered by Gordy,* had a lead singer named Smokey Robinson.
7. *Robinson was also a songwriter,* and Gordy included him in the Motown team of writers and musicians.

8. Gordy carefully managed all aspects of the Motown sound, *which is a special combination of rhythm and blues and soul.*

9. Diana Ross and the Supremes, Stevie Wonder, Marvin Gaye, the Four Tops, the Temptations, Gladys Knight and the Pips, and Michael Jackson are just some of the performers *that Gordy discovered.*

10. As you look carefully at the photographs again, *can you and your classmates recognize these music legends?*

STYLE TIP

Although short sentences can be effective, a variety of sentence structures is usually more effective. To revise choppy sentences into smoother writing, combine shorter sentences by changing some into subordinate clauses.

CHOPPY
This is our dog, Skippy. He is five years old. He is a Yorkshire terrier.

SMOOTH
This is our dog, Skippy, who is a five-year-old Yorkshire terrier.

In the example above, two of the short sentences are combined into a single subordinate clause.

Exercise 2 Identifying Subordinate Clauses

Identify the subordinate clause in each of the following sentences.

EXAMPLE   1. When you get up in the morning, do you look at your sleepy face in a mirror?

1. *When you get up in the morning*

1. A mirror is a piece of polished metal or glass that is coated with a substance such as silver.

2. The most common type of mirror is the plane mirror, which is flat.

3. The image that is reflected in a plane mirror is reversed.

4. As you look into a mirror, your left hand seems to be the image's right hand.

5. When an image is reversed, it is called a mirror image.

6. A sailor who looks through the periscope of a submarine is using a system of lenses and mirrors in a tube to see above the water's surface.

7. Right-hand rearview mirrors on cars, which show a wide area of the road behind, are usually convex, or curved outward.

8. Drivers must be careful because convex mirrors make reflected objects appear far away.

9. Because the mirror in a flashlight is concave, or curved inward, it strengthens the light from a small lightbulb.

10. When you look in a concave mirror, you sometimes see a magnified reflection of yourself.

Exercise 3 **Writing Sentences with Subordinate Clauses**

Write ten sentences by adding an independent clause to each of the following subordinate clauses. Underline the independent clause in each of your sentences. Make your sentences interesting by using a variety of independent clauses.

EXAMPLES   1. who lives next door to us

1. *Have you or Peggy met the woman who lives next door to us?*

2. that Alexander bought

2. *The sleeping bag that Alexander bought was on sale.*

1. when I bought the CD
2. who won the contest
3. if my parents agree
4. as Jessye Norman began to sing
5. because we are going to a concert
6. that you made
7. who built the pyramids
8. for which this musician is famous
9. since the introduction of the telephone
10. whose paintings are now famous

The Adjective Clause

15d. An *adjective clause* is a subordinate clause that modifies a noun or a pronoun.

Like an adjective or an adjective phrase, an adjective clause may modify a noun or a pronoun. Unlike an adjective phrase, an adjective clause contains both a verb and its subject.

ADJECTIVE	a **blue** flower
ADJECTIVE PHRASE	a flower **with blue petals** [The phrase does not have a verb and its subject.]
ADJECTIVE CLAUSE	a flower **that has blue petals** [The clause does have a verb and its subject.]

An adjective clause usually follows the word or words it modifies and tells *which one* or *what kind*.

EXAMPLES   Emma Willard was the one **who founded the first women's college in the United States.** [The adjective clause modifies the pronoun *one,* telling *which one.*]

I want a bicycle **that I can ride over rough ground.** [The adjective clause modifies the noun *bicycle,* telling *what kind.*]

│ S T Y L E ────── T I P │

The relative pronoun *that* is used to refer both to people and to things. The relative pronoun *which* is used to refer to things.

EXAMPLES

She is the person **that** I met yesterday.

This is the CD **that** you should buy.

The bus, **which** is behind schedule, stops at the next corner.

Reference Note

For information about **when to use commas to set off adjective clauses,** see page 607.

The Relative Pronoun

An adjective clause is usually introduced by a *relative pronoun.*

Commonly Used Relative Pronouns				
that	which	who	whom	whose

These words are called *relative pronouns* because they *relate* an adjective clause to the noun or pronoun that the clause modifies.

EXAMPLES   A snorkel is a hollow tube **that lets a diver breathe underwater.** [The relative pronoun *that* begins the adjective clause and relates it to the noun *tube.*]

The team's mascot, **which is a horse,** is called Renegade. [The relative pronoun *which* begins the adjective clause and relates it to the noun *mascot.*]

Gwendolyn Brooks is the writer **who is the poet laureate of Illinois.** [The relative pronoun *who* begins the adjective clause and relates it to the noun *writer.*]

Those **whose library books are overdue** must pay fines. [The relative pronoun *whose* begins the adjective clause and relates it to the pronoun *Those.*]

NOTE In some cases, the relative pronoun can be omitted.

EXAMPLE   The person [**that** or **whom**] **we met at the market** was Mrs. Herrera.

Exercise 4 Identifying Adjective Clauses

Identify the adjective clause in each of the sentences on the next page. Underline the relative pronoun that begins the clause.

EXAMPLE 1. The person who wrote the Declaration of
Independence was Thomas Jefferson.

1. *who wrote the Declaration of Independence*

1. In his later years, Jefferson lived at his home, Monticello, which he designed.
2. Jefferson planned a daily schedule that kept him busy all day.
3. He began each day by writing himself a note that recorded the morning temperature.
4. Then he did his writing, which included letters to friends and businesspeople.
5. Afterward, he ate breakfast, which was served around 9:00 A.M.
6. Jefferson, whose property included stables as well as farm fields, went horseback riding at noon.
7. Dinner, which began about 4:00 P.M., was a big meal.
8. From dinner until dark, he talked to friends and neighbors who came to visit.
9. His large family, whom he often spent time with, included twelve grandchildren.
10. Jefferson, whose interests ranged from art and architecture to biology and mathematics, read each night.

Exercise 5 Writing Appropriate Adjective Clauses

Complete each of the following sentences with an adjective clause. Then, underline the relative pronoun.

EXAMPLE 1. We read the Greek legend _____.

1. *We read the Greek legend that tells the story of the Trojan horse.*

1. You should proofread every composition _____.
2. My best friend, _____, is a good student.
3. Mrs. Rivera, _____, was my fifth-grade teacher.
4. We heard a sound _____.
5. Our neighbors _____ are from Fez, Morocco.
6. The ship, _____, carried bananas.
7. Anyone _____ is excused from the final exam.
8. Carmen, can you tell us about the scientist _____?
9. Is Victor Hugo the author _____?
10. Wow! I didn't know you had a dog _____.

┌HELP────
Remember,
to be a clause, a word
group must contain both
a verb and its subject.

The Adverb Clause

15e. An *adverb clause* is a subordinate clause that modifies a verb, an adjective, or an adverb.

Like an adverb or an adverb phrase, an adverb clause can modify a verb, an adjective, or an adverb. Unlike an adverb phrase, an adverb clause contains both a verb and its subject.

ADVERB	**Bravely,** Jason battled a fierce dragon.
ADVERB PHRASE	**With great bravery,** Jason battled a fierce dragon. [The phrase does not have both a verb and its subject.]
ADVERB CLAUSE	**Because Jason was brave,** he battled a fierce dragon. [The clause does have a verb and its subject.]

Adverb clauses answer the following questions: *How? When? Where? Why? To what extent? How much? How long?* and *Under what condition?*

EXAMPLES   I feel **as though I will never catch up.** [The adverb clause tells *how* I feel.]

After I finish painting my bookcases, I will call you. [The adverb clause tells *when* I will call you.]

I paint **where there is plenty of fresh air.** [The adverb clause tells *where* I paint.]

I have more work to do today **because I didn't paint yesterday.** [The adverb clause tells *why* I have more work to do.]

Jennifer can run faster **than Victor can.** [The adverb clause tells *to what extent* Jennifer can run faster.]

I will paint **until Mom comes home;** then I will clean my brushes and set the table for supper. [The adverb clause tells *how long* I will paint.]

If I paint for two more hours, I should be able to finish. [The adverb clause tells *under what condition* I should be able to finish.]

Notice in the preceding examples that adverb clauses may be placed in various positions in sentences. When an adverb clause comes at the beginning, it is usually followed by a comma.

STYLE   TIP

In most cases, deciding where to place an adverb clause is a matter of style, not correctness.

As he leapt across the gorge, Rex glanced back at his alien pursuers.

Rex glanced back at his alien pursuers **as he leapt across the gorge.**

Which sentence might you use in a science fiction story? The sentence to choose would be the one that looks and sounds better in context—the rest of the paragraph to which the sentence belongs.

Reference Note

For more information on **punctuating introductory adverb clauses,** see page 613.

Subordinating Conjunctions

Adverb clauses begin with *subordinating conjunctions*.

Common Subordinating Conjunctions		
after	because	though
although	before	unless
as	how	until
as if	if	when
as long as	in order that	whenever
as much as	since	where
as soon as	so that	wherever
as though	than	while

Some words that are used as subordinating conjunctions, such as *after, as, before, since,* and *until,* can also be used as prepositions.

PREPOSITION	**Before** sunrise, we left for the cabin.
SUBORDINATING CONJUNCTION	**Before** the sun had risen, we left for the cabin.

PREPOSITION	In the nineteenth century, buffalo skins were used **as** blankets and clothing.
SUBORDINATING CONJUNCTION	Around 1900, **as** the buffalo became nearly extinct, conservationists fought for its protection.

Exercise 6 — Identifying Adverb Clauses

Identify the adverb clause in each of the following sentences.

EXAMPLE
1. As long as they have been a people, the Chinese have been making kites.

1. *As long as they have been a people*

1. Although the following story is only a legend, many people believe that a kite like the one pictured on the next page may have saved the people of China's Han dynasty.
2. The Chinese were about to be attacked by an enemy army when an advisor to the emperor came up with a plan.
3. As the advisor stood beside an open window, his hat was lifted off by a strong wind.
4. He immediately called for a number of kites to be made so that they might be used to frighten the enemy.

COMPUTER TIP

A computer can help you proofread your writing. Use the computer's search function to highlight any uses of the words *after, as, before, since,* and *until.* Look at the use of such words at the beginnings of sentences. Decide whether the word begins a prepositional phrase or a subordinate clause. In most cases an introductory prepositional phrase is not set off by a comma. An introductory adverb clause, though, should be followed by a comma.

5. The kite makers had no trouble finding lightweight bamboo for their kite frames because bamboo grows widely in China.

6. As each frame was completed, silk was stretched over it.

7. The emperor's advisor attached noisemakers to the kites so that they would produce an eerie sound.

8. He ordered his men to fly the kites in the darkest hour of night because then the enemy would hear the kites but would not be able to see them.

9. Unless the advisor was wrong, the enemy would think that the kites were gods warning them to retreat.

10. According to the legend, the enemy retreated as if they were being chased by a fire-breathing dragon.

David F. Jue, *Chinese Kites, How to Make and Fly Them.* Charles E. Tuttle Co. Inc., of Tokyo, Japan.

┌HELP┐
Remember, a clause contains both a verb and its subject.

Exercise 7 Writing Adverb Clauses

Complete each of the following sentences with an adverb clause. Then, underline the subordinating conjunction.

EXAMPLE   1. _____, digital cameras will become quite popular.

1. *If I'm right, digital cameras will become quite popular.*

1. _____, everything seemed fresh and new.
2. The gears jammed _____.
3. _____, the African dancers began their routine.

4. From the trees, a Bengal tiger watched the herd ____.

5. ____, maybe he'll help you clean your room.

6. Call us ____.

7. ____, the cement mixer backed up to the wooden frame.

8. The buses have been running on time ____.

9. ____, street sweepers rolled slowly next to the curb.

10. His map looked ____.

Review A **Identifying and Classifying Subordinate Clauses**

Identify the subordinate clause in each of the following sentences. Then, classify each clause as an *adjective clause* or an *adverb clause.*

EXAMPLES   **1.** American history is filled with stories of people who performed heroic deeds.

    1. who performed heroic deeds—adjective clause

    2. As the American colonists struggled for independence, women played important roles.

    2. As the American colonists struggled for independence—adverb clause

1. When you study the American Revolution, you may learn about the adventures of a woman known as Molly Pitcher.

2. Molly Pitcher, whose real name was Mary, was the daughter of farmers.

3. Although she was born in New Jersey, she moved to the Pennsylvania colony.

4. There she married William Hays, who was a barber.

5. Hays joined the colonial army when the Revolution began.

6. Mary Hays went to be with her husband in Monmouth, New Jersey, which was the site of a battle on a hot June day in 1778.

7. At first, she carried water to the soldiers so that they would not be overcome by the intense heat.

8. The soldiers nicknamed her "Molly Pitcher" because she carried the water in pitchers.

9. Later, when her husband collapsed from the heat, she took over his cannon.

10. George Washington, who was the commander of the Continental Army, made Molly an honorary sergeant.

Review B Writing Sentences with Subordinate Clauses

Write twenty different sentences of your own. In each sentence, include a subordinate clause that begins with one of the following words or word groups. Underline the subordinate clause. After the sentence, classify the subordinate clause as an *adjective clause* or an *adverb clause*.

EXAMPLES **1.** so that

1. We hurried <u>so that we wouldn't miss the bus going downtown.</u>—adverb clause

2. whom

2. Jim Nakamura, <u>whom I met at summer camp,</u> is now my pen pal.—adjective clause

1. which	**11.** because
2. before	**12.** unless
3. since	**13.** as soon as
4. who	**14.** whom
5. than	**15.** while
6. whose	**16.** whenever
7. as though	**17.** after
8. although	**18.** where
9. that	**19.** as much as
10. if	**20.** wherever

Chapter Review

A. Identifying Independent and Subordinate Clauses

Identify the italicized clause in each of the following sentences as an *independent* or a *subordinate clause*.

1. As Jawan walked to school, *he saw a strange sight.*
2. *If you go to the library,* you should take a look at the young adult section.
3. The book *that I read last night* was very scary!
4. Long after the rain had stopped, *the ground was still wet.*
5. If the trip is cancelled, *we can play tennis.*
6. *When the spin cycle stops,* please take the laundry out of the washing machine.
7. The shells *that they found* are still in the closet.
8. *Most people are asleep* when the morning newspaper is delivered.
9. Was the movie *that the reviewers liked* sold out? adjective
10. Since we moved here from Chile, *we have met many people.*

B. Identifying Adjective and Adverb Clauses

Identify each italicized clause in the following sentences as an *adjective clause* or an *adverb clause*. Then, write the word each clause modifies.

11. We camped near Lake Arrowhead *when we went fishing last year.*
12. *Because the weather was cold,* I wore a sweater under my jacket.
13. The coat *that my mother bought for me* was blue.
14. *As she left her office,* Cletha heard the phone.
15. Vince hit the home run *that won the game!*
16. Everyone *who signed up for the marathon* should meet at 8:00 A.M. tomorrow in the school parking lot.
17. On Tuesday the Chavez family went to the Rex parade, *which is held every year in New Orleans during Mardi Gras.*

GRAMMAR

18. Larry is a little taller *than Dana is.*
19. The CD *that Rita wanted to buy* was out of stock.
20. Louise stayed home today *because she has a bad case of the flu.*
21. Play soccer *if you need more exercise.*
22. The turtle moves faster *than I expected.*
23. My older sister, *who is on the varsity basketball team,* practices after school every day.
24. *Since it was such a beautiful evening,* we decided to take a long walk.
25. Will the students *whose families observe the Jewish Sabbath* be excused early on Friday?

C. Identifying Subordinate Clauses

Identify the subordinate clause in each sentence. Then, classify the clause as an *adjective clause* or an *adverb clause.* Write *none* if the sentence does not contain a subordinate clause.

26. The denim blue jeans that are known as Levi's have an interesting history.
27. They were created in 1873 by Levi Strauss.
28. Strauss, who had immigrated to the United States from Bavaria, founded a clothing company called Levi Strauss & Co.
29. Six years after his arrival in the United States, he sailed to San Francisco because his sister and brother-in-law had a dry goods business there.
30. In 1872, Strauss had received a letter from Jacob Davis, a tailor in Nevada who was one of his regular customers.
31. Davis told Strauss about riveting the pocket corners of work pants so that the pants would be more durable.
32. Since Davis lacked the money to patent this invention, he asked Strauss to be his partner.
33. Both men were named as patent holders in 1873.
34. The copper-riveted overalls were popular with working people who needed tough but comfortable pants.
35. In 1880, the company, whose sales had reached $2.4 million, was selling denim pants to retailers for about $1.50 a pair.

36. Strauss died in 1902, four years before an earthquake and fire in San Francisco destroyed his company's factories.

37. After the earthquake, the company built a new factory that is still operating today.

38. The company suffered financially, as did many other businesses, during the Great Depression of the 1930s.

39. Since the 1940s, the pants have become increasingly fashionable among young people.

40. In the 1950s, when actors such as James Dean wore them in film roles, the jeans skyrocketed in popularity.

Writing Application
Using Clauses in a Manual

Subordinate Clauses   Your class project for National Safety Week is to write a safety manual. Each class member will write one page of instructions telling what to do in a particular emergency. Use subordinating conjunctions to show the relationships between your ideas.

Prewriting   Think of a specific emergency that you know how to handle. List the steps that someone should follow in this emergency. Number the steps in order. If you aren't sure of the order or don't know a particular step, stop writing and get the information you need.

Writing   Use your prewriting list to begin your first draft. As you write, make your instructions as clear as possible. Define or explain terms that might be unfamiliar to your readers. Be sure that your instructions are in the right order.

Revising   Read over your instructions to be sure that you've included all necessary information. Add, cut, or rearrange steps to make the instructions easy to follow. Be sure to use appropriate subordinating conjunctions to make the order of the steps clear.

Publishing   Check your work carefully for any errors in grammar, punctuation, and spelling. To publish your class safety manual, gather all the pages and make booklets out of printouts or photocopies. Organize your topics alphabetically, or group them by kinds of emergencies.

┌─HELP─
A health teacher, the school nurse, or an organization such as the Red Cross should be able to provide information.

Reference Note
For information about **punctuating introductory adverb clauses,** see page 613.

Kinds of Sentence Structure

Simple, Compound, Complex, and Compound-Complex Sentences

Diagnostic Preview

A. Identifying and Classifying Clauses

Identify each clause in the following sentences. Then, classify each clause as an *independent clause* or a *subordinate clause.*

EXAMPLE   1. Students who are interested in attending the science fair at the community college should sign up now.

          1. Students should sign up now—independent clause; who are interested in attending the science fair at the community college—subordinate clause

1. We did warm-up exercises before we practiced the routine.
2. The musical *West Side Story* is a modern version of the story of Romeo and Juliet.
3. The first poem in the book is about spring, and the second one is about autumn.
4. Molasses, which is made from sugar cane, is a thick brown liquid used for human food and animal feed.
5. Before the test we studied the chapter and did the chapter review exercises.
6. While our teacher discussed the formation of the African nation of Liberia, we took notes.

7. It rained Saturday morning, but the sun came out in time for the opening of the Special Olympics.

8. The player whose performance is judged the best receives the Most Valuable Player Award.

9. Not all stringed instruments sound alike, for their shapes and the number of their strings vary.

10. The tourists that we saw wandering up Esplanade Avenue went to the Japanese ceramics exhibit after they had reached the museum.

B. Identifying Simple, Compound, Complex, and Compound-Complex Sentences

Identify each of the following sentences as *simple, compound, complex,* or *compound-complex.*

EXAMPLE   1. The Museum of Science and Industry, which is in Chicago, features a German submarine captured during World War II.

        1. *complex*

11. Either Ana or Lee will sing the opening song for the fair.

12. We visit the Liberty Bell whenever we go to Philadelphia.

13. Have you chosen a topic for your report yet, or are you still making your decision?

14. When George Washington Carver was working on soil improvement and plant diseases, the South was recovering from the Civil War, and his discoveries gave planters a competitive edge.

15. *A Tree Grows in Brooklyn,* which was written by Betty Smith, is one of my favorite books.

16. The call of a peacock sounds very much like that of a person in distress.

17. Although it was warm enough to go swimming on Monday, snow fell the next day.

18. The student whose photographs of American Indian cliff dwellings won the contest was interviewed on the local news.

19. The house looked completely empty when I first saw it, yet a party was going on in the backyard.

20. The game was tied at the top of the ninth inning, but then Earlene hit a home run.

The Simple Sentence

Reference Note

For information on **independent and subordinate clauses**, see Chapter 15.

16a. A *simple sentence* contains one independent clause and no subordinate clauses.

EXAMPLES
         S   V
A good rain will help the farmers.

             V   S
Up for the rebound leaped Reggie.

     V   S
Where are my keys?

       V
Please put that down near the table in the corner.
[The understood subject is *you*.]

Reference Note

For information on the **understood subject**, see page 331.

    A simple sentence may have a compound subject, a compound verb, or both.

EXAMPLES
       S   S   V
Chalupas and **fajitas are** two popular Mexican dishes.
[compound subject]

      S   V   V
Kelly read *The Planet of Junior Brown* and **reported** on it last week. [compound verb]

       S   S   V   V
The **dog** and the **kitten lay** there and **napped**.
[compound subject and compound verb]

Exercise 1   Identifying Subjects and Verbs in Simple Sentences

Identify the subjects and the verbs in each of the following sentences.

EXAMPLE
    1. I enjoy urban life but need to escape from the city once in a while.

      1. I—subject; enjoy, need—verbs

┌HELP──

Some sentences in Exercise 1 have a compound subject, a compound verb, or both.

1. My favorite escape from city life is the green world of Central Park in New York City.

2. Its beautiful woods and relaxing outdoor activities are just a few minutes from our apartment.

3. The enormous size of the park, however, can sometimes be a problem.
4. Often, I take this map with me for guidance.
5. Using the map, I can easily find the zoo, the band shell, and the Lost Waterfall.
6. In the summertime my brothers and I row boats on the lake, climb huge rock slabs, and have picnics in the Sheep Meadow.
7. I also watch birds and often wander around the park in search of my favorite species.
8. Last month a pair of purple finches followed me along the pond.
9. Near Heckscher Playground, the birds tired of the game and flew off.
10. In Central Park my family and I can enjoy a little bit of nature in the middle of a bustling city.

▭ Bridge		F Food	
• Monument		R Restroom	
▬ Building		P Playground	

The Compound Sentence

16b. A *compound sentence* contains two or more independent clauses and no subordinate clauses.

INDEPENDENT CLAUSE	Melvina wrote about her mother's aunt
INDEPENDENT CLAUSE	Leroy wrote about his cousin from Jamaica
COMPOUND SENTENCE	Melvina wrote about her mother's aunt, and Leroy wrote about his cousin from Jamaica.

The independent clauses of a compound sentence are usually joined by a comma and a coordinating conjunction (*and, but, for, nor, or, so,* or *yet*).

EXAMPLES A variety of fruits and vegetables should be a part of everyone's diet**, for** they supply many important vitamins.

Kathryn's scene is in the last act of the play**, so** she must wait in the wings for her cue.

No one was injured in the fire**, but** several homes were destroyed**, and** many trees burned down.

Reference Note

For more about using **commas in compound sentences,** see page 605.

Reference Note

For more about using **semicolons in compound sentences,** see page 618.

The independent clauses of a compound sentence may be joined by a semicolon.

EXAMPLES   Pedro Menéndez de Avilés founded St. Augustine, the first permanent European settlement in the United States; he also established six other colonies in the Southeast.

           My favorite places are Miami, Florida, and Aspen, Colorado; Bernie's favorites are San Diego, California, and Seattle, Washington.

Exercise 2   Identifying Subjects and Verbs in Compound Sentences

Identify the subject and verb in each independent clause. Then, give the punctuation mark and coordinating conjunction (if there is one) that join the clauses.

EXAMPLE   1. A newspaper reporter will speak to our class next week, and we will learn about careers in journalism.

            1. *reporter—subject; will speak—verb; we—subject; will learn—verb; comma +* and

1. Ruth Benedict was a respected anthropologist, and Margaret Mead was one of her students.
2. An area's weather may change rapidly, but its climate changes very slowly.
3. Linh Phan lived in Vietnam for many years, so he could tell us about Vietnamese foods such as *nuoc mam.*
4. Students may prepare their reports on the computer, or they may write them neatly.
5. Our apartment manager is kind, yet she will not allow pets in the building.
6. Daniel Boone had no formal education, but he could read and write.
7. Sofia's favorite dance is the samba; Elena enjoys the merengue.
8. Benjamin Franklin is known for his inventions, and he should also be remembered for his work during the Constitutional Convention.
9. Sheena did not play soccer; she had sprained her ankle.
10. They did not watch the shuttle take off, nor did they watch it land.

Simple Sentence or Compound Sentence?

A simple sentence has only one independent clause. It may have a compound subject or a compound verb or both.

A compound sentence has two or more independent clauses. Each independent clause has its own subject and verb. Any of the independent clauses in a compound sentence may have a compound subject, a compound verb, or both.

SIMPLE SENTENCE	**S S V** Kim and Maureen read each other's short stories **V** and made many suggestions for improvements. [compound subject and compound verb]

COMPOUND SENTENCE	**S S V** Kim and Maureen read each other's stories, **S V** and they gave each other suggestions for improve-ments. [The first independent clause has a compound subject and a single verb. The second independent clause has a single subject and a single verb.]

NOTE When a subject is repeated after a coordinating conjunction, the sentence is not simple.

SIMPLE SENTENCE	**S V** **We studied** the artist Romare Bearden and **V** **went** to an exhibit of his paintings.

COMPOUND SENTENCE	**S V** **We studied** the artist Romare Bearden, and **S V** **we went** to an exhibit of his paintings.

Exercise 3 Distinguishing Compound Sentences from Sentences with Compound Subjects or Compound Verbs

Identify the subjects and verbs in each of the sentences on the following page. Then, identify each sentence as either *simple* or *compound*.

EXAMPLES   1. A rain forest is a tropical evergreen forest and has heavy rains throughout the year.

1. *rain forest—subject; is, has—verbs; simple*

2. The trees and other plants in a rain forest grow close together, and they rise to different heights.

2. *trees, plants—subjects; grow—verb; they—subject; rise—verb; compound*

1. The Amazon River is located in South America and is one of the longest rivers in the world.

2. The Amazon begins in Peru, and it flows across Brazil to the Atlantic Ocean.

3. This river carries more water than any other river and drains about one fifth of the earth's entire freshwater supply.

4. The Amazon is actually a network of several rivers, but most people think of these combined rivers as only one river.

5. These rivers drain the largest rainy area in the world, and during the flood season, the main river often overflows its banks.

6. In the photo at the left, the Amazon does twist and curve.

7. Generally, it follows a fairly straight course and flows at an average rate of about one and one-half miles an hour during the dry season.

8. The Amazon rain forest is only two hundred miles wide along the Atlantic, but it stretches to twelve hundred miles wide at the foot of the Andes Mountains in Peru.

9. The variety of plant life in the Amazon rain forest is remarkable; in fact, of all rain forests in the world, this area may contain the greatest number of plant species.

10. Raw materials are shipped directly from ports deep in the rain forest, for oceangoing ships can sail more than two thousand miles up the Amazon.

The Complex Sentence

16c. A *complex sentence* contains one independent clause and at least one subordinate clause.

Two kinds of subordinate clauses are adjective clauses and adverb clauses. Adjective clauses usually begin with relative pronouns such as *who, whom, whose, which,* and *that.* Adverb clauses begin with subordinating conjunctions such as *after, as, because, if, since,* and *when.*

EXAMPLES   Patricia Roberts Harris**, who served as President Carter's secretary of housing and urban development,** was the first African American woman to be a Cabinet member. [complex sentence with adjective clause]

When I hear classical music, I think of Aunt Sofia. [complex sentence with adverb clause]

One interesting annual event **that is held in the Southwest** is the Inter-Tribal Indian Ceremonial**, which involves many different American Indian peoples.** [complex sentence with two adjective clauses]

Reference Note

For more information on **adjective clauses,** see page 427. For more about **adverb clauses,** see page 430. For more about **relative pronouns,** see page 344. For more about **subordinating conjunctions,** see page 431.

Reference Note

For information on using **commas with subordinate clauses,** see page 607.

Exercise 4 **Identifying Subordinate Clauses**

Identify the subordinate clause in each of the following sentences. Then, underline the relative pronoun or the subordinating conjunction that begins the subordinate clause.

EXAMPLES   1. Helen Keller, who overcame severe physical impairments, showed great determination.

    1. who overcame severe physical impairments

    2. Keller was fortunate because she had such a skillful and loving teacher.

    2. because she had such a skillful and loving teacher

1. Helen Keller, who is shown in the photograph at right, became very ill as a small child.
2. After she recovered from the illness, she could no longer see or hear.
3. Because she could not hear, she also lost her ability to speak.

4. Helen's parents asked Alexander Graham Bell, who trained teachers of people with hearing impairments, for his advice about the child's education.

5. Upon Bell's suggestion, a special teacher, whose name was Anne Sullivan, stayed at the Kellers' home to teach Helen.

6. Sullivan spelled words into Helen's hand as the child touched the object represented by the word.

7. From this basic understanding of language, Helen went on to learn Braille, which is the alphabet used by people with visual impairments.

8. Sullivan, whose own vision had been partly restored by surgery, remained with Helen for many years.

9. Because she had triumphed over her impairments, Helen Keller was awarded the Medal of Freedom.

10. Keller's autobiography, which is titled *The Story of My Life*, tells about her remarkable achievements.

Review A   **Classifying Simple, Compound, and Complex Sentences**

Classify each of the following sentences as *simple*, *compound*, or *complex*.

EXAMPLE   1. The Mississippi River, which begins in the town of Lake Itasca, Minnesota, is the setting for many of Mark Twain's stories.

     1. *complex*

1. I drew an illustration for a poem that was written by Robert Hayden.
2. The Olympic skaters felt anxious, but they still performed their routine perfectly.
3. Kamehameha Day is an American holiday that honors the king who united the islands of Hawaii.
4. For the first time in his life, Luke saw the ocean.
5. If you had a choice, would you rather visit China or Japan?
6. The bull was donated to the children's zoo by the people who bought it at the auction.
7. Lookout Mountain, which is in Tennessee, was the site of a battle during the Civil War.
8. The guide led us through Mammoth Cave; she explained the difference between stalactites and stalagmites.
9. Wilhelm Steinitz of Austria became famous after he was officially recognized as the first world champion of chess.
10. Amy Tan is the author of the book *The Joy Luck Club*.

The Compound-Complex Sentence

16d. A *compound-complex sentence* contains two or more independent clauses and at least one subordinate clause.

In the examples below, independent clauses are underlined once. Subordinate clauses are underlined twice.

EXAMPLES

    S   **V**   **S**   **V**

The band began to play, and Clarissa was pulled onto

             S   **V**

the floor for a dance that was starting. [compound-complex sentence with adjective clause]

         S **V**   **S**   **V**

Whenever we go on vacation, our neighbors mow our

      S   **V**

yard, and they collect our mail. [compound-complex sentence with adverb clause]

STYLE   TIP

Simple sentences are best used to express single ideas. To describe more complicated ideas and to show how the ideas fit together, use compound and complex sentences.

SIMPLE SENTENCES
We went camping in the national park. Darla saw a snake. At first she was afraid. Then she looked more closely at it. [The sentences are choppy, and the ideas seem unrelated.]

COMPLEX AND COMPOUND SENTENCES
When we went camping in the national park, Darla saw a snake. At first she was afraid, but then she looked more closely at it.

Reference Note

For more about **adjective and adverb clauses,** see pages 427 and 430.

Exercise 5 Identifying Compound, Complex, and Compound-Complex Sentences

Identify each of the following sentences as either *compound, complex,* or *compound-complex.*

EXAMPLE 1. I'll sweep the porch, and Ben will start supper before Mom gets home.

1. compound-complex

1. If you've never tried Indian curry, try some of Usha's.
2. The disk drive light went on, and the drive motor whirred, but the computer would not read the disk.
3. Although the river appeared calm, crocodiles lay motionless beneath the surface.
4. Several small herds of mustangs roam these hills; we're going to find them.
5. An antique wagon, whose wheels once rolled along the Chisholm Trail, stood next to the barn.
6. You can talk to me whenever you have a problem, or you can talk to your mom.
7. Since daylight saving time started, the sky doesn't get dark until late, and that just doesn't seem right to me.
8. The plaster, which had been given a rough texture, cast shadows on itself.
9. They don't have the book that we need, so let's go to the library.
10. Did you really live in Nairobi, or are you just kidding?

COMPUTER TIP

A computer can help you focus on sentence length and structure in your writing. Programs are now available that can tell you the average number of words in your sentences. Such programs can also tell you how many different kinds of sentences you used. You can compare your numbers with the averages for students at your grade level. Using these programs, you can easily see which sentence structures you have mastered and which ones need work.

Review B Classifying Simple, Compound, Complex, and Compound-Complex Sentences

Classify each of the following sentences as *simple, compound, complex,* or *compound-complex.*

EXAMPLE 1. The Iroquois people traditionally held a Green Corn Festival in August when their crops were ready for harvesting.

1. complex

1. For the early Iroquois, the Green Corn Festival was a celebration that included many events, so it often lasted several days.
2. During the celebration, all children who had been born since midwinter received their names.

3. Iroquois leaders made speeches, and adults and children listened to them carefully.

4. In one traditional speech, the leader would give thanks for the harvest.

5. After they had heard the speeches, the people sang and danced.

6. On the second day of the festival, the people performed a special dance; during the dance they gave thanks for the sun, the moon, and the stars.

7. On the third day, the Iroquois gave thanks for the helpfulness of their neighbors and for good luck.

8. The festival ended on the fourth day when teams of young people would play a bowling game.

9. During the festival the people renewed their friendships, and they rejoiced in their harmony with nature.

10. This Iroquois festival resembles the U.S. Thanksgiving holiday, which has its roots in similar American Indian celebrations.

The Corn Dance

Review C **Writing Simple, Compound, Complex, and Compound-Complex Sentences**

Write ten sentences of your own, following the guidelines given below.

EXAMPLE 1. Write a simple sentence with a compound subject.

1. *Jorge and Pilar gave me their recipe for guacamole.*

1. Write a simple sentence with a compound verb.

2. Write a simple sentence with a compound subject and a compound verb.

3. Write a compound sentence with two independent clauses joined by a comma and the coordinating conjunction *and*.

4. Write a compound sentence with two independent clauses joined by a comma and the coordinating conjunction *but*.

5. Write a compound sentence with two independent clauses joined by a semicolon.

6. Write a compound sentence with three independent clauses.

7. Write a complex sentence with an adjective clause.

8. Write a complex sentence with an adverb clause.

9. Write a compound-complex sentence with an adjective clause.

10. Write a compound-complex sentence with an adverb clause.

16 Chapter Review

A. Identifying Independent and Subordinate Clauses

Identify each clause in the following sentences. Then, classify each clause as an *independent clause* or a *subordinate clause*.

1. Yvette raked the leaves, and Tito mowed the lawn.
2. Lupe and Ben went to the park so that they could watch the fireworks display.
3. Carl and I chose enchiladas instead of sandwiches from the cafeteria's menu.
4. The new camp that offers instruction in computer programming will be in session from August 17 through August 28.
5. The rain changed to snow that was mixed with sleet.
6. Practice your tai chi exercises when you go to the beach.
7. My grandparents, who enjoy exciting vacations, visited Nepal last year.
8. Since last year Simone has grown three inches, but she still can't reach the top shelf in the kitchen.
9. Will Martin loan me this book by Jamaica Kincaid when he is through with it?
10. Aretha hopes to be a veterinarian because she likes to be around animals.

B. Identifying Simple and Compound Sentences

Classify each of the following sentences as *simple* or *compound*.

11. Do Nathan and Shenille read only science fiction or fantasy short stories? *simple*
12. My sister and brother-in-law live in Colorado, and they raise sheep and grow fruit trees. *Compound*
13. Chai wants to walk to the theater, but I want to take the bus.
14. Aunt Evelyn and Uncle Michael are both surgeons and work at Riverside Hospital.
15. The good queen pardoned the jester, for he had meant no real harm.

16. Taking the train, Mei-Ling and her parents can be in Chicago in two hours. *[handwritten mark]*

17. Blair is interested in becoming an astronaut, so she wrote to NASA for information. *[handwritten mark]*

18. Tate laid out the patio and built it himself. *[handwritten mark]*

19. After eating, Marcia's cat Bartinka likes to take a long nap. *[handwritten mark]*

20. Mike designed and contructed the sets for the play, and Mary Anne designed the costumes and makeup. *[handwritten mark]*

C. Identifying Compound and Complex Sentences

Identify each of the following sentences as *compound* or *complex*. If the sentence is compound, write the comma and coordinating conjunction or the semicolon that joins the clauses. If the sentence is complex, write the relative pronoun or subordinating conjunction that joins the clauses.

21. Nineteenth-century shopkeepers often attracted customers by placing a carved wooden figure, which was called a shop figure, outside their shops. *Complex*

22. The shop figures were usually carved by ship carvers, who had learned to carve figures by creating ship figureheads. *complex*

23. The figures cost a great deal to make, and they were expensive to maintain. *compound*

24. Many shopkeepers were upset because the figures were so very costly. *complex*

25. Many of the wooden figures were of politicians and baseball players; others represented American Indians. *compound*

26. One surviving figure represents Father Time, and another one represents a New York City firefighter. *compound*

27. The firefighter, which commemorates Columbian Engine Company 14, now stands in the New York City Fire Museum. *complex*

28. The figures were popular between the 1840s and the 1890s, and during that time they actually became a fad. *complex*

29. By the end of the century, the carved shop figure was no longer widely used since new types of advertising had become available. *Complex*

30. People saw shop figures as old-fashioned, so shopkeepers stopped using them. *complex*

D. Classifying Compound, Complex, and Compound-Complex Sentences

Classify each of the following sentences as *compound, complex,* or *compound-complex.*

31. Islam, which originated in Arabia, is the religion of the Muslims, and it is based on a belief in one God. *compound-complex*

32. Most Muslims live in Africa, the Middle East, and Malaysia; in recent years many have come to the United States and have brought their religion with them. *complex*

33. Some American Muslims are members of the Nation of Islam, which was founded in the United States after World War II. *complex*

34. When a mosque was opened in New York in May 1991, religious leaders and other Muslims went there to pray. *complex*

35. Some worshipers wore the traditional clothing of their homelands; others were dressed in typical American clothes. *compound*

36. Muslims were particularly pleased that the new mosque opened in the spring. *complex*

37. The Muslim month of fasting, which is called Ramadan, had just ended, so the holiday after Ramadan could be celebrated in the new house of worship. *compound-complex*

38. Although Muslims share a common religion, their languages differ. *compound*

39. Many Muslims speak Arabic, but those in Iran, Turkey, and neighboring countries, for example, speak other languages as well. *compound complex*

40. Of course, Muslims who were born in the United States generally speak English, and many Muslims who are recent immigrants are learning it as a new language. *compound-complex*

E. Classifying Sentences by Structure

Classify each of the following sentences as *simple, compound, complex,* or *compound-complex.*

41. Easter Island, which is also known as Rapa Nui, is a small Polynesian island in the South Pacific. *complex*

42. The island is the most remote inhabited place on the planet. *simple*

43. The Polynesians were among the most accomplished sailors in the world; they are especially known for their skill at navigation. *compound-complex*

44. The earliest evidence of people on Easter Island dates from around A.D. 700, but the island may have been inhabited earlier than that. *complex*

45. The island is best known for its giant stone statues with long noses and pursed lips. *simple*

46. The statues, which are called *moai*, were carved out of volcanic rock, and some of them were placed upright on platforms called *ahu*. *compound-complex*

47. The *moai* that were set up on platforms were transported as far as six miles from the quarry, but no one knows for certain how the islanders moved them. *complex*

48. Several theories have been proposed, yet no single theory explains all the evidence. *complex*

49. When the British explorer Captain Cook visited the island in 1774, he noticed that many of the statues had been overturned. *compound*

50. The oral tradition of the islanders speaks of a civil war that broke out between two peoples on the island, the Hanau Eepe and the Hanau Momko. *complex*

Writing Application
Writing a Letter

Using a Variety of Sentence Structures   Anyone can enter the "Win Your Dream House" Contest. All you have to do is describe your ideal house. Write a letter to the contest judges, describing where your dream house would be and what it would look like. Use a variety of sentence structures to make your letter interesting for the judges to read.

Prewriting   Make a list of the special features of the house you want to describe. To help you think of ideas, you may want to look through magazines or books to find pictures of interesting homes. You may also find it helpful to draw a rough diagram of the rooms, yard, and other features you would want to add. Take notes on the details you want to include.

Writing   As you write your first draft, use your notes to include vivid details that will give the contest judges a clear picture of your dream house.

Revising   Read your letter to make sure it is interesting and clear. Also, check to see whether you can combine similar ideas by using either compound or complex sentences. Ask an adult to read your letter. Does he or she think your description would impress the contest judges?

Publishing   Check the grammar and spelling in your letter. Also, make sure that you have used commas correctly in compound sentences and complex sentences. You and your classmates may want to create a bulletin board display of the pictures or diagrams you used in designing your dream house and to post your descriptions next to the display.

Reference Note
For information on **using commas,** see page 602.

Agreement
Subject and Verb, Pronoun and Antecedent

Diagnostic Preview

A. Identifying Correct Subject-Verb Agreement and Pronoun-Antecedent Agreement

Choose the correct word or word group in parentheses in each of the following sentences.

EXAMPLE   1. Some of the paintings (*is, are*) dry now.
   1. *are*

1. Three hours of work (*is, are*) needed to finish the charcoal drawing for art class.
2. Everybody has offered (*his or her, their*) advice.
3. *Harlem Shadows* (*is, are*) a collection of poems by the writer Claude McKay.
4. Either Stu or Ryan can volunteer (*his, their*) skill in the kitchen.
5. Black beans, rice, and onions (*tastes, taste*) good together.
6. Not one of them has offered (*his or her, their*) help.
7. Sometimes my family (*disagrees, disagree*) with one another, but usually we all get along fairly well.
8. Five dollars (*is, are*) all you will need for the matinee.
9. (*Doesn't, Don't*) too many cooks spoil the broth?
10. One of my aunts gave me (*her, their*) silk kimono.

B. Proofreading for Subject-Verb Agreement and Pronoun-Antecedent Agreement

Most of the following sentences contain an agreement error. Write the incorrect verb or pronoun. Then, write the correct form. If the sentence is already correct, write *C*.

EXAMPLE   1. Most stargazers has seen points of light shooting across the night sky.

    1. *has—have*

11. These points of light is commonly called shooting stars.
12. Scientists who study our solar system calls these points of light *meteors.*
13. Some meteors are pieces of asteroids that exploded long ago.
14. Each of these pieces are still flying through space on the path of the original asteroid.
15. Most nights, a person is lucky if they can see a single meteor now and then.
16. Throughout the year, however, there is meteor "showers."
17. None of these showers are as big as the ones that come each year in August and November.
18. Either Katie or Carla once saw a spectacular meteor shower on their birthday.
19. In November 1833, one of the largest meteor showers in history were recorded.
20. Two hundred forty thousand meteors observed in just a few hours are a record that has never been matched!

Number

Number is the form a word takes to indicate whether the word is singular or plural.

17a. When a word refers to one person, place, thing, or idea, it is *singular* in number. When a word refers to more than one, it is *plural* in number.

Reference Note

For more about **forming plurals,** see page 663.

Singular	igloo	she	one	child	class
Plural	igloos	they	many	children	classes

Exercise 1 Classifying Nouns and Pronouns by Number

Classify each of the following words as *singular* or *plural*.

EXAMPLES
1. girl
2. rivers

1. *singular*
2. *plural*

1. evening
2. wolves
3. women
4. leaf
5. they
6. teeth
7. tacos
8. we
9. thief
10. armies
11. hoof
12. mice
13. I
14. shelf
15. geese
16. magazine
17. oxen
18. he
19. cities
20. cargo

| TIPS & TRICKS |

Most nouns ending in *–s* are plural (*cheetahs, families*). Most verbs that end in *–s* are singular (*fills, begins*). However, verbs used with the singular pronouns *I* and *you* do not end in *–s*.

EXAMPLES
Ed takes the bus.
I take the train.
You ride your bike.

Reference Note
The plurals of some nouns do not end in *–s* (*mice, teeth, deer*). For more about **irregularly formed plurals,** see page 664.

Agreement of Subject and Verb

17b. A verb should agree in number with its subject.

Two words *agree* when they have the same number. The number of a verb should agree with the number of its subject.

(1) Singular subjects take singular verbs.

EXAMPLES
The **lightning fills** the sky. [The singular verb *fills* agrees with the singular subject *lightning*.]

Jan begins her vacation today. [The singular verb *begins* agrees with the singular subject *Jan*.]

(2) Plural subjects take plural verbs.

EXAMPLES
Cheetahs run fast. [The plural verb *run* agrees with the plural subject *Cheetahs*.]

New **families move** into our neighborhood often. [The plural verb *move* agrees with the plural subject *families*.]

When a sentence contains a verb phrase, the first helping verb in the verb phrase agrees with the subject.

EXAMPLES
The **motor is** running.
The **motors are** running.

The **girl has** been delayed.
The **girls have** been delayed.

Is anyone filling the aquarium?
Are any **students** filling the aquarium?

Exercise 2 Identifying Verbs That Agree in Number with Their Subjects

Identify the form of the verb in parentheses that agrees with its subject.

EXAMPLE   1. wind (*howls, howl*)

          1. *howls*

1. people (*talks, talk*)
2. rain (*splashes, splash*)
3. birds (*flies, fly*)
4. we (*helps, help*)
5. it (*appears, appear*)

6. geese (*hisses, hiss*)
7. night (*falls, fall*)
8. roofs (*leaks, leak*)
9. baby (*smiles, smile*)
10. tooth (*aches, ache*)

Exercise 3 Identifying Verbs That Agree in Number with Their Subjects

Identify the form of the verb in parentheses that agrees with its subject.

EXAMPLE   1. Special tours (*is, are*) offered at the National Air and Space Museum in Washington, D.C.

          1. *are*

1. This museum (*has, have*) been called the best of all the Smithsonian museums.
2. This enormous building (*covers, cover*) three blocks.

3. Twenty-three galleries (*offers, offer*) visitors information and entertainment.
4. The different showrooms (*deals, deal*) with various aspects of air and space travel.
5. As you can see, the exhibits (*features, feature*) antique aircraft as well as modern spacecraft.
6. In another area, a theater (*shows, show*) films on a five-story-high screen.
7. A planetarium (*is, are*) located on the second floor.
8. Projectors (*casts, cast*) realistic images of stars on the ceiling.
9. Some tours (*is, are*) conducted by pilots.
10. In addition, the museum (*houses, house*) a large research library.

Proofreading for Errors in Subject-Verb Agreement

Most of the following sentences contain errors in subject-verb agreement. If a verb does not agree with its subject, write the correct form of the verb. If a sentence is already correct, write *C*.

EXAMPLE
1. More than fifteen million people lives in and around Mexico's capital.

1. *live*

1. Located in an ancient lake bed, Mexico City have been built on Aztec ruins.
2. Visitors admire the colorful paintings of Diego Rivera at the National Palace.
3. In one of the city's many subway stations, an Aztec pyramid still stand.
4. Sculptures grace the Alameda, which is Mexico City's main park.
5. Atop the Latin American Tower, an observatory offer a great view on a clear day.
6. At the National Autonomous University of Mexico, the library's outer walls is famous as works of art.
7. Juan O'Gorman's huge mosaics shows the cultural history of Mexico.
8. Usually, tourists is quite fascinated by the Great Temple of the Aztecs.
9. Many fiestas fills Mexico City's social calendar.
10. In addition, the city has one of the largest soccer stadiums in the world.

Problems in Agreement

Phrases Between Subject and Verb

17c. The number of a subject is not changed by a phrase following the subject.

EXAMPLES
The **hero** of those folk tales **is** Coyote. [The verb *is* agrees with the subject *hero*, not with *tales*.]

The successful **candidate,** along with two of her aides, **has entered** the auditorium. [The helping verb *has* agrees with the subject *candidate*, not with *aides*.]

Scientists from all over the world **have gathered** in Geneva. [The helping verb *have* agrees with the subject *Scientists,* not with *world.*]

The crystal **pitcher,** oozing water droplets, **was cracked** along the base. [The helping verb *was* agrees with the subject *pitcher,* not with *droplets.*]

NOTE If the subject is the indefinite pronoun *all, any, more, most, none,* or *some,* its number may be determined by the object of a prepositional phrase that follows it.

EXAMPLES   **Most** of the essays **were** graded. [*Most* refers to the plural word *essays.*]

Most of this essay **is** illegible. [*Most* refers to the singular word *essay.*]

Reference Note
For more about **indefinite pronouns,** see Rules 17d–17f on page 462.

USAGE

Exercise 5 Identifying Verbs That Agree in Number with Their Subjects

Identify the form of the verb in parentheses that agrees with its subject.

EXAMPLE   1. The water in the earth's oceans (*cover, covers*) much of the planet's surface.

1. *covers*

1. A tidal wave, despite its name, (*is, are*) not caused by the tides.
2. Earthquakes beneath the sea (*causes, cause*) most tidal waves.
3. A network of warning signals (*alert, alerts*) people in coastal areas of an approaching tidal wave.
4. The tremendous force of tidal waves sometimes (*causes, cause*) great destruction.
5. Walls of earth and stone along the shore (*is, are*) often too weak to protect coastal villages.
6. Some tidal waves, according to this encyclopedia article, (*travel, travels*) more than five hundred miles an hour.
7. Tidal waves in the open ocean generally (*do, does*) not cause much interest.
8. The height of tidal waves there often (*remain, remains*) low.
9. However, waves up to one hundred feet high (*occur, occurs*) when tidal waves hit land.
10. The scientific name for tidal waves (*are, is*) tsunamis.

Indefinite Pronouns

You may recall that personal pronouns refer to specific people, places, things, or ideas. A pronoun that does not refer to a definite person, place, thing, or idea is called an ***indefinite pronoun.***

Personal Pronouns	Indefinite Pronouns
she	anybody
them	both
we	either
you	everyone

17d. The following indefinite pronouns are singular: *anybody, anyone, anything, each, either, everybody, everyone, everything, neither, nobody, no one, nothing, one, somebody, someone,* and *something.*

EXAMPLES   **Each** of the newcomers **was welcomed** to the city.

Neither of these papayas **is** ripe.

Does anybody on the bus **speak** Arabic?

Exercise 6 **Identify Verbs That Agree in Number with Their Subjects**

Choose the form of the verb in parentheses that agrees with its subject.

EXAMPLE   **1.** One of these books (*is, are*) yours.

1. is

1. Neither of the movies (*were, was*) especially funny.
2. Everybody in those classes (*gets, get*) to leave early.
3. Someone among the store owners (*donates, donate*) the big trophy each year.
4. Each of the Jackson brothers (*study, studies*) dance.
5. No one on either team (*was, were*) ever in a playoff before.
6. Everyone with an interest in sports (*are, is*) at the tryouts.
7. Anybody with binoculars (*are, is*) popular at a large stadium.
8. Each of our neighbors (*have, has*) helped us plant the new community garden.

9. One of the new Spanish teachers (*supervises, supervise*) the language lab.
10. Nobody in our family (*speak, speaks*) Greek well, but we all can speak a little bit.

17e. The following indefinite pronouns are plural: *both, few, many, several.*

EXAMPLES **Few** of our neighbors **have** parakeets.

Many of them **keep** dogs as pets.

17f. The indefinite pronouns *all, any, more, most, none,* and *some* may be either singular or plural, depending on their meaning in a sentence.

The number of the pronouns *all, any, more, most, none,* and *some* is often determined by the number of the object in a prepositional phrase following the subject. These pronouns are singular when they refer to a singular word and are plural when they refer to a plural word.

EXAMPLES **All** of the fruit **is** ripe. [*All* is singular because it refers to the singular word *fruit.* The verb *is* is singular to agree with the subject *All.*]

All of the pears **are** ripe. [*All* is plural because it refers to the plural word *pears.* The verb *are* is plural to agree with the subject *All.*]

Some of the harvest **has been sold.** [*Some* is singular because it refers to the singular word *harvest.* The helping verb *has* is singular to agree with the subject *Some.*]

Some of the apples **have been sold.** [*Some* is plural because it refers to the plural word *apples.* The helping verb *have* is plural to agree with the subject *Some.*]

NOTE The pronouns listed in Rule 17f aren't always followed by prepositional phrases.

EXAMPLES **All are** here.

Some has spilled.

In such cases you should look at the **context**—the sentences before and after the pronoun—to see if the pronoun refers to a singular or a plural word.

USAGE

┌HELP──
Some indefinite pronouns, such as *both, each,* and *some,* can also be used as adjectives. When an indefinite adjective comes before the subject of a sentence, the verb agrees with the subject as it normally would.

Just as you would write **Children love** playing in the park.
or
The **child loves** playing in the park.

you would write **Both children love** playing in the park.
or
Each child loves playing in the park.

Identify the verb form in parentheses that agrees with its subject.

EXAMPLE 1. Somebody in the club (*want, wants*) the meetings held on a different day.

   1. *wants*

1. "Both of the tapes (*sound, sounds*) good to me," Gregory said.
2. If anyone (*know, knows*) a better way to get to Washington Square, please tell me.
3. Each of the problems (*are, is*) easy to solve if you know the correct formulas.
4. Probably everyone in the class (*remember, remembers*) how to boil an egg.
5. All of the new research on dreams (*is, are*) fascinating.
6. Most of our dreams (*occur, occurs*) toward morning.
7. Few of us really (*understand, understands*) the four cycles of sleep.
8. Most of the research (*focus, focuses*) on the cycle known as rapid eye movement, or REM.
9. None of last night's dream (*is, are*) clear to me.
10. Many of our dreams at night (*is, are*) about that day's events.

Review A Identifying Verbs That Agree in Number with Their Subjects

Identify the verb form in parentheses that agrees with its subject.

EXAMPLE 1. The flying object shown on the next page probably (*look, looks*) familiar to you.

   1. *looks*

1. Many people throughout the world (*claims, claim*) to have seen objects like this.
2. However, no one (*know, knows*) for sure what they are.
3. They (*resembles, resemble*) huge plates or saucers.
4. Not surprisingly, people (*call, calls*) them flying saucers.
5. Since 1947, they (*has, have*) been officially called unidentified flying objects, or UFOs.
6. The U.S. government (*has, have*) investigated many unusual UFO sightings.

7. The U.S. Air Force (*was, were*) responsible for conducting these investigations.

8. Government records (*shows, show*) that more than twelve thousand sightings were reported between 1948 and 1969.

9. Most reported sightings (*has, have*) turned out to be fakes, but others remain unexplained.

10. None of the official reports positively (*proves, prove*) that UFOs come from outer space.

Compound Subjects

17g. Subjects joined by *and* usually take a plural verb.

EXAMPLES   Our **dog and cat get** baths in the summer.

Mr. Duffy and his **daughter have gone** fishing.

A compound subject that names only one person or thing takes a singular verb.

EXAMPLES   **A famous singer and dancer is going** to speak at our drama club meeting. [One person is meant.]

Macaroni and cheese is my favorite supper. [One dish is meant.]

USAGE

Exercise 8   Identifying Verbs That Agree in Number with Their Subjects

Identify the correct form of the verb in parentheses. If you choose a singular verb with any of these compound subjects, be prepared to explain why.

EXAMPLE   1. Chris and her sister (*is, are*) in the school band.
            1. *are*

1. (*Is, Are*) the brown bear and the polar bear related?
2. Wind and water (*erodes, erode*) valuable farmland throughout the United States.
3. My guide and companion in Bolivia (*was, were*) Pilar.
4. New words and new meanings for old words (*is, are*) included in a good dictionary.
5. Mrs. Chang and her daughter (*rents, rent*) an apartment.
6. Iron and calcium (*needs, need*) to be included in a good diet.
7. Mr. Marley and his class (*has, have*) painted a wall-size map.
8. A horse and buggy (*was, were*) once a common way to travel.
9. Tornadoes and hurricanes (*is, are*) dangerous storms.
10. Fruit and cheese (*tastes, taste*) good together.

17h. Singular subjects joined by *or* or *nor* take a singular verb.

EXAMPLES   The chief **geologist or** her **assistant is** due to arrive tonight. [Either one *is* due, not both.]

Neither a **rabbit nor** a **mole does** that kind of damage. [Neither one *does* the damage.]

Plural subjects joined by *or* or *nor* take a plural verb.

EXAMPLES   Either **mice or squirrels are** living in our attic.

Neither the **senators nor** the **representatives want** the bill to be vetoed by the president.

17i. When a singular subject and a plural subject are joined by *or* or *nor*, the verb agrees with the subject nearer the verb.

EXAMPLES   A **book or flowers** usually **make** an appropriate gift. [The verb agrees with the nearer subject, *flowers.*]

Flowers or a **book** usually **makes** an appropriate gift. [The verb agrees with the nearer subject, *book.*]

| STYLE   TIP |

Compound subjects that have both singular and plural parts can sound awkward even though they are correct. Whenever possible, revise sentences to avoid such constructions.

AWKWARD
Two small boards or one large one is what we need to patch that hole.

REVISED
We need two small boards or one large one to patch that hole.

Exercise 9 Identifying Verbs That Agree in Number with Their Subjects

Identify the correct form of the verb in parentheses in each of the following sentences. Be prepared to explain the reason for your choice.

EXAMPLE   1. The club president or the officers (*meets, meet*) regularly with the sponsors.

     1. meet

1. Neither pens nor pencils (*is, are*) needed to mark the ballots.
2. Either my aunt or my uncle (*is, are*) going to drive us.
3. That table or this chair (*was, were*) made by hand in Portugal.
4. (*Has, Have*) the sandwiches or other refreshments been served yet?
5. Index cards or a small tablet (*is, are*) handy for taking notes.
6. Neither that clock nor my wristwatch (*shows, show*) the correct time.
7. One boy or girl (*takes, take*) the part of the narrator.
8. During our last visit to Jamaica, a map or a guidebook (*was, were*) my constant companion.
9. The dentist or her assistant (*checks, check*) my braces.
10. Either Japanese poetry or Inuit myths (*is, are*) going to be the focus of my report.

Review B Proofreading for Subject-Verb Agreement

Identify each verb that does not agree with its subject in the following sentences. Then, write the correct form of each verb.

EXAMPLE   1. The players in the photograph on the next page is competing in the most popular sport in the world—soccer.

     1. is—are

1. One expert in the field of sports have described soccer as the world's favorite type of football.
2. Some sports writers has estimated that there are over thirty million registered soccer players around the globe.
3. Youth leagues and coaching clinics has helped make amateur soccer the fastest-growing team sport in the United States.
4. In Dallas, Texas, neither baseball nor American football attract as many young players as soccer does.

5. Also, more colleges now has varsity soccer teams than have football teams.
6. This increase in soccer fans are a trend that started in 1967, when professional teams began playing in the United States.
7. Additional interest were generated when the U.S. Youth Soccer Association was formed.
8. Both males and females enjoys playing this sport.
9. In fact, by the 1980s, many of the soccer teams in the country was women's teams.
10. In the past, professional soccer were more popular abroad, but the United States hosted the World Cup in 1994.

Other Problems in Subject-Verb Agreement

Reference Note

For more information about **collective nouns,** see page 341.

17j. A collective noun may be either singular or plural, depending on its meaning in a sentence.

A *collective noun* is singular in form but names a group of persons, animals, or things.

Common Collective Nouns		
People	**Animals**	**Things**
audience	brood	batch
chorus	flock	bundle
committee	gaggle	cluster
crew	herd	collection
faculty	litter	fleet
family	pack	set
jury	pod	squadron

A collective noun takes a singular verb when the noun refers to the group as a unit. A collective noun takes a plural verb when the noun refers to the individual parts or members of the group.

EXAMPLES   The **class has decided** to have a science fair in November. [The class as a unit has decided.]

The **class were divided** in their opinions of the play. [The members of the class were divided in their opinions.]

My **family plans** to attend Beth's graduation. [The family as a unit plans to attend.]

My **family are coming** from all over the state for the reunion. [The members of the family are coming.]

17k. When the subject follows the verb, find the subject and make sure that the verb agrees with it.

The subject usually follows the verb in questions and in sentences beginning with *here* or *there*.

EXAMPLES   Where **was** the **cat**?
Where **were** the **cats**?

Does Jim know the Chens?
Do the **Chens** know Jim?

Here **is** my **umbrella**.
Here **are** our **umbrellas**.

There **is** a scary **movie** on TV.
There **are** scary **movies** on TV.

NOTE When the subject of a sentence follows part or all of the verb, the word order is said to be **inverted.** To find the subject of a sentence with inverted order, restate the sentence in normal subject-verb word order.

INVERTED   Here **are** your **gloves.**
NORMAL   Your **gloves are** here.

INVERTED   **Were you arriving** late, too?
NORMAL   **You were arriving** late, too.

INVERTED   In the pond **swim** large **goldfish.**
NORMAL   Large **goldfish swim** in the pond.

Reference Note
For more information about **contractions,** see page 641.

The contractions *here's, there's,* and *where's* contain the verb *is* and should be used only with singular subjects.

NONSTANDARD   There's our new neighbors.
STANDARD   There**'s** our new **neighbor.**
STANDARD   There **are** our new **neighbors.**

Exercise 10 **Identifying Verbs That Agree in Number with Their Subjects**

Identify the subject in each of the following sentences. Then, write the correct form of the verb in parentheses.

EXAMPLE   1. That flock of geese (*migrates, migrate*) each year.
          1. *flock—migrates*

1. There (*is, are*) at least two solutions to this complicated Chinese puzzle.
2. The soccer team (*was, were*) all getting on different buses.
3. (*Is, Are*) both of your parents from Korea?
4. Here (*comes, come*) the six members of the decorations committee for the dance.
5. Here (*is, are*) some apples and bananas for the picnic basket.
6. There (*is, are*) neither time nor money for that project.
7. (*Here's, Here are*) the social studies notes I took.
8. At the press conference, there (*was, were*) several candidates for mayor and two for governor.

9. The family (*has, have*) invited us over for a dinner to celebrate Grandma's promotion.
10. Here (*is, are*) some masks carved by the Haida people.

17l. Some nouns that are plural in form take singular verbs.

EXAMPLES **Electronics is** a branch of physics.

Civics is being taught by Ms. Gutierrez.

Measles is the most unpleasant disease I've ever had.

The **news was** not encouraging.

17m. An expression of an amount (a measurement, a percentage, or a fraction, for example) may be singular or plural, depending on how it is used.

A word or phrase stating an amount is singular when the amount is thought of as a unit.

EXAMPLES Fifteen **dollars is** enough for that CD.

Sixteen **ounces equals** one pound.

Is two **weeks** long enough for a hiking trip?

Sometimes, however, the amount is thought of as individual pieces or parts. If so, a plural verb is used.

EXAMPLES **Ten** of the dollars **were borrowed.**

Two of the hours **were spent** at the theater.

A fraction or a percentage is singular when it refers to a singular word and plural when it refers to a plural word.

EXAMPLES One fourth of the **salad is** gone.

Forty percent of the **students are** new.

NOTE Expressions of measurement (such as length, weight, and area) are usually singular.

EXAMPLES Ten **feet is** the height of a regulation basketball hoop.

Seventy-five **pounds is** the maximum baggage weight for this airline.

USAGE

17n. Even when plural in form, the title of a creative work (such as a book, song, film, or painting), the name of an organization, or the name of a country or city generally takes a singular verb.

EXAMPLES   ***World Tales*** **is** a collection of folk tales retold by Idries Shah. [one book]

Tonya's painting ***Sunflowers*** **was inspired** by the natural beauty of rural Iowa. [one painting]

Friends of the Earth was founded in 1969. [one organization]

The **Philippines is** an island country in the southwest Pacific Ocean. [one country]

Is Marble Falls a city in central Texas? [one city]

Exercise 11 Identifying Verbs That Agree in Number with Their Subjects

Identify the correct form of the verb in parentheses in each of the following sentences.

EXAMPLE   1. Three inches in height (*is, are*) a great deal to grow in one year.

    1. *is*

1. *The Friends* (*is, are*) a book about a girl from the West Indies and a girl from Harlem.
2. Two cups of broth (*seems, seem*) right for that recipe.
3. Fifteen feet (*was, were*) the length of the winning long jump.
4. Navarro and Company (*is, are*) selling those jackets.
5. The National Council of Teachers of English (*is, are*) holding its convention in our city this year.
6. Mumps (*is, are*) a highly infectious disease.
7. Three hours of practice (*is, are*) not unusual for the band.
8. *Arctic Dreams* (*was, were*) written by Barry Lopez.
9. Two weeks of preparation (*has, have*) been enough.
10. A dollar and a half (*is, are*) the cost of a subway ride.

17o. ***Don't*** and ***doesn't*** should agree in number with their subjects.

The word *don't* is a contraction of *do not*. Use *don't* with plural subjects and with the pronouns *I* and *you*.

EXAMPLES   The **children don't** seem nervous.

I don't understand.

Don't you remember?

The word *doesn't* is a contraction of *does not*. Use *doesn't* with singular subjects except the pronouns *I* and *you*.

EXAMPLES   **Kim doesn't** ride the bus.

He doesn't play tennis.

It doesn't snow here.

Oral Practice 1 **Using *Don't* and *Doesn't***

Read the following sentences aloud, stressing the italicized words.

1. My friend *doesn't* understand the problem.
2. *Doesn't* she want to play soccer?
3. The tomatoes *don't* look ripe.
4. Our school *doesn't* have a gymnasium.
5. Italy *doesn't* border Germany.
6. The geese *don't* hiss at Mr. Waverly.
7. Our Muslim neighbors, the Nassers, *don't* eat pork.
8. He *doesn't* play chess.

Review C **Identifying Verbs That Agree in Number with Their Subjects**

Write the verb form in parentheses that agrees with its subject.

EXAMPLE   1. Wheelchairs with lifts (*help, helps*) many people.
    1. *help*

1. Twenty-five cents (*is, are*) not enough to buy the Sunday newspaper.
2. Everyone in her family (*prefers, prefer*) to drink water.
3. Allen and his parents (*enjoy, enjoys*) basketball.
4. Jan (*don't, doesn't*) know the rules of volleyball.
5. Neither the cassette player nor the speakers (*work, works*) as well as we had hoped.
6. There (*is, are*) 132 islands in the state of Hawaii.
7. Many California place names (*comes, come*) from Spanish.

8. The principal or her assistant (*is, are*) the one who can help you.

9. Home economics (*is, are*) a required course in many schools.

10. A flock of sheep (*was, were*) grazing on the hill.

Review D   Proofreading for Subject-Verb Agreement

Most of the following sentences contain errors in subject-verb agreement. If a verb does not agree with its subject, write the correct form of the verb. If a sentence is already correct, write *C.*

EXAMPLE   1. Here is two pictures of Wang Yani and her artwork.

        1. are

1. There surely is few young artists as successful as Yani.

2. In fact, the People's Republic of China regard her as a national treasure.

3. She has shown her paintings throughout the world.

4. Yani don't paint in just one style.

5. Her ideas and her art naturally changes over the years.

6. The painting below shows one of Yani's favorite childhood subjects.

7. Many of her early paintings features monkeys.

8. In fact, one of her large works portray 112 monkeys.

9. However, most of her later paintings is of landscapes, other animals, and people.

10. As her smile suggests, Yani fill her paintings with energy.

Wang Yani. *Little Monkeys and Mummy.* © Byron Preiss Visual Publications, Inc. & New China Pictures Company. Photograph: Zheng Zhensun © 1991. All rights reserved. Published by Scholastic, Inc.

Wang Yani. © Byron Preiss Visual Publications, Inc. & New China Pictures Company. Photograph: Zheng Zhensun © 1991. All rights reserved. Published by Scholastic, Inc.

USAGE

Agreement of Pronoun and Antecedent

A pronoun usually refers to a noun or another pronoun called its *antecedent.* Whenever you use a pronoun, make sure that it agrees with its antecedent.

17p. A pronoun should agree in number and gender with its antecedent.

Some singular pronouns have forms that indicate gender. Feminine pronouns refer to females. Masculine pronouns refer to males. Neuter pronouns refer to things (neither male nor female) and sometimes to animals.

Feminine	she	her	hers	herself
Masculine	he	him	his	himself
Neuter	it	it	its	itself

EXAMPLES   **Carlotta** said that **she** found **her** book.

             Aaron brought **his** skates with **him.**

             The **plant** with mold on **it** is losing **its** leaves.

The antecedent of a pronoun can be another kind of pronoun. In such cases, you may need to look in a phrase that follows the antecedent to determine which personal pronoun to use.

EXAMPLES   **Each** of the **girls** has offered **her** ideas. [*Each* is the antecedent of *her.* The word *girls* tells you to use the feminine pronoun to refer to *Each.*]

             One of the **men** lost **his** key. [*One* is the antecedent of *his.* The word *men* tells you to use the masculine pronoun to refer to *One.*]

Some antecedents may be either masculine or feminine. In such cases, use both the masculine and the feminine forms.

EXAMPLES   Every **one** of the parents praised **his or her** child's efforts that day.

             No one in the senior play forgot **his or her** lines on opening night.

Reference Note

For more information on **antecedents,** see page 342.

USAGE

STYLE TIP

In conversation, people often use a plural personal pronoun to refer to a singular antecedent that may be either masculine or feminine. This nonstandard usage is becoming more common in writing, too.

NONSTANDARD
Everybody brought their swimsuit.

Every member of the club sold their tickets.

For now, however, it is best to follow the rules of standard usage in formal situations.

STYLE TIP

To avoid the awkward use of *his or her,* try to rephrase the sentence.

EXAMPLES
Everybody brought **a** swimsuit.

All the members of the club sold **their** tickets.

17q. Use a singular pronoun to refer to *anybody, anyone, anything, each, either, everybody, everyone, everything, neither, nobody, no one, nothing, one, somebody, someone,* or *something.*

EXAMPLES   **Each** of the snakes escaped from **its** cage.

                  Someone in the class left behind **his or her** pencil.

17r. Use a plural pronoun to refer to *both, few, many,* or *several.*

EXAMPLES   **Both** of the sailors asked **their** captain for shore leave.

                  Many among the others waiting below deck hoped that **they** could go, too.

17s. The indefinite pronouns *all, any, more, most, none,* and *some* may be singular or plural, depending on how they are used in a sentence.

EXAMPLES   **All** of the book is interesting, isn't **it**?
                  All of the books are interesting, aren't **they**?

                  None of the casserole is left; **it** was terrific!
                  None of the casseroles are left; **they** were terrific!

17t. Use a singular pronoun to refer to two or more singular antecedents joined by *or* or *nor.*

EXAMPLES   Either **Ralph or Carlos** will display **his** baseball cards.

                  Neither **Nina nor Mary** will bring **her** CD player.

17u. Use a plural pronoun to refer to two or more antecedents joined by *and.*

EXAMPLES   **Isaac and Jerome** told me that **they** were coming.

                  Elena and Roberto sent letters to **their** cousin.

Exercise 12 Using Pronouns in Sentences

For each of the following sentences, write a pronoun or a pair of pronouns that will correctly complete the sentence.

USAGE

EXAMPLE   1. Dominic or Martin will show _____ slides.
          1. his

1. A writer should proofread _____ work carefully.
2. One of the boys had finished _____ homework.
3. No, Joyce has not given me _____ answer.
4. The store sent Paula and Eric the posters that _____ had ordered last week.
5. Mark or Hector will arrive early so that _____ can help us.
6. Everyone read one of _____ poems aloud.
7. One of the students raised _____ hand.
8. _____ of the tennis rackets were damaged by the water leak.
9. The dogs had eaten none of _____ food.
10. Each of the dogs ate the scraps that we gave _____ .
11. The principal and the Spanish teacher announced _____ plans for the Cinco de Mayo fiesta.
12. All of the bowling pins were on _____ sides.
13. The movie made sense to _____ of the audience members.
14. Everyone in my class has _____ own writer's journal.
15. Neither recalled the name of _____ first-grade teacher.
16. _____ of the players, Sharon and P. J., agreed that the game was a draw.
17. Ms. Levine said _____ was proud of the students.
18. Frank had tried on all of the hats before _____ chose one.
19. Anyone may join if _____ collects stamps.
20. Either Vanessa or Marilyn was honored for _____ design.

COMPUTER TIP

Using indefinite pronouns correctly can be tricky. To help yourself, you may want to create an indefinite pronoun guide. First, summarize the information in Rules 17d–17f and 17q–17s.

Then, choose several examples to illustrate the rules. If you use a computer, you can create a Help file in which to store this information.

Call up your Help file whenever you run into difficulty with indefinite pronouns in your writing. If you don't use a computer, you can keep your guide in a writing notebook.

USAGE

17v. A pronoun that refers to a collective noun has the same number as the noun.

A collective noun is singular when it refers to the group as a unit and plural when it refers to the individual members of the group.

EXAMPLES   The **cast** is giving **its** final performance tonight. [The cast as a unit is giving its final performance.]

The **cast** are trying on **their** costumes. [The members of the cast are trying on their individual costumes.]

The **faculty** has prepared **its** report. [The faculty as a unit has prepared its report.]

The **faculty** are returning to **their** classrooms. [The members of the faculty are returning to their separate classrooms.]

17w. An expression of an amount may take a singular or plural pronoun, depending on how the expression is used.

EXAMPLES   **Five dollars** is all I need. I hope my sister will lend **it** to me. [The amount is thought of as a unit.]

Two dollars are torn. The vending machine won't take **them.** [The amount is thought of as individual pieces or parts.]

17x. Even when plural in form, the title of a creative work (such as a book, song, film, or painting), the name of an organization, or the name of a country or city usually takes a singular pronoun.

EXAMPLES   Have you read **Great Expectations**? **It** is on our summer reading list.

The **United Nations,** which has **its** headquarters in New York, also has offices in Geneva and Vienna.

My grandmother, who is from the **Maldives,** told us of **its** coral reefs and lagoons.

Exercise 13 Choosing Pronouns That Agree with Their Antecedents

Choose the correct word or words in parentheses in the following sentences.

EXAMPLE   1. Even a trio can have a big sound if (*it, they*) can arrange the score properly.

1. *it*

1. They are asking two hundred dollars, but (*it, they*) should be a lower price because there is no chair with the desk.
2. Darla, *The Hero and the Crown* has been checked out; however, (*it, they*) should be back next Wednesday.
3. If the high school band doesn't show up soon, (*it, they*) won't lead the parade.
4. These plans call for ten feet of African ebony, and although (*it, they*) would look great, I have no idea where we could even find ebony.
5. Seven points may not seem like much, but in jai alai, (*it, they*) can be enough to decide the game.
6. The unit took up (*its, their*) position on the hill.

USAGE

7. "Sixteen Tons" has always been one of my favorite songs, and (*it, they*) always will be.
8. Six of the sales teams exceeded (*its, their*) goals.
9. Will the board of directors alter (*its, their*) decision?
10. Try Harper Brothers Appliances first; if (*it, they*) happens to be closed, go up the street to Smith's Hardware.

Review E **Proofreading Sentences for Correct Pronoun-Antecedent Agreement**

Most of the following sentences contain errors in pronoun-antecedent agreement. Identify each error, and write the correct pronoun or pronouns. If a sentence is already correct, write *C*.

EXAMPLE
1. At the meeting, each member of the Small Business Council spoke about their concerns.

    1. *their—his or her*

1. Everybody had a chance to express their opinion about the new shopping mall.
2. Mrs. Gomez and Mr. Franklin are happy about his or her new business locations at the mall.
3. Both said that his or her profits have increased significantly.
4. Neither Mr. Chen nor Mr. Cooper, however, feels that his or her customers can find convenient parking.
5. Anyone shopping at the mall has to park their car too far from the main shopping area.
6. Several members of the council said that the mall has taken away many of their customers.
7. One of the women on the council then presented their own idea about creating a farmers' market on weekends.

8. Many members said he or she favored the plan, and a proposal was discussed.
9. Each farmer could have their own spot near the town hall.
10. The Small Business Council then agreed to take their proposal to the mayor.

Review F   Writing Sentences That Demonstrate Correct Subject-Verb and Pronoun-Antecedent Agreement

Using the following words or word groups as subjects, write twenty sentences. In each sentence, underline the verb that agrees with the subject. Then, underline twice any pronoun that agrees with the subject.

┌─HELP─┐

Not every sentence in Review F needs to have a pronoun that agrees with the subject.

EXAMPLE   1. all of the players

1. *All of the players <u>were</u> tired; <u>they</u> had had a long practice.*

1. both Jed and Bob
2. none of the puppies
3. Los Angeles
4. fifty cents
5. *Anne of Green Gables*
6. news
7. either the teacher or the students
8. the litter of kittens
9. neither Nancy nor Tim
10. everyone
11. *The Adventures of Tom Sawyer*
12. the football team
13. each of the chairs
14. athletics
15. the Masters tournament
16. few armadillos
17. most of the apple
18. several days
19. any of the orange juice
20. none of the pizza

Chapter Review

A. Determining Subject and Verb Agreement

Identify the correct form of the verb given in parentheses in each of the following sentences. Base your answers on the rules of standard, formal usage.

1. Elephants (*has, have*) worked with people for centuries.
2. A blue vase (*is, are*) the only thing in the room.
3. (*Doesn't, Don't*) Midori come here every afternoon?
4. The exhibit of drawings by John James Audubon (*was, were*) fascinating, don't you think?
5. Civics (*was, were*) only one of the classes that challenged me.
6. Since Mom repaired them, both of the radios (*work, works*).
7. Everyone (*calls, call*) Latisha by her nickname, Tish.
8. Fifty cents (*was, were*) a lot of money in 1910!
9. Ms. Sakata's former neighbor and best friend, Ms. Chang, (*writes, write*) poetry.
10. (*Is, Are*) there any other blacksmiths in town?
11. I'm sorry, but somebody (*has, have*) checked out that book.
12. (*Was, Were*) the geese in the cornfield again?
13. All of the shells in my collection (*was, were*) displayed.
14. Neither Cindy nor her cousins (*knows, know*) how to sew.
15. Outside the back door (*is, are*) a few of your friends.
16. My brother and my uncles (*plays, play*) rugby.
17. The Netherlands (*has, have*) a coastline on the North Sea.
18. Here (*is, are*) several subjects for you to consider.
19. The team (*has, have*) all received their jerseys and hats.
20. Some of Ernest Hemingway's writings (*was, were*) autobiographical.
21. This news (*was, were*) just what Barb wanted to hear.
22. *Giants of Jazz* (*is, are*) an interesting book.
23. Everyone (*is, are*) expected to attend.
24. Most of our reading (*was, were*) done on weekends.
25. Either Gordon or Ruben (*knows, know*) the right answer.

USAGE

B. Determining Pronoun and Antecedent Agreement

If the italicized pronoun in each of the following sentences does not agree with its antecedent, write the correct form of the pronoun. If the pronoun does agree with its antecedent, write *C.* Base your answers on the rules of standard, formal usage.

26. Everyone put *their* suitcases on the bus.
27. Either Marcia or Christina will bring *her* serving platter to the dinner party.
28. Both Sarah and Sue agreed with *her* counselor.
29. Several of my friends do *his or her* homework after school.
30. One of the boys used *their* bat in the game.
31. My grandfather's favorite television show is <u>The Honeymooners</u>. He watches *them* every night on cable.
32. All of the horses received *its* vaccinations.
33. Either Maria or Louise will receive *their* award today.
34. Everybody should know *their* ZIP Code.
35. Each student in the class has given *their* report on an African American folktale.
36. Every one of the dogs obeyed *its* owner.
37. I found twenty dollars in my sock drawer. Do you think I should spend *them* on Christmas presents?
38. Will either Hector or Tony read *his* paper aloud?
39. Not one of the students had finished *their* science project on time this semester.
40. After Celia finished her solo, the audience roared *their* approval for five minutes.

Writing Application
Using Agreement in a Composition

Subject-Verb Agreement   If you could be any person in history, who would you be? Why? Your social studies teacher has asked you to answer these questions in a short composition. Be sure to use correct subject-verb agreement in explaining your choice.

Prewriting First, decide what historical person you would like to be, and freewrite about that person. As you write, think about why the person is noteworthy and why you would want to be him or her.

Writing Use your freewriting ideas to write your first draft. Begin with a sentence that states the purpose of your composition and identifies your historical figure. Then, give your main reasons for wanting to be that person. Summarize your main points in a conclusion.

Revising Read through your composition, and then answer these questions: (1) Is it clear what person from history I want to be? If not, revise your main idea statement. (2) Is it clear why I want to be that person? If not, explain your reasons in more detail.

Publishing Make sure that all subjects and verbs agree in number. Check your composition for errors in spelling, capitalization, and punctuation. Your class may want to create a display using the compositions and pictures of the historical figures chosen.

18

Using Verbs Correctly

Principal Parts, Regular and Irregular Verbs, Tense, Voice

Diagnostic Preview

Proofreading Sentences for Correct Verb Forms

If a sentence contains an incorrect past or past participle form of a verb, write the correct form. If a sentence is already correct, write *C*.

EXAMPLE   1. Melissa drunk the medicine in one gulp.
                1. drank

1. We swum in the lake last weekend.
2. Carlos come from the Dominican Republic.
3. The crow just set there on the wire fence.
4. The balloon burst with a loud pop.
5. I seen that magician on television.
6. The leader raised his tambourine to begin the dance.
7. You should have went with Thomas to the game.
8. The ice cube has shrinked to half its original size.
9. Meanwhile, the water level has rose.
10. I would have wrote to you much sooner, but I lost your address after you moved.
11. Sandra throwed the ball to the shortstop.
12. Ms. Lopez has spoke before many civic groups.

13. All of these photographs were taken in Florida's Everglades National Park.
14. The bell has rang for fourth period.
15. While visiting Los Angeles last August, I run into an old friend in the city's Little Tokyo district.
16. I laid down under a tree to rest.
17. I done everything asked of me.
18. It begun to rain shortly after dusk.
19. Some of the saucers were broken.
20. Sue lay her pen down and studied the question again.

Principal Parts of Verbs

The four basic forms of a verb are called the *principal parts* of the verb.

18a. The principal parts of a verb are the *base form*, the *present participle*, the *past*, and the *past participle*.

When they are used to form tenses, the present participle and the past participle forms require helping verbs (forms of *be* and *have*).

Base Form	Present Participle	Past	Past Participle
talk	[is] talking	talked	[have] talked
draw	[is] drawing	drew	[have] drawn

Because *talk* forms its past and past participle by adding *–ed*, it is called a *regular verb*. *Draw* forms its past and past participle differently, so it is called an *irregular verb*.

The principal parts of a verb are used to express time.

PRESENT TIME   He **draws** excellent pictures.
Susan **is drawing** one now.

PAST TIME   Last week they **drew** two maps.
She **has** often **drawn** cartoons.

FUTURE TIME   Perhaps she **will draw** one for you.
By Thursday, we **will have drawn** two more.

┌HELP──
Some teachers refer to the base form as the *infinitive*. Follow your teacher's directions when you are labeling this form.

Reference Note
For information on **participles used as adjectives,** see page 410. For information on **helping verbs,** see page 361.

Most regular verbs that end in e drop the e before adding *–ing*. Some regular verbs double the final consonant before adding *–ing* or *–ed*.

EXAMPLES
shake—shak**ing**
hug—hu**gged**

Reference Note

For more about **spelling rules,** see Chapter 25. For information on **standard and nonstandard English,** see page 553.

Regular Verbs

18b. A *regular verb* forms its past and past participle by adding *–d* or *–ed* to the base form.

Base Form	Present Participle	Past	Past Participle
clean	[is] cleaning	cleaned	[have] cleaned
hope	[is] hoping	hoped	[have] hoped
inspect	[is] inspecting	inspected	[have] inspected
slip	[is] slipping	slipped	[have] slipped

One common error in forming the past or the past participle of a regular verb is to leave off the *–d* or *–ed* ending.

NONSTANDARD Our street use to be quieter.
STANDARD Our street **used** to be quieter.

Another common error is to add unnecessary letters.

NONSTANDARD The swimmer almost drownded in the riptide.
STANDARD The swimmer almost **drowned** in the riptide.

NONSTANDARD The kitten attackted that paper bag.
STANDARD The kitten **attacked** that paper bag.

Oral Practice 1 **Using Regular Verbs**

Read each of the following sentences aloud, stressing the italicized verbs.

1. We are *supposed* to meet at the track after school.
2. The twins *happened* to buy the same shirt.
3. They have already *called* me about the party.
4. Do you know who *used* to live in this house?
5. I had *hoped* they could go to the concert with us.

© 1992 by Sidney Harris.

6. The chairs have been *moved* into the hall for the dance.

7. That salesclerk has *helped* my mother before.

8. Eli may not have *looked* under the table for the cat.

Exercise 1 **Writing the Forms of Regular Verbs**

Write the correct present participle, past, or past participle form of the italicized verb given before each of the following sentences.

EXAMPLES   **1.** *learn*   Many people today are _____ folk dances from a variety of countries.

         1. learning

        2. *hope*   Dad and I had _____ to take lessons in folk dancing this summer.

         2. hoped

1. *practice*   These Spanish folk dancers must have _____ for a long time.

2. *perform*   Notice that they are _____ in their colorful native costumes.

3. *wish*   Have you ever _____ that you knew how to do any folk dances?

4. *use*   Virginia reels _____ to be popular dances in the United States.

5. *promise*   Mrs. Stamos, who is from Greece, _____ to teach her daughter the Greek chain dance.

6. *lean*   The young Jamaican dancer _____ backward before he went under the pole during the limbo dance competition.

7. *start*   The group from Estonia is _____ a dance about a spinning wheel.

8. *request*   Someone in the audience has _____ an Irish square dance called "Sweets of May."

9. *dance*   During the Mexican hat dance, the woman _____ around the brim of the sombrero.

10. *fill*   The Jewish wedding dance _____ the room with both music and movement.

USAGE

USAGE

Irregular Verbs

18c. An _irregular verb_ forms its past and past participle in some way other than by adding _–d_ or _–ed_ to the base form.

Irregular verbs form their past and past participle in various ways:

- by changing vowels

Base Form	Past	Past Participle
sing	sang	[have] sung
become	became	[have] become
drink	drank	[have] drunk

- by changing consonants

Base Form	Past	Past Participle
make	made	[have] made
build	built	[have] built
lend	lent	[have] lent

- by changing vowels _and_ consonants

Base Form	Past	Past Participle
do	did	[have] done
go	went	[have] gone
buy	bought	[have] bought

- by making no changes

Base Form	Past	Past Participle
hurt	hurt	[have] hurt
put	put	[have] put
let	let	[have] let

Common Irregular Verbs

Base Form	Present Participle	Past	Past Participle
begin	[is] beginning	began	[have] begun
bite	[is] biting	bit	[have] bitten or bit
blow	[is] blowing	blew	[have] blown
break	[is] breaking	broke	[have] broken
bring	[is] bringing	brought	[have] brought
build	[is] building	built	[have] built
burst	[is] bursting	burst	[have] burst
buy	[is] buying	bought	[have] bought
catch	[is] catching	caught	[have] caught
choose	[is] choosing	chose	[have] chosen
come	[is] coming	came	[have] come
cost	[is] costing	cost	[have] cost
cut	[is] cutting	cut	[have] cut
do	[is] doing	did	[have] done
draw	[is] drawing	drew	[have] drawn
drink	[is] drinking	drank	[have] drunk
drive	[is] driving	drove	[have] driven
eat	[is] eating	ate	[have] eaten
fall	[is] falling	fell	[have] fallen
feel	[is] feeling	felt	[have] felt
fight	[is] fighting	fought	[have] fought
find	[is] finding	found	[have] found
fly	[is] flying	flew	[have] flown
forgive	[is] forgiving	forgave	[have] forgiven
freeze	[is] freezing	froze	[have] frozen
get	[is] getting	got	[have] got or gotten
give	[is] giving	gave	[have] given
go	[is] going	went	[have] gone
grow	[is] growing	grew	[have] grown

(continued)

(continued)

Common Irregular Verbs			
Base Form	Present Participle	Past	Past Participle
have	[is] having	had	[have] had
hear	[is] hearing	heard	[have] heard
hide	[is] hiding	hid	[have] hid or hidden
hit	[is] hitting	hit	[have] hit
hold	[is] holding	held	[have] held
know	[is] knowing	knew	[have] known
lead	[is] leading	led	[have] led

Oral Practice 2 **Using Irregular Verbs**

Read the following sentences aloud, stressing the italicized verbs.

1. Edward's sister *drove* him to the mall this afternoon.
2. My parents *came* to the spelling bee last year.
3. I should have *known* the test would be difficult.
4. He's *going* to Cape Canaveral this summer.
5. Maya has been *chosen* to play on our team.
6. The water pipe *burst* during the ice storm.
7. *Did* you see the northern lights last night?
8. Wyatt *brought* his new computer game to the slumber party at Alexander's house.

Exercise 2 **Writing the Past and Past Participle Forms of Irregular Verbs**

Write the correct past or past participle form of the italicized verb given before each of the following sentences.

EXAMPLE   1. *choose*   Sara has _____ her song for the piano recital next week.

1. *chosen*

1. *drive*   Last summer we _____ to Denver, where we visited the U.S. Mint.
2. *begin*   The concert _____ an hour ago.

3. *break*   Mike Powell _____ the world long-jump record by jumping 29 feet 4½ inches.

4. *blow*   The wind has _____ the tent down.

5. *get*   We _____ tickets to ride *The Silverton*.

6. *fall*   Several people have _____ over that log.

7. *do*   Mother _____ her best, and she got a promotion.

8. *drink*   According to legend, the Aztec emperor Montezuma _____ chocolate.

9. *build*   People in Africa _____ large cities hundreds, even thousands, of years ago.

10. *go*   You've never _____ to Puerto Rico, have you?

11. *bite*   I think that Roseanne _____ into a green chile!

12. *grow*   Well, nephew, you surely have _____!

13. *catch*   You look like you just _____ the brass ring!

14. *give*   Mom had already _____ us a color copy of her grandmother's journal.

15. *eat*   The Japanese have box lunches, too, but they call them *obentos*; we have _____ them several times.

16. *feel*   They _____ better after taking a short nap.

17. *cost*   Those tickets shouldn't have _____ so much.

18. *buy*   Have you ever _____ a Greek sandwich called a *gyro*?

19. *find*   My cousin said that she has _____ a new canyon trail.

20. *freeze*   The pond _____ last winter, and we went skating.

More Common Irregular Verbs			
Base Form	Present Participle	Past	Past Participle
leave	[is] leaving	left	[have] left
lend	[is] lending	lent	[have] lent
let	[is] letting	let	[have] let
light	[is] lighting	lighted *or* lit	[have] lighted *or* lit
lose	[is] losing	lost	[have] lost
make	[is] making	made	[have] made
meet	[is] meeting	met	[have] met
pay	[is] paying	paid	[have] paid

(continued)

STYLE TIP

Some verbs have two correct past or past participle forms. However, these forms are not always interchangeable.

EXAMPLES

I **shone** the flashlight into the woods. [*Shined* also would be correct in this usage.]

I **shined** my shoes. [*Shone* would be incorrect in this usage.]

If you are unsure about which past participle form to use, check an up-to-date dictionary.

(continued)

Base Form	Present Participle	Past	Past Participle
More Common Irregular Verbs			
put	[is] putting	put	[have] put
read	[is] reading	read	[have] read
ride	[is] riding	rode	[have] ridden
ring	[is] ringing	rang	[have] rung
run	[is] running	ran	[have] run
say	[is] saying	said	[have] said
see	[is] seeing	saw	[have] seen
seek	[is] seeking	sought	[have] sought
sell	[is] selling	sold	[have] sold
send	[is] sending	sent	[have] sent
shrink	[is] shrinking	shrank or shrunk	[have] shrunk
sing	[is] singing	sang	[have] sung
sink	[is] sinking	sank or sunk	[have] sunk
speak	[is] speaking	spoke	[have] spoken
spend	[is] spending	spent	[have] spent
stand	[is] standing	stood	[have] stood
steal	[is] stealing	stole	[have] stolen
swim	[is] swimming	swam	[have] swum
swing	[is] swinging	swung	[have] swung
take	[is] taking	took	[have] taken
teach	[is] teaching	taught	[have] taught
tear	[is] tearing	tore	[have] torn
tell	[is] telling	told	[have] told
think	[is] thinking	thought	[have] thought
throw	[is] throwing	threw	[have] thrown
wear	[is] wearing	wore	[have] worn
win	[is] winning	won	[have] won
write	[is] writing	wrote	[have] written

Oral Practice 3 Using Irregular Verbs

Read the following sentences aloud, stressing the italicized verbs.

1. When the bell *rang,* we hurried out of the building.
2. The audience was quiet as the acrobats *swung* from the trapeze.
3. That dress had already *shrunk* before I washed it.
4. Otherwise, Lily would have *worn* it to the dance.
5. Have you *met* the new foreign exchange student?
6. We were late to the picnic because I *lost* the map.
7. My father *lent* me the money to buy a new watch.
8. Would you believe that Raymond *took* singing lessons?

Exercise 3 Writing the Past and Past Participle Forms of Irregular Verbs

Write the correct past or past participle form of the italicized verb given before each of the following sentences.

EXAMPLE   **1.** *see*   I have _____ that movie twice already.
           1. seen

  1. *run*   Michael _____ the 100-meter dash in excellent time.
  2. *sell*   My aunt has _____ more houses than any other real estate agent in the city.
  3. *speak* The director of the state health department _____ to our class today.
  4. *win*   The Mexican poet Octavio Paz _____ the Nobel Prize in literature.
  5. *write* I have _____ some poems, but I am shy about showing them to anyone.
  6. *ride*   Tamisha's whole family _____ mules to the bottom of the Grand Canyon.
  7. *sing*   At the concert, the group _____ my favorite song.
  8. *throw* Someone must have _____ this trash from a car.
  9. *swim* Within minutes, the two beautiful swans had _____ across the lake.
10. *sink*   King Arthur's sword Excalibur had _____ slowly to the bottom of the lake.
11. *send* My aunt in South America _____ me a fabulous sweater made from the wool of an alpaca, which is an animal similar to a llama.

12. *tell*   Mr. Noguchi _____ us that *R.S.V.P.* at the bottom of an invitation means that you should let the host know whether you are coming or not.

13. *lend*   Before the softball game, my friend Gabriela _____ me her glove.

14. *wear*   Shouldn't you have _____ a warmer jacket for the hike this morning?

15. *swim*   Soon-hee, who is training for a triathlon, _____ two miles on Saturday.

16. *ring*   I have _____ the doorbell several times, but no one has come to the door.

17. *lose*   The swan living in the pond _____ many large feathers; Tony says it must be molting.

18. *take*   It has _____ more than four hours to find the last item for the scavenger hunt.

19. *sing*   Gerald, Annie, and Trish have _____ the national anthem at assembly.

20. *say*   The weather forecast this morning _____ to expect snow flurries.

Review A   **Writing the Past and Past Participle Forms of Irregular Verbs**

Write the correct past or past participle form of the italicized verb given before each of the following sentences.

EXAMPLE   **1.** *tell*   Has Alameda _____ you about the book *The Indian Tipi: Its History, Construction, and Use*?

         1. told

1. *write*   Reginald and Gladys Laubin _____ that book and others about American Indian culture.

2. *build*   The Laubins _____ their own tepee.

3. *stand*   Tepees of various sizes once _____ all across the Great Plains.

4. *see*   I have _____ pictures of camps full of beautifully decorated tepees.

5. *make*   For many years, American Indians have _____ tepees out of cloth rather than buffalo hides.

6. *come*   The word *tepee*, or *tipi*, has _____ into English from the Sioux language.

7. *draw*   On the outside of their tepees, the Sioux and Cheyenne peoples _____ designs like the ones shown on the previous page.

8. *take*   Because the Plains Indians followed animal herds, they needed shelter that could be easily _____ from place to place.

9. *know*   Even before reading the book, I _____ that the inside of a tepee cover was rarely painted.

10. *do*   Traditionally, women _____ all the work of making tepees and putting them up.

Review B   **Writing the Past and Past Participle Forms of Irregular Verbs**

Write the correct past or past participle form of the italicized verb given before each of the following sentences.

EXAMPLE   **1.** *write*   I _____ a report on Jim Thorpe.

           1. wrote

1. *blow*   Yesterday the wind _____ the leaves into our yard.

2. *break*   My pen pal from Australia has never _____ his promise to write once a week.

3. *bring*   I _____ the wrong book to class.

4. *burst*   The children almost _____ with excitement.

5. *choose*   The director _____ James Earl Jones for the role.

6. *come*   My aunt and her friend _____ to dinner last night.

7. *do*   I have always _____ my homework right after supper.

8. *drink*   The guests _____ four quarts of fruit punch.

9. *fall*   One of Julian's Russian nesting dolls has _____ off the shelf.

10. *freeze*   Has the pond _____ yet?

11. *go*   We have never _____ to see the Parthenon in Nashville.

12. *know*   Had I _____, I would have called you sooner.

13. *ring*   Suddenly the fire alarm _____.

14. *run*   Joan Samuelson certainly _____ a good race.

15. *see*   I _____ you in line at the movies.

16. *shrink*   The apples we dried in the sun have _____.

17. *speak*   After we had _____ to George Takei, who played Mr. Sulu, we went to the *Star Trek* convention banquet.

18. *swim*   We _____ out to the float and back.

19. *write* She has ____ me several long letters.
20. *throw* You shouldn't have ____ the ball to second base.

Tense

18d. The *tense* of a verb indicates the time of the action or of the state of being that is expressed by the verb.

EXAMPLES   Yesterday, Denise **served** lox and bagels for breakfast.

Randy **has played** bass guitar for the band, but now he **plays** drums.

Once they **have painted** the signs, Jill and Cody **will finish** the decorations for the dance.

Verbs in English have six tenses.

Present	Past	Future
Present Perfect	Past Perfect	Future Perfect

The following time line shows the relationship between the six tenses.

Past
existing or
happening
in the past

Present
existing or
happening
now

Future
existing or
happening
in the future

Past Perfect
existing or
happening
before a
specific time
in the past

Present Perfect
existing or
happening
sometime
before now;
may be
continuing now

Future Perfect
existing or
happening
before a
specific time
in the future

Listing the different forms of a verb is called *conjugating* the verb.

Conjugation of the Verb *See*

Present Tense

Singular	Plural
I see	we see
you see	you see
he, she, *or* it sees	they see

Past Tense

Singular	Plural
I saw	we saw
you saw	you saw
he, she, *or* it saw	they saw

Future Tense

Singular	Plural
I will (shall) see	we will (shall) see
you will (shall) see	you will (shall) see
he, she, *or* it will (shall) see	they will (shall) see

Present Perfect Tense

Singular	Plural
I have seen	we have seen
you have seen	you have seen
he, she, *or* it has seen	they have seen

Past Perfect Tense

Singular	Plural
I had seen	we had seen
you had seen	you had seen
he, she, *or* it had seen	they had seen

Future Perfect Tense

Singular	Plural
I will (shall) have seen	we will (shall) have seen
you will (shall) have seen	you will (shall) have seen
he, she, *or* it will (shall) have seen	they will (shall) have seen

USAGE

| STYLE   TIP |

Traditionally, the helping verbs *shall* and *will* were used to mean different things. Now, however, *shall* can be used almost interchangeably with *will*.

NOTE Each tense has an additional form called the ***progressive form,*** which expresses continuing action or state of being. In each tense, the progressive form of a verb consists of the appropriate tense of *be* plus the verb's present participle.

Present Progressive	am, is, are seeing
Past Progressive	was, were seeing
Future Progressive	will (shall) be seeing
Present Perfect Progressive	has been seeing, have been seeing
Past Perfect Progressive	had been seeing
Future Perfect Progressive	will (shall) have been seeing

Consistency of Tense

18e. Do not change needlessly from one tense to another.

When writing about events that take place at the same time, use verbs that are in the same tense. When writing about events that occur at different times, use verbs that are in the different tenses.

INCONSISTENT   When we go to the movies, we bought some popcorn. [The events occur at the same time, but *go* is in the present tense and *bought* is in the past tense.]

CONSISTENT   When we **go** to the movies, we **buy** some popcorn. [Both *go* and *buy* are in the present tense.]

CONSISTENT   When we **went** to the movies, we **bought** some popcorn. [Both *went* and *bought* are in the past tense.]

Exercise 4 **Making Tenses of Verbs Consistent**

Read the following sentences, and choose whether to rewrite them in the present or past tense. Then, rewrite the sentences, changing the verb forms to correct any needless changes.

EXAMPLE   **[1]** I picked up the telephone receiver quickly, but the line is still dead.

1.   *I picked up the telephone receiver quickly, but the line was still dead.*

or

I pick up the telephone receiver quickly, but the line is still dead.

[1] Lightning struck our house, and I run straight for cover. [2] "Oh, no!" I exclaim. [3] The electricity was out! [4] My parents get out the flashlights, and we played a game. [5] Later, since the stove, oven, and microwave didn't work without electricity, we have a cold supper in the living room—picnic style! [6] My younger brother asks me what lightning is. [7] "Lightning is a big spark of electricity from a thundercloud," I tell him. [8] He nods. [9] I started to tell him about positive and negative charges creating lightning, but he doesn't understand what I'm talking about and walks away. [10] In the morning, we were all glad when the sun shone and our electricity is on again.

Active and Passive Voice

A verb in the ***active voice*** expresses an action done *by* its subject. A verb in the ***passive voice*** expresses an action done *to* its subject. In passive voice, the verb phrase always includes a form of *be* and the past participle of the main verb. Other helping verbs may also be included. Compare the following sentences:

ACTIVE VOICE	The pilot **instructed** us. [The subject, *pilot,* performs the action.]
PASSIVE VOICE	We **were instructed** by the pilot. [The subject, *we,* receives the action.]
ACTIVE VOICE	Alice **caught** a fly ball. [The subject, *Alice,* performs the action.]
PASSIVE VOICE	A fly ball **was caught** by Alice. [The subject, *ball,* receives the action.]
ACTIVE VOICE	The firefighters **have put** out the blaze. [The subject, *firefighters,* performs the action.]
PASSIVE VOICE	The blaze **has been put** out by the firefighters. [The subject, *blaze,* receives the action.]

Exercise 5 Identifying Active and Passive Voice

Tell whether the verb is in the *active voice* or *passive voice* in each of the following sentences.

EXAMPLE 1. The 10K race was won by Mikki.

   1. passive voice

1. On Sunday afternoon we painted the den.
2. Brianne was elected to the student council.
3. The CD has been misplaced by my cousin.
4. The new animation software creates vivid images.
5. Many of the yearbook photos were taken by Adrienne.
6. Shoddy work was done on the building.
7. Mike and I don't understand this algebra problem.
8. I am unloading the food and supplies at the campsite.
9. The tickets had been sold months before the concert.
10. Andre was awarded the certificate for his service to the community.

Six Troublesome Verbs

Sit and *Set*

The verb *sit* means "to be seated" or "to rest." *Sit* seldom takes an object. The verb *set* usually means "to place (something somewhere)" or "to put (something somewhere)." *Set* usually takes an object. Notice that *set* has the same form for the base form, past, and past participle.

STYLE — TIP

You may know that the word *set* has more meanings than the two given here. Check in a dictionary to see if the meaning you intend requires an object.

EXAMPLE
The sun **sets** in the West. [Here, *sets* does not take an object.]

Base Form	Present Participle	Past	Past Participle
sit	[is] sitting	sat	[have] sat
set	[is] setting	set	[have] set

EXAMPLES
Who **is sitting** on the blanket by the pool? [no object]
Theresa **is setting** the lawn chairs by the pool. [Theresa is setting what? *Chairs* is the object.]

Three boys **sat** on the platform. [no object]
The boys **set** the instruments on the platform. [The boys set what? *Instruments* is the object.]

We **had sat** on the pier for an hour before Suzanne arrived with the bait. [no object]
I **had set** the bucket of bait on the pier. [I had set what? *Bucket* is the object.]

Oral Practice 4 Using the Forms of *Sit* and *Set* Correctly

Read each of the following sentences aloud, stressing the italicized verbs.

1. Darnell and I *sat* down to play a game of chess.
2. After we had been *sitting* for a while, he decided to make bread.
3. I *set* the pan on the table.
4. After Darnell had *set* out the ingredients, he mixed them.
5. We returned to our game but could not *sit* still for long.
6. We had not *set* the pan in the oven.
7. Then, we almost *sat* too long.
8. If it had *sat* in the oven much longer, it would have burned.

Exercise 6 Writing the Forms of *Sit* and *Set* Correctly

Write the correct form of *sit* or *set* for each blank in the following sentences.

EXAMPLE   1. I _____ my suitcase on the rack.
            1. set

1. On the train to Boston, I _____ next to a woman wearing a shawl.
2. She _____ a large covered basket on the floor by her feet.
3. When the conductor asked her if she would like to _____ it in the baggage rack, she refused.
4. She insisted that the basket must _____ by her feet.
5. As I _____ beside her, I wondered what was in the basket.
6. I _____ my book down and tried to see inside the tightly woven basket.
7. Perhaps I was _____ next to a woman with a picnic lunch.
8. Maybe she had _____ next to me because I looked hungry.
9. As the woman _____ her packages down, I watched the basket.
10. A sudden movement of the train caused the basket to open, and inside it _____ a small, white rabbit.

Rise and *Raise*

The verb *rise* means "to move upward" or "to go up." *Rise* does not take an object. The verb *raise* means "to lift (something) up." *Raise* usually takes an object.

STYLE TIP

You may know that the verb *raise* has more meanings than the one given here.

EXAMPLE

The Nelsons **raise** geese. [*Raise* does not mean "lift up" here, but it still takes an object.]

USAGE

Base Form	Present Participle	Past	Past Participle
rise	[is] rising	rose	[have] risen
raise	[is] raising	raised	[have] raised

EXAMPLES   The fans **were rising** to sing the national anthem. [no object]

Fans **were raising** signs and banners. [Fans were raising what? *Signs* and *banners* are the objects.]

The student **rose** to ask a question. [no object]

The student **raised** a good question. [The student raised what? *Question* is the object.]

Prices **had risen.** [no object]

The store **had raised** prices. [The store had raised what? *Prices* is the object.]

Oral Practice 5   Using Forms of *Rise* and *Raise* Correctly

Read the following sentences aloud, stressing the italicized verbs.

1. Mount Everest *rises* over 29,000 feet.
2. He *raises* the flag at sunrise.
3. The TV reporter *raised* her voice to be heard.
4. She *rose* from her seat and looked out the window.
5. The constellation Orion had not yet *risen* in the southern sky.
6. They had *raised* the piñata high in the tree.
7. I hope the bread is *rising*.
8. He will be *raising* the bucket from the well.

Exercise 7   Identifying the Correct Forms of *Rise* and *Raise*

Identify the correct verb of the two given in parentheses in each of the following sentences.

EXAMPLE   1. After the storm, Diana (*rose, raised*) the window.
    1. *raised*

1. The entire audience quickly (*rose, raised*) to their feet to sing the "Hallelujah Chorus."

2. They used a jack to (*rise, raise*) the car so that they could change the tire.
3. The fire juggler is (*rising, raising*) two flaming batons over his head to signal the start of the show.
4. Some people have trouble remembering that the sun always (*rises, raises*) in the east.
5. He gently (*rose, raised*) the injured duckling from the lake.
6. Only half of Mauna Kea, a volcano on the island of Hawaii, (*rises, raises*) above the ocean.
7. The proud winner has (*risen, raised*) her trophy so that everyone can see it.
8. The guests have (*risen, raised*) from their seats to see the bride enter.
9. Yeast makes the dough for pizza and other baked goods, such as bread and rolls, (*rise, raise*).
10. They will (*rise, raise*) the couch while I look under it.

Lie and *Lay*

The verb *lie* generally means "to recline," "to be in a place," or "to remain lying down." *Lie* does not take an object. The verb *lay* generally means "to put (something) down" or "to place (something somewhere)." *Lay* usually takes an object.

Base Form	Present Participle	Past	Past Participle
lie	[is] lying	lay	[have] lain
lay	[is] laying	laid	[have] laid

EXAMPLES The silverware **is lying** on the table. [no object]
The waiter **is laying** silverware beside each plate. [The waiter is laying what? *Silverware* is the object.]

The apple dolls **lay** drying in the sun. [no object]
Aunt Martha **laid** her apple dolls in the sun to dry. [Aunt Martha laid what? *Dolls* is the object.]

That bicycle **had lain** in the driveway for a week. [no object]
Bill **had laid** that bicycle in the driveway. [Bill had laid what? *Bicycle* is the object.]

STYLE   TIP
The verb *lie* can also mean "to tell an untruth." Used in this way, *lie* still does not take an object.

EXAMPLE
  Don't **lie** to her, Beth.

The past and past participle forms of this meaning of *lie* are *lied* and [*have*] *lied*.

Oral Practice 6 Using Forms of *Lie* and *Lay* Correctly

Read the following sentences aloud, stressing the italicized verbs.

1. If you are tired, *lie* down for a while.
2. *Lay* your pencils down, please.
3. Two huge dogs *lay* by the fire last night.
4. The cat has been *lying* on the new bedspread.
5. Mr. Cortez *laid* the map of Puerto Rico on the table.
6. In our state, snow usually *lies* on the ground until late March or the first weeks of April.
7. He had *laid* your coats on the bed in my room.
8. After the baby had *lain* down for a nap, she still wanted to play with her new toy.

Exercise 8 Identifying the Correct Forms of *Lie* and *Lay*

Identify the correct verb of the two in parentheses for each of the following sentences.

EXAMPLE   1. Marc (*lay, laid*) his new tennis shoes on the floor.
　　　　　　 1. laid

1. The islands of American Samoa (*lie, lay*) about 4,800 miles southwest of San Francisco.
2. Dad quickly (*lay, laid*) the hermit crab down when it began to pinch him.
3. I don't know where I have (*lain, laid*) my copy of *Chinese Proverbs* by Ruthanne Lum McCunn.
4. I have often (*lain, laid*) under the oak tree and napped.
5. Many visitors (*lie, lay*) flowers and wreaths at the Vietnam Veterans Memorial in Washington, D.C.
6. My brother, who is sick, has been (*lying, laying*) in bed all day.
7. The clerk (*lay, laid*) the small package on the scale.
8. (*Lie, Lay*) your backpack down, and come see the new comic books I bought yesterday.
9. Those clothes will (*lie, lay*) on the floor until you pick them up.
10. After he had circled several times, the puppy (*lay, laid*) down and slept.

COMPUTER TIP

Most word processors can help you check your writing to be sure that you've used verbs correctly. For example, a spellchecker will highlight misspelled verb forms such as *attackted* or *drownded*.

Grammar-checking software can point out inconsistent verb tense, and it may also highlight questionable uses of problem verb pairs such as *lie* and *lay* or *rise* and *raise*. Some programs can also identify verbs in the passive voice.

Remember, though, that the computer is just a tool. As a writer, you are responsible for making all the style and content choices that affect your writing.

Identify the correct verb of the two given in parentheses in each of the following sentences.

EXAMPLE   1. The bricklayer (*rose, raised*) from the patio floor and dusted himself off.

        1. *rose*

1. These rocks have (*lain, laid*) here for centuries.
2. Please (*sit, set*) there until your name is called.
3. The nurse (*lay, laid*) her cool hand on the sick child's brow and decided to take his temperature.
4. The horses are (*lying, laying*) in the pasture.
5. The senator and her advisors had (*sat, set*) around the huge conference table.
6. After the picnic, everyone (*lay, laid*) on blankets to rest in the shade of the oak tree.
7. Smoke (*rose, raised*) from the chimney.
8. The farmhands (*sat, set*) their lunch boxes under a tree to keep them cool.
9. Have you been (*sitting, setting*) there all afternoon?
10. The sun has already (*risen, raised*).
11. Why has the stage manager (*rose, raised*) the curtains before the second act has begun?
12. A gust of hot air caused the enormous balloon to (*rise, raise*) out of sight of the spectators.
13. Be sure to (*lie, lay*) these windowpanes down carefully.
14. When the queen enters, each guest should (*rise, raise*) from his or her chair.
15. Who (*sat, set*) the glasses on my chair?
16. "(*Lie, Lay*) down!" the trainer sharply ordered the puppy, but the puppy didn't obey him.
17. If we had a pulley, we could (*rise, raise*) that stone.
18. Just (*sit, set*) those green beans by the sink; I'll get to them in a minute.
19. Mom and Aunt Opal must have been (*lying, laying*) tile in the kitchen all night.
20. You (*rise, raise*) the garage door, and I'll bring the bikes in out of the rain.

USAGE

Review D Proofreading Sentences for Correct Verb Forms

Most of the following sentences contain incorrect verb forms. If a sentence contains the wrong form of a verb, write the correct form. If a sentence is already correct, write *C*.

EXAMPLE
1. During the 1800s, many German settlers choosed to live in the Hill Country of central Texas.

1. *chose*

1. These hardy, determined pioneers builded towns and cleared land for farming.
2. I have went to the town of Fredericksburg several times with my family.
3. This interesting town lays about 80 miles west of Austin.
4. Fredericksburg use to be in Comanche territory.
5. Early on, German settlers made peace with neighboring Comanche chiefs.
6. The town then growed rapidly.
7. German-style churches, public buildings, and houses like the one shown here raised along the town's central street.
8. On one of our visits, my family set and talked about the town with a woman who had been born there.
9. She said that she had spoke German all her life.
10. When we left, she raised a hand and said, *"Auf Wiedersehen"* (until we meet again).

Chapter Review

USAGE

A. Using Irregular Verbs

Write the correct past or past participle form of the italicized irregular verb provided before each sentence.

1. *break*   The thunder ____ the silence.

2. *ring*   Who ____ the fire alarm so quickly?

3. *shrink*   Either my jeans have ____ or I've put on weight.

4. *throw*   You've ____ the ball out of bounds!

5. *lead*   Julio ____ the parade last year, so now it's my turn.

6. *rise*   The sun ____ over the pyramids of Giza in Egypt.

7. *swim*   We have ____ only three laps.

8. *choose*   Vera was ____ as captain of the volleyball team.

9. *go*   I have ____ to visit the Grand Canyon twice.

10. *sit*   The tiny tree frog ____ motionless.

11. *write*   Joan has ____ a story about aliens from the Andromeda galaxy.

12. *do*   During lunch, Jorge ____ his impersonation of Rubén Blades.

13. *steal*   Three runners ____ bases during the first inning.

14. *break*   This summer's heat wave has ____ all records.

15. *drink*   Have you ____ all of the tomato juice?

16. *sink*   The log had slowly ____ into the quicksand.

17. *lie*   The old postcards have ____ in the box for years.

18. *drive*   Have you ever ____ across the state of Texas?

19. *begin*   Our local PBS station ____ its fund-raising drive.

20. *set*   Have you ____ the paper plates and napkins on the picnic table?

21. *throw*   Who ____ the ball to first base?

22. *know*   I have ____ some of my classmates for six years.

23. *take*   Kadeem ____ the role of Frederick Douglass.

24. *tear*   My mother ____ the tag off the mattress.

25. *come*   We ____ close to winning the tournament.

B. Changing Tenses of Verbs

Rewrite each of the following sentences to change the verb or verbs to the tense indicated in italics.

26. *present perfect*   Every time Roger comes to visit me, he brings his dog Zip with him.

27. *past perfect*   The dog will sleep on the kitchen floor for the entire visit.

28. *present*   Zip moved only if he heard the sounds of food being prepared.

29. *future perfect*   Zip has broken all records for a dog not moving a muscle.

30. *past*   We had known Zip before he had grown old.

C. Making Verb Tenses Consistent

Read the following sentences, and choose whether to rewrite them in the present or past tense. Then, rewrite the sentences, changing the verb forms to make the verb tense consistent.

31. My uncle comes back to Michigan for Christmas, and he drove his vintage sports car.

32. Ava finished her assignment, but she forgets to put a title page on it.

33. The stages of the booster rocket dropped away as the space shuttle climbs into the sky.

34. Aunt Maureen jumped to her feet and cheers when Mia made the winning basket.

35. When Barbara presents her science fair project, all the judges were very impressed.

D. Identifying Active and Passive Voice

Tell whether the italicized verb is in the *active voice* or the *passive voice* in each of the following sentences.

36. The grass clippings and the kitchen scraps *were placed* on the compost pile.

37. Most of the class *had* already *gone* to see that movie.

38. All of the pencils *were sharpened* by Erica and Austin before the test began.

39. My father *was asked* for his advice on repairing the old playground equipment.

40. Every Friday night the Lopez family *invites* us to their house for dinner.

Writing Application
Using Verbs in a Story

Verb Forms and Tenses A local writers' club is sponsoring a contest for the best "cliffhanger" opening of an adventure story. Write an exciting paragraph to enter in the contest. Your paragraph should leave readers wondering, "What happens next?" In your paragraph, use at least five verbs from the lists of Common Irregular Verbs in this chapter.

Prewriting First, you will need to imagine a suspenseful situation to describe. Jot down several ideas for your story opening. Then, choose the one you like best. With that situation in mind, scan the lists of irregular verbs. Note at least ten verbs you can use. Include some lively action verbs like *burst*, *swing*, and *throw*.

Writing As you write your rough draft, think of your readers. Choose words that create a suspenseful, believable scene. Remember that you have only one paragraph to catch your readers' interest.

Revising Ask a friend to read your paragraph. Does your friend find it interesting? Can he or she picture the scene clearly? If not, you may want to add, delete, or revise some details.

Publishing Check your spelling, usage, punctuation, and grammar. Check to make sure the forms of verbs are correct and the tenses are consistent. You may want to exchange your cliffhanger with a partner, and complete each other's stories. With your teacher's permission, you can then read the completed stories aloud to the class.

19 | Using Pronouns Correctly
Nominative and Objective Case Forms

Diagnostic Preview

Correcting Errors in Pronoun Forms

Most of the following sentences contain errors in the use of pronoun forms. Identify the error, and give the correct pronoun form for each of the following sentences. If a sentence is already correct, write *C*.

EXAMPLE 1. The Garcia children and them grew up together in East Texas.
   1. *them—they*

1. Omar and him offered us some pita, a Middle Eastern bread.
2. Us basketball players know the value of warming up.
3. The computer experts in our class are Rosalinda and her.
4. There's more than a three-year age difference between Edward and I.
5. Pablo and me are planning to visit the Andes Mountains someday.
6. At Passover, my grandparents make gefilte fish and other traditional foods for my cousins and me.
7. Give Sue and him this invitation to the Japanese tea ceremony.

8. Josh made hisself a bookcase in industrial arts class.

9. Two angry hornets chased Earline and she all the way home.

10. The first actors on stage were Jesse and him.

11. Mr. Mendez and us organized a debate about the rights of students.

12. Will you attend the rally with Dominick and me?

13. I helped Kimberly and they with their play about Hiawatha.

14. Jeannette and her know a great deal about Greek myths.

15. The hickory smoke smelled good to we campers.

16. The only seventh-graders in the marching band this year are Bianca and me.

17. Liang was telling them and me about his home in Hong Kong.

18. Julia and them learned how to use hot wax to make batik patterns on cloth.

19. During the marathon, Lionel ran just behind Jim and she.

20. Thomas asked Marvella and he if they wanted to join a gospel chorus.

Case

19a. *Case* is the form that a noun or pronoun takes to show its relationship to other words in a sentence.

English has three cases for nouns and pronouns:

- nominative
- objective
- possessive

The form of a noun is the same for both the nominative and the objective cases. For example, a noun used as a subject (nominative case) will have the same form when used as a direct object (objective case).

NOMINATIVE CASE   That Ming **vase** is very old. [subject]

OBJECTIVE CASE   Who bought the **vase**? [direct object]

A noun changes its form only in the possessive case, usually by adding an apostrophe and an *s.*

POSSESSIVE CASE   The Ming **vase's** new owner is pleased.

┌HELP┐

The nominative case is sometimes referred to as the subject form. The objective case is sometimes referred to as the object form. Follow your teacher's instructions when using these terms.

Reference Note

For more about **forming the possessive case of nouns,** see page 638.

USAGE

Unlike nouns, most personal pronouns have different forms for all three cases.

Personal Pronouns		
Nominative Case	Objective Case	Possessive Case
Singular		
I	me	my, mine
you	you	your, yours
he, she, it	him, her, it	his, her, hers, its
Plural		
we	us	our, ours
you	you	your, yours
they	them	their, theirs

NOTE The personal pronouns in the possessive case—*my, mine, your, yours, his, her, hers, its, our, ours, their, theirs*—are used to show ownership or relationship.

The possessive pronouns *mine, yours, his, hers, its, ours,* and *theirs* are used as parts of sentences in the same ways in which the pronouns in the nominative and the objective cases are used.

EXAMPLES His book and **mine** are overdue.

This desk is **his.**

We completed **ours** this morning.

The possessive pronouns *my, your, his, her, its, our,* and *their* are used as adjectives before nouns.

EXAMPLES **My** shoes need to be cleaned.

Have you proofread **her** report for her yet?

There goes **their** dog Rex.

NOTE Some authorities prefer to call these words adjectives. Follow your teacher's instructions regarding these possessive forms.

The Nominative Case

19b. The *subject* of a verb should be in the nominative case.

EXAMPLES   **He** and **I** mowed lawns. [*He* and *I* are used together as the compound subject of *mowed.*]

Did **they** craft candles from antique molds? [*They* is the subject of *Did craft.*]

She took orders while **we** made change. [*She* is the subject of *took. We* is the subject of *made.*]

Reference Note

For more about **subjects,** see page 317.

TIPS & TRICKS

To help you choose the correct pronoun in a compound subject, try each form of the pronoun separately.

EXAMPLE
(*She, Her*) and (*I, me*) found them. [*She found* or *Her found? I found* or *Me found?*]

ANSWER
She and **I** found them.

USAGE

Oral Practice 1 **Using Pronouns as Subjects**

Read each of the following sentences aloud, stressing the italicized pronouns.

1. Dr. Chen and *they* discussed the usefulness of herbal medicines.
2. *He* and *I* live next door to each other.
3. *They* should try to get along better.
4. Yesterday *she* and *they* gave their reports on modern African American poets.
5. *You* and *she* left the party early.
6. Since the third grade, *we* have been friends.
7. *He* and his family are moving to Puerto Rico.
8. *I* will miss them.

Exercise 1 **Identifying Correct Pronoun Forms**

Choose the correct form of the pronoun in parentheses in each of the following sentences.

EXAMPLE   **1.** My friends and (*I, me*) like to spend time outdoors.

    1. I

1. Lou and (*me, I*) asked my mother to drive us to a nearby state park.
2. There (*he and I, him and me*) set out on a marked trail through the woods.
3. Before long, (*he and I, him and me*) were exploring a snowy area off the beaten track.
4. At midday Lou and (*me, I*) reluctantly followed our tracks back to the path.
5. (*Us, We*) had had the best time of our lives.

6. I told Mother that I thought (*she, her*) would enjoy the trail.
7. To my surprise, (*she, her*) wanted to walk part of the trail then.
8. Lou and (*she, her*) immediately started hiking down the trail.
9. (*They, Them*) knew that I would follow.
10. (*Us, We*) had fun but were ready to ride instead of walk home!

19c. A *predicate nominative* should be in the nominative case.

A *predicate nominative* is a word or word group that is in the predicate and that identifies or refers to the subject of the verb. A pronoun used as a predicate nominative completes the meaning of a linking verb, usually a form of the verb *be* (such as *am, are, is, was, were, be, been,* or *being*).

EXAMPLES   The candidates should have been **he** and **she**. [*He* and *she* follow the linking verb *should have been* and identify the subject *candidates.*]

The members of the team are **they**. [*They* follows the linking verb *are* and identifies the subject *members.*]

Oral Practice 2   Using Pronouns as Predicate Nominatives

Read each of the following sentences aloud, stressing the italicized pronouns.

1. Were the only Spanish-speaking people you and *they*?
2. The caller could have been *she*.
3. The leaders will be my mother and *he*.
4. The three candidates for class president are *she* and *we*.
5. That must be the pilot and *he* on the runway.
6. The three winners were Eduardo, Maya, and *I*.
7. The first ones on the scene were our neighbors and *they*.
8. The speakers at the rally were *she* and Jesse Jackson.

Exercise 2   **Identifying Correct Pronoun Forms**

Choose the correct form of the pronoun in parentheses in each of the following sentences.

EXAMPLE   1. Were the ones who left early (*they, them*)?
              1. *they*

1. Two witnesses claimed that the burglar was (*him, he*).

STYLE   TIP

Expressions such as *It's me* and *That's her* are acceptable in everyday speaking. However, these expressions contain the objective case pronouns *me* and *her* used incorrectly as predicate nominatives. Such expressions should be avoided in formal writing and speaking.

Reference Note

For more about **predicate nominatives**, see page 391.

TIPS & TRICKS

To choose the correct form of a pronoun used as a predicate nominative, try reversing the order of the sentence.

EXAMPLE
   The fastest runner is (*he, him*).

REVERSED
   (*He, Him*) is the fastest runner.

ANSWER
   The fastest runner is **he**.

2. The volunteers must be (*them, they*).

3. Is the last performer (*she, her*)?

4. The next speaker will be (*him, he*).

5. The guests of honor are Luther and (*us, we*).

6. I knew the one in red was (*she, her*), of course.

7. The hardest workers are Susan, Tranh, and (*me, I*).

8. Can that be (*she, her*) in the Indian sari?

9. The next batter should be (*she, her*).

10. Our newest neighbors are the Blumenthals and (*them, they*).

Review A **Writing Sentences That Contain Pronouns in the Nominative Case**

The busy scene you see on the next page was painted by the Mexican American artist Carmen Lomas Garza. It shows one of her childhood birthday parties. The fish-shaped object is a piñata, full of treats for the children. Carmen is getting ready to take a swing at the piñata. Answer each of the following questions by writing a sentence. Follow the directions after each question.

EXAMPLE   1. What are the kneeling boys in the lower right-hand corner doing? (*Use a plural personal pronoun as the subject.*)

1. *They are getting ready to play marbles.*

1. What is Carmen using to hit the piñata? (*Use a singular personal pronoun as the subject.*)

2. For whom are the presents on the table? (*Use a plural personal pronoun as the subject.*)

3. Who will get the gifts and treats inside the piñata? (*Use a person's name and a plural personal pronoun as the compound subject.*)

4. Have you and your classmates ever played a game that requires a blindfold? (*Use a plural and a singular personal pronoun as the compound subject.*)

5. Why does the boy at the far left have presents in his hand? (*Use a singular personal pronoun as the subject.*)

6. What would Carmen say if you asked her, "Who's the birthday girl?" (*Use a singular personal pronoun as a predicate nominative.*)

7. Did Carmen's parents and her grandmother plan the party? (*Use a plural and a singular personal pronoun as a compound predicate nominative.*)

8. Are the baby and his mother near the table having a good time? (*Use* the baby *and a singular personal pronoun as the compound subject.*)
9. Is Carmen's father the man holding the piñata rope? (*Use a singular personal pronoun as a predicate nominative.*)
10. Who is the one now looking at the picture of Carmen Lomas Garza's birthday party? (*Use a singular personal pronoun as a predicate nominative.*)

Reprinted by permission of GRM Associates, Inc., Agents for Children's Book Press, from the book *Family Pictures* by Carmen Lomas Garza, copyright 1990 by Carmen Lomas Garza.

The Objective Case

19d. *Direct objects* and *indirect objects* of verbs should be in the objective case.

A ***direct object*** is a noun, pronoun, or word group that tells *who* or *what* receives the action of the verb.

EXAMPLES   Mom called **me** to the phone. [*Me* tells *whom* Mom called.]

Julia bought sweet potatoes and used **them** to make filling for the empanadas. [*Them* tells *what* she used.]

Reference Note

For more about **direct and indirect objects,** see pages 386 and 388.

USAGE

An *indirect object* is a noun, pronoun, or word group that often appears in sentences containing direct objects. An indirect object tells *to whom* or *to what* or *for whom* or *for what* the action of the verb is done.

An indirect object generally comes between an action verb and its direct object.

EXAMPLES   The hostess handed **her** a name tag. [*Her* tells *to whom* the hostess handed the name tag.]

Mr. Tanaka raises large goldfish; he often feeds **them** rice. [*Them* tells to *what* Mr. Tanaka feeds rice.]

NOTE Indirect objects do not follow prepositions. If *to* or *for* precedes a pronoun, the pronoun is an object of a preposition, not an indirect object.

OBJECT OF A PREPOSITION   Send a letter to **me.**
INDIRECT OBJECT   Send **me** a letter.

Oral Practice 3 **Using Pronouns as Direct Objects and Indirect Objects**

Read each of the following sentences aloud, stressing the italicized pronouns.

1. I took Joe and *her* to a performance by French mimes.
2. The bus driver let Melba, Joe, and *me* off at the next corner.
3. An usher gave *us* programs.
4. Another usher showed *them* and *me* our seats.
5. The performers fascinated Melba and *me.*
6. Their costumes delighted the crowd and *her.*
7. No one else impressed Joe and *me* as much as the youngest mime did.
8. We watched *her* exploring the walls of an invisible room.

Exercise 3 **Writing Pronouns Used as Direct Objects and Indirect Objects**

Write an appropriate pronoun for each blank in the sentences on the following page. Use a variety of pronouns, but do not use *you* or *it.*

EXAMPLE   1. Have you seen Kim and _____?
           1. *her*

TIPS & TRICKS

To help you choose the correct pronoun in a compound object, try each form of the pronoun separately in the sentence.

EXAMPLE
The teacher chose Luisa and (*I, me*). [The teacher chose *I* or The teacher chose *me*?]

ANSWER
The teacher chose Luisa and **me.**

USAGE

1. The manager hired Susana and ____.
2. Lana sent ____ and ____ invitations.
3. We gave Grandpa López and ____ round-trip tickets to Mexico City.
4. The firefighters rescued ____ and ____.
5. Aunt Coretta showed my cousins and ____ a carved mask from Nigeria.
6. The show entertained the children and ____.
7. The waiter served ____ and ____ a variety of dumplings.
8. Our team chose ____ and ____ as representatives.
9. The election committee nominated Gerry and ____.
10. The clerk gave Misako and ____ the receipt for the paper lanterns.

Review B **Identifying Correct Pronoun Forms**

Choose the correct form of each pronoun in parentheses in the following sentences.

EXAMPLE   1. Paul told Ms. Esteban that (*he, him*) and (*I, me*) need a topic for our report.

    1. *he, I*

1. In our American history class, some of the other students and (*he, him*) thought that there should be more reports on women.
2. We were interested in Amelia Earhart and wanted to give (*she, her*) the recognition she deserves.
3. The picture on the left, showing Amelia Earhart looking relaxed and confident, interested Paul and (*I, me*).
4. Both (*he, him*) and (*I, me*) were eager to find out more about her contribution to aviation.
5. We learned that it was (*she, her*) who made the first solo flight by a woman across the Atlantic.
6. The fact that Amelia Earhart was the first pilot to fly from Hawaii to California surprised the rest of the class and (*we, us*), too.
7. In 1937, her navigator and (*she, her*) took off in a twin-engine plane for a trip around the world.
8. After (*they, them*) had completed two thirds of the trip, Earhart and her navigator lost contact with radio operators.

USAGE

9. No one ever saw (*they, them*) or the airplane again.
10. Ms. Esteban and (*we, us*) are among the many people still puzzling over this mystery.

19e. The *object of a preposition* should be in the objective case.

A noun or pronoun that follows a preposition is called the ***object of a preposition.*** Together, the preposition, its object, and any modifiers of the object make a ***prepositional phrase.***

EXAMPLES   Before **us** lay rows of green cornstalks. [*Us* is the object of the preposition *Before.*]

         The secret is between **him** and **me**. [*Him* and *me* are the compound object of the preposition *between.*]

         Please stand next to **her**. [*Her* is the object of the compound preposition *next to.*]

Reference Note

For a list of commonly used **prepositions,** see page 370. For more about **prepositional phrases,** see page 402.

Oral Practice 4   **Using Pronouns as Objects of Prepositions**

Read each of the following sentences aloud, stressing the italicized prepositions and pronouns.

1. Mr. Torres divided the burritos *among them* and *us.*
2. At the game Maria sat *near him* and *her.*
3. Rose walked *toward* Nell and *me.*
4. Sam stood *between him* and *me.*
5. Mom ordered sandwiches *for* Hannah and *her.*
6. "*Without* Squanto and *me,* the Pilgrims won't last another winter," thought Samoset.
7. I have read biographies *about him* and Martin Luther.
8. David's parents gave a bar mitzvah party *for him.*

Exercise 4   **Choosing Pronouns Used as Objects of Prepositions**

Choose the correct form of the pronoun in parentheses in each of the sentences on the following page.

EXAMPLE   1. Of all the people who traveled with Lewis and Clark, Sacagawea was particularly helpful to (*them, they*).

        1. *them*

TIPS & TRICKS

To determine the correct pronoun form when the object of a preposition is compound, use each pronoun separately in the prepositional phrase.

EXAMPLE
Maria sent a postcard to (*she, her*) and (*I, me*). [*To she* or *to her*? *To I* or *to me*?]

ANSWER
Maria sent a postcard to **her** and **me**.

USAGE

19
e

1. Sacagawea's husband, a guide named Toussaint Charbonneau, joined the expedition with (*her, she*) and their newborn baby.
2. The Shoshone were Sacagawea's people, and she longed to return to (*them, they*).
3. Captain Clark soon realized how important she would be to Lewis and (*he, him*).
4. The land they were exploring was familiar to (*she, her*).
5. Luckily for (*she, her*) and the expedition, they met a group of friendly Shoshone.
6. From (*them, they*), Sacagawea obtained the ponies that Lewis and Clark needed.
7. Sacagawea's baby boy delighted the expedition's leaders, and they took good care of (*he, him*).
8. In fact, Captain Clark made a promise to (*she, her*) and Charbonneau that he would give the boy a good education.
9. At the age of eighteen, the boy befriended a prince and traveled with (*him, he*) in Europe.
10. Although sources disagree about when Sacagawea died, a gravestone for (*she, her*) in Wyoming bears the date April 9, 1884.

Review C **Identifying Correct Pronoun Forms**

Choose the correct form of the pronoun in parentheses in each of the following sentences. Then, tell what part of the sentence each pronoun is: *subject, predicate nominative, direct object, indirect object,* or *object of a preposition*.

EXAMPLE   1. My brother Pete and (*I, me*) wanted to know more about Elizabeth Blackwell.
     1. *I—subject*

1. Mom told Pete and (*I, me*) the story of Elizabeth Blackwell, the first woman to graduate from medical school in the United States.
2. Geneva College granted (*she, her*) a degree in 1849.
3. At first, because she was a woman, no male doctor would let her work for (*he, him*).
4. Pete and (*I, me*) admire Elizabeth Blackwell for not giving up.
5. She wanted to help the poor and opened her own clinic for (*they, them*).

6. Wealthy citizens were soon supporting (*she, her*) and the clinic with donations.

7. Before long, one of the most talked-about topics in medical circles was (*she, her*) and the excellent work she was doing for the poor.

8. Mom and (*we, us*) read more about Dr. Blackwell, and we learned that she opened a medical school just for women.

9. Dr. Blackwell set high standards for students and gave (*they, them*) hard courses of study to complete.

10. Her teaching prepared (*they, them*) well, and many went on to become successful physicians.

Special Pronoun Problems

Who and *Whom*

The pronoun *who* has different forms in the nominative and objective cases. *Who* is the nominative form; *whom* is the objective form.

When you need to decide whether to use *who* or *whom* in a question, follow these steps:

STEP 1 Rephrase the question as a statement.

STEP 2 Decide how the pronoun is used in the statement—as a subject, a predicate nominative, a direct or an indirect object, or an object of a preposition.

STEP 3 Determine the case of the pronoun according to the rules of formal, standard English.

STEP 4 Select the correct form of the pronoun.

EXAMPLE (*Who, Whom*) is she?

STEP 1 The statement is *She is* (*who, whom*).

STEP 2 The pronoun is a predicate nominative that refers to the subject *She.*

STEP 3 A pronoun used as a predicate nominative should be in the nominative case.

STEP 4 The nominative form is *who.*

ANSWER: **Who** is she?

| STYLE | TIP |

In informal English, the use of *whom* is becoming less common. In fact, in informal situations, you may correctly begin any question with *who* regardless of the grammar of the sentence. In formal English, however, you should distinguish between *who* and *whom.*

EXAMPLE	(*Who, Whom*) will you invite to the dance?
STEP 1	The statement is *You will invite (who, whom) to the dance.*
STEP 2	The pronoun is the direct object of the verb *will invite*.
STEP 3	A pronoun used as a direct object should be in the objective case.
STEP 4	The objective form is *whom*.
ANSWER:	**Whom** will you invite to the dance?

Oral Practice 5 Using *Who* and *Whom*

Read each of the following sentences aloud, stressing the italicized pronouns.

1. *Who* is captain of the football team this year?
2. To *whom* did you give your old skateboard?
3. *Whom* will you call to come and pick us up after band practice?
4. *Who* were the first Americans?
5. In the last play of the game, *who* passed the ball to *whom*?
6. *Who*'s that woman in the green sari?
7. For *whom* did you buy those flowers?
8. *Who* painted that beautiful picture?

Exercise 5 Choosing *Who* or *Whom*

Choose the correct form of the pronoun in parentheses in each of the following sentences.

EXAMPLE	1.	(*Who, Whom*) helped load the hay on the wagon this morning?
	1.	*Who*
	2.	To (*who, whom*) are you going to give the award?
	2.	*whom*

1. (*Who, Whom*) will your brother invite to his birthday party?
2. (*Who, Whom*) will be our substitute teacher while Mr. Chen is away?
3. (*Who, Whom*) has Ms. Spears appointed?
4. Of the three candidates, in (*who, whom*) do you have the most confidence?
5. To (*who, whom*) do you wish these balloons sent?
6. For (*who, whom*) is the package that was delivered?

7. (*Who, Whom*) is the architect of the new library building?
8. With (*who, whom*) would you most like to talk?
9. Among your friends, (*who, whom*) has the quickest smile?
10. (*Who, Whom*) have the students elected class president?

Pronouns with Appositives

Sometimes a pronoun is followed directly by a noun that identifies the pronoun. Such a noun is called an *appositive.* To help you choose which pronoun to use before an appositive, omit the appositive and try each form of the pronoun separately.

Reference Note

For more about **appositives**, see page 609.

EXAMPLE   On Saturdays, (*we, us*) cyclists ride to Mount McCabe and back. [*Cyclists* is the appositive identifying the pronoun.] *We ride* or *Us ride*?

ANSWER   On Saturdays, **we** cyclists ride to Mount McCabe and back.

EXAMPLE   The speaker praised (*we, us*) volunteers. [*Volunteers* is the appositive identifying the pronoun.] *The speaker praised we* or *The speaker praised us*?

ANSWER   The speaker praised **us** volunteers.

Exercise 6   Choosing Correct Pronouns

Choose the correct form of the pronoun in parentheses in each of the following sentences.

EXAMPLE   1. Hanukkah is always an exciting holiday for (*we, us*) Feldmans.

   1. *us*

1. Tiger Woods is a role model for (*we, us*) golfers.
2. Miss Jefferson, (*we, us*) students want to thank you for all your help.
3. (*We, Us*) contestants shook hands warmly.
4. The woman gave (*we, us*) girls five dollars for shoveling the snow.
5. The attorneys politely answered the questions from (*we, us*) reporters.
6. For (*we, us*) volunteers, service is its own reward.
7. Frank loaned (*we, us*) fans two classical tapes.

USAGE

8. The huge dog knocked (*we, us*) joggers off the sidewalk.
9. (*We, Us*) actors need to rehearse again before Friday night.
10. The new team members were (*we, us*) boys.

┌HELP────
The pronouns *himself* and *themselves* can also be used as intensive pronouns.

EXAMPLES
Daniel **himself** will lead the parade.

They **themselves** traveled only twenty miles to get here.

┌Reference Note
For more about **reflexive and intensive pronouns,** see page 343.

Reflexive Pronouns

Do not use the nonstandard forms *hisself* and *theirselfs* or *theirselves* in place of *himself* and *themselves*.

| NONSTANDARD | The secretary voted for hisself in the last election. |
| STANDARD | The secretary voted for **himself** in the last election. |

| NONSTANDARD | The cooks served theirselves some of the hot won-ton soup. |
| STANDARD | The cooks served **themselves** some of the hot won-ton soup. |

Exercise 7 Identifying Correct Pronoun Forms

Choose the correct form of the pronoun in parentheses in each of the following sentences.

EXAMPLE 1. The contestants promised (*theirselves, themselves*) it would be a friendly competition.
1. *themselves*

1. Before he started to read, Zack asked (*hisself, himself*) three questions to set his purpose.
2. My little brother often falls down, but he never seems to hurt (*himself, hisself*).
3. The guests helped (*theirselves, themselves*) to the nuts and raisins.
4. John Yellowtail enjoys (*himself, hisself*) when he is making fine silver jewelry.
5. When the early settlers wanted cloth, they had to spin it (*theirselves, themselves*).
6. My brother was upset with (*hisself, himself*) for being rude.
7. Andrew gave (*himself, hisself*) an early birthday present— a new CD.
8. The Sartens talked (*theirselves, themselves*) out of buying a second vehicle.

USAGE

9. Uncle Allen took the last potatoes for (*hisself, himself*) and passed the onions to me.

10. Bart and Una consider (*theirself, themselves*) authorities on stamp collecting.

Review D Identifying Correct Pronoun Forms

Choose the correct form of the pronoun in parentheses in each of the following sentences.

EXAMPLE   **1.** To me, the two most interesting explorers are (*he, him*) and Vasco da Gama.

            1. he

1. The team captains will be Jack and (*he, him*).

2. The finalists in the local talent contest are Alfredo, Sylvia, and (*I, me*).

3. We were warned by our parents and (*they, them*).

4. The Washington twins and (*I, me*) belong to the same club.

5. Both (*he and she, her and him*) have promised to write us this summer.

6. Pelé and (*he, him*) both played soccer for the New York Cosmos.

7. "What do you think of (*he and I, him and me*)?" I asked.

8. "You and (*he, him*) are improving," they replied.

9. When Miriam Makeba and the troupe of African musicians arrived, we gave (*she and they, her and them*) a party.

10. Do you remember my sister and (*I, me*)?

11. The coach spoke to (*we, us*) players before the game.

12. Was the joke played on you and (*he, him*)?

13. Are you and (*she, her*) going to celebrate Kwanzaa this year?

14. Père Toussaint taught my brother and (*I, me*) several French phrases.

15. Mom, Andy gave (*himself, hisself*) the biggest piece of banana bread.
16. Who are (*they, them*), Travis?
17. They congratulated (*themselves, theirselves*) on a difficult job well done.
18. Don't leave without (*he and I, him and me*).
19. (*We, Us*) skiers had a beautiful view from the lift.
20. (*Who, Whom*) were you expecting?
21. When we met at the auditions for the school play last year, (*he and I, him and me*) got along very well right away.
22. (*Who, Whom*) recommended that book about the history of Ireland to you?
23. When Dawna, Sharon, and (*I, me*) work on homework together, we always get through it faster and remember it better.
24. (*Who, Whom*) will you be tutoring from the elementary school, Margaret Tanaka or Billy Worthington?
25. Everyone agreed that the science project designed by Shannon and (*him, he*) was the best one in the show.

USAGE

Chapter Review

A. Identifying Correct Pronoun Forms

Identify the correct form of the pronoun in parentheses in each of the following sentences.

1. One hot afternoon Mabel and (*I, me*) walked to the old mill.
2. Grandma sent a crate of apples to my family and (*I, me*).
3. The counselor chose (*we, us*) eighth-graders to give the school tour.
4. Don't worry; my stepmother will take you and (*I, me*) home.
5. Ms. Chavez sat between Kareem and (*I, me*) at the assembly.
6. It's a shame that the boys hurt (*themselves, theirselves*) last night.
7. Will you and (*I, me*) be able to reach them in time?
8. Mayor Petrakis asked my mom and (*she, her*) to help.
9. After I mailed the letter, Willie and (*they, them*) arrived.
10. Is this (*she, her*) to whom we spoke yesterday?
11. The senator (*himself, hisself*) sent me a reply.
12. Our coach sent e-mails to (*we, us*) marathon runners about the race tomorrow.
13. The fastest typists in class are Gene and (*they, them*).
14. Will you and (*she, her*) please come to my house this Wednesday?
15. While we were at the store, we saw my cousin and (*she, her*).
16. Our dog Piper will bring the ball to (*he, him*) or (*she, her*).
17. Last night Dad told Canditha and (*I, me*) a story.
18. (*Whom, Who*) wrote *The Wind in the Willows*?
19. (*We, Us*) students were not expecting the pop quiz.
20. The referee told (*we, us*) players that the game would go into overtime.
21. The best calligrapher in the school is (*she, her*).
22. (*Whom, Who*) is the better candidate?
23. To (*who, whom*) is the letter addressed?
24. Roger and (*I, me*) are studying for our lifeguard certificates.
25. Derek looked at (*hisself, himself*) in the mirror.

USAGE

B. Correcting Errors in Pronoun Forms

Most of the following sentences contain an error in the use of pronoun forms. Identify the error, and give the correct form for each of the following sentences. If a sentence is already correct, write *C*.

26. The closing procession of the powwow will be led by he and the other Dakota dancers.
27. May us choir members leave science class early today?
28. To who are you sending the flowers?
29. Please give these copies of Consuela's report to her and the committee members.
30. Him and his best friend watched *Antz* for the third time.
31. Darnell enjoyed hisself at the African Heritage Festival.
32. The last tennis player to beat my sister in straight sets was her.
33. Who have you asked for help with your math homework?
34. Tell Jennifer and I what your science project will be this year.
35. Whom did you invite to the awards ceremony?
36. Us science fiction fans are going to see *Forbidden Planet*.
37. Who will we see at the mosque?
38. Mario's mother will be driving Elena and we to the stadium.
39. Emilio and him volunteered to decorate the cafeteria.
40. The perfect person to play Lady Macbeth in the school play is she.
41. Neither Kevin nor I can decide which of Ray Bradbury's stories we like best.
42. Whom are the most famous inventors in history?
43. Last year, the best piñata was designed by the twins and she.
44. They really outdid theirselves!
45. You should hear the fight song written by us four fans this year!
46. My father and me watched *The Man Who Would Be King* on video last night.
47. Between you and I, I don't think Bill will finish his Web page in time for the contest.
48. The state trooper gave her a ticket for an illegal left turn.
49. The last people to arrive at the party were Cordelia and him.
50. Mom, will you take us tired yard workers out for dinner?

Writing Application
Using Pronouns in a Letter

Nominative and Objective Case Your favorite radio station is having a "Create a Radio Show" contest. Write a letter to the manager of the station explaining what you would like to include in a half-hour weekly radio show. In your letter, use a variety of pronouns in the nominative case and the objective case. Be sure to include enough nouns so that the meaning of all your pronouns is clear.

Prewriting Discuss your ideas for a radio program with a group of your classmates. List the kinds of entertainment and information you could present. Above all, think about what you would like to hear on the radio.

Writing As you write your first draft, follow the format for a business letter. Give specific examples of what you want to do on the show, and give reasons for your choices. Remember that even though your ideas may be very creative, your writing must be formal.

Revising Ask the other group members to read your letter to see if your ideas sound interesting and are clearly stated. Ask them if the relationship between each pronoun and its antecedent is clear. If your meaning is not clear, revise your letter.

Publishing Re-read your letter, and correct any remaining errors in usage, spelling, punctuation, or capitalization. Be sure that you have followed the correct format for a business letter. Also, make sure that you have used all pronouns according to the rules for standard written English. Your class might want to create a bulletin board display of the letters. With your teacher's permission, the class might vote on the best idea for a show and then produce and tape the pilot episode.

Reference Note

For information about **business letters,** see "Writing" in the Quick Reference Handbook.

USAGE

20 Using Modifiers Correctly
Comparison and Placement

Diagnostic Preview

Revising Sentences by Correcting Errors in the Use of Modifiers

Most of the following sentences contain errors in the use, form, or placement of modifiers. Revise each incorrect sentence to eliminate the error. If a sentence is already correct, write *C*.

EXAMPLE
1. There wasn't nothing missing.
    1. *There wasn't anything missing.*
        or
    There was nothing missing.

1. Please weigh both packages to see which of them is heaviest.
2. Alarmed, the wildfire started to spread quickly to our camp.
3. Did you read that Eduardo Mata received an award in the newspaper?
4. The bean soup tasted good.
5. We pass my aunt and uncle's restaurant walking to school.
6. I think the play *Fiddler on the Roof* is better than the movie.
7. Reading a magazine, my cat jumped up in my lap.
8. Jason tried to push the huge desk but couldn't scarcely move it.
9. The balloons startled the young children when they burst.
10. A jet taking off can sound more noisier than a jackhammer.

11. Surprised, my coin collection interested a local coin dealer.
12. He examined two old Greek coins but couldn't see no date.
13. The shinier of those two coins looked newer.
14. That coin turned out to be the oldest of the two, however.
15. I showed one coin to the dealer valued at nearly twenty dollars.
16. He said he couldn't hardly pay more than fifteen dollars for it.
17. If I had bargained good, I might have gotten more for it.
18. Those two coins come from Ireland that have images of harps on them.
19. Collecting coins, my knowledge about other countries and peoples increases.
20. I polished my Saudi Arabian fifty-halala piece careful so that I could see the Arabic writing on it.

What Is a Modifier?

A *modifier* is a word, a phrase, or a clause that makes the meaning of a word or word group more specific. The two kinds of modifiers are *adjectives* and *adverbs*.

One-Word Modifiers

Adjectives

20a. *Adjectives* make the meanings of nouns and pronouns more specific.

ADJECTIVES   Andy gave a **loud** cheer. [The adjective *loud* tells *what kind* of cheer.]

The one I made is **blue**. [The adjective *blue* tells *which one*.]

Adverbs

20b. *Adverbs* make the meanings of verbs, adjectives, and other adverbs more specific.

ADVERBS   Andy cheered **loudly.** [The adverb *loudly* makes the meaning of the verb *cheered* more specific.]

Reference Note

For more about **adjectives,** see page 346. For more about **adverbs,** see page 366.

┌ TIPS & TRICKS ┐

Many adverbs end in *–ly*, but many others do not. Furthermore, not all words with the *–ly* ending are adverbs. Some adjectives end in *–ly*.

ADVERBS
   quickly   soon
   calmly   not

ADJECTIVES
   elderly   holy
   curly   silly

To decide whether a word is an adjective or an adverb, look at how the word is used in the sentence.

The design is **very** modern. [The adverb *very* makes the meaning of the adjective *modern* more specific.]

The crocodile moved **surprisingly** quickly. [The adverb *surprisingly* makes the meaning of the adverb *quickly* more specific.]

Phrases Used as Modifiers

Reference Note

For more about different kinds of **phrases,** see Chapter 14.

Like one-word modifiers, phrases can also be used as adjectives and adverbs.

EXAMPLES   **Leaping from the step,** the toddler flapped his arms in the air. [The participial phrase *Leaping from the step* acts as an adjective that modifies the noun *toddler*.]

The Greek salad is the one **to try.** [The infinitive phrase *to try* acts as an adjective that modifies the pronoun *one*.]

Ms. Elizondo planted rosebushes **along the fence.** [The prepositional phrase *along the fence* acts as an adverb that modifies the verb *planted*.]

Clauses Used as Modifiers

Reference Note

For more about **clauses,** see Chapter 15.

Like words and phrases, clauses can also be used as modifiers.

EXAMPLES   Italian is the language **that I like best.** [The adjective clause *that I like best* modifies the noun *language*.]

Before Albert went to school, he took the trash to the curb. [The adverb clause *Before Albert went to school* modifies the verb *took*.]

Comparison of Adjectives and Adverbs

When adjectives and adverbs are used in comparisons, they take different forms. The specific form they take depends upon how many things are being compared. The different forms of comparison are called *degrees of comparison.*

20c. The three degrees of comparison of modifiers are the *positive*, the *comparative*, and the *superlative*.

(1) The *positive degree* is used when at least one thing is being described.

EXAMPLES   This suitcase is **heavy.**

Luís **cheerfully** began the job.

Those murals are **colorful.**

(2) The *comparative degree* is used when two things or groups of things are being compared.

EXAMPLES   My suitcase is **heavier** than yours.

Luís talked **more cheerfully** than Albert.

Those murals are **more colorful** than these.

(3) The *superlative degree* is used when three or more things or groups of things are being compared.

EXAMPLES   Sylvia's suitcase is the **heaviest** of all.

Of the four boys, Luís worked at the task **most cheerfully.**

Those murals are the **most colorful** that I've seen.

Regular Comparison

Most one-syllable modifiers form the comparative degree by adding *–er* and the superlative degree by adding *–est.*

Positive	Comparative	Superlative
close	clos**er**	clos**est**
slow	slow**er**	slow**est**
soon	soon**er**	soon**est**
straight	straight**er**	straight**est**

Notice that both adjectives and adverbs form their degrees of comparison in the same way.

USAGE

STYLE   TIP

In conversation, you may hear and use expressions such as *Put your best foot forward* and *May the best team win.* Such uses of the superlative are acceptable in spoken English. However, in your writing for school and other formal occasions, you should generally use superlatives only when three or more things are compared.

Reference Note

For guidelines on how to spell words when **adding –er or –est,** see page 661.

TIPS & TRICKS

Here is a way to remember which form of a modifier to use. When comparing two things, use *–er* (the two-letter ending). When comparing three or more things, use *–est* (the three-letter ending).

Many two-syllable modifiers can correctly form the comparative and superlative degrees using either the suffixes *–er* and *–est* or the words *more* and *most*. If adding *–er* or *–est* sounds awkward, use *more* or *most*.

AWKWARD
bitterer
comicest

BETTER
more bitter
most comic

Two-syllable modifiers form the comparative degree by adding *–er* or by using *more*. They form the superlative degree by adding *–est* or by using *most*.

Positive	Comparative	Superlative
simple	simpl**er**	simpl**est**
easy	easi**er**	easi**est**
jealous	**more** jealous	**most** jealous
swiftly	**more** swiftly	**most** swiftly

Modifiers that have three or more syllables form the comparative degree by using *more* and the superlative degree by using *most*.

Positive	Comparative	Superlative
powerful	**more** powerful	**most** powerful
illegible	**more** illegible	**most** illegible
joyfully	**more** joyfully	**most** joyfully
attractively	**more** attractively	**most** attractively

Exercise 1   Forming the Degrees of Comparison of Modifiers

Give the forms for the comparative and superlative degrees of the following modifiers.

EXAMPLE   1. light
1. *lighter; lightest*

1. near	6. tiny	11. healthy	16. confident
2. proud	7. timidly	12. tall	17. enthusiastically
3. carefully	8. loyal	13. grateful	18. dry
4. honestly	9. safe	14. quick	19. tasty
5. small	10. shady	15. easy	20. generous

Decreasing Comparison

To show decreasing comparisons, modifiers form the comparative degree by using *less* and the superlative degree by using *least*.

Positive	Comparative	Superlative
sharp	**less** sharp	**least** sharp
costly	**less** costly	**least** costly
often	**less** often	**least** often
frequently	**less** frequently	**least** frequently

Irregular Comparison

The comparative and superlative degrees of some modifiers are irregular in form.

Positive	Comparative	Superlative
bad	worse	worst
far	farther *or* further	farthest *or* furthest
good	better	best
well	better	best
many	more	most
much	more	most

Review A **Writing Comparative and Superlative Forms of Modifiers**

Correctly complete each of the following sentences with the comparative or superlative form of the italicized adjective or adverb given.

EXAMPLE   **1.** *unusual*   The Corn Palace in Mitchell, South Dakota, is one of the ＿＿ buildings in the United States.

　　　　　　1. most unusual

1. *big*   The Corn Palace is ＿＿ than I thought it would be.
2. *pretty* People in Mitchell try to make each year's Corn Palace decorations ＿＿ than the ones before.
3. *fresh*   The building looks the ＿＿ in September after new corn and grasses are put on it.
4. *easy*   Some workers find it ＿＿ to saw and nail the corn to panels, while others prefer to hang the finished panels on the building.

5. *well*   I could not decide which of the many corn murals on the Corn Palace I liked _____.

6. *mysterious*   The mural of the dancing figure was the _____ one to me.

7. *famous*   Until his death in 1983, Mitchell's _____ artist, Oscar Howe, helped to design and paint these murals.

8. *interesting*   The life of this Sioux artist is the _____ story I've ever heard.

9. *slowly*   My parents walked _____ around the Corn Palace than I did and studied every design.

10. *far*   I met a family from Mexico who had traveled _____ than we had to see the Corn Palace.

Special Problems in Using Modifiers

20d. Use *good* to modify a noun or a pronoun in most cases. Use *well* to modify a verb.

Reference Note

For more about **using good and well,** see page 557.

EXAMPLES   The weather was **good** on the day of the match. [*Good* modifies the noun *weather.*]

If you want a pear, here is a **good** one. [*Good* modifies the pronoun *one.*]

The trees are producing **well** this fall. [*Well* modifies the verb phrase *are producing.*]

USAGE

Good should not be used to modify a verb.

NONSTANDARD   Both teams played good.

STANDARD   Both teams played **well.**

Although *well* is usually used as an adverb, *well* may also be used as an adjective meaning "in good health" or "in good condition."

EXAMPLE   Mom feels quite **well** today. [Meaning "in good health," *well* modifies *Mom.*]

Reference Note

For a discussion of **standard and nonstandard English,** see page 553.

20e. Use adjectives, not adverbs, after linking verbs.

Linking verbs are often followed by predicate adjectives modifying the subject.

EXAMPLES   Ingrid looked **sleepy** [not *sleepily*] this morning. [The predicate adjective *sleepy* modifies the subject *Ingrid.*]

Christina felt **uncertain** [not *uncertainly*] about running in the relay race. [The predicate adjective *uncertain* modifies the subject *Christina.*]

Reference Note

For a list of **linking verbs,** see page 359.

USAGE

NOTE   Some verbs can be used as either linking or action verbs. As action verbs, they may be modified by adverbs.

EXAMPLES   Ingrid looked **sleepily** at the clock. [*Sleepily* modifies the action verb *looked.*]

Christina **uncertainly** felt her way along the hall. [*Uncertainly* modifies the action verb *felt.*]

Exercise 2   Using Adjectives and Adverbs Correctly

Choose the adjective or adverb that will make each sentence correct.

EXAMPLE   1. John seems (*nervous, nervously*) about his speech.
    1. *nervous*

1. When we came into the house after ice-skating, the fire felt (*good, well*).
2. The wind sounds (*fierce, fiercely*) at night.
3. Tino looked (*good, well*) after recovering from his operation.
4. After all, it doesn't taste (*bad, badly*).
5. Venus looks (*beautiful, beautifully*) tonight.
6. Liang cooked a (*good, well*) meal of vegetables and shrimp.

7. Is the sick child feeling (*good, well*) enough to eat something?
8. We looked (*close, closely*) at the fragile cocoon.
9. A cup of soup tastes (*good, well*) on a cold day.
10. Kudzu grows (*rapid, rapidly*) in the South.

20f. Avoid using double comparisons.

A *double comparison* is the use of both *–er* and *more* (or *less*) or *–est* and *most* (or *least*) to form a comparison. When you make a comparison, use only one form, not both.

| NONSTANDARD | This is Kathleen Battle's most finest performance. |
| STANDARD | This is Kathleen Battle's **finest** performance. |

| NONSTANDARD | His hair is more curlier than his sister's. |
| STANDARD | His hair is **curlier** than his sister's. |

| NONSTANDARD | The baby is less fussier in the morning than in the evening. |
| STANDARD | The baby is **less fussy** in the morning than in the evening. |

Exercise 3 Correcting Double Comparisons

Identify the incorrect modifier in each of the following sentences. Then, give the correct form of the modifier.

EXAMPLES 1. I have been studying more harder lately.

1. *more harder—harder*

2. Frederick Douglass was one of the most brilliantest speakers against slavery.

2. *most brilliantest—most brilliant*

1. Sunday was less rainier than Saturday.
2. That is the most saddest story I have ever heard.
3. Are you exercising more oftener than you used to?
4. That evening was the least cloudiest one in weeks.
5. Native arctic peoples have learned to survive in the most coldest weather.
6. Please show me the most finest tennis racket in the shop.
7. It is more farther from New York to Montreal than from New York to Boston.
8. Grumpkins was less jollier than the other elves.

USAGE

9. Your suitcase is more lighter since you took out the boots.
10. Is Venus the most brightest object in the sky tonight?

Double Negatives

20g. Avoid using double negatives.

A *double negative* is the use of two or more negative words to express one negative idea. Most of the negative words in the chart below are adjectives or adverbs.

Common Negative Words			
barely	never	none	nothing
hardly	no	no one	nowhere
neither	nobody	not (–n't)	scarcely

NONSTANDARD   We couldn't hardly move in the subway car.
STANDARD   We **could hardly** move in the subway car.

NONSTANDARD   Yolanda didn't eat no breakfast this morning.
STANDARD   Yolanda **didn't** eat **any** breakfast this morning.
STANDARD   Yolanda **ate no** breakfast this morning.

NONSTANDARD   Didn't she get you nothing for your birthday?
STANDARD   **Didn't** she get you **anything** for your birthday?
STANDARD   Did she get you **nothing** for your birthday?

Exercise 4   Correcting Double Negatives

Revise each of the following sentences to eliminate the double negative.

EXAMPLE   **1.** I couldn't find no one to go camping with me.
     1. I couldn't find anyone to go camping with me.

or

I could find no one to go camping with me.

1. I didn't see no one I knew at the game.
2. Early Spanish explorers searched that area of Florida for gold, but they didn't find none.

┌HELP──
Although two possible answers are given for the example in Exercise 4, you need to give only one revision for each item.

3. We couldn't hardly hear the guest speaker.
4. The cafeteria didn't serve nothing I like today.
5. Double negatives don't have no place in standard English.
6. The bird-watchers saw scarcely no bald eagles this year.
7. The club officers never do none of the work themselves.
8. We wouldn't never need three tractors on our small farm.
9. Jesse couldn't barely see the top of the waterfalls.
10. The Paynes didn't go nowhere special during the three-day holiday weekend.

Review B   Using Modifiers Correctly

Most of the following sentences contain errors in the use of modifiers. Revise each incorrect sentence to eliminate the error. If a sentence is already correct, write *C*.

EXAMPLES   1. My cold is worst today than it was yesterday.
               1. My cold is worse today than it was yesterday.

              2. There wasn't nobody willing to go into that house alone.
              2. There wasn't anybody willing to go into that house alone.

1. She is the funnier of the two comedians.
2. Kendo, a Japanese martial art, is more gracefuller than many other sports.
3. No one in our class can play volleyball as good as Sylvia Yee.
4. Time passes real slowly during the summer.
5. After a long swim, she felt good.
6. I wasn't scarcely able to hear you.
7. Which of the Rogers twins is strongest?
8. Some people don't seem to have no control over their tempers.
9. He hardly ever visit us.
10. Of all the folk dances my grandfather taught me, the polka is the most simplest.

Placement of Modifiers

20h. Place modifying words, phrases, and clauses as close as possible to the words they modify.

Notice how the meaning of the following sentence changes when the position of the phrase *from Cincinnati* changes.

EXAMPLES   The basketball player **from Cincinnati** gave a TV interview for his fans. [The phrase modifies *player.*]

The basketball player gave a TV interview for his fans **from Cincinnati.** [The phrase modifies *fans.*]

From Cincinnati the basketball player gave a TV interview for his fans. [The phrase modifies *gave.*]

A modifier that seems to modify the wrong word in a sentence is called a ***misplaced modifier.*** A modifier that does not clearly modify another word in a sentence is called a ***dangling modifier.***

MISPLACED   Ringing, everyone glared at the man with the cell phone.

CORRECT   Everyone glared at the man with the **ringing** cell phone.

DANGLING   Before moving to Philadelphia, Mexico City was their home.

CORRECT   **Before moving to Philadelphia,** they lived in Mexico City.

Prepositional Phrases

A ***prepositional phrase*** consists of a preposition, a noun or a pronoun called the *object of the preposition,* and any modifiers of that object.

A prepositional phrase used as an adjective generally should be placed directly after the word it modifies.

MISPLACED   The hat belongs to that girl with the feathers.

CLEAR   The hat **with the feathers** belongs to that girl.

A prepositional phrase used as an adverb should be placed near the word it modifies.

MISPLACED   She read that a new restaurant had opened in today's newspaper.

CLEAR   She read **in today's newspaper** that a new restaurant had opened.

USAGE

Reference Note

For more about **prepositions,** see page 370. For more about **prepositional phrases,** see page 371.

USAGE

Avoid placing a prepositional phrase so that it seems to modify either of two words. Place the phrase so that it clearly modifies the word you intend it to modify.

MISPLACED   Manuel said in the afternoon he would call Janet. [Does *in the afternoon* modify *said* or *would call*?]

CLEAR   Manuel said he would call Janet **in the afternoon.** [The phrase modifies *would call.*]

CLEAR   **In the afternoon** Manuel said he would call Janet. [The phrase modifies *said.*]

Exercise 5 Revising Sentences with Misplaced Prepositional Phrases

Each of the following sentences contains a misplaced prepositional phrase. Decide where the prepositional phrase belongs; then, revise the sentence.

EXAMPLES   1. In the United States, Zora Neale Hurston grew up in the first self-governed black township.

   1. *Zora Neale Hurston grew up in the first self-governed black township in the United States.*

   2. The cat toy rolled down the hall with a clatter.

   2. *With a clatter, the cat toy rolled down the hall.*

1. Joshua and Reginald heard that there was a destructive hailstorm on the news.
2. The poster caught my eye on the wall.
3. In the tiny bird's nest, we thought there might be eggs.
4. Our teacher said on Monday the class would put on a play.
5. Don't forget to take the box to the store with the empty bottles.
6. We saw José Clemente Orozco's beautiful murals on vacation in Guadalajara.
7. Tranh read that a wasp larva spins a cocoon in the encyclopedia.
8. A beautiful Bolivian weaving hangs on our living room wall from the town of Trinidad.
9. Did you find the kimonos worn by your grandmother in that old trunk?
10. In confusion, they watched with amusement as the puppies scrambled all over each other.

Rewrite each of the following sentences, adding the prepositional phrase given in parentheses.

EXAMPLE   1. Many paintings show strange, fantastical scenes. (*by Marc Chagall*)

1. *Many paintings by Marc Chagall show strange, fantastical scenes.*

1. Chagall's *The Green Violinist* contains many delightful mysteries and surprises. (*for the eye and mind*)
2. As you can see in the painting, a gigantic violinist sits among the buildings of a small village. (*with a green face and hand*)
3. Dark windows look just like the windows of the houses. (*on the musician's pants*)
4. A man waves to the violinist, and a dog taller than a house seems to smile at the music it hears. (*above the clouds*)
5. As you look at the painting's bright colors, perhaps you can almost hear the enchanting music. (*of the green violinist*)
6. You may be surprised to learn that the fiddler is found in many of Chagall's other works. (*in this painting*)
7. Chagall enjoyed listening to his uncle play the violin. (*during his childhood*)
8. *The Green Violinist* and other paintings of the fiddler are tributes. (*to Chagall's uncle*)
9. In a painting titled *Violinist*, Chagall painted himself standing. (*beside the violinist*)
10. In that unusual painting, Chagall has three heads turned to show enjoyment of the music. (*toward the uncle*)

The Granger Collection, New York

USAGE

Reference Note

For more information about **participles,** see page 410. For more about **participial phrases,** see page 412.

STYLE TIP

A dangling modifier often occurs when a sentence is in the passive voice. Rewriting sentences in the active voice not only eliminates many dangling modifiers but also makes your writing more interesting and lively.

PASSIVE VOICE
  Having just waxed the car, a trip to the fair was planned. [*Having just waxed the car* is a dangling modifier.]

ACTIVE VOICE
  Having just waxed the car, I planned a trip to the fair. [*Having just washed the car* modifies *I.*]

Reference Note

For more about **active voice and passive voice,** see page 499.

Reference Note

For more information on **using commas with participial phrases,** see pages 607 and 613.

USAGE

Participial Phrases

A *participial phrase* consists of a present participle or a past participle and its modifiers and complements. A participial phrase is used as an adjective to modify a noun or a pronoun. Like a prepositional phrase, a participial phrase should be placed as close as possible to the word it modifies.

EXAMPLES **Walking to school,** Celia and James found a wallet. [The participial phrase modifies *Celia* and *James.*]

I. M. Pei, **born in China,** is a gifted architect. [The participial phrase modifies *I. M. Pei.*]

A participial phrase that is not placed near the noun or pronoun that it modifies is a *misplaced modifier.*

MISPLACED Stolen from the media center, the deputies found the videocassette recorder. [Were the deputies stolen from the media center?]

CLEAR The deputies found the videocassette recorder **stolen from the media center.**

MISPLACED Sleeping on the roof, I saw the neighbor's cat. [Was I sleeping on the roof?]

CLEAR I saw the neighbor's cat **sleeping on the roof.**

MISPLACED We're used to the noise living by the airport. [Is the noise living by the airport?]

CLEAR **Living by the airport,** we're used to the noise.

A participial phrase that does not clearly and logically modify a word in the sentence is a *dangling modifier.*

DANGLING Cleaning the attic, an old trunk was found. [Who was cleaning the attic?]

CLEAR **Cleaning the attic,** we found an old trunk.

Exercise 7 Placing Participial Phrases Correctly

Rewrite each of the following sentences, adding the participial phrases given in parentheses. Be sure to use commas to set off participial phrases that begin or interrupt your sentences.

EXAMPLES
1. Finn and Darcy searched for their younger sister. (*scanning the crowd*)
1. *Scanning the crowd, Finn and Darcy searched for their younger sister.*

2. The sea turtle ducked back into its shell. (*startled by the sound of the boat's engine*)
2. *Startled by the sound of the boat's engine, the sea turtle ducked back into its shell.*

1. My older sister will be working at the garden center near my house. (*beginning next week*)
2. Our new kitten crawled under the sofa. (*exploring the house*)
3. By mistake, we sat on the swings. (*freshly painted*)
4. Lucy helped her brother find the books. (*lost somewhere in his messy room*)
5. Josie and Fred passed the playground. (*walking through the park*)
6. Ms. Surat told us about Sri Lanka and its people. (*pointing to the map*)
7. The two girls yelled loudly. (*surprised by their little brother*)
8. The horse likes to watch people. (*munching on grass*)
9. Andrea picked up the pencil and waited for the test to begin. (*sharpened moments earlier*)
10. On the beach this morning, the children found a mysterious note. (*folded in a blue bottle*)

HELP

Although some items in Exercise 7 can be revised in more than one way, you need to give only one revision for each.

Exercise 8 **Revising Sentences to Correct Misplaced and Dangling Participial Phrases**

Revise all sentences that contain misplaced or dangling participial phrases. If a sentence is already correct, write *C*.

EXAMPLE
1. Made from matzo meal, Rachel cooks tasty dumplings.
1. *Rachel cooks tasty dumplings made from matzo meal.*

1. Pacing in its cage, I watched the lion.
2. Talking on the telephone, Amanda did not hear the doorbell ringing.
3. Exploring the cave, a new tunnel was discovered.

HELP

You will need to add, delete, or rearrange some words in your revisions for Exercise 8.

USAGE

4. Wearing a bright orange suit and floppy yellow shoes, the circus featured a clown.
5. Filled with countless daisies, the two young girls walked slowly through the field.
6. Reading his part, the nervousness was hard to overcome.
7. The turkey was large enough for three families stuffed with sage and bread crumbs.
8. Tired from the long walk through the snow, food and rest were welcomed.
9. Checking the shelves, Judy found all the reference books she needed.
10. Selling the old farm, sadness welled up inside.

Adjective Clauses

Reference Note

For more about **adjective clauses,** see page 427.

An *adjective clause* modifies a noun or a pronoun. Most adjective clauses begin with a relative pronoun—*that, which, who, whom,* or *whose.* Like an adjective phrase, an adjective clause should generally be placed directly after the word it modifies.

| MISPLACED | The Labor Day picnic in the park that we had was fun. [Did we have the park?] |
| CLEAR | The Labor Day picnic **that we had** in the park was fun. |

| MISPLACED | The girls thanked their coach who had won the relay race. [Did the coach win the relay race?] |
| CLEAR | The girls **who had won the relay race** thanked their coach. |

HELP

Be sure to use commas to set off nonessential adjective clauses.

Reference Note

For information on using commas to set off **nonessential adjective clauses,** see page 607.

Exercise 9 Revising Sentences with Misplaced Clause Modifiers

Revise each of the following sentences by placing the adjective clause near the word it should modify.

EXAMPLE
1. My friend Beverly visited me who lives in Sarasota, Florida.

1. *My friend Beverly, who lives in Sarasota, Florida, visited me.*

1. The students received an *A* who made the first presentation.
2. The kitten belongs to my neighbor that is on the branch.

3. I showed the colorful cotton fabric to my sister that was made in Kenya.

4. The doctor said that the triplets were quite healthy who examined them.

5. The cleanup program was supported by all of the students that the president of the seventh-grade class suggested.

6. The flight attendant welcomed us aboard the plane whose brother I know.

7. The friend has a broken leg whom I called.

8. Donald's package is from his mother which came in the mail.

9. Quasars fascinate me which many astronomers throughout the world study.

10. The dog barked at the letter carrier that has been running loose in the neighborhood.

Review C **Correcting Errors in the Use of Modifiers**

Each of the following sentences contains an error in the use, form, or placement of a modifier. Revise each sentence by changing the form of a modifier or by adding, deleting, or rearranging words.

EXAMPLE   1. I have never been more happier in my life.
           1. *I have never been happier in my life.*

1. My stepsister plays both soccer and softball, but she likes soccer best.

2. The waiter brought plates to Terrell and me piled high with spaghetti and meat sauce.

3. Very frustrated, her locker just would not open!

4. Barking and growling loudly, the stranger was frightened by the dogs.

5. The antique German cuckoo clock still runs good after all these years.

6. I didn't do too bad on the geography quiz this morning.

7. Our puppy is much more playfuller than our older dog is.

8. We drove slow past the duck pond to see if any new ducklings had hatched.

9. They never did find no sponsor for their team.

10. The CD is the soundtrack of my favorite movie that we heard.

┌HELP─
Although some sentences in Review C can be correctly revised in more than one way, you need to give only one revision for each sentence.

Review D Proofreading Sentences for Correct Use of Modifiers

Each of the following sentences contains an error in the use, form, or placement of a modifier. Revise each sentence by changing the form of a modifier or by adding, deleting, or rearranging words.

EXAMPLE   1. Of all the important women featured in this book, Dolores S. Atencio is the one I admire more.

            1. Of all the important women featured in this book, Dolores S. Atencio is the one I admire most.

1. Her mother thought that a law career would offer her daughter the most brightest future.
2. Ms. Atencio always knew she would become a lawyer, but she didn't never expect to be so successful.
3. Looking ahead to college and law school, her grades in high school were excellent.
4. Along with two other Hispanic women, her efforts helped to launch Denver's first bilingual radio station in 1985.
5. Ms. Atencio felt quite proudly about helping to organize Colorado's first minority women lawyers' conference.
6. She decided to run for president of the Hispanic National Bar Association (HNBA) receiving encouragement from a friend.
7. Serving as president of HNBA, the legal rights of Hispanics were her main focus.
8. In 1991, she was named one of the most outstanding Hispanic women in *Hispanic Business Magazine.*
9. She also was given the Outstanding Young Woman Award from the city of Denver, which she received for all the time she had devoted to community service.
10. In addition to enjoying community service, Ms. Atencio feels really well when she is spending time with her family.

Chapter Review

A. Using the Correct Modifier

Identify the word in parentheses that will make each sentence correct.

1. I have to admit that this recording sounds (*bad, badly*).
2. Our Irish setter came (*shy, shyly*) toward the new puppy.
3. Yoki was anxious, but she appeared (*calm, calmly*).
4. Must the twins play so (*noisy, noisily*)?
5. We're pleased that you did so (*good, well*).
6. The storm ended as (*sudden, suddenly*) as it began.
7. With a little oil, the engine started (*easy, easily*).
8. Their performance is now (*good, well*) enough for any stage.
9. The kitchen counter looks (*clean, cleanly*).
10. It is (*good, well*) to be alive on a beautiful day like today.
11. Of the five designs, which one do you like (*better, best*)?
12. José Canseco played (*good, well*).
13. This ring is the (*more, most*) expensive of the two.
14. That striped tie would go (*good, well*) with your green shirt.
15. Choose the (*larger, largest*) of the two poodles.

B. Writing Comparative and Superlative Forms of Modifiers

Write the comparative or superlative form of the italicized adjective or adverb in each of the following sentences.

16. *dry*   The towels felt ____ after an afternoon on the clothesline than they had felt coming out of the washer.
17. *grateful*   We were ____ for Mr. Chang's advice than we could say.
18. *small*   The screwdriver my father used to repair my glasses was the ____ one he had.
19. *proud*   After the awards ceremony, Kerry seemed ____ of her son than she ever had before.
20. *slow*   The ____ horse of them all finished last in the race.

USAGE

21. *enthusiastically*	Pleased by all the performances, the audience applauded ____ for the dancers.
22. *tasty*	Since Dad started taking cooking classes, each dinner is ____ than the previous one.
23. *loyal*	Tadger is the ____ of our three dogs.
24. *easily*	With more practice, we solved the second puzzle ____ than the first one.
25. *tall*	Which of the five Romine girls do you think is ____?

C. Correcting Double Comparisons and Double Negatives

Rewrite the following sentences to correct errors in the use of modifiers.

26. These Hawaiian shirts don't have no pockets.

27. Pineapple juice tastes more sweeter than orange juice to me.

28. What is the most funniest thing that ever happened to you?

29. I can't hardly take another step.

30. Sakima couldn't barely catch her breath after running so far.

D. Correcting Misplaced and Dangling Modifiers

Each sentence below contains a misplaced or dangling modifier. Rewrite the sentences so that they are clear. You may need to add, delete, or rearrange words.

31. The fruit was marked for quick sale bruised by the storm.

32. Those tapes came from the library that you heard.

33. After leaving India, Singapore was the next destination.

34. Opening a savings account, a form of identification was required.

35. Skateboarding down the street, a large dog chased my brother.

36. Black Hawk was a chief of the Sauk people born in Virginia.

37. Trying to study, the noise from the chainsaw was distracting.

38. These salmon are using fish ladders, which are returning to spawn.

39. Sifting carefully through the sand, an old Spanish coin called a doubloon was found.

40. I saw the gazelles jumping through the binoculars.

Writing Application
Using Comparisons in a Letter

Comparative and Superlative Forms   An anonymous donor has given a large sum of money for improvements to your school. Write a letter to the administrators describing the improvements you would like to see. Use at least three comparative and two superlative forms of adjectives and adverbs in your writing.

Prewriting   What facilities, equipment, or supplies would make your school a better place? List your improvement ideas. You may want to discuss your ideas with a classmate or a teacher before you select the ones to include in your letter. Also, note why the improvements are needed.

Writing   As you write your first draft, use your list to help you make clear and accurate comparisons. Keep your audience in mind. The administrators need practical suggestions for how to spend the money, so let them know exactly what improvements your school needs and why.

Revising   Read your letter to a parent or other adult to see if your arguments are convincing. Add, delete, or rearrange details to make your letter more interesting and effective.

Publishing   Be sure you have used the correct comparative and superlative forms of adjectives and adverbs. Check the form of your letter to make sure it follows the guidelines for business letters. Read through your letter a final time to catch any errors in spelling, grammar, usage, or punctuation. Share your ideas for improving the school with the rest of the class, and make a chart displaying the most popular suggestions.

Reference Note

See "Writing" in the Quick Reference Handbook for guidelines on **writing business letters.**

USAGE

A Glossary of Usage
Common Usage Problems

Diagnostic Preview

Correcting Errors in Usage

Each of the following sentences contains an error in the use of formal, standard English. Revise each sentence to correct the error.

EXAMPLE   1. They did they're best to help.

          1. They did their best to help.

1. We are already for our trip to Washington, D.C.
2. They divided the crackers equally between the four toddlers.
3. Please take those packages here to me.
4. Elena had a cold, but she is feeling good now.
5. Mr. Chang he is my tai chi instructor.
6. Will you learn me how to play chess?
7. May I borrow that there collection of Cheyenne folk tales?
8. Tara might of come with us, but she had to baby-sit.
9. We use to live in Karachi, Pakistan.
10. She is the woman which owns the Great Dane.
11. I dropped the pictures, but I think they're alright.
12. I read where Mayor Alvarez will visit our school.
13. Their the best players on the team this season.
14. The pipes busted last winter during a hard freeze.
15. We cannot go sailing without we wear life jackets.
16. Her new apartment is bigger then her last one.

17. The group went everywheres together.
18. Lydia acted like she was bored.
19. *Antonyms* are when words are opposite in meaning.
20. I hope that you will except my apology.

About the Glossary

This chapter contains an alphabetical list, or *glossary,* of many common problems in English usage. You will notice throughout the chapter that some examples are labeled *nonstandard, standard, formal,* or *informal.* **Nonstandard English** is language that does not follow the rules and guidelines of standard English. **Standard English** is language that is grammatically correct and appropriate in formal and informal situations. **Formal** identifies usage that is appropriate in serious speaking and writing situations (such as in speeches and compositions for school). The label **informal** indicates standard usage common in conversation and in everyday writing such as personal letters.

The following are examples of formal and informal English.

Formal	Informal
angry	steamed
unpleasant	yucky
agreeable	cool
very impressive	totally awesome

a, an Use *a* before words beginning with a consonant sound. Use *an* before words beginning with a vowel sound. Keep in mind that the sound, not the actual letter, that a word begins with determines whether *a* or *an* should be used.

EXAMPLES They are building **a** hospital near our house.

I bought **a** one-way ticket. [Even though *o* is a vowel, the word *one* begins with a consonant sound.]

I would like **an** orange.

We worked for **an** hour. [Although *h* is a consonant, the word *hour* begins with a vowel sound. The *h* is not pronounced.]

Reference Note

For a list of **words often confused,** see page 666.

USAGE

COMPUTER TIP

The spellchecker on a computer will help you catch misspelled words such as *anywheres* and *nowheres.* The grammar checker may help you catch errors such as double negatives. However, in the case of words that are often misused, such as *than* and *then* and *between* and *among,* you will have to check your work yourself for correct usage.

HELP

In doing the exercises in this chapter, be sure to use only standard English.

accept, except   *Accept* is a verb; it means "to receive." *Except* may be used as either a verb or a preposition. As a verb, it means "to leave out." As a preposition, *except* means "excluding."

EXAMPLES   Ann **accepted** the gift. [verb]

No one will be **excepted** from writing a research paper. [verb]

All my friends will be there **except** Jorge. [preposition]

ain't   Do not use this nonstandard word in formal situations.

all right   Used as an adjective, *all right* means "satisfactory" or "unhurt." Used as an adverb, *all right* means "well enough." *All right* should be written as two words.

EXAMPLES   Your science project looks **all right** to me. [adjective]

Judy cut her toe, but she is **all right** now. [adjective]

I did **all right** in the drama club tryouts. [adverb]

| STYLE ✏ TIP |

Many writers overuse *a lot*. Whenever you run across *a lot* as you revise your own writing, try to replace it with a more exact word or phrase.

ACCEPTABLE
Emily Dickinson wrote a lot of poems.

BETTER
Emily Dickinson wrote **hundreds** of poems.

a lot   *A lot* should be written as two words.

EXAMPLE   I have read **a lot** of American Indian folk tales.

already, all ready   *Already* means "previously." *All ready* means "completely prepared."

EXAMPLES   By 5:00 P.M., I had **already** cooked dinner.

The students were **all ready** for the trip.

among   See **between, among.**

anyways, anywheres, everywheres, nowheres, somewheres   These words should have no final *s*.

EXAMPLE   I looked **everywhere** [not *everywheres*] for it!

as   See **like, as.**

as if, as though   See **like, as if, as though.**

at   Do not use *at* after *where*.

NONSTANDARD   Where are the Persian miniatures at?
STANDARD   Where are the Persian miniatures?

bad, badly   *Bad* is an adjective. It modifies nouns and pronouns. *Badly* is an adverb. It modifies verbs, adjectives, and adverbs.

EXAMPLES   The fruit tastes **bad.** [The predicate adjective *bad* modifies *fruit*.]

Don't treat him **badly.** [The adverb *badly* modifies the verb *Do treat*.]

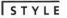
STYLE   TIP

The expression *feel badly* has become acceptable in informal situations although it is not strictly grammatical English.

INFORMAL
Carl felt badly about losing the race.

FORMAL
Carl felt **bad** about losing the race.

Exercise 1   Identifying Correct Usage

For each of the following sentences, choose the word or word group in parentheses that is correct according to the rules of formal, standard usage.

EXAMPLE   1. Navajo people came to the American Southwest from (*somewhere, somewheres*) in the North.

1. *somewhere*

1. One group of Navajos settled in the region where the Pueblo people (*lived, lived at*).
2. The Pueblo people were (*already, all ready*) farming and living in permanent dwellings by the time the Navajos arrived.
3. The Navajos may have (*excepted, accepted*) the practice of sand painting from the Pueblos and adapted it to fit their own customs.
4. When the Navajo artists are (*all ready, already*) to begin a sand painting, they gather in a circle, as shown in the picture here.
5. When creating a sand painting, (*a, an*) artist receives directions from the singer, who leads the ceremony.
6. The painter might make a certain design when things are not (*all right, allright*) in the community.

7. The Navajo sand painter may also use this art to help someone who is injured or feeling (*badly, bad*).
8. Because sand paintings used in healing ceremonies are swept away at the end of each ceremony, the designs are recorded nowhere (*accept, except*) in the artist's imagination.
9. However, the patterns used in sand painting (*ain't, aren't*) limited to this art form.
10. Variations of the sacred designs can be found almost (*anywheres, anywhere*) on items that the Navajos make.

USAGE

between, among   Use *between* when referring to two items at a time, even when they are part of a group consisting of more than two.

EXAMPLES   Who was standing **between** you and Sue?

Between the season's track meets, I trained very hard. [Although there may have been more than two meets, the training occurred between any two of them.]

There isn't much difference **between** these three brands of juice. [Although there are more than two brands, each one is being compared with the others separately.]

Use *among* when referring to a group rather than to separate individuals.

EXAMPLES   We divided the burritos **among** the five of us.

There was much discussion **among** the governors about the new tax plan. [The governors are thought of as a group.]

bring, take   *Bring* means "to come carrying something." *Take* means "to go carrying something." Think of *bring* as related to *come* (*to*), *take* as related to *go* (*from*).

EXAMPLES   Please **bring** that chair here.

Now **take** this one over there.

bust, busted   Avoid using these words as verbs in formal English. Use a form of either *burst* or *break* or *catch* or *arrest*.

EXAMPLES   The pipe **burst** [not *busted*] after the storm.

The Japanese raku vase **broke** [not *busted*] when it fell.

Mom **caught** [not *busted*] our dog Pepper digging in the garden.

Did the police **arrest** [not *bust*] the burglar?

Reference Note
For more about **double negatives,** see page 539.

can't hardly, can't scarcely   The words *hardly* and *scarcely* are negative words. They should not be used with another negative word.

EXAMPLES   I **can** [not *can't*] **hardly** wait to hear your new CD.

We **had** [not *hadn't*] **scarcely** enough food for everyone at the Juneteenth picnic.

could of Do not write *of* with the helping verb *could*. Write *could have*. Also avoid *ought to of*, *should of*, *would of*, *might of*, and *must of*.

EXAMPLES   Abdullah **could have** [not *could of*] helped us.

You **should have** [not *should of*] hung the piñata higher.

don't, doesn't See page 472.

everywheres See **anyways**, etc.

except See **accept, except.**

fewer, less *Fewer* is used with plural words. *Less* is used with singular words. *Fewer* tells "how many"; *less* tells "how much."

EXAMPLES   We had expected **fewer** guests.

Please use **less** salt.

good, well *Good* is an adjective. Do not use *good* to modify a verb; use *well*, which can be used as an adverb.

NONSTANDARD   The steel-drum band played good.

STANDARD   The steel-drum band played **well**.

Although it is usually an adverb, *well* is also used as an adjective to mean "healthy."

EXAMPLE   I did not feel **well** yesterday.

had of See **of.**

had ought, hadn't ought The verb *ought* should not be used with *had*.

NONSTANDARD   You had ought to learn to dance the polka.
You hadn't ought to be late for class.

STANDARD   You **ought** to learn to dance the polka.
or
You **should** learn to dance the polka.
You **oughtn't** to be late for class.
or
You **shouldn't** be late for class.

Reference Note

For more information about **using good and well**, see page 536.

─HELP─

Feel good and *feel well* mean different things. *Feel good* means "to feel happy or pleased." *Feel well* simply means "to feel healthy."

EXAMPLES
Helping others makes me feel **good**.

I went home because I didn't feel **well**.

Exercise 2 **Identifying Correct Usage**

For each of the following sentences, choose the word or word group in parentheses that is correct according to the rules of formal, standard usage.

EXAMPLE 1. Bike riders (*had ought, ought*) to know some simple rules of safety.

1. *ought*

1. Just about (*everywheres, everywhere*) you go these days, you see people riding bikes.
2. Riders who wear helmets have (*fewer, less*) major injuries than riders who don't.
3. When Aunt Shirley came for a visit, she (*brought, took*) her bicycle with her.
4. In choosing clothes, cyclists (*can hardly, can't hardly*) go wrong by wearing bright, easy-to-see colors.
5. On busy streets, groups of cyclists should ride in single file and leave space (*among, between*) their bikes in case of sudden stops.

6. Members of cycling clubs decide (*between, among*) themselves on special communication signals.
7. A cyclist who is involved in an accident should not try to ride home, even if he or she seems to feel (*well, good*).
8. The cyclist should call a family member or friend who can (*bring, take*) both the rider and the bike home.
9. A tire that is punctured can usually be patched, but you may not be able to fix one that has (*burst, busted*).
10. Many of the cycling accidents that have happened over the years (*could of, could have*) been avoided if cyclists and motorists had been more careful.

Review A **Proofreading for Correct Usage**

Each of the following sentences contains an error in formal, standard English usage. Identify each error. Then, write the correct word or words.

EXAMPLE 1. Don't almonds grow somewheres in Africa?

1. *somewheres—somewhere*

1. Check the hoses to see whether a seal has busted.
2. When rainfall is low here, there are less rabbits because there are not as many plants for them to eat.

3. I didn't know you could program computers that good.
4. Except for the spelling errors, you could of gotten an A.
5. Tracy's new hamster has all ready escaped.
6. Even a ten-ton truck can't hardly haul a load this size.
7. That bull ain't likely to appreciate anybody trespassing on his property.
8. Bring a glass of ice water outside to your father.
9. *Chutzpah* is a term applied to people who have alot of nerve.
10. You really had ought to hear Thelonious Monk's music.

he, she, they   Do not use a pronoun along with its antecedent as the subject of a verb. This error is called the *double subject.*

NONSTANDARD	Michael Jordan he was named Most Valuable Player.
STANDARD	Michael Jordan was named Most Valuable Player.

hisself, theirself, theirselves   These words are nonstandard English. Use *himself* and *themselves.*

EXAMPLES   Bob hurt **himself** [not *hisself*] during the game.

They served **themselves** [not *theirselves*] last.

how come   In informal English, *how come* is often used instead of *why.* In formal English, *why* is preferred.

INFORMAL	How come caribou migrate?
FORMAL	**Why** do caribou migrate?

its, it's   *Its* is a personal pronoun in the possessive case. *It's* is a contraction of *it is* or *it has.*

EXAMPLES   The kitten likes **its** new home. [possessive pronoun]

We have Monday off because **it's** Rosh Hashana. [contraction of *it is*]

It's been a long day. [contraction of *It has*]

kind, sort, type   The words *this, that, these,* and *those* should agree in number with the words *kind, sort,* and *type. This* and *that* are singular. *These* and *those* are plural.

EXAMPLES   **That kind** of watch is expensive. [singular]

Those kinds of jokes are silly. [plural]

kind of, sort of In informal English, *kind of* and *sort of* are often used to mean "somewhat" or "rather." In formal English, *somewhat* or *rather* is preferred.

INFORMAL   I feel kind of tired.

  FORMAL   I feel **somewhat** tired.

learn, teach *Learn* means "to acquire knowledge." *Teach* means "to instruct" or "to show how."

EXAMPLES   My brother is **learning** how to drive.

  The driving instructor is **teaching** him.

leave, let *Leave* means "to go away" or "to depart from." *Let* means "to allow" or "to permit."

NONSTANDARD   Leave her go to the movie.

  STANDARD   **Let** her go to the movie.

  STANDARD   Let's **leave** on time for the movie.

less See **fewer, less.**

lie, lay See page 503.

Reference Note

For more about **prepositional phrases,** see page 402. For more about **clauses,** see Chapter 15.

like, as *Like* is a preposition; it introduces a prepositional phrase. In informal English, *like* is often used before a clause as a conjunction meaning "as." In formal English, *as* is preferred.

EXAMPLES   Your uncle's hat looked **like** a sombrero. [*Like* introduces the phrase *like a sombrero.*]

  Marcia trained every day **as** the coach had suggested. [*As the coach had suggested* is a clause and needs the conjunction *as,* not the preposition *like,* to introduce it.]

like, as if, as though In formal, standard English, *like* should not be used for the subordinating conjunction *as if* or *as though.*

EXAMPLES   The Swedish limpa bread looks **as if** [not *like*] it is ready.

  The car looks **as though** [not *like*] it needs to be washed.

might of, must of See **could of.**

nowheres See **anyways,** etc.

For each of the following sentences, choose the word or word group in parentheses that is correct according to the rules of formal, standard usage.

EXAMPLE   1. Young rattlesnakes (*learn, teach*) themselves to make a rattling noise by imitating their parents.

         1. *teach*

1. (*Its, It's*) a sound that most people have learned to dread.
2. The snake's rattle consists of "buttons" of flesh at the end of (*its, it's*) tail, which are shaken against rings of loose skin.
3. The rings of skin (*themselves, theirselves*) are fragile.
4. (*Like, As*) zookeepers have discovered, snakes that rattle at visitors all day may damage their rattles.
5. (*This kind, These kind*) of snake delivers a poisonous bite, but rattlesnakes do not attack unless threatened.
6. Not all scientists agree about (*how come, why*) certain snakes have rattles.
7. According to many scientists, rattlesnakes (*they use, use*) the rattling sound to frighten enemies.
8. Some scientists believe that snakes use the rattles (*as, like*) other animals use different sounds—to communicate with each other.
9. Snakes don't have ears; however, they are (*sort of, rather*) sensitive to sound vibrations.
10. When people hear a rattlesnake, they may react (*like, as if*) the situation is an emergency—and it often is.

Each of the following sentences contains an error in formal, standard English usage. Identify each error. Then, write the correct word or words.

EXAMPLE   1. I should of known that the painting on the next page was done by Grandma Moses.

         1. *should of—should have*

1. My art teacher gave me a assignment to write a report about any artist I chose.
2. Between all the artists that I considered, Grandma Moses appealed to me the most.

USAGE

Grandma Moses, *Rockabye*. Copyright © 1987, Grandma Moses Properties Co., New York.

3. I went to the library and looked for a quiet place where I could do my research at.
4. I learned that Anna Mary Robertson Moses didn't start painting until she was all ready in her seventies.
5. By then, her children were grown, and she had less responsibilities.
6. Grandma Moses had no art teacher accept herself.
7. As you can see in the self-portrait *Rockabye*, Grandma Moses felt well about her role as a grandmother.
8. You can't hardly help feeling that Grandma Moses really loves these children.
9. My sister Kim likes this painting alot.
10. My report is already for class now, and I can't wait to tell my classmates about Grandma Moses.

of Do not use *of* with prepositions such as *inside*, *off*, and *outside*.

EXAMPLES We waited **outside** [not *outside of*] the theater for the ticket window to open.

The glass fell **off** [not *off of*] the table.

Only Muslims are allowed **inside** [not *inside of*] the city of Mecca in Saudi Arabia.

Of is also unnecessary with the verb *had*.

EXAMPLE If we **had** [not *had of*] tried harder, we would have won.

ought to of See **could of**.

real In informal English, the adjective *real* is often used as an adverb meaning "very" or "extremely." In formal English, *very*, *extremely*, or another adverb is preferred.

INFORMAL The new car is real quiet.
  FORMAL The new car is **very** quiet.

USAGE

rise, raise   See page 501.

she, he, they   See **he,** etc.

should of   See **could of.**

sit, set   See page 500.

some, somewhat   Do not use *some* for the adverb *somewhat.*

NONSTANDARD   I like classical music some.

STANDARD   I like classical music **somewhat.**

somewheres   See **anyways,** etc.

sort   See **kind,** etc.

sort of   See **kind of,** etc.

take   See **bring, take.**

teach   See **learn, teach.**

than, then   *Than* is a subordinating conjunction used in making comparisons. *Then* is an adverb meaning "next" or "after that."

EXAMPLES   I sing better **than** I act.

We'll eat first, and **then** we'll ride our bikes.

that   See **who,** etc.

that there   See **this here, that there.**

their, there, they're   *Their* is the possessive form of *they. There* is used to mean "at that place" or to begin a sentence. *They're* is a contraction of *they are.*

EXAMPLES   Do you have **their** CDs?

The lake is over **there.**

There are five movie theaters in town. [*There* begins the sentence but does not add to its meaning.]

They're writing a report on the poet Américo Paredes.

theirself, theirselves   See **hisself,** etc.

them   *Them* should not be used as an adjective. Use *these* or *those.*

EXAMPLE   Where did you put **those** [not *them*] papers?

they   See **he,** etc.

Reference Note

For information about **subordinating conjunctions,** see page 431. For more about **adverbs,** see page 366.

USAGE

this here, that there The words *here* and *there* are not needed after *this* and *that*.

EXAMPLE   I like **this** [not *this here*] Chinese dragon kite, but I like **that** [not *that there*] one better.

this kind, sort, type See **kind,** etc.

try and In informal English, *try and* is often used for *try to*. In formal English, *try to* is preferred.

INFORMAL   I will try and be there early.
FORMAL   I will **try to** be there early.

type See **kind,** etc.

Exercise 4   Identifying Correct Usage

For each of the following sentences, choose the word or word group in parentheses that is correct according to the rules of formal, standard usage.

EXAMPLE   **1.** The Amish people (*try and, try to*) maintain a simple, traditional way of life.
         1. *try to*

1. In the early 1700s, the Amish were not allowed to practice (*their, they're, there*) religion in Germany and Switzerland.
2. Hearing that there was more freedom in the Americas (*than, then*) in Europe, the Amish left their homes and settled in North America.
3. Since that time, they have remained (*outside of, outside*) the mainstream of American life.
4. The Amish work (*real, very*) hard at producing organically grown crops.
5. In Amish communities such as (*this, this here*) one, modern conveniences such as telephones, cars, and televisions are not used.
6. The closeness of Amish family life is evident in the way (*these, them*) people build their homes.
7. (*They're, There, Their*) are often three generations—grandparents, parents, and children—living in a large residence made up of several houses.

USAGE

8. Pictures and photographs are not allowed (*inside of, inside*) Amish homes, but the Amish brighten their plain houses with colorful pillows, quilts, and rugs.

9. If an Amish person gets sick, he or she is almost always cared for by family members rather (*than, then*) by a doctor.

10. The Amish way of life might surprise you (*somewhat, some*), yet Amish communities have thrived in North America for nearly three hundred years.

Review C Proofreading for Correct Usage

Each of the following sentences contains an error in the use of formal, standard English. Identify each error. Then, rewrite the sentence to correct the error.

EXAMPLE   1. It was real cold that spring!

   1. real—It was extremely cold that spring!

1. Few people commanded more respect and admiration then Mother Teresa did.

2. Nobody can dance like you do, Ariel.

3. These sort of questions can be found on every standardized test.

4. Oh, no! The baby's gotten oatmeal all over hisself.

5. The structure of molecules like these, it can most easily be understood by building a model.

6. What I want to know is how come we can't go to the concert.

7. Who learned your dog all those tricks?

8. A *howdah* is one of them seats that have a canopy and that sit on a camel or an elephant.
9. The RV campsite is just outside of town.
10. Mrs. Whitfield will try and explain how the European Economic Community is organized.

use to, used to   Don't leave off the *d* when you write *used to*. The same advice applies to *supposed to*.

EXAMPLE   Gail **used to** [not *use to*] be on the softball team.

way, ways   Use *way*, not *ways*, in referring to a distance.

EXAMPLE   Do we have a long **way** [not *ways*] to drive?

well   See **good, well.**

when, where   Do not use *when* or *where* incorrectly to begin a definition.

NONSTANDARD   A *homophone* is when a word sounds like another word but has a different meaning and spelling.

STANDARD   A *homophone* is a word that sounds like another word but has a different meaning and spelling.

where   Do not use *where* for *that*.

EXAMPLE   Did you read in the newsletter **that** [not *where*] the teen center is closing?

who, which, that   The relative pronoun *who* refers to people only. *Which* refers to things only. *That* refers to either people or things.

EXAMPLES   Jolene is the one **who** called. [person]

Here is the salad, **which** is my favorite part of the meal. [thing]

The book **that** you want is here. [thing]

This is the salesperson **that** helped me choose the gift. [person]

who, whom   See page 521.

whose, who's   *Whose* is used as the possessive form of *who* and as an interrogative pronoun. *Who's* is a contraction of *who is* or *who has.*

EXAMPLES   **Whose** book is this? [possessive pronoun]

Whose is this? [interrogative pronoun]

Who's the new student? [contraction of *who is*]

Who's read "A Walk to the Jetty"? [contraction of *who has*]

without, unless   Do not use the preposition *without* in place of the conjunction *unless*.

EXAMPLE   I can't go **unless** [not *without*] I ask Dad.

would of   See **could of.**

your, you're   *Your* is the possessive form of *you. You're* is the contraction of *you are.*

EXAMPLES   **Your** Saint Patrick's Day party was great!

You're a good friend.

Exercise 5   **Identifying Correct Usage**

For each of the following sentences, choose the word or word group in parentheses that is correct according to the rules of formal, standard usage.

EXAMPLE   1. Last week I received a letter from Sandra Joyce, (*who's, whose*) a good friend of mine.

1. *who's*

1. When I opened the envelope, I saw (*where, that*) she had sent me chopsticks and these instructions.
2. "I thought you'd like (*you're, your*) own pair of chopsticks, with instructions showing how to use them," Sandra wrote.
3. Instructions like the ones Sandra sent me are helpful because chopsticks can be hard to use (*unless, without*) you are shown how.
4. In the letter, Sandra told me (*that, where*) she and her family had been to New York.
5. Because Sandra lives in a small town, she wasn't (*use, used*) to the crowds.

6. She enjoyed visiting her grandparents, (*who's, whose*) home is near Chinatown, on Manhattan Island.

7. While her family was eating in a Chinese restaurant, one of the servers, (*which, who*) was very helpful, showed her how to use chopsticks.

8. "(*Your, You're*) not going to believe this," she wrote, "but by the end of the meal, I was using chopsticks quite well."

9. Etiquette is (*when you use good manners, the use of good manners*); Sandra wondered whether using chopsticks to eat Chinese food was a matter of etiquette or of skill.

10. I'll write Sandra that I have a long (*ways, way*) to go before I'm an expert in using chopsticks.

Review D **Proofreading for Correct Usage**

Each of the following sentences contains an error in the use of formal, standard English. Rewrite each sentence to correct the error.

EXAMPLE   1. If the quarterback can't play, whose the backup?
   1. *If the quarterback can't play, who's the backup?*

1. Are you selling you're old bike or one of theirs?
2. If they're not their, you can have their seats.
3. Don't go outside without you wear those galoshes!
4. Is Alfonso García Robles the man which was awarded the 1982 Nobel Peace Prize?
5. "Buzzing the runway" is when a plane flies low and fast over the runway.
6. I read where the word *Nippon* means "where the sun rises."
7. If this hat isn't lucky, then how come every time I wear it, I win?
8. Yes, I use to live in Madrid.
9. Please try and be ready on time tonight.
10. Listen to Lydia's new poem; its dedicated to Queen Liliuokalani.

Chapter Review

A. Identifying Correct Usage

For each of the following sentences, choose the word or word group in parentheses that is correct according to the rules of formal, standard English usage.

1. Helene made (*fewer, less*) mistakes this time.
2. That restaurant looks (*as if, like*) it might be expensive.
3. Those (*kind, kinds*) of games are easy to learn.
4. Terrance felt (*badly, bad*) about losing the house key.
5. Leticia practiced an hour every day (*like, as*) her teacher had recommended.
6. Divide the sheet music (*among, between*) the three musicians.
7. We brought the juice, but (*it's, its*) still in the car.
8. Both cars had pinstripes painted on (*their, there*) hoods.
9. The rice will feed more people (*then, than*) the bread will.
10. "(*Your, You're*) a polite young man," Aunt Henrietta told Jason.
11. There's the police officer (*which, who*) helped me yesterday.
12. Did you see in the newspaper (*that, where*) farmers are losing their crops because of the drought?
13. Chika is the woman (*whose, who's*) going to be my math tutor.
14. The child cried out when her balloon (*busted, burst*).
15. Vincent van Gogh did not receive (*a lot, alot*) of recognition during his lifetime.
16. Just do your best, and everything will be (*allright, all right*).
17. Will you (*take, bring*) that *National Geographic* to me?
18. Elyssa must (*of, have*) left her wallet here.
19. Petra likes salsa music (*somewhat, some*).
20. Can your brother (*learn, teach*) me how to play the drums?
21. Let the bread rise for (*a, an*) hour, and then put it in the oven.
22. Is Emily coming to the party, or (*ain't, isn't*) she?
23. (*Leave, Let*) me walk to the concert by myself.
24. We (*should not, hadn't ought to*) let the cat eat whatever it wants.
25. Where did you (*sit, set*) the bag of groceries?

USAGE

B. Proofreading for Correct Usage

Read each sentence below, and decide whether it contains an error in the use of formal, standard English. If the sentence contains an error in usage, rewrite the sentence correctly. If the sentence is already correct, write *C*.

26. Try to be real quiet while you are inside the library.
27. We cannot ride our bikes without it stops raining.
28. Be careful not to knock the lamp off of the table.
29. The cartoon page looks as if it got wet.
30. I told Gretchen to try and keep still.
31. Where's the salt shaker at?
32. Robbie said that the lock on the back door is busted.
33. Andrea thought we should have turned right at the stop sign.
34. Mr. Funicello seems kind of uncomfortable.
35. This here poem would be easier to memorize than that one.
36. Before 1920, farmers use to grow strawberries here.
37. My grandmother she worked in a factory when she was my age.
38. Sakura knows how come the play was canceled.
39. Those game tickets are somewheres in this drawer.
40. Before our trip, we ought to buy a map.
41. Where did Rory put them CDs?
42. Their are two bridges downriver.
43. The tollbooth will except quarters and dimes but not pennies.
44. A pronoun is when a word is used in place of a noun.
45. By noon we had all ready seen Mr. Kerr's film.
46. The class can't hardly wait to go on the field trip to the power plant.
47. The Immerguts have a long ways to drive to visit their grandparents.
48. My older sister is doing very well in law school.
49. In the final seconds of the game, Lee tripped hisself and missed the winning basket.
50. It's true: Mimi doesn't want to come to the New Year's Eve party.

Writing Application
Writing a Speech

Using Formal English   A local television station has started a new program called *Sound-Off*. Each speaker on the program gets five minutes on the air to express an opinion about a community issue. Choose a topic that you think is important, and write a speech to submit to the TV station. Use only formal, standard English in your speech.

Prewriting   First, choose a specific topic that interests you. List important facts and information about the issue. Do you have all the information you need? If not, do some research at your school or local library. Also, be sure to include your own feelings and opinions about your topic. Finally, make a rough outline of what you want to say.

Writing   Use your notes and outline to help you write a draft of your speech. Try to write a lively introduction that will grab your listeners' attention. In your introduction, give a clear statement of opinion. Then, discuss each supporting point in a paragraph or two. Conclude your speech by restating your main point.

Revising   Ask a friend to time you as you read your speech aloud. Then, ask your friend the following questions:

- Is the main idea clear?
- Does the speech give useful information?

Publishing   Proofread your speech for errors in grammar or formal, standard usage. You and your classmates may want to present your speeches to the class. You might also want to investigate whether a local TV or radio program would allow you to give your speeches on the air.

Reference Note

For more about **statements of opinion**, see page 212.

USAGE

Capital Letters
Rules for Capitalization

Diagnostic Preview

Proofreading Sentences for Correct Capitalization

Write each word that requires capitalization in the following sentences. If a sentence is already correct, write *C*.

EXAMPLE **1.** Next saturday rachel and i will get to watch the taping of our favorite TV show.

1. *Saturday, Rachel, I*

1. The curtiss soap corporation sponsors the television show called *three is two too many.*

2. The show's theme song is "you and i might get by."

3. My favorite actor on the show is joe fontana, jr., who plays the lovable dr. mullins.

4. The female lead, janelle bledsoe, used to go to our junior high school right here in houston, texas.

5. The action is set in the west just after the civil war.

6. The program is on monday nights, except during the summer.

7. One episode took place at a fourth of july picnic, at which dr. mullins challenged the sheriff to a grapefruit-eating contest.

8. Ms. Bledsoe plays a teacher who is married to Mr. reginald wilson foster II, president of the flintsville National bank.

9. Mrs. foster teaches latin, home economics, and arithmetic I at flintsville's one-room school.

10. One local character, uncle ramón, once played a practical joke on judge grimsby right outside the mayor's office.

11. Some people, including my mother, think that the program is silly, but my father enjoys watching it occasionally.

12. Even i don't think it will receive an emmy from the academy of television arts and sciences.

13. When grandma murray and aunt edna from mobile, alabama, visited us, they watched the program.

14. In that monday night's show, an alien named romax from the planet zarko stayed at the sidewinder hotel.

15. The alien, who looked like president zachary taylor, spoke english perfectly and could read people's minds.

16. He settled a dispute between the union pacific railroad and the flintsville ranchers' association.

17. In another show a united states senator and romax discussed their views of justice.

18. In the silliest show, the people in the next town, longview, thought that a sea monster was living in lake cranberry and reported it to the department of the interior.

19. A week later, mayor murdstone lost the only copy of his secret recipe for irish stew and saw the recipe in the next issue of the *flintsville weekly gazette.*

20. One time a mysterious stranger appeared, claiming he had sailed around cape horn on the ship *the gem of the ocean.*

21. Another time, the wealthy landowner mabel platt hired the law firm of crumbley, lockwood, and starr to sue mayor murdstone and threatened to take the case all the way to the united states supreme court.

22. In the next episode, a buddhist priest who just happened to be traveling through the west on his way back to china stopped off in flintsville.

23. Once, when someone mistakenly thought he had found gold down at cutter's creek, thousands of prospectors flocked to flintsville, including three bank-robbing members of the feared gumley Gang.

24. The programs are taped before a live audience in the metro theater in los angeles, california.

25. You can get tickets to be in the audience by writing to curtiss soap corporation, 151 holly avenue, deerfield, mi 49238.

Using Capital Letters Correctly

Reference Note

For more about using **capital letters** in **quotations,** see page 631.

22a. Capitalize the first word in every sentence.

EXAMPLES **M**y dog knows several tricks. **D**oes yours?

The first word of a directly quoted sentence should begin with a capital letter.

EXAMPLE Mrs. Hernandez said, "**D**on't forget to bring your contributions for the bake sale."

Traditionally, the first word of every line of poetry begins with a capital letter.

EXAMPLE **I**n the night
The rain comes down.
Yonder at the edge of the earth
There is a sound like cracking,
There is a sound like falling.
Down yonder it goes on slowly rumbling.
It goes on shaking.

A Papago poem, "In the Night"

NOTE Some modern poets do not follow this style. If you are using a quotation from a poem, be sure to use the capitalization that the poet uses.

Reference Note

For more about **writing letters,** see "Writing" in the Quick Reference Handbook. For information on using **colons in letters,** see page 620. For information on using **commas in letters,** see page 615.

22b. Capitalize the first word in both the salutation and the closing of a letter.

SALUTATIONS **D**ear Service Manager:
Dear Emily,

CLOSINGS **S**incerely,
Yours truly,

22c. Capitalize the pronoun *I*.

EXAMPLE This week **I** have to write two essays.

22d. Capitalize proper nouns.

Reference Note

For more about **common nouns** and **proper nouns,** see page 338.

A *proper noun* names a particular person, place, thing, or idea. Proper nouns are capitalized. A *common noun* names a kind or type of person, place, thing, or idea. A common noun generally is not capitalized unless it begins a sentence or is part of a title.

MECHANICS

Proper Nouns	Common Nouns
Central High School	high school
Saturday	day
Rigoberta Menchú	woman
Cambodia	country
Smokey	bear
USS *Nautilus*	submarine

Some proper nouns consist of more than one word. In these names, short words such as prepositions (those of fewer than five letters) and articles (*a, an, the*) are generally not capitalized.

EXAMPLES   House **o**f Representatives

               Ivan **t**he Terrible

(1) Capitalize the names of persons and animals.

Persons		
	Monica **S**one	**A**aron **N**eville
	Charlayne **H**unter-**G**ault	**M**ohandas **K**. **G**andhi
Animals	**S**hamu	**T**rigger
	Socks	**R**ikki-tikki-tavi

(2) Capitalize geographical names.

Type of Name	Examples	
Continents	**E**urope	**S**outh **A**merica
	Antarctica	**A**sia
Countries	**A**ustralia	**E**gypt
	El **S**alvador	**S**audi **A**rabia
Cities, Towns	**M**iami	**I**ndianapolis
	Los **A**ngeles	**M**anila
States	**T**ennessee	**D**elaware
	Rhode **I**sland	**W**yoming

(continued)

Reference Note

Abbreviations of the names of states are capitalized. See page 599 for more about using and punctuating such abbreviations.

STYLE   TIP

Some names consist of more than one part. The different parts may begin with capital letters only or with a combination of capital and lowercase letters. If you are not sure about the spelling of a name, ask the person with that name or check a reference source.

EXAMPLES
Van **d**en **A**kker, **v**an **G**ogh, **M**c**E**nroe, **L**a **F**ontaine, **d**e **l**a **G**arza, **I**bn **S**aud

COMPUTER TIP

If you use a computer, you may be able to use a spellchecker to help you capitalize names correctly. Make a list of the names you write most often. Be sure that you have spelled and capitalized each name correctly. Then, add this list to your computer's dictionary or spellchecker.

MECHANICS

STYLE TIP

A two-letter state abbreviation without periods is used only when it is followed by a ZIP Code. Both letters of the abbreviation are capitalized. No mark of punctuation is used between the abbreviation and the ZIP Code.

EXAMPLES
New Orleans, **LA** 70131-5140

New York, **NY** 10003-6981

Reference Note

In addresses, abbreviations such as *St., Blvd., Ave., Dr.,* and *Ln.* are capitalized. For more about punctuating abbreviations, see page 599.

Type of Name	Examples	
Islands	**A**leutian **I**slands **C**rete	**L**ong **I**sland **I**sle of **P**ines
Bodies of Water	**A**mazon **R**iver **C**hesapeake **B**ay **S**uez **C**anal	**L**ake **O**ntario **J**ackson's **P**ond **I**ndian **O**cean
Other Geographical Names	**M**ayon **V**olcano **P**ainted **D**esert	**S**inai **P**eninsula **M**eteor **C**rater
Streets, Highways	**M**ain **S**treet **E**ighth **A**venue	**C**anary **L**ane **H**ighway 71

NOTE In a hyphenated street number, the second part of the number is not capitalized.

EXAMPLE   West Thirty-**f**ourth Street

Type of Name	Examples	
Parks and Forests	**S**herwood **F**orest **B**rechtel **P**ark	**E**verglades **N**ational **P**ark
Mountains	**C**atskills **M**ount **F**uji	**M**ount **E**verest the **A**lps
Regions	the **M**iddle **E**ast **N**ew **E**ngland the **W**est	**S**outhern **H**emisphere **C**orn **B**elt the **S**outheast

NOTE Words such as *east, west, northern,* or *southerly* are not capitalized when the words merely indicate direction. However, they are capitalized when they name a particular region.

EXAMPLES   A car was going **s**outh on Oak Street. [direction]

The **S**outh has produced some of America's great writers. [region of the country]

Exercise 1   Writing Proper Nouns

For each common noun given below, write two proper nouns. You may need to use a dictionary and an atlas. Be sure to use capital letters correctly.

EXAMPLE   **1.** country

        1. Canada, Japan

1. lake   **5.** teacher   **8.** ocean
2. continent   **6.** athlete   **9.** city
3. president   **7.** park   **10.** region
4. highway

Exercise 2   Correcting Errors in Capitalization

Each of the following sentences contains at least one capitalization error. Correct these errors by writing the words that are incorrectly capitalized and either changing capital letters to lowercase letters or changing lowercase letters to capital letters.

EXAMPLE   **1.** The original Settlers of hawaii came from the marquesas islands and tahiti.

        1. settlers, Hawaii, Marquesas Islands, Tahiti

1. our Class is studying hawaii.
2. The Hawaiian islands are located in the pacific ocean, nearly twenty-four hundred miles West of san francisco, california.
3. Hawaii officially became the fiftieth State in the united states in 1959.
4. Our teacher, ms. Jackson, explained that the Capital City is honolulu; she said that it is located on the southeast Coast of oahu island.
5. The largest of the Islands is hawaii.
6. On the southeast shore of hawaii island is hawaii volcanoes national park.
7. Ms. Jackson asked, "can anyone name one of the Volcanoes there?"
8. Since i had been reading about National Parks, i raised my hand.
9. "The Park has two active volcanoes, mauna Loa and kilauea," I answered.

10. "These pictures show how lava from kilauea's eruption threatened everything in its path in 1989," I added.

11. Its crater, halemaumau crater, is the largest active crater in the World.

12. "we'll go into much more detail about volcanoes tomorrow," ms. jackson said.

13. then ms. jackson told us that honolulu is probably the most important business center in the pacific ocean.

14. Ever since captain William Brown sailed into the harbor in 1794, Hawaii has played an increasingly important role in business.

15. It's easy to see why—Hawaii is midway between Continents.

16. hawaii's largest city has a fine seaport; it links japan, china, and even australia with North and south America.

17. Cultural and academic studies thrive there in places such as the university of hawaii and the east-west center.

18. You can even get a look at the iolani palace where the Rulers of hawaii once lived.

19. Perhaps best of all, hawaii offers Tourists a day in the sun at waikiki beach.

20. Suddenly, i blurted out, "wouldn't it be great if we could all go there now!"

(3) Capitalize names of organizations, teams, institutions, and government bodies.

Type of Name	Examples	
Organizations	Clark Drama Club Junior League	Modern Language Association
Teams	Boston Celtics Dallas Cowboys	Los Angeles Dodgers Hutto Hippos
Institutions	Westside Regional Hospital	Roosevelt Junior High School
Government Bodies	United Nations Peace Corps	Congress York City Council

(4) Capitalize the names of historical events and periods, special events, calendar items, and holidays.

Type of Name	Examples	
Historical Events and Periods	Revolutionary War Bronze Age Holocaust	United States Bicentennial Age of Reason
Special Events	Texas State Fair Special Olympics	Super Bowl Festival of States
Calendar Items and Holidays	Monday Memorial Day	February Thanksgiving Day

NOTE Do not capitalize the name of a season unless it is part of a proper name.

EXAMPLES   the winter holidays   the Quebec Winter Carnival

(5) Capitalize the names of nationalities, races, and peoples.

EXAMPLES   Mexican   Nigerian

African American   Iroquois

┌HELP┐

The names of organizations, businesses, and government bodies are often abbreviated to a series of capital letters.

EXAMPLES

National Organization for Women	NOW
American Telephone & Telegraph	AT&T
National Science Foundation	NSF

Usually the letters in such abbreviations are not followed by periods, but always check an up-to-date dictionary or other reliable source to be sure.

MECHANICS

┌ STYLE ✏ TIP ┐

The words *black* and *white* may or may not be capitalized when they refer to races. Either way is correct.

EXAMPLE

In the 1960s, both Blacks and Whites [or blacks and whites] worked to end segregation.

Within each piece of writing, be sure to be consistent in your use of capitals or lowercase letters for these words.

(6) Capitalize the names of businesses and the brand names of business products.

Type of Name	Examples	
Businesses	**S**ears, **R**oebuck and **C**o.	**F**ields **D**epartment **S**tore
	Thirfty **D**ry **C**leaners	**F**irst **N**ational **B**ank
Business Products	**S**chwinn **M**esa	**A**pple **M**acintosh
	GMC Jimmy	**C**allaway **B**ig **B**ertha

NOTE Names of types of products are not capitalized.

EXAMPLES Schwinn **b**icycle, Apple **c**omputer, Callaway **g**olf **c**lub

(7) Capitalize the names of ships, trains, aircraft, and spacecraft.

Reference Note
For information on **using italics in names,** see page 628.

Type of Name	Examples	
Ships	*Queen Elizabeth 2*	*Kon Tiki*
Trains	*City of New Orleans*	*Silver Meteor*
Aircraft	*Memphis Belle*	*Spruce Goose*
Spacecraft	*Voyager 2*	*Sputnik*

(8) Capitalize the names of buildings and other structures.

EXAMPLES **S**ydney **O**pera **H**ouse, **S**t. **L**ouis **C**athedral, **A**swan **D**am, **E**iffel **T**ower, **B**rooklyn **B**ridge

NOTE Do not capitalize such words as *hotel, theater,* or *high school* unless they are part of the name of a particular building or institution.

EXAMPLES

Capital **T**heater	a theater
Lane **H**otel	the hotel
Taft **H**igh **S**chool	this high school

MECHANICS

(9) Capitalize the names of monuments, memorials, and awards.

Type of Name	Examples	
Monuments	Great Sphinx Navajo National Monument	Washington Monument
Memorials	Lincoln Memorial the Coronado Memorial	Tomb of the Unknown Soldier
Awards	Emmy Award Congressional Medal of Honor	Nobel Prize Pulitzer Prize

(10) Capitalize the names of religions and their followers, holy days and celebrations, sacred writings, and specific deities.

Type of Name	Examples	
Religions and Followers	Judaism Hinduism	Christian Muslim
Holy Days and Celebrations	Easter All Saints' Day	Yom Kippur Christmas Eve
Sacred Writings	Koran Bible	Dead Sea Scrolls Upanishads
Specific Deities	God Allah	Jehovah Krishna

NOTE The words *god* and *goddess* are not capitalized when they refer to a deity of ancient mythology. However, the names of specific gods and goddesses are capitalized.

EXAMPLES   The king of the Norse gods was Odin.

Athena was the Greek goddess of wisdom and warfare.

The word *earth* is not capitalized unless it is used along with the names of other heavenly bodies that are capitalized. The words *sun* and *moon* are generally not capitalized.

EXAMPLES

Oceans cover three fourths of the **e**arth's surface.

Which is larger— Saturn or **E**arth?

How many **m**oons does **J**upiter have?

(11) Capitalize the names of planets, stars, constellations, and other heavenly bodies.

Type of Name	Examples	
Planets	**M**ercury	**V**enus
Stars	**R**igel	**P**roxima **C**entauri
Constellations	**U**rsa **M**ajor	**A**ndromeda
Other Heavenly Bodies	**M**ilky **W**ay	**C**omet **K**ohoutek

Exercise 3 **Proofreading Sentences for Correct Capitalization**

Supply capital letters wherever they are needed in each of the following sentences.

EXAMPLE   **1.** Each arbor day the students at franklin junior high school plant a tree.

  1. Arbor Day, Franklin Junior High School

1. The golden gate bridge spans the entrance of san francisco bay.
2. Our muslim neighbors, the Rashads, fast during the month of ramadan.
3. The peace corps became a government agency by an act of congress.
4. Do you think the henderson hornets will win the play-offs?
5. Thousands of cherokee people live in the Smoky Mountains in and around North Carolina.
6. To stop flooding in the South, the tennessee valley authority, a government agency, built thirty-nine dams on the Tennessee River and the streams that flow into it.
7. Which biographer won the pulitzer prize this year?
8. On new year's day, many fans crowd into football stadiums for annual bowl games such as the rose bowl.
9. Can you see neptune or any of its moons through your telescope?
10. Have you read any myths about apollo, a god once worshiped by the greeks?

Review A ▶ Proofreading Sentences for Correct Capitalization

Rewrite the following sentences, using capital letters wherever they are needed.

EXAMPLE   1. according to my sister, i'm a mall rat.

           1. *According to my sister, I'm a mall rat.*

1. the branford mall is the largest in melville county.
2. It is on jefferson parkway, two miles north of duck lake state park and the big bridge that crosses duck lake.
3. Across the parkway from the mall is our new local high school with its parking lots, playing fields, and stadium, home of the branford panthers.
4. Near the mall are the american legion hall, bowlarama, and king skating rink.
5. The mall includes two jewelry stores, nicholson's department store, the palace cinema, and thirty-five other businesses.
6. They range from small stationery stores to one of the finest restaurants in the midwest.
7. The restaurant larue is run by marie and jean larue, who are from france.
8. Also in the mall is the american paper box company, which sells boxes for every packaging need.
9. My friends sharon and earl always shop at gene's jeans, which specializes in denim clothing.
10. An outlet store for northwestern leather goods of chicago sells uffizi purses and wallets.

Review B ▶ Correcting Errors in Capitalization

Each of the following sentences contains errors in capitalization. Correct these errors by changing incorrect capital letters to lowercase letters and incorrect lowercase letters to capital letters.

EXAMPLE   1. African americans in massachusetts have played an important part in American history.

           1. *Americans, Massachusetts*

1. In Boston, the Crispus attucks monument is a memorial to attucks and the other men who died in the boston Massacre.
2. According to many Historians, attucks was a former slave who fought against the british in the american Revolution.

Jan Ernst Matzeliger

W.E.B. DuBois

Crispus Attucks

The Granger Collection, New York

3. The department of the Interior has made the Home of maria baldwin a historic building in cambridge.
4. Baldwin was a Leader in the league for Community Service, an Organization to help the Needy.
5. One of the founders of the National association for the Advancement of colored people, w.e.b. DuBois, was born in great Barrington, Massachusetts.
6. A marker stands on the Spot where DuBois lived.
7. Jan ernst matzeliger, who lived in lynn, invented a machine that made Shoes easier and cheaper to manufacture.
8. The nantucket whaling Museum has information about Peter green, a Sailor on the ship *john Adams.*
9. During a storm at sea, Green saved the Ship and crew.
10. Use the Map of Massachusetts shown above to locate the Towns and Cities in which these notable african Americans lived.

22e. Capitalize proper adjectives.

A ***proper adjective*** is formed from a proper noun and is capitalized.

Reference Note

For more about **proper adjectives,** see page 349.

Proper Noun	Proper Adjective
Greece	**G**reek theater
Mars	**M**artian moons
Darwin	**D**arwinian theory
Japan	**J**apanese tea ceremony

22f. Do not capitalize the names of school subjects, except course names followed by numerals and names of language classes.

EXAMPLES   **h**istory, **t**yping, **a**lgebra, **E**nglish, **S**panish, **L**atin,
History 101, **M**usic III, **A**rt **A**ppreciation I

Exercise 4   Proofreading Sentences for Correct Capitalization

Supply capital letters where they are needed in each of the following sentences.

EXAMPLE   **1.** Rosa said we were eating mexican bread.

       1. Mexican

1. The program featured russian ballet dancers.
2. The european Common Market improves international trade.
3. The scandinavian countries include both Norway and Sweden.
4. In geography, we learned about the platypus and the koala, two australian animals.
5. We read several english plays in my literature class.
6. I am planning to take computers I next year.
7. On the floor was a large persian rug.
8. England, France, Scotland, Russia, and the United States played important roles in canadian history.
9. The backyard was decorated with chinese lanterns.
10. Are you taking french or art II?

Review C   Correcting Errors in Capitalization

Each of the sentences on the following page contains errors in capitalization. Correct these errors by writing the words that are incorrectly capitalized and changing capital letters to lowercase letters or changing lowercase letters to capital letters.

EXAMPLE   1. "what do you know about Modern architecture at the
               beginning of the Century, sean?"

           1. *What, modern, century, Sean*

1. In Social Studies, i learned about the famous Architect Frank
    Lloyd Wright.
2. One of wright's best-known works is his house, fallingwater,
    in bear run, Pennsylvania.
3. "Yes, wright still may be the best-known american architect,"
    Mrs. Lee said.
4. Louis sullivan (1856–1924) was among the first Builders in
    the united States to use a steel frame.
5. A german architect helped design the Seagram Building, an
    early Skyscraper in the east.
6. Both architects and the Public wanted new ideas after world
    war II, according to my architecture 101 teacher.
7. the use of reinforced Concrete made possible large, thin
    roofs such as the one at the Massachusetts institute of
    technology.
8. Next tuesday we will see a Film about inventive designs in
    the brazilian capital.
9. I imagine that brazilian Citizens are proud of the architect
    Oscar niemeyer.
10. Hear my report on the israeli architect Moshe Safdie during
    History today.

22g. Capitalize titles.

(1) Capitalize the title of a person when the title comes before a name.

EXAMPLES   **P**resident Lincoln   **M**rs. Oliver Wendell

            Mayor Bradley   **C**ommissioner Rodriguez

Generally, a title that is used alone or following a person's
name is not capitalized, especially if the title is preceded by
a or *the.*

EXAMPLES   The **s**ecretary of **d**efense held a news conference.

            Lien Fong, our class **s**ecretary, read the minutes.

However, a title used by itself in direct address is usually
capitalized.

Reference Note

For information
about **punctuating
abbreviations,** see
page 599.

S T Y L E   T I P

For special emphasis or
clarity, writers sometimes
capitalize a title used alone
or following a person's
name.

EXAMPLES
At the ceremony, the
Queen honored the
Royal Navy.

Mr. Biden, the **S**enator
from Delaware, called
for a committee vote.

EXAMPLES   Is it very serious, **D**octor?

               How do you do, **S**ir [or sir]?

(2) Capitalize a word showing a family relationship when the word is used before or in place of a person's name.

EXAMPLES   We expect **U**ncle Fred and **A**unt Helen soon.

               Both **M**om and **D**ad work at the hospital.

However, do not capitalize a word showing a family relationship when a possessive comes before the word.

EXAMPLE   We asked Pedro's **m**other and his **a**unt Celia to be chaperons.

(3) Capitalize the first and last words and all important words in titles and subtitles.

Unimportant words in titles include

- articles (*a, an, the*)
- coordinating conjunctions (*and, but, for, nor, or, so, yet*)
- prepositions of fewer than five letters (such as *by, for, on, with*)

Type of Name	Examples	
Books	*The **M**ask of **A**pollo* *Mules and Men*	*Long **C**laws: **A**n **A**rctic **A**dventure*
Chapters and Other Parts of Books	"**T**he **C**irculatory **S**ystem" "**L**anguage **H**andbook"	"**T**he **C**ivil **W**ar **B**egins" "**E**pilogue"
Magazines	*Popular **M**echanics* *Ebony*	*Seventeen* *Sports **I**llustrated*
Newspapers	*The **T**ennessean* the *Boston **G**lobe*	*The **W**all **S**treet **J**ournal*
Poems	"**S**eason at the **S**hore"	*Evangeline* "Birches"

(continued)

Reference Note

For more about **articles,** see page 347. For more about **coordinating conjunctions,** see page 374. For more about **prepositions,** see page 370.

Reference Note

For guidelines on **what titles are italicized,** see page 628. For guidelines on **what titles are enclosed in quotation marks,** see page 635.

MECHANICS

22 g

(continued)

Type of Name	Examples	
Short Stories	"The Purloined Letter"	"Zlateh the Goat" "Broken Chain"
Plays	*The Three Sisters* *A Midsummer Night's Dream*	*A Doll's House* *I Never Sang for My Father*
Movies and Videos	*Fairy Tale: A True Story* *Babe*	*It's a Wonderful Life* *The Wizard of Oz*
Television Series	*Home Improvement* *Kratt's Creatures*	*Star Trek: The Next Generation*
Cartoons and Comic Strips	*Jump Start* *Cathy*	*Scooby Doo* *Dilbert*
Audiotapes and CDs	*Butterfly* *Falling into You*	*Dos Mundos* *Spirit*
Computer Games and Video Games	*Sonic the Hedgehog* *Math Blaster* *Rockett's New School*	*Logical Journey* *SimCity* *Space Kids*
Works of Art	*Mona Lisa* *David*	*The Night Watch* *Mankind's Struggle*
Musical Compositions	*The Marriage of Figaro*	"America the Beautiful"
Historical Documents	Magna Carta Treaty of Paris	The Declaration of Independence

NOTE The article *the* at the beginning of a title is not capitalized unless it is the first word of the official title.

EXAMPLES My father reads *The Wall Street Journal.*

Does she work for t*he Texas Review*?

┌HELP─
The official title of a book is found on the title page. The official title of a newspaper or periodical is found on the masthead, which usually appears on the editorial page or the table of contents.

MECHANICS

Correcting Sentences by Capitalizing Words

Most of the following sentences contain at least one word that should be capitalized but is not. Correctly write each incorrect word. If a sentence is already correct, write *C*.

EXAMPLE 1. Ms. Chang is meeting with principal Hodges.

　　　　　 1. *Principal*

1. Tom Hanks' career really took off after he starred in the movie *big*.
2. In 1998, John Glenn, a former senator, became the oldest person to travel in space.
3. The assignment is to compare and contrast Amy Tan's story "Two kinds" with Bernard Malamud's "The first seven years."
4. Rummaging through the pile of used books, Marcia found a copy of *the Complete Poems Of Stephen Crane*.
5. Our English teacher, mrs. Fernandez, has a small sculpture of the globe theatre sitting on her desk.
6. Isn't it a coincidence that your aunt Jenny and my uncle Herbert work for the same company?
7. Which do you prefer, Bob Dylan's CD *Nashville skyline* or his son's *The wallflowers*?
8. Some of my friends claim that *The Empire strikes back* is the best movie of the series.
9. Did you remember to clip that article we read yesterday in *The Washington post*?
10. Mom and dad always chuckle when they read *Hagar the Horrible*.

Review D **Proofreading Sentences for Correct Capitalization**

Write the sentences on the following page, using capital letters wherever they are needed.

EXAMPLE 1. The series *all creatures great and small* is being rerun on public television.

　　　　　 1. The series *All Creatures Great and Small* is being rerun on public television.

MECHANICS

1. While waiting to interview mayor ward, I read an article in *newsweek*.
2. Have you read leslie marmon silko's poem "story from bear country"?
3. You have probably seen a picture of *the thinker,* one of rodin's best-known sculptures.
4. On television last night, we saw the movie *the return of the native.*
5. Every four years voters elect a president and several united states senators.
6. Uncle nick read aloud from francisco jiménez's short story "the circuit."
7. The reporter asked, "Can you tell us, senator inouye, when you plan to announce the committee's final decision?"
8. The main speaker was dr. andrew holt, a former president of the university of tennessee.
9. Besides uncle don, our visitors included aunt pat, aunt jean, both of my grandmothers, and my great-grandfather.
10. The soccer players listened to coach Daly as he outlined defensive strategy.

Review E **Proofreading Sentences for Correct Capitalization**

The following sentences each contain at least one capitalization error. Correctly write the words that require capital letters.

EXAMPLE 1. The waters of the caribbean are pleasantly warm.
1. Caribbean

1. The greeks believed that zeus, the king of the gods, lived on mount olympus.
2. The *titanic* sank after hitting an iceberg off the coast of newfoundland.
3. My cousin collects scandinavian pottery.
4. Stephanie is taking english, math II, and biology.
5. On friday we were cheered by the thought that monday, memorial day, would be a holiday.
6. My picture is in today's *austin American-Statesman.*
7. The quaker oats company has introduced a new corn cereal.
8. In *roots,* alex haley, a famous author, traces the history of his family.
9. She usually travels to boston on american airlines.

10. I wanted to name my persian cat after one of the justices on the supreme court.

Review F **Proofreading a Paragraph for Correct Capitalization**

Each sentence in the following paragraph contains at least one error in capitalization. Correctly write the words that require capital letters.

EXAMPLE   **[1]** Before thanksgiving, i learned some interesting facts about africa in my history II class.

    1. Thanksgiving, I, Africa, History II

[1] My teacher, mr. davidson, told us about the mighty kingdoms and empires that existed for hundreds of years in africa. [2] some of these kingdoms dated back to the time of the roman empire. [3] Others rose to power during the period known as the middle ages in europe. [4] For many years, the people in the kingdom of cush did ironwork and traded along the nile river. [5] Later, the cush were defeated by the people of axum, led by king ezana. [6] As you can see in the map below, several kingdoms in africa developed between lake chad and the atlantic ocean. [7] Three of these kingdoms were ghana, mali, and songhai. [8] These kingdoms established important trade routes across the sahara. [9] Tombouctou's famous university attracted egyptian and other arab students. [10] I read more about these african kingdoms and empires in our textbook, *world history: people and nations.*

African Kingdoms and Empires c. 200 B.C.–A.D. 1500

— Cush, c. 200 B.C.
— Axum, c. A.D. 500
— Ghana, c. A.D. 900
— Mali, c. A.D. 1300
— Songhai, c. A.D. 1500
·····► Trade route

Miles
0   250   500
0   125   250
Kilometers

ATLANTIC OCEAN

SPAIN
Strait of Gibraltar
MOROCCO
Fez
Marrakech
Tunis
Mediterranean Sea
Memphis   Cairo
EGYPT
Thebes
Arabian Peninsula
Red Sea
Memphis
Kerma
YEMEN
Napata
Meroe
Axum
Ethiopian Highlands
S A H A R A
Kumbi Saleh
Tombouctou
Lake Chad
AFRICA

Review G **Correcting Errors in Capitalization**

Each of the following sentences contains at least one error in capitalization. Correctly write each incorrect word, changing capital letters to lowercase letters or changing lowercase letters to capital letters.

EXAMPLE
1. On june 25, 1876, sioux and cheyenne warriors defeated general george a. Custer and his Troops.

1. *June, Sioux, Cheyenne, General George A., troops*

1. The Defeat of general custer occurred at the battle of the little bighorn.
2. In december of 1890, many Sioux were killed by Soldiers in a battle at wounded Knee creek in south Dakota.
3. Depicted by artists, writers, and filmmakers, both Battles have become part of american History.
4. In the late nineteenth century, the sioux Artist Kicking bear painted the *Battle Of the little Bighorn.*
5. The painting, done on muslin Cloth, is shown below.
6. Kicking bear, who himself fought in the Battle, painted at the pine Ridge agency in south Dakota, where he lived.
7. soldiers who fought against kicking Bear described him as courageous.
8. The well-known American Poet Stephen vincent benét wrote about the battle of wounded knee in a Poem called "american names."

Battle of Little Bighorn by Kicking Bear (Sioux), 1898. Courtesy of the Southwest Museum, Los Angeles

9. More recently, the author Dee brown wrote about the american indians of the west in his book *bury my Heart at Wounded knee.*
10. In 1970, the movie *Little big Man* told the story of a fictional 121-year-old character who had survived the Battle against general Custer.

Chapter Review

A. Correcting Errors in Capitalization

Each of the following sentences contains at least one error in capitalization. Correct the errors either by changing capital letters to lowercase letters or by changing lowercase letters to capital letters.

1. Please pick up a box of Tide Detergent at the store.
2. The "Battle Hymn Of The Republic" was written by Julia ward Howe.
3. Are we going to uncle Ted's house for Thanksgiving again?
4. Charing cross book shop is on Thirty-Second Street.
5. Ms. wong always stays at the Four Seasons hotel when she's in New York city on business.
6. Do you know if professor Ezekiel will be teaching Creative Writing during the spring semester?
7. In what year was the battle of gettysburg fought?
8. My aunt remembers when Mother Teresa won the Nobel Peace prize.
9. Every winter my Grandparents travel to the southwest.
10. My Uncle sid once met sir Winston Churchill.
11. Mr. Salter often remembers his old house on vine street in McAllen, Texas.
12. Father and mother traveled all over the World when they were buying furniture for their antique store.
13. The principal asked me, "how would you like to study Geography next semester?"
14. When Jim went back to New York for Christmas, he left his dog, piper, at the kennel.
15. Sometimes my Mother works at home on friday.
16. Grand Canyon National park was closed this weekend because of heavy snow.
17. Shall we renew our subscription to *national geographic*?
18. This june we plan to welcome a swedish exchange student to our home.

19. We're going to Washington, D.C., to see the white house.

20. At the Henry Ford Museum in Dearborn, Michigan, you can see a replica of the *spirit of st. louis,* the plane that Charles Lindbergh used to fly solo across the atlantic.

21. At the Crossbay Market, i bought a can of progresso soup.

22. My Aunt Janice visited Petrified Forest National Park.

23. The Rosenbach museum and library in Philadelphia is open Tuesday through Sunday.

24. dear Mr. Boylan:

    I enjoyed your book enormously.

    sincerely yours,

    Jimmy Connolly

25. In History class, we learned about queen Elizabeth I.

B. Proofreading Sentences for Correct Capitalization

Write the following sentences, and correct errors in capitalization either by changing capital letters to lowercase letters or by changing lowercase letters to capital letters.

26. Mars, Venus, and Jupiter were roman gods.

27. *The wind in the willows* is my Mother's favorite book.

28. Davis Housewares emporium has moved to Fifth street.

29. The lozi people in Africa live near the Zambezi river.

30. "Stopping By Woods On a Snowy Evening" is by Robert Frost, a Poet from New England.

31. Do you know when David Souter was appointed to the supreme court?

32. Next Monday is memorial day.

33. When we traveled through the south, we visited the Antietam National Battlefield.

34. Ms. Ling is teaching us about chinese culture.

35. Cayuga lake stretches North from Ithaca, New York.

36. The main religion in Indonesia is islam, but there are also many Indonesian buddhists.

37. My older sister is taking Spanish, Science, Mathematics II, and Art.

MECHANICS

38. Carlos and I had turkey sandwiches made with german mustard on french bread.

39. We turned west onto route 95 and stayed on it for five miles.

40. George Copway, who was born in Canada, wrote about his people, the ojibwa.

Writing Application
Using Capital Letters in a Letter

Proper Nouns   Students in your class have become pen pals with students in another country. You have been given the name of someone to write. Write your pen pal a letter introducing yourself and telling about your school and your community. In your letter, be sure to use capitalization correctly.

Prewriting   Note the information you want to give in your letter. You may wish to include information such as your age; a description of yourself; your favorite books, movies, actors, or musicians; some clubs, organizations, or special activities you participate in; some special places, events, or attractions in your community or state.

Writing   As you write your draft, keep in mind that your pen pal may not recognize names of some people, places, and things in the United States. For example, he or she may not recognize the names of your favorite movies or musical groups. Be sure to use correct capitalization to show which names are proper nouns.

Revising   Read through your letter carefully. Have you left out any important information? Are any parts of your letter confusing? If so, you may want to add, cut, or revise some details. Is the tone of your letter friendly? Have you followed the correct form for a personal letter?

Publishing   Read your letter carefully to check for any errors in grammar, spelling, and punctuation. Use the rules in this chapter to help you double-check your capitalization. With your teacher's permission, post a map of the world on the classroom wall and display the letters around the map.

Reference Note

For more about writing **personal letters,** see "Writing" in the Quick Reference Handbook.

23 Punctuation

End Marks, Commas, Semicolons, and Colons

Diagnostic Preview

Using End Marks, Commas, Semicolons, and Colons

The following sentences lack necessary periods, question marks, exclamation points, commas, semicolons, and colons. Rewrite each sentence, inserting the correct punctuation.

EXAMPLE   1. Snakes lizards crocodiles and turtles are reptiles
          1. *Snakes, lizards, crocodiles, and turtles are reptiles.*

┌─HELP─
All of the punctuation marks that are already in the sentences in the Diagnostic Preview are correct.

1. Toads and frogs on the other hand are amphibians
2. Some turtles live on land others live in lakes streams or oceans
3. Turtles have no teeth but you should watch out for their strong hard beaks
4. The words *turtle* and *tortoise* are similar in meaning but *tortoise* usually refers to a land dweller
5. The African pancake tortoise which has a flat flexible shell uses an unusual means of defense
6. Faced with a threat it crawls into a narrow crack in a rock takes a deep breath and wedges itself in tightly
7. Because some species of tortoises are endangered they cannot be sold as pets

8. Three species of tortoises that can be found in the United States are as follows the desert tortoise the gopher tortoise and the Texas tortoise

9. The gopher tortoise lives in the Southeast and the desert tortoise comes from the Southwest

10. Is the Indian star tortoise which is now an endangered species very rare

11. As this kind of tortoise grows older its shell grows larger the number of stars on the shell increases and their pattern becomes more complex

12. The Indian star tortoise requires warmth sunlight and a diet of green vegetables

13. Living in fresh water soft-shelled turtles have long flexible beaks and fleshy lips

14. Their shells are not really soft however but are covered by smooth skin

15. Sea turtles are the fastest turtles the green turtle can swim at speeds of almost twenty miles per hour.

16. Most turtles can pull their head, legs, and tail into their shell however sea turtles cannot do so.

17. Mr Kim my neighbor up the street has several turtles in his backyard pond.

18. Come to my house at 4 30 in the afternoon, and I'll show you our turtle.

19. At 7:00 P M , we can watch that new PBS documentary about sea turtles.

20. Wanda may I introduce you to Pokey my pet turtle

21. Pokey who has been part of our family for years is a red-eared turtle.

22. The book *Turtles A Complete Pet Owner's Manual* has helped me learn how to take care of Pokey.

23. Pokey has been in my family for fifteen years and my parents say that he could easily live to be fifty if he is cared for properly

24. What a great pet Pokey is.

25. Don't you agree with me Wanda that a turtle makes a good pet

End Marks

An **end mark** is a mark of punctuation placed at the end of a sentence. *Periods, question marks,* and *exclamation points* are end marks.

┌HELP──
Periods (decimal points) are also used to separate dollars from cents and whole numbers from tenths, hundredths, and so forth.

EXAMPLES
$10.23 [ten dollars and twenty-three cents]

5.7 [five and seven tenths]

23a. Use a period at the end of a statement.

EXAMPLE   Tea is grown in Sri Lanka.

23b. Use a question mark at the end of a question.

EXAMPLE   Did you see the exhibit about lightning?

23c. Use an exclamation point at the end of an exclamation.

EXAMPLE   What a high bridge that was!

23d. Use either a period or an exclamation point at the end of a request or a command.

When an imperative sentence makes a request, it is generally followed by a period. When an imperative sentence expresses a strong command, an exclamation point is generally used.

EXAMPLES   Please call the dog. [a request]

Call the dog! [a command]

Exercise 1   Adding End Marks to Sentences

Rewrite each of the following sentences, adding the necessary end marks.

EXAMPLE   1. Did you know that a choreographer is a person who creates dance steps

1. *Did you know that a choreographer is a person who creates dance steps?*

1. Why is Katherine Dunham called the mother of African American dance

2. She studied anthropology in college and won a scholarship to visit the Caribbean

3. How inspiring the dances she saw in Haiti were

4. When Dunham returned to the United States, she toured the country with her own professional dance company

5. How I admire such a talented person

6. Ask me anything about Katherine Dunham

7. How many honors has Dunham's creativity won her

8. She was named to the Hall of Fame of the National Museum of Dance in Saratoga, New York

9. She was also given the National Medal of Arts for exploring Caribbean and African dance

10. The editors of *Essence* magazine praised Dunham for helping to break down racial barriers

23e. Many abbreviations are followed by a period.

Types of Abbreviations	Examples
Personal Names	A. B. Guthrie W.E.B. DuBois Livie I. Durán
Titles Used with Names	Mr. Mrs. Ms. Jr. Sr. Dr.
Organizations and Companies	Co. Inc. Corp. Assn.

NOTE Abbreviations for government agencies and other widely used abbreviations are written without periods. Each letter of the abbreviation is capitalized.

EXAMPLES
FBI	NAACP	NIH	NPR
PTA	TV	UN	YWCA

Types of Abbreviations	Examples
Addresses	Ave. St. Rd. Blvd. P.O. Box
States	Tex. Penn. Ariz. Wash. N.C.
Times	A.M. (*ante meridiem,* used with times from midnight to noon) P.M. (*post meridiem,* used with times from noon to midnight) B.C. (before Christ) A.D. (*anno Domini,* in the year of the Lord)

STYLE   TIP

When writing the initials of someone's name, place a space between two initials (S. E. Hinton). Do not place spaces between three initials (M.F.K. Fisher).

STYLE   TIP

An **acronym** is a word formed from the first (or first few) letters of a series of words. Acronyms are written without periods.

EXAMPLES
UNICEF (**U**nited **N**ations **I**nternational **C**hildren's **E**mergency **F**und)

VISTA (**V**olunteers **i**n **S**ervice **t**o **A**merica)

MECHANICS

STYLE TIP

The abbreviations *A.D.* and *B.C.* need special attention. Place *A.D.* before the numeral and *B.C.* after the numeral.

EXAMPLES

A.D. 760   54 **B.C.**

However, for centuries expressed in words, place both A.D. and B.C. after the century.

EXAMPLES

seventh century **B.C.**

fourth century **A.D.**

┌HELP──

If you are not sure whether you should use a period with an abbreviation, look up the abbreviation in a dictionary.

NOTE A two-letter state abbreviation without periods is used only when it is followed by a ZIP Code. Both letters of such abbreviations are capitalized.

EXAMPLE   Orlando, **FL** 32819

Abbreviations for units of measure are usually written without periods and are not capitalized.

EXAMPLES   mm   kg   dl   oz   lb   ft   yd   mi

However, to avoid confusion with the word *in*, you should use a period with the abbreviation for *inch* (*in.*).

NOTE When an abbreviation with a period ends a sentence, another period is not needed. However, a question mark or an exclamation point is used as needed.

EXAMPLES   We will arrive by 3:00 P.M.
Can you meet us at 3:30 P.M.?
Oh no! It's already 3:30 P.M.!

Exercise 2 Punctuating Abbreviations

Some of the following sentences contain abbreviations that have not been correctly punctuated. Correct each error. If a sentence is already correct, write *C*.

EXAMPLE   1. Of course, we watch P.B.S.; we love the science shows it broadcasts.

1. *PBS*

1. Not everyone knows that WEB DuBois eventually became a Ghanaian citizen.
2. The writing isn't clear, but I think it says *10 ft 6 in* or *10 ft 5 in.*
3. Write me in care of Mrs. Audrey Coppola, 10 Watson Ave..
4. Yes, that's in California—Novato, C.A. 94949.
5. Were those clay statues made as far back as 500 B.C?
6. Send your check or money order to Lester's Low-Cost Computer Chips, Inc, Duluth, Minn, and receive your new chips in two days!
7. Could you be there at 7:00 P.M.?

8. I would never do business with a company whose only address was a PO box.
9. Miss Finch, Dr Bledsoe will see you now.
10. His full name is Marvin French Little Hawk, Jr., but everyone calls him Junior.

Review A **Adding Periods, Question Marks, and Exclamation Points to Sentences**

Rewrite each of the following sentences, adding the necessary periods, question marks, and exclamation points.

EXAMPLE   1. Do you ever think about how electricity is produced
             1. *Do you ever think about how electricity is produced?*

controls

water

turbine

generator

electricity

1. Electricity can come from large hydroelectric power stations
2. Wow, these stations certainly do create a lot of power
3. How do hydroelectric power stations work
4. Look at the diagram to gain a better understanding
5. Falling water from natural falls or artificial dams provides the initial power in the process
6. Have you ever been to Niagara Falls, New York, to see the famous falls
7. From 12:00 AM. to 12:00 AM.—constantly, in other words—the falls are a tremendous power source
8. As you can see, rushing water turns turbines, which then drive generators
9. What exactly are generators, and what do they do
10. J D explained that generators are the machines that turn the motion of the turbines into electricity

Commas

End marks are used to separate complete thoughts. **Commas,** however, are generally used to separate words or groups of words within a complete thought.

23f. Use commas to separate items in a series.

A *series* is a group of three or more items in a row. Words, phrases, and clauses may appear in a series.

Words in a Series

January, February, and March are all summer months in the Southern Hemisphere. [nouns]

The engine rattled, coughed, and stalled. [verbs]

The baby was happy, alert, playful, and active. [adjectives]

Phrases in a Series

There were fingerprints at the top, on the sides, and on the bottom. [prepositional phrases]

Cut into pieces, aged for a year, and well dried, the wood was ready to burn. [participial phrases]

To pitch in a World Series game, to practice medicine, and to run for mayor are all things I hope to do someday. [infinitive phrases]

Clauses in a Series

We sang, we danced, and we played trivia games. [short independent clauses]

I knew that we were late, that the ice cream was melting, and that the car was nearly out of gas. [short subordinate clauses]

NOTE Only short independent clauses in a series may be separated by commas. A series of independent clauses that are long or that contain commas should be separated by semicolons.

EXAMPLE   Yawning, Mother closed the curtains; Father, who had just come in, turned on the porch light; and my little sister, Christina, put on her pajamas.

Reference Note

For information about using **semicolons,** see page 618.

MECHANICS

Always be sure that there are at least three items in the series; two items generally do not need a comma between them.

INCORRECT   You will need a pencil, and plenty of paper.

CORRECT   You will need a pencil and plenty of paper.

When all the items in the series are joined by *and* or *or*, do not use commas to separate them.

EXAMPLES   Take water **and** food **and** matches with you.

Stephen will take a class in karate **or** judo **or** aikido next year.

Exercise 3 Proofreading Sentences for the Correct Use of Commas

Some of the following sentences need commas; others do not. If a sentence needs any commas, write the word before each missing comma and add the comma. If a sentence is already correct, write *C*.

EXAMPLES   1. Seal the envelope stamp it and mail the letter.

  1. envelope, it,

  2. You should swing the club with your knees bent and your back straight and your elbows tucked.

  2. C

1. The mountains and valleys of southern Appalachia were once home to the Cherokee people.
2. Cleveland Cincinnati Toledo and Dayton are four large cities in Ohio.
3. The captain entered the cockpit checked the instruments and prepared for takeoff.
4. Luisa bought mangos and papayas and oranges.
5. The speaker took a deep breath and read the report.
6. Rover can roll over walk on his hind feet and catch a tennis ball.
7. The neighbors searched behind the garages in the bushes and along the highway.
8. Rubén Blades is an attorney an actor and a singer.
9. Eleanor Roosevelt's courage her humanity and her service to the nation will always be remembered.
10. Tate dusted I vacuumed and Blair washed the dishes.

STYLE   TIP

In your reading, you will find that some writers omit the comma before the conjunction joining the last two items of a series. Nevertheless, you should form the habit of including this comma. Sometimes a comma is necessary to make your meaning clear. Notice how the comma affects the meaning in the following examples.

EXAMPLES

  Mom, Jody and I want to go to the movies. [Mom is being asked for her permission.]

  Mom, Jody, and I want to go to the movies. [Three people want to go to the movies.]

MECHANICS

23g. Use a comma to separate two or more adjectives that come before a noun.

EXAMPLES   A white dwarf is a tiny, dense star.

               Venus Williams played a powerful, brilliant game.

Do not place a comma between an adjective and the noun immediately following it.

INCORRECT   My spaniel is a fat, sassy, puppy.

CORRECT   My spaniel is a fat, sassy puppy.

Sometimes the final adjective in a series is thought of as part of the noun. When the adjective and the noun are linked in such a way, do not use a comma before the final adjective.

EXAMPLES   A huge **horned owl** lives in those woods.
[not *huge, horned owl*]

               An unshaded **electric light** hung from the ceiling.
[not *unshaded, electric light*]

NOTE   When an adjective and a noun are closely linked, they may be thought of as a unit. Such a unit is called a **compound noun.**

EXAMPLES   Persian cat   Black Sea   French bread

TIPS & TRICKS

To see whether a comma is needed between two adjectives, insert *and* between the adjectives (*unshaded and electric*, for example). If *and* sounds awkward there, do not use a comma.

   Another test you can use is to switch the order of the adjectives. If the sentence still makes sense when you switch them, use a comma.

Reference Note

For more information about **compound nouns**, see page 337.

Review B **Proofreading Sentences for the Correct Use of Commas**

Most of the following sentences need commas. If a sentence needs any commas, write the word before each missing comma and add the comma. If a sentence is already correct, write *C*.

EXAMPLE   1. Chen participated in debate volleyball and drama.

           1. *debate, volleyball,*

1. Carla sneaked in and left a huge gorgeous fragrant bouquet of flowers on the desk.
2. I chose the gift Michael wrapped it and Charley gave it to Gina and Kelly.
3. Smoking is a costly dangerous habit.
4. In the human ear, the hammer anvil and stirrup carry sound waves to the brain.
5. Buffalo Bill was a Pony Express rider a scout and a touring stunt performer.

6. "The Masque of the Red Death" is a famous horror story by Edgar Allan Poe.

7. According to Greek mythology, the three Fates spin the thread of life measure it and cut it.

8. LeVar Burton played the intelligent likable character Geordi on *Star Trek: The Next Generation.*

9. The fluffy kitten with the brown white and black spots is my favorite.

10. Falstaff begged for mercy in a fight ran away and later bragged about his bravery in battle.

Compound Sentences

23h. Use a comma before *and, but, for, nor, or, so,* or *yet* when it joins independent clauses in a compound sentence.

EXAMPLES   Tamisha offered me a ticket, and I accepted.

They had been working very hard, but they didn't seem especially tired.

The Mullaney twins were excited, for they were going to day care for the first time.

When the independent clauses are very short and there is no chance of misunderstanding, the comma before *and, but,* or *or* is sometimes omitted.

EXAMPLES   It rained and it rained.

Come with us or meet us there.

NOTE   Always use a comma before *for, nor, so,* or *yet* when joining independent clauses.

EXAMPLE   I was tired, yet I stayed.

Do not be misled by a simple sentence that contains a compound verb. A simple sentence has only one independent clause.

SIMPLE SENTENCE WITH COMPOUND VERB   Usually we **study** in the morning and **play** basketball in the afternoon.

COMPOUND SENTENCE   Usually we study in the morning, and we play basketball in the afternoon. [two independent clauses]

STYLE TIP

The word *so* is often overused. If possible, try to reword a sentence to avoid using *so.*

EXAMPLE
It was late, so we went home.

REVISED
Because it was late, we went home.

MECHANICS

Reference Note
For more information about **compound sentences,** see page 441. For more about **simple sentences** with **compound verbs,** see page 327.

Exercise 4 Correcting Compound Sentences by Adding Commas

If a sentence needs a comma, write the word before the missing comma and add the comma. If a comma is unnecessary, write the words before and after the comma and omit the comma. If the sentence is already correct, write *C*.

EXAMPLE   1. American Indian artists have a heritage dating back thousands of years and many of them draw on this heritage, to create modern works.

1. *years, heritage to*

1. Today's artists sometimes work with nontraditional materials but they often use traditional techniques.
2. In the photograph below, you can see the work of the Tohono O'odham artist Mary Thomas, and begin to appreciate this basket weaver's skill.
3. The baskets in the photograph are woven in the "friendship design" and show a circle of human figures in a traditional prayer ceremony.
4. Yucca and devil's claw are used to make these baskets and each plant's leaves are a different color.
5. The Navajo artist Danny Randeau Tsosie listened to his grandmother's stories, and learned about his family's heritage.
6. Tsosie's works show her influence but also express his own point of view.
7. Christine Nofchissey McHorse learned the skill of pottery making from her grandmother and now McHorse can make beautiful bowls.
8. McHorse has an unusual style for her designs combine traditional Navajo and Pueblo images.

9. American Indian jewelry makers often use pieces of turquoise and coral found in North America and they also use other stones from around the world.

10. American Indian art often looks very modern yet some of its symbols and patterns are quite old.

Interrupters

23i. Use commas to set off an expression that interrupts a sentence.

Two commas are needed if the expression to be set off comes in the middle of the sentence. One comma is needed if the expression comes first or last.

EXAMPLES	Ann Myers, **our neighbor,** is a fine golfer.
	Naturally, we expect to win.
	My answer is correct, **I think.**

(1) Use commas to set off nonessential participial phrases and nonessential subordinate clauses.

A *nonessential* (or *nonrestrictive*) phrase or clause adds information that is not needed to understand the basic meaning of the sentence. Such a phrase or clause can be omitted without changing the main idea of the sentence.

NONESSENTIAL PHRASES	My sister, **listening to her radio,** did not hear me.
	Paul, **thrilled by the applause,** took a bow.
NONESSENTIAL CLAUSES	*The Wizard of Oz,* **which I saw again last week,** is my favorite movie.
	I reported on *Secret of the Andes,* **which was written by Ann Nolan Clark.**

Each boldface clause or phrase above can be omitted because it is not essential to identify the word or phrase it modifies. Omitting such a clause or phrase will not change the meaning of the sentence.

EXAMPLES	Paul took a bow.
	I reported on *Secret of the Andes.*

PEANUTS reprinted by permission of United Feature Syndicate, Inc.

Reference Note

For more about **phrases,** see Chapter 14. For more about **subordinate clauses,** see page 424.

Do not set off an *essential* (or *restrictive*) phrase or clause. Since such a phrase or clause tells *which one(s)*, it cannot be omitted without changing the basic meaning of the sentence.

ESSENTIAL PHRASES	The people **waiting to see Michael Jordan** whistled and cheered. [Which people?]
	A bowl **made by Maria Martínez** is a collector's item. [Which bowl?]
ESSENTIAL CLAUSES	The dress **that I liked** has been sold. [Which dress?]
	The man **who tells Navajo folk tales** is Mr. Platero. [Which man?]

Notice how the meaning changes when an essential phrase or clause is omitted.

EXAMPLES	The people whistled and cheered.
	A bowl is a collector's item.
	The dress has been sold.
	The man is Mr. Platero.

NOTE A clause beginning with *that* is usually essential.

EXAMPLE   This is the birdhouse **that I made.**

Exercise 5 Adding Commas to Sentences with Nonessential Phrases and Clauses

Some of the following sentences need commas to set off nonessential phrases and clauses. Other sentences are correct without commas. If a sentence needs commas, write the word that comes before each missing comma and add the comma. If the sentence is already correct, write *C*.

EXAMPLE   **1.** My grandfather's favorite photograph which was taken near Ellis Island shows his family after their arrival from Eastern Europe.

    1. photograph, Island,

1. Millions of immigrants who came to the United States between about 1892 and 1954 stopped at Ellis Island which is in Upper New York Bay.

2. Families arriving from Europe were interviewed there.

3. The island and its buildings which were closed to the public for many years are now part of the Statue of Liberty National Monument.

4. In 1990, Ellis Island rebuilt as a museum was officially opened to the public.

5. Visitors who wish to see the museum can take a ferry ride from Manhattan Island.

6. The museum's lobby crowded with steamer trunks and other old baggage is the visitors' first sight.

7. One special attraction in the museum consists of audiotapes and videotapes that describe the immigrants' experiences.

The Granger Collection, New York.

8. The Registry Room which is on the second floor sometimes held as many as five thousand people.

9. The immigrants who came from many countries hoped to find freedom and a happier life in America.

10. Immigrants who came to the United States brought with them a strong work ethic and a variety of skills that helped to make our country great.

(2) Use commas to set off nonessential appositives and nonessential appositive phrases.

An *appositive* is a noun or a pronoun used to identify or describe another noun or pronoun.

NONESSENTIAL APPOSITIVE	My oldest sister, **Alicia,** will be at basketball practice until 6:00 P.M.
NONESSENTIAL APPOSITIVE PHRASES	Jamaica, **a popular island for tourists,** is in the Caribbean Sea.
	May I introduce you to Vernon, **my cousin from Jamaica**?

Do not use commas to set off an appositive that is essential to the meaning of a sentence.

ESSENTIAL APPOSITIVES

My sister **Alicia** is at basketball practice. [The speaker has more than one sister and must give a name to identify which sister.]

The planet **Mercury** is closer to the Sun than any other planet in our solar system. [The solar system contains more than one planet. The name is needed to identify which planet.]

Exercise 6 **Proofreading for the Correct Use of Commas with Appositives and Appositive Phrases**

┌HELP──

Not all of the appositives in Exercise 6 require commas.

Rewrite each of the following sentences, and underline the appositive or appositive phrase. Then, supply commas where needed.

EXAMPLE

1. Mars one of the planets closest to Earth can be seen without a telescope.

1. Mars, <u>one of the planets closest to Earth</u>, can be seen without a telescope.

1. The whole class has read the novel *Old Yeller*.
2. Shana Alexander a former editor of a popular magazine was the main speaker at the conference.
3. The character Sabrina is Josie's favorite.
4. The Galápagos Islands a group of volcanic islands in the Pacific Ocean were named for the Spanish word that means "tortoise."
5. Rubber an elastic substance quickly restores itself to its original size and shape.
6. This bowl is made of clay found on Kilimanjaro the highest mountain in Africa.
7. The North Sea an arm of the Atlantic Ocean is rich in fish, natural gas, and oil.
8. Jamake Highwater a Blackfoot/Eastern Band Cherokee author writes about the history of his people.
9. At Gettysburg a town in Pennsylvania an important battle of the Civil War was fought.
10. My friend Imelda is teaching me how to make empanadas.

MECHANICS

(3) Use commas to set off words that are used in direct address.

EXAMPLES   **Ben,** please answer the doorbell.

                 Mom needs you, **Francine.**

                 Would you show me, **ma'am,** where the craft store is?

Exercise 7   **Correcting Sentences by Using Commas with Words of Direct Address**

Identify the words used in direct address in the following sentences. Then, rewrite each sentence, inserting commas before, after, or both before and after the words, as needed.

EXAMPLE   1. Listen folks to this amazing announcement!

            1. *folks—Listen, folks, to this amazing announcement!*

1. Andrea when are you leaving for Detroit?
2. Pay attention now class.
3. Let us my sisters and brothers give thanks.
4. Please Dad may I use your computer?
5. Senator please summarize your tax proposal.
6. Help me move this table Marlene.
7. "Tell me both of you what movie you want to see," Jo said.
8. Hurry William and give me the phone number!
9. Mrs. Larson where is Zion National Park?
10. I'm just not sure friends that I agree with you.

(4) Use commas to set off parenthetical expressions.

A *parenthetical expression* is a side remark that adds information or shows a relationship between ideas.

EXAMPLES   Carl, **on the contrary,** prefers soccer to baseball.

            To tell the truth, Jan is one of my best friends.

Common Parenthetical Expressions		
by the way	in fact	of course
for example	in my opinion	on the contrary
however	I suppose	on the other hand
I believe	nevertheless	to tell the truth

Some of these expressions are not always used parenthetically.

EXAMPLES   **Of course** it is true. [not parenthetical]

That is**, of course,** an Indian teakwood screen. [parenthetical]

I suppose we ought to go home now. [not parenthetical]

He'll want a ride**, I suppose.** [parenthetical]

Exercise 8   Correcting Sentences by Using Commas to Set Off Parenthetical Expressions

The following sentences contain parenthetical expressions that require commas. Write the parenthetical expressions, inserting commas before, after, or both before and after the expressions, as needed.

EXAMPLES

1. Everyone I suppose has heard of the Hubble Space Telescope.
1. *, I suppose,*

2. As a matter of fact even a small refracting telescope gives a good view of Saturn's rings.
2. *As a matter of fact,*

1. You don't need a telescope however to see all the beautiful sights in the night sky.
2. For instance on a summer night you might be able to view Scorpio, Serpens, and the Serpent Bearer.
3. By the way you should not overlook the Milky Way.
4. The Milky Way in fact is more impressive in the summer than at any other time of year.
5. Hercules of course is an interesting constellation.
6. Studying the constellations is in my opinion a most interesting hobby.
7. It takes an active imagination however to spot some constellations.
8. Sagittarius for example is hard to see unless you're familiar with a constellation map.
9. Scorpio on the other hand is quite clearly outlined.
10. Astronomy is a fascinating science I think.

MECHANICS

Introductory Words, Phrases, and Clauses

23j. Use a comma after certain introductory elements.

(1) Use a comma after *yes, no,* or any mild exclamation such as *well* or *why* at the beginning of a sentence.

EXAMPLES   **Yes,** you may borrow my bicycle.

           Why, it's Lena!

           Well, I think you are wrong.

(2) Use a comma after an introductory participial phrase.

EXAMPLES   **Beginning a new school year,** Zelda felt somewhat nervous.

           Greeted with applause from the fans, Rashid ran out onto the field.

Reference Note

For information about **participial phrases,** see page 412.

(3) Use a comma after two or more introductory prepositional phrases.

EXAMPLES   **At the bottom of the hill,** you will see the baseball field.

           Until the end of the song, just keep strumming that chord.

Reference Note

For information about **prepositional phrases,** see page 402.

Use a comma after a single introductory prepositional phrase when the comma is necessary to make the meaning of the sentence clear.

EXAMPLES   In the morning they left. [clear without a comma]

           In the morning, sunlight streamed through the window. [The comma is needed so that the reader does not read "morning sunlight."]

(4) Use a comma after an introductory adverb clause.

EXAMPLES   **After I finish my homework,** I will go to the park.

           When you go to the store, could you please pick up a gallon of milk?

Reference Note

For information about **adverb clauses,** see page 430.

NOTE An adverb clause that comes at the end of a sentence does not usually need a comma.

EXAMPLE   I will go to the park **after I finish my homework.**

Exercise 9 — Using Commas with Introductory Elements

If a comma is needed in a sentence, write the word before the missing comma and add the comma. If a sentence is already punctuated correctly, write *C*.

EXAMPLE
1. Walking among the tigers and lions the trainer seemed unafraid.

1. *lions,*

1. Because pemmican remained good to eat for several years it was a practical food for many American Indians.
2. Although Jesse did not win the student council election he raised many important issues.
3. On the desk in the den you will find your book.
4. Yes I enjoyed the fajitas that Ruben made.
5. Walking home from school Rosa saw her brother.
6. When I go to bed late I sometimes have trouble waking up in the morning.
7. Well we can watch television or play checkers.
8. Attracted by the computer games in the store window George decided to go in and buy one.
9. At the stoplight on the corner of the next block they made a right turn.
10. After eating the chickens settled down.

Conventional Situations

23k. Use commas in certain conventional situations.

(1) Use commas to separate items in dates and addresses.

EXAMPLES   She was born on January 26, 1988, in Cheshire, Connecticut.

A letter dated November 26, 1888, was found in the old house at 980 West Street, Davenport, Iowa, yesterday.

Notice that a comma separates the last item in a date or in an address from the words that follow it. However, a comma does not separate a month from a day (*January 26*) or a house number from a street name (*980 West Street*).

┌HELP──
Commas are also used in numbers over 999. Use a comma before every third digit to the left of the decimal point.

EXAMPLE
3,147,425.00

NOTE Use the ZIP Code correctly on every piece of mail you address. The ZIP Code follows the two-letter state abbreviation; no punctuation separates the state abbreviation from the ZIP Code.

EXAMPLE   Fargo, ND 58102-2728

(2) Use a comma after the salutation of a personal letter and after the closing of any letter.

EXAMPLES   Dear Dad,   Dear Sharon,

     With love,   Yours truly,

Reference Note

For information about using **colons for salutations in business letters,** see page 620.

Exercise 10   Using Commas Correctly

Rewrite the following sentences, inserting commas wherever they are needed.

EXAMPLE   1. I received a package from my friend who lives in Irving Texas.

     1. *I received a package from my friend who lives in Irving, Texas.*

1. On May 25 1935 the runner Jesse Owens tied or broke six world track records.
2. The American Saddle Horse Museum is located at 4093 Iron Works Pike Lexington KY 40511-8462.
3. Marian Anderson was born on February 27 1902 in Philadelphia Pennsylvania.
4. Our new address will be 1808 Jackson Drive Ames IA 50010-4437.
5. Ocean City New Jersey is a popular seaside resort.
6. October 15 1988 is an important date because I was born then.
7. Have you ever been to Paisley Scotland?
8. We adopted our dog, King Barnabus IV, in Lee's Summit Missouri on May 9 1995.
9. The national headquarters of the Environmental Defense Fund is located at 257 Park Avenue South New York NY 10010-7304.
10. Dear Lynn
     I am fine. How are you and your family?

┌HELP─
Too much
punctuation is just as
confusing as not enough
punctuation, especially
where the use of commas
is concerned.

CONFUSING
My uncle, Doug, said he
would take me fishing,
this weekend, but now,
he tells me, he will be out
of town.

CLEAR
My uncle Doug said he
would take me fishing
this weekend, but now
he tells me he will be out
of town.

Have a reason for every
comma or other mark of
punctuation that you use.
When there is no rule
requiring punctuation and
the meaning of the sen-
tence is clear without it, do
not use any punctuation
mark.

Review C Proofreading Sentences for the Correct Use of Commas

For the following sentences, write each word that should be followed by a comma and add the comma after the word.

EXAMPLE   1. The substitute's name is Mr. Fowler I think.

1. *Fowler,*

1. What time is your appointment Kevin?
2. My aunt said to forward her mail to 302 Lancelot Drive Simpsonville SC 29681-5749.
3. George Washington Carver a famous scientist had to work hard to afford to go to school.
4. Quick violent flashes of lightning cause an average of 14,300 forest fires a year in the United States.
5. My oldest sister Kim sent a postcard from Ewa Hawaii.
6. A single branch stuck out of the water and the beaver grasped it in its paws.
7. The beaver by the way is a rodent.
8. This hard-working mammal builds dams lodges and canals.
9. Built with their entrances underwater the lodges of American beavers are marvels of engineering.
10. The beaver uses its large tail which is flat to steer.

Review D Proofreading Sentences for the Correct Use of Commas

Each of the following sentences contains at least one error in the use of commas. Write each word that should be followed by a comma, and add the comma.

EXAMPLES   1. Kyoto's palaces shrines and temples remind visitors of this city's importance in Japanese history.

1. *palaces, shrines,*

2. In Japanese Kyoto means "capital city" which is what Emperor Kammu made Kyoto in A.D. 794.

2. *Japanese, city,*

1. Kyoto a beautiful city was Japan's capital for more than one thousand years.

2. It still may be called the cultural capital of Japan for it contains many Shinto shrines Buddhist temples the Kyoto National Museum, and wonderful gardens.

3. Yes Kyoto which was called Heian-kyo during the ninth century was so important that an entire period of Japanese history, the Heian period, is named for it.

4. Originating from the monasteries outside ancient Kyoto the magnificent mandala paintings feature universal themes.

5. Oh haven't you seen the wonderful *ukiyo-e* paintings of vast mountains and tiny people?

6. Believe it or not readers there are now more than twenty colleges and universities in this treasured city.

7. Its people historic landmarks and art are respected across the globe.

8. With attractions like these it's no surprise that Kyoto is a popular tourist stop.

9. Used in industries around the world the tools of fine crafts are made in Kyoto.

10. Kyoto manufactures silk for the fashion industry copper for artists and electricians and machines for businesses.

11. Fine delicate porcelain from Kyoto graces many tables around the world.

12. The Procession of the Eras celebrated every autumn takes place in Kyoto.

13. The Procession of the Eras festival which celebrates Kyoto's history begins on October 22.

14. The beautiful solemn procession is a remarkable sight.

15. At the beginning of the festival priests offer special prayers.

16. Portable shrines are carried through the streets and thousands of costumed marchers follow.

17. Elaborate headgear and armor for example are worn by marchers dressed as ancient warriors.

18. Because the marchers near the front represent recent history they wear costumes from the nineteenth-century Royal Army Era.

19. Marching at the end of the procession archers wear costumes from the eighth-century Warrior Era.

20. The procession is in fact a rich memorial to Kyoto's long and varied history.

Semicolons are most effective when they are not overused. Sometimes it is better to separate a compound sentence or a heavily punctuated sentence into two sentences rather than to use a semicolon.

ACCEPTABLE
Garden visitors include butterflies, bats, and ladybugs; such creatures benefit gardens in various ways, some by adding color, some by controlling pests, and all by pollinating plants.

BETTER
Garden visitors include butterflies, bats, and ladybugs. Such creatures benefit gardens in various ways, some by adding color, some by controlling pests, and all by pollinating plants.

MECHANICS

Semicolons

A *semicolon* looks like a combination of a period and a comma, and that is just what it is. A semicolon can separate complete thoughts much as a period does. A semicolon can also separate items within a sentence much as a comma does.

23l. Use a semicolon between independent clauses if they are not joined by *and, but, for, nor, or, so,* or *yet.*

EXAMPLES   Jimmy took my suitcase upstairs; he left his own travel bag in the car.

             After school, I went to band practice; then I studied in the library for an hour.

Use a semicolon to link clauses only if the clauses are closely related in meaning.

INCORRECT   Uncle Ray likes sweet potatoes; Aunt Janie prefers the beach.

CORRECT   Uncle Ray likes sweet potatoes; Aunt Janie prefers peas and carrots.

or

             Uncle Ray likes the mountains; Aunt Janie prefers the beach.

23m. Use a semicolon rather than a comma before a coordinating conjunction to join independent clauses that contain commas.

CONFUSING   I wrote to Ann, Ramona, and Mai, and Jean notified Charles, Latoya, and Sue.

CLEAR   I wrote to Ann, Ramona, and Mai; and Jean notified Charles, Latoya, and Sue.

NOTE   Semicolons are also used between items in a series when the items contain commas.

EXAMPLES   They visited Phoenix, Arizona; Santa Fe, New Mexico; and San Antonio, Texas.

             Mr. Schultz, my science teacher; Ms. O'Hara, my English teacher; Mrs. Gomez, my math teacher; and Mr. Kim, my social studies teacher, attended the seventh-grade picnic.

Exercise 11 **Using Semicolons Correctly**

Most of the following sentences have a comma where there should
be a semicolon. If the sentence needs a semicolon, write the words
before and after the missing semicolon and insert the punctuation
mark. If the sentence does not need a semicolon, write *C*.

EXAMPLE   1. Human beings have walked on the moon, they have
not yet walked on any planet but earth.

      1. *moon; they*

1. Miyoko finished her homework, then she decided to go to
Sally's house.
2. Each January some people try to predict the major events of
the upcoming year, but their predictions are seldom accurate.
3. Tie these newspapers together with string, put the aluminum
cans in a bag.
4. I called Tom, Paul, and Francine, and Fred called Amy, Luis,
Carlos, and Brad.
5. Reading is my favorite pastime, I love to begin a new book.
6. In 1991, Wellington Webb was elected mayor of Denver, he
was the first African American to hold that office.
7. The two companies merged, and they became the largest
consumer goods firm in the nation.
8. Your grades have definitely improved, you will easily pass
the course.
9. Paris, France, Cairo, Egypt, and Copenhagen, Denmark, are
all places that I would like to visit someday.
10. We haven't seen the movie, for it hasn't come to our town yet.

Colons

**23n. Use a colon before a list of items, especially after
expressions such as *the following* or *as follows*.**

EXAMPLES   You will need these items for map work: a ruler, colored
pencils, and tracing paper.

Jack's pocket contained the following items: a key, a
note from a friend, a button, and two quarters.

The primary colors are as follows: red, blue, and yellow.

Do not use a colon between a verb and its object or between a preposition and its object. Omit the colon, or reword the sentence.

INCORRECT   Your heading should contain: your name, the date, and the title of your essay.

CORRECT   Your heading should contain your name, the date, and the title of your essay.

CORRECT   Your heading should contain the following information: your name, the date, and the title of your essay.

INCORRECT   This marinara sauce is made of: tomatoes, onions, oregano, and garlic.

CORRECT   This marinara sauce is made of tomatoes, onions, oregano, and garlic.

CORRECT   This marinara sauce is made of the following ingredients: tomatoes, onions, oregano, and garlic.

NOTE   Colons are also often used before long formal statements or quotations.

EXAMPLE   My opinion of beauty is clearly expressed by Margaret Wolfe Hungerford in *Molly Bawn*: "Beauty is in the eye of the beholder."

Conventional Situations

23o. Use a colon between the hour and the minute.

EXAMPLE   8:30 A.M.   10:00 P.M.

23p. Use a colon after the salutation of a business letter.

EXAMPLES   Dear Sir or Madam: Dear Mrs. Foster:

                To Whom It May Concern: Dear Dr. Christiano:

23q. Use a colon between chapter and verse in Biblical references and between all titles and subtitles.

EXAMPLES   I Chronicles 22:6–19

             "Oral Storytelling: Making the Winter Shorter"

STYLE   TIP

Use a comma after the salutation of a personal letter.

EXAMPLES
Dear Kim,
Dear Uncle Remy,

Reference Note

For information about **writing letters,** see "Writing" in the Quick Reference Handbook.

Exercise 12 **Using Colons and Commas Correctly**

Make each of the following word groups into a complete sentence by supplying the item called for in the brackets. Insert colons and commas where they are needed.

EXAMPLE   **1.** The test will begin at *[time]*.

        1. The test will begin at 9:30 A.M.

1. So far, the class has studied the following topics *[list]*.
2. You will need these supplies for your science-fair experiment *[list]*.
3. If I were writing a book about my friends and me, I would call it *[title and subtitle]*.
4. Meet me at the mall at *[time]*.
5. My classes this year are the following *[list]*.
6. You should begin your business letter with *[salutation]*.
7. The concert begins at *[time]*.
8. I need the following from the hardware store *[list]*.
9. Three countries I would like to visit are *[list]*.
10. The alarm is set to go off at *[time]*.

Review E **Using End Marks, Commas, Semicolons, and Colons Correctly**

The sentences in the following paragraph lack necessary end marks, commas, semicolons, and colons. Write each sentence, inserting the correct punctuation.

EXAMPLE   **[1]** What an unusual clever caring way to help animals that is

       1. What an unusual, clever, caring way to help animals that is!

    [1] Animal lovers have you heard about the Sanctuary for Animals **[2]** Founded by Leonard and Bunny Brook the sanctuary is a safe home for all kinds of animals **[3]** Through the years hundreds of stray unwanted and abused animals have found a home at the sanctuary **[4]** It is located on the Brooks' land in Westtown New York **[5]** On their two hundred acres the Brooks take care of the following animals dogs cats camels elephants lions and even an Australian kangaroo **[6]** Of course Mr. and

Mrs. Brook also raise chickens keep horses and look after their other farm animals [7] The Brooks their family and their friends care for animals like this young cougar they also let the animals work for themselves [8] How do the animals work [9] The Brooks formed the Dawn Animal Agency and their animals became actors and models [10] You may have seen a camel or some of the other animals in magazines movies television shows and commercials

23 Chapter Review

A. Using End Marks, Commas, Semicolons, and Colons Correctly

The following sentences lack necessary periods, question marks, exclamation points, commas, semicolons, and colons. Write each sentence, inserting the correct punctuation.

1. The following students gave reports Carlos Sue and Alan
2. Tanay carved this beautiful soapstone cooking pot
3. Walter this is Ellen who has transferred to our school
4. Calling Simon's name I ran to the door
5. The Wilsons' new address is 3100 DeSoto St New Orleans LA 70119-3251
6. Have you listened to that Bill Cosby tape Felix
7. Let me know of course if you can't attend
8. Joy our club president will conduct the meeting and Gary our recently elected secretary will take notes
9. Looking at the harsh bright glare Mai closed the blinds
10. Carlos Montoya picked up the guitar positioned his fingers and strummed a few chords of a flamenco song
11. If you hurry you can get home before 9 00
12. Help This is an emergency
13. By the way Rosa have you seen any of Alfred Hitchcock's movies
14. Dave hit a long fly ball but Phil was there to catch it
15. Flooding rapidly the gully quickly became a tremendous torrent
16. *The Grapes of Wrath* which is one of my favorite movies is about a family's struggles during the Great Depression
17. Nicaragua Panama and Honduras are in Central America and Colombia Peru and Chile are in South America
18. One of our cats Gypsy scooted through the door across the room and out the window
19. The Lock Museum of America a fascinating place in Terryville Conn has more than twenty thousand locks
20. Could the surprise gift be in-line skates a new football or tickets to a concert

B. Proofreading a Business Letter

The following business letter lacks periods, commas, semicolons, and colons. Correct each error. If a sentence is already correct, write *C*.

```
        Gable Books
        387 Monocle Lane
        Bozeman, MT  59715
        June 28, 2001
```

[21] Dear Mr Gable

[22] Please find enclosed a copy of *Edith Wharton A Biography* by R W B Lewis. **[23]** I purchased this book recently at your book shop but I have since discovered that several pages are missing **[24]** I am not happy with the book please send me a new copy.

[25] Sincerely

E. Frome

E. Frome

C. Proofreading for Correct Punctuation

Most of the following sentences lack at least one period, question mark, exclamation point, comma, semicolon, or colon. Correct each error. If a sentence is already correctly punctuated, write *C*.

26. He went shopping, cooked dinner, and washed the dishes.

27. For the good of us all please think before you act next time

28. Mr T E Hawk a friend of my mother's helps me with math.

29. Caroline have your relatives arrived

30. Yes Mario they came just last week.

31. At the center of a map of Texas you will find Brady.

32. Our new address is 72 Maple Ave Rochester NY 14612.

33. Inger designs the clothes her mother sews them

34. We followed the trail it led around the garage.

35. The world record in the long jump was held by Jesse Owens for several years but the record is now held by another outstanding athlete.

36. On June 15 1983 my father opened his first florist shop.

37. Your use of materials, for example, is very artistic.

38. My hobbies are as follows baseball ballet and magic tricks.

39. After I carry the groceries into the house my sister puts them away.

40. Stop that now Veronica

Writing Application
Using Punctuation in an Announcement

Correct Punctuation   Your class is sponsoring a carwash to raise money for a special project or trip. You have been chosen to write an announcement about the carwash for publication in a community newsletter. Write a brief announcement telling when and where the carwash will be, how much it will cost, what the money will be used for, and any other important details. Be sure to use end marks, commas, semicolons, and colons correctly in your announcement.

Prewriting   List the information that you will include in your announcement. Make sure you have included all the facts people will need to know about the purpose, time, location, and cost of the carwash.

Writing   As you write, remember that the purpose of your announcement is to attract customers. Start with an attention-grabbing first sentence that explains the purpose of the carwash. Be sure to present all your information in clear, complete sentences. Add any important details that you did not list earlier.

Revising   Ask a friend to read your announcement. Is it clear and straightforward? Does it convince your friend that the carwash is for a good cause? If not, revise, rearrange, or add details.

Publishing   As you proofread your announcement, pay special attention to your use of punctuation. Remember to check the placement of colons in expressions of time. You may wish to offer your announcement-writing services to a club or service organization at your school.

24 Punctuation

Underlining (Italics), Quotation Marks, Apostrophes, Hyphens, Parentheses, Brackets, and Dashes

Diagnostic Preview

A. Proofreading Sentences for the Correct Use of Underlining (Italics), Quotation Marks, Apostrophes, Hyphens, Parentheses, Brackets, and Dashes

Revise each of the following sentences so that underlining, quotation marks, apostrophes, hyphens, parentheses, brackets, and dashes are used correctly.

—HELP—

Sentences in the Diagnostic Preview, Part A, may contain more than one error.

EXAMPLE   1. "May I borrow your copy of 'Life' magazine?" Phil asked Alan.

        1. *"May I borrow your copy of <u>Life</u> magazine?" Phil asked Alan.*

1. Boris Karloff (his real name was William Henry Pratt played the monster in the original movie version of Frankenstein.
2. "Ive never known—do you? what the word *kith* means," Paul said.
3. "It (the new version of the software) corrects that problem," said Steve.
4. I've heard that the programs announcer and interviewer will be Connie Chung, a favorite of mine.

5. Anne said that "Norma couldn't understand why twenty two people had voted against having the dance on a Friday night.

6. "A two thirds majority said they didn't want to have it then, Shawn said.

7. Fred said, This magazine article titled Luxury Liners of the Past is interesting."

8. "Does the public library have copies of The Seminole Tribune or any other American Indian newspapers"? Tanya asked.

9. My sisters' enjoy reading folk tales like the stories in Two Ways to Count to Ten by Ruby Dee.

10. The Garcia's cat is I don't think they know living in our garage," Mary said.

B. Punctuating Quotations Correctly

Add quotation marks where they are needed in each of the following sentences.

EXAMPLE   1. I wonder why so many people enjoy collecting things, said J. D.

       1. *"I wonder why so many people enjoy collecting things," said J. D.*

11. I know I do! Julia exclaimed.

12. Tomás said, My grandmother said, It's the thrill of the hunt.

13. Do you collect anything as a hobby? Josh asked Marsha.

14. No, Marsha answered, but I know a person who collects old cameras and antique costume jewelry.

15. My aunt collects John McCormack's records, Kevin said. Do you know who he is?

16. I'm not sure, Julia said, but I think that he was an Irish singer.

17. Yes, he sang in the opera; he also sang popular Irish songs such as The Rose of Tralee, Kevin said.

18. My stepbrother has a collection of arrowheads. He hasn't been collecting them very long, Sydney said.

19. You should see Mrs. Kominek's collection of Chinese jade carvings, J. D. said. It's great!

20. Some people—I'm sure you know—have odd collections, Josh said. For instance, my aunt collects old shoelaces.

Underlining (Italics)

COMPUTER TIP

If you use a personal computer, you can probably set words in italics yourself. Most word-processing software and many printers can produce italic type.

Italics are printed letters that lean to the right—*like this*. When you write or type, you show that a word should be italicized by underlining it. If your composition were printed, the typesetter would set the underlined words in italics. For example, if you typed

```
Gary Soto wrote Pacific Crossing.
```

the sentence would be printed like this:

Gary Soto wrote *Pacific Crossing*.

Reference Note

For examples of **titles** that are not italicized but are **enclosed in quotation marks,** see page 635.

24a. Use underlining (italics) for titles and subtitles of books, plays, periodicals, films, television series, works of art, and long musical works.

Type of Name	Examples	
Books	*My Life and Hard Times*	*Life on the Mississippi*
	To Kill a Mockingbird	*Maud Martha*
Plays	*Our Town*	*I Never Sang for My Father*
	Hamlet	
Periodicals	the *Daily News*	*National Geographic*
	Essence	
Films	*The Maltese Falcon*	*Stand and Deliver*
Television Series	*Nova*	*Bill Nye the Science Guy*
	Sesame Street	
Works of Art	*Starry Night*	*The Dream*
	American Gothic	*View of Toledo*
Long Musical Works	*Carmen*	*Don Giovanni*
	An American in Paris	*Music for the Royal Fireworks*

24b. Use underlining (italics) for the names of ships, trains, aircraft, and spacecraft.

Type of Name	Examples	
Ships	HMS *Titanic* the *Pequod*	the USS *Eisenhower*
Trains	the *City of New Orleans*	the *Orient Express* *Golden Arrow*
Aircraft	the *Silver Dart*	the *Hindenburg*
Spacecraft	*Soyuz XI*	*Atlantis*

NOTE Underline (italicize) an article at the beginning of a title only if it is the first word of the official title. Check the table of contents or the masthead to find the preferred style for the title.

EXAMPLES   Would you like to subscribe to **the** *San Francisco Chronicle*?

   The *Seattle Times* is a daily newspaper.

24c. Use underlining (italics) for words, letters, and numerals referred to as such.

EXAMPLES   Double the final **n** before you add **–ing** in words like **running.**

   If your **Z's** look like **2's,** your reader may see **200** when you meant **zoo.**

Exercise 1 **Using Underlining (Italics) Correctly**

For each of the following sentences, write and underline each word or item that should be italicized.

EXAMPLE   1. Does Dave Barry write a humor column for The Miami Herald?

   1. *The Miami Herald*

1. The British spell the word humor with a u after the o.
2. In Denmark, you might see the spelling *triatlon* for the word triathlon.

MECHANICS

3. The current Newsweek has an informative article on the famine in Africa.

4. Our school paper, the Norwalk Valley News, is published weekly.

5. Luis Valdez wrote and directed La Bamba, a movie about the life of the singer Ritchie Valens.

6. Mr. Weyer said that the Oceanic is one of the ocean liners that sail to the Caribbean.

7. I think the movie The Sound of Music has some of the most beautiful photography that I have ever seen and some of the most memorable songs.

8. Our local theater group is presenting The Time of Your Life, a comedy by William Saroyan.

9. Charles Lindbergh's Spirit of St. Louis is on display at the museum, along with the Wright brothers' Flyer and NASA's Gemini IV.

10. The best novel that I read during vacation was The Summer of the Swans.

Quotation Marks

24d. Use quotation marks to enclose a *direct quotation*—a person's exact words.

Be sure to place quotation marks both before and after a person's exact words.

EXAMPLES The sonnet containing the words "Give me your tired, your poor, /Your huddled masses/ . . ." is inscribed on the Statue of Liberty.

"When the bell rings," said the teacher, "leave the room quietly."

Do not use quotation marks for an *indirect quotation*— a rewording of a direct quotation.

DIRECT QUOTATION Tom predicted, "It will be a close game." [Tom's exact words]

INDIRECT QUOTATION Tom predicted that it would be a close game. [not Tom's exact words]

24e. A direct quotation generally begins with a capital letter.

EXAMPLES   Lisa said, **"T**he *carne asada* isn't ready yet, but please help yourself to the guacamole.**"**

While he was in prison, Richard Lovelace wrote a poem containing the well-known line **"S**tone walls do not a prison make.**"**

24f. When an expression identifying the speaker interrupts a quoted sentence, the second part of the quotation begins with a lowercase letter.

EXAMPLE   "Lightning has always awed people," explained Mrs. Worthington, "**a**nd many of us are still quite frightened by it."

A quoted sentence that is divided in this way is called a **broken quotation.** Notice that each part of a broken quotation is enclosed in a set of quotation marks.

When the second part of a divided quotation is a complete sentence, it begins with a capital letter.

EXAMPLE   "I can't go today," I said. "**A**sk me tomorrow."

24g. A direct quotation can be set off from the rest of the sentence by one or more commas or by a question mark or an exclamation point, but not by a period.

To set off means "to separate." If a quotation begins a sentence, a comma follows it. If a quotation ends a sentence, a comma comes before it. If a quoted sentence is interrupted, a comma follows the first part and comes before the second part.

EXAMPLES   "I think science is more interesting than history**,**" said Bernie.

Velma commented**,** "I especially like to do the experiments."

"Yes**,**" Juan added**,** "Bernie loves experiments, too."

When a quotation at the beginning of a sentence ends with a question mark or an exclamation point, no comma is needed.

EXAMPLES   "Is that a good video game**?**" Jane wanted to know.

"I'll say it is**!**" Debbie exclaimed.

24h. A comma or a period should be placed inside the closing quotation marks.

EXAMPLES   "The Ramses exhibit begins over there**,**" said the museum guide.

Darnell replied, "I'm ready to see some ancient Egyptian jewelry and artwork**.**"

24i. A question mark or an exclamation point should be placed inside the closing quotation marks when the quotation itself is a question or an exclamation. Otherwise, it should be placed outside.

EXAMPLES   "How far have we come**?**" asked the exhausted man. [The quotation is a question.]

Who said, "Give me liberty or give me death"**?** [The sentence, not the quotation, is a question.]

"Jump**!**" ordered the firefighter. [The quotation is an exclamation.]

I couldn't believe it when he said, "No, thank you"**!** [The sentence, not the quotation, is an exclamation.]

When both the sentence and the quotation at the end of the sentence are questions (or exclamations), only one question mark (or exclamation point) is used. It is placed inside the closing quotation marks.

EXAMPLE   Did Josh really say, "What's Cinco de Mayo**?**"

Exercise 2 Punctuating and Capitalizing Quotations

Use commas, quotation marks, and capital letters where they are needed in each of the following sentences. If a sentence is already correct, write *C*.

EXAMPLE   **1.** Let's go to a movie this afternoon, said Bob.

       1. "Let's go to a movie this afternoon," said Bob.

1. When I shrieked in fear, the usher warned me to be quiet.
2. At the same time, Bob whispered it's only a movie—calm down.
3. He pointed out that the people around us were getting annoyed.

4. I quietly replied I'm sorry.

5. You shouldn't have screamed, he complained.

6. From now on I said to him I promise I'll try to be quiet.

7. When the lights came on, Bob said "it's time to go."

8. Outside the theater he muttered something about people who shouldn't go to scary movies.

9. I just couldn't help it I explained.

10. You were even afraid Bob protested during the credits!

Exercise 3 Punctuating and Capitalizing Quotations

Use capital letters, quotation marks, and other punctuation marks where they are needed in each of the following sentences.

EXAMPLE   1. Ashley Bryan wore traditional African clothes when he came to our school Elton said.

         1. *"Ashley Bryan wore traditional African clothes when he came to our school," Elton said.*

1. Oh, like the clothes Mr. Johnson showed us in class Janell exclaimed

2. Elton asked have you read any of Ashley Bryan's books about African culture

3. I've read Janell quickly replied the one titled *Beat the Story-Drum, Pum-Pum*

4. I'd like to read that again Elton said those African folk tales are wonderful

5. Mrs. Ray thinks *Walk Together Children* is excellent Janell said

6. Isn't that Elton asked about African American spirituals

7. You're right Janell answered and Bryan wrote that spirituals are America's greatest contribution to world music

8. She added he grew up in New York City and began writing stories and drawing when he was still in kindergarten

9. Did you know Elton asked that he illustrated his own books

10. Bryan made woodcuts to illustrate *Walk Together Children* he added.

Exercise 4 **Creating Direct Quotations**

Revise each of the following sentences by changing the indirect quotation to a direct quotation. Be sure to use capital letters and punctuation wherever necessary.

EXAMPLE   1. I asked my grandmother whether she would like to help us paint our float.

1. *"Grandma," I asked, "would you like to help us paint our float?"*

I will lead the pa

1. Mayor Alaniz announced that he would lead the parade this year.

what are your

2. Ms. Feldman asked me what my plans for the big parade were.
3. I answered that my brother and I were building a float.
4. She exclaimed that she thought that was terrific.
5. Ron remarked that our float probably had something to do with sports.
6. I told Ron that he was exactly right.
7. Alinda asked me what sports will be represented on the float.
8. I replied that the float will salute swimming, soccer, and tennis.
9. Ron said excitedly that he would love to help.
10. Ms. Feldman said that my brother and I would probably be glad to have help.

24j. When you write dialogue (a conversation), begin a new paragraph every time the speaker changes.

EXAMPLE   The young man smiled, and said, "My old master, now let me tell you the truth. My home is not so far away. It is quite near your temple. We have been old neighbors for many years."

The old monk was very surprised. "I don't believe it. You, young man, will have your joke. Where is there another house round here?"

"My master, would I lie to you? I live right beside your temple. The Green Pond is my home."

"You live in the pond?" The old monk was even more astonished.

"That's right. In fact," said Li Aiqi, in a perfectly serious tone, "I'm not a man at all. I am a dragon."

"Green Dragon Pond," a Bai folk tale

24k. When a quotation consists of several sentences, put quotation marks only at the beginning and the end of the whole quotation.

EXAMPLE   "Mary Elizabeth and I will wait for you at Robertson's Drugstore. Please try to get there as soon as you can. We don't want to be late for the concert," Jerome said.

24l. Use single quotation marks to enclose a quotation within a quotation.

EXAMPLES   Brandon added, "My mom always says, 'Look before you leap.'"

               "Did Ms. Neuman really say, 'It's all right to use your books and your notes during the test'?" asked Sakura.

24m. Use quotation marks to enclose the titles of short works such as short stories, poems, songs, episodes of television series, essays, articles, and chapters and other parts of books.

Reference Note

For examples of **titles that are italicized,** see page 628.

Type of Name	Examples
Short Stories	"A Day's Wait" "The Medicine Bag"
Poems	"In Time of Silver Rain" "Birdfoot's Grampa"
Songs	"The Star-Spangled Banner" "Swing Low, Sweet Chariot"
Episodes of Television Series	"This Side of Paradise" "Growing Up Hispanic"
Essays	"Self-Reliance" "The Creative Process"
Articles	"Rooting for the Home Team" "Annie Leibovitz: Behind the Images"
Chapters and Other Parts of Books	"The Natural World" "The Myths of Greece and Rome" "The Double Task of Language"

NOTE Titles that are usually set in quotation marks are set in single quotation marks when they appear within a quotation.

EXAMPLE James said, "We learned 'The Star-Spangled Banner' in music class today."

Exercise 5 Using Quotation Marks

Insert quotation marks where they are needed in each of the following items. If a sentence is already correct, write *C*.

EXAMPLE 1. Let's sing 'The Ballad of Gregorio Cortez,' suggested Jim.

1. "Let's sing 'The Ballad of Gregorio Cortez,'" suggested Jim.

1. Lani, have you seen my clarinet? asked Rob. It was on this table. I need it for my lesson this afternoon.
2. The most interesting chapter in *The Sea Around Us* is The Birth of an Island.
3. Didn't Benjamin Franklin once say, Time is money? asked Myra impatiently.
4. I believe my favorite Langston Hughes poem is As I Grew Older, said Mom.
5. Lea Evans said, One of the greatest changes in architecture has been in the design of churches. They no longer necessarily follow traditional forms. Churches have been built that are shaped like stars, fish, and ships.
6. The latest issue of *Discover* magazine has a fascinating picture of a shark that swallowed an anchor.
7. Do you know which character asked What's in a name? in *Romeo and Juliet*? I asked.
8. Yes, that was Juliet, answered Li. My mother used to say that to me when I was a little girl. That's how I first heard of Shakespeare.
9. A human hand has more than twenty-seven bones and thirty-five muscles! exclaimed Marcus. No wonder it can do so much.
10. There is an article titled The Customers Always Write in today's newspaper.

Revise the following paragraphs, adding quotation marks and other marks of punctuation wherever necessary. Remember to begin a new paragraph each time the speaker changes. If a sentence is already correct, write *C*.

┌─HELP───
The marks of punctuation that are already included in Review A are correct.

EXAMPLES   **[1]**   Mr. Brown asked Can you baby-sit tonight?

      1.   *Mr. Brown asked, "Can you baby-sit tonight?"*

      [2]   Sure I said I'd be happy to.

      2.   *"Sure," I said. "I'd be happy to."*

[**1**] Last night I baby-sat for the Browns, a new family on our block. [**2**] Come in Mrs. Brown greeted me. [**3**] You must be Lisa. [**4**] Hello, Mrs. Brown I replied. [**5**] I'm looking forward to meeting the children. [**6**] First Mrs. Brown explained I want you to meet Ludwig. [**7**] Is he a member of the family I asked. [**8**] In a way replied Mrs. Brown as she led me to the kitchen and pointed to an aging dachshund. [**9**] That is Ludwig. [**10**] He rules this house and everyone in it.

[**11**] Mr. Brown entered the kitchen and introduced himself. [**12**] I see that you've met Ludwig he said. [**13**] Yes Mrs. Brown answered for me. [**14**] Why don't you give Lisa her instructions while I go find the children?

[**15**] If Ludwig whines said Mr. Brown give him a dog biscuit. [**16**] Should I take him for a walk I asked. [**17**] No replied Mr. Brown. [**18**] Just let him out into the yard.

[**19**] Mrs. Brown came back into the kitchen with the children. [**20**] Did my husband remind you to cover Ludwig when he falls asleep she asked. [**21**] I'll remember I promised. [**22**] Also, what should I do for the children? [**23**] Don't worry said Mr. Brown. [**24**] They'll behave themselves and go to bed when they're supposed to. [**25**] As I told you laughed Mrs. Brown Ludwig rules this house and everyone in it, even the sitter!

Apostrophes

Possessive Case

The *possessive case* of a noun or a pronoun shows ownership or possession.

EXAMPLES   **Kathleen's** desk   **anybody's** guess

his bat   an **hour's** time

their car   those **horses'** manes

24n. To form the possessive case of a singular noun, add an apostrophe and an *s*.

EXAMPLES   a boy**'s** cap   Cleon**'s** pen

the baby**'s** toy   Charles**'s** opinion

> NOTE   A proper noun ending in *s* may take only an apostrophe to form the possessive case if the addition of an apostrophe and an *s* would make the name awkward to say.
>
> EXAMPLES   the Philippine**s'** government
>
> Ms. Rodger**s'** cat

Exercise 6   Using Apostrophes for Singular Possessives

Identify the word that needs an apostrophe in each of the following sentences. Then, write the word correctly punctuated.

EXAMPLE   1. The Prado in Madrid, Spain, is one of the worlds greatest museums.

1. *worlds—world's*

1. Shown on the next page is one of the Prados paintings by Diego Velázquez, *Las Meninas.*
2. Velázquezs painting is known in English as *The Maids of Honor.*
3. In the center of the canvas is Princess Margarita, the royal couples daughter.
4. To the princesss right, a kneeling maid of honor offers her something to drink.

MECHANICS

5. To the royal childs left, another maid of honor curtsies.
6. On the far left of the canvas, you can see the artists own image, for he has painted himself!
7. The palaces other important people, such as the chamberlain and a court jester, also appear.
8. The faces of Margaritas parents are reflected in the mirror on the back wall.
9. In the foreground, the royal dog ignores a young guests invitation to play.
10. This paintings fame has grown since it was painted in 1656, and each year millions of people see it when they visit the Prado.

The Granger Collection, New York

24o. To form the possessive case of a plural noun that does not end in *s*, add an apostrophe and an *s*.

EXAMPLES   mice**'s** tracks   men**'s** hats

               children**'s** games   teeth**'s** enamel

               women**'s** shoes   Sioux**'s** land

24p. To form the possessive case of a plural noun ending in *s*, add only the apostrophe.

EXAMPLES   cat**s'** basket   four day**s'** delay

               brushe**s'** bristles   the Carson**s'** bungalow

NOTE   In general, you should not use an apostrophe to form the plural of a noun.

INCORRECT   Three girl's lost their tickets.
  CORRECT   Three **girls** lost their tickets. [plural]
  CORRECT   Three **girls'** tickets were lost. [plural possessive]

Reference Note
For information on **using apostrophes to form the plurals of letters, numerals, and symbols and of words used as words,** see page 645.

MECHANICS

Exercise 7 Writing Possessives

Using the possessive case, rewrite each of the following word groups. Be sure to insert an apostrophe in the correct place.

EXAMPLE   **1.** food for the dog
      1. the dog's food

1. the nominee of the party
2. the clothes of the babies
3. the grades of my sister
4. the name tags of the guests
5. the dish for the cat

6. the yard of Mr. Granger
7. the muscles of my foot
8. the strength of the oxen
9. the computer of James
10. the members of the teams

24q. Do not use an apostrophe with possessive personal pronouns.

EXAMPLES   Is that sticker **yours** or **mine**?

               Our cat is friendlier than **theirs**.

               His report on Cherokee folk tales was as good as **hers**.

NOTE   Do not confuse the possessive pronoun *its* with the contraction *it's*. The possessive pronoun *its* means *belonging to it*. The expression *it's* is a contraction of the words *it is* or *it has*.

POSSESSIVE PRONOUN   Please give the cat **its** rubber ball.
CONTRACTIONS   **It's** time for the soccer tournament.
                   It's taken three hours.

24r. To form the possessive case of some indefinite pronouns, add an apostrophe and an *s*.

EXAMPLES   neither**'s** homework

              everyone**'s** choice

              somebody**'s** jacket

Exercise 8 Writing Possessives of Personal and Indefinite Pronouns

Rewrite each of the following expressions, using the possessive case of each pronoun.

EXAMPLE   **1.** the park for everyone
      1. everyone's park

Reference Note

For more information about **possessive personal pronouns,** see page 342.

Reference Note

For a list of **words that are often confused,** see Chapter 25.

Reference Note

For more information about **indefinite pronouns,** see page 344.

1. the opinion of them
2. the footprints of anyone
3. the fault of nobody
4. the turn of either
5. the stereo that belongs to you
6. the logo of it
7. the idea of neither
8. the backpack of someone
9. the guess of anybody
10. the land owned by no one

Contractions

24s. Use an apostrophe to show where letters, words, or numerals have been omitted (left out) in a contraction.

A *contraction* is a shortened form of a word, a numeral, or a word group. The apostrophe in a contraction shows where letters or numerals have been left out. Contractions are acceptable in informal writing, but in formal writing, you should generally avoid using them.

Common Contractions			
I am	I'm	they had	they'd
1999	'99	where is	where's
let us	let's	we are	we're
of the clock	o'clock	he is	he's
she would	she'd	you will	you'll
we have	we've	what is	what's
they are	they're	I would	I'd

STYLE TIP

In formal writing, avoid using a contraction of a year. In informal writing, if the reader cannot determine the time period from the context of the sentence, it is best to write out the year.

EXAMPLE
The famous tenor toured Europe in '01. [Did the tenor tour in 1801, 1901, or 2001?]

The famous tenor toured Europe in **2001.**

The word *not* can be shortened to *n't* and added to a verb, usually without any change in the spelling of the verb.

EXAMPLES

is not	isn't	has not	hasn't
are not	aren't	have not	haven't
does not	doesn't	had not	hadn't
do not	don't	should not	shouldn't
was not	wasn't	would not	wouldn't
were not	weren't	could not	couldn't

EXCEPTIONS

will not	won't	cannot	can't

Be careful not to confuse contractions with possessive pronouns.

Contractions	Possessive Pronouns
It's Friday. [*It is*]	**Its** nest is over there.
It's been a pleasure. [*It has*]	
Who's your server? [*Who is*]	**Whose** backpack is this?
Who's been practicing the piano? [*Who has*]	
They're arriving soon. [*They are*]	**Their** parakeet is friendly.
There's the path. [*There is*]	That rosebush is **theirs.**

Exercise 9 Using Apostrophes Correctly

HELP—

Some sentences in Exercise 9 contain more than one error.

Correct each error in the use of possessive forms and contractions in the following sentences. If a sentence is already correct, write *C*.

EXAMPLE 1. Arent you going with us at one oclock?

    1. *Aren't; o'clock*

1. Wed better chain our bicycles to the rack.
2. You're old cars seen better days, hasn't it?
3. She wasnt too happy to see us.
4. Whose ringing the doorbell?
5. We wont forget how helpful youve been.
6. Im certain youll be invited.
7. Whose turn is it to take attendance?
8. Anns an excellent swimmer, but she cant dive.
9. They're turning in their's now.
10. Shes sure theyll show up before its over.

Exercise 10 Punctuating Contractions

For each of the following sentences, identify the word that needs an apostrophe to indicate a contraction. Then, write the word correctly.

EXAMPLE 1. Whats the best route from Lawrenceville, New Jersey, to Newtown, Pennsylvania?

    1. *What's*

MECHANICS

1. Theres one especially pretty route you can take to get there.
2. I think youll enjoy the drive.
3. You shouldnt go due west directly.
4. Youve got to go north or south first.
5. Its easier to go south on Route 206 to Route U.S. 1, cross the Delaware River, and then go north on Route 32 to Yardley.
6. From Yardley, turn left on Route 322, and in a little while Im sure you will find yourself in Newtown.

7. If youd prefer a different route, go south on Route 206 to Route 546 and make a right turn to go west.
8. After you cross the Delaware River and the road becomes 532, dont turn until Linton Hill Road.
9. When you turn left onto Linton Hill Road, it wont be long before you arrive in Newtown.
10. Heres a map you can use to help you find your way.

Exercise 11 **Writing Contractions**

Write a suitable contraction to correctly complete each of the following sentences.

EXAMPLE   1. Do you know _____ for supper?

    1. *what's*

1. _____ my sweater?
2. _____ lying on the beach.
3. We _____ help you right now.
4. _____ dinner ready?
5. They _____ played that game before.
6. She was in the class of _____.
7. _____ go to the museum.
8. I _____ know that game.
9. _____ rather order the salad.
10. Is it nine _____ yet?

Exercise 12 Writing Contractions

Write the contraction of the underlined word or words in each of the following sentences.

EXAMPLE   1. If you think it <u>should have</u> been easy to visit the building shown below, guess again!

1. *should've*

1. <u>It is</u> the Potala Palace in Lhasa, Tibet, which my parents and I visited last year.
2. The city of Lhasa is two miles high in the Himalaya Mountains, and we <u>could not</u> move around much because the lack of oxygen made us tired.
3. The Potala Palace is the former residence of the Tibetan spiritual leader, <u>who has</u> been living in exile in India.
4. Because this palace is a holy shrine, pilgrims <u>do not</u> mind traveling on foot from all over the country to worship there.

5. After <u>they have</u> bought yak butter in the city square, they take it to the palace as an offering.
6. From the photograph, you <u>cannot</u> imagine how steep those stairs on the right are!
7. Because it <u>would have</u> taken a long time to climb them, our bus driver took us directly to the rear entrance on the left.
8. Once inside, we spent hours exploring the palace, but we <u>were not</u> able to visit most of its more than one thousand rooms!
9. <u>I am</u> sure we would never have found our way out without our guide, who led us to an exit on the right.
10. Walking down the stairs <u>was not</u> too hard, and soon we were in the beautiful central square in the Himalayan sunshine!

Plurals

24t. Use an apostrophe and an *s* to form the plurals of letters, numerals, and symbols, and of words referred to as words.

EXAMPLES   Your *o*'s look like *a*'s, and your *u*'s look like *n*'s.

There are three *5*'s and two *8*'s in his telephone number.

Place *$*'s before monetary amounts and *¢*'s after.

One sign of immature writing is too many *and*'s.

Review B   **Using Underlining (Italics) and Apostrophes Correctly**

For each of the following sentences, add underlining or apostrophes as necessary. The punctuation already supplied is correct.

EXAMPLE   **1.** One of my oldest brothers college textbooks is History of Art by H. W. Janson.

    1. brother's; History of Art

1. Whos the painter who inspired the musical play Sunday in the Park with George?
2. Hes Georges Seurat, one of Frances greatest painters.
3. "The young childrens reactions to Jacob Lawrences paintings were surprising," Angie said.
4. Didnt you read the review in Entertainment Weekly of the movie Vincent & Theo?
5. Its about Vincent van Gogh and his brother, who often supported him.
6. "I like Jasper Johns," Rick said, "but I cant tell if that is one of Johnss paintings."
7. Have you ever tried counting all the 2s or 4s in his painting Numbers in Color?
8. On a class trip to Chicago, we saw a bronze statue titled Horse, by Duchamp-Villon.
9. In our group, everybodys favorite painting is Cow's Skull: Red, White and Blue, by Georgia O'Keeffe.
10. "On PBS, Ive seen an American Playhouse program about O'Keeffes life," Joyce said.

Hyphens

24u. Use a hyphen to divide a word at the end of a line.

EXAMPLE   Will you and Marguerite help me put the silver-ware on the table?

When dividing a word at the end of a line, remember the following rules:

(1) Divide a word only between syllables.

INCORRECT   The man in the pinstriped suit sat bes-ide the tree, looking bewildered.

CORRECT   The man in the pinstriped suit sat be-side the tree, looking bewildered.

(2) Do not divide a one-syllable word.

INCORRECT   Exercises like push-ups help to develop stren-gth of the arm muscles.

CORRECT   Exercises like push-ups help to develop strength of the arm muscles.

(3) Do not divide a word so that one letter stands alone.

INCORRECT   The seating capacity of the new stadium is e-normous.

CORRECT   The seating capacity of the new stadium is enor-mous.

24v. Use a hyphen with compound numbers from *twenty-one* to *ninety-nine* and with fractions used as modifiers.

EXAMPLES   During a leap year, there are twenty-nine days in February.

Thirty-two species of birds are known to live in the area.

Did you know that Congress may override a president's veto by a two-thirds majority? [*Two-thirds* is an adjective that modifies *majority*.]

The pumpkin pie was so good that only one sixth of it is left. [*One sixth* is not used as a modifier. Instead, *sixth* is a noun modified by the adjective *one*. Fractions used as nouns do not have hyphens.]

COMPUTER TIP

Some word-processing programs will automatically divide a word at the end of a line and insert a hyphen. Sometimes, such hyphenation will violate one of the rules given here.

Always check a printout of your writing to see how the computer has hyphenated words at the ends of lines. If a hyphen is used incorrectly, revise the line by moving the word or by dividing the word yourself and inserting a "hard" hyphen (one that the computer cannot move).

STYLE TIP

Hyphens are often used in compound names. In such cases, the hyphen is thought of as part of the name's spelling.

EXAMPLES
Jackie Joyner-Kersee [person]

Rikki-tikki-tavi [animal]

Wilkes-Barre [city]

If you are not sure whether a compound name is hyphenated, ask the person with that name, or look in a reference source.

MECHANICS

24w. Use a hyphen with the prefixes *ex–*, *self–*, *all–*, and *great–* and with the suffixes *–elect* and *–free*.

EXAMPLES   ex-coach   president-elect   all-star

great-uncle   self-propelled   fat-free

Exercise 13 **Using Hyphens Correctly**

Write an expression—using words, not numerals—to fit the blank in each of the following sentences. Use hyphens where they are needed with compound numbers or fractions.

EXAMPLE   1. The sum of ten and fifteen is ____.

1. *twenty-five*

1. January, March, May, July, August, October, and December are the months that have ____ days.
2. ____ of the moon is visible from the earth, but the other half can be seen only from outer space.
3. In twenty years I will be ____ years old.
4. I used ____ cup, which is 25 percent of the original one cup.
5. Our seventh-grade class has ____ students.
6. The train ride is short; the route is only ____ miles long.
7. The doctor said that the heel of my shoe needs to be raised ____ of an inch.
8. Who decided that there should be ____ hours in a day?
9. ____ teaspoon of vanilla is not enough in the cake batter.
10. Only about ____ of the expected people actually attended.

Review C **Punctuating Sentences Correctly**

Rewrite the following sentences, correcting any errors in the use of underlining, quotation marks, commas, apostrophes, and hyphens.

EXAMPLE   1. For the talent show, Leila is planning to recite Poes poem The Raven.

1. *For the talent show, Leila is planning to recite Poe's poem "The Raven."*

1. Queen Hatshepsut seized the throne of Egypt in 1503 B.C. and ruled for twenty one years.
2. Whos borrowed my scissors? demanded Jean.
3. Its hard to decide which authors story I should read first.
4. A weeks vacation never seems long enough.

┌HELP─

The prefix *half* often requires a hyphen, as in *half-life*, *half-moon*, and *half-truth*. However, sometimes it is used without a hyphen, either as a part of a single word (as in *halftone*, *halfway*, and *halfback*) or as a separate word (as in *half shell*, *half pint*, and *half note*). If you are not sure how to spell a word containing *half*, look up the word in a dictionary.

┌HELP─

Hyphenate a compound adjective when it comes before the noun it modifies.

EXAMPLE
an event that is well organized

a **well-organized** event

Some compound adjectives are always hyphenated, whether they come before or after the nouns they modify.

EXAMPLE
a **full-scale** model

a model that is **full-scale**

If you are not sure whether a compound adjective is always hyphenated, look it up in a dictionary.

MECHANICS

5. After wed eaten supper, we decided to watch an old episode of Star Trek.

6. The driver shouted Move to the rear of the bus!

7. We didnt eat any salmon at all during our visit to O-regon.

8. I wasnt very sorry admitted the clerk to see those picky customers leave.

9. Very Short on Law and Order is my favorite chapter in Tough Trip Through Paradise.

10. Our new phone number starts with two 6s and ends with two 4s.

Parentheses

24x. Use parentheses to enclose material that is added to a sentence but is not considered of major importance.

EXAMPLES   Emilio Aguinaldo (1869–1964) was a Filipino patriot and statesman.

Mom and Dad bought a kilim (pronounced ki • lēm′) rug from our Turkish friend Ali.

Material enclosed in parentheses may be as short as a single word or as long as a short sentence. A short sentence in parentheses may stand alone or be contained within another sentence. Notice that a parenthetical sentence within a sentence is not capitalized and has no end mark.

EXAMPLES   Please be quiet during the performance. (Take crying babies to the lobby.)

Jack Echohawk (he's Ben's cousin) told us about growing up on a reservation.

Exercise 14   **Correcting Sentences by Adding Parentheses**

Insert parentheses where they are needed in the following sentences.

EXAMPLE   1. My bicycle I've had it for three years is a ten-speed.

1. *My bicycle (I've had it for three years) is a ten-speed.*

1. At the age of fourteen, Martina Hingis began playing tennis (my favorite sport) professionally.
2. Elijah McCoy (1843–1929) invented a way to oil moving machinery.
3. I bought a new calculator (my old one stopped working) and a notebook.
4. Charlemagne (pronounced shär′lə • mān′) was one of Europe's most famous rulers.
5. Lian Young (she's a friend of mine) told our class about her school in China.

Brackets

24y. Use brackets to enclose an explanation added to quoted or parenthetical material.

EXAMPLES   Elena said in her acceptance speech, "I am honored by this [the award], and I would like to thank the students who volunteered to help with the Special Olympics this year." [The words are enclosed in brackets to show that they have been inserted into the quotation and are not the words of the speaker.]

By a vote of 6 to 1, the council approved the petition to build a nature preserve. (See next page for a map [Diagram A] of the proposed reserve.)

Dashes

A *parenthetical expression* is a word or phrase that breaks into the main thought of a sentence. Parenthetical expressions are usually set off by commas or parentheses.

EXAMPLES   Grandma Moses, **for example,** started painting in her seventies.

In the first act of the play, the butler **(Theo Karras)** was the detective's prime suspect.

Some parenthetical elements need stronger emphasis. In such cases, a dash is used.

Reference Note

For more about using **commas with parenthetical expressions,** see page 611. For more about **using parentheses,** see page 648.

24
x, y

MECHANICS

Dashes   **649**

24z. Use a dash to indicate an abrupt break in thought or speech.

EXAMPLES   The right thing to do—I know it'll be hard—is to apologize.

"Do you think Ann will mind—I really hope she won't—if I borrow her sunglasses?" asked Melody.

Exercise 15 Correcting Sentences by Adding Dashes and Brackets

Insert dashes or brackets where they are needed in the following sentences.

EXAMPLE   1. The school lunchroom it was a dull green has been painted a cheery yellow.

1. *The school lunchroom—it was a dull green—has been painted a cheery yellow.*

1. Fireflies I can't remember where I read this make what is called cold light.
2. Roberto has always wanted to be can't you guess? an astronaut.
3. Shania Twain I really want to see her concert has a great new song out.
4. Do you mind I don't if Jill and Marcus go to the mall with us tomorrow?
5. The best way to learn how to swim that is, after you've learned the basic strokes is to practice.
6. (See page 8 Box A of the school yearbook for a list of the drama club's best performers.)
7. Where is the computer game I've looked everywhere for it that I borrowed from Alex?
8. Please hand me if you don't mind the stack of magazines on the table behind you.
9. The newspaper quoted our principal as saying, "The girls' volleyball team took both the district District 14–5A and regional championships."
10. The class trip to Chicago I've never been there will include a visit to the Art Institute.

Chapter Review

A. Using Underlining (Italics), Quotation Marks, Dashes, Parentheses, and Brackets

The following sentences contain errors in the use of underlining (italics), quotation marks, dashes, parentheses, and brackets. Rewrite the sentences correctly.

1. The song Amazing Grace has been sung for many years.
2. Garth Brooks I love his music is giving a benefit concert.
3. Did you see the article called Yogamania that appeared in last month's Seventeen magazine?
4. The poet Wallace Stevens 1879–1955 won a Pulitzer Prize.
5. (See the map of Normandy Figure D for the deployment of the German forces on June 6.)
6. The reading list included the novel Great Expectations.
7. Sharon she's my youngest cousin asked me to tell her a story.
8. The bearded man you probably guessed this is really the thief in disguise.
9. He misspelled the word accommodate by leaving out one c.
10. Aunt Rosie the aunt I told you about went to Mexico on the cruise ship Princess.

B. Proofreading for the Correct Use of Punctuation and Capitalization in Quotations

The following sentences contain errors in the use of punctuation and capitalization in quotations. Rewrite the sentences correctly. If a sentence is already correct, write C.

11. "Did you read Robert Hayden's poem "Those Winter Sundays"? asked Jorge.
12. "Who's your favorite baseball player." asked Don?
13. "Meet me at 2:30 sharp," my sister's note read.
14. Why did Ms. Redfeather say, "I need to see a doctor"?
15. Ms. Liu said, Turn to Chapter 7, 'Fractions,' now.
16. "Did you know," Katrina said, "That Robin Williams organizes fund-raisers for the homeless"?

MECHANICS

17. Akeem exclaimed, "Those giant redwoods are more than three hundred feet tall!"
18. "Are the La Vernia Bears playing tomorrow? Lorraine asked Ted.
19. Chang predicted that "it would be a rainy summer."
20. "he can work ten hours a week", said Liang.

C. Writing Dialogue Correctly

HELP

Some sentences in Part C may not require additional punctuation.

Revise the following paragraphs, adding quotation marks and other punctuation marks wherever necessary. Begin a new paragraph each time the speaker changes.

[21] A few of us are starting a reading group said Michael. [22] Would you like to join us? [23] That sounds like fun replied Audra. [24] Who is in the group? [25] Well, I am, of course Michael said and Stephanie, Jeff, and Kerry. [26] I've asked Megan to join, too, but she may be too busy. [27] She's going to let me know tomorrow.

[28] What books are you going to read asked Audra or haven't you decided that yet? [29] I'm going to suggest that we start with The Owl Service, by Alan Garner, said Michael but only if it is everyones choice. [30] I'd love to join! said Audra.

D. Using Apostrophes and Hyphens

The following sentences contain errors in the use of apostrophes and hyphens. Correctly write each incorrectly punctuated word.

31. The test includes twentytwo questions.
32. Its easy to see that you like to use &s instead of writing out the word *and* each time.
33. One fourth of the childrens toys were broken.
34. My two sisters bicycles are sporty, but neithers is as sport-y as mine.
35. Isnt this play often considered one of Shakespeares best wo-rks, Stephanie?
36. Whats the lowest common denominator of these two numbers?
37. Are those lawn chairs our's or the Millers?
38. Theyre drawings of Augusta Savages sculptures.

39. My baby brothers a good sleeper; he should have a mobile made of *Z*s instead of airplanes over his crib.

40. Whos going to help repaint the clubs float for the parade?

Writing Application
Using Quotations in Reports

Direct Quotations   Your social studies class is taking a survey of people's attitudes toward recycling. Interview at least three people from different households in your community. Ask them specific questions to find out whether they think recycling is important; what items, if any, they recycle; and how they think recycling could be made easier for people in the community. Based on the information you gather, write a brief report about recycling in your community. In your report, quote several people's exact words.

Prewriting   First, think of several questions to ask. Next, decide whom you want to interview. Begin each interview by recording the person's name, age, and occupation. When all your interviews are completed, compare your interviewees' responses. What conclusions can you draw about attitudes toward recycling in your community? Jot down some notes to help you organize your information.

Writing   In the first paragraph of your draft, give a statement that sums up the main idea of your report. Then, use your inter-viewees' answers to support your main idea.

Revising   Re-read your first draft. Does the body of your report support your main idea? If not, you may need to rethink and revise your main idea.

Publishing   As you proofread your report, check your quota-tions against your notes. Make sure that you have put quotation marks around direct quotations and that you have capitalized and punctuated all quotations correctly. Your class may want to combine the information from all the reports and create a wall chart showing the community's attitudes toward recycling.

Spelling
Improving Your Spelling

Diagnostic Preview

Proofreading Sentences for Correct Spelling

Write correctly all of the misspelled words in the following sentences.

EXAMPLE   1. Andrew carefuly lifted the massive lid and peekked inside the trunk.

1. *carefully, peeked*

1. Do you have any fresh tomatos or strawberrys?
2. Alex rides her bicycle forty miles dayly when she is in trainning.
3. The experienced tour guide lead the students to the base of the Mayan pyramid.
4. My sister made the salad while I layed the spoons and knifes on the table for dinner.
5. Would you please hand me the scissor's?
6. Mr. Escobar's too neices went to the annual family reunion.
7. Icicles formed on the park benchs when the temperature dropped below freezeing.
8. Angela's favorite classes are social studys and swiming.
9. On Wednesday our science class watched *Weavving Ants,* a film about the insect world.
10. Take out a peice of paper, and then prosede with the test.

Good Spelling Habits

Practicing the following techniques can help you spell words correctly.

1. **To learn the spelling of a word, pronounce it, study it, and write it.** Pronounce words carefully. Mispronunciation can lead to misspelling. For instance, if you say *ath•a•lete* instead of *ath•lete*, you will be more likely to spell the word incorrectly.

   • First, make sure that you know how to pronounce the word correctly, and then practice saying it.

   • Second, study the word. Notice especially any parts that might be hard to remember.

   • Third, write the word from memory. Check your spelling.

   • If you misspelled the word, repeat the three steps of this process.

2. **Use a dictionary.** When you find that you have misspelled a word, look it up in a dictionary. Do not guess about the correct spelling.

3. **Spell by syllables.** A *syllable* is a word part that is pronounced as one uninterrupted sound.

   EXAMPLES   thor•ough [two syllables]

   sep•a•rate [three syllables]

   Instead of trying to learn how to pronounce and spell a whole word, break it up into its syllables whenever possible.

Exercise 1 **Spelling by Syllables**

Look up the following words in a dictionary, and divide each one into syllables. Pronounce each syllable correctly, and learn to spell the word by syllables.

1. legislature	8. definition	15. separate
2. perspire	9. recognize	16. opportunity
3. modern	10. awkward	17. eliminate
4. temperature	11. accept	18. government
5. probably	12. interest	19. business
6. similar	13. temperament	20. appreciation
7. library	14. conscious	

─HELP─

If you are not sure how to pronounce a word, look it up in an up-to-date dictionary. In the dictionary, you will usually find the pronunciation given in parentheses after the word. The information in parentheses will show you the sounds used, the syllable breaks, and any accented syllables. A guide to the pronunciation symbols is usually found at the front of the dictionary.

STYLE TIP

In some names, marks that show how to pronounce a word are considered part of the spelling.

PEOPLE
Díaz   Rölvaag   Žižka

PLACES
Aswân   Cádiz

Compiègne

If you are not sure about the spelling of a name, ask the person with that name or look it up in a dictionary or other reference source.

MECHANICS

4. Proofread for careless spelling errors. Re-read your writing carefully, and correct any mistakes and unclear letters. For example, make sure that your *i*'s are dotted, that your *t*'s are crossed, and that your *g*'s don't look like *q*'s.

5. Keep a spelling notebook. Divide each page into four columns:

COLUMN 1   Correctly spell any word you missed. (Never enter a misspelling.)

COLUMN 2   Write the word again, dividing it into syllables and indicating which syllables are accented or stressed.

COLUMN 3   Write the word once more, circling the spot that gives you trouble.

COLUMN 4   Jot down any comments that might help you remember the correct spelling.

Here is an example of how you might make entries for two words that are often misspelled.

Correct Spelling	Syllables and Accents	Trouble Spot	Comments
attendance	at•tend´•ance	attend(a)nce	Think of attending a dance.
unnecessary	un•nec´•es•sar•y	u(nn)ecessary	un + necessary (Study rule 25c.)

COMPUTER TIP

A computer can help you catch spelling mistakes. Use the computer's spellchecker whenever you proofread your writing. Remember, though, that a computer's spellchecker points out misspellings but not misused homonyms. For example, if you use *their* when you should use *there*, a spell-checker won't catch the mistake. Always double-check your writing to make sure that your spelling is error-free.

Spelling Rules
ie and *ei*

25a. Write *ie* when the sound is long *e*, except after *c*.

EXAMPLES   ch**ie**f, br**ie**f, bel**ie**ve, y**ie**ld, rec**ei**ve, dec**ei**ve

EXCEPTIONS   s**ei**ze, l**ei**sure, **ei**ther, n**ei**ther, prot**ei**n

Write *ei* when the sound is not long *e*, especially when the sound is long *a*.

EXAMPLES sl**ei**gh, v**ei**l, fr**ei**ght, w**ei**ght, h**ei**ght, for**ei**gn

EXCEPTIONS fr**ie**nd, misch**ie**f, anc**ie**nt, p**ie**

Exercise 2 Writing Words with *ie* and *ei*

Rewrite the following words, adding the letters *ie* or *ei*.

EXAMPLE **1.** conc . . . t

  1. conceit

1. dec . . . ve
2. n . . . ther
3. rec . . . ve
4. h . . . ght
5. fr . . . nd
6. l . . . sure
7. misch . . . f
8. w . . . ght
9. . . . ght
10. sl . . . gh

11. fr . . . ght
12. n . . . ghbor
13. c . . . ling
14. shr . . . k
15. rec . . . pt
16. p . . . ce
17. r . . . gn
18. th . . . r
19. s . . . ze
20. br . . . f

Exercise 3 Proofreading Sentences to Correct Spelling Errors

Most of the following sentences contain a spelling error involving the use of *ie* or *ei*. Write each misspelled word correctly. If a sentence has no spelling error, write *C*.

EXAMPLE **1.** Last summer I recieved an airline ticket as a birthday gift.

  1. received

1. I used the ticket to fly to Puerto Rico with my freind Alicia to see my grandmother and other relatives.
2. We flew to San Juan, where my grandmother's nieghbor, Mr. Sanchez, met us and drove us to my grandmother's house.
3. When we got there, all of my relatives—aunts, uncles, cousins, neices, nephews—came to welcome us.
4. They couldn't believe that niether of us had ever been to Puerto Rico before, so they took us sightseeing the next day.

┌─────────────────────┐
│ TIPS **&** TRICKS │
└─────────────────────┘

You may find this time-tested verse a help in remembering the *ie* rule.

I before *e*
Except after *c*
Or when sounded like *a*,
As in *neighbor* and *weigh*.

If you use this rhyme, remember that "*i* before *e*" refers only to words in which these two letters are in the same syllable and stand for the sound of long *e*, as in the examples under Rule 25a.

MECHANICS

5. First, we walked through a field in Humacao, which is located on the Caribbean Sea.
6. Then, we drove along the coast to Ponce, the island's cheif city after San Juan.
7. Continuing north from Ponce, we thought that we'd take a liesurely drive on the mountain road *Ruta Panoramica,* which means "Panoramic Road."
8. However, the road turned and twisted so much that I was releived to get back on the main road.
9. After we had a breif rest that afternoon, we explored the western part of the island.
10. Within a week, Puerto Rico no longer seemed foriegn to us.

–cede, –ceed, and –sede

25b. The only English word ending in –sede is supersede. The only English words ending in –ceed are exceed, proceed, and succeed. Most other words with this sound end in –cede.

EXAMPLES   con**cede**   re**cede**

               pre**cede**   se**cede**

Prefixes and Suffixes

A *prefix* is a letter or a group of letters added to the beginning of a word to change its meaning. A *suffix* is a letter or a group of letters added to the end of a word to change its meaning.

25c. When adding a prefix to a word, do not change the spelling of the word itself.

EXAMPLES   il + legal = il**legal**

un + natural = un**natural**

dis + appear = dis**appear**

mis + spent = mis**spent**

Exercise 4 **Spelling Words with Prefixes**

Spell each of the following words, adding the given prefix.

EXAMPLE   **1.** semi + circle

        1. semicircle

1. il + legible
2. un + necessary
3. im + partial
4. in + offensive
5. im + mortal
6. mis + spell
7. dis + satisfy
8. dis + approve
9. mis + understand
10. over + rule

25d. When adding the suffix –*ness* or –*ly* to a word, do not change the spelling of the word itself.

EXAMPLES   sudden + ness = **sudden**ness

truthful + ly = **truthful**ly

EXCEPTION   For most words that end in *y,* change the *y* to *i* before adding –*ly* or –*ness.*

kindly + ness = kindl**iness**   day + ly = da**ily**

25e. Drop the final silent *e* before adding a suffix beginning with a vowel.

EXAMPLES   nice + est = **nic**est

love + ing = **lov**ing

EXCEPTION   Keep the silent *e* in words ending in *ce* and *ge* before a suffix beginning with *a* or *o.*

notice + able = notic**eable**

courage + ous = courag**eous**

┌HELP──
Vowels are the letters *a, e, i, o, u,* and sometimes *y.* The other letters of the alphabet are consonants.

MECHANICS

FRANK & ERNEST reprinted by permission of Newspaper Enterprise Association, Inc.

F W WNT T TLK RLLY GD, W'LL HV T NVNT VWLS.

THAVES 10-16

25f. Keep the final silent *e* before adding a suffix that begins with a consonant.

EXAMPLES   care + less = car**eless**

plate + ful = plat**eful**

false + hood = fals**ehood**

EXCEPTIONS   argue + ment = argu**ment**

true + ly = tru**ly**

Exercise 5   Spelling Words with Suffixes

Spell each of the following words, adding the given suffix.

EXAMPLE   1. like + able

1. *likable*

1. awful + ly
2. care + ful
3. sincere + ly
4. write + ing
5. desire + able
6. change + able
7. cross + ing

8. advance + ment
9. true + ly
10. courage + ous
11. notice + able
12. brave + est
13. accidental + ly
14. pace + ing

15. value + able
16. hope + ful
17. grateful + ly
18. pleasant + ness
19. sore + est
20. final + ly

25g. For words ending in *y* preceded by a consonant, change the *y* to *i* before any suffix that does not begin with *i*.

EXAMPLES   beauty + ful = beaut**iful**   mystery + ous = myster**ious**

carry + ing = carr**ying**   envy + able = env**iable**

EXCEPTIONS   dry + ness = dr**yness**   fry + er = fr**yer**

Words ending in *y* preceded by a vowel do not change their spelling before a suffix.

MECHANICS

EXAMPLES	key + ed = ke**yed**	buy + er = bu**yer**
	pay + ment = pa**yment**	enjoy + ing = enjo**ying**

EXCEPTIONS	lay + ed = la**id**	say + ed = sa**id**	day + ly = da**ily**

25h. Double the final consonant before adding –*ing*, –*ed*, –*er*, or –*est* to a one-syllable word that ends in a single consonant preceded by a single vowel.

EXAMPLES	sit + ing = si**tt**ing	can + er = ca**nn**er
	hop + ed = ho**pp**ed	flat + est = fla**tt**est

EXCEPTIONS	Do not double the final consonant in words ending in *w* or *x*.
	mow + ed = mo**w**ed tax + ing = ta**x**ing

For a one-syllable word ending in a single consonant that is not preceded by a single vowel, do not double the consonant before adding –*ing*, –*ed*, –*er*, or –*est*.

EXAMPLES	reap + ed = rea**p**ed	neat + est = nea**t**est
	cold + er = col**d**er	hold + ing = hol**d**ing

In words of more than one syllable, the final consonant is usually not doubled before a suffix beginning with a vowel.

EXAMPLES	final + ist = fina**l**ist	center + ed = cente**r**ed

NOTE In some cases, the final consonant may or may not be doubled.

EXAMPLES	cancel + ed = cance**l**ed *or* cance**ll**ed
	travel + er = trave**l**er *or* trave**ll**er

Most dictionaries list both spellings for each word as correct.

Exercise 6 **Spelling Words with Suffixes**

Spell each of the twenty words on the following page, adding the given suffix.

EXAMPLE	1. beauty + ful
	1. beautiful

MECHANICS

┌HELP─
When you are not sure about the spelling of a word, it is best to look it up in an up-to-date dictionary.

1. bay + ing
2. show + ed
3. drop + ed
4. deny + ing
5. pity + less
6. qualify + er
7. trip + ed

8. employ + ment
9. happy + est
10. hit + ing
11. swim + er
12. tidy + er
13. hurry + ed
14. tap + ing

15. clean + er
16. fold + ed
17. day + ly
18. bounty + ful
19. fix + ing
20. help + ful

Review A Proofreading Sentences for Correct Spelling

Most of the following sentences contain a word that has been misspelled. Write each misspelled word correctly. If a sentence is already correct, write *C*.

EXAMPLE
1. Have you seen the beautyful bonsai trees on display in the new garden center?

1. *beautiful*

1. These trees can live to be hundreds of years old, yet you can quickly create one of your own in an afternoon.
2. Simply use these pictures to help you as you procede through the following steps.
3. First, you will need an inxpensive plant (such as a juniper), some soil, some moss, and a shallow bowl.
4. When you are chooseing a plant, try to get one with a trunk that has some of its roots showing above the soil so that your tree will look old.
5. Make a carful study of your plant, and decide how you want the bonsai to look in the bowl.

MECHANICS

6. Then, cut or pinch away undesireable branches and leaves until the plant looks like a tree.

7. After triming your plant, remove most of the large roots so that the plant can stand in the bowl.

8. Cover the remaining roots with soil, and if the weather is mild, put your bonsai in a shaded place outside.

9. You don't have to water your plant dayly, but you should keep the soil moist.

10. After your plant has healed, you will have succeded in creating your very own bonsai.

Forming the Plurals of Nouns

25i. Observe the following rules for spelling the plurals of nouns.

(1) To form the plurals of most nouns, add –s.

SINGULAR	girl	cheese	task	oat	banana
PLURAL	girl**s**	cheese**s**	task**s**	oat**s**	banana**s**

NOTE Make sure that you do not confuse the plural form of a noun with its possessive form. Generally, you should not use an apostrophe to form the plural of a word.

INCORRECT	The girl's raced to the stadium for soccer practice.
CORRECT	The **girls** raced to the stadium for soccer practice. [plural]
CORRECT	The **girls'** soccer team has practice today. [possessive]

(2) Form the plurals of nouns ending in s, x, z, ch, or sh by adding –es.

SINGULAR	moss	wax	Sanchez	birch	dish
PLURAL	moss**es**	wax**es**	Sanchez**es**	birch**es**	dish**es**

NOTE Some one-syllable words ending in z double the final consonant when forming plurals.

EXAMPLES	quiz	fez
	qui**zz**es	fe**zz**es

Reference Note

For a discussion of the **possessive forms of nouns,** see page 638. For information about **using an apostrophe and an s to form the plural of a letter, a numeral, a symbol, or a word used as a word,** see page 645.

MECHANICS

Exercise 7 Spelling the Plurals of Nouns

Spell the plural form of each of the following nouns.

EXAMPLE   1. match
          1. *matches*

1. box	6. tax	11. mix	16. plate
2. crash	7. Gómez	12. clip	17. key
3. sneeze	8. ditch	13. gym	18. pass
4. address	9. miss	14. coach	19. Walsh
5. church	10. mask	15. dash	20. business

(3) Form the plurals of nouns ending in *y* preceded by a consonant by changing the *y* to *i* and adding –*es.*

SINGULAR	lady	hobby	county	strawberry
PLURAL	lad**ies**	hobb**ies**	count**ies**	strawberr**ies**

EXCEPTION   With proper nouns, simply add *s.*

the Appleby**s**   the Trilby**s**

(4) Form the plurals of nouns ending in *y* preceded by a vowel by adding –*s.*

SINGULAR	toy	journey	highway	Wednesday
PLURAL	toy**s**	journey**s**	highway**s**	Wednesday**s**

(5) Form the plurals of most nouns ending in *f* by adding –*s.* The plural form of some nouns ending in *f* or *fe* is formed by changing the *f* to *v* and adding –*es.*

SINGULAR	gulf	belief	knife	loaf	wolf
PLURAL	gulf**s**	belief**s**	kni**ves**	loa**ves**	wol**ves**

(6) Form the plurals of nouns ending in *o* preceded by a vowel by adding –*s.*

SINGULAR	video	ratio	patio	Romeo
PLURAL	video**s**	ratio**s**	patio**s**	Romeo**s**

(7) The plural form of many nouns ending in *o* preceded by a consonant is formed by adding –*es.*

SINGULAR	veto	hero	tomato	potato
PLURAL	veto**es**	hero**es**	tomato**es**	potato**es**

EXCEPTION   silo—silo**s**

However, you should form the plural of most musical terms ending in *o* preceded by a consonant by adding –s.

SINGULAR	piano	alto	solo	trio
PLURAL	piano**s**	alto**s**	solo**s**	trio**s**

SINGULAR	banjo	mosquito	flamingo
PLURAL	banjo**s**	mosquito**s**	flamingo**s**
	or	*or*	*or*
	banjo**es**	mosquito**es**	flamingo**es**

The best way to determine the plural forms of words ending in *o* preceded by a consonant is to check their spelling in an up-to-date dictionary.

(8) The plurals of some nouns are formed in irregular ways.

SINGULAR	man	mouse	foot	ox	child
PLURAL	m**en**	m**ice**	f**ee**t	ox**en**	child**ren**

Exercise 8 Spelling the Plurals of Nouns

Spell the plural form of each of the following nouns.

EXAMPLE   **1.** industry

   1. *industries*

1. turkey
2. studio
3. chief
4. soprano
5. puppy
6. self
7. chimney
8. baby
9. tomato
10. echo
11. ferry
12. joy
13. life
14. hero
15. bluff
16. radio
17. lobby
18. wife
19. foot
20. Whitby

STYLE   TIP

When it refers to the computer device, the word *mouse* can form a plural in two ways: *mouses* or *mice*. Someday one form may be the preferred style. For now, either is correct.

MECHANICS

Reference Note

For more information on **compound nouns,** see page 337.

STYLE TIP

In your reading you may notice that some writers do not use apostrophes to form the plurals of numerals, letters, symbols, and words referred to as words. However, an apostrophe is not wrong, and it may be needed for clarity. Therefore, it is best to use the apostrophe.

(9) For most compound nouns written as one word, form the plural by adding –s or –es.

SINGULAR	textbook	grandfather	toothbrush
PLURAL	textbook**s**	grandfather**s**	toothbrush**es**

(10) For compound nouns in which one word is modified by the other word or words, form the plural of the word modified.

SINGULAR	sister-in-law	coat of arms	editor in chief
PLURAL	sister**s**-in-law	coat**s** of arms	editor**s** in chief

(11) Some nouns are the same in the singular and the plural.

SINGULAR AND PLURAL	moose	sheep	salmon
	Sioux	Chinese	spacecraft

(12) Form the plurals of numerals, letters, symbols, and words referred to as words by adding an apostrophe and s.

SINGULAR	1800	*B*	*i*	*&*	*that*
PLURAL	1800**'s**	*B***'s**	*i***'s**	*&***'s**	*that***'s**

Review B **Spelling the Plurals of Nouns**

Spell the plural form of each of the following nouns.

EXAMPLE   **1.** push-up

1. *push-ups*

1. side-wheeler	**8.** governor-elect	**15.** *x*
2. deer	**9.** *0*	**16.** lean-to
3. mother-in-law	**10.** commander in chief	**17.** Swiss
4. *A*	**11.** maid of honor	**18.** *$*
5. *hello*	**12.** runner-up	**19.** Japanese
6. thirteen-year-old	**13.** bookshelf	**20.** *M*
7. aircraft	**14.** vice-president	

Words Often Confused

People often confuse the words in each of the following groups. Some of these words are *homonyms*—that is, their pronunciations are the same. However, these words have different meanings and spellings. Other words in the following groups have the same or similar spellings yet have different meanings.

accept	[verb] *to receive; to agree to* The Lanfords would not *accept* our gift.
except	[preposition] *with the exclusion of; but* Everyone *except* Lauren agreed with Selena.
advice	[noun] *a recommendation for action* What is your mother's *advice*?
advise	[verb] *to recommend a course of action* She *advises* me to take the job.
affect	[verb] *to act upon; to change* Does bad weather *affect* your health?
effect	[noun] *result; consequence* What *effect* does the weather have on your health?
already	[adverb] *previously* We have *already* studied the customs of the Navajo people.
all ready	[adjective] *all prepared; in readiness* The crew is *all ready* to set sail.
all right	[adjective] *correct; satisfactory; safe;* [adverb] *adequately* Jesse will be *all right* when his injury heals. We did *all right,* didn't we?

┌HELP┐

All right is the only acceptable spelling. The spelling *alright* is not considered standard usage.

Exercise 9 **Choosing Between Words Often Confused**

From each pair in parentheses, choose the word or words that will make the sentence correct.

EXAMPLE 1. All of us (*accept, except*) Josh forgot our tickets.
  1. *except*

1. By the time Melba arrived, Roscoe had (*already, all ready*) baked the sweet potatoes.
2. One duty of the Cabinet is to (*advice, advise*) the president.
3. The soft music had a soothing (*affect, effect*) on the child.
4. The girls were (*already, all ready*) for the sleigh ride.
5. The (*affect, effect*) of Buddhism on Japanese culture was huge.
6. By this time of year, the snow has melted everywhere (*accept, except*) in the mountains.

7. The doctor's (*advice, advise*) was to drink plenty of fluids and get a lot of rest.
8. Sarita was happy to (*accept, except*) the invitation to the party.
9. Reading the newspaper usually (*affects, effects*) my ideas about current events.
10. Do you think it would be (*alright, all right*) to leave before the end of the movie?

Reference Note

In the Glossary of Usage (Chapter 21), you can find many other words that are often confused or misused, or you can look them up in an up-to-date dictionary.

Here is a sentence to help you remember the difference between *capital* and *capitol:* There is a d**o**me on the capit**o**l.

altar	[noun] *a table or stand at which religious rites are performed* There was a bowl of flowers on the *altar.*
alter	[verb] *to change* Another hurricane may *alter* the shoreline near our town.
altogether	[adverb] *entirely* It is *altogether* too cold for swimming.
all together	[adjective] *in the same place;* [adverb] *at the same time* *All together,* the class looked bigger than it was. Sing *all together* now.
brake	[noun] *a device to stop a machine* I used the emergency *brake* to prevent the car from rolling downhill.
break	[verb] *to fracture; to shatter* Don't *break* that mirror!
capital	[noun] *a city; the location of a government* What is the *capital* of this state?
capitol	[noun] *a building; statehouse* The *capitol* is on Congress Avenue.
choose	[verb, rhymes with *lose*] *to select* We *choose* activities today in gym class.
chose	[verb, past tense of *choose*] We *chose* activities yesterday.
cloths	[noun] *pieces of cloth* I need some more cleaning *cloths.*
clothes	[noun] *wearing apparel* I decided to put on warm *clothes.*

MECHANICS

Exercise 10 **Choosing Between Words Often Confused**

From each pair in parentheses, choose the word or words that will make the sentence correct.

EXAMPLE   **1.** If it rains, we will (*altar, alter*) our plans.

       1. alter

1. My summer (*cloths, clothes*) are loose and light.
2. In England, you can still see remains of (*altars, alters*) built by ancient peoples.
3. A bicyclist can wear out a set of (*brakes, breaks*) quickly.
4. You should use soft (*cloths, clothes*) to clean silver.
5. The cold weather did not (*altar, alter*) Ling's plans for the Chinese New Year celebration.
6. Accra is the (*capital, capitol*) of Ghana.
7. Keep the pieces of the vase (*altogether, all together*), and I will try to repair it.
8. Did he (*choose, chose*) a partner during class yesterday?
9. On the dome of the (*capital, capitol*) stands a large statue.
10. The audience was (*altogether, all together*) charmed by the mime's performance.

coarse	[adjective] *rough; crude; not fine* The *coarse* sand acts as a filter.
course	[noun] *path of action; series of studies;* [also used in the expression *of course*] What is the best *course* for me to take? You may change your mind, of *course*.
complement	[verb] *to make complete;* [noun] *something that completes* The piano music *complemented* Ardene's violin solo. Red shoes are a good *complement* to that outfit.
compliment	[verb] *to praise someone;* [noun] *praise from someone* Mrs. Katz *complimented* Jean on her persuasive speech. Thank you for the *compliment*.

(continued)

council	[noun] *a group called together to accomplish a job* The mayor's *council* has seven members.
counsel	[noun] *advice;* [verb] *to give advice* He needs legal *counsel* on this matter. His attorney will *counsel* him before the hearing.
councilor	[noun] *a member of a council* The mayor appointed seven *councilors.*
counselor	[noun] *one who advises* Mr. Jackson is the guidance *counselor* for the seventh grade.
desert	[noun, pronounced des'•ert] *a dry, barren, sandy region; a wilderness* This cactus grows only in the *desert.*
desert	[verb, pronounced de•sert'] *to abandon; to leave* A good sport does not *desert* his or her teammates.
dessert	[noun, pronounced des•sert'] *a sweet, final course of a meal* Let's have fresh peaches for *dessert.*

Exercise 11 Choosing Between Words Often Confused

From each pair in parentheses, choose the word that will make the sentence correct.

EXAMPLE   **1.** At the end of dinner, we ate a (*desert, dessert*) made of fresh fruits and berries mixed with frozen yogurt.

    1. dessert

1. The city (*council, counsel*) will not meet unless seven of the ten (*councilors, counselors*) are present.
2. The patient received (*council, counsel*) from the doctor on the best (*coarse, course*) to a speedy recovery.
3. Chutney and yogurt (*complement, compliment*) an Indian meal very well.
4. When we were staying in Cairo last year, we saw the Nile River, of (*coarse, course*).

MECHANICS

5. Edward is preparing the enchiladas, and I'm making empanadas for (*desert, dessert*) tonight.
6. Marilyn made a hand puppet out of (*coarse, course*) burlap, buttons, and felt.
7. We all know the major would not (*desert, dessert*) her regiment for any reason.
8. Please, I am asking for your (*council, counsel*), not your (*complements, compliments*).
9. My mother and father both took part in the (*dessert, desert*) hiking trip last week.
10. What did you think when our camp (*councilor, counselor*) (*complemented, complimented*) us on our endurance?

formally	[adverb] *with dignity; following strict rules or procedures* We must behave *formally* at the reception.
formerly	[adverb] *previously; at an earlier date* *Formerly,* people thought travel to the moon was impossible.
hear	[verb] *to receive sounds through the ears* You can *hear* a whisper through these walls.
here	[adverb] *in this place* How long have you lived *here*?
its	[possessive form of the pronoun *it*] *belonging to it* That book has lost *its* cover.
it's	[contraction of *it is* or *it has*] *It's* [It is] the coldest winter I can remember. *It's* [It has] been a long time.
lead	[verb, rhymes with *feed*] *to go first; to be a leader* Can she *lead* us out of this tunnel?
led	[verb, past tense of *lead*] *went first* Elizabeth Blackwell *led* the movement for hospital reform.
lead	[noun, rhymes with *red*] *a heavy metal; graphite used in a pencil* There is no longer any *lead* in *lead* pencils.

(continued)

loose	[adjective, rhymes with *moose*] *not tight* This belt is too *loose*.
lose	[verb, rhymes with the verb *use*] *to suffer loss* Fran will *lose* the race if she panics.
passed	[verb, past tense of *pass*] *went by* He *passed* us five minutes ago.
past	[noun] *time that has gone by;* [preposition] *beyond;* [adjective] *ended* Good historians make the *past* come alive. We rode *past* your house. That era is *past*.

Exercise 12   Choosing Between Words Often Confused

From each pair in parentheses, choose the word that will make the sentence correct.

EXAMPLE   1. Kaya (*lead, led*) us to the ceremonial lodge.

   1. led

1. The woman who (*formally, formerly*) (*lead, led*) the band now teaches music in Alaska.
2. We do not expect to (*loose, lose*) any of our backfield players this year.
3. We (*passed, past*) three stalled cars this morning on our way to school.
4. "Why did you (*lead, led*) us (*hear, here*)?" the bewildered tourist demanded.
5. Can you (*hear, here*) the difference between the CD and the digital audio tape?
6. The workers removed the (*lead, led*) pipes from the old house and replaced them with copper ones.
7. Has the (*loose, lose*) bolt lost (*its, it's*) washer and nut?
8. The guests are to dress (*formally, formerly*) for the governor's inauguration ball.
9. "I think (*it's, its*) time for a pop spelling quiz," announced Mrs. Ferrari.
10. Has the last school bus of the morning already gone (*passed, past*) our street, Tiffany?

MECHANICS

peace	[noun] *quiet order and security* World *peace* is the goal of the United Nations.
piece	[noun] *a part of something* Lian bought that *piece* of silk in Hong Kong.
plain	[adjective] *unadorned, simple, common;* [noun] *flat area of land* Jeans were part of his *plain* appearance. A broad, treeless *plain* stretched before them.
plane	[noun] *a flat surface; a tool; an airplane* The movers pushed the couch up an inclined *plane* and into the truck. I have just used a carpenter's *plane*. Have you ever flown in a *plane*?
principal	[noun] *the head of a school;* [adjective] *chief, main* Our *principal* spoke of his *principal* duties. I outlined the *principal* ideas.
principle	[noun] *a rule of conduct; a fundamental truth* Action should be guided by *principles*.
quiet	[adjective] *still and peaceful; without noise* The forest was very *quiet*.
quite	[adverb] *wholly or entirely; to a great extent* Some students are already *quite* sure of their career plans.
shone	[verb, past tense of *shine*] *gleamed; glowed* The moon *shone* softly over the grass in the silent meadow.
shown	[verb, past participle of *show*] *revealed; demonstrated* Tamisha has *shown* me how to crochet.

┌ TIPS ┐ & ┌ TRICKS ┐

Here is a way to remember the difference between *peace* and *piece*. You eat a **pie**ce of **pie**.

┌ TIPS ┐ & ┌ TRICKS ┐

To remember the spelling of *principal*, use this sentence: The princi**pal** is your **pal.**

MECHANICS

NOTE *Shine* can mean "to direct the light of" or "to polish," but the preferred past tense form for these meanings is *shined,* not *shone.*

EXAMPLES   The firefighters **shined** a light into the attic.

Elton **shined** his shoes before the dance.

Exercise 13 **Choosing Between Words Often Confused**

From each pair in parentheses, choose the word that will make the sentence correct.

EXAMPLE   1. Mr. Ramírez used a (*plain, plane*) to smooth the board.

        1. plane

1. Each drop of water (*shone, shown*) like crystal.
2. Motor vehicles are one of the (*principal, principle*) sources of air pollution in our cities.
3. If you don't hurry, you will miss your (*plain, plane*).
4. The (*principals, principles*) of justice and trust can lead to world (*peace, piece*).
5. Jan has (*shone, shown*) me how to change a tire.
6. It is clear that Luisa is acting on (*principal, principle*), not from a personal motive.
7. On Christmas Eve we each have a (*peace, piece*) of fruitcake.
8. "The bake sale was (*quiet, quite*) successful," said Gloria.
9. "For once," the (*principal, principle*) announced with a smile, "you do not have to be (*quiet, quite*)."
10. (*Plain, Plane*) fruits and vegetables can be delicious.

Review C **Proofreading for Words Often Confused**

Identify the misspelled words in the following sentences. Then, give the correct spelling of each word.

EXAMPLE   1. Portraits of people do not have to be plane.

        1. plane—plain

1. Some portraits have a striking affect.
2. A vivid portrait can often make people from the passed seem alive.
3. The painting on the left is by Rembrandt, one of the principle painters of the seventeenth century.
4. The portrait, probably of a rabbi in the city of Amsterdam, is quiet lovely.
5. It's detail shows why Rembrandt was such a popular portrait artist.
6. The painting illustrates one of Rembrandt's main artistic principals, the strong contrast between light and dark.
7. Light has shown only on the rabbi's face, hands, and a peace of his clothing.

┌HELP──
Some sentences in Review C contain more than one spelling error.

8. The rest of the painting is quiet dark, highlighting these lighted features.

9. The rabbi is shone in a state of piece, and the lack of detail in the painting gives an impression of quite elegance.

10. Rembrandt is excepted as a great artist because of his ability to give life to the human form.

stationary	[adjective] *in a fixed position* Is that chalkboard *stationary*?
stationery	[noun] *writing paper* Do you have any white *stationery*?
than	[conjunction used in comparisons] Alaska is bigger *than* Texas.
then	[adverb] *at that time* If we meet, we can talk about it *then*.
their	[possessive form of the pronoun *they*] *belonging to them* Can you understand *their* message?
there	[adverb] *at or to that place;* [also used to begin a sentence] Let's meet *there*. *There* are toys hidden inside the piñata.
they're	[contraction of *they are*] *They're* all from Guam.
threw	[verb, past tense of *throw*] *hurled; tossed* Ted *threw* me the mitt.
through	[preposition] *in one side and out the opposite side* I can't see *through* the lens.

TIPS & TRICKS

Here is an easy way to remember the difference between *stationary* and *stationery:* You write a lett**er** on station**er**y.

Exercise 14 Choosing Between Words Often Confused

From each pair or group in parentheses, choose the word that will make the sentence correct.

EXAMPLE   1. (*Their, They're, There*) first rehearsal is after school.
     1. *Their*

1. The stars appear to be (*stationary, stationery*), but we know that (*their, there, they're*) moving at very high speeds.

2. Thailand is much larger (*than, then*) South Korea.

3. That noise is from a jet plane going (*threw, through*) the sound barrier.
4. The pitcher (*threw, through*) a curveball.
5. A (*stationary, stationery*) store usually sells paper, pencils, and other writing supplies.
6. We started our trip in Barcelona and (*than, then*) traveled west to Madrid.
7. The girls completed (*their, there, they're*) displays for the science fair.
8. Is a moving target much harder to hit (*than, then*) a (*stationary, stationery*) one?
9. Each time Chris got a free throw, he lobbed the ball neatly (*threw, through*) the net to score one point.
10. The children in the back seat kept asking, "When will we get (*their, they're, there*)?"

to	[preposition] *in the direction of; toward* [also used before the base form of a verb] We are going *to* Mexico *to* visit Gabriel.
too	[adverb] *also; more than enough* Audrey is going, *too.* Kazuo used *too* much miso, so the soup was salty.
two	[adjective or noun] *one plus one* We bought *two* sets of chopsticks before we left the restaurant.
waist	[noun] *the midsection of the body* The anchor of the tug-of-war team wrapped the rope around her *waist.*
waste	[verb] *to use foolishly;* [noun] *a needless expense* Try not to *waste* all your film now. Rodney did not agree that golf is a *waste* of time.
weak	[adjective] *feeble; not strong* Melinda's illness has left her very *weak.*
week	[noun] *seven days* We'll wait for at least a *week.*

weather	[noun] *the condition of the atmosphere* The *weather* seems to be changing.
whether	[conjunction] *if* We do not know *whether* we should expect rain.
who's	[contraction of *who is* or *who has*] *Who's* [Who is] going to the museum? "*Who's* [Who has] been eating my porridge?" asked Papa Bear.
whose	[possessive form of the pronoun *who*] *belonging to whom* *Whose* report was the most original?
your	[possessive form of the pronoun *you*] *belonging to you* What is *your* middle name?
you're	[contraction of *you are*] *You're* my best friend.

Exercise 15 **Choosing Between Words Often Confused**

From each pair or group in parentheses, choose the word that will make the sentence correct.

EXAMPLE 1. What are (*your, you're*) plans for celebrating Juneteenth?

1. *your*

1. (*Who's, Whose*) the present secretary of state of the United States, Elaine?
2. My stepsister and I built (*to, too, two*) snow forts on our front lawn yesterday.
3. "(*Your, You're*) late," my friend complained.
4. Would you be able to stand the (*weather, whether*) in Alaska?
5. That sounds like a (*weak, week*) excuse to me.
6. (*Your, You're*) dog is (*to, too, two*) sleepy to learn any new tricks today.
7. "(*Who's, Whose*) boots are these?" Mrs. Allen asked.
8. The pilot must decide very quickly (*weather, whether*) she should parachute to safety or try to land the crippled plane.

9. An obi is a sash that is worn around the (*waist, waste*).
10. My family is going (*to, too, two*) New Orleans.

Review D **Choosing Between Words Often Confused**

From each pair or group in parentheses, choose the word that will make the sentence correct.

EXAMPLE   My parents asked my **[1]** (*advice, advise*) about where we should spend our vacation.

     1. advice

My family could not decide **[1]** (*weather, whether*) to visit Boston or Philadelphia. Finally, we all agreed on Boston, the **[2]** (*capital, capitol*) of Massachusetts. We drove **[3]** (*to, too, two*) the city one week later. Even my parents could not conceal **[4]** (*their, there, they're*) excitement. We did not **[5]** (*loose, lose*) a moment. Boston **[6]** (*formally, formerly*) was "the hub of the universe," and we discovered that **[7]** (*it's, its*) still a truly fascinating city.

Everyone in my family **[8]** (*accept, except*) me had eaten lobster, and I ate it for the first time there in Boston. I was not **[9]** (*altogether, all together*) certain how to eat the lobster, but my doubt did not **[10]** (*affect, effect*) my appetite. My parents insisted that pear yogurt was a strange **[11]** (*desert, dessert*) to follow lobster, but I would not **[12]** (*altar, alter*) my order. After the pear yogurt, I thought about ordering a small **[13]** (*peace, piece*) of pie, but I decided to keep **[14]** (*quiet, quite*).

While in Boston, we walked up and down the streets just to **[15]** (*hear, here*) the Bostonians' accents. **[16]** (*Their, There, They're*) especially noted for **[17]** (*their, there, they're*) pronunciation of *a*'s and *r*'s.

We had been in Boston for only a week or so when the **[18]** (*weather, whether*) bureau predicted a big snowstorm for the area. Since we had not taken the proper **[19]** (*cloths, clothes*) for snow, we decided to return home. On the way back, we were **[20]** (*already, all ready*) making plans for another visit to Boston.

MECHANICS

25 Chapter Review

A. Identifying Misspelled Words

Identify the misspelled word in each of the following groups of words. Then, write the correct spelling of the word.

1. height, weight, cheif
2. succeed, supercede, proceed
3. unecessary, unavailable, unusual
4. happyly, finally, truly
5. said, paid, keyd
6. cleaner, tapping, driped
7. taxes, buzzes, foxs
8. switches, mixs, keys
9. knifes, tomatoes, solos
10. mothers-in-law, father-in-laws, drive-ins
11. achieve, feirce, friend
12. mowwer, followed, staying
13. acquire, arguement, always
14. tired, trys, guess
15. noticable, yield, daily
16. staying, priceless, easyer
17. halfs, coughs, princesses
18. heating, hiting, trying
19. changable, drinkable, smiling
20. misspell, ilegible, unnoticed

B. Writing the Correct Plural Form

Write the correct plural form of each of the following words.

21. boss	25. freeway	28. *3*
22. thief	26. ten-year-old	29. city
23. sheep	27. Vietnamese	30. soprano
24. woman		

MECHANICS

C. Choosing Between Words Often Confused

In each of the following sentences, choose the correct word from the pair in parentheses.

31. Have you (*already, all ready*) adopted a kitten from the animal shelter?

32. Although it's only July, the store already has a display of winter (*cloths, clothes*).

33. "I believe that both candidates for senator have very high (*principals, principles*)," my aunt said.

34. The sophomore (*councilor, counselor*) is working on next year's class schedules.

35. The moon is (*quiet, quite*) bright this evening.

36. Not getting enough exercise can (*effect, affect*) your health.

37. You must (*formally, formerly*) declare your interest in joining the club by filling out the membership card.

38. My (*advise, advice*) is that you buy a mountain bike.

39. (*Its, It's*) hard to believe that the leatherback turtle can grow to be seven feet long!

40. The fabric on the couch in Dr. Alexander's waiting room is (*course, coarse*) and scratchy.

D. Identifying Misused Words

In many of the following sentences, one word has been misused because it has been confused for another word. Write each incorrectly used word. Then, write the word that should have been used. If a sentence is already correct, write *C*.

41. An editor will altar this manuscript.

42. We had fruit and sherbet for desert.

43. I thanked Mr. Chu for the compliment.

44. While you are hear, use this towel.

45. Eventually, winter past and spring arrived.

46. Maria received a box of stationery for her birthday.

47. The blue chair is more comfortable then the green one.

48. The whether report comes on right after the news.

49. Whose the man speaking to Officer Grant?

50. The town voted to except the gift of a new library wing.

Writing Application
Using Correct Spelling in a Review

Spelling Words Correctly   Write a one- or two-paragraph review of your favorite book or movie. Be sure to use at least five of the words listed as Words Often Confused in this chapter.

Prewriting   Pick a favorite book or movie and make a list of the reasons that you prefer it over other books or movies. If you decide to write about a book, for example, you may want to compare it to a film that is based on that book.

Writing   As you write your first draft, be sure to include information about the book or film, such as who wrote it, who directed it, and who stars in it. Remember to use a dictionary to help with correct spelling.

Revising   Evaluate your draft and revise it to improve its content, organization, and style. Add sensory details that make the story come alive for the reader. Replace clichés and worn-out verbs and nouns with fresher, more precise words.

Publishing   Check your paragraph for spelling mistakes. Use a computer spellchecker if one is available, but remember that spellcheckers will not recognize a misused word (for example, *piece* for *peace*), as opposed to a misspelled word. Also, pay attention to the spelling of words in languages other than English, and consult a dictionary if you have any doubt. Exchange your report with a partner, and check each other's spelling.

You and your classmates may want to gather the class's reviews and create a bulletin board display of favorite books and movies.

Spelling Words

- offshore
  strawberry
  daylight
  seaweed
  wildlife
  grandparents
  moonlight
  chairperson
  killer whale
  watermelon
  headache
  typewrite

- shoot
  mist
  birth
  swayed
  shown
  tied
  pane
  shone
  reel
  berth
  chute
  suede

- gathered
  hammered
  controlling
  bothering
  ruined
  listening
  studying
  swallowed
  permitting
  carrying
  compelled
  groaned

- cafeteria
  alligator
  corral
  vanilla
  mosquito
  stampede
  guitar
  coyote
  jaguar
  chili

  cocoa
  tortillas

- classical
  conductor
  concert
  instrument
  clarinet
  banjo
  bugle
  harmony
  pianist
  performance
  violin
  rehearsal

- express
  envelope
  extend
  excitement
  exceed
  explode
  enthusiasm
  enclose
  expand
  exclaim
  exclude
  excel

- defeat
  destroyed
  decline
  defects
  disabled
  disappeared
  disappointment
  dependent
  deduction
  disadvantages
  disguised
  dissolved

- Spanish
  Greek
  England
  African
  French
  Spain
  Vietnam

  Australia
  Japanese
  Greece
  Australian
  Vietnamese

- arrange
  accommodate
  announced
  approaching
  accepted
  appoint
  accompanying
  array
  arrangements
  accomplish
  accelerate
  annoy

- selfish
  marine
  greenish
  awkward
  wholesome
  grayish
  childish
  masculine
  feminine
  reddish
  genuine
  awesome

- temperature
  strength
  length
  vegetable
  arctic
  twelfth
  probably
  jewelry
  literature
  boundary
  reference
  beverage

- machinery
  discovery
  nursery
  dictionary
  century
  injury
  missionary
  territory
  scenery
  revolutionary
  treasury
  luxury

- barrier
  corridor
  umbrella
  buffalo
  gorilla
  pinnacle
  syllable
  tobacco
  massacre
  opossum
  moccasins
  cinnamon

- muscular
  triangle
  muscle
  circular
  regulation
  particles
  particular
  rectangle
  vehicles
  rectangular
  triangular
  vehicular

- doubtful
  specialist
  misfortune
  fortunate
  unfortunate
  especially
  specific
  specifications
  judicial
  judgment

prejudice
undoubtedly

- organize
cooperate
congratulate
exercise
calculate
illustrate
recognize
compromise
memorize
paralyze
criticize
inaugurate

- depositing
recess
televised
revised
position
constructing
composition
opposite
structures
destruction
vision
necessary

- existence
incident
frequent
endurance
balance
intelligent
influence
reluctant
magnificent
experience
confidence
elegant

- transmission
contracted
commitment
attract
submit
references
offered
omit
admits

distract
subtraction
refer

- portrait
buffet
ballet
bouquet
dialogue
antique
unique
vague
fatigue
technique
plaque
camouflage

- fantasy
fantastic
company
companion
editor
editorial
colony
colonial
strategy
strategic
diplomacy
diplomatic

- hasten
autumn
autumnal
softly
heritage
designated
designed
reception
signature
haste
sign
resign

- diameter
graph
meters
astronomer
barometer
biography
astronaut
kilometers

astronomy
photography
centimeters
autograph

- trio
monopoly
quartet
tricycle
decade
octopus
decimal
quarters
triangles
binoculars
triple
monotonous

- desperate
lightning
adjective
penetrate
aspirin
athletes
identity
disastrous
ecstatic
platinum
incidentally
tentatively

- caravan
luncheon
champion
gymnasium
laboratory
mathematics
parachute
submarine
teenagers
memorandum
limousine
examination

- logic
biology
monologue
hydrant
technology
analogy
mythology

apologizing
periscope
telescope
dehydrated
psychology

- agricultural
identification
encyclopedia
possibility
exceptionally
responsibilities
characteristic
recommendation
rehabilitation
acceleration
simultaneously
accumulation

- inspired
convention
formula
adventure
depends
uniform
inventor
pending
invention
transformed
perform
suspended

- civilian
historian
guardian
scientist
biologist
volunteer
musician
engineer
physician
technician
politician
psychiatrist

26 | Correcting Common Errors

Key Language Skills Review

This chapter reviews key skills and concepts that pose special problems for writers.

- **Sentence Fragments and Run-on Sentences**
- **Subject-Verb and Pronoun-Antecedent Agreement**
- **Verb Forms and Pronoun Forms**
- **Comparison of Modifiers**
- **Misplaced Modifiers**
- **Standard Usage**
- **Capitalization**
- **Punctuation—End Marks, Commas, Semicolons, Colons, Quotation Marks, and Apostrophes**
- **Spelling**

Most of the exercises in this chapter follow the same format as the exercises found throughout the grammar, usage, and mechanics sections of this book. You will notice, however, that two sets of review exercises are presented in standardized test formats. These exercises are designed to provide you with practice not only in solving usage and mechanics problems but also in dealing with these kinds of problems on standardized tests.

Exercise 1   Finding and Revising Sentence Fragments

Most of the following groups of words are sentence fragments. Revise each fragment by (1) adding a subject, (2) adding a verb, or (3) attaching the fragment to a complete sentence. You may need to change the punctuation and capitalization, too. If the word group is already a complete sentence, write *S*.

EXAMPLE   1. Because she likes Chihuahuas.

         1. *My mother bought a book about dogs because she likes Chihuahuas.*

1. Wanted to study the history of Chihuahuas.
2. Small dogs with big, pointed ears.
3. When my mother's Chihuahuas begin their shrill, high-pitched barking.
4. Chihuahuas lived in ancient Mexico.
5. Ancient stone carvings showing that the Toltecs raised Chihuahuas during the eighth or ninth century A.D.
6. Are related to dogs of the Middle East.
7. Travelers may have brought Chihuahuas to the Americas as companions.
8. That Chihuahuas score poorly on canine intelligence tests.
9. However, can be trained to assist people who have hearing impairments.
10. If you want a Chihuahua.

Reference Note

For information about **correcting sentence fragments,** see page 269.

Exercise 2   Revising Sentence Fragments

Identify each of the following groups of words as a sentence fragment or a complete sentence. Write *F* if it is a sentence fragment and *S* if it is a sentence. Then, revise each sentence fragment by (1) adding a subject, (2) adding a verb, or (3) attaching the fragment to a complete sentence. You may need to change the punctuation and capitalization, too.

EXAMPLE   1. Juggling a fascinating hobby.

         1. *F—Juggling is a fascinating hobby.*

1. If you would like to be able to juggle.
2. You might start with a good, simple how-to book.
3. Most people can learn the basic moves.
4. Within a fairly short period of time.

Reference Note

For information about **correcting sentence fragments,** see page 269.

COMMON ERRORS

5. While beginners first develop a sense of how to hold one juggling bag.
6. They also practice standing in the proper, relaxed way.
7. Next, must master the ability to toss one bag back and forth.
8. Then learning the right way to throw two bags.
9. Beginners often need to practice juggling with two bags for some time.
10. Before they move up to three bags.

Reference Note
For information about **correcting sentence fragments,** see page 269.

┌HELP──

Although the example for Exercise 3 shows two possible answers, you need to give only one for each item.

Exercise 3 Finding and Revising Sentence Fragments

Some of the following groups of words are sentence fragments. Revise each sentence fragment by (1) adding a subject, (2) adding a verb, or (3) attaching the sentence fragment to a complete sentence. You may need to change the punctuation and capitalization, too. If the word group is already a complete sentence, write *S*.

EXAMPLE
1. Could have been the source of the world's legends of dragons.

1. *Could dinosaur fossils have been the source of the world's legends of dragons?*

or

Large lizards, such as monitors, could have been the source of the world's legends of dragons.

1. Eventually, taking root in the imaginations of many people.
2. Considering this.
3. The word *dinosaur* was first used around one hundred and fifty years ago.
4. That fact surprises many people.
5. Where the first dinosaur eggs were found.
6. For example, magnificent, full skeletons in museums, lifelike animations, television documentaries, and even children's toys and cartoons.
7. Can explain the sudden disappearance of these mighty creatures.
8. The remarkable work of physicists Dr. Luis Alvarez and his son Walter on this mystery.
9. Their theory based on the idea of a meteor hitting the earth.
10. Sending a huge, dark cloud around the earth, killing many plants and destroying the dinosaurs' food sources.

COMMON ERRORS

Each of the following items is a run-on sentence. Revise each sentence by following the italicized instructions in parentheses. Remember to use correct punctuation and capitalization.

Reference Note

For information about **correcting run-on sentences,** see page 271.

EXAMPLE   1. The study of shells is called malacology, shell collections are particularly popular in Japan. (*Make two sentences.*)

1. *The study of shells is called malacology. Shell collections are particularly popular in Japan.*

1. At four feet in diameter, the shell of the giant clam is the largest shell today during prehistoric times, the shell of the Nautiloidea sometimes grew to eight feet across. (*Make two sentences.*)

2. From the Mediterranean to Japan, shells have played an important part in everyday life they have functioned as money, as decoration, and even as magic charms. (*Make two sentences.*)

3. American Indians used wampum, beads cut from shells, as money West Africans and Arabs used the cowrie shell in the same way. (*Use a comma and a coordinating conjunction.*)

4. Africans prized the shell as jewelry shells are still sold as jewelry. (*Use a comma and a coordinating conjunction.*)

5. Jewelry, buttons, figurines, and all kinds of decorative objects can be purchased at tourist shops along the coasts, shells are plentiful nearby. (*Make two sentences.*)

6. The ancient Greeks boiled mollusks and created a valuable purple dye cloth treated with this dye may retain its color for hundreds of years. (*Make two sentences.*)

7. Perhaps because of their great beauty, shells have also played important parts in religious life they may be found in several belief systems. (*Make two sentences.*)

8. Quetzalcoatl, god of the Mayans, Toltecs, and Aztecs, was born from a seashell the chank shell is associated with the Hindu god Vishnu. (*Make two sentences.*)

9. Shells can be free for the taking their rarity can make them quite valuable. (*Use a comma and a coordinating conjunction.*)

10. Shells are regularly exported from the United States to Europe, Japan and the United States also ship shells back and forth. (*Make two sentences.*)

Reference Note

For information about **correcting run-on sentences,** see page 271.

Exercise 5 Correcting Run-on Sentences

Correct each of the following run-on sentences by (1) making it into two separate sentences or (2) using a comma and a coordinating conjunction to make a compound sentence. Remember to use correct punctuation and capitalization.

EXAMPLE   1. Anthony uses chopsticks skillfully I have trouble with them.

             1. *Anthony uses chopsticks skillfully, but I have trouble with them.*

1. The large crane lifted the ten-ton boxes, it set them on the concrete deck.
2. My dad does not know much about computers he has learned to surf the Internet.
3. Allen Say wrote *The Ink-Keeper's Apprentice* the events in the story are based on his boyhood in Japan.
4. Two robins landed on the ice in the birdbath one of them drank water from around the thawed edges.
5. Egyptian hieroglyphics may be written from left to right or from right to left, they may be written from top to bottom.
6. John is my youngest brother Levy is my oldest brother.
7. The nature preserve was beautiful some people had littered.
8. Grandma believes in keeping a positive attitude, she says that thinking positively is the key to a happy life.
9. Let's see that new movie from Korea I have never seen a Korean movie.
10. All my friends like to shop for bargains at the downtown mall, I do, too.

Reference Note

For information about **correcting run-on sentences,** see page 271.

Exercise 6 Revising Run-on Sentences

Revise each of the following run-on sentences by (1) making it into two separate sentences or (2) using a comma and a coordinating conjunction to make a compound sentence. Remember to use correct punctuation and capitalization.

EXAMPLE   1. James Earl Jones is a famous actor he has been in movies and plays.

             1. *James Earl Jones is a famous actor. He has been in movies and plays.*

1. You may not remember seeing James Earl Jones, you would probably recognize his voice.
2. Jones provided the voice of Darth Vader in the *Star Wars* movies, Jones's deep voice helped make the character forceful and frightening.
3. Jones has a distinctive voice he has even won a medal for his vocal delivery.
4. The prize was given by the American Academy of Arts and Letters, is that the organization that gives the Academy Awards?
5. Jones's autobiography was published in 1993 it is, quite appropriately, titled *Voices and Silences.*
6. Jones was born in Mississippi in 1931, he was raised by his grandparents on a farm in Michigan.
7. His father was a prizefighter and an actor Jones decided to be an actor, too, and studied in New York City.
8. He portrayed a boxing champion in *The Great White Hope,* he starred in both the Broadway production and the movie version of the play.
9. Jones won a Tony Award for his Broadway performance he was nominated for an Academy Award for his role in the movie.
10. Another of Jones's movies is *The Man,* in that movie he plays the first African American to be elected president of the United States.

Exercise 7 **Revising Sentence Fragments and Run-on Sentences**

Identify each of the following word groups by writing *F* if it is a sentence fragment, *R* if it is a run-on sentence, and *S* if it is a complete sentence. Revise each fragment to make it into a complete sentence. Revise each run-on to make it into one or more complete sentences. Remember to use correct capitalization and punctuation.

EXAMPLE   1. Because my ancestors were Scandinavian.

        1. *F—I have heard many stories about Vikings because my ancestors were Scandinavian.*

1. The Viking Age lasted three centuries, it started at the end of the eighth century A.D.

Reference Note

For information on **correcting sentence fragments,** see page 269. For information on **correcting run-on sentences,** see page 271.

COMMON ERRORS

2. Vikings from Scandinavian countries known today as Sweden, Denmark, and Norway.

3. Since the Vikings lived along the sea, they often became boatbuilders, sailors, and explorers.

4. The range of influence of the Vikings was enormous the Vikings developed trade routes in western Europe and also in the Middle East.

5. Also were skilled at fishing and farming.

6. All Vikings spoke the language called Old Norse they shared similar religious beliefs.

7. Odin was the chief god of the Vikings, Odin's son Thor was worshiped more widely.

8. After they were converted to Christianity, the Vikings built many wooden churches.

9. Was divided into three main social classes—royal families, free citizens, and slaves.

10. Viking women held several important rights, they could own property and land, for example.

Exercise 8 Identifying Verbs That Agree in Number with Their Subjects

Reference Note

For information about **subject-verb agreement,** see page 458.

For each of the following sentences, choose the form of the verb in parentheses that agrees with the subject.

EXAMPLE
1. The band (*play, plays*) mostly reggae.

1. *plays*

1. Samantha and Matthew (*take, takes*) art classes at the museum on weekends.

2. The card table or the folding chairs (*belong, belongs*) in that closet by the front door.

3. Earlene (*don't, doesn't*) know the exact time because her watch stopped working last week.

4. Both the stalagmites and the stalactites (*was, were*) casting eerie shadows on the cave walls.

5. Several of the exchange students at our school (*speak, speaks*) Portuguese.

6. Neither an emu nor an ostrich (*lay, lays*) eggs that look like that.

7. The members of the audience always (*clap, claps*) as soon as the star appears onstage.
8. Mike said that either the main herd or the stragglers (*is, are*) in the near canyon.
9. The coaches on the visiting team (*agree, agrees*) with the referee's decision.
10. Some of the fruit baskets (*sell, sells*) for less than three and a half dollars each.

Exercise 9 **Identifying Verbs That Agree in Number with Their Subjects**

For each of the following sentences, choose the form of the verb in parentheses that agrees with the subject.

EXAMPLE   1. (*Do, Does*) you know what a powwow is?

     1. *Do*

Reference Note

For information about **subject-verb agreement,** see page 458.

1. Each of us in my class (*has, have*) given a report about powwows, which are ceremonies or gatherings of American Indians.
2. Dancing and feasting (*is, are*) very important activities at powwows.
3. People in my family (*come, comes*) from around the country to attend the Crow Fair, which is held every August in Montana.
4. Many of the people at the powwow (*has, have*) come here from Canada.
5. Everyone here (*know, knows*) that it is the largest powwow in North America.
6. Peoples represented at the fair (*include, includes*) the Crow, Lakota, Ojibwa, Blackfoot, and Cheyenne.

7. Only one of my relatives (*dance, dances*) all four of the main kinds of dances at powwows.
8. Both skill and practice (*go, goes*) into the Traditional, Fancy, Grass, and Jingle-dress dances.
9. Last year, all of the costumes of the Fancy dancers (*was, were*) extremely colorful.
10. Either a row of porcupine quills or a band of beads (*go, goes*) all the way around some of the dancers' headdresses.

Reference Note

For information about **subject-verb agreement,** see page 458.

Exercise 10 Correcting Errors in Subject-Verb Agreement

Most of the following sentences contain errors in subject-verb agreement. Identify each error, and give the correct form of the verb. If a sentence is already correct, write *C.*

EXAMPLE   1. All of us is very excited about our Drama Club's next play.

   1. *is—are*

1. *Six Friends and One Dog* are the title of the play we are performing this fall.
2. The director and producer of the play are Mark Taylor.
3. Neither our sponsor nor the actors have ever staged a production like this.
4. Most of the actors was chosen last week.
5. Of course, the cast don't know their lines yet.
6. Many of the costumes is still being made.
7. Either Lauren or Kawanda's older brother is painting the backdrops.
8. Are five dollars too much for a ticket?
9. My friends and the crew hopes not, because the tickets are already printed!
10. Channel 6 News have promised to cover our opening night, so we'll all be famous, at least for a little while.

Reference Note

For information on **using pronouns correctly,** see Chapter 19.

Exercise 11 Choosing Correct Pronoun Forms

Choose the correct pronoun or pronouns in parentheses in each of the following sentences.

EXAMPLE   1. Tell anyone with an idea to take (*their, his or her*) suggestion to the vice-principal.

   1. *his or her*

1. Everyone on the field trip must bring (*their, his or her*) own sack lunch.
2. When my sister or mother comes back from the bakery, (*they, she*) will bring fresh-baked bread.
3. No, neither of the cowboys ever takes off (*their, his*) hat.
4. The United States was proud when (*its, their*) astronauts landed on the moon.

5. If Doug or Simon is in the clear downfield, pass (*them, him*) the ball.
6. Usually Rosita or Paula plays (*her, their*) guitar at our picnics.
7. If anybody is still in the gym, tell (*them, him or her*) to turn out the lights and shut the door.
8. The colonists and Governor William Bradford depended on Squanto as (*his or her, their*) interpreter.
9. This is a very large company, but (*they, it*) treats the employees with respect.
10. Ask Jennie or Sara what (*her, their*) middle name is.

Exercise 12 **Proofreading Sentences for Correct Pronoun-Antecedent Agreement**

Most of the following sentences contain errors in pronoun-antecedent agreement. Identify each error, and give the correct form of the pronoun. If a sentence is already correct, write *C*.

EXAMPLE   1. Jesse and Michael enjoyed his Kwanzaa activities.
               1. *his—their*

1. During Kwanzaa, which lasts from December 26 through January 1, several of our friends and neighbors celebrate his or her African heritage.
2. African American families affirm traditional values and principles during their Kwanzaa activities.
3. This year, both of my sisters made storybooks as her *zawadi,* or Kwanzaa gifts.
4. Either Uncle Willis or Uncle Roland will bring their candles for the observance.
5. One of them will bring their wooden candleholder, called a *kinara.*
6. The joyful celebration of Kwanzaa has its origins in African harvest festivals.
7. Each of my parents will discuss his or her own individual ideas about Kwanzaa.
8. Either Lily or Charlotte mentioned in their speech that Kwanzaa was created in 1966.
9. Nobody in our family likes to miss their turn to make up dances on the sixth day of Kwanzaa.
10. Jerry and Charles will volunteer his time on the third day of Kwanzaa, when collective work is celebrated.

Reference Note

For information about **pronoun-antecedent agreement,** see page 475.

Reference Note

For information about **subject-verb agreement,** see page 458. For information about **pronoun-antecedent agreement,** see page 475.

Reference Note

For information about **using verbs correctly,** see Chapter 18.

Exercise 13 Proofreading Sentences for Correct Subject-Verb and Pronoun-Antecedent Agreement

Most of the following sentences contain agreement errors. For each error, identify the incorrect verb or pronoun and supply the correct form. If a sentence is already correct, write *C*.

EXAMPLE 1. Every animal, including humans, need water to survive.

1. *need—needs*

1. The human body consist mostly of water.
2. You and I, along with everyone else, is about 65 percent water.
3. Everybody in my family tries to drink at least eight glasses of water a day.
4. "Don't Carlos usually drink more than that?" Janet asked.
5. Either Angie or Ramona said that their family usually drinks bottled water.
6. Evidence shows that drinking water helps our bodies keep its proper temperature.
7. Ian or Calinda have studied the mineral content of our local water supply.
8. Industry and agriculture depend on a good water supply for its success.
9. Most of the world's fresh water is frozen in polar icecaps and glaciers.
10. While more than 70 percent of the earth's surface are covered by water, only 3 percent of that water is not salty.

Exercise 14 Writing the Forms of Regular and Irregular Verbs

Provide the correct present participle, past, or past participle form of the given verb to complete each of the following sentences.

EXAMPLE 1. *eat*   Angela has already _____ her serving of acorn squash.

1. *eaten*

1. *install*   The shopping mall has _____ wheelchair ramps at all of the entrances.

2. *send* We have already ____ for a new crossword-puzzle magazine.

3. *see* Have you ____ the koalas at the Australian wildlife exhibit?

4. *put* Marianna is ____ together a colorful mobile.

5. *grow* My uncle ____ the largest pumpkin in the United States this year.

6. *draw* Anthony has ____ two different self-portraits.

7. *run* Both of my stepbrothers have ____ in the Cowtown Marathon.

8. *jump* Have the cats ____ out of the tree?

9. *write* Murasaki Shikibu of Japan ____ what may be the world's first novel.

10. *go* More than half of my friends ____ to the May Day parade.

Exercise 15 **Proofreading Sentences for Correct Verb Forms**

Identify any incorrect past or past participle verb forms in the following sentences, and write the correct forms. If a sentence is already correct, write *C*.

Reference Note

For information about **using verbs correctly,** see Chapter 18.

EXAMPLE   1. Many African American women maked names for themselves during the pioneer days.

    1. *made*

1. A friend of mine lended me a book called *Black Women of the Old West.*
2. It contains many biographies of African American women who leaded difficult but exciting lives.
3. For example, May B. Mason gone to the Yukon to mine gold during the Klondike Gold Rush.
4. Journalist Era Bell Thompson writed articles about the West for a Chicago newspaper.
5. In *American Daughter* she telled about her youth in North Dakota.
6. Our teacher has spoke highly of Dr. Susan McKinney Stewart, a pioneer physician.
7. During the 1800s, Cathy Williams wore men's clothes and served under the name William Cathay as a Buffalo Soldier.
8. I seen a picture of Williams at work on her farm.

9. Mary Fields choosed an exciting but sometimes hard life in the West.
10. Nicknamed "Stagecoach Mary," she drived freight wagons and stagecoaches in Montana.

Reference Note

For information about **using verbs correctly,** see Chapter 18.

Exercise 16 Proofreading Sentences for Correct Verb Forms

If any of the following sentences contains an incorrect past or past participle form of a verb, write the correct form. If a sentence is already correct, write *C*.

EXAMPLE   1. When I was ten, I begun to collect stamps.
            1. *began*

1. Over the years, my collection has growed large enough to fill three binders.
2. I have went to several stamp shows.
3. At nearly every show, I seen many rare and valuable stamps.
4. I told my friend Warren that I aim to own some of those stamps one day.
5. I once saw a picture of a rare two-cent stamp that cost one collector $1.1 million in 1987.
6. As you might imagine, that price setted a world record!
7. Stamps have appear in many shapes.
8. My uncle, a mail carrier, sended me a banana-shaped stamp.
9. He also has give me a book about the history of stamp collecting.
10. It sayed that stamp collecting was already a popular hobby by the 1860s.

Exercise 17 Choosing Correct Verb Forms

Reference Note

For information about using *rise and raise, sit and set,* and *lie and lay,* see page 500.

Choose the correct verb form in parentheses in each of the following sentences.

EXAMPLE   1. (*Set, Sit*) those packages down, and come help me catch these kittens.
            1. *Set*

1. Did Keefe (*rise, raise*) the flag for the ceremony?
2. The crowd roared when Sheila (*sit, set*) a new track record for the fifty-yard dash.
3. A giant lobster was (*laying, lying*) motionless on the seabed.

4. The incoming tide (*rose, raised*) the boat that had been beached on the sandbar.
5. An heirloom quilt (*lays, lies*) neatly folded on the bed.
6. Why is the price of housing (*rising, raising*) in this area?
7. Someone had (*laid, lain*) a row of stones carefully on either side of the path.
8. Freshly washed and brushed, the mare walked out to the corral, (*lay, laid*) down in the dust, and rolled over three or four times.
9. By noon, the fog had (*risen, raised*) and the sun had come out.
10. In the old photograph, five Sioux warriors (*sat, set*) and stared with dignity into the camera.

Exercise 18) Identifying Correct Pronoun Forms

Choose the correct form of the pronoun in parentheses in each of the following sentences.

EXAMPLE   1. Doris and (*me, I*) are planning a trip to Vietnam.
              1. *I*

Reference Note
For information on **using pronouns correctly,** see Chapter 19.

1. Will you take the first-aid class with (*we, us*)?
2. The principal gave (*he, him*) the key to the trophy case.
3. The minister gave (*they, them*) a wedding present.
4. Ulani and (*he, him*) greeted their guests with "Aloha!"
5. Mr. Galvez saved the comics especially for (*I, me*).
6. (*They, Them*) are learning how to draw with pastels.
7. R. J. asked (*she, her*) for a new CD.
8. Stan's jokes amused Martha and (*I, me*).
9. The person who called you last night was (*I, me*).
10. The captain of the debate team is (*she, her*).

Exercise 19) Identifying Correct Pronoun Forms

Choose the correct form of the pronoun in parentheses in each of the following sentences.

EXAMPLE   1. The guest speaker told (*us, we*) students many facts about Hispanic Americans in the arts.
              1. *us*

Reference Note
For information about **using pronouns correctly,** see Chapter 19.

1. Mrs. Ramirez picked out some poems by Jimmy Santiago Baca and read (*they, them*) to us.

COMMON ERRORS

2. Jan and (*he, him*) agree that Barbara Carrasco's murals are outstanding.

3. Between you and (*I, me*), Gaspar Perez de Villagra's account of an early expedition to the American Southwest sounds interesting.

4. (*He, Him*) wrote the first book to have been written in what is now the United States.

5. Our teacher showed (*we, us*) pictures of the work of the Puerto Rican artist Arnaldo Roche.

6. (*Who, Whom*) is your favorite artist?

7. The writings of Christina Garcia appeal to (*we, us*).

8. In Luz's opinion, the best writer is (*she, her*).

9. Tito Puente has recorded at least one hundred albums and has appeared in several movies; we saw (*he, him*) in *Radio Days*.

10. (*Who, Whom*) did you research for your report?

Reference Note

For information about **using pronouns correctly,** see Chapter 19.

Exercise 20 **Proofreading for Correct Pronoun Usage**

Most of the following sentences contain errors in pronoun usage. Identify each error, and give the correct pronoun. If a sentence is already correct, write *C*.

EXAMPLE   1. Who did the student council appoint?

1. *Who—Whom*

1. Let me know whom will be in charge of decorating.

2. Mr. Rodriguez gave Nicole and we shop students a handout on using the jigsaw safely.

3. Waiting for us at the door were Grandma and they.

4. For Ron and myself, geometry is easy.

5. Gina, us girls are going to the park to fly our kites; come along with us!

6. Mr. Chin, his wife, and me are going to the Mayan exhibit at the museum next weekend.

7. The big dog always keeps the bowl of food for hisself, so we feed the little dog on the porch.

8. From who could we borrow a map?

9. Yes, the team did all the planning and production of the video by theirselves.

10. The only ones who can speak French are us boys from Miss LaRouche's class.

Exercise 21   Choosing Correct Forms of Modifiers

Choose the correct form of the modifier in parentheses in each of the following sentences.

Reference Note

For information on **using modifiers correctly,** see Chapter 20.

EXAMPLE   1. Many people think that of all pets, Siamese cats are the (*better, best*).

       1. *best*

1. The boys thought that they were (*stronger, strongest*), but the girls beat them in the tug of war.
2. The (*simplest, simpler*) way to attract birds to a yard is by having water available for them.
3. Jovita is the (*most intelligent, intelligentest*) student in the seventh grade.
4. I worry about my grades (*least often, less often*) now that I do my homework every night.
5. Kim Lee has traveled (*farthest, farther*) on her bicycle than anyone else in our class has.
6. Hasn't this year's quiz-bowl team won (*more, most*) local competitions than last year's team?
7. Grandfather says that this winter is the (*colder, coldest*) one he remembers.
8. Wynton Marsalis was born in the city (*more, most*) associated with jazz—New Orleans.
9. Bicyclists who wear helmets are injured (*least, less*) often than those who do not.
10. Louisiana has (*fewer, fewest*) wetlands than it once had.

Exercise 22   Proofreading for Correct Modifiers

Most of the following sentences contain errors in the use of modifiers. Identify each incorrect modifier, and supply the correct form. If the sentence is already correct, write *C*.

Reference Note

For information about **using modifiers correctly,** see Chapter 20.

EXAMPLE   1. Low, green hills roll gentle in the dawn mist.

       1. *gentle—gently*

1. The tourists looked uncomfortably as they rode the elephant along the beach.
2. An Indian elephant calmly carried a surfboard with its trunk and did the job good, too.
3. The white waves of the Bay of Bengal smell quite well to us.

COMMON ERRORS

4. The island of Sri Lanka was once known as Ceylon, and tea grows good there.
5. At first, I felt bad for the workers up to their waists in mud.
6. I thought they had the worstest job in the world.
7. They were searching for rubies and garnets that might appear sudden in their muddy baskets.
8. I couldn't recognize a raw gem very well; could you?
9. I thought the highlands, especially Sri Pada and World's End, looked beautifully.
10. You can live simple when you are in Sri Lanka.

Exercise 23 Revising Sentences to Correct Double Comparisons and Double Negatives

Revise each of the following sentences to correct each double comparison or double negative.

EXAMPLES
1. Of the three games, the first was the least funnest.
1. *Of the three games, the first was the least fun.*

2. There are not hardly any stores near the ranch.
2. *There are hardly any stores near the ranch.*

1. The recycling center is much more busier than it used to be.
2. Sometimes even indoor water pipes freeze if they do not have no insulation around them.
3. I think that our dog Sammy is most happiest when the weather is cold.
4. I haven't received a birthday card from neither of my grandmothers yet.
5. Almost any circle that you draw by hand will be less rounder than one you draw with a compass.
6. Wearing sunscreen with a high sun-protection factor can make being in the sun more safer.
7. My second-oldest cousin, Giovanni, is not like nobody else I know.
8. We never went nowhere during spring vacation this year.
9. That was probably the most cleverest chess move I've ever seen you use, Elise.
10. When I'm old enough to vote, I'm not never going to miss a chance to do so.

Reference Note
For information about **double comparisons,** see page 538. For information about **double negatives,** see page 539.

COMMON ERRORS

The following sentences contain errors in the placement of modifiers. Revise each sentence by adding or rearranging words or by
doing both to correct the placement of each modifier.

EXAMPLE   1. My grandmother and I saw a horse on the way to
the movie.

1. *On the way to the movie, my grandmother and I
saw a horse.*

1. The party was held in the park celebrating Mary's birthday.
2. With wind-filled sails, I saw a ship approaching the harbor.
3. The tree was struck by lightning that we had pruned.
4. The Yamamotos enjoyed planting the iris that arrived from
their Japanese relatives in a box.
5. The softball team is from my hometown that won the district
championship.
6. Trying to steal home, the catcher tagged the runner.
7. Jaime told Katya about the kitten playing in a happy voice.
8. Painted bright colors, Kamal saw many houses.
9. Hanging from a clothes rack, the drama students finally
found the costumes.
10. Recently picked from the orchard, the bowl was full of fruit.

Exercise 25 Identifying Correct Usage

From the word or words in parentheses in each of the following
sentences, choose the answer that is correct according to the
rules of formal, standard English.

EXAMPLE   1. The boys carried the new recycling containers
(*themselves, theirselves*).

1. *themselves*

1. This orange marmalade smells (*bad, badly*).
2. In science class last week, we learned (*how come, why*) water
expands when it freezes.
3. The dam (*busted, burst*) because of the rising floodwaters.
4. Mario should plant (*fewer, less*) bulbs in that small flower bed.
5. This button looks (*as if, like*) it will match the material.
6. Let's (*try and, try to*) arrive at the concert early so that we can
get good seats.

Reference Note
For information about
the **correct placement
of modifiers,** see
page 540.

Reference Note
For information on
common usage errors,
see Chapter 21. For
information on **formal,
standard English,** see
page 553.

COMMON ERRORS

7. The defending champion played (*good, well*) during the chess tournament.
8. Yes, our nearest neighbor lives a long (*way, ways*) from us.
9. Those (*kind, kinds*) of fabrics are made in Madras, India.
10. Did you share the leftover chop suey (*among, between*) the three of you?

Reference Note

For information about **common usage errors,** see Chapter 21. For information about **formal, standard English,** see page 553.

Exercise 26 Identifying Correct Usage

From the word or words in parentheses in each of the following sentences, choose the answer that is correct according to the rules of formal, standard English.

EXAMPLE 1. Mrs. Lawrence is (*learning, teaching*) us about the Hohokam culture.

 1. teaching

1. The Hohokam civilization (*might of, might have*) begun around 300 B.C.
2. Where did the Hohokam people (*live, live at*)?
3. The Hohokam (*use to, used to*) live in the American Southwest.
4. Hohokam farmers grew their crops in a climate that was (*real, extremely*) dry.
5. The Hohokam irrigated the land by using (*alot, a lot*) of canals—more than six hundred miles of them!
6. (*Them, These*) canals sometimes changed the courses of rivers.
7. The Hohokam were also skilled artisans (*who's, whose*) work included jewelry, bowls, and figurines.
8. I (*can, can't*) hardly imagine what caused the culture to change so much around A.D. 1450.
9. (*Their, They're*) descendants are the Papago and the Pima peoples.
10. We read (*that, where*) one Hohokam site is known as Snaketown.

Reference Note

For information about **common usage errors,** see Chapter 21. For information about **formal, standard English,** see page 553.

Exercise 27 Proofreading Sentences for Correct Usage

Each of the following sentences contains an error in the use of formal, standard English. Identify each error. Then, write the correct usage.

EXAMPLE 1. If that ain't the proper first aid for heat exhaustion, what is?

 1. ain't—isn't

1. During the track meet last Saturday, we used a American Red Cross guidebook for first aid.
2. Fortunately, their was a handy section that was about treating heat exhaustion.
3. The day of the meet, the temperature was hotter then it had been all summer.
4. The athletes were all ready hot by the time that the track meet began.
5. Some of the runners should of been drinking more water than they were.
6. Several of the athletes which were not used to running in such high temperatures needed medical treatment for heat exhaustion.
7. We volunteers helped the runners like the first-aid guidebook instructed.
8. They soon felt alright after we led them out of the heat and helped them cool down.
9. The doctor on duty at the meet examined them and checked they're vital signs.
10. According to the doctor, even athletes in good condition must protect theirselves against heat exhaustion and heatstroke.

Grammar and Usage Test: Section 1

DIRECTIONS   Read the paragraph that follows. For each numbered blank, select the word or word group that best completes the sentence.

EXAMPLE   1.   The platypus is one of __(1)__ mammals that lays eggs.

(A) to
(B) too
(C) two
(D) 2

ANSWER   1.   (A)   (B)   C   (D)

The platypus is __(1)__ very unusual mammal. It __(2)__ external ears, __(3)__ feet are webbed, and it has thick fur. A broad tail and a fleshy bill __(4)__ to the platypus's odd appearance. Platypuses use __(5)__ bills to catch water worms and insects. Besides having a bill like a duck's, a platypus is __(6)__ like a bird than a mammal in another important way. Like a duck, the platypus __(7)__ eggs. The mother deposits __(8)__ in a nest, __(9)__ she has dug in a riverbank. If you get to Australia, you may see a platypus making its nest __(10)__ a burrow.

1. (A) an
   (B) a
   (C) the
   (D) some

2. (A) don't have no
   (B) doesn't have no
   (C) has any
   (D) has no

3. (A) its
   (B) it's
   (C) its'
   (D) their

4. (A) adds
   (B) add
   (C) added
   (D) adding

5. (A) its
   (B) it's
   (C) they're
   (D) their

6. (A) more
   (B) most
   (C) mostly
   (D) least

7. (A) lays
   (B) lies
   (C) is lying
   (D) has lain

8. (A) it
   (B) they
   (C) them
   (D) their

9. **(A)** which
   (B) it
   (C) who
   (D) whom

10. **(A)** inside of
    (B) outside of
    (C) a ways from
    (D) inside

Grammar and Usage Test: Section 2

DIRECTIONS Part or all of each of the following items is underlined. Using the rules of formal, standard English, choose the revision that most clearly expresses the meaning of the item. If there is no error, choose *A*.

EXAMPLE   1. The chopsticks that my aunt sent us made of bamboo.

   (A) The chopsticks that my aunt sent us made of bamboo.
   (B) The chopsticks that my aunt sent us are made of bamboo.
   (C) The chopsticks are made of bamboo, that my aunt sent us.
   (D) That my aunt sent us chopsticks made of bamboo.

ANSWER   1.   A   B   C   D

1. Don't buy none of that ripe fruit if you don't plan to eat it soon.

   (A) Don't buy none of that ripe fruit if you don't plan to eat it soon.
   (B) Do buy none of that ripe fruit if you don't plan to eat it soon.
   (C) Don't buy none of that ripe fruit if you do plan to eat it soon.
   (D) Don't buy any of that ripe fruit if you don't plan to eat it soon.

2. The study group meeting in the library on Wednesday?

   (A) The study group meeting in the library on Wednesday?
   (B) The study group that will be meeting in the library on Wednesday?
   (C) Is the study group meeting in the library on Wednesday?
   (D) Will the study group meeting in the library on Wednesday?

3. Some visitors to the park enjoy rock <u>climbing others prefer kayaking</u>.
   - (A) climbing others prefer kayaking
   - (B) climbing, others prefer kayaking
   - (C) climbing, others, who prefer kayaking
   - (D) climbing, and others prefer kayaking

4. Martin <u>prepares the salad, Justine sets the table</u>.
   - (A) prepares the salad, Justine sets the table
   - (B) prepares the salad, and Justine sets the table
   - (C) prepares the salad Justine sets the table
   - (D) preparing the salad, and Justine sets the table

5. Many Cherokee now live in Oklahoma, but <u>this area were not their original home</u>.
   - (A) this area were not their original home
   - (B) this area was not their original home
   - (C) this area was not they're original home
   - (D) this area were not they're original home

6. <u>Pulling weeds in the garden, a tiny toad was discovered by Ernie.</u>
   - (A) Pulling weeds in the garden, a tiny toad was discovered by Ernie.
   - (B) A tiny toad was discovered pulling weeds in the garden by Ernie.
   - (C) While pulling weeds in the garden, a tiny toad was discovered by Ernie.
   - (D) Pulling weeds in the garden, Ernie discovered a tiny toad.

7. <u>Will rehearse together for the class play.</u>
   - (A) Will rehearse together for the class play.
   - (B) Will be rehearsing together for the class play.
   - (C) We will rehearse together for the class play.
   - (D) Because we will rehearse together for the class play.

8. Some people are <u>more afraider</u> of snakes than of any other kind of animal.

   (A) more afraider

   (B) afraider

   (C) more afraid

   (D) most afraid

9. <u>Several important African kingdoms developed between Lake Chad and the Atlantic Ocean.</u>

   (A) Several important African kingdoms developed between Lake Chad and the Atlantic Ocean.

   (B) Several important African kingdoms that developed between Lake Chad and the Atlantic Ocean.

   (C) Several important African kingdoms between Lake Chad and the Atlantic Ocean.

   (D) Several important African kingdoms developing between Lake Chad and the Atlantic Ocean.

10. <u>The singer waved to some people he knew in the audience from the stage.</u>

   (A) The singer waved to some people he knew in the audience from the stage.

   (B) The singer waved to some people from the stage he knew in the audience.

   (C) The singer waved to some people from the stage in the audience he knew.

   (D) The singer waved from the stage to some people he knew in the audience.

YEAH, I'M WORRIED ALL THE TIME, TOO -- I WISH WE'D NEVER INVENTED THE FUTURE TENSE!

THAVES

┌HELP┐

Some capital letters in Exercise 28 are already used correctly.

Reference Note

For information on **capital letters,** see Chapter 22.

Exercise 28 Correcting Errors in Capitalization

The following groups of words contain errors in capitalization. Correct the errors either by changing capital letters to lowercase letters or by changing lowercase letters to capital letters.

EXAMPLE   1. a buddhist temple
   1. *a Buddhist temple*

1. appalachian state university
2. world history and math 101
3. tuesday, May 1
4. senator williams
5. Summer In texas
6. Thirty-Fifth avenue
7. saturn and the moon
8. a korean Restaurant
9. empire state building
10. will rogers turnpike

Reference Note

For information on **capital letters,** see Chapter 22.

Exercise 29 Proofreading Sentences for Correct Capitalization

For each of the following sentences, find the words that should be capitalized but are not. Then, write the words correctly.

EXAMPLE   1. American indians gave the name Buffalo Soldiers to African American troops who served in the West during the civil war.
   1. *Indians, Civil War*

1. Thirteen Buffalo Soldiers won the congressional medal of honor, which is the highest military award in the United States.
2. *Black frontiers: A history of African american heroes in the Old west,* by Lillian Schlissel, was published in 1995.
3. A chapter about mary fields tells the story of a woman known as Stagecoach Mary who drove freight wagons and stagecoaches in the west.
4. One of the museums listed in the back of the book is the great plains black museum in Omaha, Nebraska.
5. The book also tells about benjamin singleton, who was born into slavery.

6. After the Civil War, he and some others bought land and founded the communities of Nicodemus and dunlap, kansas.

7. The exciting story of the cowboy Nat Love is told in his auto-biography, *the life and adventures of Nat Love.*

8. bill pickett, who was of black, white, and American Indian ancestry, was one of the most famous rodeo competitors of all time.

9. Pickett's biography was published by the university of oklahoma press in 1977.

10. The businessman and gold miner Barney Ford became very wealthy and built ford's hotel on fifteenth street in denver, Colorado.

Exercise 30 Proofreading Sentences for the Correct Use of Commas

For each of the following sentences, write each word or numeral that should be followed by a comma and then add the comma.

EXAMPLE   1. The colors of the French flag are red white and blue.
             1. *red, white,*

Reference Note

For information about **using commas correctly,** see page 602.

1. No the mountain dulcimer is not the same as the hammered dulcimer but both of them are stringed instruments.

2. Abraham Lincoln who was the sixteenth president of the United States died on April 15 1865.

3. If you want to knit a sweater you will need to get knitting needles yarn and a pattern.

4. After oiling the wheels on his sister's wagon Tyrel oiled the wheels on his skates and on his bicycle.

5. Competing in the 10K race Nathan found that he could run faster than his friends.

6. In my opinion a person should be fined if loose trash in the back of his or her pickup truck blows out and litters the road.

7. Lupe please show us how to use the new computer program.

8. Although Cody is afraid of heights he rescued a cat that was stuck high in a tree.

9. I hope that Amy Tan my favorite author will write another book soon.

10. Many people want to conserve resources yet some of these people overlook simple ways to conserve.

COMMON ERRORS

Exercise 31 Using Periods, Question Marks, Exclamation Points, and Commas Correctly

Reference Note

For information about **end marks,** see page 598. For information about **commas,** see page 602.

The following sentences lack necessary periods, question marks, exclamation points, and commas. Write the word before each missing punctuation mark, and insert the correct punctuation.

EXAMPLE   1. When will Anita Luís Martina and Sam be back from the mall

　　　　　　1. *Anita, Luís, Martina, mall?*

1. Wow look at the size of that alligator
2. Leaning against the mast I could feel the sails catch the wind
3. Won't these new colorful curtains brighten this room
4. By the way that stack of newspapers should be recycled
5. Oil paints whether used for art projects or home improvement should be used only in well-ventilated areas
6. Hidiko watch out for that cactus
7. Was Uncle Jesse born in Cincinnati Ohio or Louisville Kentucky
8. As far as I am concerned the most interesting parts of the lecture were about the life of W E B DuBois
9. Monday Tuesday or Wednesday will be fine for our next meeting
10. Would you like to watch a movie tonight or should I bring over the model-plane kit to work on together

Exercise 32 Using Semicolons and Colons Correctly

Reference Note

For information about **semicolons and colons,** see page 618.

The following sentences lack necessary semicolons and colons. Write the words or numerals that come before and after the needed punctuation, and insert the correct punctuation.

EXAMPLE   1. Elena learned Spanish and English at home she learned French and German at school.

　　　　　　1. *home; she*

1. They should be here before 9 30 this morning.
2. Our recycling center accepts the following materials glass, newspaper, cardboard, and aluminum cans.
3. The landscape designer planted bushes around the school last fall she will plant flowers this spring.
4. Please be at the station by 2 15 P.M.

5. The children wanted to see bears, lions, and elephants but parrots, snakes, tortoises, and goats were the only animals there.

6. The sermon was based on Isaiah 61 1.

7. To refinish this dresser, we will need some supplies varnish remover, sandpaper, steel wool, wood stain, and a clear polyurethane sealant.

8. Walking is terrific exercise it improves both your stamina and your muscle tone.

9. Many children's books have beautiful illustrations some are worth having just for the art.

10. Many palaces in Europe are spectacular Linderhof in Bavaria is my favorite.

Exercise 33 Punctuating and Capitalizing Quotations and Titles

For each of the following sentences, correct any capitalization errors and add or change quotation marks and other marks of punctuation where needed.

Reference Note

For information about **punctuating and capitalizing quotations,** see page 630.

EXAMPLE
1. I learned how to play a new virtual-reality game today Pat said.

1. *"I learned how to play a new virtual-reality game today," Pat said.*

1. The most helpful chapter in my computer manual is "Search Tips" I explained to her.

2. Do Asian cobras look like African cobras Shawn asked.

3. I want to go to the fair after school Ivan said but my trumpet lesson is today.

4. The pilot said we are now beginning our descent into Orlando. Please fasten your seat belts, and return your seats to the upright position.

5. Goodness! what a surprise Taka exclaimed

6. Did some famous person say A smile is contagious

7. Cyclists should always wear helmets said the safety officer

8. Was it he who said a penny saved is a penny earned Troy asked

9. Carlos shouted, look at that dolphin near our boat!

10. During his speech at our school, the mayor said Our children are our future

Exercise 34 Punctuating and Capitalizing Quotations and Titles

For each of the following sentences, correct any capitalization errors and add or change quotation marks and other marks of punctuation where needed.

EXAMPLE   1. Sheila asked have you read about Rigoberta Menchú?

       1. Sheila asked, *"Have you read about Rigoberta Menchú?"*

1. She has lived a remarkable life Ernesto said and I admire her very much
2. Angela exclaimed yes, I know about Menchú!
3. Menchú is from Guatemala said Mrs. Harper She won the Nobel Peace Prize in 1992.
4. I once wrote about Menchú in a poem called "The Heart of a Peacemaker" Gale said.
5. I think Rigoberta Menchú is a great role model Carla said.
6. Menchú has tried to make life better for the laborers. Her own family is of Quiché heritage explained Mark
7. Did Stephanie say My dream is to meet Rigoberta Menchú asked Ryan
8. Yes, and I'd like to meet her too exclaimed Emilio.
9. Mark continued Menchú worked long hours on cotton and coffee plantations when she was a child.
10. Menchú's autobiography is *I . . . Rigoberta Menchú* said Mrs. Harper.

Exercise 35 Using Apostrophes Correctly

Add, delete, or move apostrophes where needed in the following word groups. If a word group is already correct, write *C.*

EXAMPLE   1. both boys shoes

       1. *boys'*

1. somebodys lunch
2. cant play
3. Neals motorcycle
4. better than theirs
5. womens volleyball
6. too many letter *us*
7. its engine
8. Betsy Rosss flag
9. no more *ifs*
10. the bushes branches

Exercise 36 Correcting Spelling Errors

Most of the following words are misspelled. If a word is spelled incorrectly, write the correct spelling. If a word is already spelled correctly, write *C*.

Reference Note
For information on **spelling rules,** see page 656.

EXAMPLE   1. succede

1. *succeed*

1. taxs	8. stathood	15. improper
2. vien	9. lovelyer	16. fancifuly
3. supercede	10. clearest	17. dryest
4. disallow	11. wolfs	18. cluless
5. countrys	12. sheild	19. overjoied
6. emptyness	13. preceed	20. skiping
7. tracable	14. father-in-laws	

Exercise 37 Choosing Between Words Often Confused

From each pair in parentheses, choose the word or words that make the sentence correct.

Reference Note
For information on **words often confused,** see page 666.

EXAMPLE   1. The school plans to (*except, accept*) the new computer company's offer.

1. *accept*

1. Did Coach Jefferson (*advise, advice*) you to take the first-aid course at the community center?
2. My cousins and I are (*all ready, already*) to enter the marathon.
3. Sacramento became the (*capital, capitol*) of California in 1854.
4. When garden hoses (*brake, break*), they sometimes can be mended with waterproof tape.
5. Avoid wearing (*loose, lose*) clothing when operating that equipment.
6. Many people know Mr. Perez, but I think he should be (*formerly, formally*) introduced.
7. My grandfather threw the football (*passed, past*) the trees and over the creek.
8. (*Its, It's*) a good idea to test home smoke detectors frequently to make sure the batteries are still working.
9. One basic (*principle, principal*) of our Constitution is the right to free speech.
10. Some cats are called bobtails because of (*their, there*) very short tails.

Mechanics Test: Section 1

DIRECTIONS Each numbered item below consists of an underlined word or word group. Choose the answer that shows the correct capitalization, punctuation, and spelling of the underlined part. If there is no error, choose D (Correct as is).

EXAMPLE [1] 29 South Maple street

        (A) 29 south Maple Street
        (B) 29 South Maple Street
        (C) Twenty Nine South Maple Street
        (D) Correct as is

ANSWER   1.   A   B   C   D

---

29 South Maple Street
Philadelphia, PA 19107

[1] January 15 2001

Mail-Order Sales Manager
[2] Direct Electronics, Inc.

214-C Billings Boulevard
[3] New Castle, Ken. 40050

[4] Dear Sales Manager,

The modem that I ordered from your company arrived today in [5] peices. The package was [6] open, and appeared not to have been sealed properly. [7] In addition I have not yet received the computer game that I also ordered. Please send me a new [8] modem the broken modem is enclosed.

I appreciate [9] you're prompt attention to both of these matters.

[10] Sincerely yours,

Cameron Scott

Cameron Scott

COMMON ERRORS

1. (A) January 15, 2001
   (B) January, 15 2001
   (C) January 15th 2001
   (D) Correct as is

2. (A) direct electronics, inc.
   (B) Direct electronics, inc.
   (C) Direct Electronics, inc.
   (D) Correct as is

3. (A) New Castle Ken. 40050
   (B) New Castle, KY 40050
   (C) New Castle KY, 40050
   (D) Correct as is

4. (A) Dear sales manager,
   (B) dear sales manager:
   (C) Dear Sales Manager:
   (D) Correct as is

5. (A) pieces
   (B) piece's
   (C) peaces
   (D) Correct as is

6. (A) open and appeared
   (B) open; and appeared
   (C) open, and, appeared
   (D) Correct as is

7. (A) In addition, I
   (B) In addition i
   (C) In addition, i
   (D) Correct as is

8. (A) modem, the
   (B) modem; the
   (C) modem: the
   (D) Correct as is

9. (A) youre
   (B) your,
   (C) your
   (D) Correct as is

10. (A) Sincerely Yours',
    (B) Sincerely your's,
    (C) Sincerely yours:
    (D) Correct as is

Mechanics Test: Section 2

DIRECTIONS   Each of the following sentences contains an underlined word or word group. Choose the answer that shows the correct capitalization, punctuation, and spelling of the underlined part. If there is no error, choose D (Correct as is).

EXAMPLE   1.   Rosie said that her cousin sent her that <u>soft colorful fabric</u> from Kenya.

   (A) soft, colorful, fabric
   (B) soft, colorful fabric
   (C) soft; colorful fabric
   (D) Correct as is

ANSWER   1.   A   B   C   D

1. The following people have volunteered to make <u>enchiladas, Manuel</u>, Shawn, and Anita.

   (A) enchiladas; Manuel   (C) enchiladas: Manuel
   (B) enchiladas. Manuel   (D) Correct as is

2. Our school's <u>recycling program which</u> is now three years old, has been quite successful.

   (A) recycling program, which   (C) recycling program; which
   (B) Recycling Program, which   (D) Correct as is

3. <u>Looking at the astronomical map in my science book I</u> spotted the constellations Orion, Taurus, and Pisces.

   (A) Looking at the astronomical map, in my science book I
   (B) Looking at the astronomical map, in my science book, I
   (C) Looking at the astronomical map in my science book, I
   (D) Correct as is

4. Donna <u>asked, "who</u> plans to work as a baby sitter over the summer?"

   (A) asked, "Who   (C) asked, Who
   (B) asked "who   (D) Correct as is

5. Angela and Wanda painted the <u>mural, and Jamal</u> attached it to the wall in the gym.

   (A) mural and Jamal   (C) mural, and jamal
   (B) mural: and Jamal   (D) Correct as is

6. Many television programs have closed captioning for <u>people who cant</u> hear.

   (A) people, who cant   (C) people who can't
   (B) people, who can't   (D) Correct as is

7. "What a great time we had at the <u>park"! Sandy</u> exclaimed as she got into the car.

   (A) Park"! Sandy   (C) park", Sandy
   (B) park!" Sandy   (D) Correct as is

8. <u>"Your aunt Helen</u> certainly is a fascinating person," Carla said.

   (A) "Your Aunt Helen   (C) Your aunt Helen
   (B) "Your aunt, Helen   (D) Correct as is

9. "Many of us would have gone to the picnic if we had known about <u>it</u>" Alan said.

   (A) it",
   (B) it,"
   (C) it,
   (D) Correct as is

10. The Zunigas have a new <u>puppy; its</u> a cocker spaniel.

   (A) puppy; Its
   (B) puppy; it's
   (C) puppy, its
   (D) Correct as is

11. The ants <u>carried large leafs</u> across John Henry's backyard.

   (A) carryed large leafs
   (B) carryed large leaves
   (C) carried large leaves
   (D) Correct as is

12. Has the guide <u>all ready led</u> the hikers to the top of the mesa?

   (A) all ready lead
   (B) already lead
   (C) already led
   (D) Correct as is

13. If Carlos wants to play the role of Eddie in the <u>musical, he'll have too practice</u> the solos.

   (A) musical, he'll have to practice
   (B) musical; he'll have to practice
   (C) musical he'll have too practice
   (D) Correct as is

14. <u>Sara said that the big guppy in the class aquarium is going to have babies.</u>

   (A) Sara said "That the big guppy in the class aquarium is going to have babies."
   (B) Sara said "that the big guppy in the class aquarium is going to have babies."
   (C) Sara said "That the big guppy in the class aquarium is going to have babies".
   (D) Correct as is

15. On <u>October 1 1960</u> Nigeria became an independent nation.

   (A) October, 1 1960
   (B) October 1, 1960,
   (C) October 1, 1960
   (D) Correct as is

Quick Reference Handbook

The Dictionary

Types and Contents

Types of Dictionaries Different types of dictionaries provide different kinds of information. You should choose a dictionary based on the kind of information that you need. The chart below explains the differences among three types of dictionaries; abridged, specialized, and unabridged. It also provides an example of each type of dictionary.

Dictionary Entry A dictionary entry gives more than just the meaning of a word. A sample entry from an abridged dictionary appears on the next page. The callout explanations that follow the entry explain what kinds of information an entry provides.

Types of Dictionaries	
Type	**Example**
An **abridged** dictionary is the most common type of dictionary. The word *abridged* means "shortened" or "condensed." An abridged dictionary contains most of the words you are likely to use or encounter in your writing or reading.	*Merriam-Webster's Collegiate Dictionary, Tenth Edition*
A **specialized** dictionary defines words or terms that are used in a particular profession, field, or area of interest.	*Stedman's Medical Dictionary*
An **unabridged** dictionary contains nearly all the words in use in a language.	*Webster's Third New International Dictionary*

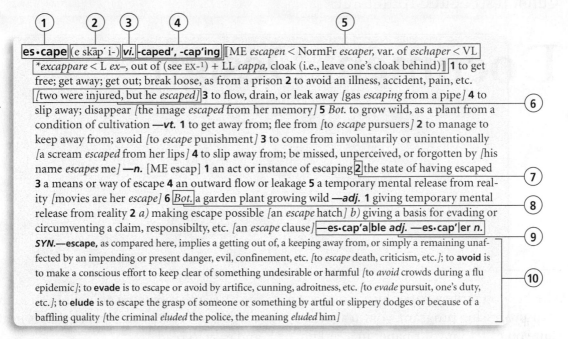

es·cape (e skāp′ i-) vi. -caped′, -cap′ing [ME escapen < NormFr escaper, var. of eschaper < VL *excappare < L ex–, out of (see EX-[1]) + LL cappa, cloak (i.e., leave one's cloak behind)] 1 to get free; get away; get out; break loose, as from a prison 2 to avoid an illness, accident, pain, etc. [two were injured, but he escaped] 3 to flow, drain, or leak away [gas escaping from a pipe] 4 to slip away; disappear [the image escaped from her memory] 5 Bot. to grow wild, as a plant from a condition of cultivation —vt. 1 to get away from; flee from [to escape pursuers] 2 to manage to keep away from; avoid [to escape punishment] 3 to come from involuntarily or unintentionally [a scream escaped from her lips] 4 to slip away from; be missed, unperceived, or forgotten by [his name escapes me] —n. [ME escap] 1 an act or instance of escaping 2 the state of having escaped 3 a means or way of escape 4 an outward flow or leakage 5 a temporary mental release from reality [movies are her escape] 6 Bot. a garden plant growing wild —adj. 1 giving temporary mental release from reality 2 a) making escape possible [an escape hatch] b) giving a basis for evading or circumventing a claim, responsibilty, etc. [an escape clause] —es·cap′a|ble adj. —es·cap′|er n.
SYN.—escape, as compared here, implies a getting out of, a keeping away from, or simply a remaining unaffected by an impending or present danger, evil, confinement, etc. [to escape death, criticism, etc.]; to avoid is to make a conscious effort to keep clear of something undesirable or harmful [to avoid crowds during a flu epidemic]; to evade is to escape or avoid by artifice, cunning, adroitness, etc. [to evade pursuit, one's duty, etc.]; to elude is to escape the grasp of someone or something by artful or slippery dodges or because of a baffling quality [the criminal eluded the police, the meaning eluded him]

1. **Entry word**   The *entry word* shows the correct spelling of a word. An alternate spelling may also be shown. The entry word shows how the word should be divided into syllables, and it may show whether the word should be capitalized.
2. **Pronunciation**   The pronunciation of a word is shown using accent marks, phonetic symbols, and diacritical marks. *Accent marks* show stress. Each *phonetic symbol* represents a specific sound. *Diacritical marks* are symbols placed above letters to show how they sound.
3. **Part-of-speech labels**   These labels are usually abbreviated and show how the entry word should be used in a sentence. Some words may be used as more than one part of speech.
4. **Other forms**   A dictionary may show spellings of plural forms of nouns, tenses of verbs, or the comparative forms of adjectives and adverbs.
5. **Etymology**   The *etymology* tells how a word (or its parts) entered the English language. The etymology also shows how the word has changed over time.
6. **Examples**   A dictionary may demonstrate how a word may be used by giving phrases or sentences containing that word.
7. **Definitions**   If there is more than one meaning for a word, the definitions are separated by numbers or letters.
8. **Special usage labels**   These labels identify the fields in which a word has a special meaning, such as *Bot.* (botany), or how it is used in special ways, such as *Slang* or *Rare.*
9. **Related word forms**   These are other forms of the entry word, such as another form of the word that is created by adding suffixes or prefixes, or a common phrase in which the entry word appears.
10. **Synonyms and antonyms**   Words that are similar in meaning are *synonyms.* Words that are opposite in meaning are *antonyms.* Dictionaries may list synonyms and antonyms at the end of some word entries.

Document Design

Manuscript Style

Whether you write a paper by hand or use a word-processing program, your teacher will want you to set up your paper in a certain way. Use the following guidelines to prepare a typed or handwritten paper that is neat and easy to read.

Guidelines for Manuscript Style

1. Use only one side of each sheet of paper.

2. Type your paper using a word processor, or write it neatly in blue or black ink.

3. For handwritten papers, ask your teacher if he or she wants you to skip lines. For typed papers or word-processed papers, many teachers prefer that you double-space your assignment.

4. Leave one-inch margins at the top, bottom, and sides of your paper.

5. The first line of every paragraph should be indented five spaces. You can set a **tab** on a word processor to indent five spaces automatically.

6. Number all pages in the top right-hand corner. Do not number the first page.

7. Make sure your pages look neat and clean. For handwritten papers, you may want to use correction fluid to correct your mistakes. If you have several mistakes on one page, however, write out the page again. For papers typed on a word processor, you can make corrections and print out a clean copy.

8. Use the heading your teacher prefers for your name, your class, the date, and the title of your paper. Your teacher may prefer that you list this information on a title page. If so, use a separate sheet of paper and place the information your teacher requests in the center of the sheet. Put only one piece of information on each line, and center-align the text. (See page 723.)

Desktop Publishing

Which would you be more likely to read: a report that contains page after page of poorly arranged text, or one that contains both neatly arranged text and eye-catching graphics? You can create attractive reports, newsletters, and other documents by using *desktop publishing*. **Desktop publishing** is a way of using a personal computer to create attractive documents that contain both text and graphics. However, even if you do not have access to a computer, you can use many of the ideas discussed below to help you design a better-looking handwritten paper.

The information in the following section will help you arrange the text of your document. For information about how you can use graphics to make your ideas clearer to readers, see also **Graphics** on page 728.

Page Layout

Page layout refers to how a page is arranged. To create an effective page layout, you must decide the best way to arrange text and graphics on the page. As you prepare to lay out the design of your page, consider the following page layout features.

Alignment   The term *alignment* refers to the arrangement of lines of text on the page. Text can be *left-*, *right-*, or *center-aligned*. Alignment can also be *ragged* or *justified*. Aligning your text properly can help you produce a neat, easy-to-read document.

- **Left-aligned**   When a section of text is *left-aligned,* each line begins at the left margin of the page or column. Since

English is read from left to right, most blocks of text are left-aligned.

EXAMPLE
These lines of text are left-aligned. Notice that each line begins at the left margin of the column.

- **Right-aligned**   Text that is *right-aligned* lines up against the right margin of the page or column. In reports, your name, the date, and page numbers may be right-aligned. Usually, only small amounts of text are right-aligned, because right-aligned text is difficult to read. Quotes pulled from poetry or other writing are sometimes right-aligned to make them stand out more. (See also **Pull-quote** on page 725.)

EXAMPLE
These lines of text are right-aligned. All of the text is lined up against the right margin of the column.

- **Center-aligned**   Text that is *center-aligned* is centered on an invisible line down the middle of the page or column. Centered text is frequently used for titles or other information, especially in posters, advertisements, and cards.

EXAMPLE
These lines are center-aligned. They are centered on an imaginary line down the middle of the column.

■ **Justified**   Text that is *justified* forms a straight edge along the right and left margins. However, spaces must be added to the lines to make sure each edge lines up. (The last line in justified text may be shorter than the other lines.) Justified text can give your document a neat, clean look.

EXAMPLE

This text is justified. The text forms a straight edge along the right and left margins of the column.

■ **Ragged**   Text that is *ragged* does not line up on both sides. When ragged text is right-aligned, each line forms a neat edge on the right but not on the left. When ragged text is left-aligned, each line forms a neat edge on the left but not on the right.

EXAMPLE

These lines are left-aligned and ragged. Each line forms a neat edge on the left but not on the right.

Bullet   A *bullet* (•) is a large dot or other symbol used to call attention to information. Brief, important pieces of information, such as instructions or lists, are easier to read when listed with bullets. The following bulleted list gives some guidelines for using bullets.

■ Make sure your bulleted list contains at least two items.

■ Be sure that each item in your list begins with the same type of wording. For example, each item in this bullet list begins with an imperative sentence, which is a sentence that gives a command.

■ Line up text within a bulleted item beneath the first letter of the first word, not beneath the bullet itself. For example, all of the text after the first line of this bulleted item lines up beneath the word *Line.*

Contrast   The balance of light and dark areas on a page is called *contrast.* Light areas have very little text and few, if any, pictures. Dark areas contain lots of text and perhaps pictures or other graphics. Pages with high contrast—or a good mix of both light and dark areas—are easier to read than pages with low contrast.

Emphasis   *Emphasis* is a designer's way of showing readers the most important information on a page. You can create emphasis by putting a box around important information or by experimenting with text size or style. Emphasis can also be created by using color and graphics. All of these techniques are used in the sample newspaper layout shown below.

THE WEEKLY TRUMPET
The Voice of Miller Middle School
January 30, 2001

Teen Triathlete Triumphs!

Millersville

What is a Triathlon?

Gutter   A *gutter* is the inner margin of space from the printed area of a page to the book's binding.

Headers and Footers   A writer uses *headers* and *footers* to provide information about a document. Headers appear in the top margin of a page, and footers appear in the bottom margin of a page. Headers and footers frequently contain information such as the following:

- author's name
- publication's name
- publication date
- chapter or section title
- page numbers

Headings and Subheadings   Titles within the sections of a document are called *headings* and *subheadings.* Headings and subheadings (also called *heads* and *subheads*) show readers how information in a document is organized.

- **Headings** are titles for major sections of text. A heading appears at the beginning of the section of text and is often in large, bold, or capital letters. (See also **Type** on page 726.)

- **Subheadings** are more specific headings within a major section. A writer uses subheadings to break a section into smaller sections so that readers can easily find the information they need. To make a subheading stand out, it may be set in a different size or design of type than that of the main text.

EXAMPLE

Information Just ———(heading)
a Click Away
The Internet Is Changing———(subheading)
How We Get the Weather
Forecast

Not so long ago, if you wanted ———(text) to find out the weather forecast, you had to flip on the television at the right time. If you turned it on five minutes too early, you had to wait; if you turned it on five minutes too late, you were out of luck. Now, with the help of the Internet, you can go online any time during the day and find out the forecast.

Indentation   When you *indent* text, you move the text a few spaces to the right of the left margin. The standard amount of indentation for beginning a new paragraph is five spaces or half an inch.

Margins   The *margin* on a page is the blank space that surrounds the text on the sides, the top, and bottom. Many word-processing programs commonly set margins at 1.25 inches for the sides and 1 inch for the top and bottom. However, you can change the margins to fit more or less text on the page. Make sure you check with your teacher before changing your margins on an assignment.

Pull-quote   A *pull-quote* is a direct quotation pulled out of a text and made into a graphic within the story. For example, an important quote may be taken from a magazine article and set in the margin of that article to attract a reader's attention. Pull-quotes should be short. They may even be just part of a sentence instead of a complete one.

EXAMPLE

Microbes, the tiny forms of life that many think of as "germs" or "bugs," are everywhere. They have been discovered living in sediments found over five hundred meters beneath the ocean bed. They even exist inside of rocks. Microbes indeed surround us.

Microbes indeed surround us.

Rules   A *rule* is a vertical or horizontal line used to set off text from other elements such as headlines and graphics. Vertical rules can separate columns on a page.

Titles and Subtitles   The *title* of a document is its name. A *subtitle* is usually longer and more descriptive than a title. You may find a title followed by a colon and a subtitle, but if the title appears on its own line, no colon is necessary. Titles and subtitles of books appear on a title page at the beginning of the book.

EXAMPLE

Going to the Extreme
A Guide to Snowboarding, Skateboarding, and Other Extreme Sports

White Space   On a page, any area where there is no text or graphics is called *white space.* Proper use of white space can make a page look neater; it can also make a page easier to read. Usually, white space is limited to the margins; the gutter; and the spaces between words, lines, and columns. (See also **Contrast** on page 724.)

Type

Type refers to the characters that make up printed text. When you create a document, you must make several decisions about type. For example, you must decide which size and design of type is best for your document. Making thoughtful decisions about type can help you produce an eye-catching, easy-to-read document.

Font   The term *font* is used to describe a set of characters (such as numbers, letters, and punctuation marks) of a particular design and size. For example, 12-point Times Roman is a font. The font size is twelve points (see below); the font design is Times Roman. Many different computer fonts are available. A font design is also called a *typeface.*

Font Size   The size of type in a document is known as the *font size,* or *point size.* The size of type is measured in points, each of which is $\frac{1}{72}$ of an inch. School assignments are usually printed in twelve-point type. Captions for pictures are usually printed in smaller sizes. Titles may be printed in point sizes that are larger than the point size of the main text.

EXAMPLE

Title ————————(24 point)
Text text text text ——(12 point)
Caption caption caption ——(9 point)

Font Style   The *font style* refers to the way the type is printed. A different font style may be used to emphasize words or phrases. For example, important words in a passage are frequently printed in *italics.* Other styles of font, such as **boldface,** can be used to set off headings, subheadings, subtitles, or other parts from the main text. Look at the examples of font styles below.

- **Boldface**   A *boldface* word is written in thick, heavy type. Boldface can be used to emphasize information.

  EXAMPLE
  This sentence is written in boldface type.

- **Capital letters**   A *capital* (or *uppercase*) *letter* signals a proper name, the beginning of a sentence, a title, and so on. Headings and subheadings may appear in all capital letters. For emphasis, a writer will sometimes put a word or a sentence in all capital letters. However, this strategy should not be overused.

- **Condensed**   When type is *condensed,* the letters in a word have less space between them. Writers may use condensed type to save space.

  EXAMPLE
  This sentence is written in condensed type.

- **Expanded**   When type is *expanded,* the letters in a word have more space between them. Writers may use expanded type to fill up space.

  EXAMPLE
  This sentence is written in expanded type.

- **Italics**   Type that is *italic* has a slanted style. Italic type can be used to emphasize information. It is also used to cite titles in text and in other conventional situations. (For more on **italics,** see page 628.)

EXAMPLE
This sentence is written in italic type.

- **Lowercase letters**   A *lowercase letter* is not a capital or a small capital. (See **Small capitals** below.) Lowercase letters are the most frequently used letters.

- **Shadow**   A word written in *shadow* style appears to cast shadows. Shadow style may be used for titles and headings.

  EXAMPLE
  This sentence is written in shadow style.

- **Small capitals**   When writing abbreviations referring to time, use *small capitals.* For example, when typing the time 12:05 P.M. and year A.D. 1066, you should use small capitals.

Leading   Another word for *line spacing,* or the distance between lines of text, is *leading* (rhymes with *wedding*). Most word-processing programs allow you to adjust the amount of space between each line. Most formal documents you create for your teacher are double-spaced. Double-spaced papers make it easier for your teacher to read your assignment and make corrections or comments on the page. Books, magazines, and newspapers, which are meant for a general audience, are single-spaced.

Legibility   A *legible* document has text and graphics that are clear and easily recognizable. A document with high legibility uses a simple, easy-to-read font size and design for the main text.

Typeface   See **Font** on page 726.

Graphics

Graphics can often communicate information more quickly and effectively than words. Graphics you can use in your documents include *charts, diagrams, graphs, illustrations,* and *tables.* Graphics can

- show information
- explain how to do something
- show how something looks, works, or is organized
- show developments over a period of time

Graphics have the most impact when they support text information on the page where they appear. When designed carefully, graphics and text work together to communicate the same message clearly.

Arrangement and Design

The following arrangement and design ideas can help you create informative and effective graphics.

Accuracy   When creating your graphic, make sure the information it contains is *accurate.* In other words, make sure your graphic contains true information.

Color   Readers are attracted to colorful graphics. You can use color to do the following:

- get readers' attention
- emphasize certain information
- group items on a page
- help organize a page or document

Keep the following tips in mind when you choose colors for your graphics.

- *Create a color scheme.* A color scheme is a collection of two or more colors that work well together. Using only one color can make your document look dull.

- *Choose complementary colors.* Colors that are too close to each other on the color wheel (see below) will tend to blend together. Instead, use colors that are opposite each other on the wheel. Colors that are opposite each other are considered *complements.* Color schemes work best when they combine complementary colors.

- *Do not overuse warm colors.* Warm colors, such as red, orange, and yellow, seem to jump off the page. Using them less often creates a more dramatic effect when you do use them.

- *Use cool colors to create a softer effect.* Cool colors, such as blue and green, can work well as backgrounds because they will not overpower your text and graphics.

Color wheels, like the one below, show how colors relate to each other. The three *primary colors* are red, blue, and yellow. All other colors are made by combining the primary colors or by mixing them with white or black.

Focus   The subject of a graphic is the graphic's *focus*. Answer these questions to make sure your graphic has a clear focus.

- *Is the graphic's subject clear?* Make sure your graphic has a clear title that describes the subject.

- *Does the graphic have any unnecessary details?* Any detail that does not make your idea clearer can be distracting. Crop or trim out the distracting details to make the graphic's focus clear.

- *Does the graphic show all of the subject, or are some parts hidden from view?* Make sure the reader can see all important parts of the subject.

- *Does the graphic need labels?* Labeling the graphic can help readers understand it better. Make sure not to use too many labels, however. Too many labels can confuse the reader and make the graphic look cluttered.

- *Is a source provided for the information in the graphic?* Telling readers where you found the facts in your visual can show that the information is trustworthy.

    Make sure that the focus of your graphic supports your text.

Labels and Captions   If your graphic needs explanation, add *labels* and *captions*. *Labels* either appear within the graphic or are connected to it by thin lines called *rules*. Labels identify important parts of a graphic. A *caption* is a sentence that explains a graphic. Photographs and illustrations often have captions. A caption appears directly beside, above, or under the graphic. If you do not use labels or captions in your graphic, make sure your graphic has a clear, descriptive title.

Types of Graphics

Use the definitions and examples that follow to choose graphics that will make your ideas clear to readers. Once you decide on the type of graphics you will use in your document, you can create the graphics by computer or by hand.

Chart   A *chart* helps show how pieces of information relate to each other. Two of the most common types of charts are flowcharts and pie charts.

- **Flowcharts**   *Flowcharts* show a sequence, or order, of events. The boxes in a flowchart contain text, and they are set in order from left to right or top to bottom. Many flowcharts contain arrows to show the direction to read.

EXAMPLE

Planning a Party

Choose a date and reason for your party.

Plan the food, drinks, and activities.

Make a list of guests and send out invitations.

Buy supplies.

Have fun!

■ **Pie charts**   *Pie charts* show percentages, or how parts of a whole relate to each other. Pie charts are often used to show comparisons. (For an example of a pie chart, see page 750.)

Diagram   A *diagram* uses pictures and symbols, such as arrows or circles, to compare abstract ideas or to provide instruction. A diagram may show how to do something or how something works. Diagrams contain only the most important information, leaving out unnecessary details. They may be drawn by hand or by using a computer program.

EXAMPLE

The Greenhouse Effect

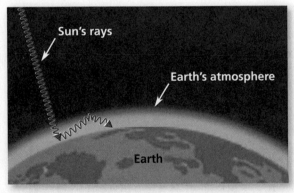

Graphs   A *graph* can show changes over time in a way that allows readers to understand the changes at a glance. A line graph is often used to show the patterns of change, or trends. Bar graphs are usually used to show comparisons. The horizontal axis (the bottom line) in a line or bar graph usually shows periods or points in time. The vertical axis (the line to the left side of the graph) usually shows amounts.

EXAMPLES

Line Graph

Bar Graph

Illustration   An *illustration* is a drawing or photograph that can show readers unfamiliar, new, or hard-to-describe items or events; the way something works; how to do something; or what something or someone looks like. (See also **Diagram** on this page; see also page 789.)

Storyboard A *storyboard* illustrates the different segments or scenes of an event or story. Storyboards are frequently used to map out a story or to plan a video. A storyboard contains several boxes, each representing one scene in the story. The boxes contain drawings and some text. If the storyboard will be used for a video, the narrator's or actors' words will appear as a caption outside the box. Most storyboards are drawn by hand, although the text may be typed. (See also page 259.)

Table A *table* provides raw information without showing trends or patterns. While readers of graphs can immediately see an increase or decrease, readers of tables must look at all of the information and draw their own conclusions. After studying the following tables, for example, a reader could conclude that teen volunteerism rose for three years in a row and that most of the volunteers were fifteen years old. A reader might also predict that teen volunteerism will continue to rise in the future.

EXAMPLES

Two-column Table

Number of Teen Volunteers in Hastings by Year	
Year	Number of Teen Volunteers
1999	15
2000	17
2001	27

Three-column Table

Number of Retirement Home Volunteers by Age and School		
Age of teens	Jamestown High	Boomer High
14	1	2
15	5	8
16	3	5
17	2	1

When making a table, be sure to organize information logically and label information clearly so that your readers will understand your point.

Time Line A *time line* shows events that happen over a period of time. The points along the horizontal axis of a time line show points in time. The events that happen during a specific year or period of years are described above or below the time line. Time lines may also include small illustrations.

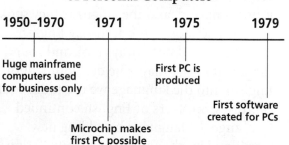

Events in the Creation of Personal Computers

The History of English

Origins and Uses

A Changing Language

A family tree shows the ancestors of a particular family. The English language has a family tree that sprang up thousands of years ago. A single early language grew into different branches. Each branch represented a different language, and one of these languages was English. No one knows exactly when English branched off as a separate language. However, we do know that a form of English was spoken by tribes of people who invaded the island of Britain in the fifth century. These tribes conquered the area that is now England, and the language they spoke was the ancestor of modern-day English.

English did not always look and sound the way it does today. The development of English into the language we use today took centuries. Speakers of English continued to change the language by adding new words and by changing the pronunciation, spelling, and meaning of existing words.

Changes in Spelling Would you recognize the words *threo, sumor,* or *sceap*?

Believe it or not, you know the meanings of these common words, but their spelling has changed over time. The modern spellings are *three, summer,* and *sheep*. Time is not the only reason that a word's spelling changes. Different spellings of a word can be standard in different places. For example, in the United States standard spellings include *color, theater,* and *tire*. In Great Britain, these words are spelled *colour, theatre,* and *tyre*.

Changes in Pronunciation By the 1300s, written English looked similar to the English we use now, but the words were pronounced differently. For example, *meek* was pronounced like *make, boot* like *boat*, and *mouse* like *moose*.

Changes in pronunciation explain why many English words are not spelled the way they sound. For example, the word *knight* used to begin with a strong *k* sound. The letter remained part of the spelling even though the *k* sound was eventually dropped.

Changes in Meaning   What if your mother accused you of being nice and your teacher complimented you for being awful? If you lived during the Middle Ages, you would understand that *awful* is appropriate for a compliment while being called *nice* would be an insult. During the Middle Ages, *nice* meant "lazy" or "foolish," and *awful* meant "very impressive." Today, these words have almost the opposite meanings.

Meanings of words are still changing today. Some words change their meaning as a result of their usage. For example, the word *cool* can mean "excellent" in informal English. Other words may change their meanings in different locations. A *bonnet* means "a hat" in the United States, but in Great Britain, it means "the hood of a car."

Word Origins   English is a multicultural language. Only about 15 percent of the words we use are native to English. The other 85 percent are words that we have borrowed from other languages and cultures. When you say you want to *munch* a *burrito* or *feast* on *chop suey*, you have borrowed words from other languages. Here are some other examples of words that English has borrowed in the past one thousand years.

AFRICAN LANGUAGES	gumbo, okra
FRENCH	beauty, dance, study
LATIN	area, candle, decorate, joke
NATIVE AMERICAN LANGUAGES	bayou, chipmunk, squash
NORSE	fellow, get, leg
SPANISH	chili, hurricane, mustang

Dialects of American English

You probably know people who pronounce words differently than you do or use words in unfamiliar ways. Maybe these same people think your English is "different," too. The variety of English comes from various **dialects,** which are the ways that different groups of people speak English. Although dialects vary widely, no dialect is better or worse than another. In this section, you will learn about two types of American English dialects, *ethnic dialects* and *regional dialects*.

Ethnic Dialects   People who share the same cultural heritage may share a dialect of English, too. The English used by a particular cultural group is called an **ethnic dialect**. Widely used American ethnic dialects include the Black English of many African Americans and the Spanish-influenced English of many people whose families come from Mexico, Central America, Cuba, and Puerto Rico.

Many words that are now part of general English usage originally came from ethnic dialects. For example, the words *afro*, *jazz*, and *jukebox* were originally Black English dialect words, and *arroyo*, *mesa*, and *taco* were originally from Hispanic English.

Regional Dialects   Do you eat *lunch* or *dinner*? Do you *wash* (or *warsh*) the *car* (or *cah*)? Do you stand *on* line or *in* line? Where you come from can help determine what words you use, how you pronounce them, and how you put words together. A dialect shared by people from the same area of the United States is called a **regional dialect**.

Not everyone who lives in a region uses that region's dialect. Someone from Alabama or Georgia might not say *y'all,* and someone from Boston may not pronounce *farm* like *fahm.* When people move from place to place, they often lose some of their old dialect and learn a new one.

Standard American English

Every variety of English has its own set of guidelines, but no variety is better or more correct than another. However, one form of English is more widely used and accepted than others in the United States. This variety is called ***standard American English.***

Standard American English is a variety that people from many different regions and cultures can understand. It is the variety you hear on radio and television and read in books and magazines, and it is the form people are expected to use in school and business situations.

Part 3: Grammar, Usage, and Mechanics in this textbook will help you understand the rules for using standard American English. The label *nonstandard* that appears next to some expressions in Part 3 indicates that the form is not considered *standard. Nonstandard* does not mean incorrect language. It identifies language that is inappropriate in situations where standard English is expected.

Formal and Informal English

The various dialects mentioned above account for some of the differences in the way people speak and write English.

Different situations also affect the way people speak or write, because you choose different words based on your purpose and audience. Look at the following sentences:

> I really enjoyed that story about the men who climbed Mount Everest.

> I really got into that story about the guys who climbed Mount Everest.

The sentences say the same things, but the first sentence uses ***formal English,*** and the other uses ***informal English.*** You might use the second sentence in a conversation with a friend. In a report, however, the formal English in the first sentence is more appropriate.

■ **Colloquialisms** *Colloquialisms* are a common type of informal English that we use in everyday conversations. These colorful expressions have understood meanings that are different from the basic meanings of the words.

EXAMPLES
My parents **hit the ceiling** when I wrecked my bike.
The plot of that movie was **hard to swallow**.

■ **Slang** *Slang* consists of made-up words or old words used in new ways. Slang is often the special language of specific groups, such as teenagers or athletes. Since slang changes very quickly, with expressions going out of style, some of the examples below may seem dated to you.

EXAMPLES
dis—to insult
my bad—an apology
weak—inadequate

The Library/Media Center

Using Print and Electronic Sources

Information is at your fingertips at your community or school library/media center. Libraries are not just for school assignments. You can find the statistics for your favorite sports team, research a place for a family vacation, or read the latest movie magazines. As long as you know how to use the library, it can bring you hours of enjoyment and information. Understanding the following terms will help you get the most out of the library.

Call Number   Every book in a library has a number and letter code known as its *call number.* The call number tells how a book has been classified and where it is shelved in the library. Most libraries use the *Dewey decimal system* to assign call numbers. (See also **Card Catalog** on this page.)

The *Dewey decimal system* assigns numbers to nonfiction books according to ten general subjects. However, biographies and autobiographies may be placed in a

separate section from other nonfiction books and arranged alphabetically according to the last name of the book's subject. Fiction books are usually separated from nonfiction books, too. Novels and short stories are grouped together under *Fiction* and arranged alphabetically by the author's last name.

Card Catalog   The traditional *card catalog* is a cabinet of small drawers containing index cards that show information about a book and where to find it in the library. These cards are arranged in alphabetical order by title, author, and subject. You do not need to know all three forms of information. You can find a book using the card catalog even if you know only the subject or only the author's name. All books have a *title card* and an *author card.* Nonfiction books will have a third card, a *subject card.* The title card is placed in the card catalog alphabetically by the first

Information in the Card Catalog

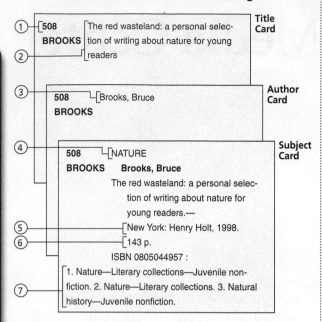

7. **Cross-references** to other headings or related topics under which you can find additional books

Many libraries now use electronic or online card catalogs instead of traditional card catalogs. (See also **Online Card Catalog** on page 737.) Even if a library has a card catalog, make sure it includes all of the books in the library. Many libraries no longer update the cards.

CD-ROMs (**C**ompact **D**isc-**R**ead **O**nly **M**emory) A **CD-ROM** is like a giant book that you see and hear using a computer with a CD-ROM drive. CD-ROMs are a compact way to store many pages of text, so many encyclopedias, dictionaries, and indexes now use this format. One CD-ROM may contain the equivalent of 250,000 pages of printed text. In addition, CD-ROMs can perform searches, provide interactive graphics, and supply audio. (For some specific CD-ROM titles, see the **Reference Sources** chart on page 739.)

Indexes When researching, you might first consult an *index*, which lists topics, sources, and authors. The *Readers' Guide to Periodical Literature*, for example, helps readers find articles, poems, and stories from more than two hundred magazines and journals. Articles are listed alphabetically by author and by subject in boldface, capitalized headings. A key located in the front of the *Readers' Guide* explains the meanings of the abbreviations used in the entries. On the next page you will find examples of entries from the print and online versions of the *Readers' Guide*.

important word in the title. The author card is alphabetized by the author's last name. The subject card is alphabetized by the first letter of the subject category. Above are examples of the title, author, and subject cards for *The Red Wasteland* by Bruce Brooks. The features of each card are explained in the following list.

1. The **call number** assigned to a book by the Dewey decimal or Library of Congress classification system
2. The full **title** and **subtitle** of a book
3. The **author's full name,** last name first
4. The general **subject** of a book; a subject card may show specific headings
5. The place and date of **publication**
6. A **description** of the book, such as its size and number of pages, and whether it is illustrated

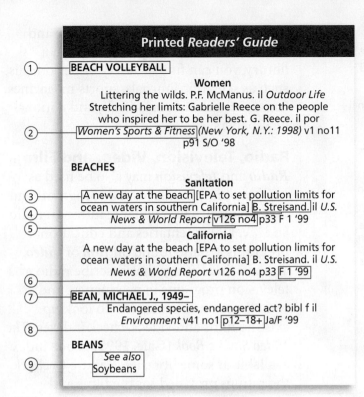

Printed *Readers' Guide*

① **BEACH VOLLEYBALL**

Women
Littering the wilds. P.F. McManus. il *Outdoor Life*
Stretching her limits: Gabrielle Reece on the people
who inspired her to be her best. G. Reece. il por
② *Women's Sports & Fitness* (New York, N.Y.: 1998) v1 no11
p91 S/O '98

BEACHES

Sanitation
③ A new day at the beach [EPA to set pollution limits for
④ ocean waters in southern California] B. Streisand. il *U.S.*
⑤ *News & World Report* v126 no4 p33 F 1 '99

California
A new day at the beach [EPA to set pollution limits for
ocean waters in southern California] B. Streisand. il *U.S.*
⑥ *News & World Report* v126 no4 p33 F 1 '99

⑦ **BEAN, MICHAEL J., 1949–**
Endangered species, endangered act? bibl f il
⑧ *Environment* v41 no1 p12–18+ Ja/F '99

BEANS
⑨ *See also*
Soybeans

① **Subject entry**
② **Name of magazine**
③ **Title of article**
④ **Author of article**
⑤ **Volume number of magazine**
⑥ **Date of magazine**
⑦ **Author entry**
⑧ **Page reference**
⑨ **Subject cross-reference**

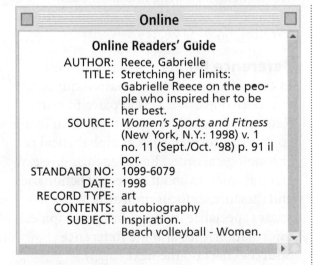

Online

Online Readers' Guide
AUTHOR: Reece, Gabrielle
TITLE: Stretching her limits:
Gabrielle Reece on the peo-
ple who inspired her to be
her best.
SOURCE: *Women's Sports and Fitness*
(New York, N.Y.: 1998) v. 1
no. 11 (Sept./Oct. '98) p. 91 il
por.
STANDARD NO: 1099-6079
DATE: 1998
RECORD TYPE: art
CONTENTS: autobiography
SUBJECT: Inspiration.
Beach volleyball - Women.

Internet   The ***Internet*** is an international
network of computers. Using the Internet,
a computer user can get information from
other computers anywhere in the world. The
Internet was first used by research scientists
in the 1960s to share data with each other.

The Internet now contains information on
almost any topic. To use the Internet, you
need access to a computer and a modem.

Microforms   ***Microforms*** are pages from
various newspapers and magazines that are
reduced on film to miniature size. The two
most common types are ***microfilm*** (a roll or
reel of film) and ***microfiche*** (a sheet of film).
You view them by using a special projector
which enlarges the images to a readable size.

Online Card Catalog   An ***online card
catalog*** is a card catalog stored on a computer. Instead of searching through individual cards, you may find a book by typing in
the book's title, author, or subject. The computer will display the results of the search
information, which you can then print out.
On the next page is an example of an online
card catalog entry.

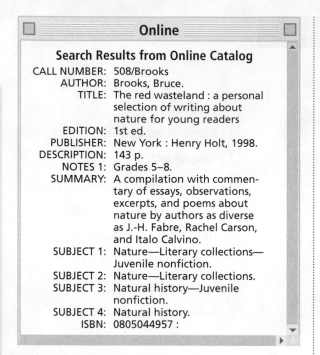

Search Results from Online Catalog

CALL NUMBER: 508/Brooks
AUTHOR: Brooks, Bruce.
TITLE: The red wasteland : a personal selection of writing about nature for young readers
EDITION: 1st ed.
PUBLISHER: New York : Henry Holt, 1998.
DESCRIPTION: 143 p.
NOTES 1: Grades 5–8.
SUMMARY: A compilation with commentary of essays, observations, excerpts, and poems about nature by authors as diverse as J.-H. Fabre, Rachel Carson, and Italo Calvino.
SUBJECT 1: Nature—Literary collections—Juvenile nonfiction.
SUBJECT 2: Nature—Literary collections.
SUBJECT 3: Natural history—Juvenile nonfiction.
SUBJECT 4: Natural history.
ISBN: 0805044957 :

Online Databases   An *online database* is a collection of information stored on a computer. Most databases are created for specific groups of people or organizations, such as universities, libraries, or businesses. Some databases require a subscription, and subscribers must pay to use the database. Other databases, including some encyclopedias, are free and may be accessed through the World Wide Web.

Online Sources   Anytime you retrieve information using the Internet, you have used an *online source*. The term *online* refers to the telephone and fiber-optic lines or satellites that allow computers to send information to each other. When computers are linked, they form a *network*. Computer networks are what make the Internet and the World Wide Web possible.

Periodicals   Magazines, journals, and newspapers are called *periodicals*. In a library, you can find a variety of periodicals, such as scientific journals, sports magazines, consumer-related periodicals, and national newspapers.

Radio, Television, Video, and Film
Radio and *television* may also be used as sources of information. News programs and documentaries are regular features on radio and TV. Documentaries and educational programs are also found on *film* or *video*. You can find listings that describe radio and television programs in newspapers and sometimes on the Internet. To look up existing films and videos, check indexes. *The Video Source Book* (Gale, 1999) is one index available at some libraries. Be sure to check the ratings provided for the films and videos before viewing them. (See also **Media Messages** on page 773 and **Critical Viewing** on page 787.)

Reference Books   When you want to check facts or get information quickly, reference books are a good place to start. Reference books arrange information in a convenient format, such as alphabetical or chronological order. Encyclopedias give general information about subjects. Dictionaries and thesauruses focus on words, while atlases specialize in maps and geographical information. (See also the **Reference Sources** chart on the next page.)

Reference Sources   Being familiar with the various kinds of reference sources can help you do research more efficiently. The chart on the next page describes common reference sources and gives examples.

Reference Sources

Types of Reference Sources	Description	Examples
Encyclopedias	<ul><li>multiple volumes</li><li>articles arranged alphabetically by subject</li><li>source for general information</li></ul>	*Collier's Encyclopedia* *Compton's Encyclopedia* *The World Book Multimedia Encyclopedia*™
General Biographical References	<ul><li>information about the lives and accomplishments of outstanding people</li></ul>	*Current Biography* *The International Who's Who* *World Biographical Index on CD-ROM*
Atlases	<ul><li>maps and geographical information</li></ul>	*Atlas of World Cultures* *National Geographic Atlas of the World*
Almanacs	<ul><li>up-to-date information about current events, facts, statistics, and dates</li></ul>	*The Information Please Almanac, Atlas & Yearbook* *The World Almanac and Book of Facts*
Books of Synonyms	<ul><li>list more interesting or more exact words to express ideas</li></ul>	*Roget's International Thesaurus* *Webster's New Dictionary of Synonyms*

Vertical File   A *vertical file* is a cabinet containing up-to-date materials. These materials may include newspaper clippings and government or information pamphlets.

World Wide Web (*WWW* or the *Web*)
The *World Wide Web* is a large system of connected documents on the Internet. These documents are known as *Web sites* or *Web pages*. They contain text, graphics, video, and sometimes sound. (See also page 740.) Documents on the World Wide Web are connected by *hyperlinks*. Clicking on a hyperlink brings a new site to the computer screen. To navigate and view the World Wide Web, you must have access to a computer with browser software installed. The following terms will help you understand the workings of the World Wide Web.

■ **Browser**   There are different ways to view material on the Internet, one of which includes using a *World Wide Web browser*. World Wide Web browsers provide access to files and documents, news and discussion groups, bulletin boards, e-mail, and the World Wide Web. The browser helps viewers to find, read, save, download, and explore Web sites and to use the links between sites.

- **Hyperlink** Users click on *hyperlinks,* or *links,* to move from one site to another. On screen, hyperlinks are usually underlined and colored words.

- **Search Engine** A search engine is a tool for finding specific information on the Web. (See also **World Wide Web, Searching** on this page.)

- **URL (*Uniform Resource Locator*)** All documents on the Web have an address called a *URL.* A typical URL includes words, abbreviations, numbers, and punctuation.

EXAMPLE

```
   1        2                    3
 ┌──┐  ┌────────┐  ┌─────────────────────────┐
http://go.hrw.com/ndNSAPI.nd/gohrw_rls1/pHome
```

1. The type of Internet service. World Wide Web sites begin with *http.*
2. The *hostname* is a group of *domains.* A domain gives a computer broad or specific information about finding a Web site. In the example above, *com* tells the computer that the site is part of a commercial network, *hrw* identifies the company where the site is located, and *go* indicates which machine within the company contains the site.

Common Networks on the World Wide Web	
com	commercial or individual
edu	educational
gov	governmental
net	administrative
org	usually nonprofit organization

3. The specific request for the file or piece of information that you want. Not all addresses will have this part.

- **Web Site (or Web Page)** Any location or document that you view on the Web is called a Web site or Web page. The *home page* is the first page on a Web site and usually gives an overview of the major areas in the site. It also lists hyperlinks, or related Web sites, and usually tells who created or sponsors the site. On the next page is a typical example of what you would see if you had located a Web site using a browser.

World Wide Web, Searching In some ways, the World Wide Web is like a massive library. The information you want is there, but you must find it before you can use it. You can search the Internet by using a *search engine* or a *directory.*

- **Search Engines** A *search engine* allows you to conduct a *keyword search* to find Web sites that contain key words or phrases. To do a keyword search, you must first decide which keyword or words to use in your search. Then, you type the keyword(s) in the search space and hit the return key or the search or find button. A list of sites will appear, with the most relevant matches at the top.

A keyword search can sometimes result in a list of hundreds or thousands of Web sites. *Refining* your search can make a search more productive. Use the strategies on the next page to help you find a manageable number of matches. Keep in mind, though, that your search engine may use slightly different commands. Consult the help section of your search engine for specific commands.

1. **Toolbar** Click the toolbar to perform functions such as searching, printing, moving forward or back to different pages, and seeing or hiding images.
2. **Location window** This box provides the address, or the URL, of the site you are looking at.
3. **Content area** This section displays the text, images, hyperlinks, and other parts of a Web page.
4. **Hyperlinks** Click these buttons to connect to other Web pages within this same site.
5. **Scroll bar** Clicking along the horizontal or vertical scroll bar (or on the arrows at either end) allows you to move left to right or up and down in the image area.

Refining a Keyword Search

Choose specific terms instead of general ones. A general keyword can produce many irrelevant matches.

EXAMPLE If you are interested in distance running, use *marathon* rather than *running* or *sports.*

Use quotation marks. Using quotation marks around your keyword or phrases will find sites that use those exact words.

EXAMPLE Enter *"Olympic gold medalists"* to find sites about medal winners rather than sites about the Olympics.

Use *AND* and *NOT*. Put the word *AND* between your keywords to narrow your search. The search engine will find only Web sites that contain all words connected by *AND*.

Use *NOT* between keywords to make sure that the search engine does not pull up sites that deal with topics that are similar but unrelated.

EXAMPLE For sites that mention both the Atlanta and the Salt Lake City Olympics, enter *Atlanta AND Salt Lake City AND Olympics.*

EXAMPLE Enter *Olympics NOT mountains* to avoid Web sites about the Olympic mountain range.

Use *OR*. To broaden your search, use *OR* to let the search engine know that you would accept sites that contain any of your keywords.

EXAMPLE If you want sites that discuss either the summer or the winter Olympics, enter *summer OR winter AND Olympics*.

■ **Directories**   A directory provides you with organized lists of Web sites on the World Wide Web. A directory organizes the sites into broad categories, such as *Recreation* and *Health*. Each category can be broken down into subcategories, which can be broken down even more into sub-subcategories. You search a subject catalog by narrowing down a general topic to a specific one.

For example, to find information about Eileen Collins, the first woman space shuttle commander, you could start with the broad category *science*, then narrow your search to *space*, *astronauts*, and finally *Eileen Collins*. Many search engine sites include directories.

World Wide Web, Web Site Evaluation   Newspapers, books, and TV news shows must check and verify information to be sure it is accurate. The World Wide Web, however, does not have the same requirements. Therefore, you must *evaluate* a Web site and the accuracy of its information. Here are some questions to help you in your evaluation.

Evaluating Web Sites	
Who created or sponsored the Web site?	You can find the site's creator or sponsor on the site's home page. You should use Web sites that are created by trustworthy organizations, such as government agencies, universities, and museums. These organizations' Web sites usually are found in the *edu, gov,* or *org* networks. National news organizations are another source of reliable information on the Web.
When was the page first posted, and is it frequently updated?	A copyright notice will tell you when a page was created. The date of the most recent update will tell you how often the information is updated. These dates are usually at the bottom of the home page. They can help you see whether a site tries to keep up with recent developments.
To what other Web pages is the site linked?	Trustworthy sites will have links to respected organizations. These links add to a site's credibility.
Does the Web site present information objectively?	Check to see if the site covers both sides of an issue. If the site uses strong language or opinions, it might not be objective.
Is the Web site well designed?	A well-designed Web site is easy to read, understand, and use. The links work properly, and the text uses proper spelling, punctuation, and grammar.

Reading and Vocabulary

Reading

Skills and Strategies

You can use the following skills and strategies to become a more effective reader.

Author's Point of View, Determining
An author's attitude about a subject is called the *author's point of view.* Point of view is also called *bias.* Recognizing an author's point of view will help you evaluate how fair the author's conclusions are. (See also page 205.)

EXAMPLE Basketball is the champion of all sports. With just five players on a team, basketball is more selective than football, baseball, or soccer. Basketball players must be better conditioned than other athletes because they are always running up and down the court playing offense and defense.

Author's point of view: Basketball is the best sport.

Author's Purpose, Determining
An author has a reason or *purpose* for writing a selection. To inform, to influence, to express oneself, and to entertain are the major purposes for writing. As a reader, determining the author's purpose will help you get more meaning from the text. (See also page 53.)

EXAMPLE Learning to play music is one reason to join the school band, but it is not the only one. By joining the school band you will meet new friends, take fun trips for concerts, and be a part of a great team of musicians. Make the smart and fun choice by joining the school band.

Author's purpose: To persuade teenagers to join the school band.

Cause-Effect Relationships, Analyzing
A *cause* makes something happen. An *effect* is what happens as a result of that cause. When you ask "Why?" and "What happened because of this?" as you read, you are examining causes and effects. (See also page 241.)

EXAMPLE Taking care of my new puppy has changed my schedule. Since the puppy has to go out first thing in the morning, I have to get up thirty minutes earlier. Then, I have to rush home from school to walk him.

Analysis: A new puppy is the *cause* that makes the following *effects* happen: getting up early and coming home quickly from school.

Clue Words, Using

Writers use certain *clue words* to connect their ideas within a text. You can use these clue words to identify the author's organizational pattern. (See also **text structures** on page 748.)

Clue Words	
Cause/effect	
as a result	because
consequently	if . . . then
since	so that
therefore	this led to
thus	
Chronological Order	
after	as
before	finally
first	not long after
now	second
then	when
Comparison/contrast	
although	as well as
but	either . . . or
however	not only . . . but also
on the other hand	similarly
unless	yet
Listing	
also	for example
in fact	most important
to begin with	

Problem/solution

as a result	nevertheless
therefore	this led to
thus	

Conclusions, Drawing

A *conclusion* is a judgment you make by combining information in a text with information you already know. As you read, you gather information, connect it to your experiences, and then draw conclusions about the text. (See also page 87.)

EXAMPLE   A flash of jagged light suddenly illuminated Keisha's bedroom. Loud booms and pelting water shook the windowpanes. Keisha sighed and covered her head with her pillow, hoping to get back to sleep.

Conclusion: A thunderstorm has awakened Keisha in the night.

Fact and Opinion, Distinguishing

A *fact* is information that can be proved true or false. An *opinion* expresses a personal belief or attitude, so it cannot be proved true or false. Facts are often used to support opinions. A reader who can tell the difference between a fact and an opinion is less likely to make false judgments. (See also page 217.)

EXAMPLE

Fact: Professional basketball player Dikembe Mutombo speaks seven languages and five African dialects.

Opinion: Americans should learn to speak more than one language.

Generalizations, Forming

A reader forms a *generalization* by combining information in a text with personal experience to make a judgment about the world in general. (See also page 236.)

EXAMPLE   More and more students at Northshore Middle School are organizing and participating in activities that help the community and other people. The student council organized a food drive to benefit Helping Hands food bank, and the students in Ms. Shaw's science classes started a recycling program. Seventh-grader Leon Miller works as a volunteer at Memorial Hospital. He said, "You really feel good about yourself when you see that something you have done makes someone else happy."

Generalization: Many young people want to help others in their community.

Implied Main Idea, Identifying

Some writers do not directly state the main idea of the text. Instead, they choose to *imply,* or suggest it. In this case, you, the reader, have to analyze the details the writer provides and decide the overall meaning of these details. (See also page 22 and **Stated Main Idea** on page 747.)

EXAMPLE   If you have Internet access, you can send an e-mail message. You do not need stationery, a pen, or a stamp. You do not have to find a post office or mailbox to send the letter. You just type in your message and hit the send button. The person will get your e-mail message, usually in minutes, rather than days.

Implied main idea: E-mail is easy to use.

Inferences, Making   An *inference* is an educated guess based on information in the text and on your prior knowledge and experience. *Conclusions, generalizations,* and *predictions* are three types of inferences. As you read, you make decisions about ideas and

details that writers do not directly reveal. (See also page 236.)

EXAMPLE   "Oh, no," Mrs. Patel said into the phone. She sat down quickly and listened intently. "When?" she asked, swallowing hard. As she listened to the reply, tears filled her eyes.

Inference: Mrs. Patel's phone call brought very bad news.

Paraphrasing   When you *paraphrase,* you restate someone else's ideas in your own words. Paraphrasing a difficult piece of writing can help you better understand that writing. A paraphrase is usually about the same length as the original text. A *summary,* on the other hand, is much shorter than a paraphrase. When you summarize, you focus only on the key ideas in a passage. Be sure to avoid *plagiarism* when you write a paraphrase or a summary. Plagiarism happens when you copy an author's exact words without using quotation marks, and then publish these words as your own. (See the chart on page 776 for **paraphrasing guidelines.**)

EXAMPLE   When Peggy Knight was just fourteen, she lost her hair due to alopecia areata, a disease of the immune system. Knight remembers the terrible teasing she got at a time when she desperately wanted to be like everyone else. Now she is helping children with the disorder by providing free, custom-made wigs of human hair. Knight's organization is called Locks of Love. People from all over the country donate their hair in ponytails, which must be at least ten inches long.

Paraphrasing: At age fourteen, Peggy Knight suffered from alopecia areata and lost all her hair. She didn't like the teasing and feeling left out. Her experience prompted her to start Locks of Love. This organization donates wigs of human hair to children with the same disease. The wigs are made from hair donated by people across America who want to help out. They must cut at least ten inches of their hair to donate it.

Persuasive Techniques, Analyzing

A writer uses *persuasive techniques* to convince readers to think or act in a certain way. Two types of persuasive techniques are *emotional appeals* and *faulty reasoning*. As you read persuasive writing, look for reasons and facts that are logical or make sense. (See also page 239.)

EXAMPLE More students need to recycle by tossing their empty soda cans into the recycling bin. Our janitor, Mr. Saunders, says that he finds many soda cans in the four trash cans near the drink machines. That means that many students do not care about the environment or our school. A school that does not recycle is a school that has no pride!

Analysis: The second sentence contains a fact that supports the opinion in the first sentence. The second-to-last sentence contains faulty reasoning. (There is not enough evidence to support the conclusion in this sentence.) The last sentence contains an emotional appeal. (It appeals to the readers' pride.)

Predicting

Predicting is deciding what will happen next in a text. As you read, you use information from the text plus your own knowledge and experience to make predictions. As you read on, you can adjust or confirm your predictions. (See also page 124.)

EXAMPLE The 200-meter freestyle relay was the next event in the swim meet, but Lauren was still not there. The coach paced nervously, trying to decide on a substitute. No one else could swim the anchor leg as well as Lauren, but the coach had no choice. "Reina!" he barked. "Take the anchor leg. Lauren has just let the team down for the last time."

Predictions: Lauren will lose her anchor position on the relay team. The coach may even kick her off the team. The team will probably not win the race.

Problem-Solution Relationships

A *problem* is an unanswered question. A *solution* is an attempt to answer that question. When an author writes about a problem, he or she may suggest one solution or several. To identify a problem, ask yourself these questions: *What is the problem? Who has the problem?* Then, look for the solution or solutions the author provides.

EXAMPLE The music program's budget at Lincoln Middle School was cut in half. As a result, the school does not have the money to buy instruments for all fifty students in the program. Mr. Nguyen, the music teacher, placed an ad in the local newspaper asking people to donate used instruments. In addition, students organized a benefit concert to raise money to buy instruments.

Analysis: The problem is that Lincoln Middle School does not have money to buy instruments because the music program's budget was cut. Students who want to participate in the music program have the problem. One solution is asking people in the community to donate used instruments. The second solution is organizing a benefit concert to raise money.

Reading Log, Using a

A *reading log* is simply a notebook or journal in which a reader writes about reading. Before you read, use the log to write down ideas about the title and the pictures in the selection. As you read, write down your honest reactions to the text: Ask questions, make connections to your own experiences, and note important passages. Because readers have different experiences, interests, beliefs, and opinions, no two reading logs will be alike.

Reading Rates According To Purpose		
Reading Rate	**Purpose**	**Example**
Scanning	Reading for specific details	Searching for the age of a character in a short story
Skimming	Reading for main points	Reviewing the headlines in a newspaper to find an interesting article
Reading for mastery	Reading to understand and remember	Taking notes and making a time line of events while reading a chapter in your history textbook
Reading at your most comfortable speed	Reading for enjoyment	Reading a book written by your favorite author

Reading Rate, Adjusting Your *reading rate* is the speed at which you read a text. How quickly or how slowly you read depends upon your purpose for reading, the difficulty of the text, and your knowledge of the text's subject. The chart above explains four possible reading rates.

SQ3R *SQ3R,* a popular reading-study strategy, stands for a five-step process:

S *Survey* the entire text. Look briefly at each page—the headings, titles, illustrations, charts, and so on.

Q *Question* yourself as you survey the text. What should you know after completing your reading? Make a list of questions to be answered.

R *Read* the entire selection. Look for answers to your questions as you read.

R *Recite* in your own words the answers you find for each of your questions.

R *Review* the material by re-reading quickly, looking over the questions, and recalling the answers.

Stated Main Idea and Supporting Details, Identifying A *main idea* is the focus or central idea in a piece of writing. Main ideas often appear as topic sentences of paragraphs or in an introduction or conclusion of a composition. *Supporting details* support or explain the main idea. (See **Implied Main Idea** on page 745.)

EXAMPLE The yo-yo has been a popular toy through many centuries and cultures. Invented in China about one thousand years ago, it appeared in England in the late eighteenth century. The troops of the French ruler Napoleon entertained themselves with the yo-yo in the nineteenth century. The yo-yo came to the United States from the Philippines in the 1920s and became a favorite toy of people of all ages.

Stated main idea: The yo-yo has appealed to many different cultures during different time periods.

Supporting details: The yo-yo was invented one thousand years ago in China. It became popular in England, France, and the United States.

Summarizing A *summary* is a short restatement of the main points of a selection. Summarizing a long passage can help you understand it. When you summarize, you try to present the key ideas in a passage without repeating every detail. A *paraphrase,* though, restates almost all of the ideas in a passage. (See also **paraphrasing** on page 745. See chart on page 777 for **summarizing guidelines**.)

> EXAMPLE Middle school students in Japan take entrance exams to get into high school. The exams are very demanding, and students study every day, including weekends, for months before the test. Parents, teachers, students, and communities focus on the upcoming test. If students fail the test, they go to a "cram school" and retake the test the next year.
>
> Summary: In Japan, entrance exams to high school are so difficult and important that students spend months preparing for them. Everyone gets involved, and students who fail go to a special school to prepare to take the test again.

Text Structures, Analyzing A *text structure* is the pattern a writer uses to organize ideas or events. Writers commonly use five major patterns of organization: *cause-effect, chronological order, comparison-contrast, listing,* and *problem-solution.* Being able to recognize these structures will help you better understand the text and its ideas. Use the following guidelines to determine the structure of a text:

1. Search the text for the main idea.

2. Look for clue words that signal a specific pattern of organization and identify one pattern. (See also **Clue Words, Using** on page 744.)

3. Look for details that support the main idea, and think about how the details and the main idea are connected to one another. Use a **graphic organizer** to map the relationship between the main idea and the supporting details. Your graphic organizer may look like one of the four following examples.

- *Cause-effect pattern* shows the relationship between results and the ideas or events that cause the results. (See also page 241.) The following example shows how faulty bicycle brakes (cause) led to a bike accident, injuries, and doctor's bills (effects).

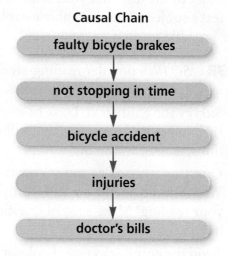

Causal Chain

faulty bicycle brakes

↓

not stopping in time

↓

bicycle accident

↓

injuries

↓

doctor's bills

- *Chronological order pattern* shows events or ideas in the order in which they happen. (See also page 55.) The example on the next page shows the sequence for washing a car.

Sequence Chain

> gather bucket, soap, rags, and hose
>
> ↓
>
> put soap into bucket and add water
>
> ↓
>
> wet car with hose
>
> ↓
>
> use rags and soapy water to wash car
>
> ↓
>
> rinse car with hose

- ***Comparison-contrast pattern*** points out similarities and/or differences. The example below compares the Mayan and Aztec people.
- ***Listing pattern*** presents material according to certain criteria such as size, location, or importance. The following example lists pets according to their size.

List

1. small: my guinea pig Little Bit

2. medium: my cat Bella

3. large: my horse Cleo

- ***Problem-solution pattern*** identifies at least one problem and offers one or more solutions to the problem. The example below shows how a school dealt with a locker shortage.

Venn Diagram

Differences	Similarities	Differences

Maya

- lived in Yucatán region
- skilled astronomers
- lived between A.D. 250–900
- civilization mysteriously disappeared

Similarities

- Native Americans
- built impressive cities
- early inhabitants of Mexico

Aztec

- lived in central Mexico
- fierce warriors
- lived between A.D. 1200 and 1521
- conquered by the Spanish

Transitional Words and Phrases, Using

Transitions are words or phrases that connect ideas. Transitions help you understand how all the ideas in a selection fit together. (See also the chart on **transitional words and phrases** on page 302.)

Visuals and Graphics, Interpreting

Visuals and *graphics* give readers information using pictures or symbols.

■ **Elements** Effective visuals and graphics contain the following elements. (See also page 192.)

1. A *title* identifies the subject or main idea of the graphic or visual.
2. The *body* presents information in the form of a graph, chart, time line, diagram, or table. The body is specific to the type of information that is presented.
3. *Labels* identify and give meaning to the information shown in the graphic or visual.
4. A *legend* identifies special symbols, colors, scales, or other features readers need to know in order to read the information. The legend usually appears as a small box near the body.
5. The *source* is where the information contained in the graphic or visual was found. Knowing the source helps readers judge whether the information in the graphic or visual is accurate.

■ **Types** The most common forms of visuals and graphics are *charts, diagrams, graphs, tables,* and *time lines.*

1. *Charts* are a compact way to show information. In the following *pie chart,* notice that the segments show the percentage of hours, not the specific number of hours.

How I Spend My Day

- GOING TO SCHOOL
- SLEEPING
- DOING HOMEWORK
- WATCHING TV
- SOCCER PRACTICE
- EATING

2%, 8%, 12%, 12%, 33%, 33%

2. *Diagrams* use symbols (such as circles or arrows) or pictures to compare ideas, show a process, or provide instruction. The example below uses pictures to show the forces of action and reaction. A *Venn diagram* uses two overlapping circles to compare two ideas or things. (See page 749 for a **Venn diagram**.)

Action Force

Reaction Force

3. *Line graphs and bar graphs* show changes over time. On the next page is an example of a bar graph and a line graph. The horizontal line, or the line

that goes from left to right, shows different points in time. The vertical line, or the line that goes up and down, shows quantities.

Miles Run by Sean and Lisa

Miles Run by Sean and Lisa

4. *Tables* provide information in a very simple way. Readers must draw their own conclusions about the information in a table.

Money Made Doing Extra Chores in the Month of June		
Date	Chore	Amount
6/4	mowed yard	$5.00
6/12	bathed dog	$2.00
6/19	washed car	$5.00
6/26	pulled weeds	$3.00

5. *Time lines* show the order of events. On a time line, you will see the event and the time in which the event happened.

Major Political Events, 1989–1995

■ **Tips**   Always read graphics or visuals carefully. Keep in mind these tips:

1. Always look at the title, labels, and legend of any visual or graphic before you start to interpret the information.
2. Draw your own conclusions about the information and compare them to those of the writer.
3. Think about information that is not included in the visual or graphic. Often, information is left out because it does not match the writer's conclusions.

Vocabulary

Skills and Strategies

You can use the following skills and strategies to become a more effective reader.

Context Clues   Sometimes you can find clues to the meaning of an unfamiliar word by examining its *context,* the group of words or sentences surrounding the unfamiliar word. The following chart shows examples of some of the common types of context clues.

How to Use Context Clues
Type of Clue
Definitions and Restatements: Look for words that define the term or restate it in other words. *The speaker was **eloquent**, persuading us with her moving stories.*
Examples: Look for examples used in context that reveal the meaning of an unfamiliar word. *Ticks, fleas, and other **parasites** can make your pet miserable.*
Synonyms: Look for clues that indicate an unfamiliar word is similar in meaning to a familiar word or phrase. *The eyewitness gave such **credible** testimony that it was easy to believe her account.*
Antonyms or Contrasts: Look for clues that indicate an unfamiliar word is opposite in meaning to a familiar word or phrase.

*His **placid** expression gave no sign of the panic he felt while taking the test.*

Cause and Effect: Look for clues that indicate an unfamiliar word is related to the cause or is the result of an action, feeling, or idea.

*Because most people use computers, typewriters have become almost **obsolete**.*

Word Bank   A *word bank* is a list of words that you gather from your reading, listening, and viewing. Storing new words in a word bank is a good way to increase your vocabulary. Check your dictionary for the meaning of each new word.

Word Meanings   Words have layers of meanings that can change depending on how the word is used. Use the following definitions and examples to help you make sure that your words say what you mean.

■ **Clichés and tired words**   *Clichés* are overused expressions that are no longer effective in writing.

EXAMPLES   *sharp as a tack, cold as ice, home sweet home, easier said than done*

A *tired word* is one that has lost its freshness and force. It has been used so often and so carelessly that it has become worn-out and almost meaningless.

EXAMPLES   *nice, good, pretty, wonderful, terrific,* and *great*

Denotation and connotation

The *denotation* of a word is its actual meaning—the one a dictionary lists. The *connotation* is the additional meaning or feeling suggested by the word. Because connotations often stir people's feelings, they can have powerful effects on the listener or reader.

EXAMPLES The words *stubborn* and *determined* have similar denotative meanings, but they connote different ideas. *Stubborn* connotes someone headstrong and difficult. *Determined,* on the other hand, has positive connotations and suggests someone who is hardworking and refuses to give up.

Euphemisms

A *euphemism* is a word or phrase that is used in place of another word that might seem too direct or blunt. Some people use euphemisms to be polite and to avoid offending others. Euphemisms are also used to mislead people—to hide unpleasant truths or misrepresent the facts.

Euphemism	More Direct Term
laid to rest	buried
stretched the truth	lied
petite	short
correctional facility	jail

Figurative language

Figurative language consists of descriptive words and phrases that are not meant to be taken literally. The following chart shows the most common types of figurative language.

Type of Figurative Language	Example
A **metaphor** says that something *is* something else.	Her smile is a neon sign.
Personification gives human characteristics to nonhuman things.	The ocean breeze whispered in my ears.
A **simile** compares two basically unlike things, using the words *like* or *as*.	The road was like a black ribbon winding through the mountains.

Idioms

Idioms are phrases that mean something different from the literal meanings of the words. Idioms often can't be explained grammatically, and they may not make sense if translated word-for-word into another language.

EXAMPLES

The two girls wanted to *hang out* at Marina's house.

I was *glued to my seat* as I watched the game.

We *plugged away* at our homework.

Jargon

Jargon is a special language used by groups of people who share the same profession, occupation, hobby, or field of study. Jargon is effective only if the reader or listener is familiar with its special meaning. Note in the following example how the word *strike* can mean different things in different fields.

EXAMPLE strike

Baseball—a pitch thrown over home plate within a "strike zone" or a pitch that the batter swings at but misses.

Bowling—knocking down ten pins with the first ball of a frame

Labor—refusal to work due to a contract disagreement

Fishing—the fish's grab at hooked bait

■ **Loaded words**   *Loaded words* are intended to provoke strong feelings, either positive or negative. A writer or speaker who wants to persuade you to share his or her opinion may use loaded words that appeal to your emotions.

EXAMPLES

The coach looked *serious* as he *paced* up and down the sidelines.

The coach looked *grim* as he *stomped* up and down the sidelines.

■ **Multiple meanings**   Many English words have more than one meaning. When using a dictionary to find a word's meaning, look at all the definitions given. Keep in mind the context in which you read or heard the word. Then, try the various definitions in that context until you find the one that fits.

EXAMPLE

With his low *threshold* for pain, even a headache sends him straight to bed.

threshold (thre**th'** ōld') *n.* **1.** the piece of wood or stone placed beneath a door **2.** an entrance **3.** the place or point of beginning **4.** the lowest point or level at which an action can be felt (The fourth definition best fits the meaning in context.)

Word Origins   See **The History of English.**

Word Parts   Most English words can be broken into smaller units called *word parts*. The three types of word parts are *roots, prefixes,* and *suffixes*. Knowing the meanings of these word parts can help you determine the meanings of many unfamiliar words.

■ **Roots**   The *root* is the main part of a word. It carries the word's meaning, and it is the part to which prefixes and suffixes are added. (See also page 57.)

Commonly Used Roots		
Roots	**Meanings**	**Examples**
–act–	do	action, react
–biblio–, –bibli–	book	bibliography, biblical
–chron–	time	chronology, chronic
–fac–	make	manufacture, factory
–log–, –logue–, –logy–	study, word	logo, biology
–magni–	large	magnitude, magnify
–mal–	bad	malpractice, dismal
–mot–	move	motion, promote
–ped–	foot	pedal, quadruped
–phon–	sound	telephone, phonograph
–sym–, –syn–	with, together	sympathy, syndrome

■ Prefixes

A *prefix* is a word part that is added before a root. (See also page 166.)

Commonly Used Prefixes

Prefixes	Meanings	Examples
de–	away from, off, down	decode, defend, defuse
dia–	through, across, between	dialogue, diameter
hemi–	half	hemicycle, hemisphere
inter–	between, among	interact, interstate
mis–	badly, not, wrongly	mislead, mistake
non–	not	nonfiction, nonstop
over–	above, excessive	overthrow, overtime
post–	after, following	postdated, postwar
pre–	before	prepare, preview
re–	back, backward, again	replay, return, reverse
sub–, suf–, sum–, sup–, sus–	under, beneath	subplot, suffocate, summon, support, suspend
trans–	across, beyond	translate, transport
un–	not, reverse of	uneven, unspoken

■ Suffixes

A *suffix* is a word part that is added after a root. Adding or changing a suffix will often change both a word's meaning and its part of speech, as in *teach/teacher*. *Teach* is a verb. *Teacher* is a noun. (See also page 166.)

Commonly Used Suffixes

Suffixes	Meanings	Examples
–ate	to become, to cause	concentrate, vaccinate
–dom	state, condition	freedom, wisdom
–en	made of, to become	sharpen, wooden
–fy	to make, to cause	magnify, terrify
–hood	state, condition	neighborhood, sisterhood
–ible	able, likely	collectible, visible
–ish	tending to be, like	childish, smallish
–ity	state, condition	activity, flexibility
–ize	to make, to cause to be	dramatize, legalize
–ment	result, act of	appointment, payment
–ness	quality, state	darkness, sadness
–ous	characterized by	generous, joyous
–tion	act of, state	flirtation, protection

Words to Learn Use the 300 words in the list below to increase your vocabulary this year. Make it a habit to learn unfamiliar words from this list regularly.

abrupt
absolute
abstract
absurd
accord
acute
adhere
adopt
aerial
aggravate
alien
ally
alternate
anguish
anticipate
antiseptic
approximate
audible
authentic
avert

banish
barbarous
baron
barren
blemish

caliber
camouflage
cancel
candid
capacity
challenge
chaos
cherish
coincide
commit
comparable
compensate

competent
compute
confirm
conform
congregate
conifer
consequence
consistent
conspicuous
constitution
contemplate
controversial
credible
crisis
crucial
cultural

dashing
debris
defiant
deliberate
designate
destiny
dialogue
diaphragm
digital
diplomatic
discrimination
dismal
distort
distract
diversity
dual

economical
ecosystem
edible
editorial
effect

efficiency
elaborate
elective
eloquent
encounter
endurance

era
eventual
exceed
excel
excess
exotic
expand

faculty
fascinate
fatigue
financial
flaw
forbidding
formal
fortress
forum
frail
fugitive
fulfill
fundamental
futile

galaxy
geological
germinate
gesture
ghastly
glacial
glucose
grammatical
grandeur
gratify
grotesque
guarantee

habitat
hardy
haunt

hesitation
hover
humane
hypocrite
hysterical

idle
ignorance
illusion
illustrious
immature
immortal
immune
impact
indefinite
indirect
indispensable
inert
inferior
infinite
inhabit
initial
inquisitive
intellect
intermediate
interpret
intolerable
intricate
invade
involuntary
irritable

journal
judicial

kernel

leash
legendary
legible
legitimate
lenient
literary
logical
loiter

luminous
lure

magnitude
maintain
mammal
maneuver
manual
manuscript
mastery
maternal
maturity
mechanism
memorandum
mere
merit
metropolitan
minimum
minority
moderate
modest
monarchy
moral
mortal
motive
myth
mythology

narration
naturalist
navigable
nocturnal
notable
notorious
nutrition

obligation
obsolete
obstacle
obstinate
offend
officially
opponent
opposition
optical
optional

organism
originality
overture

pageant
parasite
partial
participant
participate
penetrate
percentage
perilous
perpetual
persuasion
phase
photosynthesis
pigment
placid
planetary
poach
porcelain
precaution
precise
preliminary
preservation
prestige
principally
probability
proclamation
profound
prompt
propel
proportion
prose
prudent
pursue

radiate
random
reality
reception
recognition
recoil
recommend
refrain

relinquish
repel
resolve
revise
ridicule
rival

satellite
scholarship
seasonal
segregation
self-conscious
serf
signify
speculate
spontaneous
stability
stationary
stationery
status
stellar
submerged
substantial
subtle
supervise
surplus
symbolic

tactics
technique
temperate
tendency
threshold
timid
tiresome
toil
tranquil
tributary
turmoil
tutor
tyrant

undergrowth
unison
universal
unpredictable

usage
utility

vague
valiant
velocity
vengeance
versatile
veto
via
vigor
vital

wretched

yield

zoology

Speaking and Listening

Speaking

Although you speak all the time without even thinking about it, you can learn to speak more effectively. Using the strategies in this section will help you get your ideas across to listeners more clearly, in formal speeches and oral interpretations as well as in informal speaking situations.

Formal Speaking

A formal speech is given at a specific time for a specific reason. Most formal speeches are given to provide information to listeners, though they can also be given to persuade, to entertain, or even to express.

Content of a Formal Speech A formal speech must be planned carefully ahead of time. To prepare your speech, use a process similar to the writing process. The following steps can help you write an effective speech.

1. **Select a topic.** If it is up to you to choose the topic of your speech, use one of the methods below to help you find a topic that will be interesting to both you and your audience.
   - Consider turning one of your written compositions into a speech.
   - Brainstorm a list of interesting topics.
   - Ask for suggestions from your teachers, friends, and classmates.
   - Look over past journal entries.
   - Read through sources such as magazines, newspapers, and books.
   - Search the World Wide Web for ideas. (See also page 740.)

2. **Identify purpose and occasion.** The *purpose* of your speech is the reason you are giving your speech. The purpose of most speeches is to inform or to persuade an audience to do or believe something. Knowing your purpose will help you decide what ideas and words to use in your speech to achieve that purpose. The chart on the next page describes some of the most common purposes for formal speeches.

Purposes for Giving a Speech	
Purpose for Speech	**Examples of Speech Titles**
To inform gives facts or general information or explains how to do something	• Dinosaurs Once Lived in West Texas • How to Take Good Snapshots
To persuade attempts to change an opinion or attempts to get listeners to act	• Why Everyone Should Recycle • How Volunteering Can Make a Difference
To entertain relates an interesting or amusing story or incident	• My Most Embarrassing Moment • The Day I Met the President

The *occasion* of your speech is when and where it takes place. The occasion or event at which you are speaking will influence what you will say and how you will deliver your speech. Use the questions below to help you think about how the occasion of your speech will affect it.

- *Is the occasion formal or informal?* For a formal occasion, such as a school awards assembly, you will need to use **standard, formal English.** For an informal occasion, such as a friend's birthday party, you can worry less about formal language and word choice.

- *When will you give your speech?* Think about how the date and the time of day will affect your speech. Your speech may be given on a certain anniversary or holiday, and its content may be connected to that observance. The time of day can also affect your speech. If you are speaking at a time when people may be tired, such as the early morning or after a meal, plan to include lots of attention-getting information.

- *Where will your speech be given?* The place where you are speaking affects your preparation, also. Find out whether you will be using a microphone to speak or whether you will have to speak loudly to be heard.

- *What other conditions might affect your speech?* How much time will you have to speak? Can you speak on any topic? Can you use notes? Will you be able to show pictures or charts? Find out about any restrictions that may be placed on your speech.

3. **Analyze the audience.** Your speech needs to appeal to your audience. Use a vocabulary and manner of speaking that they will understand. Avoid using technical terms or jargon in your speech. Also, organize your ideas in a way that will make sense to your listeners. If you are turning a written composition into a speech, you may need to reorganize ideas or change the way you explain some concepts. The audience you had in mind when you wrote the composition may not be the same audience that will listen to your speech. Use the chart on the next page to help you analyze your audience's needs and interests.

Analyzing Your Audience		
Questions about audience	**Answer**	**Your speech will need**
What does the audience already know about this subject?	very little	to give background details to listeners
	a little	to give at least some background details
	a lot	to focus on less well-known points
How interested will the audience be in this subject?	very interested	to keep your listeners' interest with surprising information
	only a little interested	to focus on aspects most interesting to your listeners
	uninterested	to convince your listeners that this topic is important

4. **Gather information.** Once you know about the topic, purpose, occasion, and audience of your speech, your next step is to find information. For information about how to use the library or media center for research, see page 735. For information on taking notes and preparing outlines, see pages 775 and 807. (If you are turning a written piece into a speech, you will already have gathered most of the information you need. You will simply need to turn that information into speech notes.)

5. **Organize your speech notes.** You will need to organize the information you have gathered to give an effective speech that will achieve your purpose. First, organize your major ideas in an outline. Then, create a note card for each major idea in your outline. When you give your speech, you will speak directly to the audience, not read from notes. You can glance at your note cards from time to time to remind yourself of the informa-

tion you want to share with your audience. The chart below can help you create note cards for an effective speech.

How to Create Speech Note Cards

- Write each main point or idea on its own note card, with notes to remind you of evidence, elaborations, or examples you will use to clarify and support each point.

- Make a separate note card for anything you want to read word-for-word, including quotations or facts that would be difficult to memorize.

- Include a special note card to remind you when to show or refer to a visual, such as a chart, diagram, model, or illustration.

- Number your completed cards to keep them in order.

6. **Use media.** Including media such as *audiovisuals* or *electronic media* in your

speech can make your ideas clearer for listeners or provide extra information in your speech. Here are some common forms of media you might use in a presentation.

- electronic media (graphic images, audio files, and text presentations)
- audio recordings (cassettes or compact discs)
- prerecorded videotapes or videodiscs
- short films
- slides or filmstrips
- visuals such as charts, graphs, illustrations, and diagrams

Use these questions to help you decide whether to use audiovisuals or electronic media in your presentation.

Evaluating the Use of Media in Presentations

1. *Will media help you make a point more clearly?* Some ideas need a visual to help explain them. Using a chart or poster can help get your idea across more easily and clearly.

2. *Will the media help the audience remember a point?* Some points in your speech are more important than others. You can use an audiovisual to help emphasize the most important points.

3. *Will the media distract the audience while you are speaking?* Use only media that are essential to your speech. As soon as the audience has something to concentrate on besides your words, you risk losing their attention. Too many audiovisuals can distract your audience and weaken your speech.

When you use media, make sure the materials are easy for your audience to see and hear. Have audio clips cued up and ready to play. Make sure posters, charts, and other visuals are large enough for your audience to read. (See also **Graphics** on page 728.)

Delivery of a Formal Speech

1. **Rehearse.** To do your best, rehearse your speech before you give it. These strategies can help you as you practice.
   - Create a situation as much like the actual speech situation as possible. Practice your speech in front of an audience of friends and family members, and ask for feedback.
   - Present your speech just as you hope to deliver it. Use hand gestures and eye contact. You might also practice in front of a mirror to see how you come across.
   - Evaluate your performance. Ask yourself how you did, and answer honestly. Then, use your answers to help yourself improve as you keep practicing. (See also **Listening to Evaluate** on page 771.)
   - Plan for improvement with additional rehearsals. Practice can make you more confident. Make sure you plan far enough in advance to be able to practice several times before you give your speech.

2. **Deliver the speech to your audience.** To give an effective speech, you will need to use your voice and your gestures to help express your meaning to your listeners. Here are some pointers to use when you are speaking.
   - *Be prepared.* Organize your material carefully. Make sure your note cards and

Nonverbal Elements	Examples or Meanings	Functions
Eye Contact	Look directly into the eyes of your audience members	• Can communicate honesty or sincerity • Can keep audience attention
Facial Expression	Raise an eyebrow, smile, frown, or sneer	• Reveals your feelings • Can emphasize certain words or messages
Gesture	Give thumbs up (approval, encouragement), shrug (uncertainty), nod the head (agreement), shake the head (disagreement)	• Can sometimes replace words • Emphasizes words or phrases • Adds meaning to the speech
Posture	Stand tall and straight	• Gives an attitude of confidence and poise

other special information and visuals are ready before you speak.

■ *Remember your purpose.* Focus on what you want to tell your audience and how you want them to react instead of worrying about your performance. Try to give your listeners a clear and accurate perspective about your topic.

■ *Use nonverbal elements.* One way you communicate with your audience is by using nonverbal signals, sometimes called **body language.** The chart above lists some nonverbal elements you can use in your speech.

■ *Use verbal elements.* When you make your speech, use your voice's expressive qualities to communicate with your audience. You may need to vary some or all of these elements depending on your audience and on the setting of your speech. Practice the tips in the Verbal Elements chart.

Verbal Elements	Definitions
Diction	Pronounce words clearly, or *enunciate.* Speak clearly and carefully so that your listeners can understand you.
Emphasis (or stress)	Your voice *inflections*— changes in pitch and tone—naturally put stress on some words or phrases and not others. Emphasize words that are important in your message.
Mood (or tone)	Your speech may make your listeners feel certain emotions. Mood usually applies to oral interpretations of literature, but it may also apply to a speech.

Verbal Elements	Definition
Pause	Pauses are the small silences in your speech. Pauses can emphasize a point that you are making or help listeners catch up.
Pitch	Your voice modulates, or changes pitch, when you speak. If you are nervous, your voice may get higher. To control your pitch, take deep breaths and stay calm as you give your speech.
Rate	In conversations, your rate, or tempo, of speaking may be fast. When you make a speech, you should talk more slowly than you normally would to help listeners understand you.
Volume	Even if you normally speak fairly quietly, you will need to speak loudly while giving a formal speech. Listeners at the back of the room should be able to hear you clearly when you speak.

Other Formal Speaking Situations

Here are tips for getting through some additional formal speaking situations.

- **Announcements** An announcement provides a short piece of information to many people at once. Write out the message you want to get across, keeping it brief and direct. Get your audience's attention, and then read the announcement slowly, clearly, and loudly enough that everyone can hear it.

- **Introductions** Before you introduce someone to an audience, you must find out a bit about him or her. Tell the audience the person's name and title, as well as a few important or interesting facts about the person. Be respectful, and welcome the person you are introducing.

- **Oral Summaries** To summarize a book or article you have read, tell your audience about the main idea and most important points or details included in the book or article. Retell these ideas in your own words, and make connections between these ideas and your own thoughts or experiences about the topic.

Informal Speaking

Group Discussion Group discussions happen when a group of people gets together for a particular purpose. In a group discussion, members share and build on information, ideas, experiences, and insights. The elements of a group discussion are listed below.

1. **Setting a Purpose** You probably work in groups in many of your classes. Successful group discussions have a specific purpose. This purpose may be
   - to discuss and share ideas
   - to cooperate in group learning
   - to solve a problem
   - to arrive at a group decision

   Once your group has chosen a purpose, find out how much discussion time will be allowed. Then, figure out what your group will be expected to accomplish within the time allowed.

2. Understanding Roles and Responsibilities   Everyone involved in a group discussion should have a specific role. Each role has special responsibilities. For example, your group may choose a chairperson to help keep the discussion moving smoothly. Someone else may be chosen as the recorder, who has the responsibility of taking notes during the discussion. Each member of the group should actively listen to the speaker. Listeners should consider how the speaker's ideas, information, and experience relate to their own.

Many groups begin by creating a plan or outline for the order of topics to follow in a discussion. The chairperson, or sometimes the entire group, may create the plan.

Responsibilities of Group Members

Chairperson	Announce the topic and set the plan.
	Follow the plan.
	Encourage each member to participate actively.
	Keep the discussion on track. Help the group avoid disagreements and distractions.
Recorder	Take notes about important information.
	Prepare a final report.
Participant	Participate actively in the discussion both when speaking and when listening.
	Ask questions and give full attention to others.
	Cooperate and share information.

Impromptu Speaking   At times you will need to speak to a group of people without having time to plan what you will say. This is called an *impromptu speech*. Here are some suggestions.
1. Think about your purpose. Do you want to give information to your audience? Do you want to persuade them?
2. Think about your topic. What is the main thing you need to say? If you have time, add details to explain your main points.
3. Think about your audience. Does what you are saying fit the time, the place, and the people you are addressing?

Speaking Socially   Although you do not need to choose words as carefully when speaking socially as you do in more formal situations, you do need to think about how clearly you are communicating your ideas. Here are some guidelines for speaking effectively in common social situations.

1. **Giving Directions or Instructions**
   - Divide the instructions or directions into a series of clear, logical steps.
   - Tell your listener each of the steps in the process, one at a time, in order.
   - Check to be sure your listener understands all of the instructions or directions.
   - Repeat any instructions that are not clear.

2. **Making Social Introductions**
   - Have confidence. If no one else introduces you, introduce yourself to other people.

- When you introduce others, identify them by name.
- When you are introducing others, it is customary to speak first to an older person before a younger person or to the person you know best.

3. Speaking on the Telephone

- Call people at times that are convenient for them. It may not be convenient for someone to speak to you early in the morning, late at night, or around mealtimes.
- Identify yourself; then, state your reason for calling.
- Be polite, speak clearly, and keep your call to a reasonable length.

Oral Interpretation *Oral interpretation* is more like acting in a play than giving a speech. When you give an oral interpretation, you read a piece of literature expressively to your listeners. To indicate the meaning of the selection, you use facial expressions, your voice, gestures, and movements to interpret the literary work for your listeners.

1. Selecting or Adapting Material The purpose of an oral interpretation is to entertain. As you choose your selection, think about who your audience is, how much time you will have, what the occasion or situation is, and how expressive you want to be in your interpretation.

To find a literary work for your oral interpretation, consider the following suggestions.

Selecting an Oral Interpretation

Type of Literature	Description of Possible Selection
poem	a poem that tells a story, such as an epic poem a poem that has a speaker (using the word *I*) or a conversation between characters a poem that expresses a particular emotion
short story	a brief story, or portion of a story, that has - a beginning, middle, and end - either a narrator who tells the story (using *I*) or characters who talk to one another (using dialogue in quotation marks)
play	a short play, or one scene from a play, that has - a beginning, middle, and end - dialogue between two characters or a dramatic monologue
personal narrative	a piece you wrote about an experience or event in your life that has a beginning, middle, and end

You may be able to find just the right piece of literature. It may already be the perfect length. It may have just the right number of characters, with dialogue that tells the part of the story you want to tell. Sometimes, though, you need to shorten a short story, a long poem, or a play. This shortened version is called a *cutting*.

How to Make a Cutting

1. Decide where the part of the story you want to use should begin and where it should end, and follow that part of the story in time order.

2. From a short story, cut dialogue tags, such as *she whispered sadly*. Instead, use these clues to tell you how to act out the character's words.

3. Cut out parts that do not contribute to the portion of the story you are telling.

2. **Presenting an Oral Interpretation**
- *Prepare a reading script.* Once you have chosen a piece to interpret, create a *reading script*. A **reading script** is typed with double spacing, or written neatly with an extra space between each line. This space gives you a place to make marks that will help you with your reading. Underline words you want to emphasize, mark slashes where you will take a breath, or write a note to remind yourself of the emotion you want to convey.

- *Create an introduction.* You should plan to introduce your oral interpretation with a short introduction. Tell your listeners what has happened before your scene, explain whether the scene is told from the **point of view** of a certain character or an anonymous narrator, or describe the **setting** in which the action takes place.

- *Rehearse your presentation.* Rehearse in several different ways until you find the most effective way to present your scene. Practice in front of your mirror. Then, try out your reading on your friends, classmates, or relatives. Use your voice to emphasize your meaning. Vary your body movements and your voice to show that you are portraying different characters and to show important emotions.

Listening

Listening involves understanding the meaning of the sounds you hear. Listening can be especially challenging when you are listening to understand new information. This section focuses on the elements of listening.

Basics of the Listening Process

Like the reading process, the listening process includes skills you use before, during, and after you get the message.

Getting Ready to Listen You will be a more effective listener if you take steps to get focused before you begin listening.

1. **Know Why You Are Listening** Keeping your purpose in mind as you listen will help you to be a more effective listener. The way you take in information depends on your reason for listening. For example, if you are listening to the radio for enjoyment, you won't think carefully about the ideas in the songs, ads, or DJ comments. If you are listening to find out how to get tickets to see your favorite group, though, you will listen much more carefully and may even write down information you need to remember. Common purposes for listening are
   - for enjoyment or entertainment
   - to gain information or solve a problem
   - to understand information or an explanation
   - to evaluate or form an opinion

2. **Limit Distractions** Listening can be difficult if you are not focused on the speaker. Before you listen, think about the steps below.

Eliminating Barriers to Effective Listening

Keep a positive attitude, and focus your attention on the speaker.
Before you listen, make sure you feel rested and relaxed. As you sit down, remind yourself that you are going to focus on the speaker for the next few minutes. Put aside distracting thoughts, plans, or worries as you listen.

Think about the message.
As you listen to the speaker, focus on what he or she is saying. Try not to be distracted by any mannerisms or accent the speaker has.

Prepare for the setting.
Sometimes lecture halls and classrooms are too hot or cold. Wearing a sweater or jacket can help you adjust to the temperature. Also, choose a seat where you can see and hear the speaker well. Try to choose a place to sit that will minimize distractions.

Listening Communication involves give and take, both speaking and listening. Nonverbal elements, such as your facial expressions and body language, can tell the speaker when you are listening and when you are not. Follow these guidelines to listen politely and effectively to a speaker.

- **Communicate respect and attention through your body language** Look directly at the speaker, and sit up straight.

- **Listen quietly** Do not interrupt the speaker or distract others in the audience. Wait until the speaker finishes before asking questions.

- **Keep an open mind** Do not rush to judge the speaker. Listen politely to the speaker even if you do not agree with him or her. Be respectful of such possible differences as the speaker's accent, race, religion, or customs.

- **Monitor yourself as you listen** Ask yourself questions to see if you understand what the speaker is saying.

- **Take notes** Note taking will help you remember the speaker's main points and other important information. Taking notes is a way of organizing your ideas. You should not try to write down every single word, but instead capture the main points as well as your own thoughts. You may choose to organize a speaker's ideas in a graphic organizer or an outline instead. Later, use your notes to help yourself ask questions or make comments. (See also **paraphrasing** and **summarizing** on page 776.)

Responding After you finish listening to a speech, you still have a role to play. Your response can help the speaker know how the speech went. Choose one or more of these ways to respond to a speaker.

- **Ask questions** If anything the speaker said was unclear to you, ask a question about it. By rephrasing the confusing information, the speaker can help you and others to understand it better.

- **Give positive feedback** Everybody needs a pat on the back. Compliment one or two specific things that the speaker did well. Even if you do not agree with the speaker, you can praise his or her clear explanations or well-designed graphics.

- **Offer constructive criticism** One way to help speakers improve is by offering constructive, or helpful, information. Politely identify something that the speaker can improve, and call his or her attention to it.

- **Remember the power of nonverbal feedback** Sometimes the most helpful feedback is given without words. To show your appreciation, stay in your seat until after the speech is completely over. Listen attentively to questions and answers. Remember that a smile can say more than words.

- **Discuss the speech with others** Compare your understanding of the speaker's message to that of other people around you. Find out what other audience members thought of the speech. You may find that someone else got something different from the speech than you did.

Listening with a Purpose

As you listen, keep your purpose in mind. Use the strategies that follow to help you listen effectively in specific situations.

Listening to Appreciate When you listen to poetry, drama, fiction, or stories passed down through generations, you generally listen for enjoyment. Here are some ways to increase your enjoyment and appreciation as you listen.

■ **Listening to Literature**   Listening to literature is like reading literature in some ways. Readers preview a piece of literature, read it, and think about it afterward. You can use a similar process for listening to literature by following the steps below.

Before you listen

- Ask questions about the literature you are about to hear. What is the selection about? What is its title? Who wrote it? What kind of literature is it (poetry, a short story, a play)?
- Use your questions to help you make predictions about what you will hear. Don't worry about whether your predictions are correct.

As you listen

- Create mental images or pictures of what you hear as you listen.
- Write down notes, questions, or ideas you have as you listen.
- Make connections to your own life. Think about similar experiences or feelings you have had.

After you listen

- Confirm or adjust the predictions you made before you listened. How did your predictions change as you listened?
- Think about your response to the selection. What did you like about the selection? Did you learn anything? What did you feel while listening?
- Think about the literary elements used in the literature. Did the selection use imagery, alliteration, foreshadowing, repetition, or rhyme? What was the theme or message of the selection? How did the literary elements add to the theme of the selection?

- Organize your ideas. Summarize what happened in the selection and what you learned from listening to it.

■ **Listening to Oral Tradition**   *Oral tradition* refers to the way people's culture and history are passed down verbally, usually through storytelling. When you listen to oral traditions such as fairy tales or folk tales, you are participating in the process of passing that story down to a new generation. As you listen to a folk tale or fairy tale, use the following tips to be an active listener.

Strategies for Listening to Oral Tradition

Compare elements of different stories.
Many folk tales and fairy tales have elements in common, such as characters, setting, themes or messages, or plots. As you listen, think about other stories you know that have similar elements. How are the two stories alike? How are they different?

Compare versions of the same story.
Every time a story is told, the storyteller changes it in some way. By emphasizing certain parts or changing the wording, a storyteller makes the story he or she tells unique. Compare the story you hear now with the story as you have read or heard it before. How are the two stories different?

Look for similarities and differences between the story and the storyteller's regional or cultural background.
Did you know that there are hundreds of versions of the Cinderella story?

(continued)

Strategies for Listening to Oral Tradition

Each version, however, is unique to its storyteller's culture of origin or region. For example, the Egyptian Cinderella story is different from the Vietnamese Cinderella story. Listen for ways that the story you are hearing seems to match or differ from the culture or region of the storyteller.

Identify labels or sayings from specific regions and cultures.

As you listen to the story, try to identify words or phrases that are used in specific regions or by people of specific cultures. What do these phrases add to the story?

Listening to Comprehend These steps and the strategies that follow them can help you listen to get information.

Strategies for Listening for Information

Find the main idea.

What is the most important point of the speech? Listen for clue words, such as *major, main, most important,* or similar words.

Identify significant details.

What dates, names, or facts does the speaker use to support main points of the speech? What kinds of examples or explanations are used to support the main idea?

Distinguish between facts and opinions.

A *fact* is a statement that can be proved to be true. (May is the fifth month.) An *opinion* is a belief or a judgment about something. It cannot be proved. (Strawberries are better than oranges.)

Identify the order of organization.

What order does the speaker use to present ideas—time order, spatial order, logical order?

Note comparisons and contrasts.

Are some details compared or contrasted with others?

Understand cause and effect.

Does the speaker say or hint that some events cause others to occur? Or does the speaker suggest that some events are the result of others?

Predict outcomes and draw conclusions.

What reasonable conclusions or predictions can you make from the facts and evidence you have gathered from the speech?

■ **LQ2R** The LQ2R study method is especially helpful when you are listening to a speaker who is giving information or instructions.

L *Listen* carefully to information as it is being presented.

Q *Question* yourself as you listen. Make a mental list of questions as they occur to you, or write down your questions.

R *Recite* mentally in your own words the answers to your questions as they are presented, or jot down notes as you listen.

R *Relisten* as the speaker concludes the presentation. The speaker may sum up, or repeat, major points of the presentation.

■ **5W-How? Questions** When you listen for information, you need to listen for details that answer the basic *5W-How?* questions: *Who? What? When? Where? Why?* and *How?* For example, if you were listening to an invitation, you would make sure you understood these details.

- who is giving the party
- when and where the party will be held
- what kind of party it is
- how you can help with arrangements

■ **Listening to Instructions and Directions** Instructions and directions are usually given in a series of steps. It is important to make sure you understand each step as you listen.

Guidelines for Listening to Instructions

1. *Listen for the order of steps.* Listen for clue words that tell you the order of steps, including *first, next, then,* and *last.*

2. *Identify the number of steps in the process.* If the process includes many steps, make notes to help you remember all of the steps.

3. *Picture each step.* Imagine yourself completing each step of the process in order.

4. *Review the steps.* Make sure you have all the instructions and understand them. Ask questions if you are unclear about any step. Repeat the instructions back to the speaker to make sure you understand them.

Listening to Evaluate When you evaluate a speech, you judge its content, delivery, and impact on the audience. Usually when you listen to evaluate, you judge a persuasive or informative speech

based on criteria that fit the type of speech. The questions in the chart below are a starting point for interpreting and evaluating a speech. Generate more criteria for evaluation, and add your own questions to those listed. You can use the criteria to evaluate not only speeches given by others, but also your own speeches.

Points to Interpret and Evaluate

Analyze the speaker's message
- Can you summarize the main idea of the speech?
- Can you explain why the message of the speech is important?

Identify the speaker's point of view
- Can you identify the speaker's perspective or attitude toward the subject?

Evaluate the clearness of the speech
- Is the speech organized in an order that makes sense?
- Can you identify each of the main points of the speech?

Analyze the speaker's believability
- Does the speaker refer to outside sources of information?
- Are the sources respectable or credible?

Evaluate the speaker's delivery
- Does the speaker speak loudly and clearly enough to be understood easily?
- Does the speaker use eye contact, gestures, and facial expressions well?
- Does the speaker use visual materials?

Identify nonverbal messages
- Does the speaker use nonverbal elements to emphasize points?

(continued)

Points to Interpret and Evaluate	Strategies for Conducting an Interview

Points to Interpret and Evaluate

- Do the speaker's nonverbal gestures match his or her words?

Identify the speaker's purpose

- Why is the speaker giving the speech?
- Is the speech intended to inform, persuade, or entertain?

Identify the persuasive techniques

- Does the speaker try to convince you by using reasons and evidence, by appealing to your emotions, or both?
- Does the speaker use propaganda? For example, does the speaker try to make you feel that because everyone is doing something, you should, too? Does the speaker try to make you feel that he or she understands you?

Summarize the speaker's ideas

- Does the speech have a strong beginning and ending?

Special Listening Situations

In some situations, you will not only listen, but actively respond to the speaker's ideas and present new ideas or questions of your own.

Group Discussions   See **Group Discussion** on page 763.

Interviews   An interview is a one-on-one listening situation. You conduct interviews to gather information from someone who knows a great deal about a topic that interests you. This person is called the *interviewee.* Use the suggestions in the following chart to help you conduct a successful interview.

Strategies for Conducting an Interview

Before the Interview

- Decide what information you want to get from the interview.
- Make a list of questions to ask in the interview.
- Arrange an interview time and location with the person you will interview. Arrive on time.

During the Interview

- Take notes or tape-record the interview if the interviewee gives permission. If you will directly quote the person you interview, be sure you have his or her permission to do so.
- Be polite even if you disagree with the speaker's opinions. Make eye contact, and respond with facial expressions or gestures. Don't interrupt; give the interviewee time to thoroughly answer each of your questions. Then, ask follow-up questions that occur to you.
- If you do not understand an answer, ask questions to have the interviewee explain what he or she means, or repeat back to the speaker what you think he or she might have meant.
- Conclude by thanking the interviewee for his or her time.

After the Interview

- Review your notes, or make notes from your tape recording. Write a summary of the interview, and choose quotes you would like to use while the interview is still fresh in your mind.
- Send the interviewee a short note thanking him or her again for helping you gather the information you need.

Media Messages   The term *media* refers to forms of communication such as television, radio, newspapers, magazines, and the Internet. These are often called mass communication because they reach a large audience. Media may be created to inform, to persuade, or to entertain. Sometimes it is difficult to tell whether a program was created to entertain, to inform, or to persuade. Listeners must carefully analyze the messages they hear in media.

■ **Analyzing Media Messages**   In the media, persuasive messages may be disguised as entertainment or information. To understand the true purpose of a message, ask yourself the questions below.

Guidelines for Analyzing Media Messages
1. *What seems to be the purpose of the message?* Listen to the message. How is it presented? Is it presented by an authority? Does it sound true to you?
2. *Is the information in the message true and up-to-date?* Where does the information come from? If no sources are given, the information may not be trustworthy.
3. *What kind of language does the message contain?* Does it use language such as "you should . . ." to persuade you to do something? Does it compare two things using words such as *better* or *worse*?
4. *What are the underlying values or assumptions of the message?* Think about what the message is *not* saying. Sometimes what is not said in a message is as important as what is said. For example, a program on nuclear power that tells only about its positive aspects while

ignoring the dangers caused by malfunctions presents an uneven picture.

5. *What is your opinion of the message?* Use everything you know to form your own opinion about the message. If you think the message may not be accurate, you may want to find out more information on your own.

■ **Identifying Lack of Objectivity in the Media**   The chart below contains terms that you need to understand to help you evaluate media messages. These terms describe ways in which a message can be less than objective or truthful.

Bias is a preference or inclination. A biased speaker may present only one side of an issue or may downplay information that supports an opposing view. A biased listener may not pay attention to information that does not support his or her opinion.
Misleading Information means bending facts to support an idea. A speaker may use misleading information to support a point, especially if the point is already popular with the audience.
Prejudice is a pre-judgment or belief based on preconceived notions, rather than on facts or reason. Prejudiced speakers or listeners will ignore facts that go against their beliefs.
Propaganda is a systematic approach to influencing many people at once. Propaganda is found in advertisements, speeches, and other forms of persuasion. (See also page 792.)

Studying and Test Taking

Studying

Skills and Strategies

Studying helps you get good grades on assignments and tests, but good grades are not the only reason for studying. The real purpose of studying is to learn new information so that you can remember and use it later. The following section teaches skills and strategies you can use to study more effectively. (See also **Test Taking** on page 778.)

Making a Study Plan   Plan a study schedule that will help you study successfully. When you map out a schedule, stick to it. Here are some suggestions:

1. **Know your assignments.** Write down all your assignments and their due dates. Be sure you understand the instructions for each assignment.
2. **Make a plan.** Break large assignments into small steps. Keep track of when you should be finished with each step.
3. **Concentrate when you study.** Set aside time and find a quiet, well-lighted place

to study. This will help you focus your attention on your assignments.

Organizing and Remembering Information   Various study skills and strategies are simply different ways of organizing and handling information. The following are some of the most common strategies that can help you organize and remember information as you study.

■ **Classifying**   *Classifying* is arranging information into categories or groups. All the items that are in a category or group are related to each other. The name or description of the category shows the relationship among the various items in the group. If you break your notes into categories, you will have an easier time learning the material. For example, if you were studying earthquakes, you might divide your notes into these categories: the causes of earthquakes, the effects of earthquakes, and measuring earthquakes.

- **Graphic organizers** Sometimes, new information is easier to remember if you organize it visually. Using a graphic organizer, such as a map, diagram, or chart, can help you organize important details and understand their relationship to one another. Instead of trying to remember all the details in a long passage, you can simply remember the important ones you choose to include in your graphic organizer. (See also **Arranging Ideas** on page 806.)

- **Memorization** When you take tests and quizzes, you sometimes need to *memorize* the information on which you will be tested. Trying to memorize all of the study material the night before a test will not be very effective. Frequent, short, focused sessions are more likely to help you remember information. The following chart provides you with hints for memorizing effectively.

How to Memorize

1. Memorize key concepts. Whenever possible, condense the material you need to remember.

2. Rehearse the material in different ways. Copy the material by hand or recite the material out loud.

3. Invent memory games. Form a word from the first letters of important terms, or make up rhymes to help you remember facts and details.

- **Notes on reading or lectures**
Taking accurate *notes* during a reading

assignment or in class is worth the extra effort. With detailed information recorded in your notebook, you will be ready to study for even the most challenging test. It is much easier to review your study notes before a test than to review a whole chapter or series of chapters in a textbook.

How to Take Study Notes

1. Identify and take note of the main ideas in class or in your reading. These main ideas should be the headings in your notes. In class, listen for key words and phrases, such as *first, most important,* or *therefore.* These words often introduce main ideas or key concepts. In a textbook, chapter headings and related subheadings usually contain key ideas.

2. Include brief examples or details, if you can. Important examples or details can help you recall the main ideas.

3. Keep your notes brief. Develop a system of abbreviations and use it consistently. Summarize material in your own words.

4. Review your notes soon after you have written them to make sure you have included all important information.

At the top of page 776 is an example of careful study notes about an article on the history of soccer. The notes show main ideas as headings. Underneath these main headings are important details that relate to each heading. Not every detail from the passage appears. These notes list only the most important details.

Soccer is a very old game.

Evidence of games similar to soccer has been found in ancient Chinese, Mayan, Greek, and Egyptian cultures.

Modern soccer began in England in the 1800s.

"Football" was split into two games, soccer and rugby, in 1863.

The Growth of Professional Soccer

Professional soccer was first played in England and was officially recognized by the Football Association in 1885.

The first international game was played between Scotland and England in 1872.

British citizens spread soccer throughout Europe and South America.

■ **Outlines**   An *outline* helps you organize ideas that you read or hear. Outlines group the ideas in an order and in a pattern that shows relationships among the ideas. (See also **Formal** and **Informal Outlines** on page 807.)

■ **Paraphrasing**   *Paraphrasing* involves putting someone else's ideas into your own words. Putting an idea that you read or hear into your own words helps you understand it better. When you write a paraphrase of something you read, it will usually be about the same length as the original. You will probably not use paraphrasing for long passages of writing. Instead, you might *summarize* or *outline* the passage. (See also **Paraphrasing** on page 745, **Outlines** above, and **Summarizing** in the next column.)

Follow these guidelines when you write a paraphrase.

How to Paraphrase
1. Read the selection carefully before you begin.
2. Be sure you understand the main idea of the selection. Look up unfamiliar words in a dictionary.
3. Determine the tone of the selection. (What is the writer's attitude toward the subject of the selection?)
4. Identify the speaker in fictional material. (Is the writer speaking, or is a character in the selection?)
5. Write your paraphrase in your own words. Shorten long sentences or stanzas. Use your own, familiar vocabulary, but follow the same order of events or ideas that is used in the selection.
6. Check to be sure that the ideas in your paraphrase match the ideas that are expressed in the original selection.

■ **SQ3R**   *SQ3R* stands for *Survey, Question, Read, Recite,* and *Review.* This five-step method will help you read material more carefully and actively. When you read actively, you are more likely to remember what you read. (See also **SQ3R** on page 747.)

■ **Summarizing**   Like a paraphrase, a *summary* expresses another person's ideas in your own words. However, a summary shortens the original material by presenting only the most important points. (See also **Summarizing** on page 748.)

Use the following guidelines when you summarize.

How to Summarize

1. **Skim the selection** you wish to summarize.

2. **Read the passage again closely.** Look for the main ideas and notice all of the details that support each main idea.

3. **Write your summary in your own words.** Include only the main ideas and the most important supporting points.

4. **Evaluate and revise your summary,** checking to see that you have covered the most important points. Make sure you have clearly expressed the ideas in your passage.

The sample in the next column summarizes the reading selection on pages 83–85.

A recent study found that all-girl schools give girls more confidence in science and math, but not better test scores. Supporters of all-girl schools claim that girls get more attention and gain more confidence in all-girl schools. Opponents argue that all-girl schools discriminate against boys. They claim it is better to improve all schools so that girls and boys get equal, quality education in schools where they can learn to work together.

■ **Writing to learn** *Writing* can help you learn. When you write, you are forced to put your thoughts in order. For example, you can write to solve problems, record your observations, or work out the details of a plan. See the following chart for examples of different types of writing and their purposes.

Types of Writing for Different Purposes		
Type of Writing	**Purpose**	**Example**
Freewriting	To help you **focus** your thoughts	Writing for five minutes about a lecture you heard in history class
Autobiography	To help you **examine** the meaning of important events in your life	Writing about a personal experience that taught you to be thankful for what you have
Diary	To help you **recall** your impressions and **express** your feelings	Writing about your reactions to a field trip with your art class to a local art museum
Journal or Learning Log	To help you **record** your observations, descriptions, solutions, and questions	Writing down questions for your teacher as you watch a documentary on advances in math
	To help you **define** or **analyze** information, or **discover** a **solution** to a problem	Listing good and bad points of a proposed law you discussed in government class

Test Taking

Studying for Tests

As you go through school, you will take many tests. Two of the most common types are essay tests and objective tests. The following information can help you prepare for these types of tests.

Essay tests   *Essay tests* measure how well you understand a subject. Essay answers are usually a paragraph or longer.

How to Study for Essay Tests

1. Read assigned material carefully.

2. Make an outline of main points and important details.

3. Create your own essay questions and practice writing answers.

4. Evaluate and revise your practice answers. Check your answers against the information in your notes and textbook. Also, use the Writing Workshops in this textbook for help in writing.

Objective tests   *Objective tests* ask you for specific information, such as names, terms, dates, or definitions. Most objective test questions have only one correct answer.

How to Study for Objective Tests

1. Identify important terms, facts, or ideas in your textbook or class notes.

2. Review the information in more than one form. For example, if you are responsible for defining literary terms, make flash cards. Practice identifying the definition from the term; then identify the term from its definition.

3. Practice and rehearse factual information. Go over the items you have had difficulty with until you know them well.

4. If possible, briefly review all information shortly before the actual test.

Types of Test Questions

This section describes the different types of questions you may find on a test. You can use the tips and strategies for each question type to improve your performance on tests.

Analogy questions   An *analogy question* requires you to do two things. First, you must recognize the relationship between two words. Then, you must identify two other words that have a similar relationship.

EXAMPLE

Directions: Select the appropriate pair of words to complete the analogy.

1. MUG : TEA :: _____
   A. plate : bowl
   B. ice : iced water
   C. glass : milk
   D. curtain : window

How to Answer Analogy Questions

1. Create a sentence that expresses the relationship between the first pair of words. For example, you could say, "A *mug* is used to hold *tea*."

2. Use your sentence to find the answer choice with the same relationship. Test each answer choice using your sentence. Does a *plate* hold a *bowl*? Does *ice* hold *iced water*? Continue with the remaining answer choices.

3. Find the best available choice to complete the analogy. In this example, the only reasonable choice is C, since a *glass* holds *milk* just as a *mug* holds *tea*.

Essay questions *Essay questions* require thoughtful, thorough answers that are usually several paragraphs long. Prepare your essay with a topic sentence, supporting details, and a conclusion. Follow these steps to answer essay questions.

1. **Plan your approach.** Read the directions carefully to determine how many questions you are expected to answer. Decide how much time to spend on each section. Stay with your schedule. You may run out of time if you spend too much time on one question.

2. **Read the question carefully.** You may be asked for an answer that contains several parts.

3. **Pay attention to important terms in the question.** Essay questions on tests usually require an answer that accomplishes specific tasks. Each task is expressed by a verb. If you become familiar with the key verbs and the kind of response each one calls for, you can write a more successful essay. See the chart below.

Key Verbs That Appear in Essay Questions		
Key Verb	**Task**	**Sample Question**
analyze	Take something apart to see how each part works.	Analyze the water cycle.
compare	Point out likenesses.	Compare smoothies and juices.
contrast	Point out differences.	Contrast radio and TV news.
define	Give specific details that make something unique.	Define the word *culture* and give examples.
demonstrate	Provide examples to support a point.	Demonstrate the importance of voting in a democratic society.
describe	Give a picture in words.	Describe how a main character changes throughout a story.
discuss	Examine in detail.	Discuss the strategy of the Union army during the Battle of Shiloh.

(continued)

Key Verbs That Appear in Essay Questions

Key Verb	Task	Sample Question
explain	Give reasons.	Explain why a new computer lab is needed at your school.
identify	Point out specific characteristics.	Identify the different types of rock.
list	Give all steps in order or all details about a subject.	List the steps for finding the lowest common denominator of a group of numbers.
persuade	Form an opinion on an issue and give reasons to support it.	Persuade your principal that your school should or should not have vending machines.
summarize	Give a brief overview of the main points.	Summarize the tale of "Beauty and the Beast."

4. **Use prewriting strategies.** Consider the key verbs in the question. Then, jot down a few notes or an outline to help you decide what you want to say.

5. **Evaluate and revise as you write.** Look over what you have written, and find areas to improve your essay. Then, revise and edit it.

Matching questions

Matching questions ask you to match each item in one list with an item in another list.

EXAMPLE

Directions: Match the greeting in the left-hand column with its language in the right-hand column.

B	1. Guten Tag	A.	Italian
D	2. Bonjour	B.	German
A	3. Buon giorno	C.	Spanish
C	4. Buenos días	D.	French

These steps can help you answer matching questions.

How to Answer Matching Questions

1. Read the directions carefully. Sometimes you will not use all the items listed in one column. Other items may be used more than once.

2. Scan the columns. If you match items you know first, you'll have more time to evaluate items you are less sure about.

3. Complete the rest of the matching. Make your best guess on remaining items.

Multiple-choice questions

With a *multiple-choice question,* you select the best answer from a number of choices.

EXAMPLE

1. The majority of meteorites found on Earth are from
   A. Mars
   B. the asteroid belt
   C. the Moon
   D. Jupiter

The following guidelines can help you answer multiple-choice questions.

How to Answer Multiple-Choice Questions

1. Read the question or statement carefully. Make sure you understand the question or statement you are given before you look at the answer choices. Look for words such as *not* or *always*. These words limit your choice of answers.

2. Read all the choices before selecting an answer. Eliminate choices that you know are incorrect. This improves your chances of choosing correctly among the remaining choices. Think carefully about each remaining choice. Then, select the one that makes the most sense.

On-demand reading questions An on-demand test is one for which you cannot study in advance. One type of on-demand test requires reading. An *on-demand reading question* asks you to read a passage and answer questions about it. The answer may be found in the passage or may be based on your understanding of the passage.

EXAMPLE

Directions: Read the following passage and the questions after it.

People are not the only ones to get viruses. Computers also get viruses, or programs that are designed to "infect" one computer and be passed along to another. Viruses frequently scramble a computer's data. Some viruses, such as the Cascade virus, can produce spectacular effects. When the Cascade virus strikes, letters of a document appear to fall into a heap at the bottom of the screen.

1. In this passage, the author's purpose is to
   A. give information about computer viruses
   B. persuade people not to use computers
   C. compare different types of computers
   D. entertain with a story about viruses

These steps can help you answer on-demand reading questions.

How to Answer On-Demand Reading Questions

1. Read the passage carefully. As you read, identify the main idea of the passage, as well as important details. (See also **Stated Main Idea** on page 747.)

2. Read the questions that follow. Most questions after reading selections are multiple-choice.

3. Look for similar language in the questions and the reading passage. You can match words from the questions with a sentence in the reading passage and find the answer.

4. Draw your own conclusions. The example passage never states the purpose directly. However, you can tell that the author is giving information about computer viruses.

On-demand writing questions

On-demand writing questions are essay questions. You will frequently find them on state writing tests. You cannot study for the content of an on-demand writing question, but you can prepare by being familiar with different kinds of writing. These questions often ask you to write a persuasive, informative, narrative, or descriptive essay about a broad topic. Prepare by writing practice essays.

EXAMPLE

Fictional characters are often created from an author's real-life relationships. Think about a character in a book you have read. How is the character similar to someone you know? How is the character different? Write an essay comparing and contrasting a fictional character with a real-life friend or family member.

How to Answer On-Demand Writing Questions

1. Read the question carefully. Look for key terms in the question to help you determine what the question is asking. Decide whether your essay should be persuasive, informative, or descriptive. (See also **Key Verbs That Appear in Essay Questions** on page 779.)

2. Plan your answer. Use a prewriting technique to help you plan before you begin writing. (See also **Prewriting Techniques** on page 802.)

3. Evaluate and revise your answer as you write. Your essay should have a topic sentence, supporting details and examples, transitions, and a conclusion.

Reasoning or logic questions

Reasoning or *logic questions* test your reasoning abilities rather than your knowledge of a particular subject. Some reasoning questions ask you to identify the relationship among several items. For example, a reasoning question may ask you to predict the next item in a sequence.

EXAMPLE

What comes next?

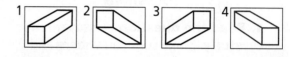

In this sequence of three drawings, the front of the block is in a different corner of the box each time. Therefore, in its final position the front of the block must be in the lower right corner of the box.

How to Answer Reasoning or Logic Questions

1. Be sure you understand the instructions. Reasoning or logic questions are often multiple-choice. On some tests, however, you may need to write a word or phrase, complete a number sequence, or even draw a picture for your answer.

2. Analyze the relationship implied in the question. Study the question carefully to gather information about the relationship of the items.

3. Draw reasonable conclusions. Evaluate the relationship of the items to decide your answer.

Sentence-completion questions

Many *sentence-completion questions* test your understanding of vocabulary words used in a sentence.

EXAMPLE

1. Because of the dry weather conditions, the tree _____ will not be as colorful and spectacular this year.

A. function   C. canopy
B. foliage   D. yacht

> ### How to Answer Sentence-Completion Questions
>
> **1. Read the sentence carefully.** Make sure you understand the words in the sentence. Some sentences may contain clues to the meaning of the word or words that go in the blanks.
>
> **2. Rule out incorrect answer choices.** If you can immediately rule out some answer choices, mark through them. In the previous example, the word *yacht* refers to a type of boat. You can immediately rule out this choice since you know the correct word has something to do with trees.
>
> **3. Fill in the blank with the remaining choices and choose the best answer.** If you are not sure which choice is correct, use each one in the blank of the sentence.

Short-answer questions

Short-answer questions ask for short, precise responses. Instead of choosing from among a set of choices, you write the answer yourself. Some short-answer questions (such as labeling a map or diagram, or fill-in-the-blank questions) can be answered with one or a few words. Other types of short-answer questions require you to give a full, written response, usually one or two sentences in length.

EXAMPLE How are suspension bridges different from other types of bridges?

Answer: Suspension bridges are supported by cables. They can cover larger distances than other types of bridges because they do not need support in the middle. Suspension bridges use less metal so they can also be cheaper to build than other types of bridges.

> ### How to Answer Short-Answer Questions
>
> **1. Read the question carefully.** Some questions have more than one part. You must answer each part.
>
> **2. Plan your answer.** Quickly decide what you need to include in the answer.
>
> **3. Be as specific as possible in your answers.** Give a full, exact answer.
>
> **4. Budget your time.** Begin by answering those questions you know.

True-false questions

In a *true-false question,* you are asked to decide whether a certain statement is true or false.

EXAMPLE

1. T   (F)   The Niagara Suspension Railway Bridge is the longest suspension bridge in the world.

> ### How to Answer True-False Questions
>
> **1. Read the statement carefully.** The statement is false if any part of it is false.
>
> **2. Look for word clues.** Words such as *always* or *never* limit a statement. A statement is true only if it is always true.

Viewing and Representing

Understanding Media Terms

Like people in many other professions, people who work in and write about the media often use *jargon*. **Jargon** is special language or terminology that helps a group of people with shared interests communicate quickly. Learning some media terms will help you analyze and evaluate the media messages you receive as well as those you create.

The terms in this section are divided into three lists: Electronic Media Terms, General Media Terms, and Print Media Terms. Terms that apply to both print media and electronic media are defined under Print Media Terms on pages 792–794. Terms relating to the Internet and the World Wide Web can be found in the "Library/Media Center" section beginning on page 735; terms relating to use of type and graphics can be found in "Document Design" beginning on page 722.

Electronic Media Terms

Advertising   See **Advertising** on page 792.

Animation   *Animation* is the technique of making photographs or drawings appear to move. Animators take a series of photographs of drawings or objects, or they generate a series of pictures on a computer. Each picture is called a frame, and each frame varies slightly from the ones before and after it. When the pictures are viewed at a rate of twenty-four frames per second, they create an illusion of movement. Many different types of media messages, including commercials and cartoons, use animation.

Broadcasting   *Broadcasting* is the sending of television or radio content over a wide area through the airwaves. *Commercial*

broadcasting is done for profit. Advertisers pay broadcasters for airtime in which to persuade the audience to buy their products or services. **Public broadcasting** is not-for-profit broadcasting. In the United States, the Public Broadcasting Service (PBS) has more than three hundred member stations. The service is funded mostly by corporations and individual viewers and listeners. The federal government also provides some funds.

Byline   See **Byline** on page 792.

Cable Television   *Cable television* is a method of delivering television signals to homes and businesses through cables. A cable service provider receives the signals using powerful antennae. Viewers pay to receive the signals in their homes and offices.

Camera Angle   The *camera angle* is the angle at which a camera is pointed at its subject. A low angle makes the subject look tall and powerful, while a high angle makes the subject look small. A tilted angle suggests that the subject is not balanced.

Camera Shot   A *camera shot* is a single, continuous image in film or video. The following shots are some of the most common shots used in film and video production.

- **Close-up shot**   a shot showing the subject up close, for example, a person's face
- **Medium shot**   a shot showing the subject from a midrange distance, for example, a person and the top of the desk at which he or she sits

- **Long shot**   a shot showing the subject from a distance, for example, a city from an airplane

Commercial Broadcasting   See **Broadcasting** on page 784.

Copy   See **Copy** on page 792.

Credits   *Credits* list the names of people who worked on a presentation. They usually appear at the end of a television program, film, or video.

Demographics   See **Demographics** on page 792.

Digital Editing   See **Digital Editing** on page 792.

Documentary   A *documentary* is a type of film or television program that interprets actual events. A documentary usually includes interviews and footage of actual events. Some documentaries include reenactments of events as well as voice-over narration. The primary purpose of a documentary may be to inform, persuade, or entertain. The purpose of some documentaries is to make money. Documentaries may have more than one purpose. For instance, a documentary about lions may be both informative (telling where lions live and what they eat) and entertaining (showing lion cubs playing together).

Editor   See **Editor** on page 792.

Feature News See **Feature News** on page 793.

Film *Film* is a medium for recording sounds and images. On film, sounds and images are clearer than they are on videotape. Filmed images and sounds last a long time, and they can be presented on a large screen. However, film is more expensive to buy and develop than videotape. (See also **Videotape** on page 787.)

Hard News See **Hard News** on page 793.

Internet The *Internet* is a network of computers that allows computer users all over the world to communicate with each other. Using the Internet requires a computer equipped with a modem, a device that connects the computer with a telephone or cable line. Internet service providers (ISPs) provide access to the Internet for a monthly fee. (See also **"The Library/Media Center."**)

Lead See **Lead** on page 793.

Marketing See **Marketing** on page 793.

Medium See **Medium** on page 793.

Message See **Message** on page 791.

News See **News** on page 793.

Newsmagazine See **Newsmagazine** on page 794.

Photography See **Photography** on page 794.

Producer A *producer* is the person who oversees the production of a movie or a television or radio program. He or she develops the overall message and finds appropriate materials. The producer also organizes a crew or staff, finds funding, budgets, and keeps the production on schedule. (See also **Production** on page 794.)

Production See **Production** on page 794.

Public Broadcasting See **Broadcasting** on page 784.

Reporter See **Reporter** on page 794.

Script A *script* is the text to be spoken during a film, a play, or a television or radio program. It may include voice-over narration as well as dialogue. Film and television scripts also include information about the images to be shown. The script for a news broadcast is called *copy*.

Soft News See **Soft News** on page 794.

Sound In film and video, *sound* is all of the recorded material that you hear, including dialogue, music, and sound effects. Producers and filmmakers use sound to achieve various goals. One role of sound is to create an illusion. For example, you may watch a movie and think it is raining even though the rain is not visible. The sounds of rain falling on a roof and the cracking of thunder convince you that it is raining. Another role of sound is to create mood. For example, the music that a video producer selects to accompany visual images can tell the audience how to feel about those images.

Source   See under **Print Media Terms**.

Storyboard   A *storyboard* is a series of drawings showing the sequence of shots and scenes in a script. It may also include audio and visual cues. (See also page 259.)

Target Audience   See **Target Audience** on page 794.

Text   See **Text** on page 794.

Videotape   *Videotape* is a medium used to record sounds and images. A videotape may be easier to make than a film because video equipment is cheaper and easier to use. However, images recorded on videotape tend to have poorer *resolution,* or less clarity, than filmed images, and videotape does not last as long as film. (See also **Film** on page 786.)

General Media Terms

Audience   An *audience* is a group of people who receive a media message. Advertisers try to reach the audience they think is most likely to buy their products or services. (See also **Advertising** on page 792, **Demographics** on page 792, and **Target Audience** on page 794.)

Authority   *Authority* refers to how knowledgeable and trustworthy the source of a message seems. When a message appears to come from an expert source, you find it authoritative. For example, a meteorologist would know more about tornadoes than a figure skater would, but a figure skater would know more about triple toe loops than a meteorologist would.

Bias   A *bias* is a preference for one side of an issue, either for it or against it. A biased speaker or writer may ignore information that does not support his or her views. (See also **Point of View** on page 791.)

Context   *Context* is the material that surrounds a media message. For example, the context of a magazine ad includes the other ads and the articles in that magazine. The context may influence how you interpret a message.

Credibility   *Credibility* is the quality of being believable. A person's credibility is decided by the audience members. (For more on **evaluating credibility**, see page 771. See also **Message** on page 791.)

Critical Viewing   *Critical viewing* means analyzing, interpreting, and evaluating visual messages in the mass media. Such messages may take a range of forms, from still photographs and editorial cartoons to films and television programs. Critical viewers keep the following five concepts in mind as they view messages in the media.

Media Concepts	
Concept 1: All messages are made by someone.	To create a visual message, an artist, photographer, or filmmaker must decide which elements (words, images, sounds) to include, which ones to leave out, and how to arrange and sequence the chosen elements. Knowing how

(continued)

Media Concepts

visual messages are constructed will help you analyze the message. It will also help you appreciate the skill that went into creating the message.

Concept 2: Messages are reflections of reality.

A visual message is a version of reality, not reality itself. For a television broadcast of a baseball game, for example, everything from the camera angles to the amount of time set aside for commercials is carefully packaged. Realizing that a visual message is a version of reality will help you evaluate how authentic (true to life) the message seems.

Concept 3: Each person interprets messages differently.

The meaning a viewer draws from a visual message depends on the viewer's prior knowledge and experience. Since people's prior knowledge and experience vary, viewers may draw different meanings from the same message. Connecting the message to your own life experiences will help you interpret the message.

Concept 4: Messages have a wide range of purposes.

Every person who creates a visual message has a purpose. Usually, that purpose is to inform, persuade, entertain, or express thoughts and feelings. Most visual messages in the mass media also have another purpose: to make money. Being aware of the underlying commercial purpose of such messages will help you understand their effects on you.

Concept 5: The medium shapes the message.

Each type of visual medium has its own strengths and weaknesses. For example, film combines motion and sound, but the action flashes by quickly. A still photograph captures only a single moment, but it can be studied at length. People who create visual messages tailor their work to take full advantage of a particular medium's strengths. Knowing how the medium shapes the message will help you understand its creator's choice of medium and its effect on you.

Evaluating Media Messages The following questions will help you analyze, interpret, and evaluate visual messages in the mass media. The questions are based on the five media concepts explained above.

- Through what medium is the message delivered?

- Who created the message?
- What seems to be the purpose of the message? Is there also an underlying purpose? If so, what is it?
- What elements (words, images, or sounds) does the message include?
- How are those elements arranged and sequenced?

- How skillfully are the elements presented?
- What may have been left out of the message?
- How is the message's version of reality similar to or different from what you know from your own experience or from other sources?
- How authentic (true to life) does the message seem? Why?
- What does the message make you think of? How does it make you feel about the world? about yourself? about other people?
- How does the medium help shape the message?

Feedback   *Feedback* is a response from an audience to the sender of a message. It can be immediate or delayed. Applauding and asking questions are examples of immediate feedback. Writing a letter to an editor and filling out a questionnaire are examples of delayed feedback.

Formula   A *formula* is an established model or approach. In television and film, it refers to a typical way of combining characters or presenting material. Situation comedies, for example, often follow the formula of pairing characters with opposite personalities and interests.

Genre   A *genre* is a category of media products that share certain characteristics. Examples of genres common on television include

- children's programming
- documentary
- drama
- game show
- infomercial
- music video
- news broadcast
- sitcom (situation comedy)
- soap opera
- talk show

Illustration   An *illustration* is a drawing, painting, photograph, or computer-generated image. Illustrations are created to decorate or explain something. Consider the following elements as you create or evaluate illustrations (or any other visual art form).

- **Color**   Illustrators use color to create a specific mood or feeling, focus attention on a certain part of the illustration, or both. The quality of color is affected by its medium: felt-tip pens, powder, paints, and watercolors, for example, all create different effects.
- **Form**   Form is the three-dimensional look of an illustration. An illustration that appears to have depth and weight can look more realistic. Artists use color, line, and shape to give form to the objects they illustrate.
- **Line**   Line is the most basic element of illustration. Although real objects do not have lines around them, illustrators can create the illusion of reality through lines. Lines can be fine and delicate, showing texture, for example, or strong and bold. Artists also use line to show depth in an illustration and to show viewers the location of the horizon line.

■ **Shape**   Lines come together to form a shape, or a two-dimensional outline of an object. An illustration may contain several shapes that are all connected to each other in some way.

Images   An **image** is a visual representation of something. A painting, a photograph, a sculpture, and a moving picture are all examples of an image. Images may be *moving* or *still.*

■ A *still image,* such as a painting or a single frame of a film, allows viewers the time to notice details and consider the meaning of the image because the image does not move. Still images may also be easier to change—through cropping or

digital editing, for example—than moving images.

■ A *moving image* is a series of still images projected quickly onto a television or film screen. Moving images that show actual events are called *documentary footage.* The evening news may include examples of documentary footage. Moving images that show an event arranged by a TV producer or filmmaker are called *dramatizations.* You can see a dramatization when you go to a movie theater. Both kinds of moving images can be incomplete or altered.

To analyze the effects of an image, consider the following techniques.

Creating Effects with Images	
Technique	**Definition/Effects**
Color	Color can create feelings or emphasize parts of an image. For example, filming a scene in black-and-white may have a sobering effect on the viewer. In a color photograph of a crowd, people wearing brightly colored clothes, such as red, orange, or yellow, will stand out compared to people wearing white or black.
Juxtaposition	Putting two or more images together creates a juxtaposition. Sometimes two images, still or moving, placed side-by-side can communicate more meaning than one image alone. For example, a detective show that cuts between images of a criminal opening a safe and a detective sneaking around a corner tells its viewers that the robbery will be interrupted by the detective.
Slow or fast motion	Moving images can be slowed down or sped up to create a certain effect. Making an image move slower than normal can create a dramatic effect, whereas speeding up an image can create a comic effect.

Media Law   The First Amendment of the U.S. Constitution guarantees the freedom of the press. Therefore, except during wartime, the United States government rarely uses *censorship*. (*Censorship* refers to any attempt by a government or other group to control people's access to literature or the mass media.) Some media regulations, however, do exist. The Federal Communications Commission (FCC) enforces laws governing electronic media. Other laws protect individuals from the media. For example, a person whose reputation has been damaged by the publication of a false statement may sue the publisher. Copyright laws guard authors or publishers against *plagiarism,* or theft, of a message.

The growing use of the Internet has raised many new questions about regulation of the media. These questions will be the subject of debate for years to come.

Media Literacy   *Media literacy* is the ability to access, analyze, evaluate, and communicate messages in a wide variety of forms. (See also **Critical Viewing** on page 787.)

Message   A *message* is a communication sent to one or more people through language, gestures, images, or sounds. The *content* of a message is the information it presents. (See also **Credibility** on page 787, **Realism** on page 792, and **Source** on page 794.)

Multimedia Presentation   *Multimedia presentations* involve the use of two or more forms of media. When you give an oral presentation that includes visuals—

such as slides, video segments, or transparencies—you are giving a multimedia presentation. One medium is your voice; the other is the visuals you use. A multimedia presentation that involves the use of presentation software or Web sites is called a *technology presentation.*

Newsworthiness   *Newsworthiness* is the quality of an event that makes it seem worth reporting. An event is considered newsworthy if it meets certain criteria (standards). News criteria include

- **impact**   events or issues that make a difference in people's lives
- **timeliness**   events or issues that are happening now
- **celebrity angle**   stories about people who are famous or in power
- **human interest**   stories that touch people's emotions

An event that meets several of these criteria is more likely to be covered by the news media.

Persuasion   See **Propaganda** on page 792.

Point of View   *Point of view* is the way a message sender approaches a topic. Everyone's point of view is shaped by his or her background and values. For example, in covering the opening of a new shopping center, one reporter might focus on the jobs the center has created. Another might focus on the locally owned stores that may lose business to the center.

In photography, point of view refers to the photographer's approach to his or her subject. The photographer's point of view affects the selection of the subject and the camera angle. (See also **Bias** on page 787 and **Propaganda** below.)

Propaganda *Propaganda* is a form of communication that influences an audience by using persuasive techniques. These techniques play on the audience's emotions and may be used to mislead audiences. You can find propaganda in television commercials, political speeches, and advertisements in magazines and newspapers. The persuasive techniques used in propaganda convince by leading the viewer to make a generalization about a person, product, or service. For instance, a commercial that shows a movie star with beautiful hair using a particular brand of shampoo may lead you to the conclusion that you can have beautiful hair if you use the shampoo, too. (See also **Advertising** below, **Bias** on page 787, and **Point of View** on page 791.)

Realism *Realism* is representing people and things just as they appear in real life, without making them seem more pleasant or acceptable.

Stereotypes *Stereotypes* are beliefs about all the members of a group. One common stereotype is that all Texans wear cowboy boots and ride horses. Such beliefs do not take into account the many differences between any two people. Usually, stereotypes are based on too little evidence or on false or misleading information.

Print Media Terms

Advertising *Advertising* is the use of images, text, or both to persuade an audi-ence to buy, use, or accept a product, service, image, or idea. Advertisers pay the media for time or space in which to promote their products and services. (See also **Marketing** on page 793.)

Byline A *byline* is the name of the reporter or writer of a newspaper or magazine article or a television or radio presentation.

Copy *Copy* is the text in a media message. (See also **Script** on page 786.)

Demographics *Demographics* are the characteristics of a particular audience. They may include gender (male or female), age, education, cultural heritage, and income. Advertisers use demographics to target certain audiences. For example, advertisers know that many women read the life and arts section of a newspaper, so they will advertise products and services in the life and arts section to capture that audience's attention. (See also **Audience** on page 787 and **Target Audience** on page 794.)

Digital Editing *Digital editing* is the use of computer technology to change a digitalized (or online) image before it is presented to an audience. When an image is converted to a digital version, it is easy to add or delete people and objects or change the original background. For example, a photograph taken in a studio can be altered so that it appears it was taken on a beach.

Editor An *editor* supervises reporters. Editors decide what news stories will appear, check facts for accuracy, and correct errors.

Editorial Cartoon   An *editorial cartoon* is a cartoon, usually found in the editorial section of a newspaper, that reflects the cartoonist's opinion on a current event. Editorial cartoonists use exaggeration and caricature to make their points in a humorous way.

Feature News   *Feature news* (also called *soft news*) refers to news stories whose primary purpose is to entertain. Such stories may or may not be timely. They may be about celebrities or ordinary people or about places, animals, events, or products. An article about a movie star's wedding would be an example of feature news. (See also **Hard News** below and **Soft News** on page 794.)

Font   A *font* is a style of lettering used for printing text. (See also **Font** on page 726.)

Hard News   *Hard news* is fact-based reporting of current events. Hard news answers the basic *5W-How?* questions about important subjects such as politics and social issues. For example, a story about factories dumping toxins into a river is hard news. (See also **Feature News** above and **Soft News** on page 794.)

Headline   A *headline* is the title of a newspaper article, usually set in large, bold-face type. It has two purposes: to catch the reader's attention and to tell the reader what the article is about. (See also **Titles and Subtitles** on page 726.)

EXAMPLE   **Senator Seeks Second Term**

Lead   A *lead* is the opening words or paragraph of a news story. It may contain the major facts of the story, or it may use a surprising or unusual fact or idea to hook the audience's attention.

EXAMPLE   Nearly one hundred volunteers helped to ease the overcrowding at the Trevor County Animal Shelter. Volunteers worked nights and weekends for an entire month repairing fences and building new dog runs. Money for the project was donated by citizens and local businesses.

Marketing   *Marketing* is the process of moving goods or services from the producer to the consumer. It includes identifying consumer wants or needs; designing, packaging, and pricing a product; and arranging for locations where the product will be sold. It also includes promoting the product to a target audience through advertising or other means. (See also **Advertising** on page 792, **Demographics** on page 792, and **Target Audience** on page 794.)

Medium   The *medium* of a message is the means through which it is communicated. *Medium* is a singular noun; its plural form is *media*. Modern media can be grouped into two general categories: *print media,* such as newspapers and magazines; and *electronic media,* such as radio, television, audio and video recordings, film, and the Internet. The *mass media* are those that reach a large audience.

Message   See **Message** on page 791.

News   *News* is the presentation of current information that will interest or affect an audience. Local news organizations focus on news of regional interest. National news organizations cover national and world issues and events.

Newsmagazine   A *newsmagazine* is a publication, usually issued weekly, that focuses on recent events and issues. In television, the term is used for a news program that airs one or more times a week and analyzes and interprets the news.

Photography   *Photography* is the process of using a camera to record an image on film. Like all media messages, photographs are selective and incomplete. Before an image is photographed, a photographer makes many decisions, including what will be in the frame and from what angle the image will be shot. The photographer will also choose a specific speed of film depending on the amount of light available. Once the photograph is developed, a photographer or editor decides whether the photograph needs to be cropped, or cut, and whether it needs a caption. (See also **Digital Editing** on page 792 and **Point of View** on page 791.)

Political Cartoon   See **Editorial Cartoon** on page 793.

Production   *Production* is the process of creating a film, video, radio or television program, or publication. There are three stages to production.

- During *preproduction,* copy or scripts are obtained and polished, funds are raised and budgeted, staff and crew are hired, and schedules are planned.
- During *production,* the work is filmed, recorded, or printed.
- During *postproduction,* finishing touches are added. Films and tapes are edited, soundtracks are recorded, and sound and special effects are added. Books and newspapers are bound or gathered. Postproduction also includes marketing and distribution. (See also **Marketing** on page 793.)

Reporter   A *reporter* is a journalist who gathers information and works with editors to create electronic or print reports.

Soft News   *Soft news* is the presentation of general-interest material, such as consumer information and sports, in a news format. A story about a local basketball team competing at a state tournament is an example of soft news. The purpose of soft news is to inform and entertain. (See also **Feature News** on page 793 and **Hard News** on page 793.)

Source   A *source* is a person or publication that supplies information or ideas. Journalists rely on sources for much of the information they report. They try to select individuals they believe are credible and have authority. (See also **Credibility** on page 787 and **Message** on page 791.)

Target Audience   A *target audience* is a segment of the population for which a product or message is designed. Children are usually the target audience for Saturday morning TV commercials, and men are often the target audience for tool ads. (See also **Demographics** on page 792.)

Text   *Text* refers to the words used to create a message. (See also **Message** on page 791.)

Writing

Skills, Structures, and Techniques

You can use the following ideas and information to become a more effective writer.

Applications   See **Forms** on page 797.

Composition   A *composition* is a piece of writing with three basic parts: *introduction, body,* and *conclusion*. The introduction is like a topic sentence in a paragraph because it states the main idea. The body develops the main idea of the composition, and the conclusion ends the composition.

■ **Introduction**   Your composition's *introduction* should do two things:

1. **Catch the readers' attention.** Your introduction should hook your readers and make them want to read more. To capture your readers' attention, try one of the following techniques. The examples show how you might use these techniques to write an introduction for a composition about summer camp.

> **How to Catch Your Readers' Attention**
>
> **Begin by asking a question.**
> *Do you find yourself bored during the summer? If so, you may want to find out what it would be like to go to summer camp.*
>
> **Begin with an anecdote or a funny story.**
> *I packed my bags, rolled up my sleeping bag, and said goodbye to my dog Max and my parents, too. I was on my way to having fun and meeting new friends. I was on my way to summer camp.*
>
> **Begin with a startling fact.**
> *For over one hundred years, YMCA camps have helped children of all ages learn new skills, make new friends, and have fun during the summer.*

2. **Present the main idea.** Include your *main idea statement,* or *thesis,* in your introduction. A *main idea statement* is

one or two sentences that announce your topic and your main point about the topic. A main idea statement works in a composition the way a topic sentence works in a paragraph. You can use your main idea statement as a guide as you plan, write, and revise your paper. Here are some strategies for writing a main idea statement.

How to Write a Main Idea Statement

1. Ask yourself, "What is my topic?"
summer camp

2. Review your prewriting notes. Think about how the facts and details fit together. Identify the idea that connects the details to one another.
Summer camp taught me much more than tennis or swimming.

3. Use specific details to make the main idea clear. Zooming in on specific details will make the main idea more focused.
Summer camp taught me to get along with new people, challenge myself, and enjoy nature.

■ **Body** Every paragraph in the *body* supports the composition's main idea by developing a part of it. To help the body paragraphs work together, use the following guidelines.

1. The ideas in your composition should be easy to follow. Give your composition *coherence* by arranging your information in an order that your readers will understand. (See also page 297.) To show how your ideas are connected, use *transitional words and phrases*. (See also pages 302–303.)

2. Give your paper *unity* by eliminating any details that do not support your thesis. (See also page 295.)

■ **Conclusion** As the final part of your paper, the *conclusion* should do two things:

1. **Let the readers feel your composition is complete.** If your composition ends too suddenly, your readers may feel dissatisfied, as if they have been left hanging.

2. **Bring the readers back to the main idea.** The conclusion should tie your composition's supporting ideas together and flow once more into your main idea.

How to Write a Conclusion

Refer to your introduction.
The girl who got off the bus and ran to greet her puppy and her parents was not the same girl who had said goodbye a month earlier. Summer camp taught me much more than swimming. I learned many valuable lessons about life.

Restate your main idea.
I might forget the songs we sang around the campfire, and maybe I won't ever get on another sailboat. However, I will never forget the real lessons that camp taught me about myself, others, and nature.

Close with a final idea or example.

I enjoyed my time at summer camp so much that I decided to help others learn life lessons, too. By volunteering at YMCA day camps, I help motivate five-year-olds to make new friends, accept new challenges, and experience nature.

E-mail Electronic mail, or *e-mail,* comes by computer rather than by a letter carrier. E-mail can be used for both personal letters and business letters. When you write a personal e-mail, you do not have to follow the usual guidelines for writing letters. However, if you are using e-mail for business or research purposes, you should follow the guidelines listed below.

E-mail Guidelines

Make sure you enter the correct address. It is easy to send e-mails to the wrong person.

Always fill in the subject line before you send a message. This helps your readers to scan and decide which e-mail messages are most important.

When writing to someone you do not know, include salutations, such as *Dear Senator Costa.* It is also polite to include a closing, such as *Sincerely* or *Thank you,* followed by your full name.

Make your message short and to the point. Be considerate of your reader by limiting yourself to one full screen or less of text.

Make sure your spelling, grammar, and punctuation are correct.

Use bulleted lists and indentation to make the document easy to read. Bulleted lists are especially helpful if you are raising more than one question or point.

Be polite in your messages—even ones to people you know well.

Avoid capitalizing entire words in your messages. USING CAPITALS IN YOUR WRITING IS SIMILAR TO SHOUTING WHEN YOU SPEAK. Constant shouting is annoying even in cyberspace. If you want to emphasize a word, try placing asterisks (*) on either side of it. For example, "Did you remember to buy the game *tickets*?"

Never use *emoticons* in formal e-mails. *Emoticons* are combinations of symbols and letters that resemble faces. They are a kind of shorthand to communicate feelings or reactions. For example, the emoticon :-) suggests laughter or the statement "I'm just kidding." Emoticons should be used only in informal e-mails.

Ask permission of the original sender before forwarding an e-mail. Private e-mails are usually intended for your eyes only.

Forms There are many kinds of forms. For example, an *application* is a form you fill out to ask or apply for something. You might fill out an application to request membership in a school organization, to open a savings account, or to apply for a job. The form on the next page is an application for a library card.

**Whitehouse Public Library System
Youth Card Application**

Date 9/21/2001

Name Shawna Washington

Address 5310 Rosemont Drive

City Whitehouse State TX

Zip 75791

Home Phone 555-0121

Birth date 4/30/90

Parent or Guardian
Signature *Eleanor Washington*

When completing forms, use the following guidelines to help you give clear, complete information.

- Look over the entire form before you begin.

- Follow special instructions (such as "Type or print" or "Use a pencil").

- Supply all the information requested. If a question does not apply to you, write *does not apply*, the symbol *N/A*, which means "not applicable," or use a dash.

- Proofread your finished form, making sure nothing is left blank. Neatly correct any errors.

Letters *Letters* are an important form of communication. Everyone likes to get letters. To receive letters, however, you usually have to write your share. Keep in mind that each type of letter has a specific purpose and an intended audience. Therefore, it is important to know a few general rules about writing different types of letters. The following chart describes the purposes and audiences of different types of letters.

Business

- The *purpose* of a business letter is to inform a business that you need its services or to tell how well or badly a service was performed.

- The *audience* of a business letter is a business or an organization.

Informal or Personal

- The *purpose* of an informal or personal letter is to express emotions, ideas, or appreciation, or to communicate information about a specific event.

- The *audience* of an informal or personal letter is a close friend, a relative, or a social acquaintance.

Letters, Business A *business letter* is a formal letter about a business-related matter, such as a request for a product or service or an application for a job. To be effective, a business letter must look and sound professional. That means you should type the letter or use your best handwriting, either print or cursive. You should also use your best English, and never use slang.

- **Envelopes** An envelope must be addressed correctly for it to arrive at its destination. Your address, or the return address, goes in the top left-hand corner of the envelope. The name and address of the person to whom you are writing go in the center of the envelope. For a business letter, the name and address on the envelope should exactly match the inside address of the letter. Use the two-letter state code on the envelope rather than writing out the state name, and always include the correct ZIP Code.

```
Tama Wuliton
2703 Bryant Road
Dana Point, CA 92629


        Clasprite Paper Clip Company
        1605 S. Noland Rd., Building 8
        San Diego, CA 92105
```

■ **Parts**   Business letters follow a particular form, which includes six parts.

1. The *heading* usually has three lines: your street address; your city, state, and ZIP Code; and the date the letter was written.

   EXAMPLE

   4516 Magnolia Drive
   Walpole, MA 02081
   November 8, 2001

2. The *inside address* gives the name and address of the person to whom you are writing. If you know the name of the person, use a courtesy title (such as *Mr.* or *Ms.*) or a professional title (such as *Dr.* or *Professor*). Include the person's business title after the name. If you do not have the person's name, use a business title or position title (such as *Store Manager* or *Complaints Department Manager*).

3. The *salutation* is your greeting to the person to whom you are writing. The salutation ends with a colon (such as in *Dear Mayor Williams:*). If you are writing to a specific person, use the person's name (such as *Dear Ms. Stokes:*). If you don't have the name of a specific person, use a general salutation (such as *Dear Sir or Madam:* or *Ladies and Gentlemen:*). You can also use a department or a position title (such as *Activity Director:* or *Head of Division:*), with or without the word *Dear.*

4. The *body* contains the message of your letter. Leave a blank line between paragraphs in the body of the letter.

5. The *closing* should end your letter politely. There are several standard phrases that are often used to close business letters, such as *Sincerely, Respectfully yours,* or *Yours truly.*

6. Your *signature* should be handwritten in ink, directly below the closing. Your name should be typed or printed neatly just below your signature.

■ **Styles**   The six parts of a letter are usually arranged in one of the two most common styles used for business letters.

The *block form* places each part of the letter at the left margin of the page. A blank space is left between each paragraph in the body of the letter. Paragraphs are not indented.

The *modified block form* arranges the heading, the closing, and your signature just to the right of the center of the page. The middle parts of the letter all begin at the left margin, and a blank space is left between each paragraph in the body of the letter. Each paragraph is indented.

Block Style

1
2
3
4
5
6

Modified Block Style

1
2
3
4
5
6

■ **Types**   Types of business letters include the following.

1. **Appreciation and commendation letters**   In an *appreciation* or *commendation letter,* you tell someone— a specific person, a group of people, a business, or an organization—that he, she, or they did a good job with a product or service. Be specific about exactly what action or idea of this person's you are praising. For example, if your city's mayor approved the construction of a skateboarding park that you and your friends enjoy, you might want to write an appreciation letter to thank him or her for being aware of

what young people in your community need.

Here is a sample appreciation letter.

Carey Middle School
12 Green Street
Chesters Corner, ME 01154
September 12, 2001

Marguerite Hong, Director
Chesters Corner Parks and
Recreation Department
251 Main Street
Chesters Corner, ME 01154

Dear Ms. Hong:

I am writing to let you know how much I enjoy the town's new skateboarding park. I have been reading the news stories about all the time and planning that went into the park. The new park shows this effort, and my friends and I think the park is definitely a winner! We are thrilled to have a place to practice our stunts.

Thank you for recognizing the need for such a park and for the work that went into creating it. I appreciate all your efforts.

Yours truly,

Benny McLean

Benny McLean

2. **Complaint and adjustment letters**   When you do not receive services or products that you expect, you may wish to write a *complaint* or *adjustment letter*. Remember these guidelines as you write.

EXAMPLE

The following is the body of a sample adjustment letter written about a faulty product.

On April 12, I ordered the CD entitled "Hip-Hop's Greatest Hits" from your catalog. However, the CD does not work properly. It skips on the third song. I have tried cleaning it with a special CD cleaner, but it keeps skipping. The CD cost $14, plus $1.95 shipping and handling, for a total of $15.95. I am returning the CD. Please send a replacement CD or a refund. Thank you for your attention to this matter.

3. **Request and order letters** In a *request letter,* you write to ask for a product or service. For example, you might write to an art museum to request a schedule of its exhibits. In an *order letter,* you ask for something specific, such as a free brochure advertised in a magazine. You may also need to write an order letter to ask for a product that appears in a magazine or advertisement without a printed order form. When you are writing a request or order letter, remember the following guidelines.

EXAMPLE

Here is an example of the salutation and body of a request letter.

Dear Professor Mack:

I would like to invite you to be one of our speakers at the Florida History Celebration at Lawton Chiles Middle Academy. This year's event will be held on October 11, from 9:00 A.M. to 12:00 noon.

The Florida History Celebration is part of the seventh-grade study of Florida history. We would like for you to give a thirty-minute talk to about one

(continued)

```
hundred seventh-graders about the
history of citrus in our state.
Your talk would take place at
10:30 A.M.

Please let me know by September
30 whether you will be able to
take part in this event. I look
forward to hearing from you soon.
```

Letters, Informal or Personal   A *personal letter* is often a gesture of friendship containing a personal message from the sender to the receiver, such as best wishes for an upcoming holiday. When you are writing a personal letter, remember to write about things that interest you and the person you are writing.

■ **Types**   There are three common types of informal or personal letters.

1. **Invitations**   An *invitation* should contain specific information about the occasion, such as the time and place and other details your guest might need to know (such as that everyone may bring a friend, should dress casually, or is expected to bring food).

2. **Letters of regret**   You write a *letter of regret* when you receive an invitation to an event that you will not be able to attend. You should make a special effort to respond in writing to invitations that include the letters *R.S.V.P.* (an abbreviation for "please reply" in French). You should always respond quickly enough so that the person who is inviting you can prepare for the number of guests. If the planned event is very soon, you may want to telephone the person to say

that you can't come. Even if you telephone to say you won't attend, it is still polite to send a follow-up letter of regret.

EXAMPLE

> 5455 Blackford Street
> Chicago, IL 60615
> February 24, 2001
>
> Dear Felicia,
>
>   I was so happy to receive your invitation to your birthday slumber party next Friday evening. I really would like to be there. Unfortunately, my parents had already made plans for the whole family for that night.
>
>   Thank you very much for inviting me. I hope you have a happy birthday and a lot of fun at your party.
>
>   Your friend,
>
>   *Bianca*
>
>   Bianca

3. **Thank-you letters**   You write *thank-you letters* when you want to thank someone for taking the time, trouble, or expense to do something for you. Thank the person, and then try to add a personal note. For example, if you are thanking someone for a gift, tell why the gift is special to you.

Prewriting Techniques   You can use the following techniques to find a subject to write about, to gather information about a subject, or to organize your ideas before you begin to write. Although the prewriting techniques are listed separately, you may use more than one technique at a time. You may also find that you prefer some techniques to others.

Many of the prewriting techniques below involve the use of *graphic organizers.* A **graphic organizer** is a visual that helps you see the ideas and details you are generating or arranging as you prewrite.

1. **Generating Ideas**   The following techniques can help you draw ideas for writing out of your own imagination.

- **Asking the *5W-How?* questions** News reporters track down information by asking the **5W-How?** questions—*Who? What? When? Where? Why?* and *How?* You can ask the same questions to find information on a topic you have chosen. For some topics, some questions won't apply. With other topics, you may think of several good answers for one question.

EXAMPLE

Who are some local people who have worked for or performed in a circus?

What are the most dangerous jobs in the circus?

When are circus animals fed?

Where do circus performers and animal trainers learn their skills?

Why are there three rings in a circus performance?

How does a person join the circus?

- **Asking "What if?" Questions** **"What if?" questions** will help you find ideas for creative writing. The following are some "What if" questions you might ask to spark your imagination.

EXAMPLES

What if I could change one thing in my life? (What if I had an identical twin? What if I grew up in India?)

What if some common thing did not exist? (What if there were no telephones? What if Earth had no water?)

What if one situation in the world could be changed? (What if everyone spoke the same language? What if there were no diseases?)

What if I could meet a historical figure? (What if I could meet Martin Luther King, Jr.? What would I ask him?)

- **Brainstorming**   You can **brainstorm** alone, but it is more fun with a partner or a group. In a group, you can bounce ideas off each other. Follow the guidelines below as you brainstorm.

How to Brainstorm

1. Write a subject at the top of a piece of paper or on a chalkboard.

2. Write down every single thought about the subject that comes to mind. Do not stop to judge ideas. (You can do that later.)

3. Keep going until you run out of ideas.

On the next page you will find some brainstorming notes on the subject *happiness.* The list contains more ideas than the writer will use, but it gives the writer a starting point.

Happiness

playing soccer
if you could drive at 12
making an A on a difficult test
getting a raise in my allowance
the dentist saying that I don't have any
    cavities
my little brother spending the night some-
    where else
splashing in a puddle of water
getting to play my stereo really loud
when my math class is not cold
if the entire world could take a nap for one
    hour every day

■ **Clustering**   *Clustering* is sometimes called *webbing* or *making connections*. When you make a cluster diagram, you break a topic into its smaller parts. The guidelines below will help you.

How to Cluster

1. Write your subject in the center of your paper and circle it.

2. Around the subject, write related ideas as you think of them. Circle these ideas, and draw lines to connect them with the subject.

3. An idea may make you think of other ideas. Connect these with circles and lines, too.

The cluster diagram in the next column shows a writer's ideas related to the topic *Titanic*.

■ **Cubing**   Visualize a cube with these six methods for investigating a subject written on each side: *(1) Describe it. (2) Compare it. (3) Associate it. (4) Analyze it. (5) Apply it. (6) Argue for or against it.* Think of a subject, and then write for three minutes about each suggestion on the cube. The example below shows a response to "associate it." (Tell what is similar to the subject.)

EXAMPLE
Rugby
Rugby is similar to American football. In both sports, you throw and kick a ball, tackle opposing players, and score by getting the ball behind the goal line.

■ **Freewriting**   *Freewriting* is writing down whatever ideas pop into your head about a subject. Think of a word or topic that is important to you. Then, write for three to five minutes about whatever your subject makes you think of or remember. Don't worry about complete sentences, spelling, or punc-tuation. If you get stuck, write anything. Don't let your pen or pencil stop, just continue writing down all your ideas. Keep writing until the time is up.

EXAMPLE

> Swim Meets: The starting whistle. Relays. My best stroke is backstroke. Wish I could make my turn faster. Like looking up and seeing the sky and clouds and then the flags that mean I'm almost to the end of the pool. Long practices with coach yelling "Go!" Swimmer's ear kept me out of one meet last year.

- **Using your five senses**   While you are awake, you receive steady input from each of your five senses (sight, hearing, smell, taste, touch). Most of the time, you ignore these sensory details. Paying attention to what your senses are telling you, however, can give you details for your writing.

EXAMPLE

> Cuban New Year's Eve celebration
> touch: warm night, breezes through open windows, embroidered tablecloth, paper plates and plastic forks and knives
> sound: record player, singing, people talking, telling jokes, laughter, children's shouts, TV in living room
> smell: spicy smells, ground coffee
> taste: crisp barbecued pork, black beans and rice, yucca, guava pastries, sweet and bitter orange
> sight: dark night, brightly lit house, about thirty family members and friends, children playing, men tending the backyard barbecue

- **Visualizing**   *Visualizing* means seeing something in your mind's eye. As you "see" your scene, try to use your other senses as well.

EXAMPLE

> I'm walking down the beach on a hot afternoon. Brightly colored beach umbrellas dot the sand. A group of small children busily builds a sand castle with a collection of toy shovels and buckets. Sea gulls swoop and cry above me. The waves splash, and the foamy, cool water covers my feet.

- **Writer's notebook or journal**   A *writer's journal* is a notebook or folder where you can record your everyday thoughts, observations, questions, and experiences. Journal entries can be very short or go on for several pages. You can use your journal as a source for writing ideas. Another type of writing journal is a *learning log*. A learning log contains thoughts and questions about things you learn from reading and participating in school discussions. A learning log helps you make connections between what you learn and what you think.

2. **Gathering Information**   To find information from outside sources on your topic to include in your composition, you can use the following techniques.

- **Listening with a focus**   Some people learn better by listening than by reading. You can gather information on a specific topic by listening to speeches, interviews, radio and TV programs, audiotapes, and videotapes. Before you begin to listen, think of questions you would like answered. These questions will give you a purpose for listening. Listen carefully with your questions in front of you, and take notes to help you remember the answers.

- **Reading with a focus**   Many people find ideas for writing by reading books, newspapers, or magazines. To find information in a book, newspaper, or magazine, check the table of contents or index. Go directly to the pages on your topic. Don't read everything. Skim the text quickly looking only for information on your topic. Don't forget to check photos and captions, too. When you find information on your topic, read the passage carefully. Then, take notes.

3. **Arranging Ideas**   Once you have chosen a subject and gathered information, you can use one or more of the following strategies to organize and summarize your ideas. These strategies can be especially helpful for organizing ideas from a number of different sources.

- **Charts**   Dividing a subject into its logical parts can help you to better analyze the subject of your writing. Organizing the information into a *chart* then helps you to understand the categories quickly. In the following example, a writer uses a type of chart called a table to organize the information she found about the three branches of government. The chart will help the writer stay organized as she begins to write a composition about the United States government.

United States Government		
Branch	Main Job	Head of the Branch
Executive	Enforces the laws	President
Legislative	Makes the laws	Congress
Judicial	Makes decisions about the laws	Supreme Court

- **Conceptual mapping**   Mapping might look like clustering, but it is more like outlining because it shows the relationship between ideas. Mapping can help you know if you have enough support for each main idea. Notice how the conceptual map on the previous page groups main ideas and supporting ideas.

- **Outlines** An *outline* helps you organize important information. In an outline, the ideas are arranged in a pattern that makes their relationship to one another clear. There are two types of outlines, *formal* and *informal*. You may need to make a formal outline for a research report. To make a formal outline like the one below, use Roman numerals for headings and capital letters for subheadings. (See also page 776.)

Formal Outline

```
Title: The Patter of Little Hooves
Main Idea: Pigs make great pets.

I.  Benefits
    A. Characteristics
       1. Ease of housebreaking
       2. Lack of fur
       3. Friendliness
    B. Enjoyment of games
       1. Fetching
       2. Swimming
       3. Rolling over
II. Drawbacks
    A. Size
    B. Inability to protect
```

To organize your ideas quickly before you begin to write, you might want to make an informal outline (sometimes called an **early plan**). An informal outline groups ideas in a logical way.

Informal Outline

Topic: Pet Pigs	
Benefits	Drawbacks
easier to housebreak than some other animals	can get very large
	can get very lazy
don't shed	can be too playful
can communicate	not a good watch animal
easy to train	
will play and do tricks	
easy to feed	

- **Sequence chain** A *sequence chain* helps you see how one event leads to another. A sequence chain works well when you are narrating or explaining a process.

- **Time line** A *time line* puts events in order on a horizontal or vertical line, with the first or earliest events usually starting on the left (in a horizontal time line) or at the top (in a vertical time line). The most recent or latest events most often will be on the right (in a horizontal time line) or at the bottom (in a vertical time line).

■ **Venn diagram**   A *Venn diagram* uses intersecting circles to show the similarities and differences between two subjects. The area where the two circles overlap shows how the two subjects are alike. The remaining areas show how they are different. (See also page 749.)

EXAMPLE

Differences   Similarities   Differences

Style   From the way you dress to the way you act, every day you make choices that reveal your unique style. When you write, you also make choices—choices such as what words to use and how to arrange those words in sentences. The sum of these choices is your writing style. You do not make choices about writing style in a vacuum, though. Your style should be determined partly by you, partly by your purpose for writing, and partly by your audience.

■ **Think about audience**   In a book report for your teacher, you will probably use a formal style. For example, you would be careful about correct grammar, use longer sentences, and try to work in some of the new vocabulary words you have been learning. In an e-mail to a friend, though, your writing might include sentence fragments, slang, and nonstandard usage. These are the types of style adjustments you make for your audience.

■ **Think about purpose**   You also adjust your style according to your purpose for writing. Informative writing, for example, goes right to the point. Describing a character for a book report, you would choose precise language to paint a clear picture in the fewest words possible. If you were writing a journal entry about the same character, however, your purpose would be to express your feelings. You might sprinkle your entry with questions, describe your emotional response, and make connections between the character and yourself—all without much attention to how briefly you made your point. This informal style is appropriate for personal correspondence between friends.

Symbols for Revising and Proofreading   When you are revising and proofreading, you will add and remove letters, words, and sentences. By using standard revising and proofreading symbols, such as the ones in the chart on the next page, your revisions will be more consistent.

Symbols for Revising and Proofreading

Symbol	Example	Meaning of Symbol
≡	Tucker's homestyle Restaurant	Capitalize a lowercase letter.
/	the City of Raleigh	Lowercase a capital letter.
∧	a cup ∧of milk	Insert a missing word, letter, or punctuation mark.
ℒ	How's the that apple?	Leave out a word, letter, or punctuation mark.
∽	fĭrst	Change the order of letters or words.
¶	¶ "Go ahead," he said.	Begin a new paragraph.
⊙	She wept⊙	Add a period.
∧	I still apologized∧ however.	Add a comma.

Transitions   When you want to show readers how ideas and details fit together, use transitions, or *transitional words and phrases*. (See page 302 for a chart of transitional words and phrases.)

Voice   Voice is the way a piece of writing "sounds." In most writing assignments, your voice should sound like you and should communicate your ideas simply and naturally. You should take care to adjust your writing voice to fit your audience and purpose for writing. As you become more experienced with writing for a variety of purposes and audiences, you will eventually develop a voice that is yours alone.

■ **Think about audience**   Writing instructions for a younger audience, you would probably want to use a friendly, reassuring voice. For example, your instructions might include easy vocabulary, examples that relate to a child's experience, and an enthusiastic conclusion. These elements would help your young readers feel confident that they can carry out the instructions you have explained. That same voice would not suit an older audience, however; they might feel that you were "talking down" to them. Your voice can go a long way toward drawing your audience in—or turning them off.

■ **Think about purpose**   When writing to express your feelings, do not try to sound like anyone else. Your voice should come as close to "the real you" as possible. When writing to inform or persuade, however, you may need to pull the reins on "the real you": Even if you feel passionately about the topic of an informative or persuasive composition, your voice should sound reasonable, not hotheaded.

Grammar at a Glance

┌H E L P─
Grammar at a Glance is an alphabetical list of special terms and expressions with examples and references to further information. When you encounter a grammar or usage problem in the revising or proofreading stage of your writing, look for help in this section first. You may find all you need to know right here. If you need more information, **Grammar at a Glance** will show you where in the book to turn for a more complete explanation. If you do not find what you are looking for in **Grammar at a Glance,** turn to the index on page 854.

abbreviation An abbreviation is a shortened form of a word or a phrase.

- **capitalization of**

TITLES USED WITH NAMES	**M**rs.	**C**apt.	**S**r.	**M.D.**
KINDS OF ORGANIZATIONS	**A**ssn.	**I**nc.	**D**ept.	**C**orp.
PARTS OF ADDRESSES	**A**ve.	**S**t.	**B**lvd.	**P.O. B**ox
NAMES OF STATES	[without ZIP Codes] **V**a.		**A**rk.	
			Mass.	**N. M**ex.
	[with ZIP Codes]	**VA**		**AR**
		MA		**NM**
TIMES	**A.M.**	**P.M.**	**B.C.**	**A.D.**

- **punctuation of** (See page 599.)

WITH PERIODS	(See preceding examples.)
WITHOUT PERIODS	CD-ROM NBC UFO FBI
	DC (D.C. without ZIP Code)
	mg qt tbsp cm yd
	[Exception: inch = in.]

action verb An action verb expresses physical or mental activity. (See page 357.)

EXAMPLE   Uncle Jim **drives** a school bus.

active voice Active voice is the voice a verb is in when it expresses an action done by its subject. (See page 499. See also **voice.**)

EXAMPLE   The dog **chased** the squirrel across the yard.

adjective An adjective modifies a noun or a pronoun. (See page 346.)

EXAMPLE   Do you see **that beautiful, old wood** house over there?

adjective clause An adjective clause is a subordinate clause that modifies a noun or a pronoun. (See page 427.)

EXAMPLE   We saw an advertisement for a car **that has aluminum wheels.** [The adjective clause modifies the noun *car.*]

adjective phrase A prepositional phrase that modifies a noun or a pronoun is called an adjective phrase. (See page 404.)

EXAMPLE   Dana prefers the backpack **with large pockets.** [The adjective phrase modifies the noun *backpack.*]

adverb An adverb modifies a verb, an adjective, or another adverb. (See page 366.)

EXAMPLE   Mom and Dad **often** drive us to the lake on weekends. [The adverb modifies the verb *drive.*]

adverb clause An adverb clause is a subordinate clause that modifies a verb, an adjective, or an adverb. (See page 430.)

EXAMPLE   Trudy's grades have improved **since she cut back her TV viewing.** [The adverb clause modifies the verb *have improved.*]

adverb phrase A prepositional phrase that modifies a verb, an adjective, or an adverb is called an adverb phrase. (See page 406.)

EXAMPLE   **After dark,** the carol singers went from house to house. [The adverb phrase modifies the verb *went.*]

agreement Agreement is the correspondence, or match, between grammatical forms. Grammatical forms agree when they have the same number and gender.

■ **of pronouns and antecedents** (See page 475.)

SINGULAR   **Desmond** often rides **his** bicycle to school.

PLURAL   Desmond's **classmates** ride **their** bicycles to school.

SINGULAR	Has **everyone** in the club paid **his** or **her** dues?
PLURAL	Have **all** of the club members paid **their** dues?
SINGULAR	Neither **Darleen** nor **Clarissa** was pleased with **her** audition.
PLURAL	**Darleen** and **Clarissa** were not pleased with **their** auditions.

■ **of subjects and verbs** (See page 458.)

SINGULAR	The music **teacher is composing** an opera.
	The music **teacher,** with the help of her students, **is composing** an opera.
PLURAL	The music **students are composing** an opera.
	The music **students,** with the help of their teacher, **are composing** an opera.
SINGULAR	**Each** of the students **is looking** forward to seeing the dinosaur exhibit.
PLURAL	**All** of the students **are looking** forward to seeing the dinosaur exhibit.
SINGULAR	Neither **Kevin** nor **I was** able to go to band camp last summer.
PLURAL	Needless to say, both **Kevin** and **I were** disappointed.
SINGULAR	Here **is** a **list** of topics from which you can choose.
PLURAL	Here **are** the **topics** from which you can choose.
SINGULAR	The social studies **class is watching** a video about the space program.
PLURAL	The social studies **class are writing** their essays on the space program.
SINGULAR	**Six dollars is** the price of the kite.
PLURAL	From this stack of bills, **six dollars are** missing.
SINGULAR	*Parallel Journeys* **was written** by Eleanor Ayer.
PLURAL	Early **journeys** to North America **were** risky.
SINGULAR	**Is measles** an infectious disease?
PLURAL	**Are** the **scissors** in your sewing basket?

antecedent An antecedent is the word or words that a pronoun stands for. (See page 342.)

EXAMPLE   **Tim** doesn't know how long his essay will be.
[*His* refers to *Tim*.]

apostrophe

- **to form contractions** (See page 641.)
  EXAMPLES   wouldn't   I'll   o'clock   '99

- **to form plurals of letters, numerals, and words used as words** (See page 645.)
  EXAMPLES   *A*'s and *B*'s   *and*'s instead of &'s   5's and 10's

- **to show possession** (See page 638.)
  EXAMPLES   player's uniform

                         players' uniforms

                         children's literature

                         someone's backpack

                         Steven Spielberg's and George Lucas's movies

                         Batman and Robin's first adventure

appositive An appositive is a noun or a pronoun placed beside another noun or pronoun to identify or describe it. (See page 609.)

EXAMPLE   My friend **Désirée** recently moved to a new house.
[*Désirée* identifies *friend*.]

appositive phrase An appositive phrase consists of an appositive and its modifiers. (See page 609.)

EXAMPLE   The first taxi in the line was driven by Stavros, **a gray-haired man with a mustache.**

article The articles, *a, an,* and *the,* are the most frequently used adjectives. (See page 347.)

EXAMPLES   **a** football   **the** farmhouse

            an antelope   **the** answer

            an honor

bad, badly (See page 554.)

NONSTANDARD   This green apple tastes badly.

STANDARD   This green apple tastes **bad.**

base form The base form, or infinitive, is one of the four principal parts of a verb. (See page 485.)

EXAMPLE   Can you help me to **find** this address?

brackets (See page 649.)

EXAMPLES   The movie critic wrote, "Leonardo DiCaprio's performance is a tour de force [an unusually skillful performance]."

Many of the Iroquois legends we know today might have been lost without the efforts of Kaiiontwa'ko (perhaps better known as Cornplanter [his Iroquois name means "by what one plants"]).

capitalization

■ **of abbreviations** (See **abbreviation.**)

■ **of first words** (See page 574.)

EXAMPLES   **M**y brother has started taking cello lessons.

Nick asked, "**W**hat does the French phrase *déjà vu* mean?"

Dear Ms. Neruda:

Yours truly,

■ **of proper nouns and proper adjectives** (See page 574.)

Proper Noun	Common Noun
North **A**merica	continent
El **S**alvador	country
Staten **I**sland	island
Chautauqua **L**ake	body of water
Jurassic **P**eriod	historical period
Mother's **D**ay	holiday

Proper Noun	Common Noun
Blue Ridge Mountains	mountain chain
Saguaro National Park	park
Bernheim Arboretum and Research Forest	forest
Mammoth Cave	cave
Kings Canyon	canyon
Southeast	region
Thirty-second Street	street
National Urban League	organization
San Diego Padres	team
Bowling Green State University	institution
Democratic Party (*or* party)	political party
Roth's Optical	business firm
Super Bowl	special event
Memorial Day	holiday
February, May, August, November	calendar items
Yavapai-Apache	people
Christianity	religion
Buddhist	religious follower
God (*but* the god Zeus)	deity
Passover	holy day
Torah	sacred writing
Jupiter	planet
Alpha Centauri	star
Ursa Major	constellation
Andrea Doria	ship
Enola Gay	aircraft
Atlantis	spacecraft
Biology I (*but* biology)	school subject
Mandarin	language
Mount Rushmore National Memorial	monument
World Trade Center	building
Heisman Trophy	award

EXAMPLES **S**enator Feinstein [preceding a name]

Feinstein, a **s**enator from California [following a name]

Thank you, **S**enator. [direct address]

Uncle Alphonse (*but* my **u**ncle Alphonse)

Anasazi: Ancient People of the Rock [book]

Mythic Warriors: Guardians of the Legend [TV program]

Arrangement in Black and Gray: The Artist's Mother [work of art]

Rhapsody in Blue [musical composition]

"**T**he **F**rog **W**ho **W**anted to **B**e a **S**inger" [short story]

"**I A**m of the **E**arth" [poem]

Reader's Digest [magazine]

the *Orlando Sentinel* [newspaper]

Family Circus [comic strip]

Back to Titanic [audiotape or CD]

case of pronouns Case is the form a pronoun takes to show how it is used in a sentence. (See page 511.)

NOMINATIVE **She** and **I** are taking tae kwon do lessons.

Two of the award winners are Erica and **he.**

Neither baby sitter, Brigitte nor **she,** is available this evening.

We students are making animal characters from our favorite books.

Is David Alfaro Siqueiros the artist **who** painted this?

We don't know **who** she is.

OBJECTIVE Did you see Jamaal and **her** at the Juneteenth festival?

Kristen invited **him** and **me** to the Natalie Merchant concert.

Are you going with **them** to the video arcade?

The Earth Day festivities are being organized by two teachers, Mr. Zapata and **her.**

Our guide gave **us** spelunkers a map of the cave we would explore.

Ms. Jennings, **whom** everyone at school admires, will retire this year.

One of the candidates **whom** I will vote for is Tamisha.

POSSESSIVE   **Their** understanding of the rules differs from **ours.**

Her making the jump shot in the final seconds sent the game into overtime.

clause A clause is a group of words that contains a subject and a verb and is used as part of a sentence. (See page 423. See also **independent clause** and **subordinate clause.**)

EXAMPLES   she arrives at work on time [independent clause]
unless the bus is late [subordinate clause]

She arrives at work on time unless the bus is late.

colon (See page 619.)

■ **before lists**

EXAMPLES   To assemble the bookcase, you will need the following tools: a crescent wrench, a small hammer, and a Phillips screwdriver.

The Bookends Club is featuring books by these authors: A. A. Milne, Laura Ingalls Wilder, and Judy Blume.

■ **in conventional situations**

EXAMPLES   7:30 P.M.

Exodus 20:3–17

The Whole Internet: User's Guide & Catalog

Dear Sir:

comma (See page 602.)

■ **in a series**

EXAMPLES   Shandra, Seth, and I spent the summer working at the animal shelter.

Alonzo's hobbies include making wind chimes, working jigsaw puzzles, and writing limericks.

- **in compound sentences**

EXAMPLES   We seventh graders performed three plays this year, but my favorite was *Androcles and the Lion* by Bernard Shaw.

My friend Albert portrayed Androcles, and I played the part of the lion.

- **with nonessential phrases and clauses**

EXAMPLES   Yu the Great, a mythical Chinese king, possessed superhuman powers. [nonessential phrase]

Yu the Great, who possessed superhuman powers, could transform himself into different animals. [nonessential clause]

- **with introductory elements**

EXAMPLES   Sitting around the bonfire, the campers told ghost stories.

If you like to read books in which animals are the main characters, you may enjoy *The Long Patrol.*

- **with interrupters**

EXAMPLES   The Gila monster, for example, is a poisonous lizard.

Most other lizards, however, are harmless.

- **in conventional situations**

EXAMPLES   On Friday, July 17, 2000, we flew from Baltimore, Maryland, to Raleigh, North Carolina, to attend my brother's graduation.

Isn't your address 728 Lakewood Boulevard, Grand Rapids, MI 49501-0827?

comma splice A comma splice is a run-on sentence in which only a comma separates two complete sentences. (See **run-on sentence.**)

COMMA SPLICE   In 1962, John H. Glenn, Jr., became the first American to orbit the earth, then in 1998, at the age of 77, Glenn made history again by becoming the oldest person to travel in space.

REVISED   In 1962, John H. Glenn, Jr., became the first American to orbit the earth, **and** then in 1998, at the age of 77, Glenn made history again by becoming the oldest person to travel in space.

REVISED In 1962, John H. Glenn, Jr., became the first American to orbit the earth; then in 1998, at the age of 77, Glenn made history again by becoming the oldest person to travel in space.

comparison of modifiers (See page 532.)

■ **comparison of adjectives and adverbs**

Positive	Comparative	Superlative
short	short**er**	short**est**
heavy	heav**ier**	heav**iest**
generous	**more (less)** generous	**most (least)** generous
slowly	**more (less)** slowly	**most (least)** slowly
bad/ill	**worse**	**worst**

■ **comparing two**

EXAMPLES Of Mars and Venus, which planet is **closer** to Earth?

In the balloon, we flew **higher** and **farther** than we had thought we would.

China is **more populous** than **any other** country.

■ **comparing more than two**

EXAMPLES Lake Superior is the **largest** of the five Great Lakes.

Of all of the figure skaters in the competition, I think that Michelle Kwan performed **most gracefully.**

complement A complement is a word or word group that completes the meaning of a verb. (See page 385. See also **direct object, indirect object, predicate nominative,** and **predicate adjective.**)

EXAMPLES All of Ms. Lozano's students admire **her.**

Bring **us** the map, please.

Do you feel **thirsty**?

Angela, this is **Ramona.**

complex sentence A complex sentence has one independent clause and at least one subordinate clause. (See page 445.)

EXAMPLES My favorite animated film was *Cinderella* [independent clause], until I saw *Jungle Book* [subordinate clause].

When my little sister wrote a letter to Santa Claus [subordinate clause], she used the address North Pole, AK 99705 [independent clause], which, by the way, is the correct address. [subordinate clause]

compound-complex sentence A compound-complex sentence has two or more independent clauses and at least one subordinate clause. (See page 447.)

EXAMPLES The Taj Mahal, which is located near Agra, India [subordinate clause], is a beautiful structure made almost entirely of white marble [independent clause]; it was built in the seventeenth century by Shah Jahan as a tomb for his wife [independent clause].

When they publish their works [subordinate clause], some writers use pseudonyms, or pen names, instead of their real names [independent clause]; for example, Theodor Geisel published most of his books for children under the pen name Dr. Seuss [independent clause].

The sweater that I bought last week [subordinate clause] was on sale [independent clause], and it fits well, too [independent clause].

compound sentence A compound sentence has two or more independent clauses but no subordinate clauses. (See page 441.)

EXAMPLES Two of the kittens are gray [independent clause], but the third one is orange [independent clause].

Yuri was born on February 29 [independent clause]; consequently, each year, except in a leap year, he celebrates his birthday on February 28 [independent clause].

Last night, Dad and I made pizza primavera [independent clause]; he prepared the dough and the Parmesan-cheese sauce [independent clause], and I diced the green onions, red peppers, carrots, and broccoli [independent clause].

conjunction A conjunction joins words or groups of words. (See page 374.)

EXAMPLES   fish **or** fowl

                not only fair **but also** firm

                through the kitchen **and** up the stairs

                Although Boris had a cold, he insisted on performing.

                They stayed on the field, **for** the game was not over.

contraction A contraction is a shortened form of a word, a numeral, or a group of words. Apostrophes in contractions indicate where letters or numerals have been omitted. (See page 641. See also **apostrophe.**)

EXAMPLES   you're [you are]   there's [there is *or* there has]

                who's [who is *or* who has]   they're [they are]

                aren't [are not]   it's [it is *or* it has]

                can't [cannot]   won't [will not]

                '14–'18 war [1914–1918 war]   o'clock [of the clock]

dangling modifier A dangling modifier is a modifying word, phrase, or clause that does not clearly and sensibly modify a word or a word group in a sentence. (See page 541.)

DANGLING   Digging a well near Xi'an, China, in 1974, thousands of ancient terra-cotta sculptures of warriors, horses, and chariots were uncovered. [Were thousands of sculptures digging a well?]

REVISED   Digging a well near Xi'an, China, in 1974, **workers** uncovered thousands of ancient terra-cotta sculptures of warriors, horses, and chariots.

dash (See page 649.)

EXAMPLE   The marine biologist spent several days—ten, I think—recording the movements of the manatee and her calf.

declarative sentence A declarative sentence makes a statement and is followed by a period. (See page 330.)

EXAMPLE   Edinburgh is the capital of Scotland.

direct object A direct object is a word or word group that receives the action of the verb or shows the result of the action. A direct object answers the question *Whom?* or *What?* after a transitive verb. (See page 386.)

EXAMPLE   Rashmi visited **them** Tuesday afternoon.

double comparison A double comparison is the nonstandard use of two comparative forms (usually *more* and *–er*) or two superlative forms (usually *most* and *–est*) to express comparison. In standard usage, the single comparative form is correct. (See page 538.)

NONSTANDARD   Olympus Mons, a volcano on Mars, is the most highest mountain in our solar system.

STANDARD   Olympus Mons, a volcano on Mars, is the **highest** mountain in our solar system.

double negative A double negative is the nonstandard use of two negative words when one is enough. (See page 539.)

NONSTANDARD   Alonzo is so very sleepy that he can't hardly keep his eyes open.

STANDARD   Alonzo is so very sleepy that he **can hardly** keep his eyes open.

NONSTANDARD   I haven't never ridden in an airplane.

STANDARD   I **have never** ridden in an airplane.

STANDARD   I **haven't ever** ridden in an airplane.

double subject A double subject occurs when an unnecessary pronoun is used after the subject of a sentence. (See page 559.)

NONSTANDARD   Abner Doubleday, contrary to popular belief, he did not create the game of baseball.

STANDARD   Abner Doubleday, contrary to popular belief, did not create the game of baseball.

end marks (See page 598.)

■ **with sentences**

EXAMPLES   In 1998, Mark McGwire broke Roger Maris's single-season home-run record**.** [declarative sentence]

How many home runs did Mark McGwire hit in 1998**?**
[interrogative sentence]

Wow**!** [interjection] McGwire hit seventy home runs**!**
[exclamatory sentence]

Don't forget that in 1998 Sammy Sosa also surpassed
Maris's record by hitting sixty-six home runs**.**
[imperative sentence]

■ **with abbreviations** (See page 599. See also **abbreviation.**)

EXAMPLES   In 1964, the Nobel Peace Prize was awarded to
Dr**.** Martin Luther King, Jr**.**

In 1964, was the Nobel Peace Prize awarded to
Dr**.** Martin Luther King, Jr**.?**

essential clause/essential phrase An essential, or
restrictive, clause or phrase is necessary to the meaning of a
sentence and is not set off by commas. (See page 608.)

EXAMPLES   The woman **who gives the lectures on Romanian art**
is Ms. Antonescu. [essential clause]

The animals **drinking at the water hole** gave the
elephants a wide berth. [essential phrase]

exclamation point (See **end marks.**)

exclamatory sentence An exclamatory sentence expresses
strong feeling and is followed by an exclamation point. (See page
331.)

EXAMPLE   What a surprise this is**!**

fragment (See **sentence fragment.**)

fused sentence A fused sentence is a run-on sentence in
which no punctuation separates complete sentences. (See **run-on
sentence.**)

FUSED   Most totems, or images, carved into a totem pole are
symbolic usually the totem at the top of the pole represents
the family's guardian spirit.

REVISED   Most totems, or images, carved into a totem pole are
symbolic**;** usually the totem at the top of the pole
represents the family's guardian spirit.

REVISED   Most totems, or images, carved into a totem pole are symbolic. Usually the totem at the top of the pole represents the family's guardian spirit.

good, well (See page 536.)

EXAMPLES   For a beginner, Julian is a **good** golfer.

Yes, for a beginner, Julian plays golf extremely **well** [*not* good].

hyphen (See page 646.)

■ **to divide words**

EXAMPLE   The Ecology Club at our school recently organ-ized a recycling campaign.

■ **in compound numbers**

EXAMPLE   The Ecology Club has ninety-seven members.

■ **with prefixes**

EXAMPLE   The Ecology Club began a recycling campaign in mid-September.

imperative sentence An imperative sentence gives a command or makes a request and is followed by either a period or an exclamation point. (See page 330.)

EXAMPLES   Please turn the TV off. [request]

Turn that TV off! [command]

independent clause An independent clause (also called a *main clause*) expresses a complete thought and can stand by itself as a sentence. (See page 424.)

EXAMPLE   Because Dad never has any spare time, **he hired a contractor to build the deck.**

indirect object An indirect object is a word or word group that often comes between a transitive verb and its direct object and tells to whom or to what or for whom or for what the action of the verb is done. (See page 388.)

EXAMPLE   Kathleen gave the **dog** a rubber toy. [The direct object is *toy.*]

infinitive An infinitive is a verb form, usually preceded by *to,* that is used as a noun, an adjective, or an adverb. (See page 414.)

EXAMPLE We all wanted **to swim,** so Mom took us to the pool.

infinitive phrase An infinitive phrase consists of an infinitive and its modifiers and complements. (See page 415.)

EXAMPLE **To help one's fellow human beings** is an admirable goal, Ronny.

interjection An interjection expresses emotion and has no grammatical relation to the rest of the sentence. (See page 377.)

EXAMPLE **Wow!** Look at those fireworks!

interrogative sentence An interrogative sentence asks a question and is followed by a question mark. (See page 331.)

EXAMPLE Have you ever seen the Rockies**?**

intransitive verb An intransitive verb is a verb that does not take an object. (See page 364.)

EXAMPLE The wind **howls** fiercely.

irregular verb An irregular verb is a verb that forms its past and past participle in some way other than by adding *–d* or *–ed* to the base form. (See page 488. See also **regular verb.**)

Base Form	Present Participle	Past	Past Participle
be	[is] being	was, were	[have] been
bring	[is] bringing	brought	[have] brought
choose	[is] choosing	chose	[have] chosen
cost	[is] costing	cost	[have] cost
eat	[is] eating	ate	[have] eaten
grow	[is] growing	grew	[have] grown
pay	[is] paying	paid	[have] paid
spread	[is] spreading	spread	[have] spread

italics (See **underlining** [**italics**].)

its, it's (See page 559.)

EXAMPLES **It's** [It is] your turn to clean **its** [the gerbil's] cage.

     It's [It has] been a long time since **it's** [it has] been cleaned.

lie, lay (See page 503.)

EXAMPLES "You look tired, Mom. Perhaps you should **lay** your work aside and **lie** down for a while," I suggested.

     Agreeing with me, Mom **laid** her reading glasses on her desk and **lay** down on the sofa.

linking verb A linking verb connects the subject with a word that identifies or describes the subject. (See page 358.)

EXAMPLE Starlings **are** determined nest-builders.

misplaced modifier A misplaced modifier is a word, phrase, or clause that seems to modify the wrong word or words in a sentence. (See page 541.)

MISPLACED The pod of humpback whales entertained the passengers aboard the tour boat, leaping gracefully out of the gentle ocean waves. [Was the tour boat leaping gracefully?]

REVISED **Leaping gracefully out of the gentle ocean waves,** the pod of humpback whales entertained the passengers aboard the tour boat.

modifier A modifier is a word or word group that makes the meaning of another word or word group more specific. (See page 531.)

EXAMPLES Harriet is **happy.**

     Laughing excitedly, the children burst the balloon.

nonessential clause/nonessential phrase A nonessential, or nonrestrictive, clause or phrase adds information not necessary to the main idea in the sentence and is set off by commas. (See page 607.)

EXAMPLES Diana discussed her trip to Florida**, which took place last month.** [nonessential clause]

The twins**, sitting quietly for a change,** posed for the picture. [nonessential phrase]

noun A noun names a person, a place, a thing, or an idea. (See page 337.)

EXAMPLES   Elizabeth Peña   Paris   mountain   knowledge

number Number is the form a word takes to indicate whether the word is singular or plural. (See page 457.)

SINGULAR   child   man   leaf   town

PLURAL   children   men   leaves   towns

object of a preposition An object of a preposition is the noun or pronoun that ends a prepositional phrase. (See page 371.)

EXAMPLE   She heard a composition on the **radio** by her **music teacher.** [*On the radio* and *by her music teacher* are prepositional phrases.]

parentheses (See page 648.)

EXAMPLES   A praying mantis **(**see Illustration C**)** is the only insect that can turn its head from side to side.

A praying mantis is the only insect that can turn its head from side to side. **(**See Illustration C.**)**

participial phrase A participial phrase consists of a participle and any complements and modifiers it has. (See page 412.)

EXAMPLE   **Admired for his courage,** my cousin George is an impressive young man.

participle A participle is a verb form that can be used as an adjective. (See page 410.)

EXAMPLE   **Blushing,** Tina accepted the award.

passive voice The passive voice is the voice a verb is in when it expresses an action done to its subject. (See page 499. See also **voice.**)

EXAMPLE   The president **was reelected** with 60 percent of the vote.

period (See **end marks.**)

phrase A phrase is a group of related words that does not contain both a verb and its subject and that is used as a single part of speech. (See page 401.)

EXAMPLES   Steve, **our champion swimmer,** will represent King Junior High **at the meet in Kansas City.** [*Our champion swimmer* is an appositive phrase. *At the meet* and *in Kansas City* are prepositional phrases.]

To make her own quilt is Maya's goal. [*To make her own quilt* is an infinitive phrase.]

The leaves, **pressed thoroughly and laminated,** will make beautiful coasters. [*Pressed thoroughly and laminated* is a participial phrase.]

predicate The predicate is the part of a sentence that says something about the subject. (See page 320.)

EXAMPLES   **Will** she **perform a solo**?

Horace **may be responsible for that prank.**

predicate adjective A predicate adjective is an adjective that completes the meaning of a linking verb and modifies the subject of the verb. (See page 393.)

EXAMPLES   The trees looked **red** in the evening light.

This rose smells **beautiful.**

predicate nominative A predicate nominative is a noun or pronoun that completes the meaning of a linking verb and identifies or refers to the subject of the verb. (See page 391.)

EXAMPLES   A lizard is a **reptile.**

My sister will be a **lawyer** soon.

prefix A prefix is a word part that is added before a base word or root. (See page 658.)

EXAMPLES   un + fair = **un**fair   il + legal = **il**legal

re + elect = **re**elect   pre + historic = **pre**historic

self + esteem =   ex + governor =
    self-esteem   **ex**-governor

mid + April =   post + Holocaust =
    mid-April   **post**-Holocaust

preposition
preposition A preposition shows the relationship of a noun or a pronoun to some other word in a sentence. (See page 370.)

EXAMPLE   Berlin, the capital **of** Germany, is located **in** the east.

prepositional phrase
prepositional phrase A prepositional phrase is a group of words beginning with a preposition and ending with its object. (See page 371. See also **object of a preposition.**)

EXAMPLE   **Before work,** Dan always feeds the birds.

pronoun
pronoun A pronoun is used in place of one or more nouns or pronouns. (See page 342.)

EXAMPLES   **His** muscles ached, **she** was sunburned, and **their** feet were sore, but all in all **they** had had a wonderful day.

                All of the guests helped **themselves** to **more** of the spinach salad.

question mark
question mark (See **end marks.**)

quotation marks
quotation marks (See page 630.)

- **for direct quotations**

  EXAMPLE   "Learning a few simple rules," said the teacher, "will help you avoid many common spelling errors."

- **with other marks of punctuation** (See also preceding example.)

  EXAMPLES   "Through which South American countries does the Amazon River flow?" asked Enrique.

            Which popular poem by Alfred Noyes begins with the line "The wind was a torrent of darkness among the gusty trees"?

            Cynthia asked, "Did Amy Tan write the short story 'Fish Cheeks'?"

■ **for titles**

EXAMPLES   "Song of the Trees" [short story]

"Mama Is a Sunrise" [short poem]

"Many Rivers to Cross" [song]

regular verb A regular verb is a verb that forms its past and past participle by adding *–d* or *–ed* to the base form. (See page 486. See also **irregular verb.**)

Base Form	Present Participle	Past	Past Participle
ask	[is] asking	asked	[have] asked
attack	[is] attacking	attacked	[have] attacked
drown	[is] drowning	drowned	[have] drowned
suppose	[is] supposing	supposed	[have] supposed
use	[is] using	used	[have] used

rise, raise (See page 501.)

EXAMPLES   The river **rose** rapidly.

The lieutenant **raised** a white flag to signal surrender.

run-on sentence A run-on sentence is two or more complete sentences run together as one. (See page 271. See also **comma splice** and **fused sentence.**)

RUN-ON   We were so impressed by the story that we said nothing he grew a little impatient.

REVISED   We were so impressed by the story that we said nothing. **H**e grew a little impatient.

REVISED   We were so impressed by the story that we said nothing; he grew a little impatient.

semicolon (See page 618.)

■ **in compound sentences with no conjunction**

EXAMPLE   My sister plays violin in her school's symphony orchestra; her goal is to become first chair.

■ **in compound sentences with conjunctive adverbs**

EXAMPLE   I play that movie's soundtrack nearly every day; consequently, I know the lyrics of all of its songs.

■ **between items in a series when the items contain commas**

EXAMPLE   The band's cross-country tour includes concerts in Seattle, Washington; Albuquerque, New Mexico; Cincinnati, Ohio; and Miami, Florida.

sentence A sentence is a group of words that contains a subject and a verb and expresses a complete thought. (See page 316.)

                S   **V**

EXAMPLE   Mr. Holland will give his presentation in the auditorium.

sentence fragment A sentence fragment is a group of words that is punctuated as if it were a complete sentence but that does not contain both a subject and a verb or that does not express a complete thought. (See pages 269 and 316.)

FRAGMENT   In 2002, the Winter Olympic Games in Salt Lake City.

SENTENCE   In 2002, the Winter Olympic Games will be held in Salt Lake City.

FRAGMENT   To find more information about the Zapotec culture.

SENTENCE   To find more information about the Zapotec culture, we searched the Internet.

simple sentence A simple sentence has one independent clause and no subordinate clauses. (See page 440.)

EXAMPLES   Both the cheetah and the chimpanzee are endangered species.

How many other species of mammals are endangered?

sit, set (See page 500.)

EXAMPLES   The science students **sat** quietly, watching the televised launch of the space shuttle *Atlantis*.

On top of the television, the science teacher **set** her model of the space shuttle *Atlantis*.

stringy sentence A stringy sentence is a sentence that has too many independent clauses. Usually, the clauses are strung together with coordinating conjunctions like *and* or *but*. (See page 282.)

STRINGY	I remember that the first time I looked through binoculars at the night sky I was surprised that I could clearly see the craters of the moon and the satellites of Jupiter, but what amazed me most was a bright object shimmering with many different colors near the horizon, and I, of course, immediately thought that I had spotted a UFO, but I learned later that the colorful object was not a UFO but the planet Venus.
REVISED	I remember the first time I looked through binoculars at the night sky. I was surprised that I could clearly see the craters of the moon and the satellites of Jupiter. What amazed me most, however, was a bright object shimmering with many different colors near the horizon. I, of course, immediately thought that I had spotted a UFO. I learned later, though, that the colorful object was not a UFO but the planet Venus.

subject The subject tells whom or what a sentence is about. (See page 317.)

EXAMPLE   Finally, **the train** entered the station.

subject complement A subject complement is a word or word group that completes the meaning of a linking verb and identifies or describes the subject. (See page 391.)

EXAMPLE   Linus was **impressive** in the play last night.

subordinate clause A subordinate clause (also called a *dependent clause*) does not express a complete thought and cannot stand alone as a sentence. (See page 424. See also **adjective clause, adverb clause.**)

EXAMPLE   Margaret and Melanie are two six-year-old girls **who live in San Marcos, Texas.**

suffix A suffix is a word part that is added after a base word or root. (See page 658.)

EXAMPLES   safe + ly =safe**ly**   fair + ness =fair**ness**

busy + ly =busi**ly**   enjoy + ing = enjoy**ing**

active + ity = activ**ity**   knowledge + able = knowledge**able**

swim + er = swimm**er**   teach + er = teach**er**

tense of verbs The tense of verbs indicates the time of the action or state of being expressed by the verb. (See page 496.)

Present

I write	we write
you write	you write
he, she, it writes	they write

Past

I wrote	we wrote
you wrote	you wrote
he, she, it wrote	they wrote

Future

I will (shall) write	we will (shall) write
you will (shall) write	you will (shall) write
he, she, it will (shall) write	they will (shall) write

Present Perfect

I have written	we have written
you have written	you have written
he, she, it has written	they have written

Past Perfect

I had written	we had written
you had written	you had written
he, she, it had written	they had written

Future Perfect

I will (shall) have written	we will (shall) have written
you will (shall) have written	you will (shall) have written
he, she, it will (shall) have written	they will (shall) have written

transitive verb A transitive verb is an action verb that takes an object. (See page 364.)

EXAMPLE   Marcia **washed** her minivan yesterday.

underlining (italics) (See page 628.)

■ **for titles**

EXAMPLES   *Thurgood Marshall: American Revolutionary* [book]

Sports Illustrated for Kids [periodical]

American Gothic [work of art]

The Water Carrier [long musical composition]

■ **for words, letters, and symbols used as such and for foreign words**

EXAMPLES   Notice that the word *Mississippi* has four *i*'s, four *s*'s, and two *p*'s.

A *fait accompli* is anything that is done that cannot be undone.

verb A verb expresses an action or a state of being. (See page 357.)

EXAMPLES   We **walked** slowly down the steep hill.

The grasshopper **is** near the fence.

verbal A verbal is a form of a verb used as a noun, an adjective, or an adverb. (See page 410. See also **participle** and **infinitive.**)

EXAMPLES   The children were amazed by the **leaping** lemurs.

To leave was hard.

verbal phrase A verbal phrase consists of a verbal and any modifiers and complements it has. (See page 410. See also **participial phrase** and **infinitive phrase.**)

EXAMPLES   **Running fast,** the squirrel reached the safety of the tree.

I don't want **to say goodbye.**

verb phrase A verb phrase consists of a main verb and at least one helping verb. (See page 323.)

EXAMPLES   **Have** you **seen** Rich today?

I **would be going** tomorrow, otherwise.

voice Voice is the form a transitive verb takes to indicate whether the subject of the verb performs or receives the action. (See page 499.)

ACTIVE VOICE   Patricia MacLachlan **wrote** the book *Sarah, Plain and Tall.*

PASSIVE VOICE   The book *Sarah, Plain and Tall* **was written** by Patricia MacLachlan.

well (See *good, well.*)

who, whom (See page 521.)

EXAMPLES   For two weeks last summer, I visited my pen pal Émile, **who** lives in Montreal, Quebec.

My pen pal Émile, **whom** I have known for five years, has taught me much about French Canadian traditions.

wordiness Wordiness is the use of more words than necessary or the use of fancy words where simple ones will do. (See page 283.)

WORDY   In the event that it rains, we will not cancel the party that we have planned in celebration of Cinco de Mayo but instead, as an alternative, will hold the party indoors, not outdoors.

REVISED   If it rains, we will hold our Cinco de Mayo party indoors.

Diagramming Appendix

Diagramming Sentences

A *sentence diagram* is a picture of how the parts of a sentence fit together. It shows how the words in the sentence are related.

Subjects and Verbs

Reference Note

For information on **subjects and verbs,** see page 317.

To diagram a sentence, first find the simple subject and the simple predicate, or verb, and write them on a horizontal line. Then, separate the subject and verb with a vertical line. Keep the capital letters, but leave out the punctuation marks, except in cases such as *Mr.* and *July 1, 1999.*

EXAMPLE   Horses gallop.

Horses	gallop

Questions

Reference Note

For information on **questions,** see page 331.

To diagram a question, first make the question into a statement. Then, diagram the sentence. Remember that in a diagram the subject always comes first, even if it does not come first in the sentence.

EXAMPLE   Are you going?

you	Are going

The examples on the previous page are easy because each sentence contains only a simple subject and a verb. Now, look at a longer sentence.

EXAMPLE   One quiet, always popular pet is the goldfish.

To diagram the simple subject and verb of this sentence, follow these steps.

Step 1:   Separate the complete subject from the complete predicate.

complete subject	complete predicate
One quiet, always popular pet	is the goldfish.

Step 2:   Find the simple subject and the verb.

simple subject	verb
pet	is

Step 3:   Draw the diagram.

Understood Subjects

To diagram an imperative sentence, place the understood subject *you* in parentheses on the horizontal line.

EXAMPLE   Clean your room.

(you)	Clean

Reference Note

For information on **understood subjects,** see page 330.

Exercise 1 **Diagramming Simple Subjects and Verbs**

Diagram only the simple subject and verb in each of the following sentences.

EXAMPLE   1. Gwendolyn Brooks has been the poet laureate of Illinois.

1.   Gwendolyn Brooks | has been

HELP

Remember that simple subjects and verbs may consist of more than one word.

1. Angela just returned from Puerto Rico.
2. She was studying Spanish in San Juan.

3. Listen to her stories about her host family.

4. She really enjoyed her trip.

5. Have you ever been to Puerto Rico?

Compound Subjects

Reference Note

For information on **compound subjects,** see page 325. For information on **conjunctions,** see page 374.

To diagram a compound subject, put the subjects on parallel lines. Then, put the connecting word (the conjunction) on a dotted line that joins the subject lines.

EXAMPLE   **Sharks** and **eels** can be dangerous.

Compound Verbs

Reference Note

For information on **compound verbs,** see page 327.

To diagram a compound verb, put the two verbs on parallel lines. Then, put the connecting word (the conjunction) on a dotted line that joins the verb lines.

EXAMPLE   The cowboy **swung** into the saddle and **rode** away.

This is how a compound verb is diagrammed when it has a helping verb that is not repeated.

EXAMPLE   Ray Bradbury **has written** many books and **received** several prizes for them.

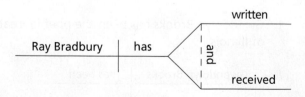

Compound Subjects and Compound Verbs

A sentence with both a compound subject and a compound verb combines the patterns for each.

EXAMPLE **Rosa Parks** and **Dr. Martin Luther King, Jr., saw** a problem and **did** something about it.

Sometimes parts of a compound subject or a compound verb are joined by correlative conjunctions, such as *both . . . and.* Correlatives are diagrammed like this:

EXAMPLE **Both** Luisa **and** Miguel can sing.

Exercise 2 **Diagramming Compound Subjects and Compound Verbs**

Diagram the simple subjects and the verbs in the following sentences. Include the conjunctions that join the compound subjects or the compound verbs.

EXAMPLE 1. Both LeAnn Rimes and Clint Black are going on tour and cutting new albums.

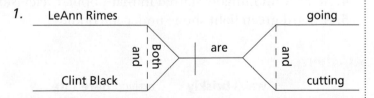

1. Everyone knows and likes Mr. Karras.
2. Hurricanes and tornadoes occur most often during the summer.
3. Julio and Rosa were cutting paper and tying string for the kites.

Reference Note

For information on **using compound subjects with compound verbs,** see page 327.

4. Both Jade Snow Wong and Amy Tan have written books about their childhoods in San Francisco's Chinatown.
5. Elena and I grabbed our jackets and took the bus to the mall.

Adjectives and Adverbs

Adjectives and adverbs are written on slanted lines connected to the words they modify. Notice that possessive pronouns are diagrammed in the same way adjectives are.

Reference Note

For information on **possessive pronouns,** see page 342.

Reference Note

For information on **adjectives,** see page 346.

Adjectives

EXAMPLES   **dark** room   **a lively** fish   **my best** friend

room	fish	friend
dark	*a* *lively*	*my* *best*

Exercise 3 **Diagramming Sentences with Adjectives**

Diagram the subjects, the verbs, and the adjectives that modify the subjects in the following sentences.

EXAMPLE   **1.** A huge silver spaceship landed in the field.

1.   spaceship | landed
     A *huge* *silver*

1. The scary movie will soon end.
2. The soft, silky kitten played with a shoelace.
3. A tall redheaded woman walked into the room.
4. Actor John Lithgow starred in that popular television show.
5. A weird green light shone under the door.

Reference Note

For information on **adverbs,** see page 366.

Adverbs

EXAMPLES   walks **briskly**   arrived **here late**

When an adverb modifies an adjective or another adverb, it is placed on a line connected to the word it modifies.

EXAMPLES   a **very** happy child   drove **rather slowly**

EXAMPLE   This **extremely** rare record will **almost certainly** cost a great deal.

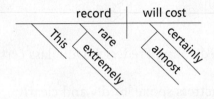

Conjunctions and Modifiers

When a modifier applies to only one part of a compound subject or compound verb, it is diagrammed like this:

EXAMPLE   Benjamin Davis, Sr., and **his** son worked **hard** and rose **quickly** through the military.

Reference Note

For information on **conjunctions,** see page 374. For information on **modifiers,** see Chapter 20.

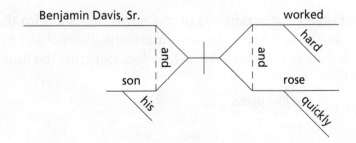

A conjunction joining two modifiers is diagrammed like this:

EXAMPLE   The **English** and **American** musicians played **slowly** and quite **beautifully.**

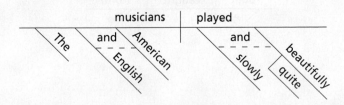

Exercise 4 Diagramming Sentences with Adjectives and Adverbs

Diagram the subjects, verbs, adjectives, adverbs, and conjunctions in the following sentences.

EXAMPLE   1. A relatively unknown candidate won the election easily and rather cheaply.

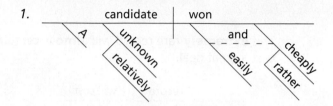

1. The determined young Frederick Douglass certainly worked hard.
2. The talented actress spoke loudly and clearly.
3. Mei-Ling and her younger sister will arrive early tomorrow.
4. The best musicians always play here.
5. That glue does not work very well.

Objects

Direct Objects

A direct object is diagrammed on the horizontal line with the subject and verb. A vertical line separates the direct object from the verb. Notice that this vertical line does not cross the horizontal line.

EXAMPLES   We like **pizza.**

The robin caught a **worm.**

Reference Note

For information on **objects,** see Chapter 13.

Reference Note

For information on **direct objects,** see page 386.

Compound Direct Objects

EXAMPLE   Lizards eat **flies** and **earthworms.**

Reference Note

For information on **compound direct objects,** see page 387.

Indirect Objects

An indirect object is diagrammed on a horizontal line beneath the verb. The verb and the indirect object are joined by a slanting line.

EXAMPLE   Marisol brought **me** a piñata.

Reference Note

For information on **indirect objects,** see page 388.

Compound Indirect Objects

EXAMPLE   Tanya gave the **singer** and the **dancer** cues.

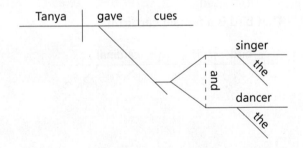

Reference Note

For information on **compound indirect objects,** see page 389.

Exercise 5   **Diagramming Direct and Indirect Objects**

Diagram the following sentences.

EXAMPLE   **1.** I gave the clerk a dollar.

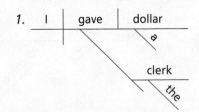

1. Kim drew us a quick sketch.
2. He sent the American Red Cross and Goodwill Industries his extra clothes.
3. My aunt knitted Violet and me sweaters.
4. Gerardo and Wendie are organizing the play and the refreshments.
5. Several businesses bought our school new computers.

Subject Complements

Reference Note

For information on **subject complements,** see page 391.

A subject complement is diagrammed on the horizontal line with the subject and the verb. It comes after the verb. A line slanting toward the verb separates the subject complement from the verb.

Predicate Nominatives

Reference Note

For information on **predicate nominatives,** see page 391.

EXAMPLES   Mariah Carey is a famous **singer.**

That bird is a female **cardinal.**

Compound Predicate Nominatives

EXAMPLE   Clara is a **student** and a volunteer **nurse.**

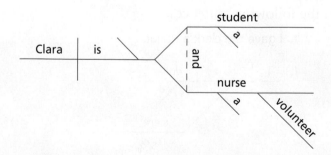

Predicate Adjectives

EXAMPLE   She was extremely **nice**.

This juice tastes **great**.

Compound Predicate Adjectives

EXAMPLE   We were **tired** but very **happy**.

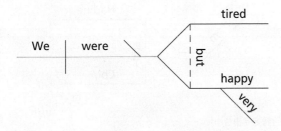

Reference Note

For information on **predicate adjectives,** see page 393.

Exercise 6 Diagramming Sentences

Diagram the following sentences.

EXAMPLE   **1.** The snake is large and shiny.

1.

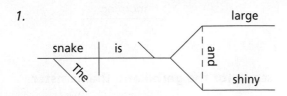

1. Turtles are reptiles.
2. Their tough beaks look sharp and strong.
3. Turtles may grow very old.
4. The alligator snapper is the largest freshwater turtle.
5. Few turtles are dangerous.

Prepositional Phrases

A prepositional phrase is diagrammed below the word it modifies. Write the preposition on a slanting line below the modified word. Then, write the object of the preposition on a horizontal line connected to the slanting line.

Reference Note

For information on **prepositional phrases,** see page 402.

Adjective Phrases

EXAMPLES   traditions **of the Sioux**

Reference Note

For information on **adjective phrases,** see page 404.

gifts **from Nadine and Chip**

Adverb Phrases

EXAMPLES   awoke early **in the morning**

Reference Note

For information on **adverb phrases,** see page 406.

search **for the gerbil and the hamster**

Two prepositional phrases may modify the same word.

EXAMPLE   The tour extends **across the country** and **around the world.**

When a prepositional phrase modifies the object of another preposition, the diagram looks like this:

EXAMPLE   Richard Wright wrote one **of the books on that subject.**

Exercise 7 **Diagramming Sentences with Prepositional Phrases**

Diagram the following sentences.

EXAMPLE   1. Our team practices **late in the afternoon.**

1. The scientist worked late into the night.
2. A play about Cleopatra will be performed tonight.
3. Leroy practices with his band and by himself.

4. Garth Brooks has written songs about love and freedom.
5. The director of that movie about the Civil War was chosen for an Academy Award.

Subordinate Clauses

Adjective Clauses

Diagram an adjective clause by connecting it with a broken line to the word it modifies. Draw the broken line between the relative pronoun and the word to which it relates.

> NOTE The words *who, whom, whose, which,* and *that* are relative pronouns.

An adjective clause is diagrammed below the independent clause.

EXAMPLE   The students **whose projects are selected** will attend the regional contest.

Adverb Clauses

Diagram an adverb clause by using a broken line to connect the adverb clause to the word it modifies. Place the subordinating conjunction that introduces the adverb clause on the broken line.

> NOTE The words *after, because, if, since, unless, when,* and *while* are common subordinating conjunctions.

Reference Note

For information on **subordinate clauses,** see page 424.

Reference Note

For information on **adjective clauses,** see page 427.

Reference Note

For information on **relative pronouns,** see page 428.

Reference Note

For information on **adverb clauses,** see page 430.

The adverb clause is diagrammed below the independent clause.

EXAMPLE   **If I study for two more hours,** I will finish my homework.

Reference Note

For information on **subordinating conjunctions,** see page 431.

Exercise 8 Diagramming Sentences with Adjective Clauses and Adverb Clauses

Diagram the following sentences.

EXAMPLE   1. Will you stop by my house after you go to the library?

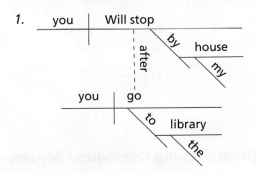

1. Most proverbs are sayings that give advice.
2. Because the day was very hot, the cool water felt good.
3. If it does not rain tomorrow, we will visit Crater Lake.
4. Janice and Linda found some empty seats as the movie started.
5. The problem that worries us now is the pollution of underground sources of water.

Reference Note

For information on the **kinds of sentence structure,** see Chapter 16.

Reference Note

For information on **simple sentences,** see page 440.

Reference Note

For information on **compound sentences,** see page 441.

The Kinds of Sentence Structure

Simple Sentences

EXAMPLE   Ray showed us his new bike. [one independent clause]

Compound Sentences

The second independent clause in a compound sentence is diagrammed below the first and usually is joined to it by a coordinating conjunction. A dotted line joins the clauses. The line is drawn between the verbs of the two clauses, and the conjunction is written on a solid horizontal line connecting the two parts of the dotted line.

EXAMPLE   Ossie Davis wrote the play, and Ruby Dee starred in it. [two independent clauses]

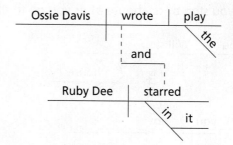

Exercise 9 **Diagramming Compound Sentences**

Diagram the following compound sentences.

EXAMPLE   **1.** Lucas likes that new CD, but I have not heard it.

1. We went to the mall, and everyone had a good time.
2. Do you like basketball, or do you prefer hockey?
3. Luis Alvarez was an atomic scientist, but his son became a geologist.
4. Miriam celebrates Hanukkah, and she told our class about the holiday.
5. Sammy Sosa is my baseball hero, but my sister prefers Randy Johnson.

Complex Sentences

Reference Note

For information on **complex sentences,** see page 445.

EXAMPLE   Altovise has a carving **that was made in Nigeria.** [one independent clause and one subordinate clause]

Exercise 10 Diagramming Complex Sentences

Diagram the following complex sentences.

EXAMPLE   1. If you see Lola, you can give her this book.

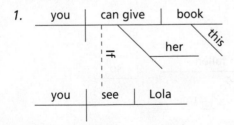

1. Valentina Tereshkova was the first woman who flew in space.
2. Because my cousins live in Toledo, they took a plane to the wedding.
3. Although Wilma Rudolph had been a very sick child, she became a top Olympic athlete.

4. All three of the children screamed as the roller coaster began its descent.

5. The amusement park that we like best offers two free rides to frequent customers.

Reference Note

For information on **compound-complex sentences,** see page 447.

Compound-Complex Sentences

EXAMPLES   Soon-Yee, whose father is a sculptor, studies art, but Mi-Kyung prefers the violin. [two independent clauses and one subordinate clause]

After the raccoon had fallen from the tree, it looked injured, so we called the Humane Society.

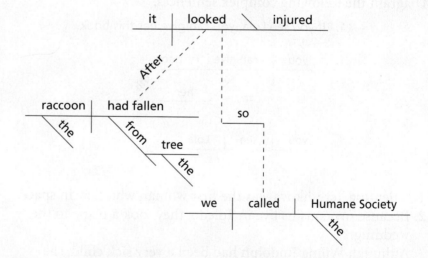

Diagramming Compound-Complex Sentences

Diagram the following compound-complex sentences.

EXAMPLE 1. The room that Carla painted had been white, but she changed the color.

1. We have a game that we bought in Korea, but we do not understand the instructions.
2. Mariella wanted frozen yogurt after she won the tennis match, but Hector and I wanted sandwiches and milk.
3. When I returned to the store, the blue backpack had been sold, so I bought the green one.
4. The restaurant that we like best serves excellent seafood, and the chef has won many awards.
5. Before we conduct the experiment, we should ask for permission from the principal and we should prepare the science lab.

INDEX

styles of, 799–800
types of, 800–802
Bust, busted, 556
Buy, **principal parts of,** 488, 489
Byline, definition of, 792

Cable television, 785. *See also* Television.
Call number, 735
Camera angles, 785
Camera lighting, 262
Camera shots, 785
Can't hardly, can't scarcely, 556
Capital, capitol, 668
Capitalization
    of abbreviations, 810
    of aircraft, 580
    of awards, 581
    of brand names/business products, 580
    of buildings/structures, 580
    of businesses, 580
    of calendar items, 579
    of common nouns, 574–75
    of constellations, 582
    in direct quotation, 39
    of *east, west, north, south,* 576
    of family relationship words, 587
    of first word of direct quotation, 574
    of first word of sentence, 574, 814
    of geographical names, 575–76
    of government bodies, 579
    of historical events/periods, 579
    of holidays, 579
    of holy days and celebrations, 581
    of institutions, 579
    of *I* pronoun, 574
    of memorials, 581
    of monuments, 581
    of names of animals, 575
    of names of persons, 575
    of nationalities/races/peoples, 579
    of organizations, 579
    of planets and heavenly bodies, 582
    in poetry, 574
    of proper adjectives, 584–85, 814
    of proper nouns, 574–75, 814
    proper nouns used as adjectives, 349
    in quoted sentences, 574, 631
    of races of people, 579
    of religions, 581
    rules for, 574–88
    of sacred writings, 581
    of school subjects, 585
    of seasons, 579

of sentence within sentence, 648
of ships, 580
of spacecraft, 580
of special events, 579
of specific deities, 581
of stars, 582
of teams, 579
of titles, 586–88, 816
of trains, 580
Capitol, capital, 668
Card catalog, 735–36
Career development activities
    collaborative news story, 47
    letter to an author, 79
    meeting authors at book signings, 155
    oral report on aspect of workplace, 115
    research and reporting on advertising careers, 265
    writing a journal entry about work activities, 199
    writing about professional uses of persuasion, 231
Case forms
    definition of, 511
    nominative case, 513–14, 816
    nouns and, 511
    objective case, 516–19, 816–17
    personal pronouns, 512
    possessive case, 511, 512, 817
    of pronouns, 816–17
Catch, **principal parts of,** 489
Categorizing ideas (writing). *See* Early plan, making an;
    Organization.
Cause-and-effect chain, 299
Cause-and-effect relationships
    analyzing, 743–44
    causal chain, 748
    identifying cause-and-effect relationships, 241
    pattern of, 748
    transitional words and phrases and, 302
CD-ROM, 736
–cede, –ceed, –sede, **spelling rule for,** 658
Celebrity angle in news, 45
Center-aligned text, 723
Characters
    book jackets and, 148
    protagonist, 133
    in short stories, 144
Chariot in the Sky: A Story of the Jubilee Singers, 298
Chart, 115
Charts
    to arrange ideas, 806
    definition of, 729
    flowcharts, 729
    interpreting ideas from, 750
    pie charts, 730, 750
Choose, **principal parts of,** 489, 825
Choose, chose, 668
Choosing a topic. *See* Topics.

creating family tree, 199
writing persuasive letter from historical
perspective, 231
Cubing, as prewriting technique, 804
Cursive writing, 75
Cut, **principal parts of,** 489

Dangling modifiers, 541, 544
definition of, 821
Dashes, uses of, 649–50
Database records, 115
Databases
on CD-ROM, 736
online databases, 738
Declarative sentences, 330
definition of, 821
Definite articles, 347
Definitions in dictionary, 721
Degrees of comparison, 532–35
Deleting (as revision strategy), 12, 69, 102, 183, 223,
253, 254
Demographics, definition of, 792
Demonstrative adjectives, 348
Demonstrative pronouns, 343, 348
Denotation, definition of, 89, 753
Dependent clauses. *See* Subordinate clauses.
Description (writing)
essay, 41–42
paragraphs, 47, 306, 307
poem, 43
Descriptive essays, 41–42
Descriptive language
definition of, 41
in eyewitness account, 18–20
figures of speech, 21, 31
metaphors, 31, 146, 753
precise words, 21
sensory language, 21
in short stories, 145
similes, 31, 146, 753
Desert, dessert, 670
Designing your writing. *See* Document design.
Desktop publishing, page layout, 723–27
Details. *See also* Evidence; Sensory details; Support.
elaboration and, 304
eyewitness account and, 29
irrelevant details, 68
relevant details, 68
using prepositional phrases to add, 421
in writing, 293
Developing
developing details, 41
writing to develop ideas, 79, 211–26

Developing ideas, writing to, 79, 211–26
Dewey, Jennifer Owings, 19–20
Diacritical marks, 721
Diagrams. *See also* Sentence diagrams.
definition of, 730
using diagrams, 750
Dialects, ethnic and regional, 733–34
Dialogue
comparing television dialogue with real-life
dialogue, 108–109
new paragraphs and, 634
punctuating dialogue, 39, 634
to show character, 145
writing for commercials, 259
Diary writing, 777
Diction, in formal speech, 762
Dictionary
dictionary entry, 720–21
function of, 240
as spelling aid, 655
types and contents of, 720–21
wordbusting strategy and, 209
Digital editing, 262, 792
Digital effects, 262
Digital reality, 262
Direct address, capitalizing the title of person in,
586–87
Direct objects
action verbs and, 392
as compound, 387
definition of, 386, 516, 822
diagram of, 842
objective case and, 516
predicate nominative distinguished from, 392
prepositional phrases and, 386
pronouns as, 386
Direct quotations
capitalization of, 574, 631
punctuating with commas, 631–32
punctuating with end marks, 632
quotation marks and, 630–35, 829
Directions
following oral, 76–78
giving oral and written, 75
Discover, writing to, 79, 155, 199
Divided quotation. *See* Broken quotations.
Dividing words, hyphens and, 646
Do
as helping verb, 362
principal parts of, 488, 489
Document design. *See also* Graphics; Illustrations; Page
layout.
desktop publishing, 723–27
guidelines for submitting papers, 722
manuscript style, 722
using text features, 187

Syntax. *See* Sentence structure.

T

ACKNOWLEDGMENTS

For permission to reprint copyrighted material, grateful acknowledgment is made to the following sources:

Annenberg/CPB Project: From "Amusement Park Physics" from *The Annenberg/CPB Project Exhibits Collections,* online, August 5, 1998. Copyright © 1998 by The Annenberg/CPB Project. Available http://www.learner.org/exhibits/parkphysics/ridesafety.html.

Johnny D. Boggs: From "Home on the Range" by Johnny D. Boggs from *Boys' Life,* June 1998. Copyright © 1998 by Johnny D. Boggs. *Boys' Life* is published by the Boy Scouts of America.

Boyds Mills Press, Inc.: From "Hopi Snake Ceremonies" from *Rattlesnake Dance: True Tales, Mysteries, and Rattlesnake Ceremonies* by Jennifer Owings Dewey. Copyright © 1997 by Jennifer Owings Dewey.

Carlinsky & Carlinsky, Inc.: From "Kites" by Dan Carlinsky from *Boys' Life,* May 1974. Copyright © 1974 by Dan Carlinsky.

Dell Publishing, a division of Random House, Inc.: Jacket cover and flap copy from *Where the Red Fern Grows* by Wilson Rawls. Copyright © 1961 by Sophie S. Rawls, Trustee, or successor for Trustee(s) of the Rawls Trust, dated July 31, 1991; copyright © 1961 by The Curtis Publishing Company.

Doubleday, a division of Random House, Inc.: From *The Richer, the Poorer* by Dorothy West. Copyright © 1995 by Dorothy West.

Farrar, Straus & Giroux, Inc.: From "A Walk to the Jetty" from *Annie John* by Jamaica Kincaid. Copyright © 1985 by Jamaica Kincaid.

Lloyd Garver: From "No, You Can't Have Nintendo" (retitled "A Veto on Video Games") by Lloyd Garver from "My Turn" from *Newsweek,* June 11, 1990, p. 8. Copyright © 1990 by Lloyd Garver.

Harcourt, Inc.: From "The No-Guitar Blues" from *Baseball in April and Other Stories* by Gary Soto. Copyright © 1990 by Gary Soto.

HarperCollins Publishers, Inc.: From *Black Elk: The Sacred Ways of a Lakota* by Wallace H. Black Elk and William S. Lyon, Ph.D. Copyright © 1990 by Wallace H. Black Elk and William S. Lyon.

Henry Holt and Company, Inc.: From "A Runaway Slave" from *Chariot in the Sky: A Story of the Jubilee Singers* by Arna Bontemps. Copyright 1951 by Arna Bontemps; copyright © 1979 by Mrs. Arna (Alberta) Bontemps.

Alfred A. Knopf, Inc.: Front cover, text from front and back flap jackets, and back cover text from *Crash* by Jerry Spinelli. Copyright © 1996 by Jerry Spinelli; jacket illustration copyright © 1996 by Eleanor Hoyt.

Lothrop, Lee & Shepard Books, a division of HarperCollins Publishers, Inc.: From "Green Dragon Pond" from *The Spring of Butterflies,* translated by He Liyi. Copyright © 1985 by William Collins Sons & Co. Ltd.

Macmillan General Reference USA: Entries, "escape" and "escaper," from *Webster's New World Dictionary,* Third Edition, Editor in Chief, Victoria Neufeldt, Editor in Chief Emeritus, David B. Guralnik. Copyright © 1988, 1991, 1994, 1996, 1997 by Simon & Schuster, Inc.

Margaret K. McElderry Books, an imprint of Simon & Schuster Children's Publishing Division: From *A Jar of Dreams* by Yoshiko Uchida. Copyright © 1981 by Yoshiko Uchida.

Millbrook Press: From "The Voice in the Attic" from *Voice Magic: Secrets of Ventriloquism & Voice Conjuring* by Ormond McGill. Copyright © 1992 by Ormond McGill.

NASA: From "NASA'S Future: Online Multimedia Presentation" by Brian Dunbar from *NASA Homepage,* online, April 6, 1999. Available http://www.nasa.gov/

National Geographic Society: "Comeback: Lions Recover from Dog Disease" by Scott Stuckey from "Geo News" from *National Geographic World,* February 1999. Copyright © 1999 by National Geographic Society. From "It's Touch and Go With Whiskers!" by Fiona Sunquist from *National Geographic World,* no. 272, June 1997. Copyright © 1997 by National Geographic Society.

Newsweek, Inc.: From "A Doll Made to Order" from *Newsweek,* December 9, 1985. Copyright © 1985 by Newsweek, Inc. All rights reserved.

People Weekly: From "On a Roll: Flipping, Flying and (Almost) Losing It on the 10 Scariest Roller Coasters in America" by Anne-Marie O'Neill from *People Weekly,* vol. 48, no. 1, July 7, 1997. Copyright © 1997 by Time Inc.

Marian Reiner for Patricia Hubbell: "Construction" from *8 A. M. Shadows* by Patricia Hubbell. Copyright © 1965, 1993 by Patricia Hubbell.

Ride Warrior, Inc.: From *Thrill Ride! 98 Preview,* online, July 1998. Copyright © 1998 by Robert Coker-Ride Warrior, Inc. Available http://www.thrillride.com/ThrillRidefrontpage.html.

Scholastic Inc.: Adaptation from "For Girls Only" by Alexandra Hanson-Harding from *Junior Scholastic,* April 27, 1998. Copyright © 1998 by Scholastic Inc. From "The Celebrated Deformed Frogs of Le Sueur County" by Susan Hayes from *Scholastic Update,* vol. 130, no. 13, April 13, 1998. Copyright © 1998 by Scholastic Inc.

Simon & Schuster Books for Young Readers, an imprint of Simon & Schuster Children's Publishing Division: From *Hatchet* by Gary Paulsen. Copyright © 1987 by Gary Paulsen.

Time for Kids, a division of Time Inc.: From *"We the People"* by Ritu Upadhyay from **TIME for Kids,** March 23, 2001. Copyright © 2001 by Time Inc.

University of California Press: From "In the Night" from *Singing for Power: The Song Magic of the Papago Indians of Southern Arizona* by Ruth Murray Underhill. Copyright © 1938, 1966 by Ruth Murray Underhill.

Viking Penguin, a division of Penguin Putnam Inc.: From *The Outsiders* by S. E. Hinton. Copyright © 1967 by S. E. Hinton.

PHOTO CREDITS

COVER: Scott Van Osdol/HRW Photo.

TABLE OF CONTENTS: Page T12, Photos by John Langford/HRW Photo (girl); Image Copyright ©2001 Photodisc, Inc. (book and electronics); T15 (tl), Gambell/SuperStock; T15 (bl), Image Copyright ©2001 Photodisc, Inc.; T16, Ron Sefton/Bruce Coleman, Inc.; T17, Courtesy of Terry Dewald/Jerry Jacka Photography; T17, Tom Prettyman/Photo Edit; T19, John Elk, III/Bruce Coleman, Inc.; xx, Image Copyright ©1998 Photodisc, Inc.; T21, Tony Arruza/Bruce Coleman, Inc.; T22, James Sugar/Black Star; T23, SuperStock; T24, Corbis-Bettmann; T25, Courtesy: Steve Cowgill, Taos, NM and McGee's Gallery, Holbrook, AZ. © Jerry Jacka Photography; T26, Image Club Graphics ©1998 Adobe Systems; T27, Sylvain Grandadam/Tony Stone Images.

INTRODUCTION: Page 7, Barbara Reed/Animals Animals/Earth Scenes.

PART OPENERS: Page xxii, 1, 266, 267, 312, 313, 718, 719, Kazu Nitta/The Stock Illustration Source, Inc.

CHAPTER 1: Page 19, MONA ©1996 d cube™ Cone Mill Corporation.

CHAPTER 3: Page 85, Nina Berman/SIPA Press.

CHAPTER 4: Page 119, From CRASH by Jerry Spinelli / Copyright © 1996 by Jerry Spinelli. Jacket Illustration / Copyright © 1996 by Eleanor Hoyt. Reprinted by permission of Alfred A. Knopf, Inc.; 123, © 1989 by Robert McGinnis.; 149 (tr), Photos by Michael Orton/Tony Stone Images (trees) and Victoria Smith (eyes)/HRW Photo; jacket design by HRW; 149 (tc), Illustrations by Jerry Dadds/Deborah Wolfe Ltd.; jacket design by HRW; 149 (br), Illustration by Mike Wimmer / Mendola Ltd. Artists Representatives; jacket design by HRW; 150, Illustration by Bill Schmidt/ Hankins & Tebenborg LTD; jacket design by HRW.

CHAPTER 5: Page 159, Diane Gentry/Black Star; 160, SuperStock; 197, NASA.

CHAPTER 7: Page 235, American Pharmaceutical Companies; 237, John Langford/HRW Photo; 237, Sam Dudgeon/HRW Photo; 244, John Langford/HRW Photo; 245, Dick Luria/FPG International; 257, Courtesy of the American Red Cross; 263, John Langford/HRW Photo; 263 (br), Sam Dudgeon/HRW Photo; 264 (tl) (tc) (tr), John Langford/HRW Photo.

CHAPTER 8: Page 270, Kim Taylor/Bruce Coleman, Inc.; 272, NASA/Nawrocki Stock Photo; 273, Image Copyright ©2001 Photodisc, Inc.; 275, SuperStock; 276, Gambell/SuperStock; 279, SuperStock; 281, Image Copyright ©2001 Photodisc, Inc.; 284, Ron Sefton/Bruce Coleman, Inc.; 285, Reuters/Mark Cardwell/Archive Photos.

CHAPTER 9: Page 289, Courtesy: Steve Cowgill, Taos, NM and McGee's Gallery, Holbrook, AZ. © Jerry Jacka Photography; 291, Image Copyright ©2001 Photodisc, Inc.; 295, People Weekly © 1986 Richard Howard; 297, David R. Frazier Photolibrary; 299, Image Copyright ©2001 Photodisc, Inc.; 301 (cr), John Shaw/Bruce Coleman, Inc.; 301 (br), Michael P. Gadomski/Bruce Coleman, Inc.; 304, UPI/Corbis-Bettmann; 305, Tim Davis/Davis/Lynn Images; 308, Archive Photos.

CHAPTER 10: Page 321, UPI/Corbis-Bettmann; 324 (cl), Paul Chesley/Tony Stone Images; 324 (bl), John Elk, III/Bruce Coleman, Inc.; 326 (bl), Tony Arruza/Bruce Coleman, Inc.; 326 (bc), John Elk, III/Bruce Coleman, Inc.; 329, Digital Stock Corp.

CHAPTER 11: Page 341, Chris Eden/Francine Seders Gallery; 351, Digital Stock Corp.

CHAPTER 12: Page 365, Image Copyright ©1998 Photodisc, Inc.; 368, Tony Kirves/Southern Exposure; 372, Culver Pictures, Inc.; 379, Fred Bruemmer/Peter Arnold, Inc.

CHAPTER 13: Page 387, ALLSPORT USA/Vandystadt Agence de Presse; 388, Nawrocki Stock Photo; 395, Image Copyright ©1998 Photodisc, Inc.; 396 (tl), Bob Daemmrich/Tony Stone Worldwide, Ltd.; 396 (cl), Jose Carrillo/Photo Edit; 396 (bl), Tom Prettyman/Photo Edit.

CHAPTER 14: Page 403, D.P. Hershkowitz/Bruce Coleman, Inc.; 405, Andrew Bernstein/ALLSPORT USA; 411, Corbis Images; 413 (c), Fielder Kownslar/IBM Corporation; 416, Image Copyright ©1998 Photodisc, Inc.; 417, Bill Aron/PhotoEdit.

CHAPTER 15: Page 425-426, Michael Och Archives/Venice, CA.

CHAPTER 16: Page 444, FPG International; 445, Corbis-Bettmann; 446, UPI/Corbis-Bettmann; 449, Culver Pictures, Inc.

CHAPTER 17: Page 459 (br), Paul S. Conklin/Nawrocki Stock Photo; 459 (cl), Paul S. Conklin/David R. Frazier Photolibrary; 460 (cl), Gerhard Gacheldle/HRW Photo; 460 (tl), Image Club Graphics ©1998 Adobe Systems; 465, SuperStock; 468, David Young Wolff/Tony Stone Images.

CHAPTER 18: Page 487, SuperStock; 499, Image Copyright ©2001 Photodisc, Inc.; 506, Bob Daemmrich/The Image Works.

CHAPTER 19: Page 518, Corbis-Bettmann; 521, Culver Pictures, Inc.

CHAPTER 20: Page 536 (c) (cr), Cameramann International; 548, H. Armstrong Roberts.

CHAPTER 21: Page 555, Paul Chesley/Tony Stone Images; 558, John Langford/HRW Photo; 561, HRW Photo Research Library; 565, Sylvain Grandadam/Tony Stone Images.

CHAPTER 22: Page 577, James Sugar/Black Star; 577, Richard Pasley/Viesti Collection; 584 (cl), Culver Pictures, Inc.; 584 (bl), Archive Photos.

ILLUSTRATION CREDITS